D0031362

PS
648
S3
S35

✓

Science fiction

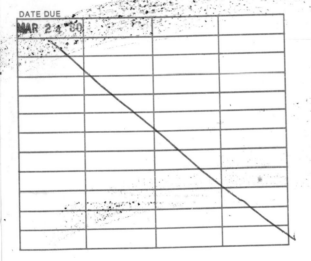

DATE DUE

MAR 24 80

001 342   000 248

SCIENCE FICTION: CONTEMPORARY MYTHOLOGY

SCIENCE FICTION: CONTEMPORARY MYTHOLOGY

The SFWA-SFRA Anthology

Editors: Patricia Warrick

Martin Harry Greenberg

Joseph Olander

HARPER & ROW, PUBLISHERS

New York, Hagerstown, San Francisco, London

SCIENCE FICTION: CONTEMPORARY MYTHOLOGY. Copyright © 1978 by Science Fiction Research Associates and Science Fiction Writers of America. All rights reserved. Printed in the United States of America. No part of this book may be used or reproduced in any manner whatsoever without written permission except in the case of brief quotations embodied in critical articles and reviews. For information address Harper & Row, Publishers, Inc., 10 East 53rd Street, New York, N.Y. 10022. Published simultaneously in Canada by Fitzhenry & Whiteside Limited, Toronto.

FIRST EDITION

Designed by Stephanie Krasnow

Library of Congress Cataloging in Publication Data

Main entry under title:
Science fiction: contemporary mythology
   Includes index.
    1. Science fiction—History and criticism—Addresses, essays, lectures. 2. Science fiction, American. 3. Science fiction, English. I. Warrick, Patricia S. II. Greenberg, Martin Harry. III. Olander, Joseph D.
PN3448.S45S275   823'.0876   76-26232
ISBN 0-06-011626-9

78 79 80 81 10 9 8 7 6 5 4 3 2 1

Acknowledgments

Grateful acknowledgment is made for permission to reprint the following:

"The Father-Thing" by Philip K. Dick. Copyright 1954 by Fantasy House, Inc. Reprinted by permission of the author and his agents, Scott, Meredith Literary Agency, Inc., 845 Third Avenue, New York, New York 10022.

"Twilight" by John W. Campbell, Jr. Copyright 1934 by Street & Smith Publications, Inc., from the November 1934 issue of *Astounding Stories*. Copyright renewed 1962 by The Condé-Nast Publications, Inc. Reprinted by permission of the author's estate and Scott Meredith Literary Agency, Inc., 845 Third Avenue, New York, New York 10022.

"Common Time" by James Blish. Reprinted by permission of the author and the author's agent, Robert P. Mills, Ltd.

"Coming Attraction" by Fritz Leiber. Reprinted by permission of the author and the author's agent, Robert P. Mills, Ltd.

"The Luckiest Man in Denv" by C. M. Kornbluth. Reprinted by permission of the author and the author's agent, Robert P. Mills, Ltd.

"Masks" by Damon Knight. Reprinted by permission of the author and the author's agent, Robert P. Mills Ltd.

"All the Last Wars At Once" by George Alec Effinger. Reprinted by permission of the author.

"Computers Don't Argue" by Gordon R. Dickson. Copyright 1965 by The Condé-Nast Publications, Inc. Reprinted by permission of the author.

"Day Million" by Frederik Pohl. Reprinted by permission of the author.

"The Dance of the Changer and the Three" by Terry Carr from *The Farthest Reachers* by Joseph Elder. Copyright © 1968 by Joseph Elder. Reprinted by permission of the author.

"Before Eden" by Arthur C. Clarke. Copyright 1961 by Ziff-Davis Publishing Company. Reprinted by permission of the author and his agents, Scott Meredith Literary Agency, Inc., 845 Third Avenue, New York, New York 10022.

"The New Father Christmas" by Brian W. Aldiss. Copyright 1969 by Mercury Press, Inc. Reprinted by permission of the author and his agents, Scott Meredith Literary Agency, Inc., 845 Third Avenue, New York, New York 10022.

"Billenium" by J. G. Ballard. Copyright 1961 by J. G. Ballard. Reprinted by permission of the author and his agents, Scott Meredith Literary Agency, Inc., 845 Third Avenue, New York, New York 10022.

"Goat Song" by Poul Anderson. Copyright 1967 by Mercury Press, Inc. Reprinted by permission of the author and his agents, Scott Meredith Literary Agency, Inc., 845 Third Avenue, New York, New York 10022.

"The Shadow of Space" by Philip José Farmer. Copyright 1972 by Robert Silverberg. Reprinted by permission of the author and his agents, Scott Meredith Literary Agency, Inc., 845 Third Avenue, New York, New York 10022.

"New York, A.D.: 2600 by Hugo Gernsback. Copyright 1911 by Modern Electrics Publication, 1925; The Stratford Co., 1950. Reprinted by permission of Forrest J. Ackerman, 2495 Glendower Avenue, Hollywood, California 90027, representing Mary Gernsback.

"The Hole Man" by Larry Niven. Reprinted by permission of the author and the author's agent, Robert P. Mills, Ltd.

"Sea Change" from *Caution: Inflammable* by Thomas N. Scortia. Copyright 1956 by Street and Smith Publications, Inc. Reprinted by permission of Doubleday & Company, Inc.

"Specialist" by Robert Sheckley. Copyright 1953 by Robert Sheckley. Reprinted by permission of The Sterling Lord Agency, Inc.

"A Happy Day in 2381" by Robert Silverberg. Copyright 1969 by Robert Silverberg. Reprinted by permission of the author and his agents, Scott Meredith Literary Agency, Inc., 845 Third Avenue, New York, New York 10022.

"The Game of Rat and Dragon" by Cordwainer Smith. Copyright 1955 by Galaxy Publishing Co. from Galaxy Science Fiction. Copyright 1963 by Cordwainer Smith. Reprinted by permission of the author's estate and Scott Meredith Literary Agency, Inc., 845 Third Avenue, New York, New York 10022.

"A Scientist Divides" by Donald A. Wandrei. Copyright 1934 by Street and Smith Publications, Inc. First published in the September 1934 issue of *Astounding Stories*. Reprinted by permission of the author and his agents, Scott Meredith Literary Agency, Inc., 845 Third Avenue, New York, New York 10022.

"The Game of Blood and Dust" by Roger Zelazny. Copyright 1975 by UPD Publishing Corporation. Reprinted by permission of the author and his agents, Henry Morrison, Inc.

"Nine Lives" by Ursula K. Le Guin. Copyright 1969, 1974 by Ursula K. Le Guin; an earlier version appeared in Playboy Magazine. Reprinted by permission of the author and her agent, Virginia Kidd.

"Memorial" by Theodore Sturgeon. Reprinted by permission of the author.

"Brightside Crossing" by Alan E. Nourse, reprinted by permission of the author and David McKay Co., Inc., New York, from *Tiger by the Tail and Other Science Fiction Stories* by Alan E. Nourse. Copyright © 1951, 1952, 1953, 1956, 1957, 1961 by Alan E. Nourse.

Contents

                                          selections by David Martwell *244*
          "Twilight"   John W. Campbell, Jr.   *254*
          "The New Father   Brian W. Aldiss   *273*
            Christmas"
          "Computers Don't   Gordon R. Dickson   *278*
            Argue"
7. More Than Human?: Androids,   George Zebrowski and
        Cyborgs, and Others   Patricia Warrick   *294*
          "Nine Lives"   Ursula K. Le Guin   *307*
          "Masks"   Damon Knight   *331*
          "Sea Change"   Thomas N. Scortia   *342*
          "Day Million"   Frederik Pohl   *354*

8. The City   Theodore R. Cogswell
                                          and Ralph S. Clem   *359*
          "Billenium"   J.G. Ballard   *365*
          "A   Happy   Day   in   Robert Silverberg   *379*
            2381"

9. Utopias and Dystopias   Frederik Pohl,
                                          Martin Harry Greenberg
                                          and Joseph D. Olander   *393*
          "New York A.D.:   Hugo Gernsback   *401*
            2660"
          "Coming Attraction"   Fritz Leiber   *412*
          "The Luckiest Man in   C. M. Kornbluth   *424*
            Denv"

10. Apocalypse   Jack Williamson
                                          and David Ketterer   *435*
          "The Game of Blood   Roger Zelazny   *441*
            and Dust"
          "All the Last Wars at   George Alec Effinger   *445*
            Once"

        Notes on the Contributors   *459*
        Index   *469*

Prefatory Comments

There are several hundred persons writing science fiction in America today. There are also several hundred persons teaching it. If there is one thing that this large, and quite disparate, group of human beings agrees on, it is that the novels and stories which are taught in science fiction courses should be the best available.

Unfortunately, at that point agreement stops. Which science fiction stories are "best"? There is no clear consensus. By what measure do we define quality? Best as literature? Best as science fiction? Are they the same? And if they are not, in what way do the standards differ?

Any one of these questions will get you a lively argument at any meeting of the Science Fiction Writers of America, Science Fiction Research Associates, Modern Language Association science fiction group or local convention—or would have, not long ago. Now, maybe a little less lively, because the questions have been debated so often and so fiercely that the juice is gone out of them.

But the questions are still there. Science fiction needs to be weighed in two different scales:

One is calibrated in the traditional literary values: graceful use of language, purity of style, perceptive illumination of persons, insight into the human condition. These are important in science fiction, as they are in any kind of writing. Science fiction readers are as appreciative of these virtues, whenever found, as any other kind of readers.

The other scale is peculiar to science fiction, and it is made up of many qualities: Does the story tell me something worth knowing, that I had not known before, about the relationship between man and technology? Does it enlighten me on some area of science where I had been in the dark? Does it open a new horizon for my thinking? Does it lead me to think new kinds of thoughts, that I would not otherwise perhaps have thought at all? Does it suggest possibilities about the alternative possible future courses my world can take? Does it illuminate events and trends of today, by showing me where they may lead tomorrow? Does it give me a fresh and objective point of view on my own world and culture, perhaps by letting me see it through the eyes of a different kind of creature entirely, from a planet light-years away?

These qualities are not only among those which make science fiction good, they are what make it unique. Be it never so beautifully written, a story is not a good *science fiction* story unless it rates high in these aspects. The content of the story is as valid a criterion as the style.

This is perhaps not true of most writing, not even of the greatest. It seems to me that if Proust and Tolstoi had been interchanged in their cradles, both would still have written masterpieces; their genius was independent of either *fin-de-siècle* Paris or Napoleon's war on Russia. It does not seem to me that Heinlein and Proust could have been so interchanged, or Clarke and Tolstoi. A French Tolstoi might easily have written about Napoleon from the other side of the battlefield, but I do not believe he could have written *Childhood's End*.

Please do not mistake me to say that Heinlein is as great a novelist as Marcel Proust. What I am saying is that, as a *science fiction* novelist, Heinlein is very great indeed; and this is because of what he says, far more than because of how well he says it.

And so, on a hot day in Chicago a year or two ago, in the coffee shop of the Palmer House Hotel, a group of us invented the idea of an anthology that was a cooperative undertaking of writer and critic. Pat Warrick contributed her outline for a collection of stories exemplifying recurring patterns or myths in science fiction.

We could anatomize science fiction this way, we schemed; and we would have the dissection of each limb and organ performed by a team, one a highly respected science fiction writer, the other an equally respected science fiction teacher.

We could not easily divide prospective editors into mandarins of style and coolies of content; but we could, we decided, divide the chores between writers and teachers very readily indeed. And so we did.

And here, endless hours of hard work later, is the result.

Have we succeeded in at last achieving a selection of stories which everyone will agree are unquestionably the best science fiction ever written?

Certainly not! For one thing, there are a large number of splendid novels and short novels or novelettes in science fiction, none of which we could include for reasons of space. And, of course, personal taste plays an important part. Any one of us could easily suggest a dozen stories we think should have been included and were not.

But what we have achieved is, I think, a collection of which three very good things can be said:

First, it is a careful sampling of the best science fiction stories available, selected by persons well qualified to decide.

Second, it is a useful teaching guide for any science fiction course, anywhere.

And third, in it you will, I am certain, find many hours of first-class reading!

Frederik Pohl
President,
Science Fiction Writers of America
1974–1976

For a variety of reasons the academic interest in science fiction has mushroomed during the 1970s in particular. One can estimate the number of courses being offered at the college and university levels— probably several hundred each term—but no one can guess accurately how many classes—"mini-courses"—are now offered at the high school level. As might be expected, in recent years some writers and devoted science fiction fans have expressed a certain skepticism at the "academic intrusion" into their favorite field. These are two of the factors which make this anthology so important. It shows that writers and teachers can work together closely and profitably.

Too often they have gone their own ways—with detrimental effects upon both writing and teaching. One need look back only to the 1930s to see the academic-critical misjudgment of such individuals as William Faulkner.

Frequently teachers and literary critics have been among those who have resisted innovation and change. One of my favorite teachers told stories of how he had to convince certain of his colleagues around the time of World War I that American literature was worthy of scholarly study and deserving of classroom attention. When I was an undergraduate in the 1940s, the survey of English literature ended abruptly with the works of Thomas Hardy because, really, one could not be certain of the value of more recent writers like Conrad and Joyce and T. S. Eliot. To a lesser extent, perhaps because of our previous experience, this same resistance greeted the emergence of the study of Popular Culture. Those of us who have worked with science fiction over the years have been haunted by individuals in the profession who ask why we give attention to work of "sub-literary" quality; at least one has asked me why I bother with "para-literature." So the writers and fans have had some cause for concern.

Several years ago at Discon—the World Science Fiction Convention in Washington, D.C.—I remember one young fan bewailing the fact that she had taken a course in science fiction the previous spring and that the syllabus was confined, by and large, to the works of Mary Shelley, Fitz-James O'Brien, Edgar Allan Poe, Jules Verne, Edward Bellamy, and H. G. Wells. She complained that not a single living author was included and that the teacher did not make use of magazines.

I tried to explain that in all probability the teacher had been instructed by a chairman or a principal or a dean to prepare a course for the next term and had not had a chance to read widely in the field. Like Fred Pohl and others, during the past decade I have received letters each week from teachers asking for help as they were faced with the problem of instant preparation. This problem was one of those at the heart of the letter columns of *Analog* during the summer of 1975.

But this is only one side of the story. Within the past few months I have heard several individuals cry out that "academe" should leave science fiction in its "ghetto"/"gutter" where it belongs. Interestingly, the individuals who have said this have not participated in the continuing Modern Language Association Seminar on Science Fiction, held each year since 1958, or in the regional or national meetings of SFRA. This summer on the last day of the SFRA meeting at the University of Montana in Missoula, one writer who had never before attended an "academic" meeting expressed pleasure that he had done so and promised to come again.

Perhaps the crucial issue can be crystallized in a single incident. A year or more ago a distinguished author wrote a rather angry letter to me asking me to confirm or deny the rumor that only English Ph.D.'s could publish articles in *Extrapolation,* the journal which has served the MLA Seminar and SFRA since 1959. I pointed out some of the writers who had published there—Judith Merril, Samuel R. Delany, Joanna Russ, Clifford D. Simak, James Gunn, and Fred Pohl, among others. He expressed surprise but was pleased.

Apparently some of those who have objected to the academic attention given to science fiction have thought that the teachers and critics were going to tell them how and what to write, were going to set forth stringent definitions which they *must* follow, were, so to speak, going to take the stories apart and not put them together again.

No one will deny that writer and teacher/critic approach the work—science fiction—from two different perspectives. The writer wishes not only to entertain but to give his readers some insight into themselves and the societies/world in which they live. As Fred Pohl has suggested, they attempt to open new horizons and give a fresh and objective point of view on the world and culture, perhaps letting the reader see it through the eyes of a different kind of creature, from a planet light-years away. The aim of the teacher/critic is the same; he acts as a guide for his students, the readers. To evaluate the work as good, better, best in purely traditional literary terms is perhaps the least part of his task. More important, as Robert E. Spiller, himself a great teacher and literary historian, has suggested, the task is to explore the work to find what "symbolic illumination" it gives man about himself and his universe.

Such matters explain why this anthology is so important. Despite the cooperation of writers and teachers previously, this anthology is in many ways the most public sign that these two groups who know the field well are working together to provide readers with a selection of some of the best science fiction written.

Thomas D. Clareson
Chairman, Science Fiction Research Associates
1970–1976

Introduction: Mythic Patterns

The Organization of the Anthology

The ten chapters of the anthology reflect what the editors regard as major patterns in science fiction. Chapters open with an essay written cooperatively by a science fiction writer and a science fiction critic. The introductory essay discusses the elements of the mythic pattern, gives some of the history of its development, and the major fictional works in that category. The essays vary somewhat in style and approach since the various pairs of writers and critics were given the freedom to develop their material as they thought appropriate. They also chose the short stories used as illustrations of the mythic pattern they were defining. In this selection, the only limitation was that the writer of the essay might not choose his own fiction. Consequently, in a few instances—such as Isaac Asimov's chapter, for example—an appropriate and well-known story is not included. An Asimov robot tale was not selected because he is the science fiction writer contributing the essay for the chapter on machines and robots. So that the range of authors could be as wide as possible, only one story by any author was used. In addition to the introductory essay and the stories, each chapter also contains a bibliography listing the outstanding fictional works using that mythic pattern. In most instances these are novels, although occasionally a short story is included if it is a very famous one. A science fiction course using this anthology might in addition select a novel from each category. The reading of the essay, the short stories, and a novel in each mythic pattern would give the student a good overall view of the ideas and literature of the science fiction genre. The bibliography at the end of the essay in Chapter 1 provides a brief list of reliable studies in science fiction history and criticism. Biographical sketches of the contributors to *Science Fiction: Contemporary Mythology* are given at the end of the anthology.

A brief description of the mythic pattern in each chapter follows:

1. *Ambiguity*

The myths portraying technological man often split in their view of his place in the universe, and the value of the science and technology that he has created. He has used his reasoning power to subdue nature and create an artificial world. His intuition tells him he may be irrational in using his reasoning ability to alienate himself from nature. And yet he marvels at his creations. So his view of technology is ambivalent. The clear-cut yes or no has disappeared from the modern world.

2. *The Remarkable Adventure*

The fictional journey is a recurring myth in literature, the journey of Odysseus, for example. The journeys of science fiction are unique in that they are never through this world, but through those worlds that lie beyond the boundaries of known reality. The adventure may be into outer space, or within the psyche—into inner space. The journeyer is a hero, like the hero of classical myth. He is a man who is able to cope in the marvelous new world created by science. In his heroic dimensions he differs from the protagonist of contemporary mainstream literature who is typically an anti-hero, unable to act in the world.

3. *Beyond Reality's Barriers: New Dimensions*

A major theme in the mythical world of science fiction is new dimensions that break the limitations of time and space as man knows them in his present reality. Time travel and space travel are prevailing myths in science fiction. This travel may take man to an alien world in outer space which turns out to be much like his own. Or the travel may take him beyond the barriers of the natural world he knows into the supernatural.

4. *Aliens*

Myths of alien creatures form a substantial part of science fiction literature. In his marvelous journeys, man encounters creatures vastly different from himself; he is pushed to define anew what it means to be human. As he journeys within, he finds alien creatures there, too. These stories reflect modern man's awareness that, on all sides, he encounters life which is different from what he has traditionally thought was "natural."

5. *The Scientist*

The world of science fiction is that universe opened up by science, and so the scientist is the protagonist in many science fiction stories. The attitude toward the scientist—and his expediter, the technologist—is ambivalent. He may be "the wise one," the prophet who has insight about and control over the future. But he may also be portrayed as demoniacal, the mad scientist whose creations unleash a power that threatens to destroy mankind.

6. *The Machine and the Robot*

The machine, continually more complex, sophisticated, and powerful, is a recurring myth. It is a product of the scientist who develops a technology to implement his theoretical constructs. The machine can accomplish all kinds of feats involving both physical and intellectual work. The attitude toward the machine, like that toward the scientist, is ambiguous. The machine may release man from the slavery of hard work, but it may also enslave man, exceeding him both in physical and mental power and control.

7. *More than Human?: Androids, Cyborgs, and Others*

Frankenstein is the prototype for a host of humanlike creatures made by man. They are biological constructions, in contrast to robots, which are built of metal, plastic, and electronic circuitry. Androids and cyborgs may be created by some mysterious, undefined process. Or they may be the result of processes like genetic manipulation, sophisticated surgery, cellular cultures, and the like. They may represent new mental, physical, or psychological patterns—either equal to, more than, or less than human. They are a radical innovation because traditional myths have pictured only the gods as capable of creating life. Since they are not quite human, it is unclear whether man's ethical standards should be extended to include them. Nor is it clear whether they are a blessing or a curse to man.

8. *The City*

The modern technological world is a world of cities. The countryside has been abandoned. Science fiction reflects this shift; it is "urban" literature, a type less common prior to the modern period.

9. *Utopias and Dystopias*

The traveler in time and space constantly encounters societies different from his own. He compares the two societies, making a judgment about which is superior. His travels present to him alternative ways of structuring a society, and make him sharply aware that his society is not the only possible society. This newfound cultural relativity means that he can never again complacently accept things the way they are, but must constantly create new versions of society. Those societies that portray a more ideal social organization are utopias; those that exaggerate present trends in his own society to an inhumane conclusion are dystopias. The myth of utopia and dystopia, as a device for social criticism, is one of the most powerful elements of science fiction.

10. *Apocalypse*

The apocalyptic imagination creates a vision of a radically altered future. This future world lies beyond and signifies a conclusion to time and conditions as we know them in the present. The word *apocalyptic* has both a positive and a negative charge: the visions that are unveiled may be heavenly or they may be demonic.

1

Science Fiction Myths and Their Ambiguity

Patricia Warrick

I

Every culture, primitive or modern, has its vision of the universe—a vision proposing an underlying system or pattern operant in the cosmos. Man has always held that, despite the appearance of randomness or chaos in the disparate phenomena we observe around us, some mysterious, hidden principle or force beneath the surface of things binds together the universe in a coherent whole. However transient the forms of matter may appear to be, constantly reshaping themselves in eternal restless movements, the movements have a pattern. The definition of the pattern and the process of its movement is the making of a myth.

What exactly is a myth? Most simply, it is a story; and the urge to tell stories just might be the quality unique to man that sets him apart from other life-forms on earth. To tell a story, man must be able to imagine things not immediately at hand or available to his sense perceptions. Next, he must have words to communicate those things he has imagined to someone else. Imagination and language; the teller and the listener; and finally, the tale of what happened—a collection of images that move in a patterned process. These are the elements of a story.

But a myth is not just any story; it is particular kind of story, a very special one that radiates an aura of mysterious power. Joseph Campbell in *The Hero With a Thousand Faces* suggests that "myth is the secret opening through which the inexhaustible energies of the cosmos pour into human manifestations.''

The word *myth* comes from the Greek root mμ, meaning to make a sound with the mouth. In the beginning, according to the Biblical account, God spoke; the first word is the word of the God of Creation. To the orthodox believer, myth is understood as the word of God, and an expression of the creative primal force in the cosmos. The story of creation is an important myth in every culture—how it all began, how heaven and earth were created, how man was made. The human mind cannot reach back far enough into the darkness of the past to be able to state with certainty how the universe began, or how life emerged from inanimate matter. But because man seems discontent to exist without any explanation, he imagines what seems to him to be a plausible explanation—he creates a myth.

When did the first man create the first myth? We can only speculate. It is as difficult to determine the origin of a myth as to describe the origins of language, or the beginnings of the universe. These ultimate origins seem likely forever to lie in a mysterious past we can never touch with our understanding. As far back as any culture can look into its past, it cannot get beyond its myth of creation—the story that stands for or symbolizes the mystery of the beginning.

We are proposing, for this anthology of stories, a definition of myth as a dynamic set of interrelated images representing or symbolizing an event for which we cannot give a more precise description. To make this definition workable we need to discard the idea of a myth as something that is not true. Truth or falsehood are not elements of our definition of a myth. Our use of the term comes close to the definition of a model: a concept, expressed either visually or mathematically, that seems to explain nature or some aspect of it, and to give a unity to what otherwise seems an incomprehensible and chaotic complexity. The model functions to explain the reality lying beneath the appearances our senses perceive. But the model is not the reality. It is not, therefore, true or false; it is functional or nonfunctional. As our perceptions change, and our knowledge accumulates, a once workable model may become nonfunctional.

A myth, then, is a complex of stories which a culture regards as demonstrating the inner meaning of the universe and of human life. Myths vary from one time to another, and from one place to another. Sir James Frazer in his monumental comparative study of myths, *The Golden Bough* (1922), made us aware of the rich diversity of myths present in the many cultures of the world. Later, the French anthropologist Claude Levi-Strauss, analyzing the myths from a variety of cultures, concluded that while the details of different myths may vary, they are all quite similar in their underlying structures. His structural analysis of myths suggests to him that primitive man thought just as logically as modern man, that the human brain has always operated in the same logical fashion. This is a system using the binary mode, where definitions are established by the use of opposites or contraries. Something either is or is not, it is alive or dead, it is male or female, it is mortal or immortal. Religious myths attempt to mediate between these opposites—to find a link between life and death, man and God, earth and Heaven. The traditional myths most familiar to us—Biblical and classical myths—are stories about gods, intermediary heroes, and man, and they are set in a cosmological framework.

What does a myth mean? The answer to this question is not a simple one. The meaning must be created by the mind of the listener as he encounters the shifting images and pictures contained in the mythic story. So there is not just one ''right'' meaning. The myth may be understood on several levels. On the literal level, it may be read as a story that means nothing more than just what it says—whose primary purpose is to entertain. When the story was first created, perhaps it was nothing more than a pleasant way to pass the time and provide entertainment. The art of storytelling may well be the oldest, and perhaps the most satisfying, art.

On a deeper level, myths—like dreams—may reflect insights and patterns of the psyche so deeply stored in the subconscious that they are not available to our waking consciousness through the probings of logic. The Swiss psychologist Carl Jung held that myths are original revelations of the pre-conscious psyche about happenings in this mental underworld of which we are unaware. Myths, like dreams, are psychically real, and myths might be called the collective dreams of mankind.

What is the function of a myth? It is a unifying force, working for cohesion in various ways, uniting into a community all who believe in the myth as a model of cosmic reality. Not only are the members of the believing community united with each other, but they are united with and a part of the cosmic pattern that structures the whole universe. They see their individual lives and the life of the community as having a purpose and meaning in the universe. The representative individual who acts out that meaning is the mythic hero. He is a man with special powers beyond the ordinary, and these supernatural qualities strengthen him to survive crises and challenges and—in a final apotheosis—

to unite in some way with the immortals. The listener to the mythic tale identifies with the hero, and thus vicariously shares in his journey through this mortal world and into the realm of the heavenly otherworld.

Western culture has for centuries shared two sets of myths, the classical myths of the Greeks and Romans, and the Judeo-Christian myths. They occurred first in the oral tradition, and later were written out. Literature surviving from these early civilizations is the best source for accounts of these myths. Homer's *Iliad* and *Odyssey,* Hesiod's *Theogony,* the poetry of Pindar, Aeschylus, and Virgil contain marvelous tales of gods, heroes, and men. How familiar are the stories of Zeus, Apollo, Prometheus, Dionysus, and all the heroes of the Trojan War. The Judeo-Christian myths use a monotheistic system rather than the polytheistic system of the Greeks and Romans. The Biblical literature preserves these myths, and they were retold again and again in the literature of the Middle Ages and Renaissance. No more brilliant account exists of the Garden of Eden myth than John Milton's in *Paradise Lost.*

But even while Milton was planning his great epic, based on the cosmic model of the medieval church, he was looking through the telescope in Italy, and discovering a new vision of the heavens that would necessitate the discarding of the then current model. The church accepted the Ptolemaic model of the universe. At the center was the earth; around it rotated the sun, and the planets, each in its crystalline sphere. The outer sphere contained the stars, and all the spheres were enclosed in a Prime Mover, keeping them in motion. Heavenly music arose from their rotation. Copernicus in Poland in the fifteenth century, then Galileo, and finally Newton in England, described quite a different model of the heavens. They used a clockwork mechanism, with the sun at the center and the earth merely one of the planets revolving about it. Modern science was born with these men in the sixteenth and seventeenth centuries. The scientific mind aimed at uniting apparently disparate phenomena by defining underlying natural laws that controlled these phenomena. In this drive to unify, the Renaissance scientist demonstrated the same impulse as had earlier myth makers.

The scientific imagination has continued to work to build models explaining the reality that lies beneath the surface appearance of things. The good scientist does more than merely collect facts. He searches for a unity in hidden likenesses between facts that superficially may seem to bear little relationship. He attempts to establish that order exists in the universe, and he builds a model to exemplify his understanding of that order. The model may be a little planetary system—as is the model of the atom; or it may be a mathematical model. What is important is to understand that it works the same way as the model we have discussed earlier, only in that discussion we used the term *myth*. Myth or model function the same way. It is a design created to explain the workings of a reality we believe to be present, but one that is not available to us for observation through our ordinary sense perceptions.

Newton's scientific model of the universe as a giant clockwork or mechanism whose movements were regulated by a few natural laws turned out to be a very productive model in terms of predicting and controlling nature. It was a cause-effect model and while it gave no clues as to the why of the universe, it was effective in explaining the how of things. Theoretical science expanded from its beginnings in astronomy and physics to incorporate chemistry, botany, geology, and biology. Next, the inventor and the engineer appeared, and technology produced the Industrial Revolution in the late eighteenth and nineteenth centuries. Our modern world was born, and it is a world radically different from the pastoral world of classical and medieval times. Science has given us new models to use in understanding: from the swirling galaxies in the heavens, to the finest subatomic particles. It has been willing to discard one model if it found another to be more functional.

II

Science fiction, first appearing in the nineteenth century, is a literary form created by the imagination as it attempted to relate man to the new models of the universe described by science, and to the new possibilities suggested by technology. What kinds of patterns appear in this new literature? How does it picture man relating to the physical universe as science models it? The germinal idea for this anthology grew from raising such questions. How does technological man in the twentieth century see himself in his relationships with the cosmos? If the mythopoeic—i.e., myth-making faculty—is inherent in man's thinking process, how does it manifest itself in science fiction? In what ways are the recurring patterns and structures in science fiction like and unlike the myths embodied in the literature of earlier ages? Can we define a set of mythic patterns unique to science fiction, and therefore reflective of technological man's world view?

Because the body of science fiction literature is large, and because it is wide ranging, since it need not limit itself to any presently existing reality, the task of defining mythic patterns or themes is not an easy one. We do not claim that those presented in this anthology are exhaustive. But nineteen science fiction writers and critics, discussing the questions together, did agree that the nine patterns presented here are major myths in science fiction. In a rich variety of permutations, they occur again and again. Some of the myths contain elements of the old Biblical and classical myths because technological man is still natural man, and he does not discard in a mere century views of himself and his place in nature that he has held for thousands of years. But science has given man a new model of the universe, and with technology he is beginning to create a new artificial environment where he now increasingly lives, so some of the myths are new and unique to the vision of man that science fiction presents.

The radical element in all the myths is their setting in the future. They describe a future time that will be different from the present in at least one significant way. In contrast, traditional myths typically are set outside time; they reflect all that is conceived to be eternal and unchanging in the universe; they propose that the order of the world and man's destiny are immutable. Although surface appearances may suggest everything is moving and changing, there is undergirding the universe a prime mover who is unchanging. But in the eighteenth and nineteenth centuries, the concept of evolution replaced that timeless view with an accelerating sense of time—from cosmic time through geological and biological, to human time. Contemporary man is sharply aware that time's arrow moves irreversibly into the future—a future that promises him only one certainty: it will be different from the present and the past. Time is no longer seen as cyclic and repetitive.

The unknown tends always to be threatening to man. He needs to find a way to cope with the novel. The science fiction imagination comes to terms with the uncertainty of the future by making up stories about what it might be like when it arrives. In the same vein, the imagination comes to terms with the vast cosmic spaces that dwarf man to a particle by making up stories about man successfully adventuring through those endless spaces sprinkled with stars and galaxies.

It seems safe to assume that in previous myths both the teller and the listener believed the story was true. In contrast, the participants in a science fiction myth are very conscious that the story is not true; however, they do believe that in the future it just might be true—for the good science fiction story always has an aura of plausibility about it. It does not violate known scientific concepts. The working of the science fiction imagination is not dissimilar to that of the modern scientist, who knows he can never transcend the human reference point in studying the universe, and so he will never really know *truth,* whatever that may be. He can only say that our experience up to the present is best represented by a particular model. Tomorrow's experience may require a new model. Quantum and relativity physics in the early twentieth century proposed new models subsuming those of Newtonian physics. This revolutionary development made it apparent to scientists that they deal with models describing reality and not with ultimate truths, as Thomas Kuhn notes in *The Structure of Scientific Revolutions* (1962). The scientist is willing to discard one model for another if he finds the new model works better. The science fiction imagination designs all the possible models it can conceive that describe how the future might be. And because this imagination has always been very inventive and fertile, a rich abundance of futures has been created.

The science fiction myths have another quality, in addition to being set in future time, that contrasts with traditional myths. These earlier myths tend to be very clear in their meanings and their concepts of good and evil. The devil may try to disguise himself, but down underneath, his qualities are known to all. The myth defines with authority what is good and evil in the universe. But science fiction myths have a quality of ambiguity about them. They are much less certain of what man's relationship to the natural world around him and to the cosmos is. Good and evil can no longer be easily labeled. This uncertainty may be a reflection of the fact that contemporary man is in transition from one cultural mode to another—from a pastoral society to an industrial and then postindustrial or information society. With this shift in cultural patterns, his values are also being transformed. But the quality of ambiguity may also reflect the awareness of science that certainty is not possible in describing the matter that comprises the material world. Max Planck in 1900 discovered that energy, like matter, is not continuous, but appears always in packets, or quanta, of definite size. In the next decade it became increasingly clear that—contrary to the earlier mechanistic view of physics—there is no way of describing the present and the future of tiny particles and events with certainty. Werner Heisenberg in 1927 formally stated this in his principle of uncertainty. Heisenberg showed that the more accurately we try to measure the speed of a particle, the less certain we will be of its precise position. For instance, we can measure either the speed of an electron accurately or its position, but not both. Therefore we can never predict the future of the particle with complete certainty.

We are coming to understand that nature is not a machine at which we peek, but a network of interconnected happenings that extend through the whole universe. Man is enmeshed in that network, and his act of observation is an event that effects a change: It alters the matter he observes from the way it would have behaved without his act of observation. Further, we begin to realize that because we are among the parts of the universal network, we cannot with certainty understand the whole. Uncertainty and a resultant ambiguity in any statement reflect the reality of man's position in a mysterious universe forever in process. The rich array of shifting science fiction images of the future catch and model that uncertainty.

Poul Anderson's "Goat Song," which follows, provides a powerful metaphor of man's ambivalent attitude toward technology and progress. The narrator of the tale is a contemporary Orpheus, singing for his dead love in a technological city world controlled by an underground computer named SUM. He recalls man's primitive Dionysian world of frenzied dreams and passions before the Apollonian computer brought order, reason, and peace to mankind. He believes man's ancient myths hold more truth than the machine's mathematics. The reader may sympathize with the song he sings; but yet, who is ready to abandon the benefits of science and technology and really return to a primitive existence in nature?

BIBLIOGRAPHY

History and Criticism

(No studies of individual authors have been included.)

Aldiss, Brain, *Billion Year Spree: The True History of Science Fiction,* 1973 (Doubleday)

Amis, Kingsely, *New Maps of Hell,* 1960 (Arno)

Bailey, James Osler, *Pilgrims through Space and Time: Trends and Patterns in Science and Utopian Fiction,* 1974 (Greenwood)

Barron, Neil, *Anatomy of Wonder: Science Fiction,* 1976 (Bowker)

Clareson, Thomas D., ed., *Many Futures, Many Worlds,* 1976 (Kent State University Press)

————, *SF: The Other Side of Realism; Essays on Modern Fantasy and Science Fiction,* 1972 (Bowling Green University Press)

Gunn, James E., *Alternate Worlds: The Illustrated History of Science Fiction,* 1975 (Prentice-Hall)

Hillegas, Mark Robert, *The Future as Nightmare: H. G. Wells and the Anti-Utopians,* 1967 (Southern Illinois University Press)

Ketterer, David, *New Worlds for Old: The Apocalyptic Imagination, Science Fiction, and American Literature,* 1974 (Anchor)

Rose, Mark, ed. *Science Fiction; A Collection of Critical Essays,* 1976 (Prentice-Hall)

Walsh, Chad, *From Utopia to Nightmare,* 1962 (Greenwood)

Wollheim, Donald, *The Universe Makers; Science Fiction Today,* 1971 (Harper & Row)

Goat Song

Poul Anderson

Three women: one is dead; one is alive; One is both and neither, and will never live and never die, being immortal in SUM.

On a hill above that valley through which runs the highroad, I await Her passage. Frost came early this year, and the grasses have paled. Otherwise the slope is begrown with blackberry bushes that have been harvested by men and birds, leaving only briars, and with certain apple trees. They are very old, those trees, survivors of an orchard raised by generations which none but SUM now remembers (I can see a few fragments of wall thrusting above the brambles)—scattered crazily over the hillside and as crazily gnarled. A little fruit remains on them. Chill across my skin, a gust shakes loose an apple. I hear it knock on the earth, another stroke of some eternal clock. The shrubs whisper to the wind.

Elsewhere the ridges around me are wooded, afire with scarlets, brasses, bronzes. The sky is huge, the westering sun wan-bright. The valley is filling with a deeper blue, a haze whose slight smokiness touches my nostrils. This is Indian summer, the funeral pyre of the year.

There have been other seasons. There have been other lifetimes, before mine and hers; and in those days they had words to sing with. We still allow ourselves music, though, and I have spent much time planting melodies around my rediscovered words. *"In the greenest growth of the Maytime—"* I unsling the harp on my back, and tune it afresh, and sing to her, straight into autumn and the waning day.

> "—You came, and the sun came after,
> And the green grew golden above;
> And the flag-flowers lightened with laughter,
> And the meadowsweet shook with love."

A footfall stirs the grasses, quite gently, and the woman says, trying to chuckle, "Why, thank you."

Once, so soon after my one's death that I was still dazed by it, I stood in the home that had been ours. This was on the hundred and first floor of a most desirable building. After dark the city flamed for us, blinked, glittered, flung immense sheets of radiance forth like banners. Nothing but SUM could have controlled the firefly dance of a million aircars among the towers: or, for that matter, have maintained the entire city, from nuclear power plants through automated factories, physical and economic distribution networks, sanitation, repair, services, education, cultures, order, everything as one immune immortal organism. We had gloried in belonging to this as well as to each other.

But that night I told the kitchen to throw the dinner it had made for me down the waste chute, and ground under my heel the chemical consolations which the medicine cabinet extended to me, and kicked the cleaner as it picked up the mess, and ordered the lights not to go on, anywhere in our suite. I stood by the vie-Wall, looking out across megalopolis, and it was tawdry. In my hands I had a little clay figure she had fashioned herself. I turned it over and over and over.

But I had forgotten to forbid the door to admit visitors. It recognized this woman and opened for her. She had come with the kindly intention of teasing me out of a mood that seemed to her unnatural. I heard her enter, and looked around through the gloom. She had almost the same height as my girl did, and her hair chanced to be bound in a way that my girl often favored, and the figurine dropped from my grasp and shattered, because for an instant I thought she was my girl. Since then I have been hard put not to hate Thrakia.

This evening, even without so much sundown light, I would not make that mistake. Nothing but the silvery bracelet about her left wrist bespeaks the past we share. She is in wildcountry garb: boots, kilt of true fur and belt of true leather, knife at hip and rifle slung on shoulder.

Her locks are matted and snarled, her skin brown from weeks of weather; scratches and smudges show beneath the fantastic zigzags she has painted in many colors on herself. She wears a necklace of bird skulls.

Now that one who is dead was, in her own way, more a child of trees and horizons than Thrakia's followers. She was so much at home in the open that she had no need to put off clothes or cleanliness, reason or gentleness, when we sickened of the cities and went forth beyond them. From this trait I got many of the names I bestowed on her, such as Wood's Colt or Fallow Hind or, from my prowlings among ancient books, Dryad and Elven. (She liked me to choose her names, and this pleasure had no end, because she was inexhaustible.)

I let my harpstring ring into silence. Turning about, I say to Thrakia, "I wasn't singing for you. Not for anyone. Leave me alone."

She draws a breath. The wind ruffles her hair and brings me an odor of her: not female sweetness, but fear. She clenches her fists and says, "You're crazy."

"Wherever did you find a meaningful word like that?" I gibe; for my own pain and—to be truthful—my own fear must strike out at something, and here she stands. "Aren't you content any longer with 'untranquil' or 'disequilibrated'?"

"I got it from you," she says defiantly, "you and your damned archaic songs. There's another word, 'damned.' And how it suits you! When are you going to stop this morbidity?"

"And commit myself to a clinic and have my brain laundered nice and sanitary? Not soon, darling." I use *that* last word aforethought, but she cannot know what scorn and sadness are in it for me, who knows that once it could also have been a name for my girl. The official grammar and pronunciation of language is as frozen as every other aspect of our civilization, thanks to electronic recording and neuronic teaching; but meanings shift and glide about like subtle serpents. (O adder that stung my Foalfoot!)

I shrug and say in my driest, most city-technological voice, "Actually, I'm the practical, nonmorbid one. Instead of running away from my emotions—via drugs, or neuroadjustment, or playing at savagery like you, for that matter—I'm about to implement a concrete plan for getting back the person who made me happy."

"By disturbing Her on Her way home?"

"Anyone has the right to petition the Dark Queen while She's abroad on Earth."

"But this is past the proper time—"

"No law's involved, just custom. People are afraid to meet Her outside a crowd, a town, bright flat lights. They won't admit it, but they are. So I came here precisely not to be part of a queue. I don't want to speak into a recorder for subsequent computer analysis of my words. How could I be sure She was listening? I want to meet Her as myself, a unique being, and look in Her eyes while I make my prayer.''

Thrakia chokes a little. "She'll be angry."

"Is She able to be angry, anymore?"

"I . . . I don't know. What you mean to ask for is so impossible, though. So absurd. That SUM should give you back your girl. You know It never makes exceptions."

"Isn't She Herself an exception?"

"That's different. You're being silly. SUM has to have a, well, a direct human liaison. Emotional and cultural feedback, as well as statistics. How else can It govern rationally? And She must have been chosen out of the whole world. Your girl, what was she? Nobody!"

"To me, she was everybody."

"You—" Thrakia catches her lip in her teeth. One hand reaches out and closes on my bare forearm, a hard hot touch, the grimy fingernails biting. When I make no response, she lets go and stares at the ground. A V of outbound geese passes overhead. Their cries come shrill through the wind, which is loudening in the forest.

"Well," she says, "you are special. You always were. You went to space and came back, with the Great Captain. You're maybe the only man alive who understands about the ancients. And your singing, yes, you don't really entertain; your songs trouble people and can't be forgotten. So maybe She will listen to you. But SUM won't. It can't give special resurrections. Once that was done, a single time, wouldn't it have to be done for everybody? The dead would overrun the living."

"Not necessarily," I say. "In any event, I mean to try."

"Why can't you wait for the promised time? Surely, then, SUM will recreate you two in the same generation."

"I'd have to live out this life, at least, without her," I say, looking away also, down to the highroad which shines through shadow like death's snake, the length of the valley. "Besides, how do you know there ever will be any resurrections? We have only a promise. No, less than that policy."

She gasps, steps back, raises her hands as if to fend me off. Her soul bracelet casts light into my eyes. I recognize an embryo exorcism. She lacks ritual; every "superstition" was patiently scrubbed out of our metal-and-energy world, long ago. But if she has no word for it, no concept, nevertheless she recoils from blasphemy.

So I say, wearily, not wanting an argument, wanting only to wait here alone: "Never mind. There could be some natural catastrophe, like a giant asteroid striking, that wiped out the system before conditions had become right for resurrections to commence."

"That's impossible," she says, almost frantic. "The homeostats, the repair functions—"

"All right, call it a vanishingly unlikely theoretical contingency. Let's declare that I'm so selfish I want Swallow Wing back now, in this life of mine, and don't give a curse whether that'll be fair to the rest of you."

You won't care either, anyway, I think. None of you. You don't grieve. It is your own precious private consciousness that you wish to preserve; no one else is close enough to you to matter very much. Would you believe me if I told you I am quite prepared to offer SUM my own death in exchange for It releasing Blossom-in-the-Sun?

I don't speak that thought, which would be cruel, nor repeat what is crueler: my fear that SUM lies, that the dead never will be disgorged. For (I am not the All-Controller; I think not with vacuum and negative energy levels but with ordinary Earth-begotten molecules; yet I can reason somewhat dispassionately, being disillusioned) consider—

The object of the game is to maintain a society stable, just, and sane. This requires satisfaction not only of somatic, but of symbolic and instinctual needs. Thus children must be allowed to come into being. The minimum number per generation is equal to the maximum: that number which will maintain a constant population.

It is also desirable to remove the fear of death from men. Hence the promise: At such time as it is socially feasible, SUM will begin to refashion us, with our complete memories but in the pride of our youth. This can be done over and over, life after life across the millennia. So death is, indeed, a sleep.

*—in that sleep of death, what dreams may come—*No. I myself dare not dwell on this. I ask merely, privately: Just when and how does SUM expect conditions (in a stabilized society, mind you) to have become so different from today's that the reborn can, in their millions, safely be welcomed back?

I see no reason why SUM should not lie to us. We, too, are objects in the world that It manipulates.

"We've quarreled about this before, Thrakia," I sigh. "Often. Why do you bother?"

"I wish I knew," she answers low. Half to herself, she goes on: "Of course I want to copulate with you. You must be good, the way that girl used to follow you about with her eyes, and smile when she touched your hand, and— But you can't be better than everyone else. That's unreasonable. There are only so many possible ways. So why do I care if you wrap yourself up in silence and go off alone? Is it that that makes you a challenge?"

"You think too much," I say. "Even here. You're a pretend primitive. You visit wildcountry to 'slake inborn atavistic impulses . . .' but you can't dismantle that computer inside yourself and simply feel, simply be."

She bristles. I touched a nerve there. Looking past her, along the ridge of fiery maple and sumac, brassy elm and great dun oak, I see others emerge from beneath the trees. Women exclusively, her followers, as unkempt as she; one has a brace of ducks lashed to her waist, and their blood has trickled down her thigh and dried black. For this movement, this unadmitted mystique has become Thrakia's by now: that not only men should forsake the easy routine and the easy pleasure of the cities, and become again, for a few weeks each year, the carnivores who begot our species; women too should seek out starkness, the better to appreciate civilization when they return.

I feel a moment's unease. We are in no park, with laid out trails and campground services. We are in wildcountry. Not many men come here, ever, and still fewer women; for the region is, literally, beyond the law. No deed done here is punishable. We are told that this helps consolidate society, as the most violent among us may thus vent their passions. But I have spent much time in wildcountry since my Morning Star went out—myself in quest of nothing but solitude—and I have watched what happens through eyes that have also read anthropology and history. Institutions are developing; ceremonies, tribalisms, acts of blood and cruelty and acts elsewhere called unnatural are becoming more elaborate and more expected every year. Then the practitioners go home to their cities and honestly believe they have been enjoying fresh air, exercise, and good tension-releasing fun.

Let her get angry enough and Thrakia can call knives to her aid.

Wherefore I make myself lay both hands on her shoulders, and meet the tormented gaze, and say most gently, "I'm sorry. I know you mean well. You're afraid She will be annoyed and bring misfortune on your people."

Thrakia gulps. "No," she whispers. "That wouldn't be logical. But I'm afraid of what might happen to you. And then—" Suddenly she throws herself against me. I feel arms, breasts, belly press through my tunic, and smell meadows in her hair and musk in her mouth. "You'd be gone!" she wails. "Then who'd sing to us?"

"Why, the planet's crawling with entertainers," I stammer.

"You're more than that," she says. "So much more. I don't like what you sing, not really—and what you've sung since that stupid girl died, oh, meaningless, horrible—but, I don't know why, I *want* you to trouble me."

Awkward, I pat her back. The sun now stands very little above the treetops. Its rays slant interminably through the booming, frosting air. I shiver and wonder what to do.

A sound rescues me. It comes off one end of the valley below us, where further view is blocked off by two cliffs; it thunders deep in our ears and rolls through the earth into our bones. We have heard that sound in the cities, and been glad to have walls and lights and multitudes around us. Now we are alone with it, the noise of Her chariot.

The women shriek, I hear them faintly across wind and rumble and my own pulse, and they vanish into the woods. They will seek their camp, dress warmly, build enormous fires; presently they will eat their ecstatics, and rumors are uneasy about what they do after that.

Thrakia seizes my left wrist, above the soul bracelet, and hauls. "Harper, come with me!" she pleads. I break loose from her and stride down the hill toward the road. A scream follows me for a moment.

Light still dwells in the sky and on the ridges, but as I descend into that narrow valley, I enter dusk, and it thickens. Indistinct bramble bushes whicker where I brush them, and claw back at me. I feel the occasional scratch on my legs, the tug as my garment is snagged, the chill that I breathe, but dimly. My perceived-outer-reality is overpowered by the rushing of Her chariot and my blood. My inner-universe is fear, yes, but exaltation too, a drunkenness which sharpens instead of dulling the senses, a psychedelia which opens the reasoning mind as well as the emotions; I have gone beyond myself, I am embodied purpose. Not out of need for comfort, but to voice what Is, I return to words whose speaker rests centuries dust, and lend them my own music. I sing:

> "—Gold is my heart, and the world's golden.
> And one peak tipped with light;
> And the air lies still above the hill
> With the first fear of night;
>
> Till mystery down the soundless valley
> Thunders, and dark is here;
> And the wind blows, and the light goes,
> And the night is full of fear.

And I know one night, on some far height,
In the tongue I never knew,
I yet shall hear the tidings clear.

They'll call the news from hill to hill,
Dark and uncomforted,
Earth and sky and the winds; and I
Shall know that you are dead.—''

But I have reached the valley floor, and She has come in sight. Her chariot is unlit, for radar eyes and inertial guides need no lamps, nor sun nor stars. Wheelless, the steel tear rides on its own roar and thrust of air. The pace is not great, far less than any of our mortals' vehicles are wont to take. Men say the Dark Queen rides thus slowly in order that She may perceive with Her own senses and so be the better prepared to counsel SUM. But now Her annual round is finished; She is homeward bound; until spring She will dwell with It Which is our lord. Why does She not hasten tonight?

Because Death has never a need of haste? I wonder. And as I step into the middle of the road, certain lines from the yet more ancient past rise tremendous within me, and I strike my harp and chant them louder than the approaching car:

"I that in heill was and gladness
Am trublit now with great sickness
And feblit with infirmitie:—
Timor mortis conturbat me.''

The car detects me and howls a warning. I hold my ground. The car could swing around; the road is wide, and in any event a smooth surface is not absolutely necessary. But I hope, I believe that She will be aware of an obstacle in Her path, and tune in Her various amplifiers, and find me abnormal enough to stop for. Who, in SUM's world—who, even among the explorers that It has sent beyond in Its unappeasable hunger for data—would stand in a cold wildcountry dusk and shout while his harp snarls:

"Our presence here is all vain glory,
This fals world is but transitory,
The flesh is bruckle, the Feynd is slee:—

The state of man does change and vary,
Now sound, now sick, now blyth, now sary,
Now dansand mirry, now like to die:—

No state in Erd here standis sicker;
As with the wynd wavis the wicker
So wannis this world's vanitie:—
Timor mortis conturbat me.—?''

The car draws alongside and sinks to the ground. I let my strings die
away into the wind. The sky overhead and in the west is gray-purple;
eastward it is quite dark and a few early stars peer forth. Here, down in
the valley, shadows are heavy and I cannot see very well.

The canopy slides back. She stands erect in the chariot, thus loom-
ing over me. Her robe and cloak are black, fluttering like restless
wings; beneath the cowl Her face is a white blur. I have seen it before,
under full light, and in how many thousands of pictures; but at this
hour I cannot call it back to my mind, not entirely. I list sharp-
sculptured profile and pale lips, sable hair and long green eyes, but
these are nothing more than words.

"What are you doing?" She has a lovely low voice; but is it, as, oh,
how rarely since SUM took Her to Itself, is it the least shaken? "What
is that you were singing?"

My answer comes so strong that my skull resonates, for I am borne
higher and higher on my tide. "Lady of Ours, I have a petition."

"Why did you not bring it before Me when I walked among men?
Tonight I am homebound. You must wait till I ride forth with the new
year."

"Lady of Ours, neither You nor I would wish living ears to hear
what I have to say."

She regards me for a long while. Do I indeed sense fear also in Her?
(Surely not of me. Her chariot is armed and armored, and would react
with machine speed to protect Her should I offer violence. And should
I somehow, incredibly, kill Her, or wound Her beyond chemosurgical
repair, She of all beings has no need to doubt death. The ordinary
bracelet cries with quite sufficient radio loudness to be heard by more
than one thanatic station, when we die; and in that shielding the soul
can scarcely be damaged before the Winged Heels arrive to bear it off
to SUM. Surely the Dark Queen's circlet can call still further, and is
still better insulated, than any mortal's. And She will most absolutely
be recreated. She has been, again and again; death and rebirth every
seven years keep Her eternally young in the service of SUM. I have
never been able to find out when She was first born.)

Fear, perhaps, of what I have sung and what I might speak?

At last She says—I can scarcely hear through the gusts and creak-
ings in the trees—"Give me the Ring, then."

The dwarf robot which stands by Her throne when She sits among men appears beside Her and extends the massive dull-silver circle to me. I place my left arm within, so that my soul is enclosed. The tablet on the upper surface of the Ring, which looks so much like a jewel, slants away from me; I cannot read what flashes onto the bezel. But the faint glow picks Her features out of murk as She bends to look.

Of course, I tell myself, the actual soul is not scanned. That would take too long. Probably the bracelet which contains the soul has an identification code built in. The Ring sends this to an appropriate part of SUM, Which instantly sends back what is recorded under that code. I hope there is nothing more to it. SUM has not seen fit to tell us.

"What do you call yourself at the moment?" She asks.

A current of bitterness crosses my tide. "Lady of Ours, why should You care? Is not my real name the number I got when I was allowed to be born?"

Calm descends once more upon Her. "If I am to evaluate properly what you say, I must know more about you than these few official data. Name indicates mood."

I too feel unshaken again, my tide running so strong and smooth that I might not know I was moving did I not see time recede behind me. "Lady of Ours, I cannot give You a fair answer. In this past year I have not troubled with names, or with much of anything else. But some people who knew me from earlier days call me Harper."

"What do you do besides make that sinister music?"

"These days, nothing, Lady of Ours. I've money to live out my life, if I eat sparingly and keep no home. Often I am fed and housed for the sake of my songs."

"What you sang is unlike anything I have heared since—" Anew, briefly, that robot serenity is shaken. "Since before the world was stabilized. You should not wake dead symbols, Harper. They walk through men's dreams."

"Is that bad?"

"Yes. The dreams become nightmares. Remember: mankind, every man who ever lived, was insane before SUM brought order, reason, and peace."

"Well, then," I say, "I will cease and desist if I may have my own dead wakened for me."

She stiffens. The tablet goes out. I withdraw my arm and the Ring is stored away by Her servant. So again She is faceless, beneath flickering stars, here at the bottom of this shadowed valley. Her voice falls cold as the air: "No one can be brought back to life before Resurrection Time is ripe."

I do not say, "What about You?" for that would be vicious. What did She think, how did She weep, when SUM chose Her of all the young on Earth? What does She endure in Her centuries? I dare not imagine.

Instead, I smite my harp and sing, quietly this time:

> "Strew on her roses, roses,
> And never a spray of yew.
> In quiet she reposes:
> Ah! would that I did too.
>
> "Her cabin'd, ample Spirit
> It flutter'd and fail'd for breath.
> To-night it doth inherit
> The vasty hall of Death."

I know why my songs strike so hard: because they bear dreads and passions that no one is used to—that most of us hardly know could exist—in SUM's ordered universe. But I had not the courage to hope She would be as torn by them as I see. Has She not lived with more darkness and terror than the ancients could conceive? She calls, "Who has died?"

"She had many names, Lady of Ours," I say. "None was beautiful enough. I can tell You her number, though."

"Your daughter? I . . . sometimes I am asked if a dead child cannot be brought back. Not often, anymore, when they go so soon to the crèche. But sometimes. I tell the mother she may have a new one; but if ever We started recreating dead infants, at what age level could We stop?"

"No, this was my woman."

"Impossible!" Her tone seeks to be not unkindly but is, instead, well-nigh frantic. "You will have no trouble finding others. You are handsome, and your psyche is, is, is extraordinary. It burns like Lucifer."

"Do You remember the name Lucifer, Lady of Ours?" I pounce. "Then You are old indeed. So old that You must also remember how a man might desire only one woman, but her above the whole world and heaven."

She tries to defend Herself with a jeer: "Was that mutual, Harper? I know more of mankind than you do, and surely I am the last chaste woman in existence."

"Now that she is gone, Lady, yes, perhaps You are. But we— Do You know how she died? We had gone to a wildcountry area. A man saw her, alone, while I was off hunting gem rocks to make her a necklace. He approached her. She refused him. He threatened force. She fled. This was desert land, viper land, and she was barefoot. One of them bit her. I did not find her till hours later. By then the poison and the unshaded sun— She died quite soon after she told me what had happened and that she loved me. I could not get her body to chemosurgery in time for normal revival procedures. I had to let them cremate her and take her soul away to SUM.''

''What right have you to demand her back, when no one else can be given their own?''

''The right that I love her, and she loves me. We are more necessary to each other than sun or moon. I do not think You could find another two people of whom this is so, Lady. And is not everyone entitled to claim what is necessary to his life? How else can society be kept whole?''

''You are being fantastic,'' She says thinly. ''Let me go.''

''No, Lady. I am speaking sober truth. But poor plain words won't serve me. I sing to You because then maybe You will understand.'' And I strike my harp anew, but it is more to her than Her that I sing.

> ''If I had thought thou couldst have died,
> I might not weep for thee;
> But I forgot, when by thy side,
> That thou couldst mortal be:
> It never through my mind had past
> The time would e'er be o'er,
> And on thee should look my last,
> And thou shouldst smile no more!''

''I cannot—'' She falters. ''I did not know such feelings existed any longer.''

''Now You do, Lady of Ours. And is that not an important datum for SUM?''

''Yes. If true.'' Abruptly She leans toward me. I see Her shudder in the murk, under the flapping cloak, and hear Her jaws clatter with cold. ''I cannot linger here. But ride with Me. Sing to Me. I think I can bear it.''

So much have I scarcely expected. But my destiny is upon me. I mount into the chariot. The canopy slides shut and we proceed.

The main cabin encloses us. Behind its rear door must be facilities for Her living on Earth; this is a big vehicle. But here is little except curved panels. They are true wood of different comely grains; so She also needs periodic escape from our machine existence, does She?

Furnishing is scant and austere. The only sound is our passage, muffled to a murmur for us; and, because their photomultipliers are not activated, the scanners show nothing outside but night. We huddle close to a glower, hands extended toward its fieriness. Our shoulders brush, our bare arms, Her skin is soft and Her hair falls loose over the thrown-back cowl, smelling of the summer which is dead. What, is She still human?

After a timeless time, She says, not yet looking at me: "The thing you sang, there on the highroad as I came near—I do not remember it. Not even from the years before I became what I am."

"It is older than SUM," I answer, "and its truth will outlive It."

"Truth?" I see Her tense Herself. "Sing me the rest."

My fingers are no longer too numb to call forth chords.

> "—Unto the Death gois all Estatis,
> Princis, Prelattis, and Potestatis,
> Baith rich and poor of all degree:—
>
> He takis the knichtis in to the field
> Enarmit under helm and scheild;
> Victor he is at all mellie:—
>
> That strong unmerciful tyrand
> Takis, on the motheris breast sowkand,
> The babe full of benignitie:—
>
> He takis the campion in the stour,
> The captain closit in the tour,
> The ladie in bout full of bewtie:—
>
> He sparis no lord for his piscence,
> Na clerk for his intelligence;
> His awful straik may no man flee:—
> Timor mortis conturbat me."

She breaks me off, clapping hands to ears and half shrieking, "No!"

I, grown unmerciful, pursue Her: "You understand now, do You not? You are not eternal either. SUM isn't. Not Earth, not Sun, not stars. We hid from the truth. Every one of us. I too, until I lost the one thing which made everything make sense. Then I had nothing left to lose, and could look with clear eyes. And what I saw was Death."

"Get out! Let Me alone!"

"I will not let the whole world alone, Queen, until I get her back. Give me her again, and I'll believe in SUM again. I'll praise It till men dance for joy to hear Its name."

She challenges me with wildcat eyes. "Do you think such matters to It?"

"Well"—I shrug—"songs could be useful. They could help achieve the great objective sooner. Whatever that is. 'Optimization of total human activity'—wasn't that the program? I don't know if it still is. SUM has been adding to Itself so long. I doubt if You Yourself understand Its purposes, Lady of Ours."

"Don't speak as if It were alive," She says harshly. "It is a computer-effector complex. Nothing more."

"Are You certain?"

"I— Yes. It thinks, more widely and deeply than any human ever did or could; but It is not alive, not aware, It has no consciousness. That is one reason why It decided It needed Me."

"Be that as it may, Lady," I tell Her, "the ultimate result, whatever It finally does with us, lies far in the future. At present I care about that; I worry; I resent our loss of self-determination. But that's because only such abstractions are left to me. Give me back my Lightfoot, and she, not the distant future, will be my concern. I'll be grateful, honestly grateful, and You Two will know it from the songs I then choose to sing. Which, as I said, might be helpful to It."

"You are unbelievably insolent," She says without force.

"No, Lady, just desperate," I say.

The ghost of a smile touches Her lips. She leans back, and murmurs, "Well, I'll take you there. What happens then, you realize, lies outside My power. My observations, My recommendations, are nothing but a few items to take into account, among billions. However . . . we have a long way to travel this night. Give Me what data you think will help you, Harper."

I do not finish the Lament. Nor do I dwell in any other fashion on grief. Instead, as the hours pass, I call upon those who dealt with the joy (not the fun, not the short delirium, but the joy) that man and woman might once have of each other.

Knowing where we are bound, I too need such comfort.

And the night deepens, and the leagues fall behind us, and finally we are beyond habitation, beyond wildcountry, in the land where life never comes. By crooked moon and waning starlight I see the plain of concrete and iron, the missiles and energy projectors crouched like beasts, the robot aircraft wheeling aloft: and the lines, the relay towers, the scuttling beetle-shaped carriers, that whole transcendent nerve-blood-sinew by which SUM knows and orders the world. For all the flitting about, for all the forces which seethe, here is altogether still.

The wind itself seems to have frozen to death. Hoarfrost is gray on the steel shapes. Ahead of us, tiered and mountainous, begins to appear the castle of SUM.

She Who rides with me does not give sign of noticing that my songs have died in my throat. What humanness She showed is departing; Her face is cold and shut; her voice bears a ring of metal; She looks straight ahead. But She does speak to me for a little while yet:

"Do you understand what is going to happen? For the next half year I will be linked with SUM, integral, another component of It. I suppose you will see Me, but that will merely be My flesh. What speaks to you will be SUM."

"I know." The words must be forced forth. My coming this far is more triumph than any man in creation before me has won; and I am here to do battle for my Dancer-on-Moonglades; but nonetheless my heart shakes me, and is loud in my skull, and my sweat stinks.

I manage, though, to add: "You *will* be a part of It, Lady of Ours. That gives me hope."

For an instant She turns to me, and lays Her hand across mine, and something makes Her again so young and untaken that I almost forget the girl who died; and She whispers, "If you knew how I hope!"

The instant is gone, and I am alone among machines.

We must stop before the castle gate. The wall looms sheer above, so high and high that it seems to be toppling upon me against the westward march of the stars, so black and black that it does not only drink down every light, it radiates blindness. Challenge and response quiver on electronic bands I cannot sense. The outer-guardian parts of It have perceived a mortal aboard this craft. A missile launcher swings about to aim its three serpents at me. But the Dark Queen answers—She does not trouble to be peremptory—and the castle opens its jaws for us.

We descend. Once, I think, we cross a river. I hear a rushing and hollow echoing and see droplets glitter where they are cast onto the viewports and outlined against dark. They vanish at once: liquid hydrogen, perhaps, to keep certain parts near absolute zero?

Much later we stop and the canopy slides back. I rise with Her. We are in a room, or cavern, of which I can see nothing, for there is no light except a dull bluish phosphorescence which streams from every solid object, also from Her flesh and mine. But I judge the chamber is enormous, for a sound of great machines at work comes very remotely, as if heard through dream, while our own voices are swallowed up by distance. Air is pumped through, neither warm nor cold, totally without odor, a dead wind.

We descend to the floor. She stands before me, hands crossed on breast, eyes half shut beneath the cowl and not looking at me nor away from me. ''Do what you are told, Harper,'' She says in a voice that has never an overtone, ''precisely as you are told.'' She turns and departs at an even pace. I watch Her go until I can no longer tell Her luminosity from the formless swirlings within my own eyeballs.

A claw plucks my tunic. I look down and am surprised to see that the dwarf robot has been waiting for me this whole time. How long a time that was, I cannot tell.

Its squat form leads me in another direction. Weariness crawls upward through me, my feet stumble, my lips tingle, lids are weighted and muscles have each their separate aches. Now and then I feel a jag of fear, but dully. When the robot indicates *Lie down here,* I am grateful.

The box fits me well. I let various wires be attached to me, various needles be injected which lead into tubes. I pay little attention to the machines which cluster and murmur around me. The robot goes away. I sink into blessed darkness.

I wake renewed in body. A kind of shell seems to have grown between my forebrain and the old animal parts. Far away I can feel the horror and hear the screaming and thrashing of my instincts; but awareness is chill, calm, logical. I have also a feeling that I slept for weeks, months, while leaves blew loose and snow fell on the upper world. But this may be wrong, and in no case does it matter. I am about to be judged by SUM.

The little faceless robot leads me off, through murmurous black corridors where the dead wind blows. I unsling my harp and clutch it to me, my sole friend and weapon. So the tranquillity of the reasoning mind which has been decreed for me cannot be absolute. I decide that It simply does not want to be bothered by anguish. (No; wrong; nothing so humanlike; It has no desires; beneath that power to reason is nullity.)

At length a wall opens for us and we enter a room where She sits enthroned. The self-radiation of metal and flesh is not apparent here, for light is provided, a featureless white radiance with no apparent source. White, too, is the muted sound of the machines which encompass Her throne. White are Her robe and face. I look away from the multitudinous unwinking scanner eyes, into Hers, but She does not appear to recognize me. Does She even see me? SUM has reached out with invisible fingers of electromagnetic induction and taken Her back into Itself. I do not tremble or sweat—I cannot—but I square my shoulders, strike one plangent chord, and wait for It to speak.

It does, from some invisible place. I recognize the voice It has chosen to use: my own. The overtones, the inflections are true, normal, what I myself would use in talking as one reasonable man to another. Why not? In computing what to do about me, and in programming Itself accordingly, SUM must have used so many billion bits of information that adequate accent is a negligible subproblem.

No . . . there I am mistaken again . . . SUM does not do things on the basis that It might as well do them as not. This talk with myself is intended to have some effect on me. I do not know what.

"Well," It says pleasantly, "you made quite a journey didn't you? I'm glad. Welcome."

My instincts bare teeth to hear those words of humanity used by the unfeeling unalive. My logical mind considers replying with an ironic "Thank you," decides against it, and holds me silent.

"You see," SUM continues after a moment that whirrs, "you are unique. Pardon Me if I speak a little bluntly. Your sexual monomania is just one aspect of a generally atavistic, superstition-oriented personality. And yet, unlike the ordinary misfit, you're both strong and realistic enough to cope with the world. This chance to meet you, to analyze you while you rested, has opened new insights for Me on human psychophysiology. Which may lead to improved techniques for governing it and its evolution."

"That being so," I reply, "give me my reward."

"Now look here," SUM says in a mild tone, "you if anyone should know I'm not omnipotent. I was built originally to help govern a civilization grown too complex. Gradually, as My program of self-expansion progressed, I took over more and more decision-making functions. They were *given* to Me. People were happy to be relieved of responsibility, and they could see for themselves how much better I was running things than any mortal could. But to this day, My authority depends on a substantial consensus. If I started playing favorites, as by recreating your girl, well, I'd have troubles."

"The consensus depends more on awe than on reason," I say. "You haven't abolished the gods, You've simply absorbed them into Yourself. If You choose to pass a miracle for me, Your prophet singer—and I will be Your prophet if You do this—why, that strengthens the faith of the rest."

"So you think. But your opinions aren't based on any exact data.

The historical and anthropological records from the past before Me are unquantitative. I've already phased them out of the curriculum. Eventually, when the culture's ready for such a move, I'll order them destroyed. They're too misleading. Look what they've done to you."

I grin into the scanner eyes. "Instead," I say, "people will be encouraged to think that before the world was, was SUM. All right. I don't care, as long as I get my girl back. Pass me a miracle, SUM, and I'll guarantee You a good payment."

"But I have no miracles. Not in your sense. You know how the soul works. The metal bracelet encloses a pseudo-virus, a set of giant protein molecules with taps directly to the bloodstream and nervous system. They record the chromosome pattern, the synapse flash, the permanent changes, everything. At the owner's death, the bracelet is dissected out. The Winged Heels bring it here, and the information contained is transferred to one of My memory banks. I can use such a record to guide the growing of a new body in the vats; a young body, on which the former habits and recollections are imprinted. But you don't understand the complexity of the process, Harper. It takes Me weeks, every seven years, and every available biochemical facility, to recreate My human liaison. And the process isn't perfect, either. The pattern is affected by storage. You might say that this body and brain you see before you remembers each death. And those are short deaths. A longer one—man, use your sense. Imagine."

I can; and the shield between reason and feeling begins to crack. I had sung, of my darling dead:

> "No motion has she now, no force;
> She neither hears nor sees;
> Roll'd round in earth's diurnal course,
> With rocks, and stones, and trees."

Peace, at last. But if the memory-storage is not permanent but circulating; if, within those gloomy caverns of tubes and wire and outer-space cold, some remnant of her psyche must flit and flicker, alone, unremembering, aware of nothing but having lost life—No!

I smite the harp and shout so the room rings: "Give her back! Or I'll kill You!"

SUM finds it expedient to chuckle; and, horribly, the smile is reflected for a moment on the Dark Queen's lips, though otherwise She never stirs. "And how do you propose to do that?" It asks me.

It knows, I know, what I have in mind, so I counter: "How do You propose to stop me?"

"No need. You'll be considered a nuisance. Someone will decide you ought to have psychiatric treatment. They'll query My diagnostic outlet. I'll recommend certain excisions."

"On the other hand, since You've sifted my mind by now, and since You know how I've affected people with my songs—even the Lady yonder, even Her—wouldn't you rather have me working for You? With words like, *'O taste, and see, how gracious the Lord is; blessed is the man that trusteth in him. O fear the Lord, ye that are his saints: for they that fear him lack nothing.'* I can make You into God."

"In a sense, I already am God."

"And in another sense not. Not yet." I can endure no more. "Why are we arguing? You made Your decision before I woke. Tell me and let me go!"

With an odd carefulness, SUM responds: "I'm still studying you. No harm in admitting to you. My knowledge of the human psyche is as yet imperfect. Certain areas won't yield to computation. I don't know precisely what you'd do, Harper. If to that uncertainty I added a potentially dangerous precedent—"

"Kill me, then. Let my ghost wander forever with hers, down in Your cryogenic dreams."

"No, that's also inexpedient. You've made yourself too conspicuous and controversial. Too many people know by now that you went off with the Lady." Is it possible that, behind steel and energy, a nonexistent hand brushes across a shadow face in puzzlement? My heartbeat is thick in the silence.

Suddenly It shakes me with decision: "The calculated probabilities do favor your keeping your promises and making yourself useful. Therefore I shall grant your request. However—"

I am on my knees. My forehead knocks on the floor until blood runs into my eyes. I hear through stormwinds:

"—testing must continue. Your faith in Me is not absolute; in fact, you're very skeptical of what you call My goodness. Without additional proof of your willingness to trust Me, I can't let you have the kind of importance which your getting your dead back from Me would give you. Do you understand?"

The question does not sound rhetorical. "Yes," I sob.

"Well, then," says my civilized, almost amiable voice, "I computed that you'd react much as you have done, and prepared for the likelihood. Your woman's body was recreated while you lay under study. The data which make personality are now being fed back into her neurones. She'll be ready to leave this place by the time you do.

"I repeat, though, there has to be a testing. The procedure is also necessary for its effect on you. If you're to be My prophet, you'll have to work pretty closely with Me; you'll have to undergo a great deal of reconditioning; this night we begin to process. Are you willing?"

"Yes, yes, yes, what must I do?"

"Only this: follow the robot out. At some point, she, your woman, will join you. She'll be conditioned to walk so quietly you can't hear her. Don't look back. Not once, until you're in the upper world. A single glance behind you will be an act of rebellion against Me, and a datum indicating you can't really be trusted . . . and that ends everything. Do you understand?"

"Is that all?" I cry. "Nothing more?"

"It will prove more difficult than you think," SUM tells me. My voice fades, as if into illimitable distances: "Farewell, worshiper."

The robot raises me to my feet. I stretch out my arms to the Dark Queen. Half blinded with tears, I nonetheless see that She does not see me. "Good-bye," I mumble, and let the robot lead me away.

Our walking is long through those murky miles. At first I am in too much of a turmoil, and later too stunned, to know where or how we are bound. But later still, slowly, I become aware of my flesh and clothes and the robot's alloy, glimmering blue in blackness. Sounds and smells are muffled; rarely does another machine pass by, unheeding of us. (What work does SUM have for them?) I am so careful not to look behind me that my neck grows stiff.

Though it is not prohibited, is it, to lift my harp past my shoulder, in the course of strumming a few melodies to keep up my courage, and see if a following illumination is reflected in this polished wood?

Nothing. Well, her second birth must take time—O SUM, be careful of her!—and then she must be led through many tunnels, no doubt, before she makes rendezvous with my back. Be patient, Harper.

Sing. Welcome her home. No, these hollow spaces swallow all music; and she is as yet in that trance of death from which only the Sun and my kiss can wake her; if indeed, she has joined me yet. I listen for other footfalls than my own.

Surely we haven't much further to go. I ask the robot, but of course I get no reply. Make an estimate. I know about how fast the chariot traveled coming down. . . . The trouble is, time does not exist here. I have no day, no stars, no clock but my heartbeat, and I have lost the count of that. Nevertheless, we must come to the end soon. What purpose would be served by walking me through this labyrinth till I die?

Well, if I am totally exhausted at the outer gate, I won't make undue trouble when I find no Rose-in-Hand behind me.

No, now that's ridiculous. If SUM didn't want to heed my plea, It need merely say so. I have no power to inflict physical damage on Its parts.

Of course, It might have plans for me. It did speak of reconditioning. A series of shocks, culminating in that last one, could make me ready for whatever kind of gelding It intends to do.

Or It might have changed Its mind. Why not? It was quite frank about an uncertainty factor in the human psyche. It may have reevaluated the probabilities and decided: better not to serve my desire.

Or It may have tried, and failed. It admitted the recording process is imperfect. I must not expect quite the Gladness I knew; she will always be a little haunted. At best. But suppose the tank spawned a body with no awareness behind the eyes? Or a monster? Suppose, at this instant, I am being followed by a half-rotten corpse?

No! Stop that! SUM would know, and take corrective measures. Would It? *Can It?*

I comprehend how this passage through night, where I never look to see what follows me, how this is an act of submission and confession. I am saying, with my whole existent being, that SUM is all-powerful, all-wise, all-good. To SUM I offer the love I came to win back. Oh, It looked more deeply into me than ever I did myself.

But I shall not fail.

Will SUM, though? If there has indeed been some grisly error . . . let me not find it out under the sky. Let her, my only, not. For what then shall we do? Could I lead her here again, knock on the iron gate, and cry, "Master, You have given me a thing unfit to exist. Destroy it and start over.''—? For what might the wrongness be? Something so subtle, so pervasive, that it does not show in any way save my slow, resisted discovery that I embrace a zombie? Doesn't it make better sense to look—make certain while she is yet drowsy with death—use the whole power of SUM to correct what may be awry?

No, SUM wants me to believe that It makes no mistakes. I agreed to that price. And to much else . . . I don't know how much else, I am daunted to imagine, but that word "recondition" is ugly. . . . Does not my woman have some rights in the matter too? Shall we not at least ask her if she wants to be the wife of a prophet; shall we not, hand in hand, ask SUM what the price of her life is to her?

Was that a footfall? Almost, I whirl about. I check myself and stand shaking; names of hers break from my lips. The robot urges me on.

Imagination. It wasn't her step. I am alone. I will always be alone.

The halls wind upward. Or so I think; I have grown too weary for much kinesthetic sense. We cross the sounding river, and I am bitten to the bone by the cold which blows upward around the bridge, and I may not turn about to offer the naked newborn woman my garment. I lurch through endless chambers where machines do meaningless things. She hasn't seen them before. Into what nightmare has she risen; and why don't I, who wept into her dying senses that I loved her, why don't I look at her, why don't I speak?

Well, I could talk to her. I could assure the puzzled mute dead that I have come to lead her back into sunlight. Could I not? I ask the robot. It does not reply. I cannot remember if I may speak to her. If indeed I was ever told. I stumble forward.

I crash into a wall and fall bruised. The robot's claw closes on my shoulder. Another arm gestures. I see a passageway, very long and narrow, through the stone. I will have to crawl through. At the end, at the end, the door is swinging wide. The dear real dusk of Earth pours through into this darkness. I am blinded and deafened.

Do I hear her cry out? Was that the final testing; or was my own sick, shaken mind betraying me; or is there a destiny which, like SUM with us, makes tools of suns and SUM? I don't know. I know only that I turned, and there she stood. Her hair flowed long, loose, past the remembered face from which the trance was just departing, on which the knowing and the love of me had just awakened—flowed down over the body that reached forth arms, that took one step to meet me and was halted.

The great grim robot at her own back takes her to it. I think it sends lightning through her brain. She falls. It bears her away.

My guide ignores my screaming. Irresistible, it thrusts me out through the tunnel. The door clangs in my face. I stand before the wall which is like a mountain. Dry snow hisses across concrete. The sky is bloody with dawn; stars still gleam in the west, and arc lights are scattered over the twilit plain of the machines.

Presently I go dumb. I become almost calm. What is there left to have feelings about? The door is iron, the wall is stone fused into one basaltic mass. I walk some distance off into the wind, turn around, lower my head and charge. Let my brains be smeared across Its gate; the pattern will be my hieroglyphic for hatred.

I am seized from behind. The force that stops me must needs be bruisingly great. Released, I crumple to the ground before a machine with talons and wings. My voice from it says, "Not here. I'll carry you to a safe place."

"What more can You do to me?" I croak.

"Release you. You won't be restrained or molested on any orders of Mine."

"Why not?"

"Obviously you're going to appoint yourself My enemy forever. This is an unprecedented situation, a valuable chance to collect data."

"You tell me this, You warn me, deliberately?"

"Of course. My computation is that these words will have the effect of provoking your utmost effort."

"You won't give her again? You don't want my love?"

"Not under the circumstances. Too uncontrollable. But your hatred should, as I say, be a useful experimental tool."

"I'll destroy You," I say.

It does not deign to speak further. Its machine picks me up and flies off with me. I am left on the fringes of a small town further south. Then I go insane.

I do not much know what happens during that winter, nor care. The blizzards are too loud in my head. I walk the ways of Earth, among lordly towers, under neatly groomed trees, into careful gardens, over bland, bland campuses. I am unwashed, uncombed, unbarbered; my tatters flap about me and my bones are near thrusting through the skin; folks do not like to meet these eyes sunken so far into this skull, and perhaps for that reason they give me to eat. I sing to them.

> "From the hag and hungry goblin
> That into rags would rend ye
> And the spirit that stan'd by the naked man
> In the Book of Moons defend ye!
> That of your five sound senses
> You never be forsaken
> Nor travel from yourselves with Tom
> Aboard to beg your bacon."

Such things perturb them, do not belong in their chrome-edged universe. So I am often driven away with curses, and sometimes I must flee those who would arrest me and scrub my brain smooth. An alley is a good hiding place, if I can find one in the oldest part of a city; I crouch there and yowl with the cats. A forest is also good. My pursuers dislike any place where any wildness lingers.

But some feel otherwise. They have visited parklands, preserves, actual wildcountry. Their purpose was overconscious—measured, planned savagery, and a clock to tell them when they must go home—but at least they are not afraid of silences and unlighted nights. As spring returns, certain among them begin to follow me. They are merely curious, at first. But slowly, month by month, especially among the younger ones, my madness begins to call to something in them.

> "With an host of furious fancies
> Whereof I am commander
> With a burning spear, and a horse of air,
> To the wilderness I wander.
> By a knight of ghosts and shadows
> I summoned am to tourney
> Ten leagues beyond the wide world's edge.
> Me thinks it is no journey."

They sit at my feet and listen to me sing. They dance, crazily, to my harp. The girls bend close, tell me how I fascinate them, invite me to copulate. This I refuse, and when I tell them why, they are puzzled, a little frightened maybe, but often they strive to understand.

For my rationality is renewed with the hawthorn blossoms. I bathe, have my hair and beard shorn, find clean raiment, and take care to eat what my body needs. Less and less do I rave before anyone who will listen; more and more do I seek solitude, quietness, under the vast wheel of the stars, and think.

What is man? Why is man? We have buried such questions; we have sworn they are dead—that they never really existed, being devoid of empirical meaning—and we have dreaded that they might raise the stones we heaped on them, rise and walk the world again of nights. Alone, I summon them to me. They cannot hurt their fellow dead, among whom I now number myself.

I sing to her who is gone. The young people hear and wonder. Sometimes they weep.

> "Fear no more the heat o' the sun,
> Nor the furious winter's rages;
> Thou thy wordly task hast done,
> Home art gone; and ta'en thy wages:
> Golden lads and girls all must
> As chimney-sweepers, come to dust."

"But this is not so!" they protest. "We will die and sleep a while, and then we will live forever in SUM."

I answer as gently as may be: "No. Remember I went there. So I know you are wrong. And even if you were right, it would not be right that you should be right."

"What?"

"Don't you see, it is not right that a thing should be the lord of man. It is not right that we should huddle through our whole lives in fear of finally losing them. You are not parts in a machine, and you have better ends than helping the machine run smoothly."

I dismiss them and stride off, solitary again, into a canyon where a river clangs, or onto some gaunt mountain peak. No revelation is given me. I climb and creep toward the truth.

Which is that SUM must be destroyed, not in revenge, not in hate, not in fear, simply because the human spirit cannot exist in the same reality as It.

But what, then, is our proper reality? And how shall we attain to it?

I return with my songs to the lowlands. Word about me has gone widely. They are a large crowd who follow me down the highroad until it has changed into a street.

"The Dark Queen will soon come to these parts," they tell me. "Abide till She does. Let Her answer those questions you put to us, which makes us sleep so badly."

"Let me retire to prepare myself," I say. I go up a long flight of steps. The people watch from below, dumb with awe, till I vanish. Such few as were in the building depart. I walk down vaulted halls, through hushed high-ceilinged rooms full of tables, among shelves made massive by books. Sunlight slants dusty through the windows.

The half memory has plagued me of late: once before, I know not when, this year of mine also took place. Perhaps in this library I can find the tale that—casually, I suppose, in my abnormal childhood—I read. For man is older than SUM: wiser, I swear; his myths hold more truth than Its mathematics. I spend three days and most of three nights in my search. There is little sound but the rustling of leaves between my hands. Folk place offerings of food and drink at the door. They tell themselves they do so out of pity, or curiosity, or to avoid the nuisance of having me die in an unconventional fashion. But I know better.

At the end of the three days I am little further along. I have too much material; I keep going off on sidetracks of beauty and fascination. (Which SUM means to eliminate.) My education was like everyone else's, science, rationality, good sane adjustment. (SUM writes our curricula, and the teaching machines have direct connections to It.) Well, I can make some of my lopsided training work for me. My reading has given me sufficient clues to prepare a search program. I sit down before an information retrieval console and run my fingers across its keys. They make a clattery music.

Electron beams are swift hounds. Within seconds the screen lights up with words, and I read who I am.

It is fortunate that I am a fast reader. Before I can press the CLEAR button, the unreeling words are wiped out. For an instant the screen quivers with formlessness, then appears:

I HAD NOT CORRELATED THESE DATA WITH THE FACTS CONCERNING YOU. THIS INTRODUCES A NEW AND INDE-TERMINATE QUANTITY INTO THE COMPUTATIONS.

The nirvana which has come upon me (yes, I found that word among the old books, and how portentous it is) is not passiveness, it is a tide more full and strong than that which bore me down to the Dark Queen those ages apast in wildcountry. I say, as coolly as may be, "An interesting coincidence. If it is a coincidence." Surely sonic receptors are emplaced here.

EITHER THAT, OR A CERTAIN NECESSARY CONSE-QUENCE OF THE LOGIC OF EVENTS.

The vision dawning within me is so blinding bright that I cannot refrain from answering, "Or a destiny, SUM?"

MEANINGLESS. MEANINGLESS. MEANINGLESS.

"Now why did You repeat Yourself in that way? Once would have sufficed. Thrice, though, makes an incantation. Are You by any chance hoping Your words will make me stop existing?"

I DO NOT HOPE. YOU ARE AN EXPERIMENT. IF I COMPUTE A SIGNIFICANT PROBABILITY OF YOUR CAUSING SERIOUS DISTURBANCE, I WILL HAVE YOU TERMINATED.

I smile. "SUM," I say, "I am going to terminate You." I lean over and switch off the screen. I walk out into the evening.

Not everything is clear to me yet, that I must say and do. But enough is that I can start preaching at once to those who have been waiting for me. As I talk, others come down the street, and hear, and stay to listen. Soon they number in the hundreds.

I have no immense new truth to offer them: nothing that I have not said before, although piecemeal and unsystematically; nothing they have not felt themselves, in the innermost darknesses of their beings. Today, however, knowing who I am and therefore why I am, I can put these things in words. Speaking quietly, now and then drawing on some forgotten song to show my meaning, I tell them how sick and starved their lives are; how they have made themselves slaves; how the enslavement is not even to a conscious mind, but to an insensate inanimate thing which their own ancestors began; how that thing is not the centrum of existence, but a few scraps of metal and bleats of energy, a few sad stupid patterns, adrift in unbounded space-time. Put not your faith in SUM, I tell them. SUM is doomed, even as you and I. Seek out mystery; what else is the whole cosmos but mystery? Live bravely, die and be done, and you will be more than any machine. You may perhaps be God.

They grow tumultuous. They shout replies, some of which are animal howls. A few are for me, most are opposed. That doesn't matter. I have reached into them, my music is being played on their nerve-strings, and this is my entire purpose.

The Sun goes down behind the buildings. Dusk gathers. The city remains unilluminated. I soon realize why. She is coming, the Dark Queen Whom they wanted me to debate with. From afar we hear Her chariot thunder. Folk wail in terror. They are not wont to do that either. They used to disguise their feelings from Her and themselves by receiving Her with grave, sparse ceremony. Now they would flee if they dared. I have lifted the masks.

The chariot halts in the street. She dismounts, tall and shadowy cowled. The people make way before Her like water before a shark. She climbs the stairs to face me. I see for the least instant that Her lips are not quite firm and Her eyes abrim with tears. She whispers, too low for anyone else to hear, "Oh, Harper, I'm sorry."

"Come join me," I invite. "Help me set the world free."

"No. I cannot. I have been too long with It." She straightens. Imperium descends upon Her. Her voice rises for everyone to hear. The little television robots flit close, bat shapes in the twilight, that the whole planet may witness my defeat. "What is this freedom you rant about?" She demands.

"To feel," I say. "To venture. To wonder. To become men again."

"To become beasts, you mean. Would you demolish the machines that keep us alive?"

"Yes. We must. Once they were good and useful, but we let them grow upon us like a cancer, and now nothing but destruction and a new beginning can save us."

"Have you considered the chaos?"

"Yes. It too is necessary. We will not be men without the freedom to know suffering. In it is also enlightenment. Through it we travel beyond ourselves, beyond Earth and stars, space and time, to Mystery.''

''So you maintain that there is some undefined ultimate vagueness behind the measurable universe?'' She smiles into the bat eyes. We have each been taught, as children, to laugh on hearing sarcasms of this kind. ''Please offer me a little proof.''

''No,'' I say. ''Prove to me instead, beyond any doubt, that there is *not* something we cannot understand with words and equations. Prove to me likewise that I have no right to seek for it.

''The burden of proof is on You Two, so often have You lied to us. In the name of rationality, You resurrected myth. The better to control us! In the name of liberation, You chained our inner lives and castrated our souls. In the name of service, You bound and blinkered us. In the name of achievement, You held us to a narrower round than any swine in its pen. In the name of beneficence, You created pain, and horror, and darkness beyond darkness.'' I turn to the people. ''I went there. I descended into the cellars. I know!''

''He found that SUM would not pander to his special wishes, at the expense of everyone else,'' cries the Dark Queen. Do I hear shrillness in her voice? ''Therefore he claims SUM is cruel.''

''I saw my dead,'' I tell them. ''She will not rise again. Nor yours, nor you. Not ever. SUM will not, cannot raise us. In Its house is death indeed. We must seek life and rebirth elsewhere, among the mysteries.''

She laughs aloud and points to my soul bracelet, glimmering faintly in the gray-blue thickening twilight. Need She say anything?

''Will someone give me a knife and an ax?'' I ask.

The crowd stirs and mumbles. I smell their fear. Street lamps go on, as if they could scatter more than this corner of the night which is rolling upon us. I fold my arms and wait. The Dark Queen says something to me. I ignore Her.

The tools pass from hand to hand. He who brings them up the stairs comes like a flame. He kneels at my feet and lifts what I have desired. The tools are good ones, a broad-bladed hunting knife and a long double-bitted ax.

Before the world, I take the knife in my right hand and slash beneath the bracelet on my left wrist. The connections to my inner body are cut. Blood flows, impossibly brilliant under the lamps. It does not hurt; I am too exalted.

The Dark Queen shrieks. ''You meant it! Harper, Harper!''

"There is no life in SUM," I say. I pull my hand through the circle and cast the bracelet down so it rings.

A voice of brass: *"Arrest that maniac for correction. He is deadly dangerous."*

The monitors who have stood on the fringes of the crowd try to push through. They are resisted. Those who seek to help them encounter fists and fingernails.

I take the ax and smash downward. The bracelet crumples. The organic material within, starved of my secretions, exposed to the night air, withers.

I raise the tools, ax in right hand, knife in bleeding left. "I seek eternity where it is to be found," I call. "Who goes with me?"

A score or better break loose from the riot, which is already calling forth weapons and claiming lives. They surround me with their bodies. Their eyes are the eyes of prophets. We make haste to seek a hiding place, for one military robot has appeared and others will not be long in coming. The tall engine strides to stand guard over Our Lady, and this is my last glimpse of Her.

My followers do not reproach me for having cost them all they were. They are mine. In me is the godhead which can do no wrong.

And the war is open, between me and SUM. My friends are few, my enemies many and mighty. I go about the world as a fugitive. But always I sing. And always I find someone who will listen, will join us, embracing pain and death like a lover.

With the Knife and the Ax I take their souls. Afterward we hold for them the ritual of rebirth. Some go thence to become outlaw missionaries; most put on facsimile bracelets and return home, to whisper my word. It makes little difference to me. I have no haste, who own eternity.

For my word is of what lies beyond time. My enemies say I call forth ancient bestialities and lunacies; that I would bring civilization down in ruin; that it matters not a madman's giggle to me whether war, famine, and pestilence will again scour the Earth. With these accusations I am satisfied. The language of them shows me that here, too, I have reawakened anger. And that emotion belongs to us as much as any other. More than the others, maybe, in this autumn of mankind. We need a gale, to strike down SUM and everything It stands for. Afterward will come the winter of barbarism.

And after that the springtime of a new and (perhaps) more human civilization. My friends seem to believe this will come in their very lifetimes: peace, brotherhood, enlightenment, sanctity. I know otherwise. I have been in the depths. The wholeness of mankind, which I am bringing back, has its horrors.

When one day
the Eater of the Gods returns
the Wolf breaks his chain
the Horsemen ride forth
the Age ends
the Beast is reborn

then SUM will be destroyed; and you, strong and fair, may go back to earth and rain.

I shall await you.

My aloneness is nearly ended, Daybright. Just one task remains. The god must die, that his followers may believe he is raised from the dead and lives forever. Then they will go on to conquer the world.

There are those who say I have spurned and offended them. They too, borne on the tide which I raised, have torn out their machine souls and seek in music and ecstasy to find a meaning for existence. But their creed is a savage one, which has taken them into wildcountry, where they ambush the monitors sent against them and practice cruel rites. They believe that the final reality is female. Nevertheless, messengers of theirs have approached me with the suggestion of a mystic marriage. This I refused; my wedding was long ago, and will be celebrated again when this cycle of the world has closed. Therefore they hate me. But I have said I will come and talk to them.

I leave the road at the bottom of the valley and walk singing up the hill. Those few I let come this far with me have been told to abide my return. They shiver in the sunset; the vernal equinox is three days away. I feel no cold myself. I stride exultant among briars and twisted ancient apple trees. If my bare feet leave a little blood in the snow, that is good. The ridges around are dark with forest, which waits like the skeleton dead for leaves to be breathed across it again. The eastern sky is purple, where stands the evening star. Overhead, against blue, cruises an early flight of homebound geese. Their calls drift faintly down to me. Westward, above me and before me, smolders redness. Etched black against it are the women.

2

The Remarkable Adventure

Philip José Farmer
and Beverly Friend

No pattern has recurred more frequently in myth and in fairy tale than that of the fictional journey. It has also been a mainstay of realistic fiction—following the adventures of the picaresque hero or, more philosophically, examining the distinct journey taken through life: from childhood on to and even through maturity.

Science fiction, however, offers the closest alignment to recognized myth, for there are strong similarities between the adventures of such a hero as Odysseus and the exploits of the twentieth-century space hero. Neither is bounded by the real. While the ancient mythic hero was ordinarily confined to earth, he might still visit the underworld. Even in his wanderings on the surface of the planet, he experienced strange adventures, unexplainable phenomena, and magic—used both for and against his prowess—transcended the limitations of reality. The science fiction adventurer has the best of both mythic and realistic traditions because an ever progressing science has melted into a magical future. Thus, what appears magic can be (and often is) explained or at least deemed explainable to one able to grasp the complicated scientific principles, and this accounts for the hero's transportation, his weaponry, his entire life-style.

What need has the space hero for a trip to the underworld if he can have access to Mercury? And as scientific knowledge has grown, the space hero stays one jump ahead of the known and predictable. Early space adventures took place on the moon. Then, when the everyday world learned of the moon's limitations (in atmosphere, in lack of habitation), the hero sought the other planets of our solar system. Now, when too much is known about them to suit the imaginative author, the entire galaxy has become ripe for exploration, a new frontier. What next? As Donald Wollheim notes in *The Universe Makers,* there is the ultimate "challenge to God. . . . The effort to match Creation and to solve the last secrets of the universe. Sometimes seeking out and confronting the Creative Force or Being or God itself, sometimes merging with that Creative First Premise."

The Great Adventure Story, in ancient times or now, is always about the individual who has a goal and makes a long and dangerous physical journey to achieve that goal. The ancient Sumerian Gilgamesh descends into the underworld to achieve immortality. Odysseus wants to get home to his wife, but he encounters many dangerous and frustrating detours. Kimball Kinnison, the Gray Lensman of E. E. Smith's vast space opera series, also has a goal. That is the destruction of the evil Eich and others even worse, all intent on total conquest of the universe.

Ancient epic, medieval romance (such as the stories of the quest for the holy grail), and much of science fiction (space opera or otherwise) can have as protagonist a heroic individual (usually a man). Until recent times the protagonist was almost always a little more than life size.

The mainstream great adventure story, that is, that outside the science fiction and western subgenres, could have as protagonist either a person of heroic mold or a "common man." Jack London's adventure stories had both. His Wolf Larsen of *The Sea Wolf* was a superman, but the narrator, an effete scholar, won out in the end. But in all great adventure stories, nonscience fiction or not, the hero, supermannish or plebeian, had to have indomitable courage. This is the second requisite for all protagonists; the first is a dangerous goal.

There are all sorts of adventures. A man may take a bus across town, or perhaps not even leave his home, and experience only inner adventures, a quest for the holy grail of mind or spirit, and end his journey a changed man. As William Barrett says in his *Irrational Man,* ". . . what counts in life is not the number of rare and exciting adventures he encounters, but the inner depths in that life, by which something great may be made out of even the paltriest and most banal of occurrences. . . ."

That is appropriate for Leopold Bloom's wanderings in *Ulysses,* but that is not what attracts us to Homer's or E. E. Smith's heroes. Neither Odysseus nor Kinnison is changed in any respect. With both, it is the hero battling to achieve his goal in the midst of exotic and dangerous forces which excites our sense of wonder.

What, then, distinguishes the great adventure of the western and mainstream from the "remarkable" adventure, as we call the science fiction adventure? All types can have a heroic or a common man. All can, should, excite a certain sense of wonder. The protagonist may or may not be changed during the adventure, though the best modern stories often show a change, for better or worse, in the protagonist.

What is it that makes the remarkable adventure differ from the others? For one thing, the mainstream and the western adventure are always of the then or the now. Only science fiction portrays the future. It is science fiction alone which uses what Joseph Campbell calls "the discipline of the parallax, for the student of binocular vision." That is, it contrasts the present, the existent, with the future or the could-be. In addition, science fiction tries to show us the shape of the future, and, if possible, shape the future.

Many remarkable adventures, however, do not do this. They are written only to evoke a sense of wonder, that is, awe and ecstasy, and sometimes horror, at the unending potentiality for strangeness in this world. Is that enough? Yes, it is for the young. That is why Smith's *Skylark* and *Lensman* stories, though primitively written and with lucite characters, still attract so many young (in age and in heart). The adventures are indeed remarkable: the imagination is boundless, evil and good are clearly differentiated, the reader knows whose side he is on; the reader *is* the hero.

Also, though there may be mysterious events and murky sinister forces behind the scenes, in the end all becomes clear. Smith's universe is made of men, monsters, and gods whose actions are intelligible. And the actions are set in a comprehensible universe. Everything is eventually explainable by logic and science.

Stanley G. Weinbaum, in his "A Martian Odyssey," a truly remarkable adventure, added what seemed to be a new element in science fiction. His hero encountered extratarrestrials whose behavior was absolutely inexplicable by human beings. Weinbaum's thesis here was that when man ventures onto other planets, he'll find that his modes of perception, the human prism through which he views the universe, won't work on alien worlds. He just won't understand much of what is going on. Stanislaw Lem, a modern Polish author, uses this theme consistently. Arthur C. Clarke used it in his *Rendezvous with Rama*.

None of the three stories in this section are intimately concerned with the shape of the future. They are, in some ways, one with the shape of ancient epic. Two are about death as challenged successfully by human protagonists. In these, men symbiotize with animals and machines or with machines to defeat death. The triumph of life is brought about by a hybridization with the lifeless. The third is about death, but the terrestrials are not threatened much by death. On the contrary, they contaminate, and so abort, Creation. But inadvertently. Through ignorance.

However these stories differ in attitude, they are similar in the basics of the remarkable adventure. They are not concerned with the inner adventure. It is the outer adventure, the remarkable, the *voyage extraordinaire,* the perilous quest, the pitting of man against dangerous and unknown forces, and his exterior triumphs or defeats, that distinguish these.

To understand how science fiction has both absorbed and added to the mythic pattern, let us examine the mythic framework as it has been delineated by Joseph Campbell, and seek the similarities and differences between his conception and the three tales to be examined: "Brightside Crossing" by Alan E. Nourse (hereafter referred to as "Brightside"), "Before Eden" by Arthur Clarke ("Eden"), and "The Game of Rat and Dragon" by Cordwainer Smith ("Game").

The mythological hero, setting forth from his commonday hut or castle, is lured, carried away, or else voluntarily proceeds, to the threshold of adventure. There he encounters a shadow presence that guards the passage. The hero may defeat or conciliate this power and go alive into the kingdom of the dark (brother-battle, dragon-battle: offering, charm), or be slain by the opponent and descend in death (dismemberment, crucifixion).*

The initial order of progression would have to be changed to fit the science fiction hero. He is seldom lured, even more seldom carried away, and almost always rushes headlong into his adventure. Moreover, like Caesar on the Ides of March, he is undeterred no matter what the warnings.

James Baron, in "Brightside," has the opportunity to learn every error-laden step which has brought disaster upon an earlier crew attempting to cross Mercury. He receives a blow-by-blow description of every hazard from a "Tiresius" who has barely survived the experience.

He was short and wiry. His face held no key to his age—he might have been thirty or a thousand—but he looked weary and immensely ugly. His cheeks and forehead were twisted and brown, with scars that were still healing.

*Joseph Campbell, *The Hero with a Thousand Faces* (Princeton, N.J.: Princeton University Press, 1968), pp. 245–246.

Thus the marks of his dreadful experience are still on him, enhancing the awful consequences he foretells. Moreover, he does not blame the failure of the expedition on human error.

It was the Sun that beat us, that surface. Perhaps we were licked the very day we started. . . . We didn't realize that, but it was *true*. There are places that men can't go, conditions men can't tolerate. The others had to die to learn that. I was lucky, I came back. But I'm trying to tell you what I found out—that *nobody* will ever make a Brightside Crossing.

Not only does Claney (the survivor from the past) fail to persuade Baron; he fails to persuade himself! As Baron rises to the inherent challenge, determined to cross the planet at all costs, Claney pleads, "When do you leave . . . I want you to take me along."

There is never any question in "Eden" or in "Game" that the characters are anywhere but where they themselves have chosen, even trained themselves, to be. Thus the science fiction hero, like the ancient hero, is a prepared man. Whether the ancient hero was lured, kidnapped, or voluntarily sought his adventure, he was able to meet it. He was sound of mind and of body, had learned the art of warfare, and was provided with both real and magic weaponry for his safekeeping. In science fiction the hero is often a scientist who has carefully studied the world he prepares to enter, and how to protect himself from its hostile environment.

In both "Brightside" and "Eden" the explorers have space suits and armored transport vehicles to protect them. However, lest the protection limit both their risk and their ability to really experience their surroundings, the characters in both stories are forced to spend much of the time proceeding on foot.

They also suffer—in spite of all their scientific gear. On Mercury, the men undergo an intolerable psychological thirst. And in both stories it is imperative that the technology fail—by breakdown, accident, or inability to master the rough terrain—so that the men are placed in peril.

A different kind of technological peril is found in "Game," where spaceships have been outfitted with a defense system combining a telepathically united man and cat in order that the combined efforts of both can serve to conquer the inimical forces living in the space between planets. What unites man and beast is a contraption, worn on the head and called a pin-set. What brings these two, and all the passengers of a spaceship, to the area where the hostile forces reside is a mechanism which causes immense jumps through space: planoforming. And it is in planoforming that the hero experiences the kind of death which marks the threshold of a new world:

> Planoforming was sort of funny. It felt like—
> Like nothing much.
> Like the twinge of a mild electric shock.
> Like the ache of a sore tooth bitten on for the first time.
> Like a slightly painful flash of light against the eyes.

Yet in that time, a forty-thousand-ton ship lifting free above the Earth disappeared somehow or other into two dimensions and appeared half a light-year or fifty light-years off.

Beyond the threshold, then, the hero journeys through a world of unfamiliar yet strangely intimate forces, some of which severely threaten him (tests), some of which give magical aid (helpers).*

It is this unfamiliar world that is the core of each story. In "Brightside" it is Mercury, hot, dry, forbidding, a true test of stamina and courage. Not only is this world totally hostile to man, but the explorers must seek to conquer it at its most hostile moment: perihelion, the moment that the bright side of the planet, the side they wish to cross, is closest to the Sun.

Why try a Crossing at aphelion? What have you done then? Four thousand miles of butcherous heat, just to have some joker come along, use your data, and drum you out of the glory by crossing at perihelion forty-four days later? No, thanks. I want Brightside without any nonsense about it. . . . I want to make a Crossing at perihelion and I want to cross on the surface. If a man can do that, he's got Mercury. Until then, *nobody's* got Mercury. I want Mercury. . . .

In actuality, he wants *more* than Mercury!

Suppose you do. . . . Suppose I'm all wrong, suppose you do make it. Then what? *What comes next?*

And Baron answers: "The Sun!"

In "Eden" the hostile world is Venus: alien yet familiar:

The green auroral light, filtering down through clouds that had rolled unbroken for a million years, gave the scene an underwater appearance, and the way in which all distant objects blurred into the haze added to the impression.

Only thirty miles from the scientists' destination, the South Pole of the planet, the scout car halts, unable to proceed further. The choices are to turn back and retrace the "four-hundred-mile journey through

*Joseph Campbell, p. 246.

this nightmare landscape'' or to proceed on foot, hoping to find (a highly doubtful) evidence of life. Protected by thermosuits, two proceed while a third stays behind with the scoutcar.

The world in ''Game'' lies between worlds, a place ''underneath space itself which is alive, capricious and malevolent.'' Psychic monsters which destroy men's minds live within this space and are perceived as dragons by the telepathic humans, as rats by their partner cats. These dragon/rats can be defeated by light. So photon bombs are carried by the cats which ride outside the ship in missile launching projectiles operated by the telepathic humans from within the ship. This partnership is akin to the magical helpers of myth.

When he arrives at the nadir of the mythological round, he undergoes a supreme ordeal and gains his reward. The triumph may be represented as the hero's sexual union with the goddess-mother of the world (sacred marriage), his recognition by the father-creator (father atonement), his own divinization (apotheosis), or again—if the powers have remained unfriendly to him—his theft of the boon he came to gain (bride-theft, fire-theft). Intrinsically it is an expansion of consciousness and therewith of being (illumination, transfiguration, frccdom).*

In ''Brightside'' and ''Eden'' the supreme ordeal is a test of endurance, the will to go on, to conquer the unknown. In ''Game'' it is a test of strength—an actual battle. However, the triumph in none of these stories, and indeed seldom if ever in science fiction, includes a woman, sexual union, or marriage. Rather, there is emphasis on the boon with different (and possibly wider) applications.

''Brightside'' can be dismissed at this point as more typically a pure adventure than the other tales, with a message primarily limited to man's ever-ready response to the same impulse that led Hilary up Everest because it was ''there.'' In ''Eden,'' however, there is a boon, and a stolen one at that, for the scientists do come upon a life-form:

He still thought of the thing as a carpet—a deep pile one, ravelled into tassles at the edges. It varied in thickness as it moved; in some parts it was a mere film; in others, it heaped up to a depth of a foot or more. As it came closer and he could see its texture, Jerry was reminded of black velvet. He wondered what it felt like to the touch, then remembered that it would burn his fingers even if it did nothing else to them. He found himself thinking, in the light-headed nervous reaction that follows a sudden shock: ''If there *are* any Venusians, we'll never be able to shake hands with them. They'd burn us, and we'd give them frost-bite.

*Joseph Campbell, p. 246.

This discovery, and the longing for communication echo J. R. R. Tolkien's list of the primordial human desires: "One of these desires is to survey the depths of space and time. Another is . . . to hold communion with other living things."

Jerry cannot communicate, but he and his colleague can attempt to study this fellow creature and bring home this new knowledge. So they snipped samples and took probes.

For life called to life, across the gulfs of space. Everything that grew or moved upon the face of any planet was a portent, a promise that Man was not alone in this universe of blazing suns and swirling nebulae. If as yet he had found no companions with whom he could speak, that was only to be expected, for the light-years and the ages still stretched before him, waiting to be explored. Meanwhile, he must guard and cherish the life he found, whether it be upon Earth or Mars or Venus.

Consciousness has been expanded. In "Game" that is communication between two life-forms—the humans and the cats—as they link to join battle:

When he had first come into contact with her mind, he was astonished at its clarity. With her he remembered her kittenhood. He remembered every mating experience she had ever had. He saw in a half-recognizable gallery all the other pinlighters with whom she had been paired for the flight. And he saw himself radiant, cheerful and desirable. He even thought he caught the edge of a longing—a very flattering and yearning thought: *What a pity he is not a cat*.

Thomas Wymer has written a provocation interpretation of the human-cat relationship as an ironic depiction of a male/female relationship.* If so, this is as close as this tale comes to offering the sexual union with a goddess that myth so often contains. Rather, the hero's expansion of consciousness separates him from his own kind at the story's end.

The final work is that of the return. If the powers have blessed the hero, he now sets forth under their protection (emissary): If not, he flees and is pursued (transformation flight, obstacle flight). At the return threshold the transcendental powers must remain behind: the hero re-emerges from the kingdom of dread (return, resurrection). The boon that he brings restores the world (elixir).†

How does the science fiction hero return? In "Brightside" the ostensible hero has not even set out on his journey as yet. Rather, he has

*Thomas Wymer, "Cordwainer Smith: Satirist or Male Chauvinist," *Extrapolation,* May 1973, pp. 157–162.
†Joseph Campbell, p. 246.

heard the tale of one survivor who wishes to try again. If the survivor is the real protagonist, the boon brought back is that of experience, a boon that he will put to use again to further his adventures. The model fits the mold poorly, and yet it is well to remember that Campbell's definition deals with works of epic scope, while the comparisons here are with brief stories, limited by length and the amount of ground to be covered. Campbell himself has commented that many tales isolate or enlarge upon only one or two of the typical elements of the full cycle. Thus, the element of return and the importance of the boon are not touched upon here, and "Brightside" offers the most limited mythic connection of the three stories under consideration.

In "Eden" the boon that is really brought back to mankind is not contained in the snippets of alien creature carried back to earth. Rather it lies in a distinct and separate message to the reader, for the point of view of the story changes at the end, the characters leave the scene: the humans return to earth, the alien returns to its foraging.

While the human scientists have been careful, even meticulous in gathering, collecting, and sealing their refuse to avoid contaminating the planet, they have failed. In this contamination they carried contagion to all the world they had left behind. "Beneath the clouds of Venus, the story of Creation was ended."

Whose consciousness is raised? Not that of the characters, but that of the reader, because he has been told "what happens next."

In "Game" the battle between the partners and their enemy has been a difficult one and the hero, Underhill, and his partner, Lady May, have been touched by the "dragon." The story does not end with a triumphant battle scene. The hero must return to the real world. He must leave the "transcendental powers" (his pin-set) behind. The final scene takes place in a hospital.

As Underhill recovers, comes back to his earthly, everyday existence, reemerges from the kingdom of dread, he is a changed man. Like Gulliver among the Houyhnhnms, like Genly Ai in Ursula K. Le Guin's *The Left Hand of Darkness,* true communication with an alien being has made him more in tune, more empathetic with that mentality and world view than with his own. Thus he looks at the nurse who tends him and sees hostility rather than a responsive chord. He longs for Lady May:

She *is* a cat, he thought. That's all she is—a *cat!* But that was not how his mind saw her—quick beyond all dreams of speed, sharp, clever, unbelievably graceful, beautiful, wordless and undemanding. Where would he ever find a woman who could compare with her?

The heroes return. Have the powers blessed or cursed them? The boon they bring is knowledge—which can be either a blessing or a curse.

Joseph Campbell once said that a complete mythology serves four functions: metaphysical-mystical, cosmological, social, and psychological.

He defined the metaphysical-mystical, stating that the function of mythology is "to waken and maintain in the individual an experience of awe, humility, and respect, in recognition of that ultimate mystery, transcending names and forms. . . ."

This is the "sense of awe" of science fiction as the science fiction hero—often a messianic hero—attempts to come to terms with the cosmos. To repeat what Donald Wollheim noted: "Sometimes [we find the hero] seeking out and confronting the Creative Force or Being or God itself, sometimes merging with that Creative First Premise. This is the shape of mythology as it appears in such works as Arthur C. Clarke's short story "The Sentinel," or his *Childhood's End,* Olaf Stapledon's *Last and First Men,* and Theodore Sturgeon's *More than Human.*

Campbell's second function of myth is to render a cosmology, an image of the universe. And one would be hard put to name a science fiction work that does not do this, to a greater or lesser extent. There's Isaac Asimov's *Foundation Trilogy,* for example, or Larry Niven and Jerry Pournell's *The Mote in God's Eye.*

Third, under the sociological function, Campbell cites the validation and maintenence of an established order. Here nearly any of the works of Robert Heinlein would apply. The very scientific laws upon which science fiction is based reflect order—and reinforce it.

And finally, Campbell's last function of myth, the psychological one, focuses on the centering and harmonization of the individual. The science fiction hero is at home in his technological world. Moreover he is a true hero—not an anti-hero. And that, indeed, is the stuff of myth!

BIBLIOGRAPHY

Aldiss, Brian, *Starship,* 1959 (Criterion)
Anderson, Poul, *War of the Wing Men,* 1958 (Ace)
Asimov, Isaac, *The End of Eternity,* 1955 (Doubleday)

Bester, Alfred, *The Stars My Destination,* 1957 (Signet)
Burroughs, Edgar Rice, *John Carter of Mars,* 1965 (Ballantine)
Clarke, Arthur C., *Rendezvous with Rama,* 1973 (Harcourt)
Clement, Hal, *Mission of Gravity,* 1954 (Doubleday)
Farmer, Philip José, *To Your Scattered Bodies Go,* 1971 (Putnam)
Gordon, Rex, *First on Mars,* 1957 (Ace)
Hamilton, Edmond, *The Star of Life,* 1959 (Doda)
Heinlein, Robert, *The Door into Summer,* 1957 (Doubleday)
————, *Glory Road,* 1962 (Putnam)
————, *Starship Troopers,* 1959 (Putnam)
Laumer, Keith, *Dinosaur Beach,* 1972 (DAW Books)
Le Guin, Ursula K., *Wizard of Earthsea,* 1968 (Parnassus)
McCaffrey, Anne, *Dragonflight,* 1968 (Ballantine)
Niven, Larry, *Ringworld,* 1970 (Ballantine)
————, and Jerry Pournelle, *The Mote in God's Eye,* 1974 (Simon and
    Schuster)
Nourse, Alan, *Raiders from the Rings,* 1962 (McKay)
Saberhagen, Fred, *Berserker,* 1967 (Ballantine)
Simak, Clifford, *Ring Around the Sun,* 1953 (Simon and Schuster)
Smith, E. E., *Gray Lensman,* 1951 (Pyramid)
Stableford, Brian M., *The Halcyon Drift,* 1972 (Daw)
Tenn, William, *Of Men and Monsters,* 1968 (Ballantine)
Van Vogt, A. E., *The World of Null-A,* 1948 (Simon and Schuster)
Verne, Jules, *20,000 Leagues Under the Sea,* 1870 (many editions)
————, *A Journey to the Center of the Earth,* 1864 (many editions)
Wright, S. Fowler, *The World Below,* 1930 (Longman's)
Wul, Stefan, *The Temple of the Past,* 1973 (Seabury)

Brightside Crossing

Alan E. Nourse

James Baron was not pleased to hear that he had had a visitor when he reached the Red Lion that evening. He had no stomach for mysteries, vast or trifling, and there were pressing things to think about at this time. Yet the doorman had flagged him as he came in from the street: "A thousand pardons, Mr. Baron. The gentleman—he would leave no name. He said you'd want to see him. He will be back by eight."

Baron drummed his fingers on the tabletop, staring about the quiet lounge. Street trade was discouraged at the Red Lion, gently but persuasively; the patrons were few in number. Across to the right was a group that Baron knew vaguely—Andean climbers, or at least two of them were. Over near the door he recognized old Balmer, who had mapped the first passage to the core of Vulcan Crater on Venus. Baron returned his smile with a nod. Then he settled back and waited impatiently for the intruder who demanded his time without justifying it.

Presently a small, grizzled man crossed the room and sat down at Baron's table. He was short and wiry. His face held no key to his age—he might have been thirty or a thousand—but he looked weary and immensely ugly. His cheeks and forehead were twisted and brown, with scars that were still healing.

The stranger said, "I'm glad you waited. I've heard you're planning to attempt the Brightside."

Baron stared at the man for a moment. "I see you can read telecasts," he said coldly. "The news was correct. We are going to make a Brightside Crossing."

"At perihelion?"

"Of course. When else?"

The grizzled man searched Baron's face for a moment without expression. Then he said slowly, "No, I'm afraid you're not going to make the Crossing."

"Say, who are you, if you don't mind?" Baron demanded.

"The name is Claney," said the stranger.

There was a silence. Then: "Claney? *Peter* Claney?"

"That's right."

Baron's eyes were wide with excitement, all trace of anger gone. "My God, man—*where have you been hiding?* We've been trying to contact you for months!"

"I know. I was hoping you'd quit looking and chuck the whole idea."

"Quit looking!" Baron bent forward over the table. "My friend, we'd given up hope, but we've never quit looking. Here, have a drink. There's so much you can tell us." His fingers were trembling.

Peter Claney shook his head. "I can't tell you anything you want to hear."

"But you've *got* to. You're the only man on Earth who's attempted a Brightside Crossing and lived through it! And the story you cleared for the news—it was nothing. We need *details*. Where did your equipment fall down? Where did you miscalculate? What were the trou-

ble spots?'' Baron jabbed a finger at Claney's face. ''That, for
instance—epithelioma? Why? What was wrong with your glass? Your
filters? We've got to know those things. If you can tell us, we can
make it across where your attempt failed—''

''You want to know why we failed?'' asked Claney.

''Of course we want to know. We *have* to know.''

''It's simple. We failed because it can't be done. We couldn't do it
and neither can you. No human beings will ever cross the Brightside
alive, not if they try for centuries.''

''Nonsense,'' Baron declared. ''We will.''

Claney shrugged. ''I was there. I know what I'm saying. You can
blame the equipment or the men—there were flaws in both quarters—
but we just didn't know what we were fighting. It was the *planet* that
whipped us, that and the *Sun*. They'll whip you, too, if you try it.''

''Never,'' said Baron.

''Let me tell you,'' Peter Claney said.

I'd been interested in the Brightside for almost as long as I can
remember (Claney said). I guess I was about ten when Wyatt and
Carpenter made the last attempt—that was in 2082, I think. I followed
the news stories like a tri-V serial, and then I was heartbroken when
they just disappeared.

I know now that they were a pair of idiots, starting off without
proper equipment, with practically no knowledge of surface conditions, without any charts—but I didn't know that then and it was a
terrible tragedy. After that, I followed Sanderson's work in the
Twilight Lab up there and began to get Brightside into my blood.

But it was Mikuta's idea to attempt a Crossing. Did you ever know
Tom Mikuta? I don't suppose you did. No, not Japanese—Polish-
American. He was a major in the Interplanetary Service for some years
and hung onto the title after he gave up his commission.

He was with Armstrong on Mars during his Service days, with a
good deal of the original mapping and surveying for the colony to his
credit. I first met him on Venus; we spent five years together up there
doing some of the nastiest exploring since the Matto Grosso. Then he
made the attempt on Vulcan Crater that paved the way for Balmer a
few years later.

I'd always liked the Major—he was big and quiet and cool, the sort
of guy who always had things figured a little further ahead than anyone
else and always knew what to do in a tight place. Too many men in this
game are all nerve and luck, with no judgment. The Major had both.

He also had the kind of personality that could take a crew of wild men and make them work like a well-oiled machine across a thousand miles of Venus jungle. I liked him and I trusted him.

He contacted me in New York, and he was very casual at first. We spent an evening here at the Red Lion, talking about old times; he told me about the Vulcan business, and how he'd been out to see Sanderson and the Twilight Lab on Mercury, and how he preferred a hot trek to a cold one any day of the year—and then he wanted to know what I'd been doing since Venus and what my plans were.

"No particular plans," I told him. "Why?"

He looked me over. "How much do you weigh, Peter?"

I told him one thirty-five.

"That's right. A hot trip." He grinned at me. "Might be dangerous, on you, at any rate. How do you take heat?"

"You should know," I said. "Venus was no ice-box."

"No, I mean *real* heat."

Then I began to get it. "You're planning a trip."

"That's right. A hot trip." He grinned at me. "Might be dangerous, too."

"What trip?"

"Brightside of Mercury," the Major said.

I whistled cautiously. "Aphelion?"

He threw his head back. "Why try a Crossing at aphelion? What have you done then? Four thousand miles of butcherous heat, just to have some joker come along, use your data, and drum you out of the glory by crossing at perihelion forty-four days later? No, thanks. I want the Brightside without any nonsense about it." He leaned toward me eagerly. "I want to make a Crossing at perihelion and I want to cross on the surface. If a man can do that, he's got Mercury. Until then, *nobody's* got Mercury. I want Mercury—but I'll need help getting it."

I'd thought of it a thousand times and never dared consider it. Nobody had, since Wyatt and Carpenter disappeared. Mercury turns on its axis in the same time that it wheels around the Sun, which means that the Brightside is always facing in. That makes the Brightside of Mercury at perihelion the hottest place in the Solar System, with one single exception: the surface of the Sun itself.

It would be a hellish trek. Only a few men had ever learned just *how* hellish and they never came back to tell about it. It was a real Hell's Crossing, but someday somebody would cross it.

I wanted to be along.

The Twilight Lab, near the northern pole of Mercury, was the obvious jumping-off place. The setup there wasn't very extensive—a rocket landing, the labs and quarters for Sanderson's crew sunk deeper into the crust, and the tower that housed the Solar 'scope that Sanderson had built up there ten years before.

Twilight Lab wasn't particularly interested in the Brightside, of course—the Sun was Sanderson's baby and he'd picked Mercury as the closest chunk of rock to the Sun that could hold his observatory. He'd chosen a good location, too. On Mercury, the Brightside temperature hits 770° F. at perihelion and the Darkside runs pretty constant at −410° F. No permanent installation with a human crew could survive at either extreme. But with Mercury's wobble, the twilight zone between Brightside and Darkside offers something closer to survival temperatures.

Sanderson built the Lab up near the pole, where the zone is about 5 miles wide, so the temperature only varies 50 to 60 degrees with the libration. The Solar 'scope could take that much change, and they'd get good clear observation of the Sun for about 70 out of the 88 days it takes the planet to wheel around.

The Major was counting on Sanderson knowing something about Mercury as well as the Sun when we camped at the Lab to make final preparations.

Sanderson did. He thought we'd lost our minds and he said so, but he gave us all the help he could. He spent a week briefing Jack Stone, the third member of our party, who had arrived with the supplies and equipment a few days earlier. Poor Jack met us at the rocket landing almost bawling, Sanderson had given him such a gloomy picture of what Brightside was like.

Stone was a youngster—hardly twenty-five, I'd say—but he'd been with the Major at Vulcan and had begged to join this trek. I had a funny feeling that Jack really didn't care for exploring too much, but he thought Mikuta was God, followed him around like a puppy.

It didn't matter to me as long as he knew what he was getting in for. You don't go asking people in this game why they do it—they're liable to get awfully uneasy, and none of them can ever give you an answer that makes sense. Anyway, Stone had borrowed three men from the Lab and had the supplies and equipment all lined up when we got there, ready to check and test.

We dug right in. With plenty of funds—tri-V money and some government cash the Major had talked his way around—our equipment was new and good. Mikuta had done the designing and testing himself, with a big assist from Sanderson. We had four Bugs, three of them the light pillow-tire models, with special lead-cooled cut-in engines when the heat set in, and one heavy-duty tractor model for pulling the sledges.

The Major went over them like a kid at the circus. Then he said, "Have you heard anything from McIvers?"

"Who's he?" Stone wanted to know.

"He'll be joining us. He's a good man—got quite a name for climbing, back home." The Major turned to me. "You've probably heard of him."

I'd heard plenty of stories about Ted McIvers and I wasn't too happy to hear that he was joining us. "Kind of a daredevil, isn't he?"

"Maybe. He's lucky and skillful. Where do you draw the line? We'll need plenty of both."

"Have you ever worked with him?" I asked.

"No. Are you worried?"

"Not exactly. But Brightside is no place to count on luck."

The Major laughed. "I don't think we need to worry about McIvers. We understood each other when I talked up the trip to him, and we're going to need each other too much to do any fooling around." He turned back to the supply list. "Meanwhile, let's get this stuff listed and packed. We'll need to cut weight sharply and our time is short. Sanderson says we should leave in three days."

Two days later, McIvers hadn't arrived. The Major didn't say much about it: Stone was getting edgy and so was I. We spent the second day studying charts of the Brightside, such as they were. The best available were pretty poor, taken from so far out that the detail dissolved into blurs on blowup. They showed the biggest ranges of peaks and craters and faults, and that was all. Still, we could use them to plan a broad outline of our course.

"This range here," the Major said as we crowded around the board, "is largely inactive, according to Sanderson. But these to the south and west *could* be active. Seismograph tracings suggest a lot of activity in that region, getting worse down toward the equator—not only volcanic, but sub-surface shifting."

Stone nodded. "Sanderson told me there was probably constant surface activity."

The Major shrugged. "Well, it's treacherous, there's no doubt of it. But the only way to avoid it is to travel over the Pole, which would lose us days and offer us no guarantee of less activity to the west. Now we might avoid some if we could find a pass through this range and cut sharp east—''

It seemed that the more we considered the problem, the further we got from a solution. We knew there were active volcanoes on the Brightside—even on the Darkside, though surface activity there was pretty much slowed down and localized.

But there were problems of atmosphere on Brightside, as well. There *was* an atmosphere and a constant atmospheric flow from Brightside to Darkside. Not much—the lighter gases had reached escape velocity and disappeared from Brightside millennia ago—but there was CO_2, and nitrogen, and traces of other heavier gases. There was also an abundance of sulfur vapor, as well as carbon disulfide and sulfur dioxide.

The atmospheric tide moved toward the Darkside, where it condensed, carrying enough volcanic ash with it for Sanderson to estimate the depth and nature of the surface upheavals on Brightside from his samplings. The trick was to find a passage that avoided those upheavals as far as possible. But in the final analysis, we were barely scraping the surface. The only way we would find out what was happening where was to be there.

Finally, on the third day, McIvers blew in on a freight rocket from Venus. He'd missed by a few hours the ship that the Major and I had taken and conned his way to Venus in hopes of getting a hop from there. He didn't seem too upset about it, as though this were his usual way of doing things, and he couldn't see why everyone should get so excited.

He was a tall, rangy man with long, wavy hair prematurely gray, and the sort of eyes that looked like a climber's—half closed, sleepy, almost indolent, but capable of abrupt alertness. And he never stood still; he was always moving, always doing something with his hands, or talking, or pacing about.

Evidently the Major decided not to press the issue of his arrival. There was still work to do, and an hour later we were running the final tests on the pressure suits. That evening, Stone and McIvers were thick as thieves, and everything was set for an early departure.

"And that," said Baron, finishing his drink and signaling the waiter for another pair, "was your first big mistake."

Peter Claney raised his eyebrows. "McIvers?"

"Of course."

Claney shrugged, glanced at the small quiet tables around them. "There are lots of bizarre personalities around a place like this, and some of the best wouldn't seem to be the most reliable at first glance. Anyway, personality problems weren't our big problem right then. *Equipment* worried us first and *route* next."

Baron nodded in agreement. "What kind of suits did you have?"

"The best insulating suits ever made," said Claney. "Each one had an inner lining of a fiberglas modification, to avoid the clumsiness of asbestos, and carried the refrigerating unit and oxygen storage which we recharged from the sledges every eight hours. Outer layer carried a monomolecular chrome-reflecting surface that made us glitter like Christmas trees. And we had a half-inch dead-air space under positive pressure between the two layers. Warning thermocouples, of course—at 770 degrees, it wouldn't take much time to fry us to cinders if the suits failed somewhere."

"How about the Bugs?"

"They were insulated, too, but we weren't counting on them too much for protection."

"You weren't!" Baron exclaimed. "Why not?"

"We'd be in and out of them too much. They gave us mobility and storage, but we knew we'd have to do a lot of forward work on foot." Claney smiled bitterly. "Which meant that we had an inch of fiberglas and a half-inch of dead air between us and a surface temperature where lead flowed like water and zinc was almost at melting point and the pools of sulfur in the shadows were boiling like oatmeal over a campfire."

Baron licked his lips. His fingers stroked the cool, wet glass.

"Go on," he said tautly. "You started on schedule?"

"Oh, yes," said Claney, "we started on schedule, all right. We just didn't quite end on schedule, that was all. But I'm getting to that."

He settled back in his chair and continued.

We jumped off from Twilight on a course due southeast, with thirty days to make it to the Center of Brightside. If we could cross an average of seventy miles a day, we could hit Center exactly at perihelion, the point of Mercury's closest approach to the Sun—which made Center the hottest part of the planet at the hottest it ever gets.

The Sun was already huge and yellow over the horizon when we started, twice the size it appears on Earth. Every day that Sun would grow bigger and whiter, and every day the surface would get hotter. But once we reached Center, the job was only half done—we would still have to travel another 2,000 miles to the opposite twilight zone. Sanderson was to meet us on the other side in the Laboratory's scout ship, approximately sixty days from the time we jumped off.

That was the plan, in outline. It was up to us to cross those seventy miles a day, no matter how hot it became, no matter what terrain we had to cross. Detours would be dangerous and time-consuming. Delays could cost us our lives. We all knew that.

The Major briefed us on details an hour before we left. "Peter, you'll take the lead Bug, the small one we stripped down for you. Stone and I will flank you on either side, giving you a hundred-yard lead. McIvers, you'll have the job of dragging the sledges, so we'll have to direct your course pretty closely. Peter's job is to pick the passage at any given point. If there's any doubt of safe passage, we'll all explore ahead on foot before we risk the Bugs. Got that?"

McIvers and Stone exchanged glances. McIvers said: "Jack and I were planning to change around. We figured he could take the sledges. That would give me a little more mobility."

The Major looked up sharply at Stone. "Do you buy that, Jack?"

Stone shrugged. "I don't mind. Mac wanted—"

McIvers made an impatient gesture with his hands. "It doesn't matter. I just feel better when I'm on the move. Does it make any difference?"

"I guess it doesn't," said the Major. "Then you'll flank Peter along with me. Right?"

"Sure, sure." McIvers pulled at his lower lip. "Who's going to do the advance scouting?"

"It sounds like I am," I cut in. "We want to keep the lead Bug as light as possible."

Mikuta nodded. "That's right. Peter's Bug is stripped down to the frame and wheels."

McIvers shook his head. "No, I mean the *advance* work. You need somebody out ahead—four or five miles, at least—to pick up the big flaws and active surface changes, don't you?" He stared at the Major. "I mean, how can we tell what sort of a hole we may be moving into, unless we have a scout up ahead?"

"That's what we have the charts for," the Major said sharply.

"Charts! I'm talking about *detail* work. We don't need to worry about the major topography. It's the little faults you can't see on the pictures that can kill us." He tossed the charts down excitedly. "Look, let me take a Bug out ahead and work reconnaissance, keep five, maybe ten miles ahead of the column. I can stay on good solid ground, of course, but scan the area closely and radio back to Peter where to avoid the flaws. Then—''

''No dice,'' the Major broke in.

''But why not? We could save ourselves days!''

''I don't care what we could save. We stay together. When we get to the Center, I want live men along with me. That means we stay within easy sight of each other at all times. Any climber knows that everybody is safer in a party than one man alone—anytime, anyplace.''

McIvers stared at him, his cheeks an angry red. Finally he gave a sullen nod. ''Okay. If you say so.''

''Well, I say so and I mean it. I don't want any fancy stuff. We're going to hit Center together, and finish the Crossing together. Got that?''

McIvers nodded. Mikuta then looked at Stone and me and we nodded, too.

''All right,'' he said slowly. ''Now that we've got it straight, let's go.''

It was hot. If I forget everything else about that trek, I'll never forget that huge yellow Sun glaring down, without a break, hotter and hotter with every mile. We knew that the first few days would be the easiest, and we were rested and fresh when we started down the long ragged gorge southeast of the Twilight Lab.

I moved out first; back over my shoulder, I could see the Major and McIvers crawling out behind me, their pillow tires taking the rugged floor of the gorge smoothly. Behind them, Stone dragged the sledges.

Even at only 30 percent Earth gravity they were a strain on the big tractor, until the ski-blades bit into the fluffy volcanic ash blanketing the valley. We even had a path to follow for the first twenty miles.

I kept my eyes pasted to the big polaroid binocs, picking out the track the early research teams had made out into the edge of Brightside. But in a couple of hours we rumbled past Sanderson's little outpost observatory and the tracks stopped. We were in virgin territory and already the Sun was beginning to bite.

We didn't *feel* that heat so much those first days out. We *saw* it. The refrig units kept our skins at a nice comfortable 75° F. inside our suits, but our eyes watched that glaring Sun and the baked yellow rocks going past, and some nerve pathways got twisted up, somehow. We poured sweat as if we were in a superheated furnace.

We drove eight hours and slept five. When a sleep period came due, we pulled the Bugs together into a square, threw up a light aluminum sun-shield and lay out in the dust and rocks. The sun-shield cut the temperature down sixty or seventy degrees, for whatever help that was. And then we ate from the forward sledge—sucking through tubes— protein, carbohydrates, bulk gelatin, vitamins.

The Major measured water out with an iron hand, because we'd have drunk ourselves into nephritis in a week otherwise. We were constantly, unceasingly thirsty. Ask the physiologists and psychiatrists why—they can give you half a dozen interesting reasons—but all we knew, or cared about, was that it happened to be so.

We didn't sleep the first few stops, as a consequence. Our eyes burned in spite of the filters and we had roaring headaches, but we couldn't sleep them off. We sat around looking at each other. Then McIvers would say how good a beer would taste, and off we'd go. We'd have butchered our grandmothers for one ice-cold bottle of beer.

After a few driving periods, I began to get my bearings at the wheel. We were moving down into desolation that made Earth's old Death Valley look like a Japanese rose garden. Huge sun-baked cracks opened up in the floor of the gorge, with black cliffs jutting up on either side; the air was filled with a barely visible yellowish mist of sulfur and sulfurous gases.

It was a hot, barren hell-hole, no place for any man to go, but the challenge was so powerful you could almost feel it. No one had ever crossed this land before and escaped. Those who had tried it had been cruelly punished, but the land was still there, so it had to be crossed. Not the easy way. It had to be crossed the hardest way possible: overland, through anything the land could throw up to us, at the most difficult time possible.

Yet we knew that even the land might have been conquered before, except for that Sun. We'd fought absolute cold before and won. We'd never fought heat like this and won. The only worse heat in the Solar System was the surface of the Sun itself.

Brightside was worth trying for. We would get it or it would get us. That was the bargain.

I learned a lot about Mercury those first few driving periods. The gorge petered out after a hundred miles and we moved onto the slope of a range of ragged craters that ran south and east. This range had shown no activity since the first landing on Mercury forty years before, but beyond it there were active cones. Yellow fumes rose from the craters constantly; their sides were shrouded with heavy ash.

We couldn't detect a wind, but we knew there was a hot, sulfurous breeze sweeping in great continental tides across the face of the planet. Not enough for erosion, though. The craters rose up out of jagged gorges, huge towering spears of rock and rubble. Below were the vast yellow flatlands, smoking and hissing from the gases beneath the crust. Over everything was gray dust—silicates and salts, pumice and lime-stone and granite ash, filling crevices and declivities—offering a soft, treacherous surface for the Bug's pillow tires.

I learned to read the ground, to tell a covered fault by the sag of the dust; I learned to spot a passable crack, and tell it from an impassable cut. Time after time the Bugs ground to a halt while we explored a passage on foot, tied together with light copper cable, digging, advanc-ing, digging some more until we were sure the surface would carry the machines. It was cruel work; we slept in exhaustion. But it went smoothly, at first.

Too smoothly, it seemed to me, and the others seemed to think so, too.

McIvers' restlessness was beginning to grate on our nerves. He talked too much, while we were resting or while we were driving: wisecracks, witticisms, unfunny jokes that wore thin with repetition. He took to making side trips from the route now and then, never far, but a little farther each time.

Jack Stone reacted quite the opposite; he grew quieter with each stop, more reserved and apprehensive. I didn't like it, but I figured that it would pass off after a while. I was apprehensive enough myself; I just managed to hide it better.

And every mile the Sun got bigger and whiter and higher in the sky and hotter. Without our ultraviolet screens and glare filters we would have been blinded; as it was our eyes ached constantly, and the skin on our faced itched and tingled at the end of an eight-hour trek.

But it took one of those side trips of McIvers' to deliver the penulti-mate blow to our already fraying nerves. He had driven down a side branch of a long canyon running off west of our route and was almost out of sight in a cloud of ash when we heard a sharp cry through our earphones.

I wheeled my Bug around with my heart in my throat and spotted him through the binocs, waving frantically from the top of his machine. The Major and I took off, lumbering down the gulch after him as fast as the Bugs could go, with a thousand horrible pictures racing through our minds. . . .

We found him standing stock-still, pointing down the gorge and, for once, he didn't have anything to say. It was the wreck of a Bug, an old-fashioned half-track model of the sort that hadn't been in use for years. It was wedged tight in a cut in the rock, an axle broken, its casing split wide open up the middle, half buried in a rock slide. A dozen feet away were two insulated suits with the white bones gleaming through the fiberglas helmets.

This was as far as Wyatt and Carpenter had gotten on *their* Brightside Crossing.

On the fifth driving period out, the terrain began to change. It looked the same, but every now and then it *felt* different. On two occasions I felt my wheels spin, with a howl of protest from my engine. Then, quite suddenly, the Bug gave a lurch; I gunned my motor and nothing happened.

I could see the dull-gray stuff seeping up around the hubs, thick and tenacious, splattering around in steaming gobs as the wheels spun. I knew what had happened the moment the wheels gave and, a few minutes later, they chained me to the tractor and dragged me back out of the mire. It looked for all the world like thick gray mud, but it was a pit of molten lead, steaming under a soft layer of concealing ash.

I picked my way more cautiously then. We were getting into an area of recent surface activity; the surface was really treacherous. I caught myself wishing that the Major had okayed McIvers' scheme for an advance scout; more dangerous for the individual, maybe, but I was driving blind now and I didn't like it.

One error in judgment could sink us all, but I wasn't thinking much about the others. I was worried about *me,* plenty worried. I kept thinking, better McIvers should go than me. It wasn't healthy thinking and I knew it, but I couldn't get the thought out of my mind.

It was a grueling eight hours, and we slept poorly. Back in the Bugs again, we moved still more slowly—edging out on a broad flat plateau, dodging a network of gaping surface cracks—winding back and forth in an effort to keep the machines on solid rock. I couldn't see far ahead, because of the yellow haze rising from the cracks, so I was almost on top of it when I saw a sharp cut ahead where the surface dropped six feet beyond a deep crack.

I let out a shout to halt the others; then I edged my Bug forward, peering at the cleft. It was deep and wide. I moved fifty yards to the left, then back to the right.

There was only one place that looked like a possible crossing: a long, narrow ledge of gray stuff that lay down across a section of the fault like a ramp. Even as I watched it, I could feel the surface crust under the Bug trembling and saw the ledge shift over a few feet.

The Major's voice sounded in my ears. "How about it, Peter?"

"I don't know. This crust is on roller skates," I called back.

"How about that ledge?"

I hesitated. "I'm scared of it, Major. Let's backtrack and try to find a way around."

There was a roar of disgust in my earphones and McIvers' Bug suddenly lurched forward. It rolled down past me, picked up speed, with McIvers hunched behind the wheel like a race driver. He was heading past me straight for the gray ledge.

My shout caught in my throat; I heard the Major take a huge breath and roar: "My God, Mac, *stop that thing,* you fool!" and then McIvers' Bug was out on the ledge, lumbering across like a juggernaut.

The ledge jolted as the tires struck it; for a horrible moment, it seemed to be sliding out from under the machine. And then the Bug was across in a cloud of dust, and I heard McIvers' voice in my ears, shouting in glee, "Come on, you slowpokes. It'll hold you!"

Something unprintable came through the earphones as the Major drew up alongside me and moved his Bug out on the ledge slowly and over to the other side. Then he said, "Take it slow, Peter. Then give Jack a hand with the sledges." His voice sounded tight as a wire.

Ten minutes later, we were on the other side of the cleft. The Major checked the whole column; then he turned on McIvers angrily. "One more trick like that," he said, "and I'll strap you to a rock and leave you. Do you understand me? *One more time—*"

McIvers' voice was heavy with protest. "Good Lord, if we leave it up to Claney, he'll have us out here forever! Any blind fool could see that that ledge would hold."

"I saw it moving," I shot back at him.

"All right, all right, so you've got good eyes. Why all the fuss? We got across, didn't we? But I say we've got to have a little nerve and use it once in a while if we're ever going to get across this lousy hotbox."

"We need to use a little judgment, too," the Major snapped. "All right, let's roll. But if you think I was joking, you just try me out once." He let it soak in for a minute. Then he geared his Bug on around to my flank again.

At the stopover, the incident wasn't mentioned again, but the Major drew me aside just as I was settling down for sleep. "Peter, I'm worried," he said slowly.

"McIvers? Don't worry. He's not as reckless as he seems—just impatient. We are over a hundred miles behind schedule, and we're moving awfully slow. We only made forty miles this last drive."

The Major shook his head. "I don't mean McIvers. I mean the kid."

"Jack? What about him?"

"Take a look."

Stone was shaking. He was over near the tractor—away from the rest of us—and he was lying on his back, but he wasn't asleep. His whole body was shaking, convulsively. I saw him grip an outcropping of rock hard.

I walked over and sat down beside him. "Get your water all right?" I said.

He didn't answer. He just kept on shaking.

"Hey, boy," I said. "What's the trouble?"

"It's hot," he said, choking out the words.

"Sure it's hot, but don't let it throw you. We're in really good shape."

"We're not," he snapped. "We're in rotten shape, if you ask me. *We're not going to make it,* do you know that? That crazy fool's going to kill us for sure—" All of a sudden, he was bawling like a baby. "I'm scared—I shouldn't be here—I'm *scared.* What am I trying to prove by coming out here, for God's sake? I'm some kind of hero or something? I tell you I'm scared—"

"Look," I said. "Mikuta's scared, *I'm* scared. So what? We'll make it, don't worry. And nobody's trying to be a hero."

"Nobody but Hero Stone," he said bitterly. He shook himself and gave a tight little laugh. "Some hero, eh?"

"We'll make it," I said.

"Sure," he said finally. "Sorry. I'll be okay."

I rolled over, but waited until he was good and quiet. Then I tried to sleep, but I didn't sleep too well. I kept thinking about that ledge. I'd known from the look of it what it was; a zinc slough of the sort Sanderson had warned us about, a wide sheet of almost pure zinc that had been thrown up white-hot from below, quite recently, just waiting for oxygen or sulfur to rot it through.

I knew enough about zinc to know that at these temperatures it gets brittle as glass. Take a chance like McIvers had taken and the whole sheet could snap like a dry pine board. But it wasn't McIvers' fault that it hadn't.

Five hours later, we were back at the wheel. We were hardly moving at all. The ragged surface was almost impassable—great jutting rocks peppered the plateau; ledges crumbled the moment my tires touched them; long, open canyons turned into lead-mires or sulfur pits.

A dozen times I climbed out of the Bug to prod out an uncertain area with my boots and pikestaff. Whenever I did, McIvers piled out behind me, running ahead like a schoolboy at the fair, then climbing back again, red-faced and panting, while we moved the machines ahead another mile or two.

Time was pressing us now, and McIvers wouldn't let me forget it.

We had made only about 320 miles in six driving periods, so we were about a hundred miles or even more behind schedule.

"We're not going to make it," McIvers would complain angrily. "That Sun's going to be out to aphelion by the time we hit the Center—"

"Sorry, but I can't take it any faster," I told him. I was getting good and mad. I knew what he wanted but didn't dare let him have it. I was scared enough pushing the Bug out on those ledges, even knowing that at least *I* was making the decisions. Put him in the lead and we wouldn't last for eight hours. Our nerves wouldn't take it, at any rate, even if the machines did.

Jack Stone looked up from the aluminum chart sheets. "Another hundred miles and we should hit a good stretch," he said. "Maybe we can make up distance there for a couple of days."

The Major agreed, but McIvers couldn't hold his impatience. He kept staring up at the Sun as if he had a personal grudge against it, and stamped back and forth under the sun-shield. "That'll be just fine," he said. "*If* we ever get that far, that is."

We dropped it there, but the Major stopped me as we climbed aboard for the next run. "That guy's going to blow wide open if we don't move faster, Peter. I don't want him in the lead, no matter what happens. He's right, though, about the need to make better time. Keep your head, but crowd your luck a little, okay?"

"I'll try," I said. It was asking the impossible and Mikuta knew it. We were on a long downward slope that shifted and buckled all around us, as though there was a molten underlay beneath the crust; the slope was broken by huge crevasses, partly covered with dust and zinc sheeting, like a vast glacier of stone and metal. The outside temperature registered 547° F. and getting hotter. It was no place to start rushing ahead.

I tried it anyway. I took half a dozen shaky passages, edging slowly out on flat zinc ledges, then toppling over and across. It seemed easy for a while and we made progress. We hit an even stretch and raced ahead. And then I quickly jumped on my brakes and jerked the Bug to a halt in a cloud of dust.

I'd gone too far. We were out on a wide, flat sheet of gray stuff, apparently solid—until I'd suddenly caught sight of the crevasse beneath in the corner of my eye. It was an overhanging shelf that trembled under me as I stopped. McIvers' voice was in my ear. "What's the trouble now, Claney?"

"Move back!" I shouted. "It can't hold us!"

"Looks solid from here."

"You want to argue about it? It's too thin, it'll snap. Move back!"

I started edging back down the ledge. I heard McIvers swear; then I saw his Bug start to creep *outward* on the shelf. Not fast or reckless, this time, but slowly, churning up dust in a gentle cloud behind him.

I just stared and felt the blood rush to my head. It seemed so hot I could hardly breathe as he edged out beyond me, farther and farther—

I think I felt it snap before I saw it. My own machine gave a sickening lurch and a long black crack appeared across the shelf—and widened. Then the ledge began to upend. I heard a scream as McIvers' Bug rose up and up and then crashed down into the crevasse in a thundering slide of rock and shattered metal.

I just stared for a full minute, I think. I couldn't move until I heard Jack Stone groan and the Major shouting, "Claney! I couldn't see— *what happened?*"

"It snapped on him, that's what happened," I roared. I gunned my motor, edged forward toward the fresh-broken edge of the shelf. The crevasse gaped; I couldn't see any sign of the machine. Dust was still billowing up blindingly from below.

We stood staring down, the three of us. I caught a glimpse of Jack Stone's face through his helmet. It wasn't pretty.

"Well," said the Major heavily, "that's that."

"I guess so." I felt the way Stone looked.

"Wait," said Stone. "I heard something."

He had. It was a cry in the earphones—faint, but unmistakable.

"Mac!" the Major called. "Mac, can you hear me?"

"Yeah, yeah. I can year you." The voice was very weak.

"Are you all right?"

"I don't know. Broken leg, I think. It's—hot." There was a long pause. Then: "I think my cooler's gone out."

The Major shot me a glance, then turned to Stone. "Get a cable from the second sledge fast. He'll fry alive if we don't get him out of there. Peter, I need you to lower me. Use the tractor winch."

I lowered him: he stayed down only a few moments. When I hauled him up, his face was drawn. "Still alive," he panted. "He won't be very long, though." He hesitated for just an instant. "We've got to make a try."

"I don't like this ledge," I said. "It's moved twice since I got out. Why not back off and lower him a cable?"

"No good. The Bug is smashed and he's inside it. We'll need

torches and I'll need one of you to help.'' He looked at me and then gave Stone a long look. ''Peter, you'd better come.''

''Wait,'' said Stone. His face was very white. ''Let me go down with you.''

''Peter is lighter.''

''I'm not so heavy. Let me go down.''

''Okay, if that's the way you want it.'' The Major tossed him a torch. ''Peter, check these hitches and lower us slowly. If you see any kind of trouble, *anything,* cast yourself free and back off this thing, do you understand? This whole ledge may go.''

I nodded. ''Good luck.''

They went over the ledge. I let the cable down bit by bit until it hit two hundred feet and slacked off.

''How does it look?'' I shouted.

''Bad,'' said the Major. ''We'll have to work fast. This whole side of the crevasse is ready to crumble. Down a little more.''

Minutes passed without a sound. I tried to relax, but I couldn't. Then I felt the ground shift, and the tractor lurched to the side.

The Major shouted, *''It's going, Peter—pull back!''* and I threw the tractor into reverse, jerked the controls as the tractor rumbled off the shelf. The cable snapped, coiled up in front like a broken clock-spring. The whole surface under me was shaking wildly now; ash rose in huge gray clouds. Then, with a roar, the whole shelf lurched and slid sideways. It teetered on the edge for seconds before it crashed into the crevasse, tearing the side wall down with it in a mammoth slide. I jerked the tractor to a halt as the dust and flame billowed up.

They were gone—all three of them, McIvers and the Major and Jack Stone—buried under thousands of tons of rock and zinc and molten lead. There wasn't any danger of anybody ever finding their bones.

Peter Claney leaned back, finishing his drink, rubbing his scarred face as he looked across at Baron.

Slowly, Baron's grip relaxed on the chair arm. ''*You* got back.''

Claney nodded. ''I got back, sure. I had the tractor and the sledges. I had seven days to drive back under that yellow Sun. I had plenty of time to think.''

''You took the wrong man along,'' Baron said. ''That was your mistake. Without him you would have made it.''

''Never.'' Claney shook his head. ''That's what I was thinking the first day or so—that it was *McIvers'* fault, that *he* was to blame. But that isn't true. He was wild, reckless, and had lots of nerve.''

''But his judgment was bad!''

"It couldn't have been sounder. We had to keep to our schedule even if it killed us, because it would positively kill us if we didn't."

"But a man like that—"

"A man like McIvers was necessary. Can't you see that? It was the Sun that beat us, that surface. Perhaps we were licked the very day we started." Claney leaned across the table, his eyes pleading. "We didn't realize that, but it was *true*. There are places that men can't go, conditions men can't tolerate. The others had to die to learn that. I was lucky, I came back. But I'm trying to tell you what I found out—that *nobody* will ever make a Brightside Crossing."

"We will," said Baron. "It won't be a picnic, but we'll make it."

"But suppose you do," said Claney, suddenly. "Suppose I'm all wrong, suppose you *do* make it. Then what? *What comes next?*"

"The Sun," said Baron.

Claney nodded slowly. "Yes. That would be it, wouldn't it?" He laughed. "Good-by, Baron. Jolly talk and all that. Thanks for listening."

Baron caught his wrist as he started to rise. "Just one question more, Claney. Why did you come here?"

"To try to talk you out of killing yourself," said Claney.

You're a liar," said Baron.

Claney stared down at him for a long moment. Then he crumpled in the chair. There was defeat in his pale blue eyes and something else. "Well?"

Peter Claney spread his hands, a helpless gesture. "When do you leave, Baron? I want you to take me along."

Before Eden

Arthur C. Clarke

"I guess," said Jerry Garfield, cutting the engines, "that this is the end of the line." With a gentle sigh, the underjets faded out; deprived of its air-cushion, the scout-car *Rambling Wreck* settled down upon the twisted rocks of the Hesperian Plateau.

There was no way forward; neither on its jets nor its tractors could S.5—to give the *Wreck* its official name—scale the escarpment that lay ahead. The South Pole of Venus was only thirty miles away, but it might have been on another planet. They would have to turn back, and retrace their four-hundred-mile journey through this nightmare landscape.

The weather was fantastically clear, with visibility of almost a thousand yards. There was no need of radar to show the cliffs ahead; for once, the naked eye was good enough. The green auroral light, filtering down through clouds that had rolled unbroken for a million years, gave the scene an underwater appearance, and the way in which all distant objects blurred into the haze added to the impression. Sometimes it was easy to believe that they were driving across a shallow sea-bed, and more than once Jerry had imagined that he had seen fish floating overhead.

"Shall I call the ship, and say we're turning back?" he asked.

"Not yet," said Dr. Hutchins. "I want to think."

Jerry shot an appealing glance at the third member of the crew, but found no moral support there. Coleman was just as bad; although the two men argued furiously half the time, they were both scientists and therefore, in the opinion of a hard-headed, engineer-navigator, not wholly responsible citizens. If Cole and Hutch had bright ideas about going forward, there was nothing he could do except register a protest.

Hutchins was pacing back and forth in the tiny cabin, studying charts and instruments. Presently he swung the car's searchlight towards the cliffs, and began to examine them carefully with binoculars. Surely, thought Jerry, he doesn't expect me to drive up there! S.5 was a hover-track, not a mountain goat. . . .

Abruptly, Hutchins found something. He released his breath in a sudden explosive gasp, then turned to Coleman.

"Look!" he said, his voice full of excitement. "Just to the left of that black mark! Tell me what you see."

He handed over the glasses, and it was Coleman's turn to stare.

"Well I'm damned," he said at length. "You were right. There *are* rivers on Venus. That's a dried-up waterfall."

"So you owe me one dinner at the Bel Gourmet when we get back to Cambridge. With champagne."

"No need to remind me. Anyway, it's cheap at the price. But this still leaves your other theories strictly on the crackpot level."

"Just a minute," interjected Jerry. "What's all this about rivers and waterfalls? Everyone knows they can't exist on Venus. It never gets cold enough on this steam-bath of a planet for the clouds to condense."

"Have you looked at the thermometer lately?" asked Hutchins with deceptive mildness.

"I've been slightly too busy driving."

"Then I've news for you. It's down to 230, and still falling. Don't forget—we're almost at the Pole, it's wintertime, and we're sixty thousand feet above the lowlands. All this adds up to a distinct nip in the air. If the temperature drops a few more degrees, we'll have rain. The water will be boiling, of course—but it will be water. And though George won't admit it yet, this puts Venus in a completely different light."

"Why?" asked Jerry, though he had already guessed.

"Where there's water, there may be life. We've been in too much of a hurry to assume that Venus is sterile, merely because the average temperature's over five hundred degrees. It's a lot colder here, and that's why I've been so anxious to get to the Pole. There are lakes up here in the highlands, and I want to look at them."

"But *boiling* water!" protested Coleman. "Nothing could live in that!"

"There are algae that manage it on Earth. And if we've learned one thing since we started exploring the planets, it's this—wherever Life has the slightest chance of surviving, you'll find it. This is the only chance it's ever had on Venus."

"I wish we could test your theory. But you can see for yourself—we can't go up that cliff."

"Perhaps not in the car. But it won't be too difficult to climb those rocks, even wearing thermosuits. All we need do is walk a few miles towards the Pole; according to the radar maps, it's fairly level once you're over the rim. We could manage in—oh, twelve hours at the most. Each of us has been out for longer than that, in much worse conditions."

That was perfectly true. Protective clothing that had been designed to keep men alive in the Venusian lowlands would have an easy job here, where it was only a hundred degrees hotter than Death Valley in midsummer.

"Well," said Coleman. "You know the regulations. You can't go by yourself, and someone has to stay here to keep contact with the ship. How do we settle it this time—chess or cards?"

"Chess takes too long," said Hutchins, "especially when you two play it." He reached into the chart table and produced a well-worn pack. "Cut them, Jerry."

"Ten of spades. Hope you can beat it, George."

"So do I. Damn—only five of clubs. Well, give my regards to the Venusians."

Despite Hutchins' assurance, it was hard work climbing the escarpment. The slope was not too steep, but the weight of oxygen gear, refrigerated thermosuit and scientific equipment came to more than a hundred pounds per man. The lower gravity—thirteen percent weaker than Earth's—gave a little help, but not much, as they toiled up screes, rested on ledges to regain breath, and then clambered on again through the submarine twilight. The emerald glow that washed around them was brighter than that of the full moon on Earth. A moon would have been wasted on Venus, Jerry told himself; it could never have been seen from the surface, there were no oceans for it to rule—and the incessant aurora was a far more constant source of light.

They had climbed over two thousand feet before the ground levelled out into a gentle slope, scarred here and there by channels that had clearly been cut by running water. After a little searching, they came across a gulley wide and deep enough to merit the name of river-bed, and started to walk along it.

"I've just thought of something," said Jerry after they had travelled a few hundred yards. "Suppose there's a storm up ahead of us? I don't feel like facing a tidal wave of boiling water."

"If there's a storm," replied Hutchins a little impatiently, "we'll hear it. There'll be plenty of time to reach high ground."

He was undoubtedly right, but Jerry felt no happier as they continued to climb the gently-shelving water-course. His uneasiness had been growing ever since they had passed over the brow of the cliff and had lost radio contact with the scout-car. In this day and age, to be out of touch with one's fellowmen was a unique and unsettling experience. It had never happened to Jerry before in all his life; even aboard the *Morning Star,* when they were a hundred million miles from Earth, he could always send a message to his family and get a reply back within minutes. But now, a few yards of rock had cut him off from the rest of mankind; if anything happened to them here, no one would ever know, unless some later expedition found their bodies. George would wait for the agreed number of hours; then he would head back to the ship— alone. I guess I'm not really the pioneering type, Jerry told himself. I like running complicated machines, and that's how I got involved in spaceflight. But I never stopped to think where it would lead, and now it's too late to change my mind.

They had travelled perhaps three miles towards the Pole, following the meanders of the river-bed, when Hutchins stopped to make observations and collect specimens. "Still getting colder!" he said. "The temperature's down to 199. That's far and away the lowest ever recorded on Venus. I wish we could call George and let him know."

Jerry tried all the wavebands; he even attempted to raise the ship—the unpredictable ups and downs of the planet's ionosphere sometimes made such long-distance reception possible—but there was not a whisper of a carrier-wave above the roar and crackle of the Venusian thunderstorms.

"This is even better," said Hutchins, and now there was real excitement in his voice. "The oxygen concentration's way up—fifteen parts in a million. It was only five back at the car, and down in the lowlands you can scarcely detect it."

"But fifteen in a *million!*" protested Jerry. "Nothing could breathe that!"

"You've got hold of the wrong end of the stick," Hutchings explained. "Nothing does breathe it. Something *makes* it. Where do you think Earth's oxygen comes from? It's all produced by life—by growing plants. Before there were plants on Earth, our atmosphere was just like this one—a mess of carbon dioxide and ammonia and methane. Then vegetation evolved, and slowly converted the atmosphere into something that animals could breathe."

"I see," said Jerry, "and you think that the same process has just started here?"

"It looks like it. *Something* not far from here is producing oxygen—and plant life is the simplest explanation."

"And where there are plants," mused Jerry, "I suppose you'll have animals, sooner or later."

"Yes," said Hutchins, packing his gear and starting up the gulley, "though it takes a few hundred million years. We may be too soon—but I hope not."

"That's all very well," Jerry answered. "But suppose we meet something that doesn't like us? We've no weapons."

"And we don't need them. Have you stopped to think what we look like? Obviously any animal would run a mile at the sight of us."

There was some truth in that. The reflecting metal foil of their thermosuits covered them from head to foot like flexible, glittering armor. No insects had more elaborate antennae than those mounted on their helmets and backpacks, and the wide lenses through which they stared out at the world looked like blank yet monstrous eyes. Yes, there were few animals on Earth that would stop to argue with such apparitions; but any Venusians might have different ideas.

Jerry was still mulling this over when they came upon the lake. Even at that first glimpse, it made him think not of the life they were seeking, but of death. Like a black mirror, it lay amid a fold of the hills; its far edge was hidden in the eternal mist, and ghostly columns of vapor swirled and danced upon its surface. All it needed, Jerry told himself, was Charon's ferry waiting to take them to the other side—or the Swan of Tuonela swimming majestically back and forth as it guarded the entrance to the Underworld. . . .

Yet for all this, it was a miracle—the first free water that men had ever found on Venus. Hutchins was already on his knees, almost in an attitude of prayer. But he was only collecting drops of the precious liquid to examine through his pocket microscopes.

"Anything there?" asked Jerry anxiously.

Hutchins shook his head.

"If there is, it's too small to see with this instrument. I'll tell you more when we're back at the ship." He sealed a test-tube and placed it in his collecting-bag, as tenderly as any prospector who had just found a nugget laced with gold. It might be—it probably was—nothing more than plain water. But it might also be a universe of unknown, living creatures on the first stage of their billion-year journey to intelligence.

Hutchins had walked no more than a dozen yards along the edge of the lake when he stopped again, so suddenly that Garfield nearly collided with him.

"What's the matter?" Jerry asked. "Seen something?"

"That dark patch of rock over there. I noticed it before we stopped at the lake."

"What about it? It looks ordinary enough to me."

"I think it's grown bigger."

All his life, Jerry was to remember this moment. Somehow he never doubted Hutchins' statement; by this time he could believe anything, even that rocks could grow. The sense of isolation and mystery, the presence of that dark and brooding lake, the never-ceasing rumble of distant storms and the green flickering of the aurora—all these had done something to his mind, had prepared it to face the incredible. Yet he felt no fear; that would come later.

He looked at the rock. It was about five hundred feet away, as far as he could estimate. In this dim, emerald light it was hard to judge distances or dimensions. The rock—or whatever it was—seemed to be a horizontal slab of almost black material, lying near the crest of a low ridge. There was a second, much smaller, patch of similar material near it; Jerry tried to measure and memorize the gap between them, so that he would have some yard-stick to detect any change.

Even when he saw that the gap was slowly shrinking, he still felt no alarm—only a puzzled excitement. Not until it had vanished completely, and he realized how his eyes had tricked him, did that awful feeling of helpless terror strike into his heart.

Here were no growing or moving rocks. What they were watching was a dark tide, a crawling carpet, sweeping slowly but inexorably towards them over the top of the ridge.

The moment of sheer, unreasoning panic lasted, mercifully, no more than a few seconds. Garfield's first terror began to fade as soon as he recognized its cause. For that advancing tide had reminded him, all too vividly, of a story he had read many years ago about the army ants of the Amazon, and the way in which they destroyed everything in their path. . . .

But whatever this tide might be, it was moving too slowly to be a real danger, unless it cut off their line of retreat. Hutchins was staring at it intently through their only pair of binoculars; he was the biologist, and he was holding his ground. No point in making a fool of myself, thought Jerry, by running like a scalded cat, if it isn't necessary.

"For heaven's sake," he said at last, when the moving carpet was only a hundred yards away and Hutchins had not uttered a word or stirred a muscle. "What *is* it?"

Hutchins slowly unfroze, like a statue coming to life.

"Sorry," he said. "I'd forgotten all about you. It's a plant, of course. At least I suppose we'd better call it that."

"But it's *moving!*"

"Why should that surprise you? So do terrestrial plants. Ever seen speeded-up movies of ivy in action?"

"That still stays in one place—it doesn't crawl all over the landscape."

"Then what about the plankton plants of the sea? *They* can swim when they have to."

Jerry gave up; in any case, the approaching wonder had robbed him of words.

He still thought of the thing as a carpet—a deep pile one, ravelled into tassles at the edges. It varied in thickness as it moved; in some parts it was a mere film; in others, it heaped up to a depth of a foot or more. As it came closer and he could see its texture, Jerry was reminded of black velvet. He wondered what it felt like to the touch, then remembered that it would burn his fingers even if it did nothing else to them. He found himself thinking, in the light-headed nervous reaction that often follows a sudden shock: "If there *are* any Venusians, we'll never be able to shake hands with them. They'd burn us, and we'd give them frost-bite."

So far, the thing had shown no signs that it was aware of their presence. It had merely flowed forward like the mindless tide that it almost certainly was. Apart from the fact that it climbed over small obstacles, it might have been an advancing flood of water.

And then, when it was only ten feet away, the velvet tide checked itself. On the right and the left, it still flowed forward; but dead ahead it slowed to a halt.

"We're being encircled," said Jerry anxiously. "Better fall back, until we're sure it's harmless."

To his relief, Hutchins stepped back at once. After a brief hesitation, the creature resumed its slow advance and the dent in its front line straightened out.

Then Hutchins stepped forward again—and the thing slowly withdrew. Half a dozen times the biologist advanced, only to retreat again, and each time the living tide ebbed and flowed in synchronism with his movements. I never imagined, Jerry told himself, that I'd live to see a man waltzing with a plant. . . .

"Thermophobia," said Hutchins. "Purely automatic reaction. It doesn't like our heat."

"Our heat!" protested Jerry. "Why, we're living icicles by comparison."

"Of course—but our suits aren't, and that's all it knows about."

Stupid of me, thought Jerry. When you were snug and cool inside your thermosuit, it was easy to forget that the refrigeration unit on your back was pumping a blast of heat out into the surrounding air. No wonder the Venusian plant had shied away.

"Let's see how it reacts to light," said Hutchins. He switched on his chest-lamp, and the green auroral glow was instantly banished by the flood of pure white radiance. Until Man had come to this planet, no white light had ever shone upon the surface of Venus, even by day. As in the seas of Earth, there was only a green twilight, deepening slowly to utter darkness.

The transformation was so stunning that neither man could check a cry of astonishment. Gone in a flash was the deep, sombre black of the thick-piled velvet carpet at their feet. Instead, as far as their lights carried, lay a glazing pattern of glorious vivid reds, laced with streaks of gold. No Persian prince could ever have commanded so opulent a tapestry from his weavers, yet this was the accidental product of biological forces. Indeed, until they had switched on their floods, these superb colors had not even existed, and they would vanish once more when the alien light of Earth ceased to conjure them into being.

"Tikov was right," murmured Hutchins. "I wish he could have known."

"Right about what?" asked Jerry, though it seemed almost a sacrilege to speak in the presence of such loveliness.

"Back in Russia, fifty years ago, he found that plants living in very cold climates tended to be blue and violet, while those from hot ones were red or orange. He predicted that the Martian vegetation would be violet, and said that if there were plants on Venus they'd be red. Well, he was right on both counts. But we can't stand here all day—we've work to do."

"You're sure it's quite safe?" asked Jerry, some of his caution reasserting itself.

"Absolutely—it can't touch our suits even if it wants to. Anyway, it's moving past us."

That was true. They could see now that the entire creature—if it was a single plant, and not a colony—covered a roughly circular area about a hundred yards across. It was sweeping over the ground, as the shadow of a cloud moves before the wind—and where it had rested, the rocks were pitted with innumerable tiny holes that might have been etched by acid.

"Yes," said Hutchins, when Jerry remarked about this. "That's how some lichens feed; they secrete acids that dissolve rock. But no questions, please—not till we get back to the ship. I've several lifetimes' work here, and a couple of hours to do it in."

This was botany on the run. . . . The sensitive edge of the huge plant-thing could move with surprising speed when it tried to evade them. It was as if they were dealing with an animated flap-jack, an acre in extent. There was no reaction—apart from the automatic avoidance of their exhaust-heat—when Hutchins snipped samples or took probes. The creature flowed steadily onwards over hills and valleys, guided by some strange vegetable instinct. Perhaps it was following some vein of mineral; the geologists could decide that, when they analyzed the rock samples that Hutchins had collected both before and after the passage of the living tapestry.

There was scarcely time to think or even to frame the countless questions that their discovery had raised. Presumably these creatures must be fairly common, for them to have found one so quickly. How did they reproduce? By shoots, spores, fission, or some other means? Where did they get their energy? What relatives, rivals or parasites did they have? This could not be the only form of life on Venus—the very idea was absurd, for if you had one species, you must have thousands. . . .

Sheer hunger and fatigue forced them to a halt at last. The creature they were studying could eat its way around Venus—though Hutchins believed that it never went very far from the lake, as from time to time it approached the water and inserted a long, tube-like tendril into it—but the animals from Earth had to rest.

It was a great relief to inflate the pressurized tent, climb in through the airlock, and strip off their thermosuits. For the first time, as they relaxed inside their tiny plastic hemisphere, the true wonder and importance of the discovery forced itself upon their minds. This world around them was no longer the same; Venus was no longer dead—it had joined Earth and Mars.

For life called to life, across the gulfs of space. Everything that grew or moved upon the face of any planet was a portent, a promise that Man was not alone in this universe of blazing suns and swirling nebulae. If as yet he had found no companions with whom he could speak, that was only to be expected, for the light-years and the ages still stretched before him, waiting to be explored. Meanwhile, he must guard and cherish the life he found, whether it be upon Earth or Mars or Venus.

So Graham Hutchins, the happiest biologist in the Solar System, told himself as he helped Garfield collect their refuse and seal it into a plastic disposal bag. When they deflated the tent and started the homeward journey, there was no sign of the creature they had been examining. That was just as well; they might have been tempted to linger for more experiments, and already it was getting uncomfortably close to their deadline.

No matter; in a few months they would be back with a team of assistants, far more adequately equipped and with the eyes of the world upon them. Evolution had labored for a billion years to make this meeting possible; it could wait a little longer.

For a while nothing moved in the greenly glimmering, fogbound landscape; it was deserted by man and crimson carpet alike. Then, flowing over the windcarved hills, the creature reappeared. Or perhaps it was another of the same strange species; no one would ever know.

It flowed past the little cairn of stones where Hutchins and Garfield had buried their wastes. And then it stopped.

It was not puzzled, for it had no mind. But the chemical urges that drove it relentlessly over the polar plateau were crying: Here, here! Somewhere close at hand was the most precious of all the food it needed—phosphorous, the element without which the spark of life could never ignite. It began to nuzzle the rocks, to ooze into the cracks and crannies, to scratch and scrabble with probing tendrils. Nothing that it did was beyond the capacity of any plant or tree on Earth—but it moved a thousand times more quickly, requiring only minutes to reach its goal and pierce through the plastic film.

And then it feasted, on food more concentrated than any it had ever known. It absorbed the carbohydrates and the proteins and the phosphates, the nicotine from the cigarette ends, the cellulose from the paper cups and spoons. All these it broke down and assimilated into its strange body, without difficulty and without harm.

Likewise it absorbed a whole microcosmos of living creatures—the bacteria and viruses which, upon an older planet, had evolved into a thousand deadly strains. Though only a very few could survive in this heat and this atmosphere, they were sufficient. As the carpet crawled back to the lake, it carried contagion to all its world.

Even as the Morning Star *set course for her distant home, Venus was dying. The films and photographs and specimens that Hutchins was carrying in triumph were more precious even than he knew. They were the only record that would ever exist of Life's third attempt to gain a foothold in the Solar System.*

Beneath the clouds of Venus, the story of Creation was ended.

The Game of Rat and Dragon

Cordwainer Smith

The Table

Pinlighting is a hell of a way to earn a living. Underhill was furious as he closed the door behind himself. It didn't make much sense to wear a uniform and look like a soldier if people didn't appreciate what you did.

He sat down in his chair, laid his head back in the headrest and pulled the helmet down over his forehead.

As he waited for the pin-set to warm up, he remembered the girl in the outer corridor. She had looked at it, then looked at him scornfully.

"Meow." That was all she had said. Yet it had cut him like a knife.

What did she think he was—a fool, a loafer, a uniformed nonentity? Didn't she know that for every half hour of pinlighting, he got a minimum of two month's recuperation in the hospital?

By now the set was warm. He felt the squares of space around him, sensed himself at the middle of an immense grid, a cubic grid, full of nothing. Out in that nothingness, he could sense the hollow aching horror of space itself and could feel the terrible anxiety which his mind encountered whenever it met the faintest trace of inert dust.

As he relaxed, the comforting solidity of the Sun, the clockwork of the familiar planets and the Moon rang in on him. Our own solar system was as charming and as simple as an ancient cuckoo clock filled with familiar ticking and with reassuring noises. The odd little moons of Mars swung around their planet like frantic mice, yet their regularity was itself an assurance that all was well. Far above the plane of the ecliptic, he could feel half a ton of dust more or less drifting outside the lanes of human travel.

Here there was nothing to fight, nothing to challenge the mind, to tear the living soul out of a body with its roots dripping in effluvium as tangible as blood.

Nothing ever moved in on the Solar System. He could wear the pin-set forever and be nothing more than a sort of telepathic astronomer, a man who could feel the hot, warm protection of the Sun throbbing and burning against his living mind.

Woodley came in.

"Same old ticking world," said Underhill. "Nothing to report. No wonder they didn't develop the pin-set until they began to planoform. Down here with the hot Sun around us, it feels so good and so quiet. You can feel everything spinning and turning. It's nice and sharp and compact. It's sort of like sitting around home."

Woodley grunted. He was not much given to flights of fantasy.

Undeterred, Underhill, went on, "It must have been pretty good to have been an Ancient Man. I wonder why they burned up their world with war. They didn't have to planoform. They didn't have to get out to earn their living among the stars. They didn't have to dodge the Rats or play the Game. They couldn't have invented pinlighting because they didn't have any need of it, did they, Woodley?"

Woodley grunted, "Uh-huh." Woodley was twenty-six years old and due to retire in one more year. He already had a farm picked out. He had gotten through ten years of hard work pinlighting with the best of them. He had kept his sanity by not thinking very much about his job, meeting the strains of the task whenever he had to meet them and thinking nothing more about his duties until the next emergency arose.

Woodley never made a point of getting popular among the Partners. None of the Partners liked him very much. Some of them even resented him. He was suspected of thinking ugly thoughts of the Partners on occasion, but since none of the Partners ever thought a complaint in articulate form, the other pinlighters and the Chiefs of the Instrumentality left him alone.

Underhill was still full of the wonder of their job. Happily he babbled on, "What does happen to us when we planoform? Do you think it's sort of like dying? Did you ever see anybody who had his soul pulled out?"

"Pulling souls is just a way of talking about it," said Woodley. "After all these years, nobody knows whether we have souls or not."

"But I saw one once. I saw what Dogwood looked like when he came apart. There was something funny. It looked wet and sort of sticky as if it were bleeding and it went out of him—and you know what they did to Dogwood? They took him away, up in that part of the hospital where you and I never go—way up at the top part where the others are, where the others always have to go if they are alive after the Rats of the Up-and-Out have gotten them."

Woodley sat down and lit an ancient pipe. He was burning something called tobacco in it. It was a dirty sort of habit, but it made him look very dashing and adventurous.

"Look here, youngster. You don't have to worry about that stuff. Pinlighting is getting better all the time. The Partners are getting better. I've seen them pinlight two Rats forty-six million miles apart in one and a half milliseconds. As long as people had to try to work the pin-sets themselves, there was always the chance that with a minimum of four hundred milliseconds for the human mind to set a pinlight, we wouldn't light the Rats up fast enough to protect our planoforming ships. The Partners have changed all that. Once they get going, they're faster than the Rats. And they always will be. I know it's not easy, letting a Partner share your mind—"

"It's not easy for them, either," said Underhill.

"Don't worry about them. They're not human. Let them take care of themselves. I've seen more pinlighters go crazy from monkeying around with Partners than I have ever seen caught by the Rats. How many do you actually know of them that got grabbed by Rats?"

Underhill looked down at his fingers, which shone green and purple in the vivid light thrown by the tuned-in pin-set, and counted ships. The thumb for the *Andromeda,* lost with crew and passengers, the index finger and the middle finger for *Release Ships* 43 and 56, found with their pin-sets burned out and every man, woman, and child on board dead or insane. The ring finger, the little finger, and the thumb of the other hand were the first three battleships to be lost to the Rats—lost as people realized that there was something out there *underneath space itself* which was alive, capricious and malevolent.

Planoforming was sort of funny. It felt like—

Like nothing much.

Like the twinge of a mild electric shock.

Like the ache of a sore tooth bitten on for the first time.

Like a slightly painful flash of light against the eyes.

Yet in that time, a forty-thousand-ton ship lifting free above Earth disappeared somehow or other into two dimensions and appeared half a light-year or fifty light-years off.

At one moment, he would be sitting in the Fighting Room, the pin-set ready and the familiar Solar System ticking around inside his head. For a second or a year (he could never tell how long it really was, subjectively), the funny little flash went through him and then he was loose in the Up-and-Out, the terrible open spaces between the stars, where the stars themselves felt like pimples on his telepathic mind and the planets were too far away to be sensed or read.

Somewhere in this outer space, a gruesome death awaited, death and horror of a kind which Man had never encountered until he reached out for interstellar space itself. Apparently the light of the suns kept the dragons away.

Dragons. That was what people called them. To ordinary people, there was nothing, nothing except the shiver of planoforming and the hammer blow of sudden death or the dark spastic note of lunacy descending into their minds.

But to the telepaths, they were Dragons.

In the fraction of a second between the telepaths' awareness of a hostile something out in the black, hollow nothingness of space and the impact of a ferocious, ruinous psychic blow against all living things within the ship, the telepaths had sensed entities something like the Dragons of ancient human lore, beasts more clever than beasts, demons more tangible than demons, hungry vortices of aliveness and hate compounded by unknown means out of the thin tenuous matter between the stars.

It took a surviving ship to bring back the news—a ship in which, by sheer chance, a telepath had a light beam ready, turning it out at the innocent dust so that, within the panorama of his mind, the Dragon dissolved into nothing at all and the other passengers, themselves non-telepathic, went about their way not realizing that their own immediate deaths had been averted.

From then on, it was easy—almost.

Planoforming ships always carried telepaths. Telepaths had their sensitiveness enlarged to an immense range by the pin-sets, which were telepathic amplifiers adapted to the mammal mind. The pin-sets in turn were electronically geared into small dirigible light bombs. Light did it.

Light broke up the Dragons, allowed the ships to reform three-dimensionally, skip, skip, skip, as they moved from star to star.

The odds suddenly moved down from a hundred to one against mankind to sixty to forty in mankind's favour.

This was not enough. The telepaths were trained to become ultra-sensitive, trained to become aware of the Dragons in less than a millisecond.

But it was found that the Dragons could move a million miles in just under two milliseconds and that this was not enough for the human mind to activate the light beams.

Attempts had been made to sheath the ships in light at all times.

This defence wore out.

As mankind learned about the Dragons, so too, apparently, the Dragons learned about mankind. Somehow they flattened their own bulk and came in on extremely flat trajectories very quickly.

Intense light was needed, light of sunlight intensity. This could be provided only by light bombs. Pinlighting came into existence.

Pinlighting consisted of the detonation of ultra-vivid miniature photonuclear bombs, which converted a few ounces of a magnesium isotope into pure visible radiance.

The odds kept coming down in mankind's favour, yet ships were being lost.

It became so bad that people didn't even want to find the ships because the rescuers knew what they would see. It was sad to bring back to Earth three hundred bodies ready for burial and two hundred or three hundred lunatics, damaged beyond repair, to be wakened, and fed, and cleaned, and put to sleep, wakened and fed again until their lives were ended.

Telepaths tried to reach into the minds of the psychotics who had been damaged by the Dragons, but they found nothing there beyond vivid spouting columns of fiery terror bursting from the primordial id itself, the volcanic sources of life.

Then came the Partners.

Man and Partner could do together what Man could not do alone. Men had the intellect. Partners had the speed.

The Partners rode in their tiny craft, no larger than footballs, outside the spaceships. They planoformed with the ships. They rode beside them in their six-pound craft ready to attack.

The tiny ships of the Partners were swift. Each carried a dozen pinlights, bombs no bigger than thimbles.

The Pinlighters threw the Partners—quite literally threw—by means of mind-to-firing relays direct at the Dragons.

What seemed to be Dragons to the human mind appeared in the form of gigantic Rats in the minds of the Partners.

Out in the pitiless nothingness of space, the Partners' minds responded to an instinct as old as life. The Partners attacked, striking with a speed faster than Man's, going from attack to attack until the Rats or themselves were destroyed. Almost all the time it was the Partners who won.

With the safety of the interstellar skip, skip, skip of the ships, commerce increased immensely, the population of all the colonies went up, and the demand for trained Partners increased.

Underhill and Woodley were a part of the third generation of pinlighters and yet, to them, it seemed as though their craft had endured forever.

Gearing space into minds by means of the pin-set, adding the Partners to those minds, keying up the mind for the tension of a fight on which all depended—this was more than human synapses could stand for long. Underhill needed his two months' rest after half an hour of fighting. Woodley needed his retirement after ten years of service. They were young. They were good. But they had limitations.

So much depended on the choice of Partners, so much on the sheer luck of who drew whom.

The Shuffle

Father Moontree and the little girl named West entered the room. They were the other two pinlighters. The human complement of the Fighting Room was now complete.

Father Moontree was a red-faced man of forty-five who had lived the peaceful life of a farmer until he reached his fortieth year. Only then, belatedly, did the authorities find he was telepathic and agree to let him late in life enter upon the career of pinlighter. He did well at it, but he was fantastically old for this kind of business.

Father Moontree looked at the glum Woodley and the musing Underhill. "How're the youngsters today? Ready for a good fight?"

"Father always wants a fight," giggled the little girl named West. She was such a little little girl. Her giggle was high and childish. She looked like the last person in the world one would expect to find in the rough, sharp duelling of pinlighting.

Underhill had been amused one time when he found one of the most sluggish of the Partners coming away happy from contact with the mind of the girl named West.

Usually the Partners didn't care much about the human minds with which they were paired for the journey. The Partners seemed to take the attitude that human minds were complex and fouled up beyond belief, anyhow. No Partner ever questioned the superiority of the human mind, though very few of the Partners were much impressed by that superiority.

The Partners liked people. They were willing to fight with them. They were even willing to die for them. But when a Partner liked an individual the way, for example, that Captain Wow or the Lady May liked Underhill, the liking had nothing to do with intellect. It was a matter of temperament, of feel.

Underhill knew perfectly well that Captain Wow regarded his, Underhill's, brains as silly. What Captain Wow liked was Underhill's friendly emotional structure, the cheerfulness and glint of wicked amusement that shot through Underhill's unconscious thought patterns, and the gaiety with which Underhill faced danger. The words, the history books, the ideas, the science—Underhill could sense all that in his own mind, reflected back from Captain Wow's mind, as so much rubbish.

Miss West looked at Underhill, "I bet you've put stickum on the stones."

"I did not!"

Underhill felt his ears grow red with embarrassment. During his novitiate, he had tried to cheat in the lottery because he got particularly fond of a special Partner, a lovely young mother named Murr. It was so much easier to operate with Murr and she was so affectionate toward him that he forgot pinlighting was hard work and that he was not instructed to have a good time with his Partner. They were both designed and prepared to go into deadly battle together.

One cheating had been enough. They had found him out and he had been laughed at for years.

Father Moontree picked up the imitation-leather cup and shook the stone dice which assigned them their Partners for the trip. By senior rights, he took first draw.

He grimaced. He had drawn a greedy old character, a tough old male whose mind was full of slobbering thoughts of food, veritable oceans full of half-spoiled fish. Father Moontree had once said that he burped cod liver oil for weeks after drawing that particular glutton, so strongly had the telepathic image of fish impressed itself upon his mind. Yet the glutton was a glutton for danger as well as for fish. He had killed sixty-three Dragons, more than any other Partner in the service, and was quite literally worth his weight in gold.

The little girl West came next. She drew Captain Wow. When she saw who it was, she smiled.

"I *like* him," she said. "He's such fun to fight with. He feels so nice and cuddly in my mind."

"Cuddly, hell," said Woodley. "I've been in his mind, too. It's the most leering mind in this ship, bar none."

"Nasty man," said the little girl. She said it declaratively, without reproach.

Underhill, looking at her, shivered.

He didn't see how she could take Captain Wow so calmly. Captain Wow's mind *did* leer. When Captain Wow got excited in the middle of a battle, confused images of Dragons, deadly Rats, luscious beds, the smell of fish, and the shock of space all scrambled together in his mind as he and CaptainWow, their consciousnesses linked together through the pin-set, became a fantastic composite of human being and Persian cat.

That's the trouble with working with cats, thought Underhill. It's a pity that nothing else anywhere will serve as Partner. Cats were all right once you got in touch with them telepathically. They were smart enough to meet the needs of the fight, but their motives and desires were certainly different from those of humans.

They were companionable enough as long as you thought tangible images at them, but their minds just closed up and went to sleep when you recited Shakespeare or Colegrove, or if you tried to tell them what space was.

It was sort of funny realizing that the Partners who were so grim and mature out here in space were the same cute little animals that people had used as pets for thousands of years back on Earth. He had embarrassed himself more than once while on the ground saluting perfectly ordinary non-telepathic cats because he had forgotten for the moment that they were not Partners.

He picked up the cup and shook out his stone dice.

He was lucky—he drew the Lady May.

The Lady May was the most thoughtful Partner he had ever met. In her, the finely bred pedigree mind of a Persian cat had reached one of its highest peaks of development. She was more complex than any human woman, but the complexity was all one of emotions, memory, hope and discriminated experience—experience sorted through without benefit of words.

When he had first come into contact with her mind, he was astonished at its clarity. With her he remembered her kittenhood. He remembered every mating experience she had ever had. He saw in a half-recognizable gallery all the other pinlighters with whom she had been paired for the fight. And he saw himself radiant, cheerful and desirable.

He even thought he caught the edge of a longing—

A very flattering and yearning thought: *What a pity he is not a cat.*

Woodley picked up the last stone. He drew what he deserved—a sullen, scared old tomcat with none of the verve of Captain Wow. Woodley's Partner was the most animal of all the cats on the ship, a low, brutish type with a dull mind. Even telepathy had not refined his character. His ears were half chewed off from the first fights in which he had engaged.

He was a serviceable fighter, nothing more.

Woodley grunted.

Underhill glanced at him oddly. Didn't Woodley ever do anything but grunt?

Father Moontree looked at the other three. "You might as well get your Partners now. I'll let the Scanner know we're ready to go into the Up-and-Out."

The Deal

Underhill spun the combination lock on the Lady May's cage. He woke her gently and took her into his arms. She humped her back luxuriously, stretched her claws, started to purr, thought better of it, and licked him on the wrist instead. He did not have the pin-set on, so their minds were closed to each other, but in the angle of her moustache and in the movement of her ears, he caught some sense of the gratification she experienced in finding him as her Partner.

He talked to her in human speech, even though speech meant nothing to a cat when the pin-set was not on.

"It's a damn shame, sending a sweet little thing like you whirling around in the coldness of nothing to hunt for Rats that are bigger and deadlier than all of us put together. You didn't ask for this kind of fight, did you?"

For answer, she licked his hand, purred, tickled his cheek with her long fluffy tail, turned around and faced him, golden eyes shining.

For a moment they stared at each other, man squatting, cat standing erect on her hind legs, front claws digging into his knee. Human eyes and cat eyes looked across an immensity which no words could meet, but which affection spanned in a single glance.

"Time to get in," he said.

She walked docilely into her spheroid carrier. She climbed in. He saw to it that her miniature pin-set rested firmly and comfortably against the base of her brain. He made sure that her claws were padded so that she could not tear herself in the excitement of battle.

Softly he said to her, "Ready?"

For answer, she preened her back as much as her harness would permit and purred softly within the confines of the frame that held her.

He slapped down the lid and watched the sealant ooze around the seam. For a few hours, she was welded into her projectile until a workman with a short cutting arc would remove her after she had done her duty.

He picked up the entire projectile and slipped it into the ejection tube. He closed the door of the tube, spun the lock, seated himself in his chair, and put his own pin-set on.

Once again he flung the switch.

He sat in a small room, *small, small, warm, warm,* the bodies of the other three people moving close around him, the tangible lights in the ceiling bright and heavy against his closed eyelids.

As the pin-set warmed, the room fell away. The other people ceased to be people and became small glowing heaps of fire, embers, dark red fire, with the consciousness of life burning like old red coals in a country fireplace.

As the pin-set warmed a little more, he felt Earth just below him, felt the ship slipping away, felt the turning Moon as it swung on the far side of the world, felt the planets and the hot, clear goodness of the Sun which kept the Dragons so far from mankind's native ground.

Finally, he reached complete awareness.

He was telepathically alive to a range of millions of miles. He felt the dust which he had noticed earlier high above the ecliptic. With a thrill of warmth and tenderness, he felt the consciousness of the Lady May pouring over into his own. Her consciousness was as gentle and clear and yet sharp to the taste of his mind as if it were scented oil. It felt relaxing and reassuring. He could sense her welcome of him. It was scarcely a thought, just a raw emotion of greeting.

At last they were one again.

In a tiny remote corner of his mind, as tiny as the smallest toy he had ever seen in his childhood, he was still aware of the room and the ship, and of Father Moontree picking up a telephone and speaking to a Scanner captain in charge of the ship.

His telepathic mind caught the idea long before his ears could frame the words. The actual sound followed the idea the way that thunder on an ocean beach follows the lightning inward from far out over the seas.

"The Fighting Room is ready. Clear to planoform, sir."

The Play

Underhill was always a little exasperated the way that the Lady May experienced things before he did.

He was braced for the quick vinegar thrill of planoforming, but he caught her report of it before his own nerves could register what happened.

Earth had fallen so far away that he groped for several milliseconds before he found the Sun in the upper rear right-hand corner of his telepathic mind.

That was a good jump, he thought. This way we'll get there in four or five skips.

A few hundred miles outside the ship, the Lady May thought back at him, "O warm, O generous, O gigantic man! O brave, O friendly, O tender and huge Partner! O wonderful with you, with you so good, good, good, warm, warm, now to fight, now to go, good with you . . ."

He knew that she was not thinking words, that his mind took the clear amiable babble of her cat intellect and translated it into images which his own thinking could record and understand.

Neither one of them was absorbed in the game of mutual greetings.

He reached out far beyond her range of perception to see if there was anything near the ship. It was funny how it was possible to do two things at once. He could scan space with his pin-set mind and yet at the same time catch a vagrant thought of hers, a lovely, affectionate thought about a son who had had a golden face and a chest covered with soft, incredibly downy white fur.

While he was still searching, he caught the warning from her.

We jump again!

And so they had. The ship had moved to a second planoform. The stars were different. The Sun was immeasurably far behind. Even the nearest stars were barely in contact. This was good Dragon country, this open, nasty, hollow kind of space. He reached farther, faster, sensing and looking for danger, ready to fling the Lady May at danger wherever he found it.

Terror blazed up in his mind, so sharp, so clear, that it came through as a physical wrench.

The little girl named West had found something—something immense, long, black, sharp, greedy, horrific. She flung Captain Wow at it.

Underhill tried to keep his own mind clear. "Watch out!" he shouted telepathically at the others, trying to move the Lady May around.

At one corner of the battle, he felt the lustful rage of Captain Wow as the big Persian tomcat detonated lights while he approached the streak of dust which threatened the ship and the people within.

The lights scored near-misses. The dust flattened itself, changing from the shape of a sting-ray into the shape of a spear.

Not three milliseconds had elapsed.

Father Moontree was talking human words and was saying in a voice that moved like cold molasses out of a heavy jar, "C-A-P-T-A-I-N." Underhill knew that the sentence was going to be "Captain, move fast!"

The battle would be fought and finished before Father Moontree got through talking.

Now, fractions of a millisecond later, the Lady May was directly in line.

Here was where the skill and speed of the Partners came in. She could react faster than he. She could see the threat as an immense Rat coming directly at her.

She could fire the light-bombs with a discrimination which he might miss.

He was connected with her mind, but he could not follow it.

His consciousness absorbed the tearing wound inflicted by the alien enemy. It was like no wound on Earth—raw, crazy pain which started like a burn at his navel. He began to writhe in his chair.

Actually he had not yet had time to move a muscle when the Lady May struck back at their enemy.

Five evenly spaced photonuclear bombs blazed out across a hundred thousand miles.

The pain in his mind and body vanished.

He felt a moment of fierce, terrible, feral elation running through the mind of the Lady May as she finished her kill. It was always disappointing to the cats to find out that their enemies whom they sensed as gigantic space Rats disappeared at the moment of destruction.

Then he felt her hurt, the pain and the fear that swept over both of them as the battle, quicker than the movement of an eyelid, had come and gone. In the same instant, there came the sharp and acid twinge of planoform.

Once more the ship went skip.

He could hear Woodley thinking at him. "You don't have to bother much. This old son of a gun and I will take over for a while."

Twice again the twinge, the skip.

He had no idea where he was until the lights of the Caledonia space board shone below.

With a weariness that lay almost beyond the limits of thought, he threw his mind back into rapport with the pin-set, fixing the Lady May's projectile gently and neatly in its launching tube.

She was half dead with fatigue, but he could feel the beat of her heart, could listen to her panting, and he grasped the grateful edge of a thanks reaching from her mind to his.

The Score

They put him in the hospital at Caledonia.

The doctor was friendly but firm. "You actually got touched by that Dragon. That's as close a shave as I've ever seen. It's all so quick that it'll be a long time before we know what happened scientifically, but I suppose you'd be ready for the insane asylum now if the contact had lasted several tenths of a millisecond longer. What kind of cat did you have out in front of you?"

Underhill felt the words coming out of him slowly. Words were such a lot of trouble compared with the speed and the joy of thinking, fast and sharp and clear, mind to mind! But words were all that could reach ordinary people like this doctor.

His mouth moved heavily as he articulated words, "Don't call our Partners cats. The right thing to call them is Partners. They fight for us in a team. You ought to know we call them Partners, not cats. How is mine?"

"I don't know," said the doctor contritely. "We'll find out for you. Meanwhile, old man, you take it easy. There's nothing but rest that can help you. Can you make yourself sleep, or would you like us to give you some kind of sedative?"

"I can sleep," said Underhill. "I just want to know about the Lady May."

The nurse joined in. She was a little antagonistic. "Don't you want to know about the other people?"

"They're okay," said Underhill. "I knew that before I came in here."

He stretched his arms and sighed and grinned at them. He could see they were relaxing and were beginning to treat him as a person instead of a patient.

"I'm all right," he said. "Just let me know when I can go see my Partner."

A new thought struck him. He looked wildly at the doctor. "They didn't send her off with the ship, did they?"

"I'll find out right away," said the doctor. He gave Underhill a reassuring squeeze of the shoulder and left the room.

The nurse took a napkin off a goblet of chilled fruit juice.

Underhill tried to smile at her. There seemed to be something wrong with the girl. He wished she would go away. First she had started to be friendly and now she was distant again. It's a nuisance being tele-pathic, he thought. You keep trying to reach even when you are not making contact.

Suddenly she swung around on him.

"You pinlighters! You and your damn cats!"

Just as she stamped out, he burst into her mind. He saw himself a radiant hero, clad in his smooth suede uniform, the pin-set crown shining like ancient royal jewels around his head. He saw his own face, handsome and masculine, shining out of her mind. He saw himself very far away and he saw himself as she hated him.

She hated him in the secrecy of her own mind. She hated him

because he was—she thought—proud, and strange, and rich, better and more beautiful than people like her.

He cut off the sight of her mind and, as he buried his face in the pillow, he caught an image of the Lady May.

"She *is* a cat," he thought. "That's all she is—a *cat!*"

But that was not how his mind saw her—quick beyond all dreams of speed, sharp, clever, unbelievably graceful, beautiful, wordless and undemanding.

Where would he ever find a woman who could compare with her?

3

Beyond Reality's Barriers: New Dimensions

Robert Silverberg and Charles Elkins

These two remarkable stories do not make sense; at least, they do not make "common sense." They frustrate and contradict some of our common-sense notions of space and time. In introducing them, we could focus our analysis on trying to explain the meaning of each narrative; however, this would diminish the challenge facing the reader. Another alternative would be a search to discover what prompted the writers to create such marvelous space-time fictions, but this, too, seems futile. Motives can be as elusive as they are numerous, and, in the long run, they are probably irrelevant for understanding and appreciating the work. Instead, we decided that one might profit more by examining the social functions of these fictions and trying to understand what stories such as these do for those reading them. This approach does not ignore the works themselves. Quite the contrary, since form follows function, we can better penetrate the stories' structures by grasping their social utility. Our basic thesis is this: inventing new fictions of time and space permits those who experience these novel forms not only to think about other worlds and various modalities of time but also to come to terms (intellectually, emotionally, and imaginatively) with their own space-time situations.

In order to act, there must be a *coming to terms* with one's situation, an act of definition to create order. The major constituent of any situation is its "scene," and the basic components of any scene are its space-time coordinates. Changing these coordinates changes the scene. One must be able to reorient oneself to confront new circumstances. Thus, it is not surprising that "adaptation" is a basic and recurring theme in science fiction. Adaptation is essential for survival: we must know *how* we are expected to cope with the unexpected. All action is problematic because it moves into a future which, by definition, will be different from the present. Actions which served us well in the past may not work in handling new challenges. Hence, we continually create new images of the past and future in order to act in the present. The writer gives us completed acts, which we experience in the imagination before we commit ourselves in irrevocable, overt actions.

And so creating alternative space-time fictions helps us act in the present. Consider the creation of alternative worlds: to put it theologically, each writer has his own Heaven and, by implication, his own Hell; to put it sociologically, he has his own utopia and dystopia. Does technology conjure up a society where we have won our age-old dream of freedom from deadening labor and are now at liberty to exercise our creativity? Or does it suggest a society in which we have become slaves, dominated or even replaced by machines? Science fiction cannot give us the Truth about this problem. It does, however, convey that future society in such a way that the writer communicates a *present* attitude toward technology for the reader to accept, question, or reject; the reader's response, in turn, will influence the kind of future they both will inhabit. Once published, the work is no longer a private fantasy but a statement using consensually validated symbols to describe possible futures. Science fiction becomes a public form for coping with tomorrow.

Often, science fiction grapples with the problem of the future itself. What form will it take? What roles are needed to insure the survival of the individual and his society? What means and methods are available for us to meet and cope with tomorrow? To what end are we moving? Can we, for example, use roles which have been legitimated by the past, sanctified by tradition and custom, to meet novel situations? There is only one thing we know for *certain* about the future: it will be different from today. One of the functions of science fiction, then, is to create alternative scenes with novel space-times which entail reinforcing, testing, doubting and/or subverting traditional roles. If new roles are needed, then the writer must demystify old roles and create new metaphors enabling us to pass from one role to another, and finally make legitimate, by symbolically sanctifying, the new roles considered appropriate for a new space-time. By the same token, there are certain values, purposes, and roles embodying these norms, which we believe necessary for order (social, political, aesthetic, moral, scientific, etc.) and which we believe must survive in any conceivable future. We are so committed to their survival that we may sacrifice our own lives to these values, e.g. "Give me liberty, or give me death!" "Better dead than red." In this case, science fiction will depict the kinds of space-times and the appropriate roles necessary for the endurance of these values.

One major problem we may encounter in the future is the metamorphosis of space-time itself. Our common-sense notions of space and time may have to be discarded if we are to take any voyages (either imaginatively or literally) beyond our solar system. The common-sense notion of physical space is independent of the flow of time; it has three dimensions; it is isotropic (the condition of a medium whose measurable physical properties are the same in every direction), homogeneous, and continuous. Indeed, the great French mathematician Poincaré, reflecting on how we experience our physical surroundings, observed that, constructed as we are, with our senses and memories of earlier experiences, we must necessarily come to conceive of physical space as isotropic, homogeneous, continuous, and ruled by Euclidian laws. As for time, our common sense tells us that it is independent of space; it is one-dimensional; it is anisotropic (i.e. has a definite direction—forward); it is homogeneous and continuous. Common sense assumes that time flows with constant velocity; one second is always one second, the same everywhere and always. Its duration is independent of the observer and his position. So saith common sense.

But what does common sense have to do with the work of Lobachevsky, Minkowski, Riemann, or Möbius? What good is common sense in explaining the implications of Lorentz's transformations, anti-matter, black holes, space warps, tachyons, negative mass, time contractions or time tunneling? What about relativity? What are we to make of this:

> There was a young lady called Bright
> Who travelled much faster than light.
> She took off one day
> On her relative way
> and returned on the previous night.

or this:

> There was a young man named Fisk
> Whose fencing was exceedingly brisk.
> So fast was his action,
> The Einsteinian contraction
> Reduced his rapier to a disk.

Impossible? The hero of Farmer's story says, ''Forget about that remark. What is possible? What happens is possible.''

Testing the effects of faster-than-light travel, Farmer's and Blish's heroes are both drastically withdrawn from familiar environments and thrust into and invaded by disorientating space-time coordinates. It is a terrifying experience because, as Garrard (Blish's hero) points out, ''Our very personalities, really, depend on large part upon *all* the things in our environment, large and small, that exist outside our skins.'' Some cannot survive the experience. The two others who had preceded Garrard had ''both been excellent men, intelligent, resourceful . . . the best men in the Project,'' but they had not returned. As the hero of ''The Shadow of Space'' reminds us: ''It takes a special type of man or woman to loose himself from Earth or his native planet, to go out among the stars so far that the natal sun is not even a faint glimmer.''

However, it is not merely that by writing about the human encounter with novel forms of space and time the writer equips man to go to the stars. It may be that, as Arthur C. Clarke's Overlords say, ''The stars are not for man.'' On the other hand, the very presentation of the problem serves to shake the reader up, to boggle his mind a bit, to subvert and frustrate his normal, common-sense mode of imaging some very basic categories of existence. Einstein was supposed to have said that ''common sense'' is the layer of prejudice built up before the age of eighteen. Common sense is often the cognitive aspect of myth; it is the customary way of ordering experience. In this connection, by depicting a hero who embodies certain values (e.g. discipline, curiosity, openness, creativity, courage, ingenuity, etc.) which allow him to confront and survive the disruption of common-sense space-time, the science fiction writer is creating models or ideal types which may have much wider applications: What kind of man will best survive the challenge of the future? The question should not be brushed aside, for in one way or another we all make fantastic voyages which bring us face to face with the inexplicable.

Classical myths, by contrast, do not prepare us to face novel situations, and that is why science fiction writers are not myth makers in the traditional sense; they create fictions. Fictions and classical myths, while similar in some respects, are different in several crucial areas. Fictions become myths when they are apprehended as reality and not as consciously created fictions. Myth is the stuff of religion; it assumes a total, sufficient explanation of things as they were, are, and will be. The mode of myth is ritual. Fiction is the stuff of art; it assumes patterns of experience but is tentative, hypothetical in its approach to experience. While myth speaks of the eternal and unchanging, fictions speak of permanence in change. Fictions can be agents of change; they call for a willing suspension of disbelief—what if?—rather than unconditional assent. Indeed, myths are reality, or they are taken for reality by those who live with them. While myths presuppose, indeed, have their *raison d'être* in, an adequate and sufficient explanation of experience, fictions are for discovering and coming to terms with the possibilities of human experience. As Aristotle pointed out, poetry (by which he meant all art) relates not what has happened (i.e., history) but what may happen according to the ways of probability or necessity. Unlike myths, which legitimate their truths in history, tradition, custom, revelation, charisma, etc., literary fictions never claim Truth. They are consciously false and operate in the domain of the hypothetical rather than the dogmatic.

Writers create fictive scenes rather than mythological scenes. These scenes where man acts are the symbolization of time and place; they are the setting of the act and lay down the conditions of all action. *Man's environment is symbolic.* Even physical space and time are symbolized in spatial and temporal *imagery.* As C. S. Lewis once pointed out: "Literalness we cannot have." It is not that our metaphors and models merely illustrate otherwise obtainable knowledge, but rather they constitute it in such a way that a diagram, formula, description, image, or metaphor is part of the object or event. We do not think and then apply a metaphor to our thoughts; we learn to think by using metaphor. In order to act at all, we must *define our situation,* but our ability to construct definitions is determined by the symbol system available to us or by one which we can only partially create. We symbolize time and space not merely in order to "think about" our world but to act in it. The symbolization of time and space constitutes one of the elements in the construction of human relationships because the form of space and time shapes the ways in which we relate. We cannot hold intimate conversations in vast lecture halls, nor can we plan for a future if we believe the apocalypse is upon us. The scene determines the act. As the crew of the *Sleipnir* entered the body of Mrs. Wellington—in the other super-universe they have penetrated—they "return . . . to the womb," and "the officers and crew lost their feeling of dissociation. Grettir's stomach expanded with relief; the dreadful fragmenting was gone. He now felt as if something had been attached, or reattached, to his navel." A new scene entails a different set of possibilities for human action. Back on earth, "in Haertel's *cramped old* office, in the Project's administration *shack,* he [Garrard] felt both strange and as *old,* as *compressed, constricted.* . . . He had returned to humanity's common time and would never leave it again'' (emphasis ours).

The *names* we give to space and time—the basic context of our situation—determine how we can act. Names are not simply signs for cognitions, they are goads to action. Is this universe a result of God's handiwork as described in the first chapters of Genesis, or of a ''big bang'' described by an Expanding universe theory and Einstein's field equations, or is it a universe in continuous creation, a ''steady state'' universe, or all of these? What happens when men no longer believe that planets are fixed, embedded in their respective spheres and preserved and continued by their love of God, who moves them indirectly as an object of that love, or no longer believe that the divine planets, in their ardent desire to come as close to God as possible, move around and around in a circular motion, in a celestial dance? What happens, after Copernicus, when the Earth is viewed as simply a minor star in an infinite host of stars, and man anything but the center of creation? In 1611, John Donne records his confusion:

> The New Philosophy calls all in doubt,
> the Element of fire is quite put out;
> The Sun is lost, and th'Earth, and no man's wit
> Can well direct him where to look for it.
>
> . . .
> 'Tis all in pieces, all coherence gone;
> All just supply, and all Relation.

A new name, a new image entails a new attitude, and an attitude is an incipient act.

One of the major social functions of all art is to come to terms with our ruling myths. In this process, these myths are either reinforced, called into question, or destroyed and replaced by other myths. At the same time, it is obvious that some myths are easier to deal with than others; for example, myths that are tied to a specific context and culture give way when the times change and that society undergoes certain transformations which make these myths unworkable. Myths about the nature of war, about the role of business and government, the nature of the American presidency, and the like, have undergone rather substantial changes in our lifetime. By contrast, other myths—those that seem to deal with universal phenomena—are much more difficult to confront. These myths that seem grounded in the very biological makeup of man—sexual differentiation, perceptual categories, for example—are particularly difficult to handle. In this connection, nowhere is this difficulty more vividly seen than in our thinking about time and space.

All human activity takes place in time and space. These categories are so basic to experience that many thinkers believe that space and time are not real things in their own right but forms of our sensibility—forms under which alone our sensations and, hence, physical objects, revealed by these sensations, can be given to our human minds. Our minds impose space on what we sense much as sunglasses impose their color on what we see. We cannot think about time and space without using metaphor.

However, just because they are so basic to experience, it is absolutely crucial that these metaphors—the terms we use for ordering time and space—are made conscious and subject to critical scrutiny. For example, does time "flow"? Is it like the Heraclitean "flux" or Thomas Wolfe's "river"? In English, *time* has the same root as "tide," and we tend to think of time as a "river," "stream," "cycle," "linear flow." Can we conceive of it in entirely different metaphors? Another example: we can see now that those early stream-of-consciousness novelists—Marcel Proust, James Joyce, Virginia Woolf and others like them—helped reclaim and give significance and integrity to human *subjective* time, which appeared to be overwhelmed by the fragmented, quantified, "scientific" time of nineteenth-century industrial society, with its need for precise coordination.

What about space and its relationship to time? Does space arise from our dissection of time? Is space, as Henri Bergson argued, a mode of our "intellect" and time a mode of our "intuition," with space arising from a dissection of the flux and, hence, illusionary? Is time the essential characteristic of life? Is mathematical time, scientific time, merely a form of space? And how are we to understand Einsteinian time? Both Blish's and Farmer's stories depict individuals confronting spatial and temporal anomalies and coming to grips with this experience. It is not a technical but a human problem: How are we to confront the problematic? What is the status of the past, the present, and the future?

Particularly the future. Do we adopt the point of view of science, the perspective of the great physicist C. D. Broad, who argues in his *Scientific Thought* (1925) that the past and the present but *not* the future are "real." What role can the concept of the future play in science? Certainly the future is of overriding importance in our lives. A personal time and social time is interpenetrated with the future. Without some tacit belief in tomorrow, nearly everything we do today would be meaningless. In fact, we could not act at all. Expectations, intentions, anticipations, premonitions, presentiments, goals, purposes—all of these have a forward reference in time and structure our acts in the present. The future is fraught with the sense of the distance between desire and satisfaction. Implicit in all our acts are schemes, however vague and inarticulate. Our entire psychic and social life is shot through with the hope of things to come. Is not a defining feature of human existence to be able to transcend the immediate boundaries of time—the present—to view ourselves in the light of a distant past and future and to act and react in terms of those images? In what sense is the future "unreal"? These are some of the questions which science fiction tries to answer.

However, the main point of all of these questions is this: the terms we give, the symbols we create for naming time and space are the basic coordinates in the organization of all human action. They are *terms,* terms which we must have to order action, but terms nonetheless which we can change. We create the symbols we use for ordering our existence. While these terms may be the result of the dialectical interplay between our symbols and a nonsymbolic "reality," it is to the symbols which contain the "meaning" of that reality that we react. Change the symbols of time and space and you change the conditions, the stage upon which human action takes place; change the symbols and you change the possibilities of human action because *situation* is another term for "motives."

This brings us back to the question of Truth. What is our "real" situation? What coordinates of time and space should we adopt to define our scene? Science fiction cannot provide the answer because, like other forms of literature, it is not solely or even mainly concerned with Truth (especially if we mean empirical truth). It is not concerned with making propositions about phenomena which must be verified empirically, perceptually, cognitively, etc. Rather, like all art, science fiction presents the phenomena itself. It offers the reader imagined explorations of the possibilities of human action; it presents a dramatic rehearsal in the imagination of the alternatives of actions. The writer not only gives us the symbols by which we can *think about* the world, but he creates the symbolic forms which embody the roles and goals, as well as the scenes we *use* in the symbolic phases of action. We do not simply think about action: we act, and to act we must have forms which fuse the imaginative, emotional, instinctual as well as the cognitive aspects of experience. This is the task of art.

In terms of creating fictions of time and space, for example, the writer knows that scientific time and space are vastly different from both subjective, social, and cosmological time. Scientific time and space have no sensuous content; they are a set of coordinates, a structure of mathematically ordered points, dates, or numbers. There is no passage in scientific time and space; it is a time and space of "events," of motion but not of "acts." The "present" of scientific time is the boundary between two infinite series of numbers. Scientific time does not embrace a past or future. It does not even contain a "present," if by that term one means something at once extended, perceivable, and encounterable. The writer, then, must insert scientific space-time into perceptual, eventful, subjective, social, historical, and cosmological times, and he must show his audience reasons and methods for inserting their subjective time and space into his spatial and temporal constructs and the ultimate consequences of his match. In the stories which follow, two of science fiction's most gifted writers tackle some of these most difficult but crucially important problems.

BIBLIOGRAPHY

de Camp, Sprague, *Lost Darkness*, 1941 (Holt); Revised Edition, 1949 (Prime)

Dick, Philip K., *The Man in the High Castle*, 1962 (Putnam)

Edmondson, G. C., *The Ship That Sailed the Time Stream*, 1965 (Ace)

Eklund, Gordon, *All Times Possible*, 1974 (Daw)

Finney, Jack, *Time and Again*, 1970 (Simon and Schuster)

Hamilton, Edmond, *Crashing Sons*, 1965 (Ace)

Hoyle, Fred, *October the First Is Too Late*, 1966 (Harper)

Jones, Raymond F., *This Island Earth*, 1952 (Shasta)

Moorcock, Michael, *Behold the Man*, 1970 (Avon)

Moore, Ward, *Bring the Jubilee*, 1953 (Farrar)

Roberts, Keith, *Pavane*, 1968 (Doubleday)

Shaw, Bob, *The Two-Timers*, 1968 (Ace)

Silverberg, Robert, *Up the Line*, 1969 (Ballantine)

Smith, E. E., *Skylark Three*, 1948 (Fantasy Press)

Stapledon, Olaf, *Last and First Men*, 1930 (Methuen)

Wells, H. G., *The Time Machine*, 1895.

Williamson, Jack, *The Legion of Time*, 1953 (Fantasy Press)

Common Time

James Blish

> ... the days went slowly round and round, endless and
> uneventful as cycles in space. Time, and time-pieces!
> How many centuries did my hammock tell, as
> pendulum-like it swung to the ship's dull roll, and ticked
> the hours and ages.
> —HERMAN MELVILLE, in *Mardi*

Don't move.

It was the first thought that came into Garrard's mind when he awoke, and perhaps it saved his life. He lay where he was, strapped against the padding, listening to the round hum of the engines. That in itself was wrong; he should be unable to hear the overdrive at all.

He thought to himself: *Has it begun already?*

Otherwise everything seemed normal. The DFC-3 had crossed over into interstellar velocity, and he was still alive, and the ship was still functioning. The ship should at this moment be traveling at 22.4 times the speed of light—a neat 4,157,000 miles per second.

Somehow Garrard did not doubt that it was. On both previous tries, the ships had whiffed away toward Alpha Centauri at the proper moment when the overdrive should have cut in; and the split second of residual image after they had vanished, subjected to spectroscopy, showed a Doppler shift which tallied with the acceleration predicted for that moment by Haertel.

The trouble was not that Brown and Cellini hadn't gotten away in good order. It was simply that neither of them had ever been heard from again.

Very slowly, he opened his eyes. His eyelids felt terrifically heavy. As far as he could judge from the pressure of the couch against his skin, the gravity was normal; nevertheless, moving his eyelids seemed almost an impossible job.

After long concentration, he got them fully open. The instrument chassis was directly before him, extended over his diaphragm on its elbow joint. Still without moving anything but his eyes—and those only with the utmost patience—he checked each of the meters. Velocity: 22.4 c. Operating temperature: normal. Ship temperature: 37° C. Air pressure: 778 mm. Fuel: No. 1 tank full, No. 2 tank full, No. 3 tank full, No. 4 tank nine-tenths full. Gravity: 1 g. Calendar: stopped.

He looked at it closely, though his eyes seemed to focus very slowly, too. It was, of course, something more than a calendar—it was an all-purpose clock, designed to show him the passage of seconds, as well as of the ten months his trip was supposed to take to the double star. But there was no doubt about it: the second-hand was motionless.

That was the second abnormality. Garrard felt an impulse to get up and see if he could start the clock again. Perhaps the trouble had been temporary and safely in the past. Immediately there sounded in his head the injunction he had drilled into himself for a full month before the trip had begun—

Don't move!

Don't move until you know the situation as far as it can be known without moving. Whatever it was that had snatched Brown and Cellini irretrievably beyond human ken was potent, and totally beyond anticipation. They had both been excellent men, intelligent, resourceful, trained to the point of diminishing returns and not a micron beyond that point—the best men in the Project. Preparations for every knowable kind of trouble had been built into their ships, as they had been built into the DFC-3. Therefore, if there was something wrong nevertheless, it would be something that might strike from some commonplace quarter—and strike only once.

He listened to the humming. It was even and placid, and not very loud, but it disturbed him deeply. The overdrive was supposed to be inaudible, and the tapes from the first unmanned test vehicles had recorded no such hum. The noise did not appear to interfere with the overdrive's operation, or to indicate any failure in it. It was just an irrelevancy for which he could find no reason.

But the reason existed. Garrard did not intend to do so much as draw another breath until he found out what it was.

Incredibly, he realized for the first time that he had not in fact drawn one single breath since he had first come to. Though he felt not the slightest discomfort, the discovery called up so overwhelming a flash of panic that he very nearly sat bolt upright on the couch. Luckily—or so it seemed, after the panic had begun to ebb—the curious lethargy which had affected his eyelids appeared to involve his whole body, for the impulse was gone before he could summon the energy to answer it. And the panic, poignant though it had been for an instant, turned out to be wholly intellectual. In a moment, he was observing that his failure to breathe in no way discommoded him as far as he could tell—it was just there, waiting to be explained. . . .

Or to kill him. But it hadn't, yet.

Engines humming; eyelids heavy; breathing absent; calendar stopped. The four facts added up to nothing. The temptation to move something—even if it were only a big toe—was strong, but Garrard fought it back. He had been awake only a short while—half an hour at most—and already had noticed four abnormalities. There were bound to be more, anomalies more subtle than these four; but available to close examination before he had to move. Nor was there anything in particular that he had to do, aside from caring for his own wants; the Project, on the chance that Brown's and Cellini's failure to return had resulted from some tampering with the overdrive, had made everything in the DFC-3 subject only to the computer. In a very real sense, Garrard was just along for the ride. Only when the overdrive was off could he adjust—

Pock.

It was a soft, low-pitched noise, rather like a cork coming out of a wine bottle. It seemed to have come just from the right of the control chassis. He halted a sudden jerk of his head on the cushions toward it with a flat fiat of will. Slowly, he moved his eyes in that direction.

He could see nothing that might have caused the sound. The ship's temperature dial showed no change, which ruled out a heat noise from differential contraction or expansion—the only possible explanation he could bring to mind.

He closed his eyes—a process which turned out to be just as difficult as opening them had been—and tried to visualize what the calendar had looked like when he had first come out of anesthesia. After he got a clear and—he was almost sure—accurate picture, Garrard opened his eyes again.

The sound had been the calendar, advancing one second. It was now motionless again, apparently stopped.

He did not know how long it took the second-hand to make that jump, normally; the question had never come up. Certainly the jump, when it came at the end of each second, had been too fast for the eye to follow.

Belatedly, he realized what all this cogitation was costing him in terms of essential information. The calendar had moved. Above all and before anything else, he *must* know exactly how long it took it to move again. . . .

He began to count, allowing an arbitrary five seconds lost. *One-and-a-six, one-and-a-seven, one-and-an-eight—*

Garrard had gotten only that far when he found himself plunged into hell.

First, and utterly without reason, a sickening fear flooded swiftly through his veins, becoming more and more intense. His bowels began to knot, with infinite slowness. His whole body became a field of small, slow pulses—not so much shaking him as putting his limbs into contrary joggling motions, and making his skin ripple gently under his clothing. Against the hum another sound became audible, a nearly subsonic thunder which seemed to be inside his head. Still the fear mounted, and with it came the pain, and the tenesmus—a boardlike stiffening of his muscles, particularly across his abdomen and his shoulders, but affecting his forearms almost as grievously. He felt himself beginning, very gradually, to double at the middle, a motion about which he could do precisely nothing—a terrifying kind of dynamic paralysis. . . .

It lasted for hours. At the height of it, Garrard's mind, even his very personality, was washed out utterly; he was only a vessel of horror. When some few trickles of reason began to return over that burning desert of reasonless emotion, he found that he was sitting up on the cushions, and that with one arm he had thrust the control chassis back on its elbow so that it no longer jutted over his body. His clothing was wet with perspiration, which stubbornly refused to evaporate or to cool him. And his lungs ached a little, although he could still detect no breathing.

What under God had happened? Was it this that had killed Brown and Cellini? For it would kill Garrard, too—of that he was sure—if it happened often. It would kill him even if it happened only twice more, if the next two such things followed the first one closely. At the very best it would make a slobbering idiot of him; and though the computer might bring Garrard and the ship back to Earth, it would not be able to tell the Project about his tornado of senseless fear.

The calendar said that the eternity in hell had taken three seconds. As he looked at it in academic indignation, it said *pock* and condescended to make the total seizure four seconds long. With grim determination, Garrard began to count again.

He took care to establish the counting as an absolutely even, automatic process which would not stop at the back of his mind no matter what other problem he tackled along with it, or what emotional typhoons should interrupt him. Really compulsive counting cannot be stopped by anything—not the transports of love nor the agonies of empires. Garrard knew the dangers in deliberately setting up such a mechanism in his mind, but he also knew how desperately he needed to time that clock tick. He was beginning to understand what had happened to him—but he needed exact measurement before he could put that understanding to use.

Of course there had been plenty of speculation on the possible effect of the overdrive on the subjective time of the pilot, but none of it had come to much. At any speed below the velocity of light, subjective and objective time were exactly the same as far as the pilot was concerned. For an observer on Earth, time aboard the ship would appear to be vastly slowed at near-light speeds; but for the pilot himself there would be no apparent change.

Since flight beyond the speed of light was impossible—although for slightly differing reasons—by both the current theories of relativity, neither theory had offered any clue as to what would happen on board a translight ship. They would not allow that any such ship could even exist. The Haertel transformation, on which, in effect, the DFC-3 flew, was nonrelativistic: it showed that the apparent elapsed time of a translight journey should be identical in ship-time, and in the time of observers at both ends of the trip.

But since ship and pilot were part of the same system, both covered by the same expression in Haertel's equation, it had never occurred to anyone that the pilot and the ship might keep different times. The notion was ridiculous.

One-and-a-sevenhundred one, one-and-a-sevenhundred two, one-and-a-sevenhundred three, one-and-a-sevenhundred four . . .

The ship was keeping ship-time, which was identical with observer-time. It would arrive at the Alpha Centauri system in ten months. But the pilot was keeping Garrard-time, and it was beginning to look as though he wasn't going to arrive at all.

It was impossible, but there it was. Something—almost certainly an unsuspected physiological side effect of the overdrive field on human metabolism, an effect which naturally could not have been detected in the preliminary, robot-piloted tests of the overdrive—had speeded up Garrard's subjective apprehension of time, and had done a thorough job of it.

The second-hand began a slow, preliminary quivering as the calendar's innards began to apply power to it. *Seventy-hundred-forty-one, seventy-hundred-forty-two, seventy-hundred-forty-three . . .*

At the count of 7,058 the second-hand began the jump to the next graduation. It took it several apparent minutes to get across the tiny distance, and several more to come completely to rest. Later still, the sound came to him:

Pock.

In a fever of thought, but without any real physical agitation, his mind began to manipulate the figures. Since it took him longer to count an individual number as the number became larger, the interval between the two calendar ticks probably was closer to 7,200 seconds than to 7,058. Figuring backward brought him quickly to the equivalence he wanted:

One second in ship-time was two hours in Garrard-time.

Had he really been counting for what was, for him, two whole hours? There seemed to be no doubt about it. It looked like a long trip ahead.

Just how long it was going to be struck him with stunning force. Time had been slowed for him by a factor of 7,200. He would get to Alpha Centauri in just 72,000 months.

Which was—

Six thousand years!

2

Garrard sat motionless for a long time after that, the Nessusshirt of warm sweat swathing him persistently, refusing even to cool. There was, after all, no hurry.

Six thousand years. There would be food and water and air for all that time, or for sixty or six hundred thousand years; the ship would synthesize his needs, as a matter of course, for as long as the fuel lasted, and the fuel bred itself. Even if Garrard ate a meal every three seconds of objective, or ship, time (which, he realized suddenly, he wouldn't be able to do, for it took the ship several seconds of objective time to prepare and serve up a meal once it was ordered; he'd be lucky if he ate once a day, Garrard-time), there would be no reason to fear any shortage of supplies. That had been one of the earliest of the possibilities for disaster that the Project engineers had ruled out in the design of the DFC-3.

But nobody had thought to provide a mechanism which would indefinitely refurbish Garrard. After six thousand years, there would be nothing left of him but a faint film of dust on the DFC-3's dully gleaming horizontal surfaces. His corpse might outlast him a while, since the ship itself was sterile—but eventually he would be consumed by the bacteria which he carried in his own digestive tract. He needed those bacteria to synthesize part of his B-vitamin needs while he lived, but they would consume him without compunction once he had ceased to be as complicated and delicately balanced a thing as a pilot—or as any other kind of life.

Garrard was, in short, to die before the DFC-3 had gotten fairly away from Sol; and when, after 12,000 apparent years, the DFC-3 returned to Earth, not even his mummy would be still aboard.

The chill that went through him at that seemed almost unrelated to the way he thought he felt about the discovery; it lasted an enormously long time, and insofar as he could characterize it at all, it seemed to be a chill of urgency and excitement—not at all the kind of chill he should be feeling at a virtual death sentence. Luckily it was not as intolerably violent as the last such emotional convulsion; and when it was over, two clock ticks later, it left behind a residuum of doubt.

Suppose that this effect of time-stretching was only mental? The rest of his bodily processes might still be keeping ship-time; Garrard had no immediate reason to believe otherwise. If so, he would be able to move about only on ship-time, too; it would take many apparent months to complete the simplest task.

But he would live, if that were the case. His mind would arrive at Alpha Centauri six thousand years older, and perhaps madder, than his body, but he would live.

If, on the other hand, his bodily movements were going to be as fast as his mental processes, he would have to be enormously careful. He would have to move slowly and exert as little force as possible. The normal human hand movement, in such a task as lifting a pencil, took the pencil from a state of rest to another state of rest by imparting to it an acceleration of about two feet per second—and, of course, decelerated it by the same amount. If Garrard were to attempt to impart to a two-pound weight, which was keeping ship-time, an acceleration of $14,440$ ft/sec^2 in his time, he'd have to exert a force of 900 pounds on it.

The point was not that it couldn't be done—but that it would take as much effort as pushing a stalled jeep. He'd never be able to lift that pencil with his forearm muscles alone; he'd have to put his back into the task.

And the human body wasn't engineered to maintain stresses of that magnitude indefinitely. Not even the most powerful professional weight-lifter is forced to show his prowess throughout every minute of every day.

Pock.

That was the calendar again; another second had gone by. Or another two hours. It had certainly seemed longer than a second, but less than two hours, too. Evidently subjective time was an intensively recomplicated measure. Even in this world of micro-time—in which Garrard's mind, at least, seemed to be operating—he could make the lapses between calendar ticks seem a little shorter by becoming actively interested in some problem or other. That would help, during the waking hours, but it would help only if the rest of his body were *not* keeping the same time as his mind. If it were not, then he would lead an incredibly active, but perhaps not intolerable, mental life during the many centuries of his awake-time, and would be mercifully asleep for nearly as long.

Both problems—that of how much force he could exert with his body, and how long he could hope to be asleep in his mind—emerged simultaneously into the forefront of his consciousness while he still sat inertly on the hammock, their terms still much muddled together. After the single tick of the calendar, the ship—or the part of it that Garrard could see from here—settled back into complete rigidity. The sound of the engines, too, did not seem to vary in frequency or amplitude, at least as far as his ears could tell. He was still not breathing. Nothing moved, nothing changed.

It was the fact that he could still detect no motion of his diaphragm or his rib cage that decided him at last. His body had to be keeping ship-time, otherwise he would have blacked out from oxygen starvation long before now. That assumption explained, too, those two incredibly prolonged, seemingly sourceless saturnalias of emotion through which he had suffered: they had been nothing more nor less than the response of his endocrine glands to the purely intellectual reactions he had experienced earlier. He had discovered that he was not breathing, had felt a flash of panic and had tried to sit up. Long after his mind had forgotten those two impulses, they had inched their way from his brain down his nerves to the glands and muscles involved, and actual, *physical* panic had supervened. When that was over, he actually *was* sitting up, though the flood of adrenalin had prevented his noticing the motion as he had made it. The later chill—less violent, and apparently associated with the discovery that he might die long before the trip was completed—actually had been his body's response to a much earlier mental command; the abstract fever of interest he had felt while computing the time differential had been responsible for it.

Obviously, he was going to have to be very careful with apparently cold and intellectual impulses of any kind—or he would pay for them later with a prolonged and agonizing glandular reaction. Nevertheless, the discovery gave him considerable satisfaction, and Garrard allowed it free play; it certainly could not hurt him to feel pleased for a few hours, and the glandular pleasure might even prove helpful if it caught him at a moment of mental depression. Six thousand years, after all, provided a considerable number of opportunities for feeling down-in-the-mouth; so it would be best to encourage all pleasure moments, and let the after-reaction last as long as it might. It would be the instants of panic, of fear, of gloom, which he would have to regulate sternly the moment they came into his mind; it would be those which would otherwise plunge him into four, five, six, perhaps even ten, Garrard-hours of emotional inferno.

Pock.

There now, that was very good: there had been two Garrard-hours which he had passed with virtually no difficulty of any kind, and without being especially conscious of their passage. If he could really settle down and become used to this kind of scheduling, the trip might not be as bad as he had at first feared. Sleep would take immense bites out of it; and during the waking periods he could put in one hell of a lot of creative thinking. During a single day of ship-time, Garrard could get in more thinking than any philosopher of Earth could have managed during an entire lifetime. Garrard could, if he disciplined himself sufficiently, devote his mind for a century to running down the consequences of a single thought, down to the last detail, and still have millennia left to go on to the next thought. What panoplies of pure reason could he not have assembled by the time 6,000 years had gone by? With sufficient concentration, he might come up with the solution to the Problem of Evil between breakfast and dinner of a single ship's day, and in a ship's month might put his finger on the First Cause!

Pock.

Not that Garrard was sanguine enough to expect that he would remain logical or even sane throughout the trip. The vista was still grim, in much of its detail. But the opportunities, too, were there. He felt a momentary regret that it hadn't been Haertel, rather than himself, who had been given such an opportunity—

Pock.

—for the old man could certainly have made better use of it than Garrard could. The situation demanded someone trained in the highest rigors of mathematics to be put to the best conceivable use. Still and all Garrard began to feel—

Pock.

—that he would give a good account of himself, and it tickled him to realize that (as long as he held on to his essential sanity) he would return—

Pock.

—to Earth after ten Earth months with knowledge centuries advanced beyond anything—

Pock.

—that Haertel knew, or that anyone could know—

Pock.

—who had to work within a normal lifetime. *Pck.* The whole prospect tickled him. *Pck.* Even the clock tick seemed more cheerful. *Pck.* He felt fairly safe now *Pck* in disregarding his drilled-in command *Pck* against moving *Pck,* since in any *Pck* event the *Pck* had already *Pck* moved *Pck* without *Pck* being *Pck* harmed *Pck Pck Pck Pck Pck pckpckpckpckpckpckpck....*

He yawned, stretched, and got up. It wouldn't do to be too pleased, after all. There were certainly many problems that still needed coping with, such as how to keep the impulse toward getting a ship-time task performed going, while his higher centers were following the ramifications of some purely philosophical point. And besides . . .

And besides, he had just moved.

More than that, he had just performed a complicated maneuver with his body *in normal time!*

Before Garrard looked at the calendar itself, the message it had been ticking away at him had penetrated. While he had been enjoying the protracted, glandular backwash of his earlier feeling of satisfaction, he had failed to notice, at least consciously, that the calendar was accelerating.

Good-bye, vast ethical systems which would dwarf the Greeks. Good-bye, calculuses aeons advanced beyond the spinor calculus of Dirac. Good-bye, cosmologies by Garrard which would allot the Almighty a job as third-assistant-waterboy in an *n*-dimensional backfield.

Good-bye, also, to a project he had once tried to undertake in college—to describe and count the positions of love, of which, according to under-the-counter myth, there were supposed to be at least forty-eight. Garrard had never been able to carry his tally beyond twenty, and he had just lost what was probably his last opportunity to try again.

The micro-time in which he had been living had worn off, only a few objective minutes after the ship had gone into overdrive and he had come out of the anesthetic. The long intellectual agony, with its glandular counterpoint, had come to nothing. Garrard was now keeping ship-time.

Garrard sat back down on the hammock, uncertain whether to be bitter or relieved. Neither emotion satisfied him in the end; he simply felt unsatisfied. Micro-time had been bad enough while it lasted; but now it was gone, and everything seemed normal. How could so transient a thing have killed Brown and Cellini? They were stable men, more stable, by his own private estimation, than Garrard himself. Yet he had come through it. Was there more to it than this?

And if there was—what, conceivably, could it be?

There was no answer. At his elbow, on the control chassis which he had thrust aside during that first moment of infinitely protracted panic, the calendar continued to tick. The engine noise was gone. His breath came and went in natural rhythm. He felt light and strong. The ship was quiet, calm, unchanging.

The calendar ticked, faster and faster. It reached and passed the first hour, ship-time, of flight in overdrive.

Pock.

Garrard looked up in surprise. The familiar noise, this time, had been the hour-hand jumping one unit. The minute-hand was already sweeping past the past half-hour. The second-hand was whirling like a propeller—and while he watched it, it speeded up to complete invisibility—

Pock.

Another hour. The half-hour already passed. *Pock.* Another hour. *Pock.* Another, *Pock. Pock. Pock, Pock, Pock, Pock, pck-pck-pck-pck-pckpckpckpck. . . .*

The hands of the calendar swirled toward invisibility as time ran away with Garrard. Yet the ship did not change. It stayed there, rigid, inviolate, unvulnerable. When the date tumblers reached a speed at which Garrard could no longer read them, he discovered that once more he could not move—and that, although his whole body seemed to be aflutter like that of a hummingbird, nothing coherent was coming to him through his senses. The room was dimming, becoming redder; or no, it was . . .

But he never saw the end of the process, never was allowed to look from the pinnacle of macro-time toward which the Haertel overdrive was taking him.

Pseudo-death took him first.

3

That Garrard did not die completely, and within a comparatively short time after the DFC-3 had gone into overdrive, was due to the purest of accidents; but Garrard did not know that. In fact, he knew nothing at all for an indefinite period, sitting rigid and staring, his metabolism slowed down to next to nothing, his mind almost utterly inactive. From time to time, a single wave of low-level metabolic activity passed through him—what an electrician might have termed a "maintenance turnover"—in response to the urgings of some occult survival urge; but these were of so basic a nature as to reach his consciousness not at all. This was the pseudo-death.

When the observer actually arrived, however, Garrard woke. He could make very little sense out of what he saw or felt even now; but one fact was clear: the overdrive was off—and with it the crazy alterations in time rates—and there was strong light coming through one of the ports. The first leg of the trip was over. It had been these two changes in his environment which had restored him to life.

The thing (or things) which had restored him to consciousness, however, was—it was what? It made no sense. It was a construction, a rather fragile one, which completely surrounded his hammock. No, it wasn't a construction, but evidently something alive—a living being, organized horizontally, that had arranged itself in a circle about him. No, it was a number of beings. Or a combination of all of these things.

How it had gotten into the ship was a mystery, but there it was. Or there they were.

"How do you hear?" the creature said abruptly. Its voice, or their voices, came at equal volume from every point in the circle, but not from any particular point in it. Garrard could think of no reason why that should be unusual.

"I—" he said. "Or we—we hear with our ears. Here."

His answer, with its unintentionally long chain of open vowel sounds, rang ridiculously. He wondered why he was speaking such an odd language.

"We-they wooed to pitch you-yours thiswise," the creature said. With a thump, a book from the DFC-3's ample library fell to the deck beside the hammock. "We wooed there and there and there for a many. You are the being-Garrard. We-they are the clinesterton beademung, with all of love."

"With all of love," Garrard echoed. The beademung's use of the language they both were speaking was odd; but again Garrard could find no logical reason why the beademung's usage should be considered wrong.

"Are—are you-they from Alpha Centauri?" he said hesitantly.

"Yes, we hear the twin radioceles, that show there beyond the gift-orifices. We-they pitched that the being-Garrard with most adoration these twins and had mind to them, soft and loud alike. How do you hear?"

This time the being-Garrard understood the question. "I hear Earth," he said. "But that is very soft, and does not show."

"Yes," said the beademung. "It is a harmony, not a first, as ours. The All-Devouring listens to lovers there, not on the radioceles. Let me-mine pitch you-yours so to have mind of the rodalent beademung and other brothers and lovers, along the channel which is fragrant to the being-Garrard."

Garrard found that he understood the speech without difficulty. The thought occurred to him that to understand a language on its own terms—without having to put it back into English in one's own mind—is an ability that is won only with difficulty and long practice. Yet, instantly his mind said, "But it *is* English," which of course it was. The offer the clinesterton beademung had just made was enormously hearted, and he in turn was much minded and of love, to his own delighting as well as to the beademungen; that almost went without saying.

There were many matings of ships after that, and the being-Garrard pitched the harmonies of the beademungen, leaving his ship with the many gift-orifices in harmonic for the All-Devouring to love, while the beademungen made show of they-theirs.

He tried, also, to tell how he was out of love with the overdrive, which wooed only spaces and times, and made featurelings. The rodalent beademung wooed the overdrive, but it did not pitch he-them.

Then the being-Garrard knew that all the time was devoured, and he must hear Earth again.

"I pitch you-them to fullest love," he told the beademungen, "I shall adore the radioceles of Alpha and Proxima Centauri, 'on Earth as it is in Heaven.' Now the overdrive my-other must woo and win me, and make me adore a featureling much like silence."

"But you will be pitched again," the clinesterton beademung said. "After you have adored Earth. You are much loved by Time, the All-Devouring. We-they shall wait for this othering."

Privately Garrard did not faith as much, but he said, "Yes, we-they will make a new wooing of the beademungen at some other radiant. With all of love.''

On this the beademungen made and pitched adorations, and in the midst the overdrive cut in. The ship with the many gift-orifices and the being-Garrard him-other saw the twin radioceles sundered away.

Then, once more, came the pseudo-death.

4

When the small candle lit in the endless cavern of Garrard's pseudo-dead mind, the DFC-3 was well inside the orbit of Uranus. Since the Sun was still very small and distant, it made no spectacular display through the nearby port, and nothing called him from the post-death sleep for nearly two days.

The computers waited patiently for him. They were no longer immune to his control; he could now tool the ship back to Earth himself if he so desired. But the computers were also designed to take into account the fact that he might be truly dead by the time the DFC-3 got back. After giving him a solid week, during which time he did nothing but sleep, they took over again. Radio signals began to go out, tuned to a special channel.

An hour later, a very weak signal came back. It was only a directional signal, and it made no sound inside the DFC-3—but it was sufficient to put the big ship in motion again.

It was that which woke Garrard. His conscious mind was still glazed over with the icy spume of the pseudo-death; and as far as he could see the interior of the cabin had not changed one whit, except for the book on the deck—

The book. The clinesterton beademung had dropped it there. But what under God was a clinesterton beademung? And what was he, Garrard, crying about? It didn't make sense. He remembered dimly some kind of experience out there by the Centauri twins—

—*the twin radioceles*—

There was another one of those words. It seemed to have Greek roots, but he knew no Greek—and besides, why would Centaurians speak Greek?

He leaned forward and actuated the switch which would roll the shutter off the front port, actually a telescope with a translucent viewing screen. It showed a few stars, and a faint nimbus off on one edge which might be the Sun. At about one o'clock on the screen was a planet about the size of a pea which had tiny projections, like teacup handles, on each side. The DFC-3 hadn't passed Saturn on its way out; at that time it had been on the other side of the Sun from the route the starship had had to follow. But the planet was certainly difficult to mistake.

Garrard was on his way home—and he was still alive and sane. Or was he still sane? These fantasies about Centaurians—which still seemed to have such a profound emotional effect upon him—did not argue very well for the stability of his mind.

But they were fading rapidly. When he discovered, clutching at the handiest fragments of the "memories," that the plural of *beademung* was *beademungen,* he stopped taking the problem seriously. Obviously a race of Centaurians who spoke Greek wouldn't also be forming weak German plurals. The whole business had obviously been thrown up by his unconscious.

But what *had* he found by the Centaurus stars?

There was no answer to that question but that incomprehensible garble about love, the All-Devouring, and beademungen. Possibly, he had never seen the Centaurus stars at all, but had been lying here, cold as a mackerel, for the entire twenty months.

Or had it been 12,000 years? After the tricks the overdrive had played with time, there was no way to tell what the objective date actually was. Frantically Garrard put the telescope into action. Where was the Earth? After 12,000 years—

The Earth was there. Which, he realized swiftly, proved nothing. The Earth had lasted for many millions of years; 12,000 years was nothing to a planet. The Moon was there, too; both were plainly visible, on the far side of the Sun—but not too far to pick them out clearly, with the telescope at highest power. Garrard could even see a clear sun-highlight on the Atlantic Ocean, not far east of Greenland; evidently the computers were bringing the DFC-3 in on the Earth from about 23° north of the plane of the ecliptic.

The Moon, too, had not changed. He could even see on its face the huge splash of white, mimicking the sun-highlight on Earth's ocean, which was the magnesium hydroxide landing beacon, which had been dusted over the Mare Vaporum in the earliest days of space flight, with a dark spot on its southern edge which could only be the crater Monilius.

But that again proved nothing. The Moon never changed. A film of dust laid down by modern man on its face would last for millennia—what, after all, existed on the Moon to blow it away? The Mare

Vaporum beacon covered more than 4,000 square miles; age would not dim it, nor could man himself undo it—either accidentally, or on purpose—in anything under a century. When you dust an area that large on a world without atmosphere, it stays dusted.

He checked the stars against his charts. They hadn't moved; why should they have, in only 12,000 years? The pointer stars in the Dipper still pointed to Polaris. Draco, like a fantastic bit of tape, wound between the two Bears, and Cepheus and Cassiopeia, as it always had done. These constellations told him only that it was spring in the northern hemisphere of Earth.

But spring of what year?

Then, suddenly, it occurred to Garrard that he had a method of finding the answer. The Moon causes tides in the Earth, and action and reaction are always equal and opposite. The Moon cannot move things on Earth without itself being affected—and that effect shows up in the Moon's angular momentum. The Moon's distance from the Earth increases steadily by 0.6 inch every year. At the end of 12,000 years, it should be 600 feet farther away from the Earth.

Was it possible to measure? Garrard doubted it, but he got out his ephemeris and his dividers anyhow, and took pictures. While he worked, the Earth grew nearer. By the time he had finished his first calculation—which was indecisive, because it allowed a margin of error greater than the distances he was trying to check—Earth and Moon were close enough in the telescope to permit much more accurate measurements.

Which were, he realized wryly, quite unnecessary. The computer had brought the DFC-3 back, not to an observed sun or planet, but simply to a calculated point. That Earth and Moon would not be near that point when the DFC-3 returned was not an assumption that the computer could make. That the Earth was visible from here was already good and sufficient proof that no more time had elapsed than had been calculated for from the beginning.

This was hardly new to Garrard; it had simply been retired to the back of his mind. Actually he had been doing all this figuring for one reason, and one reason only: because deep in his brain, set to work by himself, there was a mechanism that demanded counting. Long ago, while he was still trying to time the ship's calendar, he had initiated compulsive counting—and it appeared that he had been counting ever since. That had been one of the known dangers of deliberately starting such a mental mechanism; and now it was bearing fruit in these perfectly useless astronomical exercises.

The insight was healing. He finished the figures roughly, and that unheard moron deep inside his brain stopped counting at last. It had been pawing its abacus for twenty months now, and Garrard imagined that it was as glad to be retired as he was to feel it go.

His radio squawked, and said anxiously, "DFC-3, DFC-3. Garrard, do you hear me? Are you still alive? Everybody's going wild down here. Garrard, if you hear me, call us!"

It was Haertel's voice. Garrard closed the dividers so convulsively that one of the points nipped into the heel of his hand. "Haertel, I'm here. DFC-3 to the Project. This is Garrard." And then, without knowing quite why, he added: "With all of love."

Haertel, after all the hoopla was over, was more than interested in the time effects. "It certainly enlarges the manifold in which I was working," he said. "But I think we can account for it in the transformation. Perhaps even factor it out, which would eliminate it as far as the pilot is concerned. We'll see, anyhow."

Garrard swirled his highball reflectively. In Haertel's cramped old office, in the Project's administration shack, he felt both strange and as old, as compressed, constricted. He said, "I don't think I'd do that, Adolph. I think it saved my life."

"How?"

"I told you that I seemed to die after a while. Since I got home, I've been reading; and I've discovered that the psychologists take far less stock in the individuality of the human psyche than you and I do. You and I are physical scientists, so we think about the world as being all outside our skins—something which is to be observed, but which doesn't alter the essential *I*. But evidently, that old solipsistic position isn't quite true. Our very personalities, really, depend on large part upon *all* the things in our environment, large and small, that exist outside our skins. If by some means you could cut a human being off from every sense impression that comes to him from outside, he would cease to exist as a personality within two or three minutes. Probably he would die."

"Unquote: Harry Stack Sullivan," Haertel said, dryly. "So?"

"So," Garrard said, "think of what a monotonous environment the inside of a spaceship is. It's perfectly rigid, still, unchanging, lifeless. In ordinary interplanetary flight, in such an environment, even the most hardened spaceman may go off his rocker now and then. You know the typical spaceman's psychosis as well as I do, I suppose. The man's personality goes rigid, just like his surroundings. Usually he recovers as soon as he makes port, and makes contact with a more-or-less normal world again.

"But in the DFC-3, I was cut off from the world around me much more severely. I couldn't look outside the ports—I was in overdrive, and there was nothing to see. I couldn't communicate with home, because I was going faster than light. And then I found I couldn't move either, for an enormous long while; and that even the instruments that are in constant change for the usual spaceman wouldn't be in motion for me. Even those were fixed.

"After the time rate began to pick up, I found myself in an even more impossible box. The instruments moved, all right, but then they moved too *fast* for me to read them. The whole situation was now utterly rigid—and, in effect, I died. I froze as solid as the ship around me, and stayed that way as long as the overdrive was on."

"By that showing," Haertel said dryly, "the time effects were hardly your friends."

"But they were, Adolph. Look. Your engines act on subjective time; they keep it varying along continuous curves—from far-too-slow to far-too-fast—and, I suppose, back down again. Now, this is a *situation of continuous change.* It wasn't marked enough, in the long run, to keep me out of pseudo-death; but it was sufficient to protect me from being obliterated altogether, which I think is what happened to Brown and Cellini. Those men knew that they could shut down the overdrive if they could just get to it, and they killed themselves trying. But I knew that I just had to sit and take it—and, by my great good luck, your sine-curve time variation made it possible for me to survive."

"Ah, ah," Haertel said. "A point worth considering—though I doubt that it will make interstellar travel very popular!"

He dropped back into silence, his thin mouth pursed. Garrard took a grateful pull at his drink.

At last Haertel said: "Why are you in trouble over these Centaurians? It seems to me that you have done a good job. It was nothing that you were a hero—any fool can be brave—but I see also that you *thought,* where Brown and Cellini evidently only reacted. Is there some secret about what you found when you reached those two stars?"

Garrard said, "Yes, there is. But I've already told you what it is. When I came out of the pseudo-death, I was just a sort of plastic palimpsest upon which anybody could have made a mark. My own environment, my ordinary Earth environment, was a hell of a long way off. My present surroundings were nearly as rigid as they had ever been. When I met the Centaurians—if I did, and I'm not at all sure of that—*they* became the most important thing in my world, and my personality changed to accommodate and understand them. That was a change about which I couldn't do a thing.

"Possibly I did understand them. But the man who understood them wasn't the same man you're talking to now, Adolph. Now that I'm back on Earth, I don't understand that man. He even spoke English in a way that's gibberish to me. If I can't understand myself during that period—and I can't; I don't even believe that that man was the Garrard I know—what hope have I of telling you or the Project about the Centaurians? They found me in a controlled environment, and they altered me by entering it. Now that they're gone, nothing comes through; I don't even understand why I think they spoke English!"

"Did they have a name for themselves?"

"Sure," Garrard said. "They were the beademungen."

"What did they look like?"

"I never saw them."

Haertel leaned forward. "Then . . ."

"I heared them. I think." Garrard shrugged, and tasted his Scotch again. He was home, and on the whole he was pleased.

But in his malleable mind he heard someone say. *On Earth, as it is in Heaven;* and then, in another voice, which might also have been his own (why had he thought "him-other"?), *It is later than you think.*

"Adolph," he said, "is this all there is to it? Or are we going to go on with it from here? How long will it take to make a better starship, a DFC-4?"

"Many years," Haertel said, smiling kindly. "Don't be anxious, Garrard. You've come back, which is more than the others managed to do, and nobody will ask you to go out again. I really think that it's hardly likely that we'll get another ship built during your lifetime; and even if we do, we'll be slow to launch it. We really have very little information about what kind of playground you found out there."

"I'll go," Garrard said. "I'm not afraid to go back—I'd like to go. Now that I know how the DFC-3 behaves, I could take it out again, bring you back proper maps, tapes, photos."

"Do you really think," Haertel said, his face suddenly serious, "that we could let the DFC-3 go out again? Garrard, we're going to take that ship apart practically molecule by molecule; that's preliminary to the building of any DFC-4. And no more can we let you go. I don't mean to be cruel, but has it occurred to you that this desire to go back may be the result of some kind of posthypnotic suggestion? If so, the more badly you want to go back, the more dangerous to us all you may be. We are going to have to examine you just as thoroughly as we do the ship. If these beademungen wanted you to come back, they must have had a reason—and we have to know that reason.''

Garrard nodded, but he knew that Haertel could see the slight movement of his eyebrows and the wrinkles forming in his forehead, the contractions of the small muscles which stop the flow of tears only to make grief patent on the rest of the face.

"In short," he said, *"don't move."*

Haertel looked politely puzzled. Garrard, however, could say nothing more. He had returned to humanity's common time and would never leave it again.

Not even, for all his dimly remembered promise, with all there was left in him of love.

The Shadow of Space

Philip José Farmer

The klaxon cleared its plastic throat and began to whoop. Alternate yellow and reds pulsed on the consoles wrapped like bracelets around the wrists of the captain and the navigator. The huge auxiliary screens spaced on the bulkheads of the bridge also flashed red and yellow.

Captain Grettir, catapulted from his reverie, and from his chair, stood up. The letters and numerals 20-G-DZ-R hung burning on a sector of each screen and spurted up from the wrist-console, spread out before his eyes, then disappeared, only to rise from the wrist-console again and magnify themselves and thin into nothing. Over and over again. 20-G-DZ-R. The code letters indicating that the alarm originated from the corridor leading to the engine room.

He turned his wrist and raised his arm to place the lower half of the console at the correct viewing and speaking distance.

"20-G-DZ-R, report!"

The flaming, expanding, levitating letters died out, and the long high-cheekboned face of MacCool, chief engineer, appeared as a tiny image on the sector of the console. It was duplicated on the bridge bulkhead screens. It rose and grew larger, shooting towards Grettir, then winking out to be followed by a second ballooning face.

Also on the wrist-console's screen, behind MacCool, were Comas, a petty officer, and Grinker, a machinist's mate. Their faces did not float up because they were not in the central part of the screen. Behind them was a group of marines and an 88-K cannon on a floating sled.

"It's the Wellington woman," MacCool said. "She used the photer, lowpower setting, to knock out the two guards stationed at the engine-room port. Then she herded us—me, Comas, Grinker—out. She said she'd shoot us if we resisted. And she welded the grille to the bulkhead so it can't be opened unless it's burned off.

"I don't know why she's doing this. But she's reconnected the drive wires to a zander bridge so she can control the acceleration herself. We can't do a thing to stop her unless we go in after her."

He paused, swallowed and said, "I could send men outside and have them try to get through the engine room airlock or else cut through the hull to get her. While she was distracted by this, we could make frontal attack down the corridor. But she says she'll shoot anybody that gets too close. We could lose some men. She means what she says."

"If you cut a hole in the hull, she'd be out of air, dead in a minute," Grettir said.

"She's in a spacesuit," MacCool replied. "That's why I didn't have this area sealed off and gas flooded in."

Grettir hoped his face was not betraying his shock. Hearing an exclamation from Wang, seated near him, Grettir turned his head. He said. "How in the hell did she get out of sick bay?"

He realized at the same time that Wang could not answer that question. MacCool said, "I don't know, sir. Ask Doctor Wills."

"Never mind that now!"

Grettir stared at the sequence of values appearing on the navigator's auxiliary bulkhead-screen. The 0.5 of light speed had already climbed to 0.96. It changed every 4 seconds. The 0.96 became 0.97, then 0.98, 0.99 and then 1.0. And then 1.1 and 1.2.

Grettir forced himself to sit back down. If anything was going to happen, it would have done so by now; the TSN-X cruiser *Sleipnir,* 280 million tons, would have been converted to pure energy.

A nova, bright but very brief, would have gouted in the heavens. And the orbiting telescopes of Earth would see the flare in 20.8 light-years.

"What's the state of the *emc* clamp and acceleration-dissipaters?" Grettir said.

"No strain—yet," Wang said. "But the power drain . . . if it continues . . . 5 megakilowatts per 2 seconds, and we're just beginning."

"I think," Grettir said slowly, "that we're going to find out what we intended to find out. But it isn't going to be under the carefully controlled conditions we had planned."

The Terran Space Navy experimental cruiser *Sleipnir* had left its base on Asgard, eighth planet of Altair (alpha Aquilae), 28 shipdays ago. It was under orders to make the first attempt of a manned ship to exceed the velocity of light. If its mission was successful, men could travel between Earth and the colonial planets in weeks instead of years. The entire galaxy might be opened to Earth.

Within the past two weeks, the *Sleipnir* had made several tests at 0.8 times the velocity of light, the tests lasting up to two hours at a time.

The *Sleipnir* was equipped with enormous motors and massive clamps, dissipaters and space-time structure expanders ("hole-openers") required for near-lightspeeds and beyond. No ship in Terrestrial history had ever had such power or the means to handle such power.

The drive itself—the cubed amplification of energy produced by the controlled mixture of matter, antimatter and half-matter—gave an energy that could eat its way through the iron core of a planet. But part of that energy had to be diverted to power the energy-mass conversion "clamp" that kept the ship from being transformed into energy itself. The "hole-opener" also required vast power. This device—officially the Space-Time Structure Expander, or Neutralizer—"unbent" the local curvature of the universe and so furnished a "hole" through which the *Sleipnir* traveled. This hole nullified 99.3 per cent of the resistance the *Sleipnir* would normally have encountered.

Thus the effects of speeds approaching and even exceeding light-speed would be modified, even if not entirely avoided. The *Sleipnir* should not contract along its length to zero nor attain infinite mass when it reached the speed of light. It contracted, and it swelled, yes, by only 1/777,777th what it should have. The ship would assume the shape of a disk—but much more slowly than it would without its openers, clamps and dissipaters.

Beyond the speed of light, who knew what would happen? It was the business of the *Sleipnir* to find out. But, Grettir thought, not under these conditions. Not willy-nilly.

"Sir!" MacCool said, "Wellington threatens to shoot anybody who comes near the engine room."

He hesitated, then said, "Except you. She wants to speak to you. But she doesn't want to do it over the intercom. She insists that you come down and talk to her face to face." Grettir bit his lower lip and made a sucking sound.

"Why me?" he said, but he knew why, and MacCool's expression showed that he also knew.

"I'll be down in a minute. Now, isn't there any way we can connect a bypass, route a circuit around her or beyond her and get control of the drive again?"

"No, sir!"

"Then she's cut through the engine-room deck and gotten to the redundant circuits also?"

MacCool said, "She's crazy, but she's clear-headed enough to take all precautions. She hasn't overlooked a thing."

Grettir said, "Wang! What's the velocity now?"

"2.3 sl/pm, sir!"

Grettir looked at the huge starscreen on the "forward" bulkhead of the bridge. Black except for a few glitters of white, blue, red, green, and the galaxy called xD-2 that lay dead ahead. The galaxy had been the size of an orange, and it still was. He stared at the screen for perhaps a minute, then said, "Wang, am I seeing right? The red light from xD-2 is shifting towards the blue, right?"

"Right, sir!"

"Then . . . why isn't xD-2 getting bigger? We're overhauling it like a fox after a rabbit."

Wang said, "I think it's getting closer, sir. But we're getting bigger."

II

Grettir rose from the chair. "Take over while I'm gone. Turn off the alarm; tell the crew to continue their normal duties. If anything comes up while I'm in the engine area, notify me at once."

The exec saluted. "Yes, sir!" she said huskily.

Grettir strode off the bridge. He was aware that the officers and crewmen seated in the ring of chairs in the bridge were looking covertly at him. He stopped for a minute to light up a cigar. He was glad that his hands were not shaking, and he hoped that his expression was confident. Slowly, repressing the impulse to run, he continued across the bridge and into the jump-shaft. He stepped off backward into the shaft and nonchalantly blew out smoke while he sank out of sight of the men in the bridge. He braced himself against the quick drop and then the thrusting deceleration. He had set the controls for Dock 14; the doors slid open; he walked into a corridor where a g-car and operator waited for him. Grettir climbed in, sat down and told the crewman where to drive.

Two minutes later, he was with MacCool. The chief engineer pointed down the corridor. Near its end on the floor were two still unconscious Marines. The door to the engine room was open. The secondary door, the grille, was shut. The lights within the engine room had been turned off. Something white on the other side of the grille moved. It was Donna Wellington's face, visible through the helmet.

"We can't keep this acceleration up," Grettir said. "We're already going far faster than even unmanned experimental ships have been allowed to go. There are all sorts of theories about what might happen to a ship at these speeds, all bad."

"We've disproved several by now," MacCool said. He spoke evenly, but his forehead was sweaty and shadows hung under his eyes.

MacCool continued, "I'm glad you got here, sir. She just threatened to cut the *emc* clamp wires if you didn't show within the next two minutes."

He gestured with both hands to indicate a huge expanding ball of light.

"I'll talk to her," Grettir said. "Although I can't imagine what she wants."

MacCool looked dubious. Grettir wanted to ask him what the hell he was thinking but thought better of it. He said, "Keep your men at this post. Don't even look as if you're coming after me."

"And what do we do, sir, if she shoots you?"

Grettir winced. "Use the cannon. And never mind hesitating if I happen to be in the way. Blast her! But make sure you use a beam short enough to get her but not long enough to touch the engines."

"May I ask why we don't do that before you put your life in danger?" MacCool said.

Grettir hesitated, then said, "My main responsibility is to the ship and its crew. But this woman is very sick; she doesn't realize the implications of her actions. Not fully anyway. I want to talk her out of this, if I can.''

He unhooked the communicator from his belt and walked down the corridor toward the grille and the darkness behind it and the whiteness that moved. His back prickled. The men were watching him intently. God knew what they were saying, or at least thinking, about him. The whole crew had been amused for some time by Donna Wellington's passion for him and his inability to cope with her. They had said she was mad about him, not realizing that she really was mad. They had laughed. But they were not laughing now.

Even so, knowing that she was truly insane, some of them must be blaming him for this danger. Undoubtedly, they were thinking that if he had handled her differently, they would not now be so close to death.

He stopped just one step short of the grille. Now he could see Wellington's face, a checkerboard of blacks and whites. He waited for her to speak first. A full minute passed, then she said, ''Robert!''

The voice, normally low-pitched and pleasant, was now thin and strained.

''Not Robert. Eric,'' he said into the communicator. ''Captain Eric Grettir, Mrs. Wellington.''

There was a silence. She moved closer to the grille. Light struck one eye, which gleamed bluely.

''Why do you hate me so, Robert?'' she said plaintively. ''You used to love me. What did I do to make you turn against me?''

''I am *not* your husband,'' Grettir said. ''Look at me. Can't you see that I am not Robert Wellington? I am Captain Grettir of the *Sleipnir*. You *must* see who I *really* am, Mrs. Wellington. It is very important.''

''You don't love me!'' she screamed. ''You are trying to get rid of me by pretending you're another man! But it won't work! I'd know you anywhere, you beast! You beast! I hate you, Robert!''

Involuntarily, Grettir stepped back under the intensity of her anger. He saw her hand come up from the shadows and the flash of light on a handgun. It was too late then; she fired; a beam of whiteness dazzled him.

Light was followed by darkness.

Ahead, or above, there was a disk of grayness in the black. Grettir traveled slowly and spasmodically towards it, as if he had been swallowed by a whale but was being ejected towards the open mouth, the muscles of the Leviathan's throat working him outwards.

Far behind him, deep in the bowels of the whale, Donna Wellington spoke.

"Robert?"

"Eric!" he shouted. "I'm *Eric!*"

The *Sleipnir,* barely on its way out from Asgard, dawdling at 6200 kilometers per second, had picked up the Mayday call. It came from a spaceship midway between the 12th and 13th planet of Altair. Although Grettir could have ignored the call without reprimand from his superiors, he altered course, and he found a ship wrecked by a meteorite. Inside the hull was half the body of a man. And a woman in deep shock.

Robert and Donna Wellington were second-generation Asgardians, Ph.D.'s in biotatology, holding master's papers in astrogation. They had been searching for specimens of "space plankton" and "space hydras," forms of life born in the regions between Altair's outer planets.

The crash, the death of her husband and the shattering sense of isolation, dissociation and hopelessness during the eighty-four hours before rescue had twisted Mrs. Wellington. Perhaps twisted was the wrong word. Fragmented was a better description.

From the beginning of what at first seemed recovery, she had taken a superficial resemblance of Grettir to her husband for an identity. Grettir had been gentle and kind with her at the beginning and had made frequent visits to sick bay. Later, advised by Doctor Wills, he had been severe with her.

And so the unforeseen result.

Donna Wellington screamed behind him and, suddenly, the twilight circle ahead became bright, and he was free. He opened his eyes to see faces over him. Doctor Wills and MacCool. He was in sick bay.

MacCool smiled and said, "For a moment, we thought . . ."

"What happened?" Grettir said. Then "I know what she did. I mean—"

"She fired full power at you," MacCool said. "But the bars of the grille absorbed most of the energy. You got just enough to crisp the skin off your face and to knock you out. Good thing you closed your eyes in time."

Grettir sat up. He felt his face; it was covered with a greasy ointment, pain-deadening and skin-growing *resec.*

"I got a hell of a headache."

Doctor Wills said, "It'll be gone in a minute."

"What's the situation?" Grettir said. "How'd you get me away from her?"

MacCool said, "I had to do it, Captain. Otherwise, she'd have taken another shot at you. The cannon blasted what was left of the grille. Mrs. Wellington—"

"She's dead?"

"Yes. But the cannon didn't get her. Strange. She took her suit off, stripped to the skin. Then she went out through the airlock in the engine room. Naked, as if she meant to be the bride of Death. We almost got caught in the outrush of air, since she fixed the controls so that the inner port remained open. It was close, but we got the port shut in time."

Grettir said, "I . . . never mind. Any damage to the engine room?"

"No. And the wires are reconnected for normal operation. Only—"

"Only what?"

MacCool's face was so long he looked like a frightened bloodhound.

"Just before I reconnected the wires, a funny . . . peculiar . . . thing happened. The whole ship, and everything inside the ship, went through a sort of distortion. Wavy, as if we'd all become wax and were dripping. Or flags flapping in a wind. The bridge reports that the fore of the ship seemed to expand like a balloon, then became ripply, and the entire effect passed through the ship. We all got nauseated while the waviness lasted."

There was silence, but their expressions indicated that there was more to be said.

"Well?"

MacCool and Wills looked at each other. MacCool swallowed and said, "Captain, we don't know where in hell we are!"

III

On the bridge, Grettir examined the forward EXT. screen. There were no stars. Space everywhere was filled with a light as gray and as dull as that of a false dawn on Earth. In the gray glow, at a distance as yet undetermined, were a number of spheres. They looked small, but if they were as large as the one immediately aft of the *Sleipnir,* they were huge.

The sphere behind them, estimated to be at a distance of fifty kilometers, was about the size of Earth's moon, relative to the ship. Its surface was as smooth and as gray as a ball of lead.

Darl spoke a binary code into her wrist-console, and the sphere on the starscreen seemed to shoot towards them. It filled the screen until Darl changed the line-of-sight. They were looking at about 20 degrees of arc of the limb of the sphere.

"There it is!" Darl said. A small object floated around the edge of the sphere and seemed to shoot towards them. She magnified it, and it became a small gray sphere.

"It orbits round the big one," she said.

Darl paused, then said, "We—the ship—came *out* of that small sphere. *Out* of it. *Through* its skin."

"You mean we had been inside it?" Grettir said. "And now we're outside it?"

"Yes, sir! Exactly!"

She gasped and said, "Oh, oh—sir!"

Around the large sphere, slightly above the plane of the orbit of the small sphere but within its sweep in an inner orbit, sped another object. At least fifty times as large as the small globe, it caught up with the globe, and the two disappeared together around the curve of the primary.

"Wellington's body!" Grettir said.

He turned away from the screen, took one step, and turned around again. "It's not right! She should be trailing along behind us or at least parallel with us, maybe shooting off at an angle but still moving in our direction.

"But she's been grabbed by the big sphere! She's in orbit! And her size; Gargantuan! It doesn't make sense! It shouldn't be!"

"Nothing should," Wang said.

"Take us back," Grettir said. "Establish an orbit around the primary, on the same plane as the secondary but further out, approximately a kilometer and a half from it."

Darl's expression said, "Then what?"

Grettir wondered if she had the same thought as he. The faces of the others on the bridge were doubtful. The fear was covered but leaking out. He could smell the rotten bubbles. Had they guessed, too?

"What attraction does the primary have on the ship?" he said to Wang.

"No detectable influence whatsoever, sir. The *Sleipnir* seems to have a neutral charge, neither positive nor negative in relation to any of the spheres. Or to Wellington's . . . body."

Grettir was slightly relieved. His thoughts had been so wild that he had not been able to consider them as anything but hysterical fantasies.

But Wang's answer showed that Grettir's idea was also his. Instead of replying in terms of gravitational force, he had talked as if the ship were a subatomic particle.

But if the ship was not affected by the primary, why had Wellington's corpse been attracted by the primary?

"Our velocity in relation to the primary?" Grettir said.

"We cut off the acceleration as soon as the wires were reconnected," Wang said.

"This was immediately after we came out into this... this space. We didn't apply any retrodrive. Our velocity, as indicated by power consumption, is ten megaparsecs per minute. That is," he added after a pause, "what the instruments show. But our radar, which should be totally ineffective at this velocity, indicates 50 kilometers per minute, relative to the big sphere."

Wang leaned back in his chair as if he expected Grettir to explode into incredulity. Grettir lit up another cigar. This time, his hands shook. He blew out a big puff of smoke and said, "Obviously, we're operating under different quote laws unquote *out here*."

Wang sighed softly. "So you think so, too, Captain? Yes, different *laws*. Which means that every time we make a move through this space, we can't know what the result will be. May I ask what you plan to do, sir?"

By this question, which Wang would never have dared to voice before, though he had doubtless often thought it, Grettir knew that the navigator shared his anxiety. The umbilical had been ripped out; Wang was hurting and bleeding inside. Was he, too, beginning to float away in a gray void? Bereft as no man had even been bereft?

It takes a special type of man or woman to loose himself from Earth or his native planet, to go out among the stars so far that the natal sun is not even a faint glimmer. It also takes special conditioning for the special type of man. He has to believe, in the deepest part of his unconscious, that his ship is a piece of Mother Earth. He has to believe; otherwise, he goes to pieces.

It can be done. Hundreds do it. But nothing had prepared even these farfarers for absolute divorce from the universe itself.

Grettir ached with the dread of the void. The void was coiling up inside him, a gray serpent, a slither of nothingness. Coiling. And what would happen when it uncoiled?

And what would happen to the crew when they were informed—as they must be—of the utter dissociation?

There was only one way to keep their minds from slipping their moorings. They must believe that they could get back into the world. Just as he must believe it.

"I'll play it by ear," Grettir said.

"What? Sir?"

"Play it by ear!" Grettir said more harshly than he had intended. "I was merely answering your question. Have you forgotten you asked me what I meant to do?"

"Oh, no, sir," Wang said. "I was just thinking . . ."

"Keep your mind on the job," Grettir said. He told Darl he would take over. He spoke the code to activate the ALL-STATIONS; a low rising-falling sound went into every room of the *Sleipnir,* and all screens flashed a black-and-green checked pattern. Then the warnings, visual and audible, died out, and the captain spoke.

He talked for two minutes. The bridgemen looked as if the lights had been turned off in their brains. It was almost impossible to grasp the concept of their being outside their universe. As difficult was thinking of their unimaginably vast native cosmos as only an "electron" orbiting around the nucleus of an "atom." If what the captain said was true (how could it be?), the ship was in the space between the superatoms of a supermolecule of a superuniverse.

Even though they knew that the *Sleipnir* had ballooned under the effect of nearly 300,000 times the speed of light, they could not wrap the fingers of their minds around the concept. It turned to smoke and drifted away.

It took ten minutes, ship's time, to turn and to complete the maneuvers which placed the *Sleipnir* in an orbit parallel to but outside the secondary, or, as Grettir thought of it, "our universe." He gave his chair back to Darl and paced back and forth across the bridge while he watched the starscreen.

If they were experiencing the sundering, the cutting-off, they were keeping it under control. They had been told by their captain that they *were* going back in, not that they would make a *try* at re-entry. They had been through much with him, and he had never failed them. With this trust, they could endure the agony of dissolution.

As the *Sleipnir* established itself parallel to the secondary, Wellington's body curved around the primary again and began to pass the small sphere and ship. The arms of the mountainous body were extended stiffly to both sides, and her legs spread out. In the gray light, her skin was bluish-black from the ruptured veins and arteries below the skin. Her red hair, coiled in a Psyche knot, looked black. Her eyes, each of which was larger than the bridge of the *Sleipnir,* were open, bulging clots of black blood. Her lips were pulled back in a grimace, the teeth like a soot-streaked portcullis.

Cartwheeling, she passed the sphere and the ship.

Wang reported that there were three "shadows" on the surface of the primary. Those were keeping pace with the secondary, the corpse and the ship. Magnified on the bridge-bulkhead screen, each "shadow" was the silhouette of one of the three orbiting bodies. The shadows were only about one shade darker than the surface and were caused by a shifting pucker in the primary skin. The surface protruded along the edges of the shadows and formed a shallow depression within the edges.

If the shadow of the *Sleipnir* was a true indication of the shape of the vessel, the *Sleipnir* had lost its needle shape and was a spindle, fat at both ends and narrow-waisted.

When Wellington's corpse passed by the small sphere and the ship, her shadow or "print" reversed itself in shape. Where the head of the shadow should have been, the feet now were and vice versa.

She disappeared around the curve of the primary and, on returning on the other side, her shadow had again become a "true" reflection. It remained so until she passed the secondary, after which the shadow once more reversed itself.

Grettir had been informed that there seemed to be absolutely no matter in the space outside the spheres. There was not one detectable atom or particle. Moreover, despite the lack of any radiation, the temperature of the hull, and ten meters beyond the hull, was a fluctuating 70° plus-or-minus 20° F.

IV

Three orbits later, Grettir knew that the ship had diminished greatly in size. Or else the small sphere had expanded. Or both changes occurred. Moreover, on the visual screen, the secondary had lost its spherical shape and become a fat disk during the first circling of the ship to establish its orbit.

Grettir was puzzling over this and thinking of calling Van Voorden, the physicist chief, when Wellington's corpse came around the primary again. The body caught up with the other satellites, and for a moment the primary, secondary, and the *Sleipnir* were in a line, strung on an invisible cord.

Suddenly, the secondary and the corpse jumped toward each other.

They ceased their motion when within a quarter kilometer of each other. The secondary regained its globular form as soon as it had attained its new orbit. Wellington's arms and legs, during this change in position, moved in as if she had come to life. Her arms folded themselves across her breasts, and her legs drew up so that her thighs were against her stomach.

Grettir had been told of the distorting in the ship when it had left the cabin boy—if we had one—knows as much as I do about what's going on or what to expect. The data, such as they are, are too inadequate, too confusing. I can only suggest that there was an interchange of energy between Wellington and the secondary.''

''A quantum jump?'' Grettir said. ''If that's so, why didn't the ship experience a loss or gain?''

Darl said, ''Pardon, sir. But it did. There was a loss of 50 megakilowatts in 0.8 second.''

Van Voorden said, ''The *Sleipnir* may have decreased in relative size because of decrease in velocity. Or maybe velocity had nothing to do with it or only partially, anyway. Maybe the change in spatial interrelationships among bodies causes other changes. In shape, size, energy transfer and so forth. I don't know. Tell me, how big is the woman—corpse—relative to the ship now?''

''The radar measurements say she's eighty-three times as large. She increased. Or we've decreased.''

Van Voorden's eyes grew even larger. Grettir thanked him and cut him off. He ordered the *Sleipnir* to be put in exactly the same orbit as the secondary but ten dekameters ahead of it.

Van Voorden called back. ''The jump happened when we were in line with the other three bodies. Maybe the *Sleipnir* is some sort of *geometrical catalyst* under certain conditions. That's only an analogy, of course.''

Wang verbally fed the order into the computer-interface, part of his wrist-console. The *Sleipnir* was soon racing ahead of the sphere. Radar reported that the ship and secondary were now approximately equal in size. The corpse, coming around the primary again, was still the same relative size as before.

Grettir ordered the vessel turned around so that the nose would be facing the sphere. This accomplished, he had the velocity reduced. The retrodrive braked them while the lateral thrusts readjusted forces to keep the ship in the same orbit. Since the primary had no attraction for the *Sleipnir,* the ship had to remain in orbit with a constant rebalancing of thrusts. The sphere, now ballooning, inched towards the ship.

"Radar indicates we're doing 26.6 dekameters per second relative to the primary," Wang said. "Power drain indicates we're making 25,000 times the speed of light. That, by the way, is not proportionate to what we were making when we left our world."

"More braking," Grettir said. "Cut it down to 15 dm."

The sphere swelled, filled the screen, and Grettir involuntarily braced himself for the impact, even though he was so far from expecting one that he had not strapped himself into a chair. There had been none when the ship had broken through the "skin" of the universe.

Grettir had been told of the distorting in the ship when it had left the universe and so was not entirely surprised. Nevertheless, he could not help being both frightened and bewildered when the front part of the bridge abruptly swelled and then rippled. Screen, bulkheads, deck and crew waved as if they were cloth in a strong wind. Grettir felt as if he were being folded into a thousand different angles at the same time.

Then Wang cried out, and the others repeated his cry. Wang rose from his seat and put his hands out before him. Grettir, standing behind and to one side of him, was frozen as he saw dozens of little objects, firefly-size, burning brightly, slip *through* the starscreen and bulkhead and drift towards him. He came out of his paralysis in time to dodge one tiny whitely glowing ball. But another struck his forehead, causing him to yelp.

A score of the bodies passed by him. Some were white; some blue; some green; one was topaz. They were at all levels, above his head, even with his waist, one almost touching the deck. He crouched down to let two pass over him, and as he did so, he saw Nagy, the communications officer, bent over and vomiting. The stuff sprayed out of his mouth and caught a little glow in it and snuffed it out in a burst of smoke.

Then the forepart of the bridge had reasserted its solidity and constancy of shape. There were no more burning objects coming through.

Grettir turned to see the aft bulkheads of the bridge quivering in the wake of the wave. And they, too, became normal. Grettir shouted the "override" code so that he could take control from Wang, who was screaming with pain. He directed the ship to change its course to an "upward vertical" direction. There was no "upward" sensation, because the artificial g-field within the ship readjusted. Suddenly, the forward part of the bridge became distorted again, and the waves reached through the fabric of the ship and the crew.

The starscreen, which had been showing nothing but the blackness of space, speckled by a few stars, now displayed the great gray sphere in one corner and the crepuscular light. Grettir, fighting the pain in his forehead and the nausea, gave another command. There was a delay of possibly thirty seconds, and then the *Sleipnir* began the turn that would take it back into a parallel orbit with the secondary.

Grettir, realizing what was happening shortly after being burned, had taken the *Sleipnir* back out of the universe. He put in a call for corpsmen and Doctor Wills and then helped Wang from his chair. There was an odor of burned flesh and hair in the bridge which the air-conditioning system had not as yet removed. Wang's face and hands were burned in five or six places, and part of the long coarse black hair on the right side of his head was burned.

Three corpsmen and Wills ran into the bridge. Wills started to apply a pseudoprotein jelly on Grettir's forehead, but Grettir told him to take care of Wang first. Wills worked swiftly and then, after spreading the jelly over Wang's burns and placing a false-skin bandage over the burns, treated the captain. As soon as the jelly was placed on his forehead, Grettir felt the pain dissolve.

"Third degree," Wills said. "It's lucky those things—whatever they are—weren't larger."

Grettir picked up his cigar, which he had dropped on the deck when he had first seen the objects racing towards him. The cigar was still burning. Near it lay a coal, swiftly blackening. He picked it up gingerly. It felt warm but could be held without too much discomfort.

Grettir extended his hand, palm up, so that the doctor could see the speck of black matter in it. It was even smaller than when it had floated into the bridge through the momentarily "opened" interstices of the molecules composing the hull and bulkheads.

"This is *a galaxy*," he whispered.

Doc Wills did not understand. "A galaxy of our universe," Grettir added.

Doc Wills paled, and he gulped loudly.

"You mean . . . ?"

Grettir nodded.

Wills said, "I hope . . . not our . . . Earth's . . . Galaxy!"

"I doubt it," Grettir said. "We were on the edge of the star fields farthest out, that is, the closest to the—skin?—of our universe. But if we had kept on going . . ."

Wills shook his head. Billions of stars, possibly millions of inhabitable, hence inhabited, planets, were in that little ball of fire, now cool and collapsed. Trillions of sentient beings and an unimaginable number of animals had died when their world collided with Grettir's forehead.

Wang, informed of the true cause of his burns, became ill again. Grettir ordered him to sick bay and replaced him with Gomez. Van Voorden entered the bridge. He said, "I suppose our main objective has to be our reentry. But why couldn't we make an attempt to penetrate the primary, the nucleus? Do you realize what an astounding. . .?"

Grettir interrupted. "I realize. But our fuel supply is low, very low. If—I mean, *when* we get back through the 'skin,' we'll have a long way to go before we can return to Base. Maybe too long. I don't dare exceed a certain speed during reentry because of our size. It would be too dangerous. . . . I don't want to wipe out any more galaxies. God knows the psychological problems we are going to have when the guilt really hits. Right now, we're numbed. *No!* We're not going to do any exploring!"

"But there may be no future investigations permitted!" Van Voorden said. "There's too much danger to the universe itself to allow any more research by ships like ours!"

"Exactly," Grettir said. "I sympathize with your desire to do scientific research. But the safety of the ship and crew comes first. Besides, I think that if I were to order an exploration, I'd have mutiny on my hands. And I couldn't blame my men. Tell me, Van Voorden, don't you feel a sense of . . . dissociation?"

Van Voorden nodded and said, "But I'm willing to fight it. There is so much . . ."

"So much to find out," Grettir said. "Agreed. But the authorities will have to determine if that is to be done."

Grettir dismissed him. Van Voorden marched off. But he did not give the impression of a powerful anger. He was, Grettir thought, secretly relieved at the captain's decision. Van Voorden had made his protest for Science's sake. But as a human being, Van Voorden must want very much to get "home."

V

At the end of the ordered maneuver, the *Sleipnir* was in the same orbit as the universe but twenty kilometers ahead and again pointed toward it. Since there was no attraction between ship and primary, the *Sleipnir* had to use power to maintain the orbit; a delicate readjustment of lateral thrust was constantly required.

Grettir ordered braking applied. The sphere expanded on the star-screen, and then there was only a gray surface displayed. To the viewers the surface did not seem to spin, but radar had determined that the globe completed a revolution on its polar axis once every 33 seconds.

Grettir did not like to think of the implications of this. Van Voorden undoubtedly had received the report, but he had made no move to notify the captain. Perhaps, like Grettir, he believed that the fewer who thought about it, the better.

The mockup screen showed, in silhouette form, the relative sizes of the approaching spheres and the ship. The basketball was the universe; the toothpick, the *Sleipnir*. Grettir hoped that this reduction would be enough to avoid running into any more galaxies. Immediately after the vessel penetrated the ''skin,'' the *Sleipnir* would be again braked, thus further diminishing it. There should be plenty of distance between the skin and the edge of the closest star fields.

''Here we go,'' Grettir said, watching the screen which indicated in meters the gap between ship and sphere. Again he involuntarily braced himself.

There was a rumble, a groan. The deck slanted upwards, then rolled to port. Grettir was hurled to the deck, spun over and over and brought up with stunning impact against a bulkhead. He was in a daze for a moment, and by the time he had recovered, the ship had reasserted its proper attitude. Gomez had placed the ship into ''level'' again. He had a habit of strapping himself into the navigator's chair although regulations did not require it unless the captain ordered it.

Grettir asked for a report on any damage and, while waiting for it, called Van Voorden. The physicist was bleeding from a cut on his forehead.

''Obviously,'' he said, ''it requires a certain force to penetrate the outer covering or energy shield or whatever it is that encloses the universe. We didn't have it. So—''

''Presents quite a problem,'' Grettir said. ''If we go fast enough to rip through, we're too large and may destroy entire galaxies. If we go too slow, we can't get through.''

He paused, then said, ''I can think of only one method. But I'm ignorant of the consequences, which might be disastrous. Not for us but for the universe. I'm not sure I should even take such a chance.''

He was silent so long that Van Voorden could not restrain himself.

"Well?"

"Do you think that if we could make a hole in the skin, the rupture might result in some sort of collapse or cosmic disturbance?"

"You want to beam a hole in the skin?" Van Voorden said slowly. His skin was pale, but it had been that color before Grettir asked him the question. Grettir wondered if Van Voorden was beginning to crumble under the "dissociation."

"Never mind," Grettir said. "I shouldn't have asked you. You can't know what the effects would be any more than anyone else. I apologize. I must have been trying to make you share some of the blame if anything went wrong. Forget it."

Van Voorden stared, and he was still looking blank when Grettir cut off his image. He paced back and forth, once stepping over a tiny black object on the deck and then grimacing when he realized that it was too late for care. Millions of stars, billions of planets, trillions of creatures. All cold and dead. And if he experimented further in trying to get back into the native cosmos, then what? A collapsing universe?

Grettir stopped pacing and said aloud, "We came through the skin twice without harm to it. So we're going to try the beam!"

Nobody answered him, but the look on their faces was evidence of their relief. Fifteen minutes later, the *Sleipnir* was just ahead of the sphere and facing it. After an unvarying speed and distance from the sphere had been maintained for several minutes, laser beams measured the exact length between the tip of the cannon and the surface of the globe.

The chief gunnery officer, Abdul White Eagel, set one of the fore cannons. Grettir delayed only a few seconds in giving the next order. He clenched his teeth so hard he almost bit the cigar in two, groaned slightly, then said, "Fire!"

Darl transmitted the command. The beam shot out, touched the skin and vanished.

The starscreen showed a black hole in the gray surface at the equator of the sphere. The hole moved away and then was gone around the curve of the sphere. Exactly 33 seconds later, the hole was in its original position. It was shrinking. By the time four rotations were completed, the hole had closed in on itself.

Grettir sighed and wiped the sweat off his forehead. Darl reported that the hole would be big enough for the ship to get through by the second time it came around. After that, it would be too small.

"We'll go through during the second rotation," Grettir said. "Set up the compigator for an automatic entry; tie the cannon in with the compigator. There shouldn't be any problem. If the hole shrinks too fast, we'll enlarge it with the cannon.''

He heard Darl say, ''Operation begun, sir!'' as Gomez spoke into his console. The white beam spurted out in a cone, flicked against the ''shell'' or ''skin'' and disappeared. A circle of blackness three times the diameter of the ship came into being and then moved to one side of the screen. Immediately, under the control of the compigator, the retrodrive of the *Sleipnir* went into action. The sphere loomed; a gray wall filled the starscreen. Then the edge of the hole came into view, and a blackness spread over the screen.

''We're going to make it,'' Grettir thought. ''The compigator can't make a mistake.''

He looked around him. The bridgemen were strapped to their chairs now. Most of the faces were set, they were well disciplined and brave. But if they felt as he did—they must—they were shoving back a scream far down in them. They could not endure this ''homesickness'' much longer. And after they got through, were back in the womb, he would have to permit them a most unmilitary behavior. They would laugh, weep, shout. And so would he.

The nose of the *Sleipnir* passed through the hole. Now, if anything went wrong, the fore cannon could not be used. But it was impossible that . . .

The klaxon whooped. Darl screamed, ''Oh, my God! Something's wrong! The hole's shrinking too fast!''

Grettir roared, ''Double the speed! No! Halve it!''

Increasing the forward speed meant a swelling in size of the *Sleipnir* but a contraction of the longitudinal axis and a lengthening of the lateral. The *Sleipnir* would get through the hole faster, but it would also narrow the gap between its hull and the edges of the hole.

Halving the speed, on the other hand, though it would make the ship smaller in relation to the hole, would also make the distance to be traversed greater. This might mean that the edges would still hit the ship.

Actually, Grettir did not know what order should be given or if any order would have an effect upon their chance to escape. He could only do what seemed best.

The grayness spread out from the perimeter of the starscreen. There was a screech of severed plastic running through the ship, quivering the bulkheads and decks, a sudden push forward of the crew as they felt the inertia, then a release as the almost instantaneous readjustment of the internal g-field canceled the external effects.

Everybody in the bridge yelled. Grettir forced himself to cut off his shout. He watched the starscreen. They were out in the gray again. The huge sphere shot across the screen. In the corner was the secondary and then a glimpse of a giant blue-black foot. More grayness. A whirl of other great spheres in the distance. The primary again. The secondary. Wellington's hand, like a malformed squid of the void.

When Grettir saw the corpse again, he knew that the ship had been deflected away from the sphere and was heading towards the corpse. He did not, however, expect a collision. The orbital velocity of the dead woman was greater than that of the secondary or of the *Sleipnir*.

Grettir, calling for a damage report, heard what he had expected. The nose of the ship had been sheared off. Bearing 45 crewmen with it, it was now inside the "universe," heading toward a home it would never reach. The passageways leading to the cut-off part had been automatically sealed, of course, so that there was no danger of losing air.

But the retrodrives had also been sliced off. The *Sleipnir* could drive forward but could not brake itself unless it was first turned around to present its aft to the direction of motion.

VI

Grettir gave the command to stabilize the ship first, then to reverse it. MacCool replied from the engine room that neither maneuver was, at the moment, possible. The collision and the shearing had caused malfunctions in the control circuits. He did not know what the trouble was, but the electronic trouble-scanner was searching through the circuits. A moment later, he called back to say that the device was itself not operating properly and that the troubleshooting would have to be done by his men until the device had been repaired.

MacCool was disturbed. He could not account for the breakdown because, theoretically, there should have been none. Even the impact and loss of the fore part should not have resulted in loss of circuit operation.

Grettir told him to do what he could. Meanwhile, the ship was tumbling and was obviously catching up with the vast corpse. There had been another inexplainable interchange of energy, position and momentum, and the *Sleipnir* and Mrs. Wellington were going to collide.

Grettir unstrapped himself and began walking back and forth across the bridge. Even though the ship was cartwheeling, the internal g-field neutralized the effect for the crew. The vessel seemed level and stable unless the starscreen was looked at.

Grettir asked for a computation of when the collision would take place and of what part of the body the *Sleipnir* would strike. It might make a difference whether it struck a soft or hard part. The difference would not result in damage to the ship, but it would affect the angle and velocity of the rebound path. If the circuits were repaired before the convergence, or just after, Grettir would have to know what action to take.

Wang replied that he had already asked the compigator for an estimate of the area of collision if conditions remained as they were. Even as he spoke, a coded card issued from a slot in the bulkhead. Wang read it, handed it to Grettir.

Grettir said, "At any other time, I'd laugh. So we will return— literally—to the womb."

The card had also indicated that, the nearer the ship got to Wellington, the slower was its velocity. Moreover, the relative size of the ship, as reported by radar, was decreasing in direct proportion to its proximity to the body.

Gomez said, "I think we've come under the influence of that . . . woman, as if she's become a planet and had captured a satellite. Us. She doesn't have any gravitational attraction or any charge in relation to us. But—"

"But there are other factors," Grettir said to her. "Maybe they are spatial relations, which, in this 'space,' may be the equivalent of gravity."

The *Sleipnir* was now so close that the body entirely filled the starscreen when the ship was pointed towards it. First, the enormous head came into view. The blood-clotted and bulging eyes stared at them. The nose slid by like a Brobdingnagian guillotine; the mouth grinned at them as if it were to enjoy gulping them down. Then the neck, a diorite column left exposed by the erosion of softer rock; the cleavage of the blackened Himalayan breasts; the navel, the eye of a hurricane.

Then she went out of sight, and the secondary and primary and the gray-shrouded giants far off wheeled across the screen.

Grettir used the ALL-STATIONS to tell the nonbridge personnel what was happening. "As soon as MacCool locates the trouble, we will be on our way out. We have plenty of power left, enough to blast our way out of a hundred corpses. Sit tight. Don't worry. It's just a matter of time."

He spoke with a cheerfulness he did not feel, although he had not lied to them. Nor did he expect any reaction, positive or negative. They must be as numb as he. Their minds, their entire nervous systems, were boggling.

Another card shot out from the bulkhead-slot, a corrected impact prediction. Because of the continuing decrease in size of the vessel, it would strike the corpse almost dead-center in the navel. A minute later, another card predicted impact near the coccyx. A third card revised that to collision with the top of the head. A fourth changed that to a strike on the lower part on the front of the right leg.

Grettir called Van Voorden again. The physicist's face shot up from the surface of Grettir's wrist-console but was stationary on the auxiliary bulkhead-screen. This gave a larger view and showed Van Voorden looking over his wrist-console at a screen on his cabin-bulkhead. It offered the latest impact report in large burning letters.

"Like the handwriting on the wall in the days of King Belshazzar," Van Voorden said. "And I am a Daniel come to judgment. So we're going to hit her leg, heh, *Many, many tickle up her shin.* Hee, hee!"

Grettir stared uncomprehendingly at him, then cut him off. A few seconds later, he understood Van Voorden's pun. He did not wonder at the man's levity at a moment so grave. It was a means of relieving his deep anxiety and bewilderment. It might also mean that he was already cracking up, since it was out of character with him. But Grettir could do nothing for him at that moment.

As the *Sleipnir* neared the corpse, it continued to shrink. However, the dwindling was not at a steady rate nor could the times of shrinkage be predicted. It operated in spurts of from two to thirty seconds' duration at irregular intervals. And then, as the 300th card issued from the slot, it became evident that, unless some new factor entered, the *Sleipnir* would spin into the gaping mouth. While the head rotated "downward," the ship would pass through the great space between the lips.

And so it was. On the starscreen, the lower lip, a massive ridge, wrinkled with mountains and pitted with valleys, appeared. Flecks of lipstick floated by, black-red Hawaiis. A tooth like a jagged skyscraper dropped out of sight.

The *Sleipnir* settled slowly into the darkness. The walls shot away and upwards. The blackness outside knotted. Only a part of the gray "sky" was visible during that point of the cartwheel when the fore part of the starscreen was directed upwards. Then the opening became a thread of gray, a strand, and was gone.

Strangely—or was it so odd?—the officers and crew lost their feeling of dissociation. Grettir's stomach expanded with relief; the dreadful fragmenting was gone. He now felt as if something had been attached, or reattached, to his navel. Rubb, the psychology officer, reported that he had taken a survey of one out of fifty of the crew, and each described similar sensations.

Despite this, the personnel were free of only one anxiety and were far from being out of danger. The temperature had been slowly mounting ever since the ship had been spun off the secondary and had headed towards the corpse. The power system and air-conditioning had stabilized at 80°F for a while. But the temperature of the hull had gone upwards at a geometric progression, and the outer hull was now 2500 K. There was no danger of it melting as yet; it could resist up to 56,000 K. The air-conditioning demanded more and more power, and after thirty minutes ship's time, Grettir had had to let the internal temperature rise to 98.2°F to ease the load.

Grettir ordered everybody into spacesuits, which could keep the wearers at a comfortable temperature. Just as the order was carried out, MacCool reported that he had located the source of malfunction.

"The Wellington woman did it!" he shouted. "She sure took care of us! She inserted a monolith subparticle switch in the circuits; the switch had a timer which operated the switch after a certain time had elapsed. It was only coincidence that the circuits went blank right after we failed to get back into our world!"

VII

"So she wanted to be certain that we'd be wrecked if she was frustrated in her attempts in the engine room," Grettir said. "You'd better continue the search for other microswitches or sabotage devices."

MacCool's face was long.

"We're ready to operate now only... hell! We can't spare any power now because we need all we can get to keep the temperature down. I can spare enough to cancel the tumble. But that's all."

"Forget it for now," Grettir said. He had contacted Van Voorden, who seemed to have recovered. He confirmed the captain's theory about the rise in temperature. It was the rapid contraction of the ship that was causing the emission of heat.

"How is this contraction possible?" Grettir said. "Are the atoms of the ship, and of our bodies, coming closer together? If so, what happens when they come into contact with each other?"

"We've already passed that point of diminishment," Van Voorden said. "I'd say that our atoms are shrinking also."

"But that's not possible," Grettir replied. Then, "Forget about that remark. What is possible? Whatever happens is possible."

Grettir cut him off and strode back and forth and wished that he could smoke a cigar. He had intended to talk about what the *Sleipnir* would find if it had managed to break back into its native universe. It seemed to Grettir that the universe would have changed so much that no one aboard the ship would recognize it. Every time the secondary—the universe—completed a revolution on its axis, trillions of Earth years, maybe quadrillions, may have passed. The Earth's sun may have become a lightless clot in space or even have disappeared altogether. Man, who might have survived on other planets, would no longer be homo sapiens.

Moreover, when the *Sleipnir* attained a supercosmic mass on its way out of the universe, it may have disastrously affected the other masses in the universe.

Yet none of these events may have occurred. It was possible that time inside that sphere was absolutely independent of time outside it. The notion was not so fantastic. God Almighty! Less than seventy minutes ago, Donna Wellington had been inside the ship. Now the ship was inside her.

And when the electrons and the nuclei of the atoms composing the ship and the crew came into contact, what then? Explosion?

Or were the elements made up of divisible subelements, and collapse would go on towards the inner infinity? He thought of the 20th-century stories of a man shrinking until the molecules became clusters of suns and the nuclei were the suns and the electrons were the planets. Eventually, the hero found himself on an electron-planet with atmosphere, seas, rivers, plains, mountains, trees, animals and aboriginal sentients.

These stories were only fantasies. Atomic matter was composed of wavicles, stuff describable in terms of both waves and particles. The parahomunculus hero would be in a cosmos as bewildering as that encountered by the crew of the *Sleipnir* on breaking into the extra-universe space.

That fantasy galloping across the sky of his mind, swift as the original *Sleipnir,* eight-legged horse of All-Father Odin of his ancestor's religion, would have to be dismissed. Donna Wellington was not a female Ymir, the primeval giant out of whose slain corpse was formed the world, the skull the sky, the blood the sea, the flesh the Earth, the bones the mountains.

No, the heat of contraction would increase until the men cooked in their suits. What happened after that would no longer be known to the crew and hence of no consequence.

"Captain!"

MacCool's face was on the auxiliary screen, kept open to the engine room. "We'll be ready to go in a minute."

Sweat mingled with tears to blur the image of the engineer's face. "We'll make it then," Grettir said.

Four minutes later, the tumble was stopped, the ship was pointed upwards and was on its way out. The temperature began dropping inside the ship at one degree F per 30 seconds. The blackness was relieved by a gray thread. The thread broadened into ribbon, and then the ribbon became the edges of two mountain ridges, one below and the one above hanging upside down.

"This time," Grettir said, "we'll make a hole more than large enough."

Van Voorden entered the bridge as the *Sleipnir* passed through the break. Grettir said, "The hole repairs itself even more quickly than it did the last time. That's why the nose was cut off. We didn't know that the bigger the hole the swifter the rate of reclosure."

Van Voorden said, "Thirty-six hundred billion years old or even more! Why bother to go home when home no longer exists?"

"Maybe there won't be that much time gone," Grettir said. "Do you remember Minkowski's classical phrase? *From henceforth space in itself and time in itself sink to mere shadows, and only a kind of union of the two preserves an independent existence.*

"That phrase applied to the world inside the sphere, our world. Perhaps *out here* the union is somehow dissolved, the marriage of space and time is broken. Perhaps no time, or very little, has elapsed in our world."

"It's possible," Van Voorden said. "But you've overlooked one thing, Captain. If our world has not been marked by time while we've been gone, *we* have been marked. Scarred by unspace and untime. I'll never believe in cause and effect and order throughout the cosmos again. I'll always be suspicious and anxious. I'm a ruined man."

Grettir started to answer but could not make himself heard. The men and women on the bridge were weeping, sobbing, or laughing shrilly. Later, they would think of that *out there* as a nightmare and would try not to think of it at all. And if other nightmares faced them here, at least they would be nightmares they knew.

4

Aliens

Pamela Sargent and James Gunn

Those who have never seen a living Martian can scarcely imagine the strange horror of its appearance. The peculiar V-shaped mouth with its pointed upper lip, the absence of brow ridges, the absence of a chin beneath the wedgelike lower lip, the incessant quivering of this mouth, the Gorgon groups of tentacles, the tumultuous breathing of the lungs in a strange atmosphere, the evident heaviness and painfulness of movement due to the greater gravitational energy of the earth—above all, the extraordinary intensity of the immense eyes—were at once vital, intense, inhuman, crippled and monstrous. There was something fungoid in the oily brown skin, something in the clumsy deliberation of the tedious movements, unspeakably nasty. Even at this first encounter, this first glimpse, I was overcome with disgust and dread.

When H. G. Wells unscrewed the end of his metal cylinder, he released upon an unsuspecting world a new kind of nightmare creature, the first horrible vision of what might await man on the other worlds his astronomers were beginning to describe—or that might not wait for man to reach him, that might arrive on earth before man reached those other worlds, before he even suspected they might be inhabited by beings unlike himself in appearance but perhaps too much like himself in greed and aggression.

The alien of science fiction made a dramatic entrance in Wells's *The War of the Worlds,* and Western civilization was entranced by the fantastic concept of horrible things from Mars, more advanced in science and technology than humanity, devastating the earth, brushing aside its puny weapons, using people as food. This delight in the conquering alien was understood by Wells even as he was writing the book. He wrote to a friend: ''I'm doing the dearest little serial for

Pearson's new magazine, in which I completely wreck and destroy Woking—killing my neighbors in painful and eccentric ways—then proceed via Kingston and Richmond to London, which I sack, selecting South Kensington for feats of peculiar atrocity.''

Often when the novel was serialized elsewhere, the locale of the destruction was changed to the new neighborhood, as Orson Welles did in his celebrated 1938 radio adaptation, and as George Pal did in his film version.

Stories about aliens have been a major theme in science fiction ever since *The War of the Worlds* was first serialized in 1897. Wells's novel probably was not the first description of aliens. Literary historians may find earlier examples, and certainly Fitz-James O'Brien's invisible creature in "What Was It?" (1859) had an unnatural, if not indeed an unearthly, origin, as did the beings in those stories which were influenced by it, Guy de Maupassant's "The Horla" (1887) and Ambrose Bierce's "The Damned Thing" (1898). Wells himself had a story published in 1897 called "The Crystal Egg," which described an apparent effort by strange creatures on Mars to spy on earth; the story may have been prefatory to *The War of the Worlds*.

Stories about aliens of another sort, however, go back to the beginnings of humanity, and one measure of the growing humanity of the species may be the distance from the individual the concept of alien is pushed.

With the occurrence of the first awareness of self must have come the first definition of the alien: every separate creature. But gradually the concession of mutual humanity was extended to the family, the village, the tribe, and finally to the entire culture group. The alien was the creature who lives over there, who is not as we are; perhaps civilization begins with the recognition that those who live over there, who may not be what we are, still may be human.

The Greeks and Romans delighted in stories about witches and one-eyed giants and lotus-eaters, about people who lived in strange places and had stranger customs, like Hyperborea, where happiness was a birthright, and the Fortunate Isles, where men had elastic bones and bifurcated tongues; like the Valley of Ismaus, where wild men had feet turned inwards, and Albania, where people had pink eyes and white hair, and Libya, where people's bodies had a poison deadly to snakes. In distant lands, the storytellers said, lived races of hermaphrodites and fascinators and women who killed with their eyes, men who wore their heads underneath their shoulders and people who dressed in the down of feathers and lived on the scent of the rose.

Some of these differences, clearly, were no more than reversals of appearance or custom, or merely the strange practices we attribute to our neighbors, but some of the fascination of the stories came from the cherished notion that distant places are marvelous and there may live creatures who are so different that they may not even be human. This interest in far places still survives in modern form, in the stories of alleged sightings of unidentified flying objects.

The first stories about travel off the earth, mostly to the moon, can be discounted in any serious consideration of the alien. Works like Lucian of Samosata's "A True History" and Cyrano de Bergerac's *Voyages to the Moon and the Sun* were satires, and the strange creatures their heroes met are not so much aliens as reflections of the societies the authors intended to criticize. But an early Renaissance book, *The Voiage and Travaile of Sir John Mandeville,* had the same basic interest in strange races and their strange doings as the Greek and Roman stories, and Marco Polo's account of his experiences in the East was just as remarkable even though substantially real.

The many later stories about the moon, from Kepler's *Somnium* through Poe's "Hans Pfaall" and Locke's "The Moon Hoax" to Verne's *From the Earth to the Moon,* added little to the concept of the alien because none of them, with the possible exception of Verne, considered space travel feasible, and Verne's capsule never landed.

The world was ready, then, to be captured by the concept of the alien in *The War of the Worlds.* Like Wells himself, Western civilization had been prepared by the technological advances of the Industrial Revolution, by a growing interest in astronomy, and by the discovery of new details about Mars. An Italian astronomer named Giovanni Schiaparelli had described in 1877 what he called *canali* (channels) on Mars; Percival Lowell founded his observatory at Flagstaff and published his first observations of Mars and its so-called canals by 1895.

Wells already had begun to write his new "stories of science" for the *Pall Mall Budget* and by 1895 he was selling his stories to the *Gazette* and the *Strand* as well, and the other mass magazines that were providing a new reading experience for the developing middle class. Always watchful for opportunities to shake the complacency of his Victorian contemporaries, Wells took the concept of life on other worlds and added to it his inspiration—a more advanced civilization on Mars whose need for water and other resources might drive the Martians to attack earth.

Although *The War of the Worlds* inspired a number of imitations and sequels, including Garrett P. Serviss's *Edison's Conquest of Mars,* the concept of the alien developed little in the decade that followed.

Stories in the mass magazines and the all-fiction pulp magazines that followed the lead of *Argosy* after 1896 occasionally involved space travel but alien creatures were seldom encountered, and those few were usually human though less technologically advanced, as in the lost race story that was so popular during the Victorian era and reached its peak with H. Rider Haggard's *She* and *Allan Quatermain*.

Edgar Rice Burroughs made a significant contribution to the concept of alien creatures on other worlds beginning in 1911 with *Under the Moons of Mars* and continuing John Carter's adventures through ten sequels. He also described other alien life-forms in his seven books about Pellucidar, his world in the center of the earth. Although most of his characters were sufficiently human that they could mate with his heroes, Burroughs included enough significantly different kinds of creatures to inspire later imitators and successors.

A. Merritt's most colorful creations were even more alien, beginning with the Dweller in *The Moon Pool* in 1919, and continuing through the Snake Mother and the Face in the Abyss and the Metal Monster, but Merritt stayed on earth, and the adventures of his heroes seemed to belong more to the lost-race tradition with some embellishment from the elder-gods concept that H. P. Lovecraft would develop into a mythos.

The founding of the science fiction magazines, beginning in 1926, coincided with discoveries about the size of our galaxy and the universe itself that made it substantially bigger than it had ever seemed before and, because it was expanding, growing larger all the time. The creatures who might live in that infinite space were potentially stranger and more diverse than any author had ever imagined.

The new breed of science fiction writers being developed by the science fiction magazines, like Edward Elmer Smith and Edmond Hamilton and Jack Williamson, began to explore that vast new territory with scientist-heroes in shiny spaceships and people it with strange creatures often organized into galactic civilizations.

The most important contribution to the concept of aliens in the 1930s was made by Stanley Weinbaum, whose "A Martian Odyssey" would initiate a new movement toward believable though totally alien creatures to which Weinbaum himself would contribute for the remainder of his tragically short fifteen-month career. A couple of years later John W. Campbell provided aliens who were completely different from humanity in "The Brain Stealers of Mars" and "Who Goes There?"

By the end of the thirties John Campbell began developing the writing of science fiction into a profession through his editorship of

Astounding Science Fiction, and the various themes of science fiction, including the alien, began to be explored professionally, analytically. Through conferences with writers, letters, editorials, and his letter section, "Brass Tacks," Campbell encouraged writers to consider different angles until they had virtually exhausted the possible permutations. Not all such stories appeared in *Astounding* or its successor, *Analog,* but they were the natural outgrowth of the analytic process begun in *Astounding.*

The different kinds of encounters that might occur between man and alien may be infinite, but they can be categorized according to three major considerations: (1) relationship between man and alien; (2) attitude of alien toward man, and sometimes of man toward alien; and (3) outcome of the encounter.

The most important relationship is the relative stage of civilization, sometimes defined by technological development. Aliens can be (1) superior, (2) inferior, (3) equal, or (4) none of the above, simply different. If superior, the alien threatens us with conquest of one kind or another: physical, psychological, technological, economic. Sometimes humanity fights back and wins; when humanity is inferior in technology, it must win by dogged determination or by ingenuity. Often, however, such a story ends with an O. Henry-like twist, the revelation that a presumed inferiority is actually a superiority, that the superior alien has a fatal flaw, or that for some unforeseen reason conquest is impossible.

A big group of stories, particularly popular during the late forties and fifties when the threat of a nuclear World War III seemed closer than it does now, speculated that an alien attack, sometimes real but often contrived, might unite humanity against a common enemy, solve its ancient problems, and resolve its ancient feuds. This was the beginning of Arthur C. Clarke's *Childhood's End.*

The way a story developed usually depended upon the author's reading of alien psychology. Aliens can be (1) envious, like Wells's Martians, (2) fearful, like Larry Niven's Puppeteers, (3) aggressive, like humanity, (4) innocent, like James Blish's Lithians, (5) benevolent, like Clarke's Overlords, or (6) incomprehensible, like Terry Carr's Loarra.

Envy and fear can make aliens wish to occupy or destroy our world, or manipulate us so that we are not a threat to them; an aggressive attitude can make aliens attack us simply because we are a potential threat, as they are to us. Most science fiction stories have assumed that we dare not risk the survival of the race; when in doubt we cannot reveal the location of earth, or if we have the chance we must destroy the potentially dangerous alien opponent or even the alien race itself. A mistake, a sentimental withholding of the death blow, might mean the destruction of humanity.

Murray Leinster's "First Contact" was received with delight because it demonstrated that races of goodwill and sufficient ingenuity could meet and part in friendship and mutual trust. Like many such "solution" stories, however, "First Contact" demanded special circumstances: the races had to be at almost identical stages of development, and they had to meet far from the home planet of either, where there could be no possibility of guessing where either came from.

If the aliens we meet are inferior and/or innocent, the stories usually reenact the experience of European civilization in the New World, conquering and destroying the rich civilizations of South America and Mexico, pushing the Amerindians from their lands, or bringing a superior and culture-destroying civilization, with its twin blessings of smallpox and the Christian religion, to the Polynesians.

Sometimes, however, a story of alien contact in which the aliens are inferior may wish to make a political or sociological point, as in Poul Anderson's "The Double-Dyed Villains," which says that an inferior race may be wise to refuse the gift of civilization until it is ready. Sometimes theology is the issue: in *A Case of Conscience* Blish tested a priest's faith by letting him come to know an alien race living in a state of grace without having experienced original sin or redemption; in "The Streets of Ashkalon" Harry Harrison exposed fundamentalism to the test of a completely literal alien tribe.

Sometimes, as in Robert Sheckley's "Specialist," the point may be about human nature, and the point is made through fable or parable as Aesop would have made it.

Of course the question of superiority or inferiority is not always clear-cut; sometimes, as in real life, the relationships are mixed. This is often true in science fiction when human beings go to the aliens. In two early A. E. Van Vogt stories, "Black Destroyer" and "Discord in Scarlet," the alien creatures are superior individually but inferior to the collective wisdom and experience of the crew of the Space Beagle. In Robert Heinlein's novel of attack by parasitic monsters from Titan, *The Puppet Masters,* humanity almost is conquered and destroyed, but man's superior aggressiveness and determination win in the end. Sometimes the outcome is doubtful; in Lester del Rey's "For I Am a Jealous People" humanity fights on in spite of desperate odds—the invaders have on their side not only technological superiority but God.

The most frequent single outcome of man-alien meeting has been war (although it has fallen out of favor in the last decade or two as both trite and of debatable logic). If humanity and aliens battle, they must be roughly equal. Occasionally, however, humanity is caught up in a larger struggle between alien races far in advance of man, as in Raymond F. Jones's *This Island Earth*. Why do man and alien fight? Sometimes because they are dangerous to each other, sometimes because they want the same territory, sometimes for domination. Sometimes simply because they are different; they cannot understand each other, or perhaps even communicate. Thus the reasons for the wars in Heinlein's *Starship Troopers* are never clear (also because the subject is not warfare but citizenship), and Joe Haldeman's citizen soldiers in *The Forever War* never know why they are fighting.

When the aliens are truly alien, the story may develop around the difficulties of understanding them, or just picking up their messages, as in James Gunn's *The Listeners*. Some stories have linguistics as their method—the finding of a Martian Rosetta stone such as a periodic table of the elements. Terry Carr's "The Dance of the Changer and the Three" suggests that the alien mind and alien customs will be so completely baffling that we will never be able to understand each other.

An even more disturbing possibility is proposed in Stanislaw Lem's *Solaris*. The sentient ocean depicted in this novel is one of the finest portraits of a truly alien being in science fiction. Although the humans studying this being have developed many possible theories to explain it, the alien remains as incomprehensible as those in Carr's story. Rather than being simply alienated from this being, the human characters are led by it to confront themselves. Lem is asserting that, in dealing with an alien intelligence, we will react to it according to our own preconceptions. Ambiguity will always be present; complete knowledge will remain out of reach. Man will travel into space, and meet himself.

Communication is not always the problem of the story, and then science fiction avoids the question by supplying a thought-wave transmitter or automatic translator, or English-speaking aliens who have learned the language by telepathy or from radio and television broadcasts while they traveled to earth, or by spending some years or generations among us without notice. Sometimes the aliens do not want to be understood; they may seem benevolent but are really hiding darker motives, as in Damon Knight's "To Serve Man."

An entire group of stories about aliens deals with the ways they differ from us, having evolved on other planets under different conditions, and how we can gain perspective on ourselves by seeing how others have been shaped. Hal Clement has specialized in stories about alien life-forms as they have adapted to unusual environments: in *Iceworld* creatures who came from a hot planet must cope with the comparatively icy conditions of earth; in *Mission of Gravity* creatures who evolved to cope with a gravity many hundred times that of earth must conquer their natural fears when they encounter a gravity only two or three times ours.

In a novel like Ursula K. Le Guin's *The Left Hand of Darkness,* aliens on the planet of Gethen, though human in origin, are hermaphrodites, as in the ancient Roman tales; sexless most of the month, they come into heat for a few days and may assume either sex and, therefore, may either father or bear a child. From the effects of this sexual situation on the social and political customs of Gethen, we can better understand how our bisexuality has shaped our institutions, our culture, and ourselves.

Aliens may be depicted as humanoid or non-humanoid. Isaac Asimov has in the past written primarily about humanoids, reasoning that on Earth-like planets (the ones with which we would most likely have contact) beings like ourselves would evolve. Ursula K. Le Guin's novels are set against a background in which one humanoid race has populated many other worlds, including Earth, in the distant past. Such a hypothesis would also explain the presence of humanoids on other worlds. It is not altogether unlikely that extraterrestrials will be like ourselves; this thought may be either comforting or frightening, depending upon how one views humanity.

Generally, if we visit the aliens, we are superior, though we must beware of underestimating the potential of seemingly harmless aliens, as in Jerry Pournelle and Larry Niven's *The Mote in God's Eye;* they may be more sophisticated or smarter than we think, they may breed too fast or too irresponsibly (like humans?), or they may have unsuspected new talents; or they may learn too fast, as in F. L. Wallace's "Student Body," or learn to pass as human, as in Murray Leinster's "If You Was a Moklin."

In any case, the rules of the contact services, as science fiction has evolved them, usually insist that native cultures must be protected; the introduction of tools or technology beyond their capacities is forbidden. Stories often develop around the breaking of such rules by unscrupulous companies or entrepreneurs, or by foolish do-gooders.

If aliens visit earth first, they must be superior, and they represent danger. They may consider that we have about as much right to earth as the Amerindians had to the forests of North America. Some stories emphasize the necessity of turning back the first exploratory contact: Anthony Boucher's "Expedition" showed how a clever photographer tricked insectlike invaders into believing that he was a midget and real humans were many times his size; in Murray Leinster's "Nobody Saw the Ship," an exploring ship is destroyed by common terrestrial pests; in Philip K. Dick's "The Father-Thing," children see through and destroy the menace. Some stories, on the other hand, like Ray Bradbury's "Zero Hour" and Cyril Kornbluth's "The Silly Season," illustrate how easily earth could be conquered.

There is another battle in the pages of science fiction, between romance and realism.

Even if aliens are superior, they need not necessarily (1) threaten us or (2) invade us. They might (3) tempt us, (4) judge us, or (5) teach us.

In some stories the affluence and opportunities of galactic civilization destroy humanity; in others events seem to be going poorly for humanity until a way is found to give man back his self-esteem and his own culture; for this reason the great gifts of alien cultures often are withheld from man by benevolent aliens until man is ready. But sometimes simply the fact of alternate forms of existence may be a temptation too great to resist. In Clifford Simak's "Desertion," men have the opportunity to transfer their consciousnesses into "lopers," wolflike natives of Jupiter with superior senses and abilities; eventually in the novel *City,* all humanity transforms itself into lopers, leaving earth to the dogs.

Aliens may come here to judge man's right to enter the galactic community, or even to exist, offering an author the opportunity to measure humanity and its values against more permanent and less parochial standards than the here and now. In Heinlein's juvenile novel *Have Space Suit—Will Travel,* humanity is condemned before a Council of Three Galaxies as a dangerous, warmaking, destructive race that ought to be exterminated before it becomes a menace to other civilized beings in the universe; and our sun is saved only by the eloquence of a boy.

In Jack Williamson's *The Trial of Terra,* earth's sun again is in peril: a galactic civilization wants to use it as a celestial beacon and finds humanity's destruction of little importance since it has not developed toward galactic citizenship in five thousand years. In Gordon Dickson's "Dolphin's Way," aliens who wish to make contact with the most civilized creatures on earth walk past man to greet the dolphins.

Science fiction can teach us humility.

Sometimes it is only alien artifacts we find and marvel at, as in Leinster's "The Ethical Equations," Niven's *Ringworld,* or Clarke's "The Sentinel" or *Rendezvous with Rama.* Sometimes the aliens marvel at, or misunderstand, our artifacts, as in Ross Rocklynne's "Jackdaw" or Clarke's "History Lesson."

Sometimes aliens teach us, and we learn from them as students, as equals exchanging goods and ideas, or as superiors learning from totally different forms of life. Sometimes the stories involve only individuals rather than the race; they are personal successes or personal tragedies, as in Roger Zelazny's "A Rose for Ecclesiastes."

When the stories are conceived properly and written well, what they do best is teach us about ourselves, what it is to be human, and, what may be more important, what it is to be intelligent and aware in an unfeeling universe. As Clifford Simak wrote in *Time and Again,* "There is no thing, no matter how created, how born or conceived or made, which knows the pulse of life, that goes alone. . . ." Science fiction has come a long way from Wells's unspeakably nasty Martians.

The alien is the familiar come from afar. What is familiar to us will be alien to an extraterrestrial; what is ordinary to him will be strange to us. Yet, as Arthur C. Clarke has written: "Among the stars lies the proper study of mankind; Pope's aphorism gave only part of the truth, for the proper study of mankind is not merely Man, but Intelligence." We can hope that the intelligence we may share with alien beings will provide a bridge to understanding each other; that in spite of possibly vast differences, we will be able to communicate. For in facing the alien, we will, in a sense, be facing ourselves. The final lesson the alien can teach us is that nothing is finally alien.

BIBLIOGRAPHY

Short fiction

Aldiss, Brian, *The Dark Light-Years,* 1964 (Signet)
Blish, James, *A Case of Conscience,* 1958 (Ballantine)
Budrys, Algis, *Rogue Moon,* 1960 (Fawcett)
Clarke, Arthur C., *Childhood's End,* 1953 (Ballantine)
Clement, Hal, *Mission of Gravity,* 1954 (Doubleday)
Farmer, Philip José, *The Lovers,* 1961 (Ballantine)
Gunn, James, *The Listeners,* 1972 (Scribners)

Heinlein, Robert A., *The Puppet Masters,* 1951 (Doubleday)
Jones, Raymond F., *This Island Earth,* 1952 (Shasta)
Le Guin, Ursula K., *The Left Hand of Darkness,* 1969 (Walker)
Leiber, Fritz, *The Wanderer,* 1964 (Ballantine)
Lem, Stanislaw, *Solaris,* 1970 (Walker)
Merritt, A., *The Moon Pool,* 1919 (Putnam)
Niven, Larry, *Ringworld,* 1970 (Ballantine)
Pournelle, Jerry, and Larry Niven, *The Mote in God's Eye,* 1974 (Simon and
    Schuster)
Wells, H. G., *The War of the Worlds,* 1897 (*Pearson's Magazine*)
Wolfe, Gene, *The Fifth Head of Cerberus,* 1972 (Scribners)

Short Fiction

Anderson, Poul, "The Double-Dyed Villains," *Astounding,* 1949
Benford, Gregory, and Gordon Eklund, "If the Stars are Gods," *Universe 4,*
    ed. by Terry Carr, 1974 (Random House)
Bishop Michael, "Death and Designation Among the Asadi," *If* magazine,
    1973
Campbell, John W., Jr. (as Don A. Stuart), "Who Goes There?" *Astounding,*
    1938
Clarke, Arthur C., "The Sentinel," 1951 (Avon Periodicals)
Dick, Philip K., "Faith of Our Fathers," *Dangerous Visions,* ed. by Harlan
    Ellison, 1967 (Doubleday)
Farmer, Philip José, "Mother," *Thrilling Wonder Stories,* 1953
Heinlein, Robert A., "Goldfish Bowl," *Astounding,* 1942
Knight, Damon, "Stranger Station," *Fantasy & Science Fiction,* 1956
Kornbluth, C. M., "The Silly Season," *Fantasy & Science Fiction,* 1950
Le Guin, Ursula K., "The Author of the Acacia Seeds and Other Extracts
    From the *Journal of the Association of Therolinguistics,*" *Fellowship of
    the Stars,* ed. by Terry Carr, 1974 (Simon and Schuster)
———, "The Word for World Is Forest," *Again, Dangerous Visions,* ed.
    by Harlan Ellison, 1972 (Doubleday)
Leinster, Murray, "First Contact," *Astounding,* 1945
Martin, George R. R., "A Song For Lya," *Analog,* 1974
Moore, C. L., "Shambleau," *Weird Tales,* 1933
Pangborn, Edgar, "Angel's Egg," *Galaxy,* 1951
Piper, H. Beam, "Omnilingual," *Astounding,* 1958
Russell, Eric Frank, "Dear Devil," *Other Worlds,* 1950
Silverberg, Robert, "Passengers," *Orbit 4,* ed. by Damon Knight, 1968
    (Putnam)
Sturgeon, Theodore, "The Hurkle Is a Happy Beast," *Fantasy & Science
    Fiction,* 1949

Tiptree, James, Jr., "Filomena & Greg & Rikki-Tikki & Barlow & the Alien," *New Dimensions II,* ed. by Robert Silverberg, 1972 (Doubleday)
Van Vogt, A. E., "The Rull," *Astounding,* 1948
Weinbaum, Stanley G., "A Martian Odyssey," *Wonder Stories,* 1934
Wells, H. G., "The Crystal Egg," *Tales of Space and Time,* 1911
Zelazny, Roger, "A Rose for Ecclesiastes," *Fantasy & Science Fiction,* 1963

Specialist

Robert Sheckley

The photon storm struck without warning, pouncing upon the Ship from behind a bank of giant red stars. Eye barely had time to flash a last second warning through Talker before it was upon them.

It was Talker's third journey into deep space, and his first light-pressure storm. He felt a sudden pang of fear as the Ship yawed violently, caught the force of the wave-front and careened end for end. Then the fear was gone, replaced by a strong pulse of excitement.

Why should he be afraid, he asked himself—hadn't he been trained for just this sort of emergency?

He had been talking to Feeder when the storm hit, but he cut off the conversation abruptly. He hoped Feeder would be all right. It was the youngster's first deep space trip.

The wirelike filaments that made up most of Talker's body were extended throughout the Ship. Quickly he withdrew all except the ones linking him to Eye, Engine, and the Walls. This was strictly their job now. The rest of the Crew would have to shift for themselves until the storm was over.

Eye had flattened his disklike body against a Wall, and had one seeing organ extended outside the Ship. For greater concentration, the rest of his seeing organs were collapsed, clustered against his body.

Through Eye's seeing organ, Talker watched the storm. He translated Eye's purely visual image into a direction for Engine, who shoved the Ship around to meet the waves. At appreciably the same time, Talker translated direction into velocity for the Walls who stiffened to meet the shocks.

The coordination was swift and sure—Eye measuring the waves, Talker relaying the messages to Engine and Walls, Engine driving the ship nose-first into the waves, and Walls bracing to meet the shock.

Talker forgot any fear he might have had in the swiftly functioning teamwork. He had no time to think. As the Ship's communication system, he had to translate and flash his messages at top speed, coordinating information and directing action.

In a matter of minutes, the storm was over.

"All right," Talker said. "Let's see if there was any damage." His filaments had become tangled during the storm, but he untwisted and extended them through the Ship, plugging everyone into circuit. "Engine?"

"I'm fine," Engine said. The tremendous old fellow had dampened his plates during the storm, easing down the atomic explosions in his stomach. No storm could catch an experienced spacer like Engine unaware.

"Walls?"

The Walls reported one by one, and this took a long time. There were almost a thousand of them, thin, rectangular fellows making up the entire skin of the Ship. Naturally, they had reinforced their edges during the storm, giving the whole Ship resiliency. But one or two were dented badly.

Doctor announced that he was all right. He removed Talker's filament from his head, taking himself out of circuit, and went to work on the dented Walls. Made mostly of hands, Doctor had clung to an Accumulator during the storm.

"Let's go a little faster now," Talker said, remembering that there still was the problem of determining where they were. He opened the circuit to the four Accumulators. "How are you?" he asked.

There was no answer. The Accumulators were asleep. They had had their receptors open during the storm and were bloated on energy. Talker twitched his filaments around them, but they didn't stir.

"Let me," Feeder said. Feeder had taken quite a beating before planting his suction cups to a Wall, but his cockiness was intact. He was the only member of the Crew who never needed Doctor's attention; his body was quite capable of repairing itself.

He scuttled across the floor on a dozen or so tentacles, and booted the nearest Accumulator. The big, conical storage unit opened one eye, then closed it again. Feeder kicked him again, getting no response. He reached for the Accumulator's safety valve and drained off some energy.

"Stop that," the Accumulator said.

"Then wake up and report," Talker told him.

The Accumulators said testily that they were all right, as any fool could see. They had been anchored to the floor during the storm.

The rest of the inspection went quickly. Thinker was fine, and Eye was ecstatic over the beauty of the storm. There was only one casualty.

Pusher was dead. Bipedal, he didn't have the stability of the rest of the Crew. The storm had caught him in the middle of a floor, thrown him against a stiffened Wall, and broken several of his important bones. He was beyond Doctor's skill to repair.

They were silent for a while. It was always serious when a part of the Ship died. The Ship was a cooperative unit, composed entirely of the Crew. The loss of any member was a blow to all the rest.

It was especially serious now. They had just delivered a cargo to a port several thousand light-years from Galactic Center. There was no telling where they might be.

Eye crawled to a Wall and extended a seeing organ outside. The Walls let it through, then sealed around it. Eye's organ pushed out, far enough from the Ship so he could view the entire sphere of stars. The picture traveled through Talker, who gave it to Thinker.

Thinker lay in one corner of the room, a great shapeless blob of protoplasm. Within him were all the memories of his space-going ancestors. He considered the picture, compared it rapidly with others stored in his cells, and said, "No galactic planets within reach."

Talker automatically translated for everyone. It was what they had feared.

Eye, with Thinker's help, calculated that they were several hundred light-years off their course, on the galactic periphery.

Every Crew member knew what that meant. Without a Pusher to boost the Ship to a multiple of the speed of light, they would never get home. The trip back, without a Pusher, would take longer than most of their lifetimes.

"What would you suggest?" Talker asked Thinker.

This was too vague a question for the literal-minded Thinker. He asked to have it rephrased.

"What would be our best line of action," Talker asked, "to get back to a galactic planet?"

Thinker needed several minutes to go through all the possibilities stored in his cells. In the meantime, Doctor had patched the Walls and was asking to be given something to eat.

"In a little while we'll all eat," Talker said, twitching his tendrils nervously. Even though he was the second youngest Crew member— only Feeder was younger—the responsibility was largely on him. This was still an emergency; he had to coordinate information and direct action.

One of the Walls suggested that they get good and drunk. This unrealistic solution was vetoed at once. It was typical of the Walls' attitude, however. They were fine workers and good shipmates, but happy-go-lucky fellows at best. When they returned to their home planets, they would probably blow all their wages on a spree.

"Loss of the Ship's Pusher cripples the Ship for sustained faster-than-light speeds," Thinker began without preamble. "The nearest galactic planet is four hundred and five light-years off."

Talker translated all this instantly along his wave-packet body.

"Two courses of action are open. First, the Ship can proceed to the nearest galactic planet under atomic power from Engine. This will take approximately two hundred years. Engine might still be alive at this time, although no one else will.

"Second, locate a primitive planet in this region, upon which are latent Pushers. Find one and train him. Have him push the Ship back to galactic territory."

Thinker was silent, having given all the possibilities he could find in the memories of his ancestors.

They held a quick vote and decided upon Thinker's second alternative. There was no choice, really. It was the only one which offered them any hope of getting back to their homes.

"All right," Talker said. "Let's eat. I think we all deserve it."

The body of the dead Pusher was shoved into the mouth of Engine, who consumed it at once, breaking down the atoms to energy. Engine was the only member of the Crew who lived on atomic energy.

For the rest, Feeder dashed up and loaded himself from the nearest Accumulator. Then he transformed the food within him into the substances each member ate. His body chemistry changed, altered, adapted, making the different foods for the Crew.

Eye lived entirely on a complex chlorophyl chain. Feeder reproduced this for him, then went over to give Talker his hydrocarbons, and the Walls their chlorine compound. For Doctor he made a facsimile of a silicate fruit that grew on Doctor's native planet.

Finally, feeding was over and the Ship back in order. The Accumulators were stacked in a corner, blissfully sleeping again. Eye was extending his vision as far as he could, shaping his main seeing organ for high-powered telescopic reception. Even in this emergency, Eye couldn't resist making verses. He announced that he was at work on a new narrative poem, called *Peripheral Glow*. No one wanted to hear it, so Eye fed it to Thinker, who stored everything, good or bad, right or wrong.

Engine never slept. Filled to the brim on Pusher, he shoved the Ship along at several times the speed of light.

The Walls were arguing among themselves about who had been the drunkest during their last leave.

Talker decided to make himself comfortable. He released his hold on the Walls and swung in the air, his small round body suspended by his crisscrossed network of filaments.

He thought briefly about Pusher. It was strange. Pusher had been everyone's friend and now he was forgotten. That wasn't because of indifference; it was because the Ship was a unit. The loss of a member was regretted, but the important thing was for the unit to go on.

The Ship raced through the suns of the periphery.

Thinker laid out a search spiral, calculating their odds on finding a Pusher planet at roughly four to one. In a week they found a planet of primitive Walls. Dropping low, they could see the leathery, rectangular fellows basking in the sun, crawling over rocks, stretching themselves thin in order to float in the breeze.

All the Ship's Walls heaved a sigh of nostalgia. It was just like home.

These Walls on the planet hadn't been contacted by a galactic team yet, and were still unaware of their great destiny—to join in the vast Cooperation of the Galaxy.

There were plenty of dead worlds in the spiral, and worlds too young to bear life. They found a planet of Talkers. The Talkers had extended their spidery communication lines across half a continent.

Talker looked at them eagerly, through Eye. A wave of self-pity washed over him. He remembered home, his family, his friends. He thought of the tree he was going to buy when he got back.

For a moment, Talker wondered what he was doing here, part of a Ship in a far corner of the Galaxy.

He shrugged off the mood. They were bound to find a Pusher planet, if they looked long enough.

At least, he hoped so.

There was a long stretch of arid worlds as the Ship speeded through the unexplored periphery. Then a planetful of primeval Engines, swimming in a radioactive ocean.

"This is rich territory," Feeder said to Talker. "Galactic should send a Contact party here."

"They probably will, after we get back," Talker said.

They were good friends, above and beyond the all-enveloping friendship of the Crew. It wasn't only because they were the youngest Crew members, although that had something to do with it. They both had the same kind of functions and that made for a certain rapport. Talker translated languages; Feeder transformed foods. Also, they looked somewhat alike. Talker was a central core with radiating filaments; Feeder was a central core with radiating tentacles.

Talker thought that Feeder was the next most aware being on the Ship. He was never really able to understand how some of the others carried on the processes of consciousness.

More suns, more planets. Engine started to overheat. Usually, Engine was used only for taking off and landing, and for fine maneuvering in a planetary group. Now he had been running continuously for weeks, both over and under the speed of light. The strain was telling on him.

Feeder, with Doctor's help, rigged a cooling system for him. It was crude, but it had to suffice. Feeder rearranged nitrogen, oxygen and hydrogen atoms to make a coolant for the system. Doctor diagnosed a long rest for Engine. He said that the gallant old fellow couldn't stand the strain for more than a week.

The search continued, with the Crew's spirits gradually dropping. They all realized that Pushers were rather rare in the Galaxy, as compared to the fertile Walls and Engines.

The Walls were getting pock-marked from interstellar dust. They complained that they would need a full beauty treatment when they got home. Talker assured them that the company would pay for it.

Even Eye was getting bloodshot from staring into space so continuously.

They dipped over another planet. Its characteristics were flashed to Thinker, who mulled over them.

Closer, and they could make out the forms.

Pushers! Primitive Pushers!

They zoomed back into space to make plans. Feeder produced twenty-three different kinds of intoxicants for a celebration.

The Ship wasn't fit to function for three days.

"Everyone ready now?" Talker asked, a bit fuzzily. He had a hangover that burned all along his nerve ends. What a drunk he had thrown! He had a vague recollection of embracing Engine, and inviting him to share his tree when they got home.

He shuddered at the idea.

The rest of the Crew were pretty shaky, too. The Walls were letting air leak into space; they were just too wobbly to seal their edges properly. Doctor had passed out.

But the worst off was Feeder. Since his system could adapt to any type of fuel except atomic, he had been sampling every batch he made, whether it was an unbalanced iodine, pure oxygen or a supercharged ester. He was really miserable. His tentacles, usually a healthy aqua, were shot through with orange streaks. His system was working furiously, purging itself of everything, and Feeder was suffering the effects of the purge.

The only sober ones were Thinker and Engine. Thinker didn't drink, which was unusual for a spacer, though typical of Thinker, and Engine couldn't.

They listened while Thinker reeled off some astounding facts. From Eye's pictures of the planet's surface, Thinker had detected the presence of metallic construction. He put forth the alarming suggestion that these Pushers had constructed a mechanical civilization.

"That's impossible," three of the Walls said flatly, and most of the Crew were inclined to agree with them. All the metal they had ever seen had been buried in the ground or lying around in worthless oxidized chunks.

"Do you mean that they make things out of metal?" Talker demanded. "Out of just plain dead metal? What could they make?"

"They couldn't make anything," Feeder said positively. "It would break down constantly. I mean metal doesn't *know* when it's weakening."

But it seemed to be true. Eye magnified his pictures, and everyone could see that the Pushers had made vast shelters, vehicles, and other articles from inanimate material.

The reason for this was not readily apparent, but it wasn't a good sign. However, the really hard part was over. The Pusher planet had been found. All that remained was the relatively easy job of convincing a native Pusher.

That shouldn't be too difficult. Talker knew that cooperation was the keystone of the Galaxy, even among primitive peoples.

The Crew decided not to land in a populated region. Of course, there was no reason not to expect a friendly greeting, but it was the job of a Contact Team to get in touch with them as a race. All they wanted was an individual.

Accordingly, they picked out a sparsely populated land-mass, drifting in while that side of the planet was dark.

They were able to locate a solitary Pusher almost at once.

Eye adapted his vision to see in the dark, and they followed the Pusher's movements. He lay down, after a while, beside a small fire. Thinker told them that this was a well-known resting habit of Pushers.

Just before dawn, the Walls opened, and Feeder, Talker and Doctor came out.

Feeder dashed forward and tapped the creature on the shoulder. Talker followed with a communication tendril.

The Pusher opened his seeing organs, blinked them, and made a movement with his eating organ. Then he leaped to his feet and started to run.

The three Crew members were amazed. The Pusher hadn't even waited to find out what the three of them wanted!

Talker extended a filament rapidly, and caught the Pusher, fifty feet away, by a limb. The Pusher fell.

"Treat him gently," Feeder said. "He might be startled by our appearance." He twitched his tendrils at the idea of a Pusher—one of the strangest sights in the Galaxy, with his multiple organs—being startled at someone else's appearance.

Feeder and Doctor scurried to the fallen Pusher, picked him up and carried him back to the Ship.

The Walls sealed again. They released the Pusher and prepared to talk.

As soon as he was free, the Pusher sprang to his limbs and ran at the place where the Walls had sealed. He pounded against them frantically, his eating organ open and vibrating.

"Stop that," the Wall said. He bulged, and the Pusher tumbled to the floor. Instantly, he jumped up and started to run forward.

"Stop him," Talker said. "He might hurt himself."

One of the Accumulators woke up enough to roll into the Pusher's path. The Pusher fell, got up again, and ran on.

Talker had his filaments in the front of the Ship also, and he caught the Pusher in the bow. The Pusher started to tear at his tendrils, and Talker let go hastily.

"Plug him into the communication system!" Feeder shouted. "Maybe we can reason with him!"

Talker advanced a filament toward the Pusher's head, waving it in the universal sign of communication. But the Pusher continued his amazing behavior, jumping out of the way. He had a piece of metal in his hand and he was waving it frantically.

"What do you think he's going to do with that?" Feeder asked. The Pusher started to attack the side of the Ship, pounding at one of the Walls. The Wall stiffened instinctively and the metal snapped.

"Leave him alone," Talker said. "Give him a chance to calm down."

Talker consulted with Thinker, but they couldn't decide what to do about the Pusher. He wouldn't accept communication. Every time Talker extended a filament, the Pusher showed all the signs of violent panic. Temporarily, it was an impasse.

Thinker vetoed the plan of finding another Pusher on the planet. He considered this Pusher's behavior typical; nothing would be gained by approaching another. Also, a planet was supposed to be contacted only by a Contact Team.

If they couldn't communicate with this Pusher, they never would with another on the planet.

"I think I know what the trouble is," Eye said. He crawled up on an Accumulator. "These Pushers have evolved a mechanical civilization. Consider for a minute how they went about it. They developed the use of their fingers, like Doctor, to shape metal. They utilized their seeing organs, like myself. And probably countless other organs." He paused for effect.

"These Pushers have become unspecialized!"

They argued over it for several hours. The Walls maintained that no intelligent creature could be unspecialized. It was unknown in the Galaxy. But the evidence was before them—the Pusher cities, their vehicles . . . This Pusher, exemplifying the rest, seemed capable of a multitude of things.

He was able to do everything except Push!

Thinker supplied a partial explanation. "This is not a primitive planet. It is relatively old and should have been in the Cooperation thousands of years ago. Since it was not, the Pushers upon it were robbed of their birthright. Their ability, their specialty was to Push, but there was nothing *to* Push. Naturally, they have developed a deviant culture.

"Exactly what this culture is, we can only guess. But on the basis of the evidence, there is reason to believe that these Pushers are— uncooperative."

Thinker had a habit of uttering the most shattering statement in the quietest possible way.

"It is entirely possible," Thinker went on inexorably, "that these Pushers will have nothing to do with us. In which case, our chances are approximately 283 to one against finding another Pusher planet."

"We can't be sure he won't cooperate," Talker said, "until we get him into communication." He found it almost impossible to believe that any intelligent creature would refuse to cooperate willingly.

"But how?" Feeder asked. They decided upon a course of action. Doctor walked slowly up to the Pusher, who backed away from him. In the meantime, Talker extended a filament outside the Ship, around, and in again, behind the Pusher.

The Pusher backed against a Wall—and Talker shoved the filament through the Pusher's head, into the communication socket in the center of his brain.

The Pusher collapsed.

When he came to, Feeder and Doctor had to hold the Pusher's limbs, or he would have ripped out the communication line. Talker exercised his skill in learning the Pusher's language.

It wasn't too hard. All Pusher languages were of the same family, and this was no exception. Talker was able to catch enough surface thoughts to form a pattern.

He tried to communicate with the Pusher.

The Pusher was silent.

"I think he needs food," Feeder said. They remembered that it had been almost two days since they had taken the Pusher on board. Feeder worked up some standard Pusher food and offered it.

"My God! A steak!" the Pusher said.

The Crew cheered along Talker's communication circuits. The Pusher had said his first words!

Talker examined the words and searched his memory. He knew about two hundred Pusher languages and many more simple variations. He found that this Pusher was speaking a cross between two Pusher tongues.

After the Pusher had eaten, he looked around. Talker caught his thoughts and broadcast them to the Crew.

The Pusher had a queer way of looking at the Ship. He saw it as a riot of colors. The walls undulated. In front of him was something resembling a gigantic spider, colored black and green, with his web running all over the Ship and into the heads of all the creatures. He saw Eye as a strange, naked little animal, something between a skinned rabbit and an egg yolk—whatever those things were.

Talker was fascinated by the new perspective the Pusher's mind gave him. He had never seen things that way before. But now that the Pusher was pointing it out, Eye *was* a pretty funny-looking creature.

They settled down to communication.

"What in hell *are* you things?" the Pusher asked, much calmer now than he had been during the two days. "Why did you grab me? Have I gone nuts?"

"No," Talker said, "you are not psychotic. We are a galactic trading ship. We were blown off our course by a storm and our Pusher was killed."

"Well, what does that have to do with me?"

"We would like you to join our Crew," Talker said, "to be our new Pusher."

The Pusher thought it over after the situation was explained to him. Talker could catch the feeling of conflict in the Pusher's thoughts. He hadn't decided whether to accept this as a real situation or not. Finally, the Pusher decided that he wasn't crazy.

"Look, boys," he said, "I don't know what you are or how this makes sense. I have to get out of here. I'm on a furlough, and if I don't get back soon, the U.S. Army's going to be very interested."

Talker asked the Pusher to give him more information about "army," and he fed it to Thinker.

"These Pushers engage in personal combat," was Thinker's conclusion.

"But *why?*" Talker asked. Sadly he admitted to himself that Thinker might have been right; the Pusher didn't show many signs of willingness to cooperate.

"I'd like to help you lads out," Pusher said, "but I don't know where you get the idea that I could push anything this size. You'd need a whole division of tanks just to budge it."

"Do you approve of these wars?" Talker asked, getting a suggestion from Thinker.

"Nobody likes war—not those who have to do the dying at least."

"Then why do you fight them?"

The Pusher made a gesture with his eating organ, which Eye picked up and sent to Thinker. "It's kill or be killed. You guys know what war is, don't you?"

"We don't have any wars," Talker said.

"You're lucky," the Pusher said bitterly. "We do. Plenty of them."

"Of course," Talker said. He had the full explanation from Thinker now. "Would you like to end them?"

"Of course I would."

"Then come with us. Be our Pusher."

The Pusher stood up and walked up to an Accumulator. He sat down on it and doubled the ends of his upper limbs.

"How the hell can I stop all wars?" the Pusher demanded. "Even if I went to the big shots and told them—"

"You won't have to," Talker said. "All you have to do is come with us. Push us to our base. Galactic will send a Contact Team to your planet. That will end your wars.''

"The hell you say,'' the Pusher replied. "You boys are stranded here, huh? Good enough. No monsters are going to take over Earth.''

Bewildered, Talker tried to understand the reasoning. Had he said something wrong? Was it possible that the Pusher didn't understand him?

"I thought you wanted to end wars,'' Talker said.

"Sure I do. But I don't want anyone *making* us stop. I'm no traitor. I'd rather fight.''

"No one will make you stop. You will just stop because there will be no further need for fighting.''

"Do you know why we're fighting?''

"It's obvious.''

"Yeah? What's your explanation?''

"You Pushers have been separated from the main stream of the Galaxy,'' Talker explained. "You have your specialty—pushing—but nothing to Push. Accordingly, you have no real jobs. You play with things—metal, inanimate objects—but find no real satisfaction. Robbed of your true vocation, you fight from sheer frustration.

"Once you find your place in the galactic Cooperation—and I assure you that it is an important place—your fighting will stop. Why should you right, which is an unnatural occupation, where you can Push? Also, your mechanical civilization will end, since there will be no need for it.''

The Pusher shook his head in what Talker guessed was a gesture of confusion. "What is this pushing?''

Talker told him as best he could. Since the job was out of his scope, he had only a general idea of what a Pusher did.

"You mean to say that *that* is what every Earthman should be doing?''

"Of course,'' Talker said. "It is your great specialty.''

The Pusher thought about it for several minutes. "I think you want a physicist or a mentalist or something. I could never do anything like that. I'm a junior architect. And besides—well, it's difficult to explain.''

But Talker had already caught Pusher's objection. He saw a Pusher female in his thoughts. No, two, three. And he caught a feeling of loneliness, strangeness. The Pusher was filled with doubts. He was afraid.

"When we reach galactic," Talker said, hoping it was the right thing, "you can meet other Pushers. Pusher females, too. All you Pushers look alike, so you should become friends with them. As far as loneliness in the Ship goes—it just doesn't exist. You don't understand the Cooperation yet. No one is lonely in the Cooperation."

The Pusher was still considering the idea of there being other Pushers. Talker couldn't understand why he was so startled at that. The Galaxy was filled with Pushers, Feeders, Talkers, and many other species, endlessly duplicated.

"I can't believe that anybody could end all war," Pusher said. "How do I know you're not lying?"

Talker felt as if he had been struck in the core. Thinker must have been right when he said these Pushers would be uncooperative. Was this going to be the end of Talker's career? Were he and the rest of the Crew going to spend the rest of their lives in space, because of the stupidity of a bunch of Pushers?

Even thinking this, Talker was able to feel sorry for the Pusher. It must be terrible, he thought. Doubting, uncertain, never trusting anyone. If these Pushers didn't find their place in the Galaxy, they would exterminate themselves. Their place in the Cooperation was long overdue.

"What can I do to convince you?" Talker asked.

In despair, he opened all the circuits to the Pusher. He let the pusher see Engine's good-natured gruffness, the devil-may-care humor of the Walls; he showed him Eye's poetic attempts, and Feeder's cocky good nature. He opened his own mind and showed the Pusher a picture of his home planet, his family, the tree he was planning to buy when he got home.

The pictures told the story of all of them, from different planets, representing different ethics, united by a common bond—the galactic Cooperation.

The Pusher watched it all in silence.

After a while, he shook his head. The thought accompanying the gesture was uncertain, weak—but negative.

Talker told the Walls to open. They did, and the Pusher stared in amazement.

"You may leave," Talker said. "Just remove the communication line and go."

"What will you do?"

"We will look for another Pusher planet."

"Where? Mars? Venus?"

"We don't know. All we can do is hope there is another in this region."

The Pusher looked at the opening, then back at the Crew. He hesitated and his face screwed up in a grimace of indecision.

"All that you showed me was true?"

No answer was necessary.

"All right," the Pusher said suddenly. "I'll go. I'm a damned fool, but I'll go. If this means what you say—it *must* mean what you say!"

Talker saw that the agony of the Pusher's decision had forced him out of contact with reality. He believed that he was in a dream, where decisions are easy and unimportant.

"There's just one little trouble," Pusher said with the lightness of hysteria. "Boys, I'll be damned if I know how to Push. You said something about faster-than-light? I can't even run the mile in an hour."

"Of course you can Push," Talker assured him, hoping he was right. He knew what a Pusher's abilities were; but this one . . .

"Just try it."

"Sure," Pusher agreed. "I'll probably wake up out of this, anyhow."

They sealed the ship for takeoff while Pusher talked to himself.

"Funny," Pusher said. "I thought a camping trip would be a nice way to spend a furlough and all I do is get nightmares!"

Engine boosted the Ship into the air. The Walls were sealed and Eye was guiding them away from the planet.

"We're in open space now," Talker said. Listening to Pusher, he hoped his mind hadn't cracked. "Eye and Thinker will give a direction, I'll transmit it to you, and you Push along it."

"You're crazy," Pusher mumbled. "You must have the wrong planet. I wish you nightmares would go away."

"You're in the Cooperation now," Talker said desperately. "There's the direction. Push!"

The Pusher didn't do anything for a moment. He was slowly emerging from his fantasy, realizing that he wasn't in a dream, after all. He felt the Cooperation. Eye to Thinker, Thinker to Talker, Talker to Pusher, all intercoordinated with Walls, and with each other.

"What is this?" Pusher asked. He felt the oneness of the Ship, the great warmth, the closeness achieved only in the Cooperation.

He Pushed.

Nothing happened.

"Try again," Talker begged.

Pusher searched his mind. He found a deep well of doubt and fear. Staring into it, he saw his own tortured face.

Thinker illuminated it for him.

Pushers had lived with this doubt and fear for centuries. Pushers had fought through fear, killed through doubt.

That was where the Pusher organ was!

Human—specialist—Pusher—he entered fully into the Crew, merged with them, threw mental arms around the shoulders of Thinker and Talker.

Suddenly, the Ship shot forward at eight times the speed of light. It continued to accelerate.

The Dance of the Changer and The Three

Terry Carr

This all happened ages ago, out in the depths of space beyond Dark-edge, where galaxies lumber ponderously through the black like so many silent bright rhinoceroses. It was so long ago that when the light from Loarr's galaxy finally reached Earth, after millions of light-years, there was no one here to see it except a few things in the oceans that were too mindlessly busy with their monotonous single-celled reactions to notice.

Yet, as long ago as it was, the present-day Loarra still remember this story and retell it in complex, shifting wave-dances every time one of the newly-changed asks for it. The wave-dances wouldn't mean much to you if you saw them, nor I suppose would the story itself if I were to tell it just as it happened. So consider this a translation, and don't bother yourself that when I say "water" I don't mean our hydrogen-oxygen compound, or that there's no "sky" as such on Loarr, or for that matter that the Loarra weren't—aren't—creatures that "think" or "feel" in quite the way we understand. In fact, you could take this as a piece of pure fiction, because there are damned few real facts in it—but I know better (or worse), because I know how true it is. And that has a lot to do with why I'm back here on Earth, with forty-two friends and co-workers left dead on Loarr. They never had a chance.

There was a Changer who had spent three life cycles planning a particular cycle climax and who had come to the moment of action. He wasn't really named Minnearo, but I'll call him that because it's the closest thing I can write to approximate the tone, emotional matrix, and associations that were all wrapped up in his designation.

When he came to his decision, he turned away from the crag on which he'd been standing overlooking the Loarran ocean, and went quickly to the personality-homes of three of his best friends. To the first friend, Asterrea, he said, "I am going to commit suicide," wave-dancing this message in his best festive tone.

His friend laughed, as Minnearo had hoped, but only for a short time. Then he turned away and left Minnearo alone, because there had already been several suicides lately and it was wearing a little thin.

To his second friend, Minnearo gave a pledge-salute, going through all sixty sequences with exaggerated care, and wave-danced, "Tomorrow I shall immerse my body in the ocean, if anyone will watch."

His second friend, Fless, smiled tolerantly and told him he would come and see the performance.

To his third friend, with many excited leapings and boundings, Minnearo described what he imagined would happen to him after he had gone under the lapping waters of the ocean. The dance he went through to give this description was intricate and even imaginative, because Minnearo had spent most of that third life cycle working it out in his mind. It used motion and color and sound and another sense something like smell, all to communicate descriptions of falling, impact with the water, and then the quick dissolution and blending in the currents of the ocean, the dimming and loss of awareness, then darkness, and finally the awakening, the completion of the change. Minnearo had a rather romantic turn of mind, so he imagined himself recoalescing around the life-mote of one of Loarr's greatest heroes, Krollim, and forming on Krollim's old pattern. And he even ended the dance with suggestions of glory and imitation of himself by others, which was definitely presumptuous. But the friend for whom the dance was given did nod approvingly at several points.

"If it turns out to be half what you anticipate," said this friend, Pur, "then I envy you. But you never know."

"I guess not," Minnearo said, rather morosely. And he hesitated before leaving, for Pur was what I suppose I'd better call female, and Minnearo had rather hoped that she would join him in the ocean jump.

But if she thought of it she gave no sign, merely gazing at Minnearo calmly, waiting for him to go; so finally he did.

And at the appropriate time, with his friend Fless watching him from the edge of the cliff, Minnearo did his final wave-dance as Minnearo—rather excited and ill-coordinated, but that was understandable in the circumstances—and then performed his approach to the edge, leaped and tumbled downward through the air, making fully two dozen turns this way and that before he hit the water.

Fless hurried back and described the suicide to Asterrea and Pur, who laughed and applauded in most of the right places, so on the whole it was a success. Then the three of them sat down and began plotting Minnearo's revenge.

—All right, I *know* a lot of this doesn't make sense. Maybe that's because I'm trying to tell you about the Loarra in human terms, which is a mistake with creatures as alien as they are. Actually, the Loarra are almost wholly an energy life-form, their consciousnesses coalescing in each life cycle around a spatial center which they call a "life-mote," so that, if you could see the patterns of energy they form (as I have, using a sense filter our expedition developed for that purpose), they'd look rather like a spiral nebula sometimes, or other times like iron filings gathering around a magnet, or maybe like a half-melted snowflake. (That's probably what Minnearo looked like on that day, because it's the suicides and the aged who look like that.) Their forms keep shifting, of course, but each individual usually keeps close to one pattern.

Loarr itself is a gigantic gaseous planet with an orbit so close to its primary that its year has to be only about thirty-seven Earthstandard Days long. (In Earthsystem, the orbit would be considerably inside that of Venus.) There's a solid core to the planet, and a lot of hard outcroppings like islands, but most of the surface is in a molten or gaseous state, swirling and bubbling and howling with winds and storms. It's not a very inviting planet if you're anything like a human being, but it does have one thing that brought it to Unicentral's attention: mining.

Do you have any idea what mining is like on a planet where most metals are fluid from the heat and/or pressure? Most people haven't heard much about this, because it isn't a situation we encounter often, but it was there on Loarr, and it was very, very interesting. Because our analyses showed some elements that had been until then only computer-theory—elements that were supposed to exist only in the hearts of suns, for one thing. And if we could get hold of some of them . . . Well, you see what I mean. The mining possibilities were very interesting indeed.

Of course, it would take half the wealth of Earthsystem to outfit a full-scale expedition there. But Unicentral hummed for two-point-eight seconds and then issued detailed instructions on just how it was all to be arranged. So there we went.

And there I was, a Standard Year later (five Standard Years ago), sitting inside a mountain of artificial Earth welded onto one of Loarr's "islands" and wondering what the hell I was doing there. Because I'm not a mining engineer, not a physicist or comp-technician or, in fact, much of anything that requires technical training. I'm a public-relations man; and there was just no reason for me to have been assigned to such a hellish, impossible, godforsaken, inconceivable, and plain damned *unlivable* planet as Loarr.

But there was a reason, and it was the Loarra, of course. They lived ("lived") there, and they were intelligent, so we had to negotiate with them. Ergo: me.

So in the next several years, while I negotiated and we set up operations and I acted as a go-between, I learned a lot about them. Just enough to translate, however clumsily, the wave-dance of the Changer and the Three, which is their equivalent of a classic folk-hero myth (or would be if they had anything honestly equivalent to anything of ours).

To continue:

Fless was in favor of building a pact among the Three by which they would, each in turn and each with deliberate lack of the appropriate salutes, commit suicide in exactly the same way Minnearo had. "Thus we can kill this suicide," Fless explained in excited waves through the air.

But Pur was more practical. "Thus," she corrected him, "we would kill *only* this suicide. It is unimaginative, a thing to be done by rote, and Minnearo deserves more."

Asterrea seemed undecided; he hopped about, sparking and disappearing and reappearing inches away in another color. They waited for him to comment, and finally he stabilized, stood still in the air, settled to the ground, and held himself firmly there. Then he said, in slow, careful movements, "I'm not sure he deserves an original revenge. It wasn't a new suicide, after all. And who is to avenge us?" A single spark leaped from him. "Who is to avenge us?" he repeated, this time with more pronounced motions.

"Perhaps," said Pur slowly, "we will need no revenge—if our act is great enough."

The other two paused in their random wave-motions, considering this. Fless shifted from blue to green to a bright red which dimmed to yellow; Asterrea pulsed a deep ultraviolet.

"Everyone has always been avenged," Fless said at last. "What you suggest is meaningless."

"But if we do something great enough," Pur said; and now she began to radiate heat which drew the other two reluctantly toward her. "Something which has never been done before, in *any* form. Something for which there can *be* no revenge, for it will be a *positive* thing—not a death-change, not a destruction or a disappearance or a forgetting, even a great one. A *positive* thing."

Asterrea's ultraviolet grew darker, darker, until he seemed to be nothing more than a hole in the air. "Dangerous, dangerous, dangerous," he droned, moving torpidly back and forth. "You know it's impossible to ask—we'd have to give up all our life cycles to come. Because a positive in the world . . ." He blinked into darkness, and did not reappear for long seconds. When he did he was perfectly still, pulsing weakly but gradually regaining strength.

Pur waited till his color and tone showed that consciousness had returned, then moved in a light wave-motion calculated to draw the other two back into calm, reasonable discourse. "I've thought about this for six life cycles already," she danced. "I must be right—*no* one has worked on a problem for so long. A positive would *not* be dangerous, no matter what the three- and four-cycle theories say. It would be beneficial." She paused, hanging orange in midair. "And it would be *new,*" she said with a quick spiral. "Oh, how *new!*"

And so, at length, they agreed to follow her plan. And it was briefly this: On a far island outcropping set in the deepest part of the Loarran ocean, where crashing, tearing storms whipped molten metal-compounds into blinding spray, there was a vortex of forces that was avoided by every Loarra on pain of inescapable and final death-change. The most ancient wave-dances of that ancient time said that the vortex had always been there, that the Loarra themselves had been born there or had escaped from there or had in some way cheated the laws that ruled there. Whatever the truth about that was, the vortex was an eater of energy, calling and catching from afar any Loarra or other beings who strayed within its influence. (For all the life on Loarr is energy-based, even the mindless, drifting foodbeasts—creatures of uniform dull color, no inertal motion, no scent or tone, and absolutely no self-volition. Their place in the Loarran scheme of things is and was literally nothing more than that of food; even though there were countless foodbeasts drifting in the air in most areas of the planet, the Loarra hardly ever noticed them. They ate them when they were hungry, and looked around them at any other time.)

"Then you want us to destroy the *vortex?*" cried Fless, dancing and dodging to right and left in agitation.

"Not *destroy,*" Pur said calmly. "It will be a *life*-change, not a destruction."

"Life-change?" said Asterrea faintly, wavering in the air.

And she said it again: "*Life*-change." For the vortex had once created, or somehow allowed to be created, the Oldest of the Loarra, those many-cycles-ago beings who had combined and split, reacted and changed countless times to become the Loarra of this day. And if creation could happen at the vortex once, then it could happen again.

"But how?" asked Fless, trying now to be reasonable, dancing the question with precision and holding a steady green color as he did so.

"We will need help," Pur said, and went on to explain that she had heard—from a windbird, a creature with little intelligence but perfect memory—that there was one of the Oldest still living his first life cycle in a personality-home somewhere near the vortex. In that most ancient time of the race, when suicide had been considered extreme as a means of cycle-change, this Oldest had made his change by a sort of negative suicide—he had frozen his cycle, so that his consciousness and form continued in a never-ending repetition of themselves, on and on while his friends changed and grew and learned as they ran through life cycle after life cycle, becoming different people with common memories, moving forward into the future by this method while he, the last Oldest, remained fixed at the beginning. He saw only the beginning, remembered only the beginning, understood only the beginning.

And for that reason his had been the most tragic of all Loarran changes (and the windbird had heard it rumored, in eight different ways, each of which it repeated word-for-word to Pur, that in the ages since that change more than a hundred hundred Loarra had attempted revenge for the Oldest, but always without success) and it had never been repeated, so that this Oldest was the only Oldest. And for that reason he was important to their quest, Pur explained.

With a perplexed growing and shrinking, brightening and dimming, Asterrea asked, "But how can he live anywhere near the vortex and not be consumed by it?"

"That is a crucial part of what we must find out," Pur said. And after the proper salutes and rituals, the Three set out to find the Oldest.

The wave-dance of the Changer and the Three traditionally at this point spends a great deal of time, in great splashes of color and bursts of light and subtly contrived clouds of darkness all interplaying with hops and swoops and blinking and dodging back and forth, to describe the scene as Pur, Fless and Asterrea set off across that ancient molten sea. I've seen the dance countless times, and each viewing has seemed to bring me maddeningly closer to understanding the meaning that this has for the Loarra themselves. Lowering clouds flashing bursts of aimless, lifeless energy, a rumbling sea below, whose swirling depths pulled and tugged at the Three as they swept overhead, darting around each other in complex patterns like electrons playing cat's-cradle around an invisible nucleus. A droning of lamentation from the changers left behind on their rugged home island, and giggles from those who had recently changed. And the colors of the Three themselves: burning red Asterrea and glowing green Fless and steady, steady golden Pur. I see and hear them all, but I feel only a weird kind of alien beauty, not the grandeur, excitement and awesomeness they have for the Loarra.

When the Three felt the vibrations and swirlings in the air that told them they were coming near to the vortex, they paused in their flight and hung in an interpatterned motion-sequence above the dark, rolling sea, conversing only in short flickerings of color because they had to hold the pattern tightly in order to withstand the already-strong attraction of the vortex.

"Somewhere near?" asked Asterrea, pulsing a quick green.

"Closer to the vortex, I think," Purr said, chancing a sequence of reds and violets.

"Can we be sure?" asked Fless; but there was no answer from Pur and he had expected none from Asterrea.

The ocean crashed and leaped; the air howled around them. And the vortex pulled at them.

Suddenly they felt their motion-sequence changing, against their wills, and for long moments all three were afraid that it was the vortex's attraction that was doing it. They moved in closer to each other, and whirled more quickly in a still more intricate pattern, but it did no good. Irresistibly they were drawn apart again, and at the same time the three of them were moved toward the vortex.

And then they felt the Oldest among them.

He had joined the motion-sequence; this must have been why they had felt the sequence changed and loosened—to make room for him. Whirling and blinking, the Oldest led them inward over the frightening sea, radiating warmth through the storm and, as they followed, or were pulled along, they studied him in wonder.

He was hardly recognizable as one of them, this ancient Oldest. He was . . . not quite energy any longer. He was half matter, carrying the strange mass with awkward, aged grace, his outer edges almost rigid as they held the burden of his congealed center and carried it through the air. (Looking rather like a half-dissolved snowflake, yes, only dark and dismal, a snowflake weighed with coal-dust.) And, for now at least, he was completely silent.

Only when he had brought the Three safely into the calm of his barren personality-home on a tiny rock jutting at an angle from the wash of the sea did he speak. There, inside a cone of quiet against which the ocean raged and fell back, the sands faltered and even the vortex's power was nullified, the Oldest said wearily, "So you have come." He spoke with a slow waving back and forth, augmented by only a dull red color.

To this the Three did not know what to say; but Pur finally hazarded, "Have you been waiting for us?"

The Oldest pulsed a somewhat brighter red, once, twice. He paused. Then he said, "I do not *wait*—there is nothing to wait *for*." Again the pulse of a brighter red. "One waits for the future. But there is no future, you know."

"Not for him," Pur said softly to her companions, and Fless and Asterrea sank wavering to the stone floor of the Oldest's home, where they rocked back and forth.

The Oldest sank with them, and when he touched down he remained motionless. Pur drifted over the others, maintaining movement but unable to raise her color above a steady blue-green. She said to the Oldest, "But you knew we would come."

"Would come? *Would* come? Yes, and *did* come, and *have* come, and *are* come. It is today only, you know, for me. I will be the Oldest, when the others pass me by. I will never change, nor will my world."

"But the others have already passed you by," Fless said. "We are many life cycles after you, Oldest—so many it is beyond the count of windbirds."

The Oldest seemed to draw his material self into a more upright posture, forming his energy-flow carefully around it. To the red of his color he added a low hum with only the slightest quaver as he said, "*Nothing* is after me, here on Rock. When you come here, you come out of time, just as I have. So now you have always been here and will always be here, for as long as you are here."

Asterrea sparked yellow suddenly, and danced upward into the be-calmed air. As Fless stared and Pur moved quickly to calm him, he drove himself again and again at the edge of the cone of quiet that was the Oldest's refuge. Each time he was thrown back and each time he returned to dash himself once more against the edge of the storm, trying to penetrate back into it. He flashed and burned countless colors, and strange sound-frequencies filled the quiet, until at last, with Pur's stern direction and Fless's blank gaze upon him, he sank back wearily to the stone floor. "A trap, a trap," he pulsed. "This is it, this is the vortex itself, we should have known, and we'll never get away."

The Oldest had paid no attention to Asterrea's display. He said slowly, "And it is because I am not in time that the vortex cannot touch me. And it is because I am out of time that I know what the vortex is, for I can remember myself born in it."

Pur left Asterrea then, and came close to the Oldest. She hung above him, thinking with blue vibrations, then asked, "Can you tell us how you were born?—what is creation?—how new things are made?" She paused a moment, and added, "And what *is* the vortex?"

The Oldest seemed to lean forward, seemed tired. His color had deepened again to the darkest red, and the Three could clearly see every atom of matter within his energy-field, stark and hard. He said, "So many questions to ask one question." And he told them the answer to that question.

—And I can't tell you that answer, because I don't know it. No one knows it now, not even the present-day Loarra who are the Three after a thousand million billion life cycles. Because the Loarra really do become different . . . different "persons," when they pass from one cycle to another, and after that many changes, memory becomes meaningless. ("Try it sometime," one of the Loarra once wave-danced to me, and there was no indication that he thought this was a joke.)

Today, for instance, the Three themselves, a thousand million billion times removed from themselves but still, they maintain, *themselves,* often come to watch the Dance of the Changer and the Three, and even though it is about them they are still excited and moved by it as though it were a tale never even heard before, let alone lived through. Yet let a dancer miss a movement or color or sound by even the slightest nuance, and the Three will correct him. (And yes, many times the legended Changer himself, Minnearo, he who started the story, has attended these dances—though often he leaves after the re-creation of his suicide dance.)

It's sometimes difficult to tell one given Loarra from all the others, by the way, despite the complex and subtle technologies of Unicentral, which had provided me with sense filters of all sorts, plus frequency simulators, pattern scopes, special gravity inducers, and a minicomp that takes up more than half of my very tight little island of Earth pasted onto the surface of Loarr and which can do more thinking and analyzing in two seconds than I can do in fifty years. During my four years on Loarr, I got to ''know'' several of the Loarra, yet even at the end of my stay I was still never sure just who I was ''talking'' with at any time. I could run through about seventeen or eighteen tests, linking the sense-filters with the minicomp, and get a definite answer that way. But the Loarra are a bit short on patience and by the time I'd get done with all that whoever it was would usually be off bouncing and sparking into the hellish vapors they call air. So usually I just conducted my researches or negotiations or idle queries, whichever they were that day, with whoever would pay attention to my antigrav ''eyes,'' and I discovered that it didn't matter much just who I was talking with: none of them made any more sense than the others. They were all, as far as I was and am concerned, totally crazy, incomprehensible, stupid, silly, and plain damn no good.

If that sounds like I'm bitter, it's because I am. I've got forty-two murdered men to be bitter about. But back to the unfolding of the greatest legend of an ancient and venerable alien race:

When the Oldest had told them what they wanted to know, the Three came alive with popping and flashing and dancing in the air, Pur just as much as the others. It was all that they had hoped for and more; it was the entire answer to their quest and their problem. It would enable them to create, to transcend any negative cycle-climax they could have devised.

After a time the Three came to themselves and remembered the rituals.

''We offer thanks in the name of Minnearo, whose suicide we are avenging,'' Fless said gravely, waving his message in respectful deep-blue spirals.

''We thank you in our own names as well,'' said Asterrea.

''And we thank you in the name of no one and nothing,'' said Pur, ''for that is the greatest thanks conceivable.''

But the Oldest merely sat there, pulsing his dull red, and the Three wondered among themselves. At last the Oldest said, ''To accept thanks is to accept responsibility, and in only-today, as I am, there can be none of that because there can be no new act. I am outside time, you know, which is almost outside life. All this I have told you is something told to you before, many times, and it will be again.''

Nonetheless, the Three went through all the rituals of thanks-giving, performing them with flawless grace and care—color-and-sound demonstrations, dances, offerings of their own energy, and all the rest. And Pur said, "It is possible to give thanks for a long-past act or even a mindless reflex, and we do so in the highest."

The Oldest pulsed dull red and did not answer, and after a time the Three took leave of him.

Armed with the knowledge he had given them, they had no trouble penetrating the barrier protecting Rock, the Oldest's personality-home, and in moments were once again alone with themselves in the raging storm that encircled the vortex. For long minutes they hung in midair, whirling and darting in their most tightly linked patterns while the storm whipped them and the vortex pulled them. Then abruptly they broke their patterns and hurled themselves deliberately into the heart of the vortex itself. In a moment they had disappeared.

They seemed to feel neither motion nor lapse of time as they fell into the vortex. It was a change that came without perception or thought—a change from self to unself, from existence to void. They knew only that they had given themselves up to the vortex, that they were suddenly lost in darkness and a sense of surrounding emptiness which had no dimension. They knew without thinking that if they could have sent forth sound there would have been no echo, that a spark or even a bright flare would have brought no reflection from anywhere. For this was the place of the origin of life, and it was empty. It was up to them to fill it, if it was to be filled.

So they used the secret the Oldest had given them, the secret those at the Beginning had discovered by accident and which only one of the Oldest could have remembered. Having set themselves for this before entering the vortex, they played their individual parts automatically— selfless, unconscious, almost random acts such as even non-living energy can perform. And when all parts had been completed precisely, correctly, and at just the right time and in just the right sequence, the creating took place.

It was a foodbeast. It formed and took shape before them in the void, and grew and glowed its dull, drab glow until it was whole. For a moment it drifted there, then suddenly it was expelled from the vortex, thrown out violently as though from an explosion—away from the nothingness within, away from darkness and silence into the crashing, whipping violence of the storm outside. And with it went the Three, vomited forth with the primitive bit of life they had made.

Outside, in the storm, the Three went automatically into their tightest motion sequence, whirling and blinking around each other in desperate striving to maintain themselves amid the savagery that roiled around them. And once again they felt the powerful pull of the vortex behind them, gripping them anew now that they were outside, and they knew that the vortex would draw them in again, this time forever, unless they were able to resist it. But they found that they were nearly spent; they had lost more of themselves in the vortex than they had ever imagined possible. They hardly felt alive now, and somehow they had to withstand the crushing powers of both the storm and the vortex, and had to forge such a strongly interlinked motion-pattern that they would be able to make their way out of this place, back to calm and safety.

And there was only one way they could restore themselves enough for that.

Moving almost as one, they converged upon the mindless foodbeast they had just created, and they ate it.

That's not precisely the end of the Dance of the Changer and the Three—it does go on for a while, telling of the honors given the Three when they returned, and of Minnearo's reaction when he completed his change by reappearing around the life-mote left by a dying windbird, and of how all of the Three turned away from their honors and made their next changes almost immediately—but my own attention never quite follows the rest of it. I always get stuck at that one point in the story, that supremely contradictory moment when the Three destroyed what they had made, when they came away with no more than they had brought with them. It doesn't even achieve irony, and yet it is the emotional highpoint of the Dance as far as the Loarra are concerned. In fact, it's the *whole* point of the Dance, as they've told me with brighter sparkings and flashes than they ever use when talking about anything else, and if the Three had been able to come away from there *without* eating their foodbeast, then their achievement would have been duly noted, applauded, giggled at by the newly-changed, and forgotten within two life cycles.

And these are the creatures with whom I had to deal and whose rights I was charged to protect. I was ambassador to a planetful of things that would tell me with a straight face that two and two are orange. And yes, that's why I'm back on Earth now—and why the rest of the expedition, those who are left alive from it, are back here too.

If you could read the fifteen-microtape report I filed with Unicentral (which you can't, by the way: Unicentral always Classifies its failures), it wouldn't tell you anything more about the Loarra than I've just told you in the story of the Dance. In fact, it might tell you less, because although the report contained masses of hard data on the Loarra, plus every theory I could come up with or coax out of the minicomp, it didn't have much about the Dance. And it's only in things like that, attitude-data rather than I.Q. indices, psych reports and so on, that you can really get the full impact of what we were dealing with on Loarr.

After we'd been on the planet for four Standard Years, after we'd established contact and exchanged gifts and favors and information with the Loarra, after we'd set up our entire mining operation and had had it running without hindrance for over three years—after all that, the raid came. One day a sheet of dull purple light swept in from the horizon, and as it got closer I could see that it was a whole colony of the Loarra, their individual colors and fluctuations blending into that single purple mass. I was in the mountain, not outside with the mining extensors, so I saw all of it, and I lived through it.

They flashed in over us like locusts descending, and they hit the crawlers and dredges first. The metal glowed red, then white, then it melted. Then it was just gas that formed billowing clouds rising to the sky. Somewhere inside those clouds was what was left of the elements which had comprised seventeen human beings, who were also vapor now.

I hit the alarm and called everyone in, but only a few made it. The rest were caught in the tunnels when the Loarra swarmed over them, and they went up in smoke too. Then the automatic locks shut, and the mountain was sealed off. And six of us sat there, watching on the screen as the Loarra swept back and forth outside, cleaning up the bits and pieces they'd missed.

I sent out three of my "eyes," but they too were promptly vaporized.

Then we waited for them to hit the mountain itself . . . half a dozen frightened men huddled in the comp-room, none of us saying anything. Just sweating.

But they didn't come. They swarmed together in a tight spiral, went three times around the mountain, made one final salute-dip and then whirled straight up and out of sight. Only a handful of them were left behind out there.

After a while I sent out a fourth "eye." One of the Loarra came over, flitted around it like a firefly, blinked through the spectrum, and settled down to hover in front for talking. It was Pur—a Pur who was a thousand million billion life cycles removed from the Pur we know and love, of course, but nonetheless still pretty much Pur.

I sent out a sequence of lights and movements that translated, roughly, as, ''What the hell did you do that for?''

And Pur glowed pale yellow for several seconds, then gave me an answer that doesn't translate. Or, if it does, the translation is just ''Because.''

Then I asked the question again, in different terms, and she gave me the same answer in different terms. I asked a third time, and a fourth, and she came back with the same thing. She seemed to be enjoying the variations on the Dance; maybe she thought we were playing.

Well . . . We'd already sent out our distress call by then, so all we could do was wait for a relief ship and hope they wouldn't attack again before the ship came, because we didn't have a chance of fighting them—we were miners, not a military expedition. God knows what any military expedition could have done against energy things, anyway. While we were waiting, I kept sending out the ''eyes,'' and I kept talking to one Loarra after another. It took three weeks for the ship to get there, and I must have talked to over a hundred of them in that time, and the sum total of what I was told was this:

Their reason for wiping out the mining operation was untranslatable. No, they weren't mad. No, they didn't want us to go away. Yes, we were welcome to the stuff we were taking out of the depths of the Loarran ocean.

And, most importantly: No, they couldn't tell me whether or not they were likely ever to repeat their attack.

So we went away, limped back to Earth, and we all made our reports to Unicentral. We included, as I said, every bit of data we could think of, including an estimate of the value of the new elements on Loarr—which was something on the order of six times the wealth of Earthsystem. And we put it up to Unicentral as to whether or not we should go back.

Unicentral has been humming and clicking for ten months now, but it hasn't made a decision.

The Father-Thing

Philip K. Dick

"Dinner's ready," commanded Mrs. Walton. "Go get your father and tell him to wash his hands. The same applies to you, young man." She carried a steaming casserole to the neatly set table. "You'll find him out in the garage."

Charles hesitated. He was only eight years old, and the problem bothering him would have confounded Hillel. "I . . .," he began uncertainly.

"What's wrong?" June Walton caught the uneasy tone in her son's voice and her matronly bosom fluttered with sudden alarm. "Isn't Ted out in the garage? For heaven's sake, he was sharpening the hedge shears a minute ago. He didn't go over to the Andersons', did he? I told him dinner was practically on the table."

"He's in the garage," Charles said. "But he's . . . talking to himself."

"Talking to himself!" Mrs. Walton removed her bright plastic apron and hung it over the doorknob. "Ted? Why, he never talks to himself. Go tell him to come in here." She poured boiling black coffee in the little blue-and-white china cups and began ladling out creamed corn. "What's wrong with you? Go tell him!"

"I don't know which of them to tell," Charles blurted out desperately. "They both look alike."

June Walton's fingers lost their hold on the aluminum pan; for a moment the creamed corn slushed dangerously. "Young man—" she began angrily, but at that moment Ted Walton came striding into the kitchen, inhaling and sniffing and rubbing his hands together.

"Ah," he cried happily. "Lamb stew."

"Beef stew," June murmured. "Ted, what were you doing out there?"

Ted threw himself down at his place and unfolded his napkin. "I got the shears sharpened like a razor. Oiled and sharpened. Better not touch them—they'll cut your hand off." He was a good-looking man in his early thirties; thick blond hair, strong arms, competent hands, square face, and flashing brown eyes. "Man, this stew looks good. Hard day at the office—Friday, you know. Stuff piles up and we have to get all the accounts out by five. Al McKinley claims the department could handle twenty percent more stuff if we organized our lunch hours; staggered them so somebody was there all the time.'' He beckoned Charles over. ''Sit down and let's go.''

Mrs. Walton served the frozen peas. ''Ted,'' she said, as she slowly took her seat, ''is there anything on your mind?''

''On my mind?'' He blinked. ''No, nothing unusual. Just the regular stuff. Why?''

Uneasily June Walton glanced over at her son. Charles was sitting bolt-upright at his place, face expressionless, white as chalk. He hadn't moved, hadn't unfolded his napkin or even touched his milk. A tension was in the air; she could feel it. Charles had pulled his chair away from his father's; he was huddled in a tense little bundle as far from his father as possible. His lips were moving, but she couldn't catch what he was saying.

''What is it?'' she demanded, leaning toward him.

''The other one,'' Charles was muttering under his breath. ''The other one came in.''

''What do you mean, dear?'' June Walton asked out loud. ''What other one?''

Ted jerked. A strange expression flitted across his face. It vanished at once; but in the brief instant Ted Walton's face lost all familiarity. Something alien and cold gleamed out, a twisting, wriggling mass. The eyes blurred and receded, as an archaic sheen filmed over them. The ordinary look of a tired, middle-aged husband was gone.

And then it was back—or nearly back. Ted grinned and began to wolf down his stew and frozen peas and creamed corn. He laughed, stirred his coffee, kidded, and ate. But something terrible was wrong.

''The other one,'' Charles muttered, face white, hands beginning to tremble. Suddenly he leaped up and backed away from the table. ''Get away!'' he shouted. ''Get out of here!''

''Hey,'' Ted rumbled ominously. ''What's got into you?'' He pointed sternly at the boy's chair. ''You sit down there and eat your dinner, young man. Your mother didn't fix it for nothing.''

Charles turned and ran out of the kitchen, upstairs to his room. June Walton gasped and fluttered in dismay. ''What in the world—''

Ted went on eating. His face was grim; his eyes were hard and dark. ''That kid,'' he grated, ''is going to have to learn a few things. Maybe he and I need to have a little private conference together.''

Charles crouched and listened.

The father-thing was coming up the stairs, nearer and nearer. ''Charles!'' it shouted angrily. ''Are you up there?''

He didn't answer. Soundlessly he moved back into his room and pulled the door shut. His heart was pounding heavily. The father-thing had reached the landing; in a moment it would come in his room.

He hurried to the window. He was terrified; it was already fumbling in the dark hall for the knob. He lifted the window and climbed out on the roof. With a grunt he dropped into the flower garden that ran by the front door, staggered and gasped, then leaped to his feet and ran from the light that streamed out the window, a patch of yellow in the evening darkness.

He found the garage; it loomed up ahead, a black square against the skyline. Breathing quickly, he fumbled in his pocket for his flashlight, then cautiously slid the door up and entered.

The garage was empty. The car was parked out front. To the left was his father's workbench. Hammers and saws on the wooden walls. In the back were the lawnmower, rake, shovel, hoe. A drum of kerosene. License plates nailed up everywhere. Floor was concrete and dirt; a great oil slick stained the center, tufts of weeds greasy and black in the flickering beam of the flashlight.

Just inside the door was a big trash barrel. On top of the barrel were stacks of soggy newspapers and magazines, moldy and damp. A thick stench of decay issued from them as Charles began to move them around. Spiders dropped to the cement and scampered off; he crushed them with his foot and went on looking.

The sight made him shriek. He dropped the flashlight and leaped wildly back. The garage was plunged into instant gloom. He forced himself to kneel down, and for an ageless moment, he groped in the darkness for the light, among the spiders and greasy weeds. Finally he had it again. He managed to turn the beam down into the barrel, down the well he had made by pushing back the piles of magazines.

The father-thing had stuffed it down in the very bottom of the barrel. Among the old leaves and torn-up cardboard, the rotting remains of magazines and curtains, rubbish from the attic his mother had lugged down here with the idea of burning someday. It still looked a little like his father enough for him to recognize. He had found it—and the sight made him sick at his stomach. He hung onto the barrel and shut his eyes until finally he was able to look again. In the barrel were the remains of his father, his real father. Bits the father-thing had no use for. Bits it had discarded.

He got the rake and pushed it down to stir the remains. They were dry. They cracked and broke at the touch of the rake. They were like a discarded snake skin, flaky and crumbling, rustling at the touch. *An empty skin*. The insides were gone. The important part. This was all that remained, just the brittle, cracking skin, wadded down at the bottom of the trash barrel in a little heap. This was all the father-thing had left; it had eaten the rest. Taken the insides—and his father's place.

A sound.

He dropped the rake and hurried to the door. The father-thing was coming down the path, toward the garage. Its shoes crushed the gravel; it felt its way along uncertainly. "Charles!" it called angrily. "Are you in there? Wait'll I get my hands on you, young man!"

His mother's ample, nervous shape was outlined in the bright door-way of the house. "Ted, please don't hurt him. He's all upset about something."

"I'm not going to hurt him," the father-thing rasped; it halted to strike a match. "I'm just going to have a little talk with him. He needs to learn better manners. Leaving the table like that and running out at night, climbing down the roof—"

Charles slipped from the garage; the glare of the match caught his moving shape, and with a bellow the father-thing lunged forward.

"Come here!"

Charles ran. He knew the ground better than the father-thing, it knew a lot, had taken a lot when it got his father's insides, but nobody knew the way like *he* did. He reached the fence, climbed it, leaped into the Andersons' yard, raced past their clothesline, down the path around the side of their house, and out on Maple Street.

He listened, crouched down and not breathing. The father-thing hadn't come after him. It had gone back. Or it was coming around the sidewalk.

He took a deep, shuddering breath. He had to keep moving. Sooner or later it would find him. He glanced right and left, made sure it wasn't watching, and then started off at a rapid dog-trot.

"What do you want?" Tony Peretti demanded belligerently. Tony was fourteen. He was sitting at the table in the oak-paneled Peretti dining room, books and pencils scattered around him, half a ham-and-peanut-butter sandwich and a coke beside him. "You're Walton, aren't you?"

Tony Peretti had a job uncrating stoves and refrigerators after school at Johnson's Appliance Shop, downtown. He was big and blunt-faced. Black hair, olive skin, white teeth. A couple of times he had beaten up Charles; he had beaten up every kid in the neighborhood.

Charles twisted. "Say, Peretti. Do me a favor?"

"What do you want?" Peretti was annoyed. "You looking for a bruise?"

Gazing unhappily down, his fists clenched, Charles explained what had happened in short, mumbled words.

When he had finished, Peretti let out a low whistle. "No kidding."

"It's true." He nodded quickly. "I'll show you. Come on and I'll show you."

Peretti got slowly to his feet. "Yeah, show me. I want to see."

He got his b.b. gun from his room, and the two of them walked silently up the dark street, toward Charles's house. Neither of them said much. Peretti was deep in thought, serious and solemn-faced. Charles was still dazed; his mind was completely blank.

They turned down the Anderson driveway, cut through the back-yard, climbed the fence, and lowered themselves cautiously into Charles's backyard. There was no movement. The yard was silent. The front door of the house was closed.

They peered through the living room window. The shades were down, but a narrow crack of yellow streamed out. Sitting on the couch was Mrs. Walton, sewing a cotton T-shirt. There was a sad, troubled look on her large face. She worked listlessly, without interest. Opposite her was the father-thing. Leaning back in his father's easy chair, its shoes off, reading the evening newspaper. The TV was on, playing to itself in the corner. A can of beer rested on the arm of the easy chair. The father-thing sat exactly as his own father had sat; it had learned a lot.

"Looks just like him," Peretti whispered suspiciously. "You sure you're not bulling me?"

Charles led him to the garage and showed him the trash barrel. Peretti reached his long tanned arms down and carefully pulled up the dry, flaking remains. They spread out, unfolded, until the whole figure of his father was outlined. Peretti laid the remains on the floor and pieced broken parts back into place. The remains were colorless. Almost transparent. An amber yellow, thin as paper. Dry and utterly lifeless.

"That's all," Charles said. Tears welled up in his eyes. "That's all that's left of him. The thing has the insides."

Peretti had turned pale. Shakily he crammed the remains back in the trash barrel. "This is really something," he muttered. "You say you saw the two of them together?"

"Talking. They looked exactly alike. I ran inside." Charles wiped the tears away and sniveled; he couldn't hold it back any longer. "It ate him while I was inside. Then it came in the house. It pretended it was him. But it isn't. It killed him and ate his insides.''

For a moment Peretti was silent. ''I'll tell you something,'' he said suddenly. ''I've heard about this sort of thing. It's a bad business. You have to use your head and not get scared. You're not scared, are you?''

''No,'' Charles managed to mutter.

''The first thing we have to do is figure out how to kill it.'' He rattled his b.b. gun. ''I don't know if this'll work. It must be plenty tough to get hold of your father. He was a big man.'' Peretti considered. ''Let's get out of here. It might come back. They say that's what a murderer does.''

They left the garage. Peretti crouched down and peeked through the window again. Mrs. Walton had got to her feet. She was talking anxiously. Vague sounds filtered out. The father-thing threw down its newspaper. They were arguing.

''For God's sake!'' the father-thing shouted. ''Don't do anything stupid like that.''

''Something's wrong,'' Mrs. Walton moaned. ''Something terrible. Just let me call the hospital and see.''

''Don't call anybody. He's all right. Probably up the street playing.''

''He's never out this late. He never disobeys. He was terribly upset—afraid of you! I don't blame him.'' Her voice broke with misery. ''What's wrong with you? You're so strange.'' She moved out of the room, into the hall. ''I'm going to call some of the neighbors.''

The father-thing glared after her until she had disappeared. Then a terrifying thing happened. Charles gasped; even Peretti grunted under his breath.

''Look,'' Charles muttered. ''What—''

''Golly,'' Peretti said, black eyes wide.

As soon as Mrs. Walton was gone from the room, the father-thing sagged in its chair. It became limp. Its mouth fell open. Its eyes peered vacantly. Its head fell forward, like a discarded rag doll.

Peretti moved away from the window. ''That's it,'' he whispered. ''That's the whole thing.''

''What is it?'' Charles demanded. He was shocked and bewildered. ''It looked like somebody turned off its power.''

''Exactly.'' Peretti nodded slowly, grim and shaken. ''It's controlled from outside.''

Horror settled over Charles. ''You mean, something outside our world?''

Peretti shook his head with disgust. "Outside the house! In the yard. You know how to find?"

"Not very well." Charles pulled his mind together. "But I know somebody who's good at finding." He forced his mind to summon the name. "Bobby Daniels."

"That little colored kid? Is he good at finding?"

"The best."

"All right," Peretti said. "Let's go get him. We have to find the thing that's outside. That made *it* in there, and keeps it going..."

"It's near the garage," Peretti said to the small, thin-faced Negro boy who crouched beside them in the darkness. "When it got him, he was in the garage. So look there."

"In the garage?" Daniels asked.

"*Around* the garage. Walton's already gone over the garage, inside. Look around outside. Nearby."

There was a small bed of flowers growing by the garage, and a great tangle of bamboo and discarded debris between the garage and the back of the house. The moon had come out; a cold, misty light filtered down over everything. "If we don't find it pretty soon," Daniels said, "I got to go back home. I can't stay up much later." He wasn't any older than Charles. Perhaps nine.

"All right," Peretti agreed. "Then get looking."

The three of them spread out and began to go over the ground with care. Daniels worked with incredible speed; his thin little body moved in a blur of motion as he crawled among the flowers, turned over rocks, peered under the house, separated stalks of plants, ran his expert hands over leaves and stems, in tangles of compost and weeds. No inch was missed.

Peretti halted after a short time. "I'll guard. It might be dangerous. The father-thing might come and try to stop us." He posted himself on the back step with his b.b. gun while Charles and Bobby Daniels searched. Charles worked slowly. He was tired, and his body was cold and numb. It seemed impossible, the father-thing and what had happened to his own father, his real father. But terror spurred him on; what if it happened to his mother, or to him? Or to everyone? Maybe the whole world.

"I found it!" Daniels called in a thin, high voice. "You all come around here quick!"

Peretti raised his gun and got up cautiously. Charles hurried over; he turned the flickering yellow beam of his flashlight where Daniels stood.

The Negro boy had raised a concrete stone. In the moist, rotting soil the light gleamed on a metallic body. A thin, jointed thing with endless crooked legs was digging frantically. Plated, like an ant; a red-brown bug that rapidly disappeared before their eyes. Its rows of legs scabbled and clutched. The ground gave rapidly under it. Its wicked-looking tail twisted furiously as it struggled down the tunnel it had made.

Peretti ran into the garage and grabbed up the rake. He pinned down the tail of the bug with it. "Quick! Shoot it with the b.b. gun!"

Daniels snatched the gun and took aim. The first shot tore the tail of the bug loose. It writhed and twisted frantically; its tail dragged uselessly and some of its legs broke off. It was a foot long, like a great millipede. It struggled desperately to escape down its hole.

"Shoot again," Peretti ordered.

Daniels fumbled with the gun. The bug slithered and hissed. Its head jerked back and forth; it twisted and bit at the rake holding it down. Its wicked specks of eyes gleamed with hatred. For a moment it struck futilely at the rake; then abruptly, without warning, it thrashed in a frantic convulsion that made them all draw away in fear.

Something buzzed through Charles's brain. A loud humming, metallic and harsh, a billion metal wires dancing and vibrating at once. He was tossed about violently by the force; the banging crash of metal made him deaf and confused. He stumbled to his feet and backed off; the others were doing the same, white-faced and shaken.

"If we can't kill it with the gun," Peretti gasped, "we can drown it. Or burn it. Or stick a pin through its brain." He fought to hold onto the rake, to keep the bug pinned down.

"I have a jar of formaldehyde," Daniels muttered. His fingers fumbled nervously with the b.b. gun. "How does this thing work? I can't seem to—"

Charles grabbed the gun from him. "I'll kill it." He squatted down, one eye to the sight, and gripped the trigger. The bug lashed and struggled. Its force-field hammered in his ears, but he hung onto the gun. His finger tightened. . . .

"All right, Charles," the father-thing said. Powerful fingers gripped him, a paralyzing pressure around his wrists. The gun fell to the ground as he struggled futilely. The father-thing shoved against Peretti. The boy leaped away and the bug, free of the rake, slithered triumphantly down its tunnel.

"You have a spanking coming, Charles," the father-thing droned on. "What got into you? Your poor mother's out of her mind with worry."

It had been there, hiding in the shadows. Crouched in the darkness watching them. Its calm, emotionless voice, a dreadful parody of his father's, rumbled close to his ear as it pulled him relentlessly toward the garage. Its cold breath blew in his face, an icy-sweet odor, like decaying soil. Its strength was immense; there was nothing he could do.

"Don't fight me," it said calmly. "Come along, into the garage. This is for your own good. I know best, Charles."

"Did you find him?" his mother called anxiously, opening the back door.

"Yes, I found him."

"What are you going to do?"

"A little spanking." The father-thing pushed up the garage door. "In the garage." In the half-light a faint smile, humorless and utterly without emotion, touched its lips. "You go back in the living room, June. I'll take care of this. It's more in my line. You never did like punishing him."

The back door reluctantly closed. As the light cut off, Peretti bent down and groped for the b.b. gun. The father-thing instantly froze.

"Go on home, boys," it rasped.

Peretti stood undecided, gripping the b.b. gun.

"Get going," the father-thing repeated. "Put down that toy and get out of here." It moved slowly toward Peretti, gripping Charles with one hand, reaching toward Peretti with the other. "No b.b. guns allowed in town, sonny. Your father know you have that? There's a city ordinance. I think you better give me that before—"

Peretti shot it in the eye.

The father-thing grunted and pawed at its ruined eye. Abruptly it slashed out at Peretti. Peretti moved down the driveway, trying to cock the gun. The father-thing lunged. Its powerful fingers snatched the gun from Peretti's hands. Silently the father-thing mashed the gun against the wall of the house.

Charles broke away and ran numbly off. Where could he hide? It was between him and the house. Already, it was coming back toward him, a black shape creeping carefully, peering into the darkness, trying to make him out. Charles retreated. If there were only some place he could hide...

The bamboo.

He crept quickly into the bamboo. The stalks were huge and old. They closed after him with a faint rustle. The father-thing was fumbling in its pocket; it lit a match, then the whole pack flared up. "Charles," it said, "I know you're here, someplace. There's no use hiding. You're only making it more difficult."

His heart hammering, Charles crouched among the bamboo. Here, debris and filth rotted. Weeds, garbage, papers, boxes, old clothing, boards, tin cans, bottles. Spiders and salamanders squirmed around him. The bamboo swayed with the night wind. Insects and filth.

And something else.

A shape, a silent, unmoving shape that grew up from the mound of filth like some nocturnal mushroom. A white column, a pulpy mass that glistened moistly in the moonlight. Webs covered it, a moldy cocoon. It had vague arms and legs. An indistinct half-shaped head. As yet, the features hadn't formed. But he could tell what it was.

A mother-thing. Growing here in the filth and dampness, between the garage and the house. Behind the towering bamboo.

It was almost ready. Another few days and it would reach maturity. It was still a larva, white and soft and pulpy. But the sun would dry and warm it. Harden its shell. Turn it dark and strong. It would emerge from its cocoon, and one day when his mother came by the garage . . .

Behind the mother-thing were other pulpy white larvae, recently laid by the bug. Small. Just coming into existence. He could see where the father-thing had broken off; the place where it had grown. It had matured here. And in the garage, his father had met it.

Charles began to move numbly away, past the rotting boards, the filth and debris, the pulpy mushroom larvae. Weakly he reached out to take hold of the fence—and scrambled back.

Another one. Another larva. He hadn't seen this one, at first. It wasn't white. It had already turned dark. The web, the pulpy softness, the moistness, were gone. It was ready. It stirred a little, moved its arm feebly.

The Charles-thing.

The bamboo separated, and the father-thing's hand clamped firmly around the boy's wrist. "You stay right here," it said. "This is exactly the place for you. Don't move." With its other hand it tore at the remains of the cocoon binding the Charles-thing. "I'll help it out—it's still a little weak."

The last shred of moist gray was stripped back, and the Charles-thing tottered out. It floundered uncertainly, as the father-thing cleared a path for it toward Charles.

"This way," the father-thing grunted. "I'll hold him for you. When you're fed you'll be stronger."

The Charles-thing's mouth opened and closed. It reached greedily toward Charles. The boy struggled wildly, but the father-thing's immense hand held him down.

"Stop that, young man," the father-thing commanded. "It'll be a lot easier for you if you—"

It screamed and convulsed. It let go of Charles and staggered back. Its body twitched violently. It crashed against the garage, limbs jerking. For a time it rolled and flopped in a dance of agony. It whimpered, moaned, tried to crawl away. Gradually it became quiet. The Charles-thing settled down in a silent heap. It lay stupidly among the bamboo and rotting debris, body slack, face empty and blank.

At last the father-thing ceased to stir. There was only the faint rustle of the bamboo in the night wind.

Charles got up awkwardly. He stepped down onto the cement driveway. Peretti and Daniels approached, wide-eyed and cautious. "Don't go near it," Daniels ordered sharply. "It ain't dead yet. Takes a little while."

"What did you do?" Charles muttered.

Daniels set down the drum of kerosene with a gasp of relief. "Found this in the garage. We Daniels always used kerosene on our mosquitoes, back in Virginia."

"Daniels poured kerosene down the bug's tunnel," Peretti explained, still awed. "It was his idea."

Daniels kicked cautiously at the contorted body of the father-thing. "It's dead, now. Died as soon as the bug died."

"I guess the others'll die too," Peretti said. He pushed aside the bamboo to examine the larvae growing here and there among the debris. The Charles-thing didn't move at all, as Peretti jabbed the end of a stick into its chest. "This one's dead."

"We better make sure," Daniels said grimly. He picked up the heavy drum of kerosene and lugged it to the edge of the bamboo. "It dropped some matches in the driveway. You get them, Peretti."

They looked at each other.

"Sure," Peretti said softly.

"We better turn on the hose," Charles said. "To make sure it doesn't spread."

"Let's get going," Peretti said impatiently. He was already moving off. Charles quickly followed him and they began searching for the matches, in the moonlit darkness.

5

The Scientist

L. Sprague de Camp
and Thomas D. Clareson

From the Gothic labyrinth emerged Mary Shelley's *Frankenstein* (1818), an updating of the Faustus legend, which provides the most persevering myth of the modern scientist. Whether or not one accepts the reading of the novel that makes the nameless monster the protagonist as he pleads that all creatures be accepted for themselves—a tempting interpretation against the context of the Shelley circle, Dr. Frankenstein, crazed with guilt as a result of his experiment, established the convention of the scientist who transgresses both natural and moral law in his pursuit of knowledge. His madness was echoed in such a tale as Fitz-James O'Brien's "The Diamond Lens" (1858), in which a "mad microscopist" inadvertently destroys the beautiful woman whom he discovers in a subatomic world.

Frankenstein's experiment was repeated in such stories as William C. Morrow's "The Monster Maker" (1902) and Harle Owen Cummins's "The Man Who Made a Man" (1902). Most notably, perhaps, the monster-making experiment was performed in H. G. Wells's *The Island of Dr. Moreau,* in which the protagonist seeks to transform beasts into men, a plot that Edgar Rice Burroughs used at least twice, in *Tarzan and the Lion Man* (1934) and in the early story published in book form as *The Monster Men* (1929), in which the heroine accuses her father of playing God. Nor should one forget that the Faustus figure, acting with no regard for moral responsibility, has survived as late as Thon Taddeo in Walter Miller, Jr.'s *A Canticle for Leibowitz* (1959).

So much a part of early science fiction—or scientific romance—did the concept of the monster become that in Roy Norton's *The Vanishing Fleets* (1908), when an admiral observes an experiment involving an anti-gravity device, he can exclaim, "Frankenstein's under control!"

In American literature, the "evil" scientist assumed his more frequent guise as early as 1871 in William Rhodes's "The Case of Summerfield." The protagonist has no choice but to kill the chemist Summerfield, who threatens to ignite the oceans of the world with "a pill of my own composition and discovery" if the citizens of San Francisco do not pay him a million dollars. In Stewart Edward White's *The Sign at Six* (1912), a crazed physicist warns that he will annihilate New York City by using wireless waves to cut off the ether vibrations which carry heat and light, unless a notorious capitalist is surrendered to him for judgment. In George Allan England's *The Air Trust* (1915), a scientist in the hire of the Trusts perfects a device to remove oxygen from the air so that his employers can monopolize and sell even the air people breathe. A socialist revolution is necessary to overthrow such tyranny. On the other hand, England's protagonist in *The Golden Blight* (1916) invents a machine capable of disintegrating gold and thus helps to rid society of the Trusts. Earlier, Dr. Syx, in Garrett P. Serviss's *The Moon Metal* (1900), had gained control of the international monetary system after the discovery of vast gold fields in the Antarctic made that metal no more valuable than iron. Syx offers the world artesium as a basis for its coinage so long as he is allowed to maintain a monopoly on this material which he draws from the moon by means of a special ray. A final example from the early works is the "mad" scientist of Arthur Train and Robert Wood's *The Man Who Rocked the Earth* (1914, 1915), who unsuccessfully uses atomic power and the threat of shifting the earth's axis in an attempt to end a stalemated European war.

By and large, however, the "evil" scientist was early relegated to the pages of those innumerable series of dime, juvenile novels celebrating the adventures of boy-inventors, beginning with Frank Reade, Jr. (1884–1892) and continuing through Tom Swift and Tom Edison, Jr., to various later "Boy Adventurers" and "Boy Inventors." As antagonist, the wicked fellow bedeviled the teen-age hero with his schemes to steal the latest invention and place it in the hands of a foreign power or a monopoly. He became everything that middle-class, Anglo-Saxon America of the period detested: a paid agent of a foreign power, a Slav, a physical coward, and a nihilist—at least a socialist.

Perhaps the most memorable portrait of the evil scientist is that of the Pole, Rovinski, in Frank Stockton's *The Great Stone of Sardis* (1898), a novel intended for an adult audience. And, of course, with superficial changes, he has survived; one thinks of the heinous gadgets with which Herr Doktor Kreuger attempted to overcome the Allies in the pulp magazine *G-8 and His Battle Aces* during the 1930s, to say nothing of the devices of the stereotyped cruel scientist in present-day TV and motion pictures.

Yet, however much a role these descendants of Dr. Frankenstein have played in science fiction, the writers have not usually pictured the scientist as either insane or deliberately evil. At times he and his work have been spoofed, as in some of the fiction of Robert W. Chambers; sometimes he has been drawn as a delightfully comic individual, as in the Henry Kuttner–C. L. Moore "Gallagher" stories (published under the pseudonym Lewis Padgett). Occasionally, even in science fiction itself, he has been bitterly attacked simply because he is a scientist and holds scientific/materialistic views, as perhaps most notably in C. S. Lewis's *That Hideous Strength* (1945).

More often, because he is devoted to his work and because his specialized knowledge removes him from the everyday world of the layman, the scientist has been portrayed as an eccentric—as early as Samuel E. Chapman's *Doctor Jones' Picnic* (1898). In William Wallace Cook's *The Eighth Wonder* (1906–1907), a genius, cheated out of his patents, hopes to avenge himself by cornering "the electrical supply of the country" in giant electromagnets that he has set up in the Black Hills of South Dakota. An even worse vengeance is planned by an eccentric atomic scientist in L. Sprague de Camp's "Judgment Day" (1955) when, embittered by the teasing of his childhood peers and the indifference of his colleagues, he decides to publish a nuclear discovery that will, he believes, result in the destruction of the earth. This image of the eccentric has also been perpetuated in TV and the films, as in the classic *Them* (1953) and the recent characterization of Edgar Rice Burroughs's Abner Parry in the film travesty of *At the Earth's Core* (1976).

When the scientist has been emphasized as much as or more than his invention, some of the finest work in science fiction has portrayed an individual who experiments with—indeed, tampers with—forces which he does not fully comprehend, forces which may lead him to destruction. The classic examples are Robert Louis Stevenson's *Dr. Jekyll and Mr. Hyde* (1886) and H. G. Wells's *The Invisible Man* (1897). Realizing from his youth onward that there is a certain wickedness in his nature, Henry Jekyll develops a potion which brings that evil side of his personality into dominance and transforms him literally into the monstrous Hyde. Too late he understands that his experiment will destroy him.

Stevenson's tale of good and evil within the human being became the prototype for the many tales of dual and multiple personality that have proved so popular since the turn of the century, and that have survived in many of the explorations of "inner space" conducted by contemporary writers. Similarly, the protagonist of *The Invisible Man,* Griffin of University College, did not know that his work with molecular physics and refraction would drive him mad. He originally "beheld, unclouded by doubt, a magnificent vision of all that invisibility might mean to a man,—the mystery, the power, the freedom." These variations upon the Faustus theme must be apparent.

Of lesser proportion, the brilliant chemist of Helen Stark's *The Bacillus of Beauty* (1900) gives an outstanding student an injection which transforms her into the most beautiful woman in the world. The chemist does not realize that she will also become proud, selfish, and greedy. She finally dies of the infection. The protagonist of Richard Slee and Cornelia Atwood's *Dr. Berkeley's Discovery* (1899) develops a method by which to photograph the content of memory cells; he must use the process to prove that his murdered wife was innocent of infidelity. The experience so exhausts him that he flees to his old tutor and dies without revealing the secrets of his discovery. Donald Wandrei's "A Scientist Divides" (1934), included here, is a horror story of a scientist who does not foresee the consequences of his experiment.

One may ask why so many of the stories cited thus far are of a date preceding the appearance of the specialist magazines associated with science fiction. There are, basically, two answers. Several years ago, when asked why Freud still held so strong a grip upon the literary imagination a generation after he had lost much influence within psychological circles, a professor of psychology smiled and remarked that Freudian materials made a better story than did reinforcement theory. So it has proved with the scientist and his inventions.

Beginning with the voyages of Jules Verne—with the famous Captain Nemo, for example—a major role of the scientist in science fiction has been to play the man of reason, providing both the hardware necessary to instigate the adventure and any explanation—scientific, geographical, or otherwise—needed in the course of the plot. For example, in Ray Cummings's *The Sea Girl* (1930), Dr. Plantet remains available in the wings to comment upon the earth's receding oceans and to report the reactions of the government. His son and a companion are the ones who venture into a subterranean world, fall in love, and confront the cruel Rhana, who would destroy the surface nations. In his *The Man Who Mastered Time* (1929), Loto, son of the chemist Rogers, explains molecular theory (and thereby, supposedly, the rationale of time travel) and develops the time machine (in antecedent, off-stage action), but the majority of the narrative concerns his venture into the future to rescue a girl with whom he has fallen in love and his subsequent involvement in a civil war. Clifford D. Simak's *The Cosmic Engineers* (1939, 1950) travel to the edge of the universe but act primarily as observers of the titanic struggle taking place. One thinks, too, of Dr. Huer from *Buck Rogers* and Dr. Zarkov from *Flash Gordon*.

Not only did this role as man of reason-informant-inventor make the portrayal of the scientist as an eccentric an easier task, but it also emphasized his similarity to the detective—a fact made apparent by the creation of that literary hybrid, the scientific detective so well exemplified by Arthur B. Reeve's Craig Kennedy, once called America's Sherlock Holmes. From December 1910 through 1915, his cases were featured monthly in *Cosmopolitan,* which hailed him as "the professor of criminal science . . . Edison and Tesla rolled into one."

Because so much attention was given to current theory (as well as to the invention of imaginary gadgets, many of which anticipated subsequent developments), Craig Kennedy well represents American treatment of the scientist as hero—particularly in view of the mass audience that followed his adventures.

The portrayal of the scientist as unquestioned hero began in the 1870s and 1880s. On the one hand, especially in the emphasis given the medical doctor, the theme became a commonplace of realistic fiction. It has led through Sinclair Lewis's *Arrowsmith* to C. P. Snow's *New Men*. On the other hand, it helped to create science fiction; for had the public not been fascinated with the men and the work which were transforming America during that generation, there would have been no demand for science fiction as such. Those developments—together with the social criticism which made the last decades of the nineteenth century the great age of the literary utopia—promised some kind of paradise and opened the popular imagination to the concept of change and a promising future.

From the 1870s and 1880s until at least the end of World War I, the inventor—rather than the pure scientist—was the culture hero. Edison himself was the hero of at least one novel, Garrett P. Serviss's *Edison's Conquest of Mars* (1898), a sequel to Wells's *The War of the*

Worlds. In science fiction, the adulation took three basic forms. The first emphasized an inventor far in advance of his contemporaries who perfected some "wonderful machine." One of the earliest of these appeared in Edward Bellamy's *Dr. Heidenhoff's Process* (1880), in which the good doctor used the galvanic battery in a treatment not unlike modern shock therapy to erase from his patient's mind all memory of sin and guilt. The patient, of course, had already repented so that Heidenhoff only completed "physically what was already done morally." Although the period gave much attention to man's morality and spirit, the great majority of new inventions had as their end some material improvement.

On one end of the spectrum, as in Charles E. Bolton's *The Harris-Ingram Experiment* (1905), the finest steel mill in the world might be produced; on the other, as in Clement Fezandie's *Through the Earth* (1898), a tunnel might be bored to connect New York and Australia. Aluminum and electricity boggled the imagination; thus, countless protagonists sought some super-metal or ultimate form of energy which would profoundly affect the future of civilization. In Stewart Edward White and Samuel Hopkins Adams's *The Mystery* (1907), Karl Augustus Schermirhorn of 1409½ Spruce Street, Philadelphia, dreamed of combining rare volcanic gases with such radioactives as uranium and radium to produce *celestium,* which would provide "light, heat, motive power in incredible degrees and under such control as has never been known." Alas, the inventor was killed in the South Pacific by superstitious sailors who thought he had transformed base metal into gold; and his secret died with him.

The epitome of the treatment of the inventor as hero occurred in *Ralph 124 C 41+* (1911) by Hugo Gernsback, who, in 1926, founded *Amazing Stories.* In a sense, the story line (a triangle in which the other man is a Martian and in which Ralph revives his beloved after she dies) degenerates into a catalogue describing the wondrous machines of this future world. The attention to technology in this motif, incidentally, as well as the continued public fascination with gadgetry, explains why so many persons still hold to the erroneous idea that science fiction is concerned primarily with the prediction of things to come. The filming of Wells's forecast in the 1930s helped, of course, to fix that impression.

At one point in Gernsback's narrative, the head of state informs Ralph: "You are a great inventor... and a tremendous factor in the world's advancement. You are invaluable to humanity, and—you are irreplaceable. You belong to the world—not to yourself." No writer praised the scientist-inventor more highly; others could only increase the dramatic impact of his accomplishments.

This they did in two motifs. The first concerned the dramatization of a possible future war, a theme arising from the imperialistic arms race at the end of the century, as I. F. Clarke has shown. For example, in Stanley Waterloo's *Armageddon* (1898), American know-how produces a dirigible-type bomber to destroy the foreign navies attacking the United States, while an American inventor insists that he and his colleagues will continue the search for some ultimate weapon so terrible as to bring all war to an end. In Cleveland Moffett's *The Conquest of America* (1916), Thomas Edison emerges from his laboratory long enough to engineer the defeat of German hosts who have invaded the United States.

J. Stewart Barney's *L.P.M.: The End of the Great War* (1915) predicts a future dominated by science. Its protagonist, Edestone, discovers an ultimate energy and builds a fortresslike airship as an ultimate weapon. Assembling the nations at a conference table, he announces that henceforth the world will be ruled by ''the Aristocracy of Intelligence''—surely an echo of Wells's men of good intention. He establishes an authoritarian state with little, if any, regard for conventional morality or the individual; for him the good equals the efficient. He fulfills Schermirhorn's earlier dream of a ''dynasty of science.''

Stories of future conflicts survived World War I; but they lost their concern for conference tables and their vision of a bright tomorrow. On the one hand, they portrayed revolutions and civil wars in the far-distant future—a framework for love and adventure, as in Ray Cummings's *Tarrano, the Conqueror* (1930) and Stanley G. Weinbaum's ''The Black Flame'' (1939). American science did save the Western Hemisphere from unnamed Mongol hordes who tunneled through the earth in Gawain Edwards's *The Earth Tube* (1929), but during the 1930s in America, the motif found itself enmeshed in the endless battles of such pulp magazines as *Dusty Ayres and His Battle Birds* and *Operator #5,* in which Asiatic armies invaded the mainland of the United States. In retrospect, one realizes that it was less a question of *if* than of *when* the United States fought ''the yellow menace.'' Then, too, one wonders whether or not the easy victories in fiction and the sudden victory at Hiroshima contributed somehow to Vietnam.

The final development of the scientist-inventor as hero took place in the so-called catastrophe motif. Although it may be traced through such stories as H. G. Wells's ''The Star'' (1896) and the novels of John Wyndham and John Christopher in Britain, the motif became uniquely American in its treatment of the protagonist. Two examples may suffice. In Garrett P. Serviss's *The Second Deluge* (1912), the eccentric genius, Cosmos Versal, predicts that the world will be engulfed by a watery nebula. While his colleagues scoff, he proceeds to build a great ark in order to save a chosen few, beginning ''with the men of science [who] are the true leaders.'' Although his projected society is augmented by other survivors—a geological phenomenon saves the Rocky Mountain area from inundation—Versal remains the primary influence upon the new world, for he has ''taught the principles of eugenics and implanted deep the germs of science.''

In George Allan England's trilogy, *Darkness and Dawn* (1914), centuries after an explosion of natural gases rips the American continent and poisons the atmosphere, one man and one woman awaken from suspended animation to rebuild civilization. Of his protagonist, England remarks, ''Something drove him inexorably, for he was an engineer—and an American.'' This new Adam and Eve plan ''a kinder and saner world this time. No misery, no war, no poverty, woe, strife, creeds, oppression, tears—for we are wiser than those other folk, and there shall be no error.''

The evolution of the scientist as hero was completed. A man apart (often a daughter assisted him and fell in love, as the plot demanded), a man dealing with the ultimate secrets of nature, a man serving a public which—both in the worlds of fiction and the world of fact—did not comprehend the mysteries he worked with, he gave up his seclusion at a moment of critical danger. Be it a final war to end all wars or a threatened world cataclysm, he emerged from his laboratory to lead mankind ''onward and upward'' to the utopian millennium. (One must recall the many utopian novels of the period, as well as the science fiction of George Allan England, in which the scientist used his inventions to overthrow the ''capitalist oppressors.'') As portrayed in the early twentieth century, he may be compared to the epic or mythic hero. For he became the saviour of society, the father of a new race of men, taking unto himself powers ''no less than godlike'' to guide and rule mankind.

This vision of the scientist did not long endure. True, on a lesser scale, it did survive through the 1930s in the characterization of the Man of Bronze, Doc Savage. But one must acknowledge at once that the most enduring portrait of a scientist from the early period was British, not American. The irascible George Challenger dominated Arthur Conan Doyle's *The Lost World* (1912) and *The Poison Belt* (1913); he found a prehistoric remnant on a plateau in South America and helped friends survive the apparent end of the world. A vivid individual, he was not cut from the same cloth as his American counterparts, and by 1926, in *The Land of Mist,* he stepped into the background as Doyle indulged himself in a mixture of psychic forces and mysticism.

One can conjecture why the vision lasted so briefly. The *Titanic* sank; World War I destroyed the old order; and the Great Depression dimmed man's hope of an earthly paradise. Then came World War II, ending in Hiroshima. As early as Victor Rousseau's *The Messiah of the Cylinder* (1917) and Eugene Zamiatin's *We* (1921), the basic premise that science would lead to a better world was questioned. This rejection has led through Huxley and Orwell to the flood of dystopian nightmares that haunt both science fiction and modern fiction in general.

One should note that the impetus of this anti-utopian view was more British than American. Brian Aldiss said it well a few years ago when he remarked that suddenly it was the date when Wells had said such-and-such would take place. But it did not take place. The wars and the Depression had made impossible the world Wells and his contemporaries foresaw.

This is not to say that the scientist and his inventions were no longer celebrated. One has only to turn to the works of Dr. David H. Keller or to such individual stories as Ray Cummings's "The Secret of the Sun" (1939), C. W. Diffin's "The Power and the Glory" (1930), J. R. Fearn's "The Man Who Stopped the Dust (1934), D. W. Hall's "A Scientist Rises" (1932), or Calvin Peregoy's "The Short Wave Experiment" (1935)—all published in the magazines specializing in science fiction. In John W. Campbell's classic "Who Goes There?" (1938), the main interest lies with the efforts of the scientists to identify and restrain the alien; but in his "Twilight" (1934), the emphasis was already changing. The concern is with the effect upon the narrator of his discovery that man, cradled by a perfected technology, has lost his intellectual curiosity; his own invention is dismissed within several paragraphs. The reader is told of it; it is not dramatized.

The effect upon the narrator—herein lies the key to the changes which have taken place in science fiction since the 1930s and 1940s and, consequently, to the literary explanation of the demise of the celebration of the scientist as hero. Perhaps needed to escape the already existent emphasis upon love and adventure demanded by popular fiction, this shift also made possible the creation and exploration of innumerable alternate societies and alternate futures bearing little resemblance to the present-day world. It released science fiction from the pulp formulas and from the *cul-de-sac* of a linear extrapolation of probable developments within a single, known society. That is, the mere extension of the present into the future. On one end of the spectrum, it made possible Heinlein's future history, for even those most ardent of his engineers are concerned with the effects of their efforts, while of late even Lazarus Long has become something of a philosopher. It made possible Simak's *City* (1952); note that the Websters' experiments with the dogs—as well as the mutant's experiment with the ants—are only talked about, never presented onstage; yet they make possible a narrative structure and story line which carry a thematic denunciation of man's surrender to technology. Nor without this freedom could Frank Herbert have created his Dune trilogy.

Hiroshima completed the change in attitude toward science and the scientist. Simak has acknowledged that *City* grew out of his anger at that holocaust. Theodore Sturgeon's "Memorial" (1946), included here, well represents the reaction of the science fiction community to that holocaust. The protagonist Grenfell is certainly not Faustus; he is too aware of the moral responsibility of science and the scientist for that. But he does bring back the image of scientific man who tampers with forces he does not comprehend and cannot control. Only desolation remains; however inadvertently, man has destroyed his world. That warning lies at the heart of the dystopian mood of so much contemporary science fiction.

Despite the difference in tone, something of the same image is evoked by Larry Niven's "The Hole Man" (1973), the third story included here. The degree to which that tone is controlled by the matter-of-fact narrator can be underscored if one tries to imagine the story from any other point of view. Andrew Lear is neither hero nor villain in the eyes of the narrator; he has characteristics which in other hands or at another period could make him another stereotype of the eccentric scientist far in advance of his contemporaries. He differs from other scientists represented here in that he acknowledges making a mistake; yet it is perhaps that admission itself which complicates the implications of the ending. Whatever he did, now he can continue his studies. Thus, although Niven's characterization portrays Lear as the most human of the scientists, the reader cannot be certain how much of that humanity he has surrendered to his quest for knowledge.

Full circle.

Without the scientist there could be no science fiction, whether the reader and audience are more interested in his specific accomplishments—his gadgetry—or in the effect of those accomplishments upon society. One might well argue that the portrayal of the scientist himself provides the most telling index to society's changing attitudes toward science.

BIBLIOGRAPHY

Aldiss, Brian, *Frankenstein Unbound,* 1974 (Random House)
Asimov, Isaac, *I, Robot,* 1968 (Panther)
Campell, John, *Who Goes There? and Other Stories,* 1955 (Dell)
Clarke, Arthur C., *Prelude to Space,* 1954 (Gnome Press)
Compton, D. G., *The Steel Crocodile,* 1970 (Ace)
Cummins, Ray, *The Man Who Mastered Time,* 1929 (McClurg)
de Camp, Sprague, *Judgment Day,* 1956 (Fredrick Fell) (in *The Best SF
    Stories and Novels,* ed. by T. E. Ditkay)
Gernsback, Hugo, *Ralph 124 C 41 +,* 1925 (Stratford)
Herbert, Frank, *Destination: Void,* 1966 (Berkley)
Lewis, C. S., *That Hideous Strength,* 1945 (Bodley Head)
Malzberg, Barry N., *Beyond Apalla,* 1972 (Random House)
Miller, Walter M., Jr., *A Canticle for Leibowitz,* 1960 (Lippincott)
Oliver, Chad, *Shadows in the Sun,* 1954 (Ballantine)
Shelley, Mary, *Frankenstein,* 1818
Simak, Clifford D., *The Cosmic Engineers,* 1950 (Gnome Press)
Stevenson, Robert Louis, *The Strange Case of Dr. Jekyll and Mr. Hyde,*
Weinbaum, Stanley, *The Black Flame,* 1948 (Fantasy Press)
Wells, H. G., *The Invisible Man,* 1897 (Pearson)

A Scientist Divides

Donald Wandrei

I shall always remember him as he stood there by the slides and microscope that summer afternoon three years ago. His face was enkindled with the glow that is present only at the immediate moment of a great discovery. He held the beaker in his hands and looked at it with all the loving pride of a mother studying the first babe.

Yet it was characteristic of Dr. Weylith that his eyes wore a far-away look. It was never the discovery that mattered so much to him, as it was the potential and far-reaching effects that future generations might enjoy.

Dr. R. L. Weylith was then one of the country's brilliant biologists. He had made a name for himself by his exhaustive researches into the nature of cells and cell structures, chromosomes, hæmin, and more esoteric minutiae of the human organism. He was one of the men who developed the hyperoxygenic treatment for schizophrenia. He successfully isolated, identified, and photographed the first of the nonfilterable viruses. Yet he had scarcely reached thirty when he received the highest honor, the most distinguished medal, that science bestows on its own. And he was only thirty-five that afternoon three years ago.

A slender, quiet man, he carried himself with a curious and disconcerting air of alert detachment, as though he saw everything, but could not pause in his progress toward ultimate goals. Always tolerant, gracious, and generous, he encouraged and helped others even when his own work suffered. Gifted with a keen mind and vivid imagination, he took advantage of every educational facility to specialize in the methods of science, making biology his particular field.

He was no mere grubber of facts. His work was precise, elaborately documented, but also linked to the great dreams that lured him on. He was that rare and enviable type—the pure scientist in his technique, the pure visionary in his mind, the successful joiner of both in his work.

Does this sound as if I was writing his epitaph? I am. Or I hope I am, since I cannot be positive.

Our relationship was somewhat unusual but readily understandable. I had long been interested in all phases of modern science, but without the aptitude or the interest in specializing in any given field. I was fascinated by the possibilities of new discoveries and naturally turned to writing. Professor Weylith, on the other hand, confined his published work to material that would bear the strictest and most technical scrutiny.

It was difficult for me to find laymen sufficiently versed in various categories of science to talk to, and it would have been suicidal for Weylith to expound some of his more fanciful ideas to his colleagues. But the two of us got along famously, for in him I found a man I could deeply admire, and in me I hope he at least enjoyed an enthusiastic listener.

I advanced the idea that caught his imagination and set him off on the years of investigation which culminated that afternoon. Now I regret ever having mentioned it.

For the years that I knew him, I saw him regularly and discussed everything above the sun and beneath the clouds. I was the only person who knew the nature of his last experiment. It is just as well that he permitted no one else to share the secret. The world would be a less complacent globe.

Yet in spite of our numerous conversations, I did not go with a full understanding of what might ensue that afternoon when Dr. Weylith telephoned and asked me to drop in at his laboratory. I had originally thrown off my suggestion as the germ for a fictional romance.

"Science tells us," I had once remarked, "that the higher organisms all evolved from a single-celled animalcule or amœba which represented the first life-bud eons ago. From that humble beginning came vertebrates and man. Why may not man himself now be only a similar basic cell out of which even vaster and more complex organisms will evolve in the course of ages? Imagine what would happen if a superscientist treated a man as such a cell and then, in the laboratory, constructed from one or dozens of men a creature of the year one billion!"

That was the thought which fired Weylith's imagination, but not quite in the way I believed. Through nearly five years of work, he kept his real objective to himself, while discussing my suggestion as if he was making progress on it. Since the idea was merely fictional, and rather far-fetched, I did not seriously think he would turn it into reality.

Then, too, he was noncommittal over the phone. He merely suggested that I drop around if I would like to see something interesting. From his casual tone, I suspected that his request had to do with the topic we had often discussed. I decided he had probably made an important new discovery in the matter of cellular structure or an allied subject. I knew he had been making extensive researches of late in cosmic radiations, chlorophyll, hæmin, hormones, and glandular secretions.

It was about three in the afternoon when I walked into his laboratory and saw him with the beaker in his hands. The westward-slanting sun poured a flood of light through the windows, hot light, molten light, but the air-conditioned laboratory was cool and dustless. The window-staves split the light into rectangles. They left a cross on the side of his smock. His face seemed a little tired, evidently from days and nights of arduous work, but weariness never prevented a quick smile of welcome.

"It's worth being half cooked in that sun just to bask in the coolness here," I remarked.

"Is it hot out? I hadn't noticed. But come over and look at this."

I made my way between the tables of chemicals, slides, tissues, tinted specimens, microscopes, and other apparatus.

"What is it?" I asked when I reached his side.

He held the little beaker toward me. Inside it nestled a drop of opaque, reddish-gray stuff. There was only a drop, but nothing ever before gave me the creeps like that tiny nodule. It seemed to quiver with a strange and restless motion. It elongated, contracted, rested, made an abortive effort to roll up the side of the glass toward Weylith's hand.

The reflected sunlight glistened on it. It looked pinkish, like an albino's eyes, slimy, like an angleworm's tip. It suggested in no single or specific way such diabolic and distorted anthropomorphic traits, so sinister a human nature in so subhuman a way, that I made no effort to take the beaker. The drop almost mesmerized me.

I bent over, and it slid up the side of the beaker so swiftly that I shrank away. The globule fell back, palpitated faintly and restlessly like a heart endlessly beating for a body to clothe it.

"What is it? I can tell you right now I don't like it, I won't touch it, and I refuse to have anything to do with it."

Weylith smiled. "That is why you write fiction. You romanticize things, I investigate them and find out their nature. Then they lose their mystery and neither repel nor attract. They are reduced to facts."

"Yes, but then *you* romanticize them by planning their ultimate possible use in the furthest future world. You haven't told me what this is."

Weylith looked at the beaker thoughtfully. He shook it a trifle. The drop raced madly around the spot where his hand held the glass. "Hungry little devil, isn't it? It hasn't eaten since I made it."

"Made it? Out of what? What for? How?"

"Not so fast! I'll go back a little. Do you remember the day, years ago, when you suggested the idea that man might be only the basic cell of an immensely more complicated organism yet to develop?"

"Of course! I said also that it would be wonderful if some scientist could only speed up the cell and produce overnight the homunculus of the year one billion. Don't tell me that this is it?"

Weylith shook his head. "Hardly! No; that isn't quite the line I was following. Your suggestion captured my fancy, but I went after it in a different way. After you left that time, I thought a good deal about the idea. Science has accepted as truth the evolution of multicellular organisms such as man from an ancient, original, single cell. You suggested that man himself might be, so to speak, only the real basic cell of which the primeval cell was only a part, and that out of man might evolve a complex being almost beyond our power to envision. Right?''

''Yes. Then what?''

''It occurred to me that a reduction instead of expansion might be equally interesting for speculation. The simple cell produced, through countless mutations, man, and was itself changed. Why, therefore, might not man carry within himself a different kind of cell, substance, or essence, which was his full being expressed in its least compass? I don't mean sperm, of course; I mean something that was the minimum refinement of blood, bone, tissue, organs, glands, secretions, and so on; perhaps inert, but at least possessed of the capacity for life; a modern cell that was the counterpart to the ancient, simple cell.

''Perhaps it might be found in extracts of each part of him, interfused into a unit. Perhaps he contained a hitherto-undiscovered gland or secretion that had the latent capacity of summarizing his nature. Perhaps one could construct a centimeter model of man, from tiny parts of the brain, the nervous system, the skeleton, the muscles, the organs, the blood system, the glands, the hair, the cartilage, and imbue it with life. Perhaps one might take cells and subject them to enzymic, metabolistic, biochemical, or other changes that would convert them into what might be called homoplasm.''

''Homoplasm?'' I queried.

''To distinguish it from protoplasm. And here it is.''

I looked at the malignant little drop with intensified curiosity and dislike. To tell the truth, Dr. Weylith's comments had partly escaped me, I was so fascinated by the actions of the globule. I heard without comprehension. One graphic picture is mightier than a thousand words. I saw the result of his experiment, and I had only half ears for the cause, the explanation.

But I managed to ask, simply for lack of any more intelligent comment that I might make: ''What does it do?''

Weylith answered candidly. ''I don't know. I isolated homoplasm this morning, and I haven't had time to go further. It appears to be sentient, animate, and locomotory, as you can see. What its other properties are, I don't know. I can't even say for sure that it is what I believe it is. It may be just a particularly voracious bit of protoplasm-plus, without any individual or special characteristics. I called you because I thought you would be interested in any case, since it was your suggestion that set me on my way. There are a good many tests yet to be made.

"For instance, how long will it last in its present state? Does it require food? If so, what kind? If not, why not? Are its actions spontaneous or deliberate? Instinctive or rational? Can it exist without air? And by what magic is it replacing the energy that it burns in its motions? It has hardly stayed still a minute in the last eight hours, yet it is as active as at creation. Is it directly converting natural or artificial light, or both, into energy If so, it is the most wonderful little machine devised up to now and opens visions of immeasurable energies that can be harnessed for man.

"What everlasting dreams hover around this simple bit of homoplasm! Just to think at it, you wouldn't think that this one globule is the full complexity of man reduced to a minimum, would you?"

"No," I said frankly. "I wouldn't, and I don't want to think so. My idea wasn't so hot after all, if this is what it boiled down to."

"On the contrary, it was a brilliant speculation. One thing you writers of science-fiction possess that most scientists lack is freedom from fact. You can start out with almost any concept, expand it to its most imaginative limits, even take liberties with science, and produce a vision of the years to come. But we who work in the laboratory must always offer substantial proof, back up every step with fact, and document our theories or claims by evidence that can stand the laboratory test.

"Domination by fact is both science's greatest safeguard and its worst drag. X discovers a cure for cancer. He knows it is a cure, but cannot prove it immediately. He tests it for years in every conceivable way on all sorts of animal tissues before he announces his results to the public and permits application to human sufferers. In the meantime, tens of thousands of victims die.

"Or take homoplasm. I know what it is. I've a good understanding of what it will do, and what its functions, properties, and actions are. That's why I keep it tightly stoppered. But I could no more announce its discovery to the world without perhaps irreparable loss of prestige now than I could make time run backward."

"It wouldn't surprise me if you even succeeded in doing that," I remarked, and sincerely. "All I can say about your homoplasm I've already said. I refuse to have anything to do with it. You could extol its virtues till doomsday, and I still wouldn't like it. See how it's quivering? It's been squirting around the beaker like a crazy thing while you've been talking. It goes wild every time it gets near your fingers and that seems to be as often as it can. No. I'd get rid of it if it was my choice.''

''You may be even nearer the truth than you think,'' Dr. Weylith answered ambiguously.

A ray of sunlight slanted through the glass of the beaker and turned the living stuff to a drop of scarlet flame, glistening like a bead of blood, beautiful in its own evil way. I shrugged my shoulders in dislike of it.

''Put it up on that shelf out of harm's way,'' Dr. Weylith suggested with a hint of good-natured banter we often indulged in.

''Not I, thanks. I wouldn't touch that beaker for a million dollars. Or a thousand, anyway.''

Dr. Weylith, his sensitive features again wearing a rapt expression as his dreaming mind was absorbed by the homoplasm and fascination over the endless fields of conjecture it opened, stood on tiptoe and placed the beaker on a shelf.

I looked out of the window and saw the sun burn across pavements with a glare that bubbled asphalt and sent the heat waves dancing.

A faint tinkle and a heavier thud came from behind me. I whirled around.

Dr. Weylith sprawled on the floor, face up. A gash laid open his right forehead. I sprang to his side, saw that the fragments of glass were imbedded in the wound, decided instantly it was a case for medical care. He must have lost his balance in attempting to place the beaker on the shelf, and it fell, shattering on his forehead and knocking him unconscious. I cursed myself for my reluctance to heed his request, even though it had been made in jest. The flow of blood was steady, but not large.

For fear of driving the splinters of glass deeper, I merely placed a clean handkerchief on the injury to act as a clotting agent while I raced to the phone in another room.

I called the office of Dr. Weylith's personal physician, but was told he was in the midst of an operative case. To save time, I then called an ambulance and asked for immediate service. Weylith's name worked magic. I could expect the ambulance in fifteen minutes at most. I hurried back to the laboratory.

It does not seem to me that I could have been more than a half minute, but perhaps the telephone delayed me two or three minutes in all. It really makes no difference since there is nothing I might possibly have done had I returned sooner.

When I entered the laboratory and rounded the tables obstructing my view, I received a shock of horror such as I hope may never be repeated. Weylith's head was gone. The upper half of his clothing sagged, but a squirming and hellish motion affected it from some amorphous substance within. Almost as fast as my eyes could follow, the rippling spread down the torso and limbs. I was paralyzed in my tracks. I remembered the pinkish nodule, but that dreadful thought only served to stun me more.

Then, out of that loose and shapeless heap of clothing slid a mass a million times the size of that original drop of ooze; a reddish-gray pulp of heaving and awful life which left not the tiniest bone behind, not the least particle except the glass splinters and the now flat clothing. The stuff quivered damnably, shivered as in a wind, split in two by simple fission. The sun imbued those two mounds of jelly with a smoky and sinister glow. And now they began to eddy and swirl and extend upward. They elongated here, contracted there, filled out elsewhere, assumed new forms of terrifying significance.

"No! No!" I shrieked.

Before me stood two identical Weyliths, naked, each half the size of the original man. There was a duller luster on the faces. In the eyes there was nothing whatever of Weylith's intelligent and friendly gaze. They were dangerous, menacing, primeval eyes, and they stared at me. I wondered madly if each creature had only half the brain of Weylith, or no brain at all.

The homoplasmic drop, having absorbed every germ of Weylith's body, had divided, and each mass had built up a new body from the image of man that was inherent in it. That reproduction was faithful even to the cut on the forehead. And now a stranger occurrence deepened the spell upon me.

The two Weyliths took a step forward, but out of the cuts oozed a rapidly swelling flood of the pink stuff that deliquesced the bodies almost as soon as they had been formed.

The sweat trickled from my face, but my eyes burned and my forehead was hot, dry.

The two heaps quivered hellishly again, and I thanked the stars that no one else had witnessed the transformation. Or was I mad? Perhaps corroboration was the saving grace I needed lest I find this to be only a hideous hallucination. And still I stared, utterly incapable of motion.

The strange life puddles stirred eerily. They narrowed in the middle and separated into four. They swirled into mounting shapes until four grisly phantoms, four pigmy Weyliths, glared at me from eyes ferocious with basic, subhuman, food desire. The four demons tottered toward me, their pink-white eyes blank of any intelligence. They were eyes neither of man nor vertebrate nor fish, neither insane nor sane— just hungry eyes.

I acted as I certainly did not wish to act. I wanted to leave that laboratory forever behind. Something drove me, some subconscious but lightning intuition of what might happen, some unreasoned desire to do what my dead friend would have preferred. I sprang to the door, locked it, whirled around.

Already the four Weyliths were headless. They stood in their tracks like so many decapitated monstrosities, while the streams of ooze pouring down took with them the chests, torsos, limbs, every vestige of those abominable entities.

The speed of the cycle increased perceptibly and proportionately as the mass diminished. The two scientists had divided into four and the four into eight in only three fourths the time that the scientist had first divided. The life of the eight little things was correspondingly shorter, but they moved a step closer.

Then, always more rapidly and horribly, the fission and reproduction of form, the deliquescence and fission again, swept through the cycle. No nightmare was ever more gripping or terrifying by its distortion of the familiar than this travesty of the highest type of human being.

With every fission, the characteristics of the body became coarser, less human, more corrupt and devolutionary, until there was not even a remote resemblance. Weylith, divided and redivided, swept into the ceaselessly changing reduction of this appalling life-cycle, became so many naked little animals ravening for food.

They closed in on all sides. I lost my head. I kicked at one of the new knee-high creatures. My shoe plowed into it, and it clung like glue. Panic seized me, but the return to plasmic state caused the stuff to fall to the floor by gravity.

I dashed for the window and leaped on a radiator coil. It was two stories to the cement sidewalk.

I faced the laboratory. It swarmed with the ever-increasing horde of that ever-contracting spawn—128, 256, 512—I lost count of the doubling and redoubling. They were moving now. They made wailing cries. A shrill and abysmal moan of hunger swept from their ranks when they assumed their momentary and minute imitation of man's estate. A sucking sibilance filled the laboratory when they returned to the homoplasmic stage of their brief life-cycle. Hummocks of reddish jelly. Little ratlike things of human semblance. Surge toward the radiator. Deliquescence. Smaller balls of homoplasm. Retreat into slime, advance into anthropoid form. I saw a million centuries bridged in seconds.

For a few minutes I felt comparatively safe. But I had only begun to consider the peril of my situation when a new menace rose. A great swarm of the viscous plasms turned into inch-high caricatures of Weylith at the foot of the radiator. Instantly they locked, scrambled up, shot a living pyramid toward me. The wriggling mass with all its thousands of intertwined limbs and pin-point eyes shining with baleful luster fell short of me by so small a distance that I was on the verge of leaping out of the window. Then the column collapsed, and I shivered, for I knew the next cycle would not fail of its objective.

What could I do? No matter what the cost, I could not escape from the laboratory, could not loose that demoniacal horde upon the world. Somehow I must destroy it. Somehow I must save myself and obliterate every trace of these subhuman monsters. And every moment the task grew more difficult. I was still reasonably certain that the stuff could not get out. The laboratory had a concrete floor. The windows were weather-stripped, and the door soundproofed. The ventilators were in the ceiling. But if the things became much smaller, they might seep out through invisible cracks and crevices.

The column of myriad, terrible little beasts, like human beetles, shot toward me again in a rising geyser. The nearest table was fifteen feet away. I leaped in panic. The column swerved instantly. Even terror did not give me strength enough. I landed on a cluster of the plasms and felt them squirt in all directions as if I had splashed in a puddle.

I bounded to the table. A jar of hydrochloric acid stood on it. I sloshed the acid over my shoe, wiped it with a piece of waste cloth. My hands burned. I poured the container on the floor. The acid spread, ate its way in a widening pool. A thin but sharply reedy wail crept up. The whole laboratory was paved with a film of ceaselessly undulating slime that alternated with antlike things, save where the acid lay.

There came a pounding on the door. "Ambulance for Dr. Weylith!"

"Just a minute!" I shouted, and made no effort to move.

In the stress of that moment, my senses must have become preternaturally keen, my mind clear as seldom before. I was in so tight a spot that no matter what happened, I must lose out somewhere. My only choice lay between trying to save my own skin for what it was worth, or accepting all risks and doing what I could to annihilate every last mote of the homoplasm.

The beating on the door repeated. "Open!"

"Dr. Weylith has gone elsewhere! I'll be there in a few seconds if you want to wait!" I called.

On the next table lay an electric furnace, gas burners, thermite and cordite. And a blowtorch. I don't know what Weylith used them for. The moment I saw them, I sprang over, pumped the torch, and lighted it. The flame hissed forth with the roaring sound peculiar to gasoline blowtorches. And suddenly I felt protected.

I seared the floor. Foot by foot, I went over the laboratory. I burned my way ahead in swinging swaths. I scorched the legs of every table, the base of each wall. All surfaces in contact with the floor, I subjected to that crisping flame. And a dim, hideous, murmuring cry squealed constantly in my ears, punctuated by the pounding on the door. There was a sickening smell in the air which the ventilators were powerless to carry off.

Nauseated, shaking like the jelly I had destroyed, and on the verge of collapse, I finally extinguished the blowtorch and tossed it on a table. I scarcely cared what happened now. Then I opened the door.

Probably most people are familiar with the incidents of the next six months. The circumstances were highly suspicious. I have no complaint against the authorities for trying to establish a case against me. It was out of the question for me even to hint at what I had seen. I took no one, not even the lawyer, into my confidence.

The case became one of headlines through no fault of my own except the desire to protect the memory of Weylith, who was as dear a friend as I ever had. Perhaps I was foolish. I am in no position to say. But I feel absolutely certain that the case would have been far more notorious and given over to infinitely greater reams of speculation had I tried to explain exactly what happened.

So I botched the tragedy. I told the ambulance men that Dr. Weylith had already been taken away. I would not tell them where. The police became inquisitive, questioned me. They wanted to know why I had called a physician, then an ambulance, why the laboratory floor was seared. Weylith was listed as missing. Suspicion of murder developed.

Doubts of my sanity arose when I gave confused explanations or none at all. There were detentions, specialists, grillings, examinations. A grand jury investigated and handed up a presentment. But there were no witnesses, no proof of homicide, and no trace of a body. Eventually the indictment was quashed for lack of evidence. I was a free, but discredited, man.

That was nearly three years ago. And what saved me as much as anything was an occasional rumor that Weylith had been seen in other parts of the country.

To me, this is the most heartbreaking aspect of the tragedy. I did my best to give Weylith the absolute oblivion he would have wished, but I must have failed. I thought I was thorough, but evidently I was not thorough enough. The division and subdivision and fission of that strange plasm must have reached such minute degrees and such immense numbers that the blowtorch was inadequate.

Perhaps some of the plasm adhered to my shoes in spite of the acid. Or it may have crept up the walls. Or a few flecks might have found some opening invisible to human eyes and thus made their way out of the laboratory. Even so, I think the stuff might have worn itself out—if vertebrate forms had not been susceptible to wounds and injuries; for the homoplasm would apparently never have spread had it not been for direct blood openings.

A child, scratched by brambles, was seen to cross a field near Greenwich one morning. She was never seen again. A caretaker pulling weeds claimed he looked up and saw a naked man, brutally resembling the missing Dr. Weylith, suddenly appear in a field. The child would have reached there about the time.

But the caretaker unfortunately added that he was so shocked that he rubbed his eyes. When he looked again, there were two naked men, and they seemed smaller because they were making toward a clump of woods. His story would have been completely discounted except that the child's clothing was later found near the spot.

A butcher in Chillicothe left his store one noon to deliver an order around the corner. When he returned, he saw a strange little naked boy climbing out of a window. He ran shouting toward his store and asserted that a gang of brats swarmed from every opening. His narrative would also have been met with disbelief except for the fact that not an ounce of meat remained in his shop, with one exception. Cuts, loins, quarters, whole carcasses, liver, even suet, were stolen. Only sausage in casings were left. He thought he had recently seen a picture of the first youth, but he could not remember where.

At various times, in the years since, and in widely scattered parts not only of North America but of the world, the missing Dr. Weylith has been reported seen. A legend grew up about him, rivaling that of

Ambrose Bierce. Sometimes the news dispatches carried items about his reappearance simultaneously in opposite countries of the globe, and in places thousands of miles apart.

And with disturbing frequency, the press also carried accounts of phantom scavengers that looted food markets; of hordes of debased, naked, wild boys who vanished as suddenly as they were seen, leaving no trace behind them; of anthropoid, adult footprints that successively and mysteriously became youth's footprints, children's steps, the marks of babes, and finally ended in mid-fields.

A party of explorers came upon an African village where stew was still cooking over a hot fire. But not a trace of any man, woman, child, or animal was found, nor were the villagers ever discovered. There were dwindling footprints, no other clue. I alone knew what had happened, and I preserved my silence.

To this lengthy, and still-growing list, I will add but one more incident, the incident that caused me to record these facts for the guidance of people, before I, too, disappear of my own choice.

The episode occurred last night. It had been a hot day, and I went for a long walk in the country. As evening drew near, I found myself sauntering down a narrow road that wound between pastures and fields and hills and an occasional farmhouse. The sun hung just above the horizon, and was already half set, when I paused to rest against the wooden fence inclosing a pasture.

Cows munched in the field. Most of them lay under the shade of trees on the far side of the field, but a couple of Jerseys grazed near by and lazily switched off the attack of flies and gnats. It was a peaceful, rural scene that I admired.

Then one of the Jerseys bellowed. The other moved away. The rest of the herd shifted uneasily. The first Jersey mooed plaintively. Sickness and nausea overcame me when I saw it melt down into a swelling puddle, but horror kept me watching though I could have predicted what was coming. The cow ceased struggling, and its eyes glazed while the fore half of its carcass still remained, but that, too, swiftly dissolved into the reddish heap.

Then that shapeless pile took form, and against the dark and lurid western sky stood outlined the gigantic and naked figure of a man. Man? It was a dreadful parody, a grotesque and misshapen monster, of bestial head, apelike hands, and animal feet, whose body was only faintly human in nature, and of a blackish hue.

For seconds the giant stood there, before plodding sluggishly toward the rest of the herd, and it lowered its head to utter a sound, a throatless and primeval food howl, the like of which I never heard before. The huge shape collapsed into slime, and the slime fissioned, and I fled on my way while twin but smaller monsters rose behind.

There is nothing more to add. There is nothing that I or anyone can do, now. The homoplasm carries within it some instinctive or hereditary or vestigial image of man. Because its human manifestations are invariably cast in the likeness of Dr. Weylith, I must assume that he created the original stuff from his own body. So long as one drop of that now world-migrated homoplasm survives, so long will there be theft of animal food throughout the globe, and so long will the everlasting figure of Dr. Weylith be re-created, though it be till the end of time.

Memorial

Theodore Sturgeon

The Pit, in A.D. *5000, had changed little over the centuries. Still it was an angry memorial to the misuse of great power; and because of it, organized warfare was a forgotten thing. Because of it, the world was free of the wasteful smoke and dirt of industry. The scream and crash of bombs and the soporific beat of marching feet were never heard, and at long last the earth was at peace.*

To go near The Pit was slow, certain death, and it was respected and feared, and would be for centuries more. It winked and blinked redly at night, and was surrounded by a bald and broken tract stretching out and away over the horizon; and around it flickered a ghostly blue glow. Nothing lived there. Nothing could.

With such a war memorial, there could only be peace. The earth could never forget the horror that could be loosed by war.

That was Grenfell's dream.

Grenfell handed the typewritten sheet back. ''That's it, Jack. My idea, and—I wish I could express it like that.'' He leaned back against the littered workbench, his strangely asymmetrical face quizzical. "Why is it that it takes a useless person adequately to express an abstract?"

Jack Roway grinned as he took back the paper and tucked it into his breast pocket. "Interestin' question, Grenfell, because this *is* your expression, the words *are* yours. Practically verbatim. I left out the 'er's and 'Ah's' that you play conversation hopscotch with, and strung together all the effects you mentioned without mentioning any of the technological causes. Net result: you think I did it, when you did. You think it's good writing, and I don't."

"You don't?"

Jack spread his bony length out on the hard little cot. His relaxation was a noticeable act, like the unbuttoning of a shirt collar. He laughed.

"Of course I don't. Much too emotional for my taste. I'm just a fumbling aesthete—useless, did you say? Mm-m-m—yeah. I suppose so." He paused reflectively. "You see, you cold-blooded characters, you scientists, are the true visionaries. Seems to me the essential difference between a scientist and an artist is that the scientist mixes his hopes with patience.

"The scientist visualizes his ultimate goal, but pays little attention to it. He is all caught up with the achievement of the next step upward. The artist looks so far ahead that more often than not he can't see what's under his feet; so he falls flat on his face and gets called useless by scientists. But if you strip all of the intermediate steps away from the scientist's thinking, you have an artistic concept to which the scientist responds distantly and with surprise, giving some artist credit for deep perspicacity purely because the artist repeated something the scientist said."

"You amaze me," Grenfell said candidly. "You wouldn't be what you are if you weren't lazy and superficial. And yet you come out with things like that. I don't know that I understand what you just said. I'll have to think—but I do believe that you show all the signs of clear thinking. With a mind like yours, I can't understand why you don't use it to build something instead of wasting it in these casual interpretations of yours."

Jack Roway stretched luxuriously. "What's the use? There's more waste involved in the destruction of something which is already built than in dispersing the energy it would take to help build something. Anyway, the world is filled with builders—and destroyers. I'd just as soon sit by and watch, and feel things. I like my environment, Grenfell. I want to feel all I can of it, while it lasts. It won't last much longer. I want to touch all of it I can reach, taste of it, hear it, while there's time. What is around me, here and now, is what is important to me. The acceleration of human progress, and the increase of its mass—to use your terms—are taking humanity straight to Limbo. You, with your work, think you are fighting humanity's inertia. Well, you are. But it's the kind of inertia called momentum. You command no force great enough to stop it, or even to change its course appreciably.''

"I have atomic power."

Roway shook his head, smiling. "That's not enough. No power is enough. It's just too late."

"That kind of pessimism does not affect me," said Grenfell. "You can gnaw all you like at my foundations, Jack, and achieve nothing more than the loss of your front teeth. I think you know that."

"Certainly I know that. I'm not trying to. I have nothing to sell, no one to change. I am even more impotent than you and your atomic power; and you are completely helpless. Uh—I quarrel with your use of the term 'pessimist,' though. I am nothing of the kind. Since I have resolved for myself the fact that humanity, as we know it, is finished, I'm quite resigned to it. Pessimism from me, under the circumstances, would be the pessimism of a photophobiac predicting that the sun would rise tomorrow."

Grenfell grinned. "I'll have to think about that, too. You're such a mass of paradoxes that turn out to be chains of reasoning. Apparently you live in a world in which scientists are poets and the grasshopper has it all over the ant."

"I always did think that ant was a stinker."

"Why do you keep coming here, Jack? What do you get out of it? Don't you realize I'm a criminal?"

Roway's eyes narrowed. "Sometimes I think you wish you were a criminal. The law says you are, and the chances are very strong that you'll be caught and treated accordingly. Ethically, you know you're not. It sort of takes the spice out of being one of the hunted."

"Maybe you're right," Grenfell said thoughtfully. He sighed. "It's so completely silly. During the war years, the skills I had were snatched up and the government flogged me into the Manhattan Project, expecting, and getting, miracles. I have never stopped working along the same lines. And now the government has changed the laws, and pulled legality from under me."

"Hardly surprising. The government deals rather severely with soldiers who go on killing other soldiers after the war is over." He held up a hand to quell Grenfell's interruption. "I know you're not killing anyone, and are working for the opposite result. I was only pointing out that it's the same switcheroo. We the people," he said didactically, "have, in our sovereign might, determined that no atomic research be done except in government laboratories. We have then permitted our politicians to allow so little for maintenance of those laboratories— unlike our overseas friends—that no really exhaustive research can be done in them. We have further made it a major offense to operate such a bootleg lab as yours." He shrugged. "Comes the end of mankind. We'll get walloped first. If we put more money and effort into nuclear research than any other country, some other country would get walloped first. If we last another hundred years—which seems doubtful—some poor, spavined, underpaid government researcher will stumble on the aluminum-isotope space-heating system you have already perfected."

"That was a little rough," said Grenfell bitterly. "Driving me underground just in time to make it impossible for me to announce it. What a waste of time and energy it is to heat homes and buildings the way they do now! Space heating—the biggest single use for heat-energy—and I have the answer to it over there." He nodded toward a compact cube of lead alloys in the corner of the shop. "Build it into a foundation, and you have controllable heat for the life of the building, with not a cent for additional fuel and practically nothing for maintenance." His jaw knotted. "Well, I'm glad it happened that way."

"Because it got you started on your war memorial—The Pit? Yeah. Well, all I can say is, I hope you're right. It hasn't been possible to scare humanity yet. The invention of gunpowder was going to stop war, and didn't. Likewise the submarine, the torpedo, the airplane, and that two-by-four bomb they pitched at Hiroshima."

"None of that applies to The Pit," said Grenfell. "You're right; humanity hasn't been scared off war yet; but the Hiroshima bomb rocked 'em back on their heels. My little memorial is the real stuff. I'm not depending on a fission effect, you know, with a release of one-tenth of one percent of the energy of the atom. I'm going to disrupt it completely, and get all the energy there is in it. And it'll be *more* than a thousand times as powerful as the Hiroshima bomb, because I'm going to use twelve times as much explosive; and it's going off on the ground, not fifteen hundred feet above it." Grenfell's brow, over suddenly hot eyes, began to shine with sweat. "And then—The Pit," he said softly. "The war memorial to end war, and all other war memorials. A vast pit, alive with bubbling lava, radiating death for ten thousand years. A living reminder of the devastation mankind has prepared for itself. Out here on the desert, where there are no cities, where the land has always been useless, will be the scene of the most useful thing in the history of the race—a never-ending sermon, a warning, an example of the dreadful antithesis of peace.'' His voice shook to a whisper, and faded.

"Sometimes," said Roway, "you frighten me, Grenfell. It occurs to me that I am such a studied sensualist, tasting everything I can, because I am afraid to feel any one thing that much." He shook himself, or shuddered. "You're a fanatic, Grenfell. Hyperemotional. A monomaniac. I hope you can do it."

"I can do it," said Grenfell.

Two months passed, and in those two months Grenfell's absorption in his work had been forced aside by the increasing pressure of current events. Watching a band of vigilantes riding over the waste to the south of his little buildings one afternoon, he thought grimly of what Roway had said. "Sometimes I think you wish you were a criminal." Roway, the sensualist, would say that. Roway would appreciate the taste of danger, in the same way that he appreciated all other emotions. As it intensified, he would wait to savor it, no matter how bad it got.

Twice Grenfell shut off the instigating power of the carbon-aluminum pile he had built, as he saw government helicopters hovering on the craggy skyline. He knew of hard-radiation detectors; he had developed two different types of them during the war; and he wanted no questions asked. His utter frustration at being unable to announce the success of his space-heating device, for fear that he would be punished as a criminal and his device impounded and forgotten—that frustration had been indescribable. It had canalized his mind, and intensified the devoted effort he had put forth for the things he believed in during the war. Every case of neural shock he encountered in men who had been hurt by war and who despised it made him work harder on his monument—on The Pit. For if humans could be frightened by war, humanity could be frightened by The Pit.

And those he met who had been hurt by war and who still hated the late enemy—those who would have been happy to go back and kill some more, reckoning vital risk well worth it—those he considered mad, and forgot them.

So he could not stand another frustration. He was the center of his own universe, and he realized it dreadfully, and he had to justify his position there. He was a humanitarian, a philanthropist in the world's truest sense. He was probably as mad as any man who has, through his own efforts, moved the world.

For the first time, then, he was grateful when Jack Roway arrived in his battered old convertible, although he was deliriously frightened at the roar of the motor outside his laboratory window. His usual reaction to Jack's advent was a mixture of annoyance and gratification, for it was a great deal of trouble to get out to his place. His annoyance was not because of the interruption, for Jack was certainly no trouble to have around. Grenfell suspected that Jack came out to see him partly to get the taste of the city out of his mouth, and partly to be able to feel superior to somebody he considered of worth.

But the increasing fear of discovery, and his race to complete his work before it was taken from him by an hysterical public, had had the unusual effect of making him lonely. For such a man as Grenfell to be lonely bordered on the extraordinary; for in his daily life there were simply too many things to be done. There had never been enough hours in a day nor days in a week to suit him, and he deeply resented the . encroachments of sleep, which he considered a criminal waste.

"Roway!" he blurted, as he flung the door open, his tone so warm that Roway's eyebrows went up in surprise. "What dragged you out here?"

"Nothing in particular," said the writer, as they shook hands. "Nothing more than usual, which is a great deal. How goes it?"

"I'm about finished." They went inside, and as the door closed, Grenfell turned to face Jack. "I've been finished for so long I'm ashamed of myself," he said intently.

"Ha! Ardent confession so early in the day! What are you talking about?"

"Oh, there have been things to do," said Grenfell restlessly. "But I could go ahead with the . . . with the big thing at almost any time."

"You hate to be finished. You've never visualized what it would be like to have the job done." His teeth flashed. "You know, I've never heard a word from you as to what your plans are after the big noise. You going into hiding?"

"I . . . haven't thought much about it. I used to have a vague idea of broadcasting a warning and an explanation before I let go with the disruptive explosion. I've decided against it, though. In the first place, I'd be stopped within minutes, no matter how cautious I was with the transmitter. In the second place—well, this is going to be so big that it won't need any explanation."

"No one will know who did it, or why it was done."

"Is that necessary?" asked Grenfell quietly.

Jack's mobile face stilled as he visualized The Pit spewing its ten-thousand-year hell. "Perhaps not," he said. "Isn't it necessary, though, to you?"

"To me?" asked Grenfell, surprised. "You mean, do I care if the world knows I did this thing, or not? No, of course I don't. A chain of circumstance is occurring, and it has been working through me. It goes directly to The Pit; The Pit will do all that is necessary from then on. I will no longer have any part in it."

Jack moved, clinking and splashing, around the sink in the corner of the laboratory. "Where's all your coffee? Oh—here. Uh . . . I have been curious about how much personal motive you had for your work. I think that answers it pretty well. I think, too, that you believe what you are saying. Do you know that people who do things for impersonal motives are as rare as fur on a fish?"

"I hadn't thought about it."

"I believe that, too. Sugar? And milk. I remember. And have you been listening to the radio?"

"Yes. I'm . . . a little upset, Jack," said Grenfell, taking the cup. "I don't know where to time this thing. I'm a technician, not a Machiavelli."

"Visionary, like I said. You don't know if you'll throw this gadget of your into world history too soon or too late—is that it?"

"Exactly. Jack, the whole world seems to be going crazy. Even fission bombs are too big for humanity to handle."

"What else can you expect," said Jack grimly, "with our dear friends across the water sitting over their push buttons waiting for an excuse to punch them?"

"And we have our own set of buttons, of course."

Jack Roway said: "We've got to defend ourselves."

"Are you kidding?"

Roway glanced at him, his dark brows plotting a V. "Not about this. I seldom kid about anything, but particularly not about this." And he—shuddered.

Grenfell stared amazedly at him and then began to chuckle. "Now," he said, "I've seen everything. My iconoclastic friend Jack Roway, of all people, caught up by a . . . a fashion. A national pastime, fostered by uncertainty and fed by yellow-journalism—fear of the enemy."

"This country is not at war."

"You mean, we have no enemy? Are you saying that the gentlemen over the water, with their itching fingers hovering about the push buttons, are not our enemies?"

"Well—"

Grenfell came across the room to his friend, and put a hand on his shoulder. "Jack—what's the matter? You can't be so troubled by the news—not *you!*"

Roway stared out at the brazen sun, and shook his head slowly. "International balance is too delicate," he said softly; and if a voice could glaze like eyes, his did. "I see the nations of the world as masses balanced each on its own mathematical point, each with its center of gravity directly above. But the masses are fluid, shifting violently away from the center lines. The opposing trends aren't equal: they can't cancel each other; the phasing is too slow. One or the other is going to topple, and then the whole works is going to go."

"But you've known that for a long time. You've known that ever since Hiroshima. Possibly before. Why should it frighten you now?"

"I didn't think it would happen so soon."

"Oh-ho! So that's it! You have suddenly realized that the explosion is going to come in your lifetime. Hm-m-m? And you can't take that. You're capable of all of your satisfying aesthetic rationalizations as long as you keep the actualities at arm's length!"

"*Whew!*" said Roway, his irrepressible humor passing close enough to nod him. "Keep it clean, Grenfell!"

Grenfell smiled. "Y'know, Jack, you remind me powerfully of some erstwhile friends of mine who write science fiction. They had been living very close to atomic power for a long time—years before the man on the street—or the average politician, for that matter—knew an atom from Adam. Atomic power was handy to these specialized word-merchants because it gave them a limitless source of power for background to a limitless source of story material. In the heyday of the Manhattan Project, most of them suspected what was going on, some of them knew—some even worked on it. All of them were quite aware of the terrible potentialities of nuclear energy. Practically all of them were scared silly of the whole idea. They were afraid for humanity, but they themselves were not really afraid, except in a delicious drawing room sort of way, because they couldn't conceive of this Buck Rogers event happening to anything but posterity. But it happened, right smack in the middle of their own sacrosanct lifetimes.

"And I will be doggoned if you're not doing the same thing. You've gotten quite a bang out of figuring out the doom humanity faces in an atomic war. You've consciously risen above it by calling it inevitable, and in the meantime, leave us gather rosebuds before it rains. You thought you'd be safe home—dead—before the first drops fell. Now social progress has rolled up a thunderhead and you find yourself a mile from home with a crease in your pants and no umbrella. And you're scared.''

Roway looked at the floor and said, "It's so soon. It's so soon." He looked at up Grenfell, and his cheekbones seemed too large. He took a deep breath. "You ... we can stop it, Grenfell. The war ... the ... this thing that's happening to us. The explosion that will come when the strains get too great in the international situation. And it's *got* to be stopped!''

"That's what The Pit is for.''

"The Pit!'' Roway said scornfully. "I've called you a visionary before. Grenfell, you've got to be more practical! Humanity is not going to learn anything by example. It's got to be kicked and carved. Surgery.''

Grenfell's eyes narrowed. "Surgery? What you said a minute ago about my stopping it ... do you mean what I think you mean?''

"Don't you see it?'' said Jack urgently. "What you have here— total disruptive energy—the peak of atomic power. One or two wallops with this, in the right place, and we can stop anybody.''

"This isn't a weapon. I didn't make this to be a weapon.''

"The first rock ever thrown by a prehistoric man wasn't made to be a weapon, either. But it was handy and it was effective, and it was certainly used because it had to be used.'' He suddenly threw up his hands in a despairing gesture. "You don't understand. Don't you realize that this country is likely to be attacked at any second—that diplomacy is now hopeless and helpless, and the whole world is just waiting for the thing to start? It's probably too late even now—but it's the least we can do.''

"What, specifically, is the least thing we can do?''

"Turn your work over to the War Department. In a few hours the government can put it where it will do the most good.'' He drew his finger across his throat. "Anywhere we want to, over the ocean.''

There was a taut silence. Roway looked at his watch and licked his lips. Finally Grenfell said. "Turn it over to the government. Use it for a weapon—and what for? To stop war?''

"Of course!'' blurted Roway. "To show the rest of the world that our way of life ... to scare the daylights out of ... to—''

"*Stop it!*'' Grenfell roared. "Nothing of the kind. You think—you hope anyway—that the use of total disruption as a weapon will stall off the inevitable—at least in your lifetime. Don't you?''

"No. I—''

"Don't you?''

"Well, I—''

"You have some more doggerel to write,'' said Grenfell scathingly. "You have some more blondes to chase. You want to go limp over a few more Bach fugues.''

Jack Roway said: "No one knows where the first bomb might hit. It might be anywhere. There's nowhere I . . . we . . . can go to be safe.'' He was trembling.

"Are the people in the city quivering like that?'' said Grenfell.

"Riots,'' breathed Roway, his eyes bright with panic. "The radio won't announce anything about the riots.''

"Is that what you came out here for today—to try to get me to give disruptive power to *any* government?''

Jack looked at him guiltily. "It was the only thing to do. I don't know if your bomb will turn the trick, but it has to be tried. It's the only thing left. We've got to be prepared to hit first, and hit harder than anyone else.''

"No.'' Grenfell's one syllable was absolutely unshakable.

"Grenfell—I thought I could argue you into it. Don't make it tough for yourself. You've got to do it. Please do it on your own. Please, Grenfell.'' He stood up slowly.

"Do it on my own—or what? *Keep away from me!*''

"No . . . I—'' Roway stiffened suddenly, listening. From far above and to the north came the whir of rotary wings. Roway's fear-slackened lips tightened into a grin, and with two incredibly swift strides he was across to Grenfell. He swept in a handful of the smaller man's shirt front and held him half off the floor.

"Don't try a thing,'' he gritted. There was not a sound then except their harsh breathing, until Grenfell said wearily: "There was somebody called Judas—''

"You can't insult me,'' said Roway, with a shade of his old cockiness, "And you're flattering yourself.''

A helicopter sank into its own roaring dust cloud outside the building. Men poured out of it and burst in the door. There were three of them. They were not in uniform.

"Dr. Grenfell,'' said Jack Roway, keeping his grip, "I want you to meet—''

"Never mind that,'' said the taller of the three in a brisk voice.

"You're Roway? Hm-m-m Dr. Grenfell, I understand you have a nuclear energy device on the premises."

"Why did you come by yourself?" Grenfell asked Roway softly. "Why not just send those stooges?"

"For you, strangely enough. I hoped I could argue you into giving the thing freely. You know what will happen if you resist?"

"I know." Grenfell pursed his lips for a moment, and then turned to the tall man. "Yes. I have some such thing here. Total atomic disruption. Is that what you were looking for?"

"Where is it?"

"Here, in the laboratory, and then there's the pile in the other building. You'll find—" He hesitated. "You'll find two samples of the concentrate. One's over there—" he pointed to a lead case on a shelf behind one of the benches. "And there's another like it in a similar case in the shed back of the pile building."

Roway sighed and released Grenfell. "Good boy. I knew you'd come through."

"Yes," said Grenfell. "Yes—"

"Go get it," said the tall man. One of the others broke away.

"It will take two men to carry it," said Grenfell in a shaken voice. His lips were white.

The tall man pulled out a gun and held it idly. He nodded to the second man. "Go get it. Bring it here and we'll strap the two together and haul 'em to the plane. Snap it up."

The two men went out toward the shed.

"Jack?"

"Yes, doc."

"You really think humanity can be scared?"

"It will be—now. This thing will be used right."

"I hope so. Oh, I hope so," Grenfell whispered.

The men came back. "Up on the bench," said the leader, nodding toward the case the men carried between them.

As they climbed up on the bench and laid hands on the second case, to swing it down from the shelf, Jack Roway saw Grenfell's face spurt sweat, and a sudden horror swept over him.

"Grenfell!" he said hoarsely. "It's—"

"Of course," Grenfell whispered. "Critical mass."

Then it let go.

It was like Hiroshima, but much bigger. And yet, that explosion did not create The Pit. It was the pile that did—the boron-aluminum lattice which Grenfell had so arduously pieced together from parts bootlegged over the years. Right there at the heart of the fission explosion, total disruption took place in the pile, for that was its function. This was slower. It took more than an hour for its hellish activity to reach a peak, and in that time a huge crater had been gouged out of the earth, a seething, spewing mass of volatilized elements, raw radiation, and incandescent gases. It was—The Pit. Its activity curve was plotted abruptly—up to peak in an hour and eight minutes, and then a gradual subsidence as it tried to feed further afield with less and less fueling effect, and as it consumed its own flaming wastes in an effort to reach inactivity. Rain would help to blanket it, through energy lost in volatilizing the drops; and each of the many elements involved went through its respective secondary radioactivity, and passed away its successive half-lives. The subsidence of The Pit would take between eight and nine thousand years.

And like Hiroshima, this explosion had effects which reached into history and into men's hearts in places far separated in time from the cataclysm itself.

These things happened:

The explosion could not be concealed; and there was too much hysteria afoot for anything to be confirmed. It was easier to run headlines saying WE ARE ATTACKED. There was an instantaneous and panicky demand for reprisals, and the government acceded, because such "reprisals" suited the policy of certain members who could command emergency powers. And so the First Atomic War was touched off.

And the Second.

There were no more atomic wars after that. The Mutant's War was a barbarous affair, and the mutants defeated the tattered and largely sterile remnants of humanity, because the mutants were strong. And then the mutants died out becuase they were unfit. For a while there was some very interesting material to be studied on the effects of radiation on heredity, but there was no one to study it.

There were some humans left. The rats got most of them, after increasing in fantastic numbers; and there were three plagues.

After that there were half-stooping, naked things whose twisted heredity could have been traced to humankind; but these could be frightened, as individuals and as a race, so therefore they could not progress. They were certainly not human.

The Pit, in A.D. 5000, had changed little over the centuries. Still it was an angry memorial to the misuse of great power; and because of it, organized warfare was a forgotten thing. Because of it, the world was free of the wasteful smoke and dirt of industry. The scream and crash of bombs and the soporific beat of marching feet were never heard, and at long last the earth was at peace.

To go near The Pit was slow, certain death, and it was respected and feared, and would be for centuries more. It winked and blinked redly at night, and was surrounded by a bald and broken tract stretching out and away over the horizon; and around it flickered a ghostly blue glow. Nothing lived there. Nothing could.

With such a war memorial, there could only be peace. The earth could never forget the horror that could be loosed by war.

That was Grenfell's dream.

The Hole Man

Larry Niven

One day Mars will be gone.

Andrew Lear says that it will start with violent quakes, and end hours or days later, very suddenly. He ought to know. It's all his fault.

Lear also says that it won't happen for from years to centuries. So we stay, Lear and the rest of us. We study the alien base for what it can tell us, while the center of the world we stand on is slowly eaten away. It's enough to give a man nightmares.

It was Lear who found the alien base.

We had reached Mars: fourteen of us, in the cramped bulbous life-support system of the *Percival Lowell*. We were circling in orbit, taking our time, correcting our maps and looking for anything that thirty years of Mariner probes might have missed.

We were mapping mascons, among other things. Those mass concentrations under the lunar maria were almost certainly left by good-sized asteroids, mountains of rock falling silently out of the sky until they struck with the energies of thousands of fusion bombs. Mars has been cruising through the asteroid belt for four billion years. Mars would show bigger and better mascons. They would affect our orbits.

So Andrew Lear was hard at work, watching pens twitch on graph paper as we circled Mars. A bit of machinery fell alongside the *Percival Lowell,* rotating. Within its thin shell was a weighted double lever system, deceptively simple: a Forward Mass Detector. The pens mapped its twitchings.

Over Sirbonis Palus they began mapping strange curves.

Another man might have cursed and tried to fix it. Andrew Lear thought it out, then sent the signal that would stop the free-falling widget from rotating.

It had to be rotating to map a stationary mass.

But now it was mapping simple sine waves.

Lear went running to Captain Childrey.

Running? It was more like trapeze artistry. Lear pulled himself along by handholds, kicked off from walls, braked with a hard push of hands or feet. Moving in free fall is hard work when you're in a hurry, and Lear was a forty-year-old astrophysicist, not an athlete. He was blowing hard when he reached the control bubble.

Childrey—who was an athlete—waited with a patient, slightly contemptuous smile while Lear caught his breath.

He already thought Lear was crazy. Lear's words only confirmed it. "Gravity for sending signals? Doctor Lear, will you please quit bothering me with your weird ideas. I'm busy. We all are."

This was not entirely unfair. Some of Lear's enthusiasms were peculiar. Gravity generators. Black holes. He thought we should be searching for Dyson spheres: stars completely enclosed by an artificial shell. He believed that mass and inertia were two separate things: that it should be possible to suck the inertia out of a spacecraft, say, so that it could accelerate to near lightspeed in a few minutes. He was a wide-eyed dreamer, and when he was flustered he tended to wander from the point.

"You don't understand," he told Childrey. "Gravity radiation is harder to block than electromagnetic waves. Patterned gravity waves would be easy to detect. The advanced civilizations in the galaxy may all be communicating by gravity. Some of them may even be modulating pulsars—rotating neutron stars. That's where Project Ozma went wrong: they were only looking for signals in the electromagnetic spectrum."

Childrey laughed. "Sure. Your little friends are using neutron stars to send you messages. What's that got to do with us?"

"Well, look!" Lear held up the strip of flimsy, nearly weightless paper he'd torn from the machine. "I got this over Sirbonis Palus. I think we ought to land there."

"We're landing in Mare Cimmerium, as you perfectly well know. The lander is already deployed and ready to board. Doctor Lear, we've spent four days mapping this area. It's flat. It's in a green-brown area. When spring comes next month, we'll find out whether there's life there! And everybody wants it that way except you!"

Lear was still holding the graph paper before him like a shield. "Please. Take one more circuit over Sirbonis Palus."

Childrey opted for the extra orbit. Maybe the sine waves convinced him. Maybe not. He would have liked inconveniencing the rest of us in Lear's name, to show him for a fool.

But the next pass showed a tiny circular feature in Sirbonis Palus. And Lear's mass indicator was making sine waves again.

The aliens had gone. During our first few months we always expected them back any minute. The machinery in the base was running smoothly and perfectly, as if the owners had only just stepped out.

The base was an inverted pie plate two stories high, and windowless. The air inside was breathable, like Earth's air three miles up, but with a bit more oxygen. Mars's air is far thinner, and poisonous. Clearly they were not of Mars.

The walls were thick and deeply eroded. They leaned inward against the internal pressure. The roof was somewhat thinner, just heavy enough for the pressure to support it. Both walls and roof were of fused Martian dust.

The heating system still worked—and it was also the lighting system: grids in the ceiling glowing brick red. The base was always ten degrees too warm. We didn't find the off switches for almost a week: they were behind locked panels. The air system blew gusty winds through the base until we fiddled with the fans.

We could guess a lot about them from what they'd left behind. They must have come from a world smaller than Earth, circling a red dwarf star in close orbit. To be close enough to be warm enough, the planet would have to be locked in by tides, turning one face always to its star. The aliens must have evolved on the lighted side, in a permanent red day, with winds constantly howling over the border from the night side.

And they had no sense of privacy. The only doorways that had doors in them were airlocks. The second floor was a hexagonal metal gridwork. It would not block you off from your friends on the floor below.

The bunk room was an impressive expanse of mercury-filled waterbed, wall to wall. The rooms were too small and cluttered, the furniture and machinery too close to the doorways, so that at first we were constantly bumping elbows and knees. The ceilings were an inch short of six feet high on both floors, so that we tended to walk stooped even if we were short enough to stand upright. Habit. But Lear was just tall enough to knock his head if he stood up fast, anywhere in the base.

We thought they must have been smaller than human. But their padded benches seemed human-designed in size and shape. Maybe it was their minds that were different: they didn't need psychic elbow room.

The ship had been bad enough. Now this. Within the base was instant claustrophobia. It put all of our tempers on hair triggers.

Two of us couldn't take it.

Lear and Childrey did not belong on the same planet.

With Childrey, neatness was a compulsion. He had enough for all of us. During those long months aboard *Percival Lowell,* it was Childrey who led us in calisthenics. He flatly would not let anyone skip an exercise period. We eventually gave up trying.

Well and good. The exercise kept us alive. We weren't getting the healthy daily exercise anyone gets walking around the living room in a one gravity field.

But after a month on Mars, Childrey was the only man who still appeared fully dressed in the heat of the alien base. Some of us took it as a reproof, and maybe it was, because Lear had been the first to doff his shirt for keeps. In the mess Childrey would inspect his silverware for water spots, then line it up perfectly parallel.

On Earth, Andrew Lear's habits would have been no more than a character trait. In a hurry, he might choose mismatched socks. He might put off using the dishwasher for a day or two if he were involved in something interesting. He would prefer a house that looked "lived in." God help the maid who tried to clean up his study. He'd never be able to find anything afterward.

He was a brilliant but one-sided man. Backpacking or skin diving might have changed his habits—in such pursuits you learn not to forget any least trivial thing—but they would never have tempted him. An expedition to Mars was something he simply could not turn down. A pity, because neatness is worth your life in space.

You don't leave your fly open in a pressure suit.

A month after the landing, Childrey caught Lear doing just that.

The "fly" on a pressure suit is a soft rubber tube over your male member. It leads to a bladder and there's a spring clamp on it. You open the clamp to use it. Then you close the clamp and open an outside spigot to evacuate the bladder into vacuum.

Similar designs for women involve a catheter, which is hideously uncomfortable. I presume the designers will keep trying. It seems wrong to bar half the human race from our ultimate destiny.

Lear was addicted to long walks. He loved the Martian desert scene: the hard violet sky and the soft blur of whirling orange dust, the sharp close horizon, the endless emptiness. More: he needed the room. He was spending all his working time on the alien communicator, with the ceiling too close over his head and everything else too close to his bony elbows.

He was coming back from a walk, and he met Childrey coming out. Childrey noticed that the waste spigot on Lear's suit was open, the spring broken. Lear had been out for hours. If he'd had to go, he might have bled to death through flesh ruptured by vacuum.

We never learned all that Childrey said to him out there. But Lear came in very red about the ears, muttering under his breath. He wouldn't talk to anyone.

The NASA psychologists should not have put them both on that small planet. Hindsight is wonderful, right? But Lear and Childrey were each the best choice for competence coupled to the kind of health they would need to survive the trip. There were astrophysicists as competent and as famous as Lear, but they were decades older. And Childrey had a thousand spaceflight hours to his credit. He had been one of the last men on the Moon.

Individually, each of us was the best possible man. It was a damn shame.

The aliens had left the communicator going, like everything else in the base. It must have been hellishly massive, to judge by the thick support pillars slanting outward beneath it. It was a bulky tank of a thing, big enough that the roof had to bulge slightly to give it room. That gave Lear about a square meter of the only head room in the base.

Even Lear had no idea why they'd put it on the second floor. It would send through the first floor, or through the bulk of a planet. Lear learned that by trying it, once he knew enough. He beamed a dot-dash message through Mars itself to the Forward Mass Detector aboard *Lowell*.

Lear had set up a Mass Detector next to the communicator, on an extremely complex platform designed to protect it from vibration. The Detector produced waves so sharply pointed that some of us thought they could *feel* the gravity radiation coming from the communicator.

Lear was in love with the thing.

He skipped meals. When he ate he ate like a starved wolf. "There's a heavy point-mass in there," he told us, talking around a mouthful of food, two months after the landing. "The machine uses electromagnetic fields to vibrate it at high speed. Look—" He picked up a toothpaste tube of tuna spread and held it in front of him. He vibrated it rapidly. Heads turned to watch him around the zigzagged communal table in the alien mess. "I'm making gravity waves now. But they're too mushy because the tube's too big, and their amplitude is virtually zero. There's something very dense and massive in that machine, and it takes a hell of a lot of field strength to keep it there."

"What is it?" someone asked. "Neutronium? Like at the heart of a neutron star?"

Lear shook his head and took another mouthful. "That size, neutronium wouldn't be stable. I think it's a quantum black hole. I don't know how to measure its mass yet."

I said, "A *quantum* black hole?"

Lear nodded happily. "Luck for me. You know, I was against the Mars expedition. We could get a lot more for our money by exploring the asteroids. Among other things, we might have found if there are really quantum black holes out there. But this one's already captured!" He stood up, being careful of his head. He turned in his tray and went back to work.

I remember we stared at each other along the zigzag mess table. Then we drew lots . . . and I lost.

The day Lear left his waste spigot open, Childrey had put a restriction on him. Lear was not to leave the base without an escort.

Lear had treasured the aloneness of those walks. But it was worse than that. Childrey had given him a list of possible escorts: half a dozen men Childrey could trust to see to it that Lear did nothing dangerous to himself or others. Inevitably they were the men most thoroughly trained in space survival routines, most addicted to Childrey's own compulsive neatness, least likely to sympathize with Lear's way of living. Lear was as likely to ask Childrey himself to go walking with him.

He almost never went out any more. I knew exactly where to find him.

I stood beneath him, looking up through the gridwork floor.

He'd almost finished dismantling the protective panels around the gravity wave communicator. What showed inside looked like parts of a computer in one spot, electromagnetic coils in most places, and a square array of pushbuttons that might have been the aliens' idea of a typewriter. Lear was using a magnetic induction sensor to try to trace wiring without actually tearing off the insulation.

I called, "How you making out?"

"No good," he said. "The insulation seems to be one hundred percent perfect. Now I'm afraid to open it up. No telling how much power is running through there, if it needs shielding that good." He smiled down at me. "Let me show you something."

"What?"

He flipped a toggle above a dull grey circular plate. "This thing is a microphone. It took me awhile to find it. I am Andrew Lear, speaking to whomever may be listening." He switched it off, then ripped paper from the Mass Indicator and showed me squiggles interrupting smooth sine waves. "There. The sound of my voice in gravity radiation. It won't disappear until it's reached the edges of the universe."

"Lear, you mentioned quantum black holes back there. What's a quantum black hole?"

"Um. You know what a black hole is."

"I ought to." Lear had educated us on the subject, at length, during the months aboard *Lowell*.

When a not too massive star has used up its nuclear fuel, it collapses into a white dwarf. A heavier star—say, 1.44 times the mass of the sun and larger—can burn out its fuel, then collapse into itself until it is ten kilometers across and composed solely of neutrons packed edge to edge: the densest matter in this universe.

But a big star goes further than that. When a really massive star runs its course . . . when the radiation pressure within is no longer strong enough to hold the outer layers against the star's own ferocious gravity . . . then it can fall into itself entirely, until gravity is stronger than any other force, until it is compressed past the Swartzchild radius and effectively leaves the universe. What happens to it then is problematical. The Swartzchild radius is the boundary beyond which nothing can climb out of the gravity well, not even light.

The star is gone then, but the mass remains: a lightless hole in space, perhaps a hole into another universe.

"A collapsing star can leave a black hole," said Lear. "There may be bigger black holes, whole galaxies that have fallen into themselves.

But there's no other way a black hole can form, now.''

"So?"

"There was a time when black holes of all sizes could form. That was during the Big Bang, the explosion that started the expanding universe. The forces in that blast could have compressed little local vortices of matter past the Swartzchild radius. What that left behind—the smallest ones, anyway—we call quantum black holes."

I heard a distinctive laugh behind me as Captain Childrey walked into view. The bulk of the communicator would have hidden him from Lear, and I hadn't heard him come up. He called, "Just how big a thing are you talking about? Could I pick one up and throw it at you?"

"You'd disappear into one that size," Lear said seriously. "A black hole the mass of the Earth would only be a centimeter across. No, I'm talking about things from ten-to-the-minus-fifth grams on up. There could be one at the center of the sun—"

"Eek!"

Lear was trying. He didn't like being kidded, but he didn't know how to stop it. Keeping it serious wasn't the way, but he didn't know that either. "Say, ten-to-the-seventeenth grams in mass and ten-to-the-minus-eleven centimeters across. It would be swallowing a few atoms a day."

"Well, at least you know where to find it," said Childrey. "Now all you have to do is go after it."

Lear nodded, still serious. "There could be quantum black holes in asteroids. A small asteroid could capture a quantum black hole easily enough, especially if it was charged; a black hole can hold a charge, you know—"

"Ri-ight."

"All we'd have to do is check out a small asteroid with the Mass Detector. If it masses more than it should, we push it aside and see if it leaves a black hole behind."

"You'd need little teeny eyes to see something that small. Anyway, what would you do with it?"

"You put a charge on it, if it hasn't got one already, and electromagnetic fields. You can vibrate it to make gravity; then you manipulate it with radiation. I think I've got one in here," he said, patting the alien communicator.

"Ri-ight," said Childrey, and he went away laughing.

Within a week the whole base was referring to Lear as the Hole Man, the man with the black hole between his ears.

It hadn't sounded funny when Lear was telling me about it. The rich variety of the universe ... but when Childrey talked about the black hole in Lear's Anything Box, it sounded hilarious.

Please note: Childrey did not misunderstand anything Lear had said. Childrey wasn't stupid. He merely thought Lear was crazy. He could not have gotten away with making fun of Lear, not among educated men, without knowing exactly what he was doing.

Meanwhile the work went on.

There were pools of Marsdust, fascinating stuff, fine enough to behave like viscous oil, and knee deep. Wading through it wasn't dangerous, but it was very hard work, and we avoided it. One day Brace waded out into the nearest of the pools and started feeling around under the dust. Hunch, he said. He came up with some eroded plastic-like containers. The aliens had used the pool as a garbage dump.

We were having little luck with chemical analysis of the base materials. They were virtually indestructible. We learned more about the chemistry of the alien visitors themselves. They had left traces of themselves on the benches and on the communal waterbed. The traces had most of the chemical components of protoplasm, but Arsvey found no sign of DNA. Not surprising, he said. There must be other giant organic molecules suitable for gene coding.

The aliens had left volumes of notes behind. The script was a mystery, of course, but we studied the photographs and diagrams. A lot of them were notes on anthropology!

The aliens had been studying Earth during the first Ice Age.

None of us were anthropologists, and that was a damn shame. We never learned if we'd found anything new. All we could do was photograph the stuff and beam it up to *Lowell*. One thing was sure: the aliens had left very long ago, and they had left the lighting and air systems running and the communicator sending a carrier wave.

For us? Who else?

The alternative was that the base had been switched off for some six hundred thousand years, then come back on when something detected *Lowell* approaching Mars. Lear didn't believe it. "If the power had been off in the communicator," he said, "the mass wouldn't be in there any more. The fields have to be going to hold it in place. It's smaller than an atom; it'd fall through anything solid."

So the base power system had been running for all that time. What the hell could it be? And where? We traced some cables and found that it was under the base, under several yards of Marsdust fused to lava. We didn't try to dig through that.

The source was probably geophysical: a hole deep into the core of the planet. The aliens might have wanted to dig such a hole to take core samples. Afterward they would have set up a generator to use the temperature difference between the core and the surface.

Meanwhile, Lear spent some time tracing down the power sources in the communicator. He found a way to shut off the carrier wave. Now the mass, if there was a mass, was at rest in there. It was strange to see the Forward Mass Detector pouring out straight lines instead of drastically peaked sine waves.

We were ill equipped to take advantage of these riches. We had been fitted out to explore Mars, not a bit of civilization from another star. Lear was the exception. He was in his element, with but one thing to mar his happiness.

I don't know what the final argument was about. I was engaged on another project.

The Mars lander still had fuel in it. NASA had given us plenty of fuel to hover while we looked for a landing spot. After some heated discussion, we had agreed to take the vehicle up and hover it next to the nearby dust pool on low thrust.

It worked fine. The dust rose up in a great soft cloud and went away toward the horizon, leaving the pond bottom covered with otherworldly junk. And more! Arsvey started screaming at Brace to back off. Fortunately Brace kept his head. He tilted us over to one side and took us away on a gentle curve. The backblast never touched the skeletons.

We worked out there for hours, being very finicky indeed. Here was another skill none of us would own to, but we'd read about how careful an archeologist has to be, and we did our best. Traces of water had had time to turn some of the dust to natural cement, so that some of the skeletons were fixed to the rock. But we got a couple free. We put them on stretchers and brought them back. One crumbled the instant the air came hissing into the lock. We left the other outside.

The aliens had not had the habit of taking baths. We'd set up a bathtub with very tall sides, in a room the aliens had reserved for some incomprehensible ritual. I had stripped off my pressure suit and was heading for the bathtub, very tired, hoping that nobody would be in it.

I heard the voices before I saw them.

Lear was shouting.

Childrey wasn't, but his voice was a carrying one. It carried mockery. He was standing between the supporting pillars. His hands were on his hips, his teeth gleamed white, his head was thrown back to look up at Lear.

He finished talking. For a time neither of them moved. Then Lear made a sound of disgust. He turned away and pushed one of the buttons on what might have been an alien typewriter keyboard.

Childrey looked startled. He slapped at his right thigh and brought the hand away bloody. He stared at it, then looked up at Lear. He started to ask a question.

He crumpled slowly in the low gravity. I got to him before he hit the ground. I cut his pants open and tied a handkerchief over the blood spot. It was a small puncture, but the flesh was puckered above it on a line with his groin.

Childrey tried to speak. His eyes were wide. He coughed, and there was blood in his mouth.

I guess I froze. How could I help if I couldn't tell what had happened? I saw a blood spot on his right shoulder, and I tore the shirt open and found another tiny puncture wound.

The doctor arrived.

It took Childrey an hour to die, but the doctor had given up much earlier. Between the wound in his shoulder and the wound in his thigh, Childrey's flesh had been ruptured in a narrow line that ran through one lung and his stomach and part of his intestinal tract. The autopsy showed a tiny, very heat hole drilled through the hip bones.

We looked for, and found, a hole in the floor beneath the communicator. It was the size of a pencil lead, and packed with dust.

"I made a mistake," Lear told the rest of us at the inquest. "I should never have touched that particular button. It must have switched off the fields that held the mass in place. It just dropped. Captain Childrey was underneath."

And it had gone straight through him, eating the mass of him as it went.

"No, not quite," said Lear. "I'd guess it massed about ten-to-the-fourteenth grams. That only makes it ten-to-the-minus-sixth Angstrom across, much smaller than an atom. It wouldn't have absorbed much. The damage was done to Childrey by tidal effects as it passed through him. You saw how it pulverized the material of the floor."

Not surprisingly, the subject of murder did come up.

Lear shrugged it off. "Murder with what? Childrey didn't believe there was a black hole in there at all. Neither did many of you." He smiled suddenly. "Can you imagine what the trial would be like? Imagine the prosecuting attorney trying to tell a jury what he thinks happened. First he's got to tell them what a black hole is. Then a quantum black hole. Then he's got to explain why he doesn't have the murder weapon, and where he left it, freely falling through Mars! And if he gets that far without being laughed out of court, he's still got to explain how a thing smaller than an atom could hurt anyone!''

But didn't Doctor Lear know the thing was dangerous? Could he not have guessed its enormous mass from the way it behaved?

Lear spread his hands. ''Gentlemen, we're dealing with more variables than just mass. Field strength, for instance. I might have guessed its mass from the force it took to keep it there, but did any of us expect the aliens to calibrate their dials in the metric system?''

Surely there must have been safeties to keep the fields from being shut off accidentally. Lear must have bypassed them.

''Yes, I probably did, accidentally. I did quite a lot of fiddling to find out how things worked.''

It got dropped there. Obviously there would be no trial. No ordinary judge or jury could be expected to understand what the attorneys would be talking about. A couple of things never did get mentioned.

For instance: Childrey's last words. I might or might not have repeated them if I'd been asked to. They were: ''All right, show me! Show it to me or admit it isn't there!''

As the court was breaking up I spoke to Lear with my voice lowered. ''That was probably the most unique murder weapon in history.''

He whispered, ''If you said that in company I could sue for slander.''

''Yeah? Really? Are you going to explain to a jury what you think I implied happened?''

''No, I'll let you get away with it this time.''

''Hell, you didn't get away scot free yourself. What are you going to study now? The only known black hole in the universe, and you let it drop through your fingers.''

Lear frowned. ''You're right. Partly right, anyway. But I knew as much about it as I was going to, the way I was going. Now... I stopped it vibrating in there, then took the mass of the entire setup with the Forward Mass Sensor. Now the black hole isn't in there any more. I can get the mass of the black hole by taking the mass of the communicator alone.''

''Oh.''

''And I can cut the machine open, see what's inside. How they controlled it. Damn it, I wish I were six years old.''

''What? Why?''

"Well ... I don't have the times straightened out. The math is chancy. Either a few years from now, or a few centuries, there's going to be a black hole between Earth and Jupiter. It'll be big enough to study. I think about forty years."

When I realized what he was implying, I didn't know whether to laugh or scream. "Lear, you can't think that something that small could absorb Mars!"

"Well, remember that it absorbs everything it comes near. A nucleus here, an electron there ... and it's not just waiting for atoms to fall into it. Its gravity is ferocious, and it's falling back and forth through the center of the planet, sweeping up matter. The more it eats, the bigger it gets, with its volume going up as the cube of the mass. Sooner or later, yes, it'll absorb Mars. By then it'll be just less than a millimeter across—big enough to see."

"Could it happen within thirteen months?"

"Before we leave? Hmm." Lear's eyes took on a faraway look. "I don't think so. I'll have to work it out. The math is chancy ..."

6

The Machine and the Robot

Isaac Asimov

To a physicist, a machine is any device that transfers a force from the point where it is applied to another point where it is used and, in the process, changes its intensity or direction.

In this sense it is difficult for a human being to make use of anything that is not part of his body without, in the process, using a machine. A couple of million years ago, when one could scarcely decide whether the most advanced hominids were more humanlike than apelike, pebbles were already being chipped and their sharp edges used to cut or scrape.

And even a chipped pebble is a machine, for the force applied to the blunt edge by the hand is transmitted to the sharp end and, in the process, intensified. The force spread over the large area of the blunt end, is equal to the force spread over the small area of the sharp end. The pressure (force per area) is therefore increased, and without ever increasing the total force, that force is intensified in action. The sharp-edge pebble could, by the greater pressure it exerts, force its way through an object, as a rounded pebble (or a man's hand) could not.

In actual practice, however, few people, other than physicists at their most rigid, would call a chipped pebble a machine. In actual practice, we think of machines as relatively complicated devices, and are more likely to use the name if the device is somewhat removed from direct human guidance and manipulation.

The further a device is removed from human control, the more authentically mechanical it seems, and the whole trend in technology has been to devise machines that are less and less under direct human control and more and more seem to have the beginning of a will of their own. A chipped pebble is almost part of the hand it never leaves. A thrown spear declares a sort of independence the moment it is released.

The clear progression away from direct and immediate control made it possible for human beings, even in primitive times, to slide forward into extrapolation, and to picture devices still less controllable, still more independent than anything of which they had direct experience. Immediately we have a form of fantasy—which some, defining the term more broadly than I would, might even call science fiction.

Man can move on his feet by direct and intimate control; or on horseback, controlling the more powerful animal muscles by rein and heel; or on ship, making use of the invisible power of the wind. Why not progress into further etherealization by way of seven-league boots, flying carpets, self-propelled boats. The power used in these cases was ''magic,'' the tapping of the superhuman and transcendental energies of gods or demons.

Nor did these imaginings concern only the increased physical power of inanimate objects, but even increased mental power of objects which were still viewed as essentially inanimate. Artificial intelligence is not really a modern concept.

Hephaistos, the Greek god of the forge, is pictured in the *Iliad* as having golden mechanical women, which were as mobile and as intelligent as flesh-and-blood women, and which helped him in his palace.

Why not? After all, if a human smith makes inanimate metal objects of the base metal iron, why should not a god-smith make far more clever inanimate metal objects of the noble metal gold? It is an easy extrapolation, of the sort that comes as second nature to science fiction writers (who, in primitive times, had to be myth-makers, in default of science).

But human artisans, if clever enough, could also make mechanical human beings. Consider Talos, a bronze warrior made by that Thomas Edison of the Greek myths, Daedalus. Talos guarded the shores of Crete, circling the island once each day and keeping off all intruders. The fluid that kept him alive was kept within his body by a plug at his heel. When the Argonauts landed on Crete, Medea used her magic to pull out the plug and Talos lost all his pseudo-animation.

(It is easy to ascribe a symbolic meaning to this myth. Crete, starting in the fourth century, before the Greeks had yet entered Greece, had a navy, the first working navy in human history. The Cretan navy made it possible for the islanders to establish an empire over what became the nearby islands and mainland. The Greek barbarians, invading the land, were more or less under Cretan dominion to begin with. The bronze-armored warriors carried by the ships guarded the Cretan mainland for two thousand years—and then failed. The plug was pulled, so to speak, when the island of Thera exploded in a vast volcanic eruption in 1500 B.C. and a tsunami destroyed the Cretan civilization—and the Greeks took over. Still, the fact that a myth is a sort of vague and distorted recall of something actual does not alter its function of indicating a way of human thinking.)

From the start, then, the machine has faced mankind with a double aspect. As long as it is completely under human control, it is useful and good and makes a better life for people. However, it is the experience of mankind (and was already his experience in quite early times) that technology is a cumulative thing, that machines are invariably improved, and that the improvement is always in the direction of etherealization, always in the direction of less human control and more auto-control—and at an accelerating rate.

As the human control decreases, the machine becomes frightening in exact proportion. Even when the human control is not visibly decreasing, or is doing so at an excessively low rate, it is a simple task for human ingenuity to look forward to a time when the machine may go out of control altogether, and the fear of that can be felt in advance.

What is the fear?

The simplest and most obvious fear is that of the possible harm that comes from machinery out of control. In fact, any technological advance, however fundamental, has this double aspect of good/harm and, in response, is viewed with a double aspect of love/fear.

Fire warms you, gives you light, cooks your food, smelts your ore—and, out of control, burns and kills. Your knives and spears kill your animal enemies and your human foes and, out of *your* control, are used by your foes to kill you. You can run down the list and build examples indefinitely and there has never been any human activity which, on getting out of control and doing harm, has not raised the sigh among many of, "Oh, if we had only stuck to the simple and virtuous lives of our ancestors who were not cursed with this new-fangled misery."

Yet is this fear of piecemeal harm from this advance or that the kind of deep-seated terror so difficult to express that it finds its way into the myths?

I think not. Fear of machinery for the discomfort and occasional harm it brings has (at least until very recently) not moved humanity to more than that occasional sigh. The love of the uses of machinery has always far overbalanced such fears, as we might judge if we consider that at no time in the history of mankind has any culture *voluntarily* given up significant technological advance because of the inconvenience or harm of its side effects. There have been involuntary retreats from technology as a result of warfare, civil strife, epidemics, or natural disasters, but the results of that are precisely what we call a "dark age" and the population suffering from one does its best over the generations to get back on the track and restore the technology.

Mankind has always chosen to counter the evils of technology, not by abandonment of technology, but by additional technology. The smoke of an indoor fire was countered by the chimney. The danger of the spear was countered by the shield. The danger of the mass army was countered by the city wall.

This attitude, despite the steady drizzle of backwardist outcries, has continued to the present. Thus the characteristic technological product of our present life is the automobile. It pollutes the air, assaults our eardrums, kills fifty thousand Americans a year and inflicts survivable injuries on hundreds of thousands.

Does anyone seriously expect Americans to give up their murderous little pets voluntarily? Even those who attend rallies to denounce the mechanization of modern life are quite likely to reach those rallies by automobile.

The first moment when the magnitude of possible evil was seen by *many* people as uncounterable by *any* conceivable good, came with the fission bomb in 1945. Never before had any technological advance set off demands for abandonment by so large a percentage of the population.

In fact, the reaction to the fission bomb set a new fashion. People were readier to oppose other advances they saw as unacceptably harmful in their side effects—biological warfare, the SST, certain genetic experiments on micro-organisms, breeder reactors, spray cans.

And even so, not one of these items has yet been given up.

But we're on the right track. The fear of the machine is not at the deepest level of the soul if the harm it does is accompanied by good, too; or if the harm is merely to some people—the few who happen to be on the spot in a vehicular collision, for instance.

The majority, after all, escape, and reap the good of the machine.

No, it is when the machine threatens all mankind in any way so that each individual human being begins to feel that he, *himself,* will not escape, that fear overwhelms love.

But since technology has begun to threaten the human race as a whole only in the last thirty years, were we immune to fear before that—or has the human race always been threatened?

After all, is physical destruction by brute energy of a type only now in our first the only way in which human beings can be destroyed? Might not the machine destroy the essence of humanity, our minds and souls, even while leaving our bodies intact and secure and comfortable?

It is a common fear, for instance, that television makes people unable to read and pocket computers will make them unable to add. Or think of the Spartan king who, on observing a catapult in action, mourned that that would put an end to human valor.

Certainly such subtle threats to humanity have existed and been recognized through all the long ages when man's feeble control over nature made it impossible for him to do himself very much physical harm.

The fear that machinery might make men effete is not yet, in my opinion, the basic and greatest fear. The one (it seems to me) that hits closest to the core is the general fear of irreversible change. Consider:

There are two kinds of change that we can gather from the universe about us. One is cyclic and benign.

Day both follows and is followed by night. Summer both follows and is followed by winter. Rain both follows and is followed by clear weather, and the net result is, therefore, no change. That may be boring, but it is comfortable and induces a feeling of security.

In fact, so comfortable is the notion of short-term cyclic change implying long-term changelessness, that human beings labor to find it everywhere. In human affairs, there is the notion that one generation both follows and is followed by another, that one dynasty both follows and is followed by another, that one empire both follows and is followed by another. It is not a good analogy to the cycles of nature since the repetitions are not exact, but it is good enough to be comforting.

So strongly do human beings want the comfort of cycles that they will seize upon one even when the evidence is insufficient—or even when it actually points the other way.

With respect to the universe, what evidence we have points to a hyperbolic evolution; a universe that expands forever out of the initial big bang and ends as formless gas and black holes. Yet our emotions drag us, against the evidence, to notions of oscillating, cyclic, repeating universes, in which even the black holes are merely gateways to new big bangs.

But then there is the other change, to be avoided at all costs—the irreversible, malignant change; the one-way change; the permanent change; the change-never-to-return.

What is so fearful about it? The fact is that there is one such change that lies so close to ourselves that it distorts the entire universe for us.

We are, after all, old, and though we were once young we shall never be young again. Irreversible! Our friends are dead, and though they were once alive, they shall never be alive again. Irreversible! The fact is that life ends in death and that is not a cyclic change and we fear that end and know it is useless to fight it.

What is worse is that the universe doesn't die with us. Callously and immortally it continues onward in its cyclic changes, adding to the injury of death the insult of indifference.

And what is still worse is that other human beings don't die with us. There are younger human beings, born later, who were helpless and dependent on us to start with, but who grow into supplanting nemeses and take our places as we age and die. To the injury of death is added the insult of supplantation.

Did I say it is useless to fight this horror of death accompanied by indifference and supplantation? Not quite. The uselessness is apparent only if we cling to the rational, but there is no law that says we must cling to it, and human beings do not, in fact, do so.

Death can be avoided by simply denying it exists. We can suppose that life on Earth is an illusion, a short testing period prior to entry into some afterlife where all is eternal and there is no question of irreversible change. Or we can suppose that it is only the body that is subject to death and that there is an immortal component of ourselves, not subject to irreversible change, which might, after the death of one body, enter another, in indefinite, cyclic repetitions of life.

These mythic inventions of afterlife and transmigration may make life tolerable for many human beings and enable them to face death with reasonable equanimity—but the fear of death and supplantation is only masked and overlaid; it is not removed.

In fact, the Greek myths involve the successive supplantation of one set of immortals by another—in what seems to be a despairing admission that not even eternal life and superhuman power can remove the danger of irreversible change and the humiliation of being supplanted.

To the Greeks it was disorder (Chaos) that first ruled the universe, and it was supplanted by Ouranos (the sky), whose intricate powdering of stars and complexly moving planets symbolized order (''Kosmos'').

But Ouranos was castrated by Kronos, his son. Kronos, his brothers, his sisters, and their progeny then ruled the universe.

Kronos feared that he would be served by his children as he had served his father (a kind of cycle of irreversible changes) and devoured his children as they were born. He was duped by his wife, however, who managed to save her last-born, Zeus, and spirit him away to safety. Zeus grew to adult godhood, rescued his siblings from his father's stomach, warred against Kronos and those who followed him, defeated him, and replaced him as ruler.

(There are supplantation myths among other cultures, too, even in our own—as the one in which Satan tried to supplant God and failed; a myth that reached its greatest literary expression in John Milton's *Paradise Lost*.)

And was Zeus safe? He was attracted to the sea nymph Thetis and would have married her had he not been informed by the Fates that Thetis was destined to bear a son mightier than his father. That meant it was not safe for Zeus, or for any other god, either, to marry her. She was therefore forced (much against her will) to marry Peleus, a mortal, and bear a mortal son, the only child the myths describe her as having. That son was Achilles, who was certainly far mightier than his father (and, like Talos, had only his heel as his weak point through which he might be killed).

Now, then, translate this fear of irreversible change and of being supplanted into the relationship of man and machine and what do we have? Surely the *great* fear is not that machinery will harm us—but that it will supplant us. It is not that it will render us ineffective—but that it will make us obsolete.

The ultimate machine is an intelligent machine and there is only one basic plot to the intelligent-machine story—that it is created to serve man, but that it ends by dominating man. It cannot exist without threatening to supplant us, and it must therefore be destroyed or we will be.

There is the danger of the broom of the sorcerer's apprentice, the golem of Rabbi Löw, the monster created by Dr. Frankenstein. As the child born of our body eventually supplants us, so does the machine born of our mind.

Mary Shelley's *Frankenstein,* which appeared in 1818, represents a peak of fear, however, for, as it happened, circumstances conspired to reduce that fear, at least temporarily.

Between the year 1815, which saw the end of a series of general European wars, and 1914, which saw the beginning of another, there was a brief period in which humanity could afford the luxury of optimism concerning its relationship to the machine. The Industrial Revolution seemed suddenly to uplift human power and to bring on dreams of a technological utopia on Earth in place of the mythic one in Heaven. The good of machines seemed to far outbalance the evil and the response of love far outbalance the response of fear.

It was in that interval that modern science fiction began—and by modern science fiction I refer to a form of literature that deals with societies differing from our own specifically in the level of science and technology, and into which we might conceivably pass from our own society by appropriate changes in that level. (This differentiates science fiction from fantasy or from "speculative fiction," in which the fictional society cannot be connected with our own by any rational set of changes.)

Modern science fiction, because of the time of its beginning, took on an optimistic note. Man's relationship to the machine was one of use and control. Man's power grew and man's machines were his faithful tools, bringing him wealth and security and carrying him to the farthest reaches of the universe.

This optimistic note continues to this day, particularly among those writers who were molded in the years before the coming of the fission bomb—notably, Robert Heinlein, Arthur C. Clarke, and myself.

Nevertheless, with World War I, disillusionment set in. Science and technology, which promised an Eden, turned out to be capable of delivering Hell was well. The beautiful airplane that fulfilled the age-old dream of flight could deliver bombs. The chemical techniques that produced anesthetics, dyes, and medicines produced poison gas as well.

The fear of supplantation rose again. In 1921, not long after the end of World War I, Karel Čapek's drama *R.U.R.* appeared and it was the tale of Frankenstein again, escalated to the planetary level. Not a single monster was created but millions of robots (Čapek's word, meaning "worker," a mechanical one, that is). And it was not a single monster turning upon his single creator, but robots turning on humanity, wiping them out and supplanting them.

From the beginning of the science fiction magazine in 1926 to 1959 (a third of a century or a generation) optimism and pessimism battled each other in science fiction, with optimism—thanks chiefly to the influence of John W. Campbell, Jr.—having the better of it.

Beginning in 1939, I wrote a series of influential robot stories that self-consciously combated the "Frankenstein complex" and made of the robots the servants, friends, and allies of humanity.

It was pessimism, however, that won in the end, and for two reasons:

First, machinery grew more frightening. The fission bomb threatened physical destruction, of course, but worse still was the rapidly advancing electronic computer. Those computers seemed to steal the human soul. Deftly they solved our routine problems and more and more we found ourselves placing our questions in the hands of these machines with increasing faith, and accepting their answers with increasing humility.

All that fission and fusion bombs can do is destroy us, the computer might supplant us.

The second reason is more subtle, for it involved a change in the nature of the science fiction writer.

Until 1959, there were many branches of fiction, with science fiction perhaps the least among them. It brought its writers less in prestige and money than almost any other branch, so that no one wrote science fiction who wasn't so fascinated by it that he was willing to give up any chance at fame and fortune for its sake. Often that fascination stemmed from an absorption in the romance of science so that science fiction writers would naturally picture men as winning the universe by learning to bend it to their will.

In the 1950s, however, competition with TV gradually killed the magazines that supported fiction, and by the time the 1960s arrived the only form of fiction that was flourishing, and even expanding, was science fiction. Its magazines continued and an incredible paperback boom was initiated. To a lesser extent it invaded movies and television, with its greatest triumphs undoubtedly yet to come.

This meant that in the 1960s and 1970s, young writers began to write science fiction not because they wanted to, but because it was there—and because nothing else was there. It meant that many of the new generation of science fiction writers had no knowledge of science, no sympathy for it—and were in fact rather hostile to it. Such writers were far more ready to accept the fear half of the love/fear relationship of man to machine.

As a result, contemporary science fiction, far more often than not, is presenting us, over and over, with the myth of the child supplanting the parent, Zeus supplanting Kronos, Satan supplanting God, the machine supplanting humanity.

Here are three examples in frightening and convincing detail: John W. Campbell's "Twilight," Gordon R. Dickson's "Computers Don't Argue," and Brian W. Aldiss's "The New Father Christmas."

Nightmares they are, and they are to be read as such.

—But allow me my own cynical commentary at the end. Remember that although Kronos foresaw the danger of being supplanted, and though he destroyed his children to prevent it—he was supplanted anyway, and rightly so, for Zeus was the better ruler.

So it may be that although we will hate and fight the machines, we will be supplanted anyway, and rightly so, for the intelligent machines to which we will give birth may, better than we, carry on the striving toward the goal of understanding and using the universe, climbing to heights we ourselves could never aspire to.

BIBLIOGRAPHY

Asimov, Isaac, *I, Robot,* 1950 (Gnome)
————, *The Caves of Steel,* 1954 (Doubleday)
————, *The Naked Sun,* 1957 (Doubleday)
————, *The Rest of the Robots,* 1964 (Doubleday)
————, *The Bicentennial Man,* 1976 (Doubleday)
Bester, Alfred, *The Computer Connection,* 1975 (Berkley)
Boyd, John, *The Last Starship from Earth,* 1968 (Berkley Medallion)
Clarke, Arthur C., *2001: A Space Odyssey,* 1968 (New American Library)
Compton, D. G., *The Steel Crocodile,* 1970 (Ace)
Conklin, Groff, ed., *Science Fiction Thinking Machines,* 1954 (Vanguard)
Delany, Samuel R., *Nova,* 1968 (Doubleday)
Gerrold, David, *When Harlie Was One,* 1972 (Nelson Doubleday)
Greenberg, Martin, ed., *The Robot and The Man,* 1953 (Gnome)
Heinlein, Robert, *The Moon Is a Harsh Mistress,* 1966 (Berkley Medallion)
Herbert, Frank, *Destination: Void,* 1966 (Berkley Medallion)
Hodder-Williams, Christopher, *Fistful of Digits,* 1968 (Hodder and Staughton)
Hoyle, Fred, and John Elliot, *A for Andromeda,* 1962 (Harper & Row)
Jones, D. F., *Colossus,* 1967 (Putnam)
Lem, Stanislaw, *The Cyberiad,* 1974 (Seabury)

Levin, Ira, *This Perfect Day,* 1970 (Random House)
Moskowitz, Sam, ed., *The Coming of the Robots,* 1963 (Collier)
Reynolds, Mack, *Computer World,* 1970 (Ace)
Roshwald, Mordecai, *Level 7,* 1959 (New American Library)
Silverberg, Robert, ed., *Men and Machines,* 1968 (Meredith)
Vonnegut, Kurt, Jr., *Player Piano,* 1952 (Holt, Rinehart, and Winston)
Williamson, Jack, *The Humanoids,* 1949 (Simon and Schuster)
Wolfe, Bernard, *Limbo,* 1952 (Ace)
Zamiatin, Yevgeny, *We,* 1921 (Bantam)

Twilight

John W. Campbell, Jr.

"Speaking of Hitchhikers," said Jim Bendell in a rather bewildered way, "I picked up a man the other day that certainly was a queer cuss." He laughed, but it wasn't a real laugh. "He told me the queerest yarn I ever heard. Most of them tell you how they lost their good jobs and tried to find work out here in the wide spaces of the West. They don't seem to realize how many people we have out here. They think all this great beautiful country is uninhabited."

Jim Bendell's a real estate man, and I knew how he could go on. That's his favorite line, you know. He's real worried because there's a lot of homesteading plots still open out in our state. He talks about the beautiful country, but he never went farther into the desert than the edge of town. 'Fraid of it actually. So I sort of steered him back on the track.

"What did he claim, Jim? Prospector who couldn't find land to prospect?"

"That's not very funny, Bart. No; it wasn't only what he claimed. He didn't even claim it, just said it. You know, he didn't say it was true, he just said it. That's what gets me. I know it ain't true, but the way he said it— Oh, I don't know."

By which I knew he didn't. Jim Bendell's usually pretty careful about his English—real proud of it. When he slips, that means he's disturbed. Like the time he thought the rattlesnake was a stick of wood and wanted to put it on the fire.

Jim went on: And he had funny clothes, too. They looked like silver, but they were soft as silk. And at night they glowed just a little.

I picked him up about dusk. Really picked him up. He was lying off about ten feet from the South Road. I thought, at first, somebody had hit him, and then hadn't stopped. Didn't see him very clearly, you know. I picked him up, put him in the car, and started on. I had about three hundred miles to go, but I thought I could drop him at Warren Spring with Doc Vance. But he came to in about five minutes, and opened his eyes. He looked straight off, and he looked first at the car, then at the Moon. "Thank God!" he says, and then looks at me. It gave me a shock. He was beautiful. No; he was handsome.

He wasn't either one. He was magnificent. He was about six feet two, I think, and his hair was brown, with a touch of red-gold. It seemed like fine copper wire that's turned brown. It was crisp and curly. His forehead was wide, twice as wide as mine. His features were delicate, but tremendously impressive; his eyes were gray, like etched iron, and bigger than mine—a lot.

That suit he wore—it was more like a bathing suit with pajama trousers. His arms were long and muscled smoothly as an Indian's. He was white, though, tanned lightly with a golden, rather than a brown, tan.

But he was magnificent. Most wonderful man I ever saw. I don't know, damn it!

"Hello!" I said. "Have an accident?"

"No; not this time, at least."

And his voice was magnificent, too. It wasn't an ordinary voice. It sounded like an organ talking, only it was human.

"But maybe my mind isn't quite steady yet. I tried an experiment. Tell me what the date is, year and all, and let me see," he went on.

"Why—December 9, 1932," I said.

And it didn't please him. He didn't like it a bit. But the wry grin that came over his face gave way to a chuckle.

"Over a thousand—" he says reminiscently. "Not as bad as seven million. I shouldn't complain."

"Seven million what?"

"Years," he said, steadily enough. Like he meant it. "I tried an experiment once. Or I will try it. Now I'll have to try again. The experiment was—in 3059. I'd just finished the release experiment. Testing space then. Time—it wasn't that, I still believe. It was space. I felt myself caught in that field, but I couldn't pull away. Field gamma-H 481, intensity 935 in the Pellman range. It sucked me in, and I went out.

"I think it took a short cut through space to the position the solar system will occupy. Through a higher dimension, effecting a speed exceeding light and throwing me into the future plane."

He wasn't telling me, you know. He was just thinking out loud. Then he began to realize I was there.

"I couldn't read their instruments, seven million years of evolution changed everything. So I overshot my mark a little coming back. I belong in 3059.

"But tell me, what's the latest scientific invention of this year?"

He startled me so, I answered almost before I thought.

"Why, television, I guess. And radio and airplanes."

"Radio—good. They will have instruments."

"But see here—who are you?"

"Ah—I'm sorry. I forgot," he replied in that organ voice of his. "I am Ares Sen Kenlin. And you?"

"James Waters Bendell."

"Waters—what does that mean? I do not recognize it."

"Why—it's a name, of course. Why should you recognize it?"

"I see—you have not the classification, then. 'Sen' stands for science."

"Where did you come from, Mr. Kenlin?"

"Come from?" He smiled, and his voice was slow and soft. "I came out of space across seven million years or more. They had lost count—the men had. The machines had eliminated the unneeded service. They didn't know what year it was. But before that—my home is Neva'th City in the year 3059."

That's when I began to think he was a nut.

"I was an experimenter," he went on. "Science, as I have said. My father was a scientist, too, but in human genetics. I myself am an experiment. He proved his point, and all the world followed suit. I was the first of the new race."

"The new race—oh, holy destiny—what has—what will—"

"What is its end? I have seen it—almost. I saw them—the little men—bewildered—lost. And the machines."

"Must it be—can't anything sway it?"

"Listen—I heard this song."

He sang the song. Then he didn't have to tell me about the people. I knew them. I could hear their voices, in the queer, crackling, un-

English words. I could read their bewildered longings. It was in a minor key, I think. It called, it called and asked, and hunted hopelessly. And over it all the steady rumble and whine of the unknown, forgotten machines.

The machines that couldn't stop, because they had been started, and the little men had forgotten how to stop them, or even what they were for, looking at them and listening—and wondering. They couldn't read or write any more, and the language had changed, you see, so that the phonic records of their ancestors meant nothing to them.

But that song went on, and they wondered. And they looked out across space and they saw the warm, friendly stars—too far away. Nine planets they knew and inhabited. And locked by infinite distance, they couldn't see another race, a new life.

And through it all—two things. The machines. Bewildered forgetfulness. And maybe one more. Why?

That was the song, and it made me cold. It shouldn't be sung around people of today. It almost killed something. It seemed to kill hope. After that song—I—well, I believed him.

When he finished the song, he didn't talk for a while. Then he sort of shook himself.

You won't understand (he continued). Not yet—but I have seen them. They stand about, little misshapen men with huge heads. But their heads contain only brains. They had machines that could think—but somebody turned them off a long time ago, and no one knew how to start them again. That was the trouble with them. They had wonderful brains. Far better than yours or mine. But it must have been millions of years ago when they were turned off, too, and they just haven't thought since then. Kindly little people. That was all they knew.

When I slipped into that field it grabbed me like a gravitational field whirling a space transport down to a planet. It sucked me in—and through. Only the other side must have been seven million years in the future. That's where I was. It must have been in exactly the same spot on Earth's surface, but I never knew why.

It was night then, and I saw the city a little way off. The Moon was shining on it, and the whole scene looked wrong. You see, in seven million years, men had done a lot with the positions of the planetary bodies, what with moving space liners, clearing lanes through the asteroids, and such. And seven million years is long enough for natural things to change positions a little. The Moon must have been fifty thousand miles farther out. And it was rotating on its axis. I lay there a while and watched it. Even the stars were different.

There were ships going out of the city. Back and forth, like things sliding along a wire, but there was only a wire of force, of course. Part of the city, the lower part, was brightly lighted with what must have been mercury-vapor glow, I decided. Blue-green. I felt sure men didn't live there—the light was wrong for eyes. But the top of the city was so sparsely lighted.

Then I saw something coming down out of the sky. It was brightly lighted. A huge globe, and it sank straight to the center of the great black-and-silver mass of the city.

I don't know what it was, but even then I knew the city was deserted. Strange that I could even imagine that, I who had never seen a deserted city before. But I walked the fifteen miles over to it and entered it. There were machines going about the streets, repair machines, you know. They couldn't understand that the city didn't need to go on functioning, so they were still working. I found a taxi machine that seemed fairly familiar. It had a manual control that I could work.

I don't know how long that city had been deserted. Some of the men from the other cities said it was a hundred and fifty thousand years. Some went as high as three hundred thousand years. Three hundred thousand years since human foot had been in that city. The taxi machine was in perfect condition, functioned at once. It was clean, and the city was clean and orderly. I saw a restaurant and I was hungry. Hungrier still for humans to speak to. There were none, of course, but I didn't know.

The restaurant had the food displayed directly, and I made a choice. The food was three hundred thousand years old, I suppose. I didn't know, and the machines that served it to me didn't care, for they made things synthetically, you see, and perfectly. When the builders made those cities, they forgot one thing. They didn't realize that things shouldn't go on forever.

It took me six months to make my apparatus. And near the end I was ready to go; and, from seeing those machines go blindly, perfectly, on in orbits of their duties with the tireless, ceaseless perfection their designers had incorporated in them, long after those designers and their sons, and their sons' sons had no use for them—

When Earth is cold, and the Sun has died out, those machines will go on. When Earth begins to crack and break, those perfect, ceaseless machines will try to repair her—

I left the restaurant and cruised about the city in the taxi. The machine had a little, electric-power motor, I believe, but it gained its power from the great central power radiator. I knew before long that I was far in the future. The city was divided into two sections, a section of many strata where machines functioned smoothly, save for a deep humming beat that echoed through the whole city like a vast unending song of power. The entire metal framework of the place echoed with it, transmitted it, hummed with it. But it was soft and restful, a reassuring beat.

There must have been thirty levels above ground, and twenty more below, a solid block of metal walls and metal floors and metal and glass and force machines. The only light was the blue-green glow of the mercury-vapor arcs. The light of mercury vapor is rich in high-energy quanta, which stimulate the alkali metal atoms to photoelectric activity. Or perhaps that is beyond the science of your day? I have forgotten.

But they had used that light because many of their worker machines needed sight. The machines were marvelous. For five hours I wandered through the vast power plant on the very lowest level, watching them, and because there was motion, and that pseudo-mechanical life, I felt less alone.

The generators I saw were a development of the release I had discovered—when? The release of the energy of matter, I mean, and I knew when I saw that for what countless ages they could continue.

The entire lower block of the city was given over to the machines. Thousands. But most of them seemed idle, or, at most, running under light load. I recognized a telephone apparatus, and not a single signal came through. There was no life in the city. Yet when I pressed a little stud beside the screen on one side of the room, the machine began working instantly. It was ready. Only no one needed it any more. The men knew how to die, and be dead, but the machines didn't.

Finally I went up to the top of the city, the upper level. It was a paradise.

There were shrubs and trees and parks, glowing in the soft light that they had learned to make in the very air. They had learned it five million years or more before. Two million years ago they forgot. But the machines didn't, and they were still making it. It hung in the air, soft, silvery light, slightly rosy, and the gardens were shadowy with it. There were no machines here now, but I knew that in daylight they must come out and work on these gardens, keeping them a paradise for masters who had died, and stopped moving, as they could not.

In the desert outside the city it had been cool, and very dry. Here the air was soft, warm and sweet with the scent of blooms that men had spent several hundreds of thousands of years perfecting.

Then somewhere music began. It began in the air, and spread softly through it. The Moon was just setting now, and as it set, the rosy-silver glow waned and the music grew stronger.

It came from everywhere and from nowhere. It was within me. I do not know how they did it. And I do not know how such music could be written.

Savages make music too simple to be beautiful, but it is stirring. Semisavages write music beautifully simple, and simply beautiful. Your Negro music was your best. They knew music when they heard it and sang it as they felt it. Semicivilized peoples write great music. They are proud of their music, and make sure it is known for great music. They make it so great it is top-heavy.

I had always thought our music good. But that which came through the air was the song of triumph, sung by a mature race, the race of man in its full triumph! It was man singing his triumph in majestic sound that swept me up; it showed me what lay before me; it carried me on.

And it died in the air as I looked at the deserted city. The machines should have forgotten that song. Their masters had, long before.

I came to what must have been one of their homes; it was a dimly seen doorway in the dusky light, but as I stepped up to it, the lights which had not functioned in three hundred thousand years illuminated it for me with a green-white glow, like a firefly, and I stepped into the room beyond. Instantly something happened to the air in the doorway behind me; it was opaque as milk. The room in which I stood was a room of metal and stone. The stone was some jet-black substance with the finish of velvet, and the metals were silver and gold. There was a rug on the floor, a rug of just such material as I am wearing now, but thicker and softer. There were divans about the room, low and covered with these soft metallic materials. They were black and gold and silver, too.

I had never seen anything like that. I never shall again, I suppose, and my language and yours were not made to describe it.

The builders of that city had right and reason to sing that song of sweeping triumph, triumph that swept them over the nine planets and the fifteen habitable moons.

But they weren't there any more, and I wanted to leave. I thought of a plan and went to a subtelephone office to examine a map I had seen. The old World looked much the same. Seven or even seventy million years don't mean much to old Mother Earth. She may even succeed in wearing down those marvelous machine cities. She can wait a hundred million or a thousand million years before she is beaten.

I tried calling different city centers shown on the map. I had quickly learned the system when I examined the central apparatus.

I tried once—twice—thrice—a round dozen times. Yawk City, Lunon City, Paree, Shkago, Singpor, others. I was beginning to feel that there were no more men on all Earth. And I felt crushed, as at each city the machines replied and did my bidding. The machines were there in each of those far vaster cities, for I was in the Neva City of their time. A small city. Yawk City was more than eight hundred kilometers in diameter.

In each city I had tried several numbers. Then I tried San Frisco. There was someone there, and a voice answered and the picture of a human appeared on the little glowing screen. I could see him start and stare in surprise at me. Then he started speaking to me. I couldn't understand, of course. I can understand your speech, and you mine, because your speech of this day is largely recorded on records of various types and has influenced our pronunciation.

Some things are changed; names of cities, particularly, because names of cities are apt to be polysyllabic, and used a great deal. People tend to elide them, shorten them. I am in—Nee-vah-dah—as you would say? We say only Neva. And Yawk State. But it is Ohio and Iowa still. Over a thousand years, effects were small on words, because they were recorded.

But seven million years had passed, and the men had forgotten the old records, used them less as time went on, and their speech varied till the time came when they could no longer understand the records. They were not written any more, of course.

Some men must have arisen occasionally among that last of the race and sought for knowledge, but it was denied them. An ancient writing can be translated if some basic rule is found. An ancient voice though—and when the race has forgotten the laws of science and the labor of mind.

So his speech was strange to me as he answered over that circuit. His voice was high in pitch, his words liquid, his tones sweet. It was almost a song as he spoke. He was excited and called others. I could not understand them, but I knew where they were. I could go to them.

So I went down from the paradise of gardens, and as I prepared to leave, I saw dawn in the sky. The strange-bright stars winked and twinkled and faded. Only one bright rising star was familiar—Venus.

She shone golden now. Finally, as I stood watching for the first time that strange heaven, I began to understand what had first impressed me with the wrongness of the view. The stars, you see, were all different.

In my time—and yours—the solar system is a lone wanderer that by chance is passing across an intersection point of Galactic traffic. The stars we see at night are the stars of moving clusters, you know. In fact our system is passing through the heart of the Ursa Major group. Half a dozen other groups center within five hundred light-years of us.

But during those seven millions of years, the Sun had moved out of the group. The heavens were almost empty to the eye. Only here and there shone a single faint star. And across the vast sweep of black sky swung the band of the Milky Way. The sky was empty.

That must have been another thing those men meant in their songs—felt in their hearts. Loneliness—not even the close, friendly stars. We have stars within half a dozen light-years. They told me that their instruments, which gave directly the distance to any star, showed that the nearest was one hundred and fifty light-years away. It was enormously bright. Brighter even than Sirius of our heavens. And that made it even less friendly, because it was a blue-white supergiant. Our sun would have served as a satellite for that star.

I stood there and watched the lingering rose-silver glow die as the powerful blood-red light of the Sun swept over the horizon. I knew by the stars now that it must have been several millions of years since my day; since I had last seen the Sun sweep up. And that blood-red light made me wonder if the Sun itself was dying.

An edge of it appeared, blood-red and huge. It swung up, and the color faded, till in half an hour it was the familiar yellow-gold disk.

It hadn't changed in all that time.

I had been foolish to think that it would. Seven million years—that is nothing to Earth, how much less to the Sun? Some two thousand thousand thousand times it had risen since I last saw it rise. Two thousand thousand thousand days. If it had been that many years—I might have noticed a change.

The universe moves slowly. Only life is not enduring; only life changes swiftly. Eight short millions of years. Eight days in the life of Earth—and the race was dying. It had left something: machines. But they would die, too, even though they could not understand. So I felt. I—may have changed that. I will tell you. Later.

For when the Sun was up, I looked again at the sky and the ground, some fifty floors below. I had come to the edge of the city.

Machines were moving on that ground, leveling it, perhaps. A great wide line of gray stretched off across the level desert straight to the east. I had seen it glowing faintly before the Sun rose—a roadway for ground machines. There was no traffic on it.

I saw an airship slip in from the east. It came with a soft, muttering whine of air, like a child complaining in sleep; it grew to my eyes like an expanding balloon. It was huge when it settled in a great port-slip in the city below. I could hear now the clang and mutter of machines, working on the materials brought in, no doubt. The machines had ordered raw materials. The machines in other cities had supplied. The freight machines had carried them here.

San Frisco and Jacksville were the only two cities on North America still used. But the machines went on in all the others, because they couldn't stop. They hadn't been ordered to.

Then high above, something appeared, and from the city beneath me, from a center section, three small spheres rose. They, like the freight ship, had no visible driving mechanisms. The point in the sky above, like a black star in a blue space, had grown to a moon. The three spheres met it high above. Then together they descended and lowered into the center of the city, where I could not see them.

It was a freight transport from Venus. The one I had seen land the night before had come from Mars, I learned.

I moved after that and looked for some sort of a taxiplane. They had none that I recognized in scouting about the city. I searched the higher levels, and here and there saw deserted ships, but far too large for me, and without controls.

It was nearly noon—and I ate again. The food was good.

I knew then that this was a city of the dead ashes of human hopes. The hopes not of *a* race, not the whites, nor the yellow, nor the blacks, but the human race. I was mad to leave the city. I was afraid to try the ground road to the west, for the taxi I drove was powered from some source in the city, and I knew it would fail before many miles.

It was afternoon when I found a small hangar near the outer wall of the vast city. It contained three ships. I had been searching through the lower strata of the human section—the upper part. There were restaurants and shops and theaters there. I entered one place where, at my entrance, soft music began, and colors and forms began to rise on a screen before me.

They were the triumph songs in form and sound and color of a mature race, a race that had marched steadily upward through five millions of years—and didn't see the path that faded out ahead, when they were dead and had stopped, and the city itself was dead—but hadn't stopped. I hastened out of there—and the song that had not been sung in three hundred thousand years died behind me.

But I found the hangar. It was a private one, likely. Three ships. One must have been fifty feet long and fifteen in diameter. It was a yacht, a space yacht, probably. One was some fifteen feet long and five feet in diameter. That must have been the family air machine. The third was a tiny thing, little more than ten feet long and two in diameter. I had to lie down within it, evidently.

There was a periscopic device that gave me a view ahead and almost directly above. A window that permitted me to see what lay below—and a device that moved a map under a frosted-glass screen and projected it onto the screen in such a way that the cross-hairs of the screen always marked my position.

I spent half an hour attempting to understand what the makers of that ship had made. But the men who made that were men who held behind them the science and knowledge of five millions of years and the perfect machines of those ages. I saw the release mechanism that powered it. I understood the principles of that and, vaguely, the mechanics. But there were no conductors, only pale beams that pulsed so swiftly you could hardly catch the pulsations from the corner of the eye. They had been glowing and pulsating, some half dozen of them, for three hundred thousand years at least; probably more.

I entered the machine, and instantly half a dozen more beams sprang into being; there was a slight suggestion of a quiver, and a queer strain ran through my body. I understood in an instant, for the machine was resting on gravity nullifiers. That had been my hope when I worked on the space fields I discovered after the release.

But they had had it for millions of years before they built that perfect deathless machine. My weight entering it had forced it to readjust itself and simultaneously to prepare for operation. Within, an artificial gravity equal to that of Earth had gripped me, and the neutral zone between the outside and the interior had caused the strain.

The machine was ready. It was fully fueled, too. You see they were equipped to tell automatically their wants and needs. They were almost living things, every one. A caretaker machine kept them supplied, adjusted, even repaired them when need be, and when possible. If it was not, I learned later, they were carried away in a service truck that came automatically; replaced by an exactly similar machine; and carried to the shops where they were made, and automatic machines made them over.

The machine waited patiently for me to start. The controls were simple, obvious. There was a lever at the left that you pushed forward to move forward, pulled back to go back. On the right a horizontal, pivoted bar. If you swung it left, the ship spun left; if right, the ship spun right. If tipped up, the ship followed it, and likewise for all motions other than backward and forward. Raising it bodily raised the ship, as depressing it depressed the ship.

I lifted it slightly, a needle moved a bit on a gauge comfortably before my eyes as I lay there, and the floor dropped beneath me. I pulled the other control back, and the ship gathered speed as it moved gently out into the open. Releasing both controls into neutral, the machine continued till it stopped at the same elevation, the motion absorbed by air friction. I turned it about, and another dial before my eyes moved, showing my position. I could not read it, though. The map did not move, as I had hoped it would. So I started toward what I felt was west.

I could feel no acceleration in that marvelous machine. The ground simply began leaping backward, and in a moment the city was gone. The map unrolled rapidly beneath me now, and I saw that I was moving south of west. I turned northward slightly, and watched the compass. Soon I understood that, too, and the ship sped on.

I had become too interested in the map and the compass, for suddenly there was a sharp buzz and, without my volition, the machine rose and swung to the north. There was a mountain ahead of me; I had not seen, but the ship had.

I noticed then what I should have seen before—two little knobs that could move the map. I started to move them and heard a sharp clicking, and the pace of the ship began decreasing. A moment and it had steadied at a considerably lower speed, the machine swinging to a new course. I tried to right it, but to my amazement the controls did not affect it.

It was the map, you see. It would either follow the course, or the course would follow it. I had moved it and the machine had taken over control of its own accord. There was a little button I could have pushed—but I didn't know. I couldn't control the ship until it finally came to rest and lowered itself to a stop six inches from the ground in the center of what must have been the ruins of a great city, Sacramento, probably.

I understood now, so I adjusted the map for San Frisco, and the ship went on at once. It steered itself around a mass of broken stone, turned back to its course, and headed on, a bullet-shaped, self-controlled dart.

It didn't descend when it reached San Frisco. It simply hung in the air and sounded a soft musical hum. Twice. Then it waited. I waited, too, and looked down.

There were people here. I saw the humans of that age for the first time. They were little men—bewildered—dwarfed, with heads disproportionately large. But not extremely so.

Their eyes impressed me most. They were huge, and when they looked at me there was a power in them that seemed sleeping, but too deeply to be roused.

I took the manual controls then and landed. And no sooner had I got out, than the ship rose automatically and started off by itself. They had automatic parking devices. The ship had gone to a public hangar, the nearest, where it would be automatically serviced and cared for. There was a little call set I should have taken with me when I got out. Then I could have pressed a button and called it to me—wherever I was in that city.

The people about me began talking—singing almost—among themselves. Others were coming up leisurely. Men and women—but there seemed no old and few young. What few young there were, were treated almost with respect, carefully taken care of lest a careless foot step on their toes or a careless step knock them down.

There was reason, you see. They lived a tremendous time. Some lived as long as three thousand years. Then—they simply died. They didn't grow old, and it never had been learned why people died as they did. The heart stopped, the brain ceased thought—and they died. But the young children, children not yet mature, were treated with the utmost care. But one child was born in the course of a month in that city of one hundred thousand people. The human race was growing sterile.

And I have told you that they were lonely? Their loneliness was beyond hope. For, you see, as man strode toward maturity, he destroyed all forms of life that menaced him. Disease. Insects. Then the last of the insects, and finally the last of the man-eating animals.

The balance of nature was destroyed then, so they had to go on. It was like the machines. They started them—and now they can't stop. They started destroying life—and now it wouldn't stop. So they had to destroy weeds of all sorts, then many formerly harmless plants. Then the herbivora, too, the deer and the antelope and the rabbit and the horse. They were a menace, they attacked man's machine-tended crops. Man was still eating natural foods.

You can understand. The thing was beyond their control. In the end they killed off the denizens of the sea, also, in self-defense. Without the many creatures that had kept them in check, they were swarming beyond bounds. And the time had come when synthetic foods replaced natural. The air was purified of all life about two and a half million years after our day, all microscopic life.

That meant that the water, too, must be purified. It was—and then came the end of life in the ocean. There were minute organisms that lived on bacterial forms, and tiny fish that lived on the minute organisms, and small fish that lived on the tiny fish, and big fish that lived on the small fish—and the beginning of the chain was gone. The sea was devoid of life in a generation. That meant about one thousand and five hundred years to them. Even the sea plants had gone.

And on all Earth there was only man and the organisms he had protected—the plants he wanted for decoration, and certain ultrahygienic pets, as long-lived as their masters. Dogs. They must have been remarkable animals. Man was reaching his maturity then, and his animal friend, the friend that had followed him through a thousand millenniums to your day and mine, and another four thousand millenniums to the day of man's early maturity, had grown in intelligence. In an ancient museum—a wonderful place, for they had, perfectly preserved, the body of a great leader of mankind who had died five and a half million years before I saw him—in that museum, deserted then, I saw one of those canines. His skull was nearly as large as mine. They had simple ground machines that dogs could be trained to drive, and they held races in which the dogs drove those machines.

Then man reached his full maturity. It extended over a period of a full million years. So tremendously did he stride ahead, the dog ceased to be a companion. Less and less were they wanted. When the million years had passed, and man's decline began, the dog was gone. It had died out.

And now this last dwindling group of men still in the system had no other life form to make its successor. Always before when one civilization toppled, on its ashes rose a new one. Now there was but one civilization, and all other races, even other species, were gone save in the plants. And man was too far along in his old age to bring intelligence and mobility from the plants. Perhaps he could have in his prime.

Other worlds were flooded with man during that million years—the million years. Every planet and every moon of the system had its quota of men. Now only the planets had their populations, the moons had been deserted. Pluto had been left before I landed, and men were coming from Neptune, moving in toward the Sun, and the home planet, while I was there. Strangely quiet men, viewing, most of them, for the first time, the planet that had given their race life.

But as I stepped from that ship and watched it rise away from me, I saw why the race of man was dying. I looked back at the faces of those men, and on them I read the answer. There was one single quality gone from the still-great minds—minds far greater than yours or mine. I had to have the help of one of them in solving some of my problems. In space, you know, there are twenty coordinates, ten of which are zero, six of which have fixed values, and the four others represent our changing, familiar dimensions in space-time. That means that integrations must proceed in not double, or triple, or quadruple—but ten integrations.

It would have taken me too long. I would never have solved all the problems I must work out. I could not use their mathematics machines; and mine, of course, were seven million years in the past. But one of those men was interested and helped me. He did quadruple and quintuple integration, even quadruple integration between varying exponential limits—in his head.

When I asked him to. For the one thing that had made man great had left him. As I looked in their faces and eyes on landing I knew it. They looked at me, interested at this rather unusual-looking stranger—and went on. They had come to see the arrival of a ship. A rare event, you see. But they were merely welcoming me in a friendly fashion. They were not curious! Man had lost the instinct of curiosity.

Oh, not entirely! They wondered at the machines, they wondered at the stars. But they did nothing about it. It was not wholly lost to them yet, but nearly. It was dying. In the six short months I stayed with them, I learned more than they had learned in the two or even three thousand years they had lived among the machines.

Can you appreciate the crushing hopelessness it brought to me? I, who love science, who see in it, or have seen in it, the salvation, the raising of mankind—to see those wondrous machines, of man's triumphant maturity, forgotten and misunderstood. The wondrous, perfect machines that tended, protected, and cared for those gentle, kindly people who had—forgotten.

They were lost among it. The city was a magnificent ruin to them, a thing that rose stupendous about them. Something not understood, a thing that was of the nature of the world. It was. It had not been made; it simply was. Just as the mountains and the deserts and the waters of the seas.

Do you understand—can you see that the time since those machines were new was longer than the time from our day to the birth of the race? Do we know the legends of our first ancestors? Do we remember their lore of forest and cave? The secret of chipping a flint till it had a sharp-cutting edge? The secret of trailing and killing a saber-toothed tiger without being killed oneself?

They were now in similar straits, though the time had been longer, because the language had taken a long step towards perfection, and because the machines maintained everything for them through generation after generation.

Why, the entire planet of Pluto had been deserted—yet on Pluto the largest mines of one of their metals were located; the machines still functioned. A perfect unity existed throughout the system. A unified system of perfect machines.

And all those people knew was that to do a certain thing to a certain lever produced certain results. Just as men in the Middle Ages knew that to take a certain material, wood, and place it in contact with other pieces of wood heated red, would cause the wood to disappear, and become heat. They did not understand that wood was being oxidized with the release of the heat of formation of carbon dioxide and water. So those people did not understand the things that fed and clothed and carried them.

I stayed with them there for three days. And then I went to Jacksville. Yawk City, too. That was enormous. It stretched over— well, from well north of where Boston is today to well south of Washington—that was what they called Yawk City.

I never believed that, when he said it, said Jim, interrupting himself. I knew he didn't. If he had I think he'd have bought land somewhere along there and held for a rise in value. I know Jim. He'd have the idea that seven million years was something like seven hundred, and maybe his great-grandchildren would be able to sell it.

Anyway, went on Jim, he said it was all because the cities had spread so. Boston spread south. Washington, north. And Yawk City spread all over. And the cities between grew into them.

And it was all one vast machine. It was perfectly ordered and perfectly neat. They had a transportation system that took me from the North End to the South End in three minutes. I timed it. They had learned to neutralize acceleration.

Then I took one of the great space liners to Neptune. There were still some running. Some people, you see, were coming the other way.

The ship was huge. Mostly it was a freight liner. It floated up from Earth, a great metal cylinder three quarters of a mile long, and a quarter of a mile in diameter. Outside the atmosphere it began to accelerate. I could see Earth dwindle. I have ridden one of our own liners to Mars, and it took me, in 3048, five days. In half an hour on this liner Earth was just a star, with a smaller, dimmer star near it. In an hour we passed Mars. Eight hours later we landed on Neptune. M'reen was the city. Large as the Yawk City of my day—and no one living there.

The planet was cold and dark—horribly cold. The sun was a tiny, pale disk, heatless and almost lightless. But the city was perfectly comfortable. The air was fresh and cool, moist with the scent of growing blossoms, perfumed with them. And the whole giant metal framework trembled just slightly with the humming, powerful beat of the mighty machines that had made and cared for it.

I learned from records I deciphered, because of my knowledge of the ancient tongue that their tongue was based on, and the tongue of that day when man was dying, that the city was built three million, seven hundred and thirty thousand, one hundred and fifty years after my birth. Not a machine had been touched by the hand of man since that day.

Yet the air was perfect for man. And the warm, rose-silver glow hung in the air here and supplied the only illumination.

I visited some of their other cities where there were men. And there, on the retreating outskirts of man's domain, I first heard the Song of Longings, as I called it.

And another, The Song of Forgotten Memories. Listen:

He sang another of those songs. There's one thing I know, declared Jim. That bewildered note was stronger in his voice, and by that time I guess I pretty well understood his feelings. Because, you have to remember, I heard it only secondhand from an ordinary man, and Jim had heard it from an eye-and-ear witness that was not ordinary, and heard it in that organ voice. Anyway, I guess Jim was right when he said: "He wasn't any ordinary man." No ordinary man could think of those songs. They weren't right. When he sang that song, it was full of more of those plaintive minors. I could feel him searching his mind for something he had forgotten, something he desperately wanted to remember—something he knew he should have known—and I felt it eternally elude him. I felt it get further away from him as he sang. I heard that lonely, frantic searcher attempting to recall that thing—that thing that would save him.

And I heard him give a little sob of defeat—and the song ended. Jim tried a few notes. He hasn't a good ear for music—but that was too powerful to forget. Just a few hummed notes. Jim hasn't much imagination, I guess, or when that man of the future sang to him he would have gone mad. It shouldn't be sung to modern men; it isn't meant for them. You've heard those heart-rending cries some animals give, like human cries, almost? A loon, now—he sounds like a lunatic being murdered horribly.

That's just unpleasant. That song made you feel just exactly what the singer meant—because it didn't just sound human—it was human. It was the essence of humanity's last defeat, I guess. You always feel sorry for the chap who loses after trying hard. Well, you could feel the whole of humanity trying hard—and losing. And you knew they couldn't afford to lose, because they couldn't try again.

He said he'd been interested before. And still not wholly upset by those machines that couldn't stop. But that was too much for him.

I knew after that, he said, that these weren't men I could live among. They were dying men, and I was alive with the youth of the race. They looked at me with the same longing, hopeless wonder with which they looked at the stars and the machines. They knew what I was, but couldn't understand.

I began to work on leaving.

It took six months. It was hard because my instruments were gone, of course, and theirs didn't read in the same units. And there were few instruments, anyway. The machines didn't read instruments; they acted on them. They were sensory organs to them.

But Reo Lantal helped where he could. And I came back.

I did just one thing before I left that may help. I may even try to get back there sometime. To see, you know.

I said they had machines that could really think? But that someone had stopped them a long time ago, and no one knew how to start them?

I found some records and deciphered them. I started one of the latest and best of them and started it on a great problem. It is only fitting it should be done. The machine can work on it, not for a thousand years, but for a million, if it must.

I started five of them actually, and connected them together as the records directed.

They are trying to make a machine with something that man had lost. It sounds rather comical. But stop to think before you laugh. And remember that Earth as I saw it from the ground level of Neva City just before Reo Lantal threw the switch.

Twilight—the sun has set. The desert out beyond, in its mystic, changing colors. The great, metal city rising straight-walled to the human city above, broken by spires and towers and great trees with scented blossoms. The silvery-rose glow in the paradise of gardens above.

And all the great city-structure throbbing and humming to the steady gentle beat of perfect, deathless machines built more than three million years before—and never touched since that time by human hands. And they go on. The dead city. The men that have lived, and hoped, and built—and died to leave behind them those little men who can only wonder and look and long for a forgotten kind of companionship. They wander through the vast cities their ancestors built, knowing less of them than the machines themselves.

And the songs. Those tell the story best, I think. Little, hopeless, wondering men amid vast unknowing, blind machines that started three million years before—and just never knew how to stop. They are dead—and can't die and be still.

So I brought another machine to life, and set it to a task which, in time to come, it will perform.

I ordered it to make a machine which would have what man had lost. A curious machine.

And then I wanted to leave quickly and go back. I had been born in the first full light of man's day. I did not belong in the lingering, dying glow of man's twilight.

So I came back. A little too far back. But it will not take me long to return—accurately this time.

"Well, that was his story," Jim said. "He didn't *tell* me it was true—didn't say anything about it. And he had me thinking so hard I didn't even see him get off in Reno when we stopped for gas.

"But—he wasn't an ordinary man," repeated Jim, in a rather belligerent tone.

Jim claims he doesn't believe the yarn, you know. But he does; that's why he always acts so determined about it when he says the stranger wasn't an ordinary man.

No, he wasn't, I guess. I think he lived and died, too, probably, sometime in the thirty-first century. And I think he saw the twilight of the race, too.

The New Father Christmas

Brian W. Aldiss

Little old Roberta took the clock down off the shelf and put it on the Hotpoint; then she picked up the kettle and tried to wind it. The clock was almost on the boil before she realised what she had done. Shrieking quietly, so as not to wake old Robin, she snatched up the clock with a duster and dropped it onto the table. It ticked furiously. She looked at it.

Although Roberta wound the clock every morning when she got up, she had neglected to look at it for months. Now she looked and saw it was 7.30 on Christmas Day, 2388.

"Oh dear," she exclaimed. "It's Christmas Day already! It seems to have come very soon after Lent this year."

She had not even realised it was 2388. She and Robin had lived in the factory so long. The idea of Christmas excited her, for she liked surprises—but it also frightened her, because she thought about the New Father Christmas and that was something she preferred not to think about. The New Father Christmas was reputed to make his rounds on Christmas morning.

"I must tell Robin," she said. But poor Robin had been very touchy lately; it was conceivable that having Christmas suddenly forced upon him would make him cross. Roberta was unable to keep anything to herself, so she would have to go down and tell the tramps. Apart from Robin, there were only the tramps.

Putting the kettle on to the stove, she left her living-quarters and went into the factory, like a little mouse emerging from its mincepie-smelling nest. Roberta and Robin lived right at the top of the factory and the tramps had their illegal home right at the bottom. Roberta began tiptoeing down many, many steel stairs.

The factory was full of the sort of sounds Robin called "silent noise." It continued day and night, and the two humans had long ago ceased to hear it; it would continue when they had become incapable of hearing anything. This morning, the machines were as busy as ever, and looked not at all Christmassy. Roberta noticed in particular the two machines she hated most: the one with loomlike movements which packed impossibly thin wire into impossibly small boxes, and the one which threshed about as if it were struggling with an invisble enemy and did not seem to be producing anything.

The old lady walked delicately past them and down into the basement. She came to a grey door and knocked at it. At once she heard the three tramps fling themselves against the inside of the door and press against it, shouting hoarsely across to each other.

Roberta was unable to shout, but she waited until they were silent and then called through the door as loudly as she could, "It's only me, boys."

After a moment's hush, the door opened a crack. Then it opened wide. Three seedy figures stood there, their faces anguished: Jerry, the ex-writer, and Tony and Dusty, who had never been and never would be anything but tramps. Jerry, the youngest, was forty, and so still had half his life to drowse through, Tony was fifty-five and Dusty had sweat rash.

"We thought you was the Terrible Sweeper!" Tony exclaimed.

The Terrible Sweeper swept right through the factory every morning. Every morning, the tramps had to barricade themselves in their room, or the sweeper would have bundled them and all their tawdry belongings into the disposal chutes.

"You'd better come in," Jerry said. "Excuse the muddle."

Robert entered and sat down on a crate, tired after her journey. The tramps' room made her uneasy, for she suspected them of bringing Women in here occasionally; also, there were pants hanging in one corner.

"I had something to tell you all," she said. They waited politely, expectantly. Jerry cleaned out his nails with a tack.

"I've forgotten just now what it is," she confessed.

The tramps sighed noisily with relief. They feared anything which threatened to disturb their tranquillity. Tony became communicative.

"It's Christmas Day," he said, looking round furtively.

"Is it really!" Roberta exclaimed. "So soon after Lent?"

"Allow us," Jerry said, "to wish you a safe Christmas and a persecution-free New Year."

This courtesy brought Roberta's latent fears to the surface at once.

"You—you don't believe in the New Father Christmas, do you?" she asked them. They made no answer, but Dusty's face went the colour of lemon peel and she knew they did believe. So did she.

"You'd better all come up to the flat and celebrate this happy day," Roberta said. "After all, there's safety in numbers."

"I can't go through the factory: the machines bring on my sweat rash," Dusty said. "It's a sort of allergy."

"Nevertheless, we will go," Jerry said. "Never pass a kind offer by."

Like heavy mice, the four of them crept up the stairs and through the engrossed factory. The machines pretended to ignore them.

In the flat, they found pandemonium loose. The kettle was boiling over and Robin was squeaking for help. Officially bed-ridden, Robin could get up in times of crisis; he stood now just inside the bedroom door, and Roberta had to remove the kettle before going to placate him.

"And why have you brought those creatures up here?" he demanded in a loud whisper.

"Because they are our friends, Robin," Roberta said, struggling to get him back to bed.

"They are no friends of mine!" he said. He thought of something really terrible to say to her; he trembled and wrestled with it and did not say it. The effort left him weak and irritable. How he loathed being in her power! As caretaker of the vast factory, it was his duty to see that no undesirables entered, but as matters were at present he could not evict the tramps while his wife took their part. Life really was exasperating.

"We came to wish you a safe Christmas, Mr. Proctor," Jerry said, sliding into the bedroom with his two companions.

"Christmas, and I got sweat rash!" Dusty said.

"It isn't Christmas," Robin whined as Roberta pushed his feet under the sheets. "You're just saying it to annoy me." If they could only know or guess the anger that stormed like illness through his veins.

At that moment, the delivery chute pinged and an envelope catapulted into the room. Robin took it from Roberta, opening it with trembling hands. Inside was a Christmas card from the Minister of Automatic Factories.

"This proves there are other people still alive in the world," Robin said. These other fools were not important enough to receive Christmas cards.

His wife peered short-sightedly at the Minister's signature.

"This is done by a rubber stamp, Robin," she said. "It doesn't prove anything."

Now he was really enraged. To be contradicted in front of these scum! And Roberta's cheeks had grown more wrinkled since last Christmas, which also annoyed him. As he was about to flay her, however, his glance fell on the address on the envelope; it read, *"Ro-*

bin Proctor, A.F.X10.''

"But this factory isn't X10!'' he protested aloud. "It's SC541.''

"Perhaps we've been in the wrong factory for thirty-five years,'' Roberta said. "Does it matter at all?''

The question was so senseless that the old man pulled the bedclothes out of the bottom of the bed.

"Well, go and find out, you silly old woman!'' he shrieked. "The factory number is engraved over the output exit. Go and see what it says. If it does not say SC541, we must leave here at once. Quickly!''

"I'll come with you,'' Jerry told the old lady.

"You'll all go with her,'' Robin said. "I'm not having you stay here with me. You'd murder me in my bed!''

Without any particular surprise—although Tony glanced regretfully at the empty teapot as he passed it—they found themselves again in the pregnant layers of factory, making their way down to the output exit. Here, conveyor belts transported the factory's finished product outside to waiting vehicles.

"I don't like it much here,'' Roberta said uneasily. "Even a glimpse of outside aggravates my agoraphobia.''

Nevertheless, she looked where Robin had instructed her. Above the exit, a sign said "X10.''

"Robin will never believe me when I tell him,'' she wailed.

"My guess is that the factory changed its own name,'' Jerry said calmly. "Probably it has changed its product as well. After all, there's nobody in control; it can do what it likes. Has it always been making these eggs?''

They stared silently at the endless, moving line of steel eggs. The eggs were smooth and as big as ostrich eggs; they sailed into the open, where robots piled them into vans and drove away with them.

"Never heard of a factory laying eggs before,'' Dusty laughed, scratching his shoulder. "Now we'd better get back before the Terrible Sweeper catches up with us.''

Slowly they made their way back up the many, many steps.

"I think it used to be television sets the factory made,'' Roberta said once.

"If there are no more men—there'd be no more need for television sets,'' Jerry said grimly.

"I can't remember for sure. . . .''

Robin, when they told him, was ill with irritation, rolling out of bed in his wrath. He threatened to go down and look at the name of the factory himself, only refraining because he had a private theory that the factory itself was merely one of Roberta's hallucinations.

"And as for *eggs* . . ." he stuttered.

Jerry dipped into a torn pocket, produced one of the eggs, and laid it on the floor. In the silence that followed, they could all hear the egg ticking.

"You didn't oughta done that, Jerry," Dusty said hoarsely. "That's . . . interfering." They all stared at Jerry, the more frightened because they did not entirely know what they were frightened about.

"I brought it because I thought the factory ought to give us a Christmas present," Jerry told them dreamily, squatting down to look at the egg. "You see, a long time ago, before the machines declared all writers like me redundant, I met an old robot writer. And this old robot writer had been put out to scrap, but he told me a thing or two. And he told me that as machines took over man's duties, so they took over his myths too. Of course, they adapt the myths to their own beliefs, but I think they'd like the idea of handing out Christmas presents."

Dusty gave Jerry a kick which sent him sprawling.

"That's for your idea!" he said. "You're mad, Jerry boy! The machine'll come up here to get that egg back. I don't know what we ought to do."

"I'll put the tea on for some kettle," Roberta said brightly.

The stupid remark made Robin explode.

"Take the egg back, all of you!" he shrieked. "It's stealing, that's what it is, and I won't be responsible. And then you tramps must leave the factory!"

Dusty and Tony looked at him helplessly, and Tony said, "But we got nowhere to go."

Jerry, who had made himself comfortable on the floor, said without looking up, "I don't want to frighten you, but the New Father Christmas will come for you, Mr. Proctor, if you aren't careful. That old Christmas myth was one of the ones the machines took over and changed; the New Father Christmas is all metal and glass, and instead of leaving new toys he takes away old people and machines."

Roberta, listening at the door, went as white as a sheet. "Perhaps that's how the world has grown so depopulated recently," she said. "I'd better get us some tea."

Robin had managed to shuffle out of bed, a ghastly irritation goading him on. As he staggered towards Jerry, the egg hatched.

It broke cleanly into two halves, revealing a pack of neat machinery. Four tiny, busy mannikins jumped out and leapt into action. In no time, using minute welders, they had forged the shell into a double dome; sounds of hammering came from underneath.

"They're going to build another factory right in here, the saucy things!" Roberta exclaimed. She brought the kettle crashing down on the dome and failed even to dent it. At once a thin chirp filled the room.

"My heavens, they are wirelessing for help!" Jerry exclaimed. "We've got to get out of here at once!"

They got out, Robin twittering with rage, and the New Father Christmas caught them all on the stairs.

Computers Don't Argue

Gordon R. Dickson

Treasure Book Club
PLEASE DO NOT FOLD,
SPINDLE OR MUTILATE
THIS CARD

Mr: Walter A. Child Balance: $4.98 Dear Customer: Enclosed is your latest book selection. "Kidnapped," by Robert Louis Stevenson.

Woodlawn Drive
Panduk, Michigan
Nov. 16, 1965

Treasure Book Club
1823 Mandy Street
Chicago, Illinois

Dear Sirs:

I wrote you recently about the computer punch card you sent, billing me for "Kim," by Rudyard Kipling. I did not open the package containing it until I had already mailed you my check for the amount on the card. On opening the package, I found the book missing half its pages. I sent it back to you, requesting either another copy or my money back. Instead, you have sent me a copy of "Kidnapped," by Robert Louis Stevenson. Will you please straighten this out?

I hereby return the copy of "Kidnapped."

Sincerely yours,
Walter A. Child

Treasure Book Club
SECOND NOTICE
PLEASE DO NOT FOLD,
SPINDLE OR MUTILATE
THIS CARD

Mr: Walter A Child Balance: $4.98 For "Kidnapped," by Robert Louis Stevenson

(If remittance has been made for the above, please disregard this notice)

437 Woodlawn Drive
Panduk, Michigan
Jan. 21, 1966

Treasure Book Club
1823 Mandy Street
Chicago, Illinois

Dear Sirs:

May I direct your attention to my letter of November 16, 1965? You are still continuing to dun me with computer punch cards for a book I did not order. Whereas, actually, it is your company that owes *me* money.

Sincerely yours,
Walter A. Child

Treasure Book Club
1823 Mandy Street
Chicago, Illinois
Feb. 1, 1966

Mr. Walter A. Child
437 Woodlawn Drive
Panduk, Michigan

Dear Mr. Child:

We have sent you a number of reminders concerning an amount owing to us as a result of book purchases you have made from us. This amount, which is $4.98 is now long overdue.

This situation is disappointing to us, particularly since there was no hesitation on our part in extending you credit at the time original arrangements for these purchases were made by you. If we do not receive payment in full by return mail, we will be forced to turn the matter over to a collection agency.

Very truly yours,
Samuel P. Grimes
Collection Mgr.

437 Woodlawn Drive
Panduk, Michigan
Feb. 5, 1966

Dear Mr. Grimes:

Will you stop sending me punch cards and form letters and make me some kind of a direct answer from a human being?

I don't owe you money. *You* owe me money. Maybe I should turn your company over to a collection agency.

Walter A. Child

FEDERAL COLLECTION
OUTFIT

88 Prince Street
Chicago, Illinois
Feb. 28, 1966

Mr. Walter A. Child
437 Woodlawn Drive
Panduk, Michigan

Dear Mr. Child:

Your account with the Treasure Book Club, of $4.98 plus interest and charges has been turned over to our agency for collection. The amount due is now $6.83. Please send your check for this amount or we shall be forced to take immediate action.

Jacob N. Harshe
Vice President

FEDERAL COLLECTION
OUTFIT

88 Prince Street
Chicago, Illinois
April 8, 1966

Mr. Walter A. Child
437 Woodlawn Drive
Panduk, Michigan

Dear Mr. Child:

You have seen fit to ignore our courteous requests to settle your long overdue account with Treasure Book Club, which is now with accumulated interest and charges, in the amount of $7.51.

If payment in full is not forthcoming by April 11, 1966 we will be forced to turn the matter over to our attorneys for immediate court action.

Ezekiel B. Harshe
President

MALONEY, MAHONEY,
MACNAMARA AND PRUITT
Attorneys

89 Prince Street
Chicago, Illinois
April 29, 1966

Mr. Walter A. Child
437 Woodlawn Drive
Panduk, Michigan

Dear Mr. Child:

Your indebtedness to the Treasure Book Club has been referred to us for legal action to collect.

This indebtedness is now in the amount of $10.01. If you will send us this amount so that we may receive it before May 5, 1966, the matter may be satisfied. However, if we do not receive satisfaction in full by that date, we will take steps to collect through the courts.

I am sure you will see the advantage of avoiding a judgment against you, which as a matter of record would do lasting harm to your credit rating.

Very truly yours,
Hagthorpe M. Pruitt, Jr.
Attorney at law

437 Woodlawn Drive
Panduk, Michigan
May 4, 1966

Mr. Hagthorpe M. Pruitt, Jr.
Maloney, Mahoney, MacNamara and Pruitt
89 Prince Street
Chicago, Illinois

Dear Mr. Pruitt:

You don't know what a pleasure it is to me in this matter to get a letter from a live human being to whom I can explain the situation.

This whole matter is silly. I explained it fully in my letters to the Treasure Book Company. But I might as well have been trying to explain to the computer that puts out their punch cards, for all the good it seemed to do. Briefly, what happened was I ordered a copy of "Kim," by Rudyard Kipling, for $4.98. When I opened the package they sent me, I found the book had only half its pages, but I'd previously mailed a check to pay them for the book.

I sent the book back to them, asking either for a whole copy or my money back. Instead, they sent me a copy of "Kidnapped," by Robert Louis Stevenson—which I had not ordered; and for which they have been trying to collect from me.

Meanwhile, I am still waiting for the money back that they owe me for the copy of ''Kim'' that I didn't get. That's the whole story. Maybe you can help me straighten them out.

Relievedly yours,
Walter A. Child

P.S.: I also sent them back their copy of ''Kidnapped,'' as soon as I got it, but it hasn't seemed to help. They have never even acknowledged getting it back.

MALONEY, MAHONEY,
MACNAMARA AND PRUITT
Attorneys

89 Prince Street
Chicago, Illinois
May 9, 1966

Mr. Walter A. Child
437 Woodlawn Drive
Panduk, Michigan

Dear Mr. Child:

I am in possession of no information indicating that any item purchased by you from the Treasure Book Club has been returned.

I would hardly think that, if the case had been as you stated, the Treasure Book Club would have retained us to collect the amount owing from you.

If I do not receive your payment in full within three days, by May 12, 1966, we will be forced to take legal action.

Very truly yours,
Hagthorpe M. Pruitt, Jr.

COURTS OF MINOR CLAIMS
Chicago, Illinois

Mr. Walter A. Child:
437 Woodlawn Drive,
Panduk, Michigan

Be informed that a judgment was taken and entered against you in this court this day of May 26, 1966 in the amount of $15.66 including court costs.

Payment in satisfaction of this judgment may be made to this court or to the adjudged creditor. In the case of payment being made to the creditor, a release should be obtained from the creditor and filed with this court in order to free you of legal obligation in connection with this judgment.

Under the recent Reciprocal Claims Act, if you are a citizen of a different state, a duplicate claim may be automatically entered and judged against you in your own state so that collection may be made there as well as in the State of Illinois.

COURT OF MINOR CLAIMS
Chicago, Illinois
PLEASE DO NOT FOLD,
SPINDLE OR MUTILATE THIS CARD

Judgment was passed this day of May 27, 1966 under Statute $15.66
Against: Child, Walter A. of 437 Woodlawn Drive, Panduk, Michigan. Pray to enter a duplicate claim for judgment
In: Picayune Court—Panduk, Michigan
For Amount: Statute 941

437 Woodlawn Drive
Panduk, Michigan
May 31, 1966

Samuel P. Grimes
Vice President, Treasure Book Club
1823 Mandy Street
Chicago, Illinois

Grimes:

This business has gone far enough. I've got to come down to Chicago on business of my own tomorrow. I'll see you then and we'll get this straightened out once and for all, about who owes what to whom, and how much!

Yours,
Walter A. Child

From the desk of the Clerk
Picayune Court

June 1, 1966

Harry:

The attached computer card from Chicago's Minor Claims Court against A. Walter has a 1500-series Statute number on it. That puts it over in Criminal with you, rather than Civil, with me. So I herewith submit it for your computer instead of mine. How's business?

Joe

CRIMINAL RECORDS
Panduk, Michigan
PLEASE DO NOT FOLD,
SPINDLE OR MUTILATE THIS CARD

Convicted: (Child) A. Walter
On: May 26, 1966
Address: 437 Woodlawn Drive, Panduk, Mich.
Crim: Statute: 1566 (Corrected) 1567
Crime: Kidnap
Date: Nov. 16, 1965
Notes: At large. To be picked up at once.

POLICE DEPARTMENT, PANDUK, MICHIGAN. TO POLICE DEPARTMENT CHICAGO ILLINOIS. CONVICTED SUBJECT A. (COMPLETE FIRST NAME UNKNOWN) WALTER, SOUGHT HERE IN CONNECTION REF. YOUR NOTIFICATION OF JUDGMENT FOR KIDNAP OF CHILD NAMED ROBERT LOUIS STEVENSON, ON NOV. 16, 1965. INFORMATION HERE INDICATES SUBJECT FLED HIS RESIDENCE, AT 437 WOODLAWN DRIVE, PANDUK, AND MAY BE AGAIN IN YOUR AREA.

POSSIBLE CONTACT IN YOUR AREA: THE TREASURE BOOK CLUB, 1823 MANDY STREET, CHICAGO, ILLINOIS. SUBJECT NOT KNOWN TO BE ARMED, BUT PRESUMED DANGEROUS. PICK UP AND HOLD, ADVISING US OF CAPTURE . . .

TO POLICE DEPARTMENT, PANDUK, MICHIGAN, REFERENCE YOUR REQUEST TO PICK UP AND HOLD A. (COMPLETE FIRST NAME UNKNOWN) WALTER, WANTED IN PANDUK ON STATUTE 1567, CRIME OF KIDNAPPING.

SUBJECT ARRESTED AT OFFICES OF TREASURE BOOK CLUB, OPERATING THERE UNDER ALIAS WALTER ANTHONY CHILD AND ATTEMPTING TO COLLECT $4.98 FROM ONE SAMUEL P. GRIMES, EMPLOYEE OF THAT COMPANY.

DISPOSAL: HOLDING FOR YOUR ADVICE.

POLICE DEPARTMENT PANDUK, MICHIGAN TO POLICE DEPARTMENT CHICAGO, ILLINOIS.

REF: A. WALTER (ALIAS WALTER ANTHONY CHILD) SUBJECT WANTED FOR CRIME OF KIDNAP, YOUR AREA, REF: YOUR COMPUTER PUNCH CARD NOTIFICATION OF JUDGMENT, DATED MAY 27, 1966. COPY OUR CRIMINAL RECORDS PUNCH CARD HEREWITH FORWARDED TO YOUR COMPUTER SECTION.

CRIMINAL RECORDS
Chicago, Illinois
PLEASE DO NOT FOLD,
SPINDLE OR MUTILATE THIS CARD

SUBJECT (CORRECTION—
OMITTED RECORD SUPPLIED)
APPLICABLE STATUTE NO. 1567
JUDGMENT NO. 456789
TRIAL RECORD: APPARENTLY MISFILED AND UNAVAILABLE
DIRECTION: TO APPEAR FOR SENTENCING BEFORE JUDGE JOHN ALEXANDER MCDIVOT, COURTROOM A JUNE 9, 1966
From the Desk of Judge Alexander J. McDivot

June 2, 1966

Dear Tony:

I've got an adjudged criminal coming up before me for sentencing Thursday morning—but the trial transcript is apparently misfiled.

I need some kind of information (Ref: A. Walter—Judgment No. 456789, Criminal). For example, what about the victim of the kidnapping. Was victim harmed?

Jack McDivot

June 3, 1966

Records Search Unit

Re: Ref: Judgment No. 456789—victim is dead.

Tonio Malagasi
Records Division

June 3, 1966

To: United States Statistics Office
Attn.: Information Section
Subject: Robert Louis Stevenson
Query: Information concerning

Records Search Unit
Criminal Records Division
Police Department
Chicago, Ill.

June 5, 1966

To: Records Search Unit
Criminal Records Division
Police Department
Chicago, Illinois
Subject: Your query re Robert Louis Stevenson (File no. 189623)
Action: Subject deceased. Age at death, 44 yrs. Further information requested'?

A.K.
Information Section
U.S. Statistics Office

June 6, 1966

To: United States Statistics Office
Attn.: Information Division
Subject: Re: File no. 189623
  No further information required.

Thank you.
Records Search Unit
Criminal Records Division
Police Department
Chicago, Illinois

June 7, 1966

To: Tonio Malagasi
Records Division
Re: Ref: judgment No. 456789—victim is dead.

Records Search Unit

June 7, 1966

To: Judge Alexander J. McDivot's Chambers

Dear Jack:

Ref: Judgment No. 456789. The victim in this kidnap case was apparently slain.

From the strange lack of background information on the killer and his victim, as well as the victim's age, this smells to me like a gangland killing. This for your information. Don't quote me. It seems to me; though, that Stevenson—the victim—has a name that rings a faint bell with me. Possibly, one of the East Coast Mob, since the association comes back to me as something about pirates—possibly New York dockage hijackers—and something about buried loot.

As I say, above is only speculation for your private guidance.

Any time I can help . . .

Best,
Tony Malagasi
Records Division

MICHAEL R. REYNOLDS
Attorney-at-law

49 Water Street
Chicago, Illinois
June 8, 1966

Dear Tim:

Regrets: I can't make the fishing trip. I've been court-appointed here to represent a man about to be sentenced tomorrow on a kidnapping charge.

Ordinarily, I might have tried to beg off, and McDivot, who is doing the sentencing, would probably have turned me loose. But this is the damndest thing you ever heard of.

The man being sentenced has apparently been not only charged, but adjudged guilty as a result of a comedy of errors too long to go into here. He not only isn't guilty—he's got the best case I ever heard of for damages against one of the larger Book Clubs headquartered here in Chicago. And that's a case I wouldn't mind taking on.

It's inconceivable—but damnably possible, once you stop to think of it in this day and age of machine-made records—that a completely innocent man could be put in this position.

There shouldn't be much to it. I've asked to see McDivot tomorrow before the time of sentencing, and it'll just be a matter of explaining to him. Then I can discuss the damage suit with my freed client at his leisure.

Fishing next weekend?

Yours,
Mike

MICHAEL R. REYNOLDS
Attorney-at-law

49 Water Street
Chicago, Illinois
June 10

Dear Tim:

In haste—

No fishing this coming week either. Sorry.

You won't believe it. My innocent-as-a-lamb-and-I'm-not-kidding client has just been sentenced to death for first-degree murder in connection with the death of his kidnap victim.

Yes, I explained the whole thing to McDivot. And when he explained his situation to me, I nearly fell out of my chair.

It wasn't a matter of my not convincing him. It took less than three minutes to show him that my client should never have been within the walls of the Court Jail for a second. But—get this—McDivot couldn't do a thing about it.

The point is, my man had already been judged guilty according to the computerized records. In the absence of a trial record—of course there never was one (but that's something I'm not free to explain to you now)—the judge has to go by what records are available. And in the case of an adjudged prisoner, McDivot's only legal choice was whether to sentence to life imprisonment, or execution.

The death of the kidnap victim, according to the statute, made the death penalty mandatory. Under the new laws governing length of time for appeal, which has been shortened because of the new system of computerizing records, to force an elimination of unfair delay and mental anguish to those condemned, I have five days in which to file an appeal, and ten to have it acted on.

Needless to say, I am not going to monkey with an appeal. I'm going directly to the Governor for a pardon—after which we will get this farce reversed. McDivot has already written the Governor, also, explaining that his sentence was ridiculous, but that he had no choice. Between the two of us, we ought to have a pardon in short order.

Then, I'll make the fur fly . . .

And we'll get in some fishing.

Best,
Mike

OFFICE OF THE GOVERNOR OF ILLINOIS

June 17, 1966

Mr. Michael R. Reynolds
49 Water Street
Chicago, Illinois

Dear Mr. Reynolds:

In reply to your query about the request for pardon for Walter A. Child (A. Walter), may I inform you that the Governor is still on his trip with the Midwest Governors Committee, examining the Wall in Berlin. He should be back next Friday.

I will bring your request and letters to his attention the minute he returns.

Very truly yours,
Clara B. Jilks
Secretary to the Governor

June 27, 1966

Michael R. Reynolds
49 Water Street
Chicago, Illinois

Dear Mike:

Where is that pardon?
My execution date is only five days from now!

Walt

June 29, 1966

Walter A. Child (A. Walter)
Cell Block E
Illinois State Penitentiary
Joliet, Illinois

Dear Walt:

The Governor returned, but was called away immediately to the White House in Washington to give his views on interstate sewage.

I am camping on his doorstep and will be on him the moment he arrives here.

Meanwhile, I agree with you about the seriousness of the situation. The warden at the prison there, Mr. Allen Magruder, will bring this letter to you and have a private talk with you. I urge you to listen to what he has to say; and I enclose letters from your family also urging you to listen to Warden Magruder.

Yours,
Mike

June 30, 1966

Michael R. Reynolds
49 Water Street
Chicago, Illinois

Dear Mike: (This letter being smuggled out by Warden Magruder)
As I was talking to Warden Magruder in my cell, here, news was

brought to him that the Governor has at last returned for a while to Illinois, and will be in his office early tomorrow morning, Friday. So you will have time to get the pardon signed by him and delivered to the prison in time to stop my execution on Saturday.

Accordingly, I have turned down the Warden's kind offer of a chance to escape; since he told me he could by no means guarantee to have all the guards out of my way when I tried it; and there was a chance of my being killed escaping.

But now everything will straighten itself out. Actually, an experience as fantastic as this had to break down sometime under its own weight.

> Best,
> Walt

FOR THE SOVEREIGN STATE OF ILLINOIS

I, Hubert Daniel Willikens, Governor of the State of Illinois, and invested with the authority and powers appertaining thereto, including the power to pardon those in my judgment wrongfully convicted or otherwise deserving of executive mercy, do this day of July 1, 1966 announce and proclaim that Walter A. Child (A. Walter) now in custody as a consequence of erroneous conviction upon a crime of which he is entirely innocent, is fully and freely pardoned of said crime. And I do direct the necessary authorities having custody of the said Water A. Child (A. Walter) in whatever place or places he may be held, to immediately free, release, and allow unhindered departure to him . . .

Interdepartmental Routing Service

PLEASE DO NOT FOLD, MUTILATE, OR SPINDLE THIS CARD

Failure to route Document properly.
To: Governor Hubert Daniel Willikens
Re: Pardon issued to Walter A. Child, July 1, 1966

Dear State Employee:
You have failed to attach your Routing Number.
PLEASE: Resubmit document with this card and form 876, explaining your authority for placing a TOP RUSH category on this document. Form 876 must be signed by your Departmental Superior.

RESUBMIT ON: Earliest possible date ROUTING SERVICE office is open. In this case, Tuesday, July 5, 1966

WARNING: Failure to submit form 876 WITH THE SIGNATURE OF YOUR SUPERIOR may make you liable to prosecution for misusing a Service of the State Government. A warrant may be issued for your arrest.

There are NO exceptions. YOU have been WARNED.

7

More Than Human?: Androids, Cyborgs, and Others

George Zebrowski and Patricia Warrick

I

Robots are machine systems made of nonbiological materials like metal, plastic, and electronic devices. Androids are presented as newly designed humanlike entities made of biological materials. Although lacking the evolutionary history of human bodies, androids share with us many of the same biological and psychological features—self-conscious thought and the capacity for mental development (for example, *Tower of Glass* by Robert Silverberg). The concept of the cyborg (the word is a portmanteau of the words cybernetic and organism) describes the joining of mechanism and biological organism (see "Masks" by Damon Knight). A simple example of a cyborg is a man wearing a hearing aid; an advanced example might involve a subtle homeostatic linkage between an astronaut and his ship, or the placing of a human brain and nervous system into an artificial body, as in "Masks."

Definitions or descriptions of robots, androids, and cyborgs must not be drawn too tightly; one should always examine the sophistication of a particular writer's use of the concepts. The word android means "resembling a man," and may be used to refer to thinking machines in general—automatons, robots, computers. Many writers see a robot's actions as being of a finitary;deductive character (purely mechanical and limited), while an android may be capable of thought in the manner of

an open system (non-finitary-deductive, intuitive, emotional, crea-
tively unpredictable). Other writers are guided by less technical considerations: a robot looks like a machine; an android is humanlike, if
not human.

These considerations lead to a number of problems. Isaac Asimov's
robots, for example, though mechanical in construction, possess brain
centers exhibiting conscious acts, at least in the behavioral sense. A
good case might be made that they are humanlike, an alternate form of
humanity. Karel Čapek's robots in his play *R.U.R.* would today be
considered androids, since they were made of biological materials, or
software, and quickly developed into an alternate humanity. Clearly,
the concept of the robot stands for a purely mechanical, unconscious,
deterministic system designed to do certain set tasks, both human and
superhuman, like the automatic pilot in aircraft and the super-fast
computer. Science fiction writers have not always used the term consistently, but this points up the difficulties of defining concepts like
intelligence, consciousness, or *aliveness.* Robots, androids, and
cyborgs belong to a continuum of concepts representing the modeling
of various aspects of life, including intelligent life. The divisions that
exist between the concepts as presented in science fiction are imposed
by the writer's needs in a particular story.

II

Biology has exploded into a host of specialties, a number of which
promise to influence the course of our civilization in a radical way. The
discovery of the structure of DNA by Watson and Crick in the early
1950s heralded the real possibility of biological engineering—the idea
that man might be modified, improved, or that physical defects might
be eliminated from future generations through an active quality control
of the present human genetic code. The same thing might be done with
animals, as in Robert A. Heinlein's story, ''Jerry Was a Man.''

One form of bio-engineering is the technique of cloning, by which a
twin is made of any organism, animal or human. The twin, an *exact*
twin (natural twins are only mirror images of each other), is usually
seen as coming to term in the usual way, in a host mother, or in an
artificial womb. Contrary to popular superstition and some poor science fiction, a clone is not the person from whom the genetic materials
are taken; a clone is an exact twin, sharing the same genetic heritage as
the donor. A clone will certainly develop in his or her own way, as

would any brother or sister. A clone is simply another chance for the same genetic inheritance. Of course, if a clone is deliberately raised in a way similar to the life of the parent-donor, then he or she might recapitulate certain patterns of behavior—a talent for physics, or music, for example; but this is not a strange possibility.

Cloning may have uses in our society: the preservation of extraordinary abilities; single-parent families, where the child is actually a brother or sister; the creation of highly cooperative teams (as in Ursula K. Le Guin's "Nine Lives") for specialized tasks in exploration, construction, or in sports. If cloning became a major method of reproduction, it might lead to a stratification of society and an end to evolution through natural selection. It is possible that we are no longer evolving, except socially; although this seems likely, it has not been established beyond question. Cloning would preserve exceptional genetic combinations from the past; by storing the cells of various animal species, we could guard them against extinction; by combining the inheritances of more than one person, we may produce favorable combinations not possible through sexual reproduction.

Organ transplantation, another piece of the biological time bomb, has forced us to examine the nature of death, the ethics of biological experimentation, and the use of extraordinary procedures in medical care; it has raised the problem of donors, and come face to face with the fact of each person's biological individuality through the problem of donor organ rejection.

There appear to be at least three ways to go with organ transplants: (1) solve the problems of rejection and donors (the first may be possible through chemical means, or through a more subtle manipulation of the immune system of the body; donors, however, will always be in short supply); (2) solve the problem of donors by developing sophisticated artificial organs that will function homeostatically in the patient (automatically, without attention, like the real organ), thus making the subject a true cyborg; (3) use clones of the patient as a source of rejection-free organs (presumably the clone would have to be rapidly matured to the age of organ usability, but this would make it a person, even if it were kept unconscious; organs might be removed from fetuses and grown separately, thus raising a problem akin to abortion). The moral difficulties here are certainly too much for us now. An answer to this kind of unlikely gruesomeness might be to clone individual organs from the patient's own cells and grow them to the age of usability, instead of using one's own twins for spare parts. Organs might be cloned at an individual's birth and kept on ice; in time we would all need them.

Besides application in the freezing of sperm, ova, and organs for later use, cryonic techniques might be used for short-term suspended animation of accident victims who must be transported a great distance to receive proper care. The technique might be used to suspend the lives of terminally ill persons, until such time as there is a remedy for their problems. Cryonic suspension is just one application of cryogenics, low-temperature technology as it affects a variety of substances, both living and nonliving. Cryonics may become more credible when the first person is frozen and revived successfully, without freezing damage, and when it is known that a few years will make the difference in the solution of a certain medical problem; in such a case it would become murder not to freeze a patient. After this time it will become natural to attempt longer freezing periods, with applications in long-term space voyages, or for one-way travel into the future, as suggested by Robert A. Heinlein in his novel *The Door into Summer*.

Psychosurgery to correct psychological difficulties seems to be in severe disrepute, as is electroshock; both are akin to shaking or kicking a machine to fix it. Brain implants, however, may become useful as communications links for astronauts (as in ''Sea Change'' by Thomas N. Scortia); the idea might in time be extended to create integrated ship-embodied human cyborgs (as in Henry Kuttner's pioneering story ''Camouflage'').

The area of awesome implications involves the manipulation of the genetic code, not just to correct hereditary defects, but to create new and positive qualities. The creation of successful human mutations would lead to a proliferation of human types, and would radically transform humanity into a different psychosocial being, perhaps possessing a greater degree of adaptability (failure in this direction might make us more specialized and less adaptable, in the manner of Wells's selenites in *The First Men in the Moon*). A humanity engaged in participant evolution would not be known by any particular form, but by its intelligence and capacity for change. The subject was brilliantly treated in a critical way by James Blish in *The Seedling Stars,* and in *A Torrent of Faces* written by Blish with Norman L. Knight.

In view of all these very real possibilities, concepts of the android and cyborg, as projected by science fiction writers, can be given a clearer meaning. Androids imply the creation of humanlike life. Cyborgs stand for the alteration of human form through sophisticated devices (hardware). Manfred Clynes and Nathan S. Kline, who coined the term cyborg in 1960, define the cyborg as a self-regulating man-machine system functioning without the benefit of consciousness in order to cooperate with the body's own autonomous homeostatic controls. Cyborgs would involve the modification of a mature or growing individual. Androids would involve the creation of a cousin humanity, our equals, our superiors, or our inferior slaves (assuming human perversity). In the case of unconscious machines, slavery is not an ethical issue, but with a cousin humanity the issue would be agonizing, especially if the humanity of the androids was to be genuinely, or falsely, in doubt.

Clearly, science fiction has often paralleled, anticipated or reflected developments in biology; ironically, however, the recent situation finds science fiction looking more conservative than many serious speculations coming out of biology. *The Biological Time Bomb* by Gordon Rattray Taylor seems more fantastic than most science fiction in this area. Realistic science fiction deals with the human impact of developments in science and technology; if this kind of science fiction is failing, it follows that the crucial relationship between science and science fiction, much denied in recent years, should be restored more effectively. The human face of science, explored by science fiction, is also the face of human creativity, the same face we find in art and the humanities.

III

The bio-technical developments discussed so far raise vast problems of value and possibility; these problems easily recall the mythic models of mortal human identity, the moral ideals of godhood, the limits of the natural world. The old myths sought to present the nature of human identity. Myths of origin gave a partial sense of identity, a sense of history which answered the absurdity of a sudden appearance of man in time, as well as presenting origins that were not demeaning, and essentially true: we are not strangers in the universe; we are made of the same stuff as nature; we have a role to play, a certain context. Myths of metamorphosis told us where we were going. The creation of human life, as in the stories of Prometheus or Adam and Eve, was seen as a mysterious act; creation was the province of a god. The incomprehensibility of man's appearance in time is taken out of the realm of absurdity and made into an act of god, who by virtue of godhood can accomplish creation, even though we cannot understand how it is done. Actually, the general idea that great wisdom, knowledge, and power are necessary to be a creator is not unreasonable, despite its vagueness. The point is not to leave the process with chance or chaos, which would be demeaning if not impossible, since it would be difficult to see how chance could ever muster the necessities of creation (being disorganized). The story is told that Charles Darwin did not publish *Origin of Species* for more than twenty years because, among other things, he thought it would embarrass his wife to consider man's origin from apelike ancestors through natural selection. A more critical scientific view of man's origins no longer despairs over the role of chance in the equation of evolution; rather, it sees man as existing in a natural context, and though standing apart from nature in the reach of his reason and imagination, still belonging to nature.

But the myth of creation could not be left to stand on the fact of man's divine origin alone. A full sense of identity demands that a continuing relationship exist between humankind and the gods; otherwise the original act of creation would seem isolated, without purpose, a meaningless affair between heaven and earth. Heroes, or supermen, mediate between gods and men. The hero is also the result of a mysterious mating, often between an immortal god and a mortal woman, as in the story of Leda and the swan, or Mary and the dove. The myths of the heroes carry a moral component. Heroes are moral examples, or teachers of mankind; even when they come among us through a god's indiscretion, it is because the god was drawn to his creatures by love.

Myths represent our relationship with the divine as a way of dealing with death. The fear of death is rationalized within a system of meanings. Immortality is often promised, but in another life, after great changes have taken place, physical and moral—dying and a deserving way of life; to gain immortality in any other way would be seen as an act against the gods.

It might seem that evil and devil figures are absent from most science fictional works; in reality they have only become secularized. Ignorance is seen as evil; the human drives of greed, jealousy, and hatred are depicted as leading society, science, and religion astray; scientific creativity and the pursuit of knowledge are seen as good, if used properly.

It is a natural step to go from being godlike in our origins to doing godlike things, though the stories of golem and homunculus clearly suggest that we cannot do as well as the gods do such things; but the statement is clear that knowledge is involved, however much of the supernatural is still needed to shore up the gaps in our knowledge. Doing without full knowledge is a fact of technology; doing often precedes knowledge. In the making of steel, for example, or the use of electricity, we knew how long before we knew fully why; practice came before adequate theory. Some would argue that this is not always a good way to do things, though necessary to stimulate discovery. In the absence of perfect knowledge, mistakes offer the greatest lessons. The adolescence of technology includes much of the twentieth century; yet doing without full knowledge is the only road to knowledge, at the beginning. The old mythic models teach caution, though they suggest that knowledge does exist; gradually the supernatural becomes knowledge, seeming magical only to the ignorant. That may seem a very modern statement about the past, but the thing to note is that modern developments in biological science give us the kind of knowledge that may produce the wonders or terrors of earlier myths.

IV

We can now show how the myth models of modern biologically oriented science fiction depart from the traditional story models. The changeover can be illustrated by Mary Shelley's novel *Frankenstein* (1818). The story may be regarded as science fiction because the elements of the supernatural are at a minimum. The monster is built up entirely out of spare parts, a mess of transplants. He is activated by electricity, which by this time had been linked with muscular functions. This aspect of the story is not well explained, but the notion is naturalistic in principle and goes beyond the science of the day in a genuinely science fictional way. Technically, the monster is not an android, since all his parts are human; they are not freshly made from raw materials. The monster is a revived corpse.

The moral aspect of the story lies in the fact that a person has been brought back to life. The experimenter is responsible for the kind of life he has brought the person back to live, and for what effect this life may have on others. The model of the sorcerer's apprentice is clearly applicable, as it is to all science and technology, to politics and social life, and to the individual life foiled by its own devices.

In *Frankenstein* the element of the supernatural has become that part of reality which is unforeseen, mysterious to some degree. The forces of chaos in myth are present as the unpredictable, though natural, aspects of the world and the actions we take in it; there is an irrational aspect to the world. The novel is a work of science fiction because it deals with the human impact of science and technology and the limits of knowledge. The story secularizes the supernatural, leaving it as the level of uncertainty to be found in the world and in our knowledge of it. Perfect knowledge is to be found nowhere; only probability is left, the measure of imperfection.

But a vast area of competence is now open to us. If life came about through natural means, and if we can gain knowledge of those means (being natural creatures also), then we too can create life, bestow immortality, and radically alter and improve ourselves. Creation is a misleading word to use, since it can imply creation *ex nihilo;* but the creation of life in a laboratory implies nothing more than the manipulation of already existing materials. One might even synthesize life by accident; or by knowing what to do, not why it succeeds. There is nothing godlike about it.

Science teaches that we can gain understanding somewhere in the middle of things: we can do considerably more than nothing, but we cannot do everything. How elastic this assertion may be must be left to future developments. Forms of science fiction which seek to dispense with limits, where too much can happen too easily, exhibit the hubris of wish fulfillment; works of this kind are not only bad science fiction, but bad fantasy, where alternate ontological limits must prevail. At best these works are symptoms of power fantasies, valuable in the clinical sense, as examples of our desire for omniscience and omnipotence.

Science fiction based on serious biological themes is now coming into its own. In the same way that physics acquired a social dimension in science fiction through the release of atomic energy, so biology acquired a social dimension in science fiction through the discovery of the structure of DNA. Writing in the introduction to her anthology *Bio-Futures,* Pamela Sargent describes the development of biological science fiction:

The treatment of biological change ... in science fiction describes a line of development that moves from individual cases and accidents to a view of a future in which biological change is normal and creative. This suggests the analogy of evolution, in which sports or mutations appear, most fail, and viable organisms survive ... As far as science fiction is concerned, we are talking about both the evolution of ideas (some of which are sports and do not survive) and the larger reality of biological innovation. Most readers of science fiction have come to accept the idea of biological change, suggesting that wider public acceptance is possible. ... Science fiction has warned us of the dangers of such change and at the same time legitimized the concept.

Earlier science fiction stories dealt with biological anomalies, exceptions showing no tendency to alter life on a large scale. Stories of superpeople, like *Seeds of Life* by John Taine (Eric Temple Bell), *Odd John* by Olaf Stapledon, or Philip Wylie's *Gladiator,* showed us persons who only pass through our world, but do not lastingly affect it. These works and others were harbingers of the new biology, as the early stories of the physical exploration of space and matter were suggestive of the great changes coming in physics and astronomy.

Today, physics and biology are not far apart, as we learn that the dividing line between living and nonliving matter is not clear cut. Biological organisms are elaborate synergistic structures, capable in their complexity of producing such states as self-awareness and intelligence. In many ways they are machines, but the word can no longer mean an assembly of parts that affect each other in a simple determined way, as in a clockwork. Biology is reducible to physics, but we must not seek to find simpler qualities at higher levels of complexity; we must not commit the fallacy of saying that a living creature is no more than a few chemicals. Complexity of structure and function make the difference between a human being and a rock. Intelligence may be found in a suitably complex machine as in a man, an android, or an alien being. Intelligent self-awareness, the mythic concept of soul, makes for humanity, not the physical form; any life-form reaching this state must be treated as an example of humanity.

In confronting our biological selves, we learn more about our human possibilities, the potential humanity of beings we may create or meet on far worlds; we learn that we are not tied to our form or our sex. *Humanity is an adaptive, intelligent life-form that takes itself as its own project.* "Day Million" by Frederik Pohl illustrates this view with a wry humor that owes much to the outlook of comparative anthropology and modern science fiction's qualified rejection of Faustian views of science and technology. The story is the natural heir of earlier works, especially Stapledon's *Last and First Men* and *The Star Maker,* novels which depict the myriad permutations of intelligence in the universe, the relatedness of all intelligence, its common humanity. In Stapledon's view the word "humanity" must have countless synonyms among the stars.*

*Stapledon early saw the universe as filled with life, including intelligent life, a view which has prevailed in biology, creating the new branch called exobiology—the study of life beyond the earth. Scientific discussions routinely accept the idea of the natural place of intelligence in nature, denying that we are strangers in the universe. As we write this, the Viking Mars Probe nears the red planet, making exobiology an experimental science; those who read this know what the probe has found.

How, then, do the models of biological science fiction depart from traditional bio-myths? The answer clearly shows a radical departure from earlier fictions on the part of modern science fiction; but the rift is not complete. Although much biological science fiction owes images and patterns to traditional myths about human origin, life, death, and destiny, it is obvious that past models are not fully adequate to support realistic projections about the future, especially the pluralistic futures of current writers. Stanislaw Lem summarizes the situation in his essay "Robots in Science Fiction" (included in *SF: The Other Side of Realism,* edited by Thomas D. Clareson):

... it isn't possible to construct a reflection of the future with clichés. It isn't the archetypes of Jung, nor the structures of the myth, nor irrational nightmares which cause the central problems of the future and determine them. And should the future be full of dangers, those dangers cannot be reduced to the known patterns of the past. They have a unique quality, as a variety of factors of a new type. That is the most important thing for the writer of science fiction.

The success of this open-ended view of science fiction lies in the source of the science fiction writer's inputs. Good science fiction forms itself not so much out of the moral universe of traditional myths, but out of the limits of knowledge and possibility; yet it maintains a relationship with past myths when it recognizes that projections of the future must be related to the possibilities of human frailty and failure in order to have a communicable meaning. Man is often the doer in science fiction, sometimes superhuman and godlike; there are other gods, powerful aliens, sometimes superior to humanity; but in contrast to his previous place in myth, man now is at least one of the new gods, despite his imperfect knowledge of himself and nature. Modern science fiction is most itself when it insists on real possibilities, combining them with a morally critical humanistic outlook to create a rich background of speculations against which to view human destiny.

V

Biological innovations raise many psychosocial and ethical problems. What should we become? Should we alter the human form at all? Perhaps genetic engineering should be restricted entirely to the repair of ailments like diabetes and hemophilia, thus making it a branch of preventive medicine. What effect would biological changes have on economics? What weight should we give to changing environmental factors before we consider genetic endowment? Is biological transformation necessary for human happiness? How should we use our new plasticity? And most important, what do we want to be?

Science fiction writers have dealt with these and other questions only superficially. James Gunn's novel *The Immortals* attacks the potential for dehumanization of values present in biological innovation. Developments such as transplants, efficient medical care, immortality, etc., become the property of a wealthy class and a corrupt medical establishment. To some degree this tendency already exists.

The abortion debate foreshadows future debates that will make the current formulation of the problem seem very mild. The Supreme Court has used ''viability'' outside the womb as a legal criterion for abortion—therefore abortions are a problem only when the fetus can survive outside the mother's body. What happens when it becomes possible for the fetus to survive, perhaps as early as conception, outside a human womb? Should the mother always have the final decision? Views of the problem run the gamut from Plato's idea that a fetus is not human until birth, to the notion held in certain sectors today that a fetus is a person from the moment of conception. Ironically, it is historically true that anti-abortion laws were originally designed to *protect the woman* during a time when abortion was riskier than birth. Our respect for human life is itself a result of advanced medicine. Children do not die often, so we value them more—even *in utero*.

When is a person dead? The case of Karen Quinlan has affected the views we have of extraordinary measures to preserve life; it will affect the possible use of cryonics, both short- and long-term suspended animation.

How much of our improved health is due to environmental improvements (food, sanitation, etc.) and how much to medical developments? Vaccination and antibiotics have helped, but what about the new diseases that may resist our drugs? What about the possibility of new plagues coming out of the laboratory, either deliberately or through an accident?

The questions proliferate into a critical mass of problems, making comprehensive discussions in science fiction and elsewhere extremely difficult. Although the possibilities for science fiction have been only slightly explored, the writers have taken diverse approaches to the problems, and this seems the best way to present these issues to the public, in fiction and in nonfiction. Specific solutions will belong to each generation of those who struggle with the problems.

The Seedling Stars by the late James Blish comes to mind as the work which conveys the sense of biological choice surrounding the possible diversification of the human form. Doubtless there will be tragedies as well as miracles and wonders. Arthur C. Clarke's *The City and the Stars* is critically Wellsian in its depiction of a stagnating immortalist society. Thomas N. Scortia's novella "The Weariest River" examines our views of dying and the traps waiting for those who take a facile approach to biological creativity.

A genuinely creative view of cyborg technology appears in Samuel R. Delany's novel *Nova.* His approach is notable because it deals with the issue of dehumanization through technology, and comes up with a surprising answer. Algis Budrys writes:

What about taking the cyborg idea, and painting a picture of a civilization where everyone plugs directly into his tools? What about then making you realize that a socketed man plugged into a factory literally puts the raw materials in with his bare hands and nudges and pushes the product along the processing line.

His brain, after all, cannot tell the difference between telling his hand to scoop and telling an automated train of ore cars to roll into the unloading dock... then such a factory worker has a sense of accomplishment and identity with his product that is now lost to the 20th century and has in fact been lost to us all since the disappearance of the artisan... this becomes a major social fact in the world of the future... a redeeming fact of technology, with all its intense humanistic implications arrived at via the route of playing on the sensorium. (*Galaxy,* January 1969).

Douglas Barbour sees Delany as presenting the end of the worker's alienation from his work (*Foundation* 7–8, March 1975).

A more recent book, Pamela Sargent's *Cloned Lives,* depicts the problematical lives of five clones, as they grow and come to maturity within a larger context of biological change; the details of this larger context and the depth of the various problems presented are unusual in a science fiction novel.

We have seen that science fiction based on biological projections cannot avoid touching on older myths of human behavior, as well as discussing genuine possibilities and creating newer models. Biology gives new meaning to old dreams and new power to old fears; but it also shifts the ground of symbolic thought, showing it to be, in its catalog of stories, moral and psychological models, perhaps a prophetic effort to see the powers we are now acquiring, a pre-vision of the impact of science and technology on human life and the transformation that this "real magic" is bringing to our way of life and our view of life in the universe.

"The chemical or physical inventor is always a Prometheus," J. B. S. Haldane once wrote. "There is no great invention from fire to flying, which has not been hailed as an insult to some god. But if every physical invention is a blasphemy, every biological invention is a perversion." We have had our physical Prometheans, and biology has given us its Proteans. We are no longer unanimous about insults to gods, but we have a human conscience, a human intellect which raises problems. The answers to our ethical doubts about the biological time bomb will emerge from the quality of our creative acts and from the planned foresight of our moral choices. A secular mythology demands that we do not offend against ourselves. As a literature of foresight, science fiction attempts to live up to this model.

BIBLIOGRAPHY

Novels

Blish, James, *The Seedling Stars,* 1957 (Gnome Press)
————, *Titan's Daughter,* 1961 (Berkley)
————, and Norman L. Knight, *A Torrent of Faces,* 1967 (Doubleday)
Clarke, Arthur C., *The City and the Stars,* 1956 (Harcourt)
————, *2001: A Space Odyssey,* 1968 (New American Library)
Dick, Philip K., *Ubik,* 1969 (Doubleday)
Gunn, James, *The Immortals,* 1962 (Bantam)
Huxley, Aldous, *Brave New World,* 1932 (Doubleday)
Sargent, Pamela, *Cloned Lives,* 1976 (Gold Medal)
Silverberg, Robert, *Tower of Glass,* 1970 (Scribner's)
Stapledon, Olaf, *Last and First Men,* 1968 (Dover), 1930 (London)
————, *Odd John,* 1972 (Dover), 1935 (London)
Sturgeon, Theodore, *Venus Plus X,* 1960 (Pyramid)
Taine, John, *Seeds of Life,* 1951 (Fantasy Press)
Wallace, F. L., *Address: Centauri,* 1955 (Gnome Press)
Wells, H. G., *The Island of Doctor Moreau,* 1896 (Chicago)
————, *The Time Machine,* 1895 (New York)
Wolfe, Bernard, *Limbo,* 1952 (Random House)

Anthologies

Conklin, Groff, ed., *Science Fiction Adventures in Mutation,* 1955 (Vanguard Press)
Dann, Jack, ed., *Immortal,* (Harper & Row)
Greenberg, Martin, ed., *Travelers of Space,* 1951 (Gnome Press)
Sargent, Pamela, ed., *Bio-Futures,* 1976 (Vintage Books)
Scortia, Thomas N. and George Zebrowski, eds., *Human-Machines: Stories about Cyborgs,* 1975 (Vintage Books)
Zebrowski, George, ed., *Biogenesis,* 1977 (Unity Press)

Short Fiction

Heinlein, Robert A., "Jerry Was a Man," 1947, in *Assignment in Eternity,* ed. by Robert A. Heinlein (Fantasy Press)
Keyes, Daniel, "Flowers for Algernon," 1959, in *The Year's Best SF,* ed. by Judith Merril (Simon and Schuster, 1960).
Scortia, Thomas N., "The Weariest River," in *Bio-Futures,* ed. by Pamela Sargent (Vintage Books, 1976)

ACKNOWLEDGMENT

We would like to thank Pamela Sargent for showing us the extensive and annotated bibliography of biological SF which appears in her anthology *Bio-Futures.* The interested reader is urged to consult this bibliography, which contains numerous listings of nonfiction, novels, anthologies, and short stories in this area of science fiction.

NINE LIVES

Ursula K. Le Guin

She was alive inside, but dead outside, her face a black and dun net of wrinkles, tumors, cracks. She was bald and blind. The tremors that crossed Libra's face were mere quiverings of corruption: underneath, in the black corridors, the halls beneath the skin, there were crepitations in darkness, ferments, chemical nightmares that went on for centuries. "Oh the damned flatulent planet," Pugh murmured as the dome shook and a boil burst a kilometer to the southwest, spraying silver pus across the sunset. The sun had been setting for the last two days. "I'll be glad to see a human face."

"Thanks," said Martin.

"Yours is human to be sure," said Pugh, "but I've seen it so long I can't see it."

Radvid signals cluttered the communicator which Martin was operating, faded, returned as face and voice. The face filled the screen, the nose of an Assyrian king, the eyes of a samurai, skin bronze, eyes the color of iron: young, magnificent. "Is that what human beings look like?" said Pugh with awe. "I'd forgotten."

"Shut up, Owen, we're on."

"Libra Exploratory Mission Base, come in please, this is *Passerine* launch."

"Libra here. Beam fixed. Come on down, launch."

"Expulsion in seven E-seconds. Hold on." The screen blanked and sparkled.

"Do they all look like that? Martin, you and I are uglier men than I thought."

"Shut up, Owen. . . ."

For twenty-two minutes Martin followed the landing-craft down by signal and then through the cleared dome they saw it, small star in the blood-colored east, sinking. It came down neat and quiet, Libra's thin atmosphere carrying little sound. Pugh and Martin closed the headpieces of their imsuits, zipped out of the dome airlocks, and ran with soaring strides, Nijinsky and Nureyev, toward the boat. Three equipment modules came floating down at four-minute intervals from each other and hundred-meter intervals east of the boat. "Come on out," Martin said on his suit radio, "we're waiting at the door."

"Come on in, the methane's fine," said Pugh.

The hatch opened. The young man they had seen on the screen came out with one athletic twist and leaped down onto the shaky dust and clinkers of Libra. Martin shook his hand, but Pugh was staring at the hatch, from which another young man emerged with the same neat twist and jump, followed by a young woman who emerged with the same neat twist, ornamented by a wriggle, and the jump. They were all tall, with bronze skin, black hair, high-bridged noses, epicanthic fold, the same face. They all had the same face. The fourth was emerging from the hatch with a neat twist and jump. "Martin bach," said Pugh, "we've got a clone."

"Right," said one of them, "we're a ten-clone. John Chow's the name. You're Lieutenant Martin?"

"I'm Owen Pugh."

"Alvaro Guillen Martin," said Martin, formal, bowing slightly. Another girl was out, the same beautiful face; Martin stared at her and his eye rolled like a nervous pony's. Evidently he had never given any thought to cloning, and was suffering technological shock. "Steady," Pugh said in the Argentine dialect, "it's only excess twins." He stood close by Martin's elbow. He was glad himself of the contact.

It is hard to meet a stranger. Even the greatest extrovert meeting even the meekest stranger knows a certain dread, though he may not know he knows it. Will he make a fool of me wreck my image of myself invade me destroy me change me? Will he be different from me? Yes, that he will. There's the terrible thing: the strangeness of the stranger.

After two years on a dead planet, and the last half year isolated as a team of two, oneself and one other, after that it's even harder to meet a stranger, however welcome he may be. You're out of the habit of difference, you've lost the touch; and so the fear revives, the primitive anxiety, the old dread.

The clone, five males and five females, had got done in a couple of minutes what a man might have got done in twenty: greeted Pugh and Martin, had a glance at Libra, unloaded the boat, made ready to go. They went, and the dome filled with them, a hive of golden bees. They hummed and buzzed quietly, filled up all silences, all spaces with a honey-brown swarm of human presence. Martin looked bewilderedly at the long-limbed girls, and they smiled at him, three at once. Their smile was gentler than that of the boys, but no less radiantly self-possessed.

"Self-possessed," Owen Pugh murmured to his friend, "that's it. Think of it, to be oneself ten times over. Nine seconds for every motion, nine ayes on every vote. It would be glorious!" But Martin was asleep. And the John Chows had all gone to sleep at once. The dome was filled with their quiet breathing. They were young, they didn't snore. Martin sighed and snored, his hershey-bar-colored face relaxed in the dim afterglow of Libra's primary, set at last. Pugh had cleared the dome and stars looked in, Sol among them, a great company of lights, a clone of splendors. Pugh slept and dreamed of a one-eyed giant who chased him through the shaking halls of Hell.

From his sleeping-bag Pugh watched the clone's awakening. They all got up within one minute except for one pair, a boy and a girl, who lay snugly tangled and still sleeping in one bag. As Pugh saw this there was a shock like one of Libra's earthquakes inside him, a very deep tremor. He was not aware of this, and in fact thought he was pleased at the sight; there was no other such comfort on this dead hollow world, more power to them who made love. One of the others stepped on the pair. They woke and the girl sat up flushed and sleepy, with bare golden breasts. One of her sisters murmured something to her; she shot a glance at Pugh and disappeared in the sleeping-bag, followed by a giant giggle, from another direction a fierce stare, from still another direction a voice: "Christ, we're used to having a room to ourselves. Hope you don't mind, Captain Pugh."

"It's a pleasure," Pugh said half-truthfully. He had to stand up then, wearing only the shorts he slept in, and he felt like a plucked rooster, all white scrawn and pimples. He had seldom envied Martin's compact brownness so much. The United Kingdom had come through the Great Famines well, losing less than half its population: a record achieved by rigorous food-control. Black-marketeers and hoarders had been executed. Crumbs had been shared. Where in richer lands most had died and a few had thriven, in Britain fewer died and none throve. They all got lean. Their sons were lean, their grandsons lean, small, brittle-boned, easily infected. When civilization became a matter of standing in lines, the British had kept queue, and so had replaced the survival of the fittest with the survival of the fair-minded. Owen Pugh was a scrawny little man. All the same, he was there.

At the moment he wished he wasn't.

At breakfast a John said, "Now if you'll brief us, Captain Pugh—"

"Owen, then."

"Owen, we can work out our schedule. Anything new on the mine since your last report to your Mission? We saw your reports when *Passerine* was orbiting Planet V, where they are now."

Martin did not answer, though the mine was his discovery and project, and Pugh had to do his best. It was hard to talk to them. The same faces, each with the same expression of intelligent interest, all leaned toward him across the table at almost the same angle. They all nodded together.

Over the Exploitation Corps insignia on their tunics each had a nameband, first name John and last name Chow of course, but the middle names different. The men were Aleph, Kaph, Yod, Gimel, and

Samedh; the women Sadhe, Daleth, Zayin, Beth, and Resh. Pugh tried to use the names but gave it up at once; he could not even tell sometimes which one had spoken, for the voices were all alike.

Martin buttered and chewed his toast, and finally interrupted: "You're a team. Is that it?"

"Right," said two Johns.

"God, what a team! I hadn't seen the point. How much do you each know what the others are thinking?"

"Not at all, properly speaking," replied one of the girls, Zayin. The others watched her with the proprietary, approving look they had. "No ESP, nothing fancy. But we think alike. We have exactly the same equipment. Given the same stimulus, the same problem, we're likely to be coming up with the same reactions and solutions at the same time. Explanations are easy—don't even have to make them, usually. We seldom misunderstand each other. It does facilitate our working as a team."

"Christ yes," said Martin. "Pugh and I have spent seven hours out of ten for six months misunderstanding each other. Like most people. What about emergencies, are you as good at meeting the unexpected problem as a nor... an unrelated team?"

"Statistics so far indicate that we are," Zayin answered readily. Clones must be trained, Pugh thought, to meet questions, to reassure and reason. All they said had the slightly bland and stilted quality of answers furnished to the Public. "We can't brainstorm as singletons can, we as a team don't profit from the interplay of varied minds; but we have a compensatory advantage. Clones are drawn from the best human material, individuals of IIQ 99th percentile, Genetic Constitution alpha double A, and so on. We have more to draw on than most individuals do."

"And it's multiplied by a factor of ten. Who is—who was John Chow?"

"A genius surely," Pugh said politely. His interest in cloning was not so new and avid as Martin's.

"Leonardo Complex type," said Yod. "Biomath, also a cellist, and an undersea hunter, and interested in structural engineering problems, and so on. Died before he'd worked out his major theories."

"Then you each represent a different facet of his mind, his talents?"

"No," said Zayin, shaking her head in time with several others. "We share the basic equipment and tendencies, of course, but we're all engineers in Planetary Exploitation. A later clone can be trained to develop other aspects of the basic equipment. It's all training; the genetic substance is identical. We *are* John Chow. But we were differently trained.''

Martin look shell-shocked. ''How old are you?''

''Twenty-three.''

''You say he died young. Had they taken germ cells from him beforehand or something?''

Gimel took over: ''He died at twenty-four in an aircar crash. They couldn't save the brain, so they took some intestinal cells and cultured them for cloning. Reproductive cells aren't used for cloning since they have only half the chromosomes. Intestinal cells happen to be easy to despecialize and reprogram for total growth.

''All chips off the old block,'' Martin said valiantly. ''But how can... some of you be women...?''

Beth took over: ''It's easy to program half the clonal mass back to the female. Just delete the male gene from half the cells and they revert to the basic, that is, the female. It's trickier to go the other way, have to hook in artificial Y chromosomes. So they mostly clone from males, since clones function best bisexually.

Gimel again: ''They've worked these matters of technique and function out carefully. The taxpayer wants the best for his money, and of course clones are expensive. With the cell-manipulations, and the incubation in Ngama Placentae, and the maintenance and training of the foster-parent groups, we end up costing about three million apiece.''

''For your next generation,'' Martin said, still struggling, ''I suppose you... you breed?''

''We females are sterile,'' said Beth with perfect equanimity; ''you remember that the Y chromosome was deleted from our original cell. The male can interbreed with approved singletons, if they want to. But to get John Chow again as often as they want, they just reclone a cell from this clone.''

Martin gave up the struggle. He nodded and chewed cold toast. ''Well,'' said one of the Johns, and all changed mood, like a flock of starlings that change course in one wingflick, following a leader so fast that no eye can see which leads. They were ready to go. ''How about a look at the mine? Then we'll unload the equipment. Some nice new models in the roboats; you'll want to see them. Right?'' Had Pugh or Martin not agreed they might have found it hard to say no. The Johns were polite but unanimous; their decisions carried. Pugh, Commander of Libra Base 2, felt a qualm. Could he boss around this superman-woman-entity-of-ten? and a genius at that? He stuck close to Martin as they suited for outside. Neither said anything.

Four apiece in the three large jetsleds, they slipped off north from the dome, over Libra's dun rugose skin, in starlight.

"Desolate," one said.

It was a boy and girl with Pugh and Martin. Pugh wondered if these were the two that had shared a sleeping-bag last night. No doubt they wouldn't mind if he asked them. Sex must be as handy as breathing, to them. Did you two breathe last night?

"Yes," he said, "it is desolate."

"This is our first time Off, except training on Luna." The girl's voice was definitely a bit higher and softer.

"How did you take the big hop?"

"They doped us. I wanted to experience it." That was the boy; he sounded wistful. They seemed to have more personality, only two at a time. Did repetition of the individual negate individuality?

"Don't worry," said Martin, steering the sled, "you can't experience no-time because it isn't there."

"I'd just like to once," one of them said. "So we'd know."

The Mountains of Merioneth showed leprotic in starlight to the east, a plume of freezing gas trailed silvery from a vent-hole to the west, and the sled tilted groundward. The twins braced for the stop at one moment, each with a slight protective gesture to the other. Your skin is my skin, Pugh thought, but literally, no metaphor. What would it be like, then, to have someone as close to you as that? Always to be answered when you spoke, never to be in pain alone. Love your neighbor as you love yourself. . . . That hard old problem was solved. The neighbor was the self: the love was perfect.

And here was Hellmouth, the mine.

Pugh was the Exploratory Mission's ET geologist, and Martin his technician and cartographer; but when in the course of a local survey Martin had discovered the U-mine, Pugh had given him full credit, as well as the onus of prospecting the lode and planning the Exploitation Team's job. These kids had been sent out from Earth years before Martin's reports got there, and had not known what their job would be until they got here. The Exploitation Corps simply sent out teams regularly and blindly as a dandelion sends out its seeds, knowing there would be a job for them on Libra or the next planet out or one they hadn't even heard about yet. The Government wanted uranium too urgently to wait while reports drifted home across the light-years. The

stuff was like gold, old-fashioned but essential, worth mining extrater-
restrially and shipping interstellar. Worth its weight in people, Pugh
thought sourly, watching the tall young men and women go one by
one, glimmering in starlight, into the black hole Martin had named
Hellmouth.

As they went in their homeostatic forehead-lamps brightened.
Twelve nodding gleams ran along the moist, wrinkled walls. Pugh
heard Martin's radiation counter peeping twenty to the dozen up
ahead. "Here's the drop-off," said Martin's voice in the suit intercom,
drowning out the peeping and the dead silence that was around them.
"We're in a side-fissure; this is the main vertical vent in front of us."
The black void gaped, its far side not visible in the headlamp beams.
"Last vulcanism seems to have been a couple of thousand years ago.
Nearest fault is twenty-eight kilos east, in the Trench. This region
seems to be as safe seismically as anything in the area. The big basalt-
flow overhead stabilizes all these substructures, so long as it remains
stable itself. Your central lode is thirty-six meters down and runs in a
series of five bubble-caverns northeast. It is a lode, a pipe of very
high-grade ore. You saw the percentage figures, right? Extraction's
going to be no problem. All you've got to do is get the bubbles
topside."

"Take off the lid and let 'em float up." A chuckle. Voices began to
talk, but they were all the same voice and the suit radio gave them no
location in space. "Open the thing right up. —Safer that way. —But
it's a solid basalt roof, how thick, ten meters here? —Three to twenty,
the report said. —Blow good ore all over the lot. —Use this access
we're in, straighten it a bit and run slider-rails for the robos. —Import
burros. —Have we got enough propping material? —What's your
estimate of total payload mass, Martin?"

"Say over five million kilos and under eight."

"Transport will be here in ten E-months. —It'll have to go pure.
—No, they'll have the mass problem in NAFAL shipping licked by
now; remember it's been sixteen years since we left Earth last Tuesday. —Right, they'll send the whole lot back and purify it in Earth
orbit. —Shall we go down, Martin?"

"Go on. I've been down."

The first one—Aleph? (Heb., the ox, the leader)—swung onto the
ladder and down; the rest followed. Pugh and Martin stood at the
chasm's edge. Pugh set his intercom to exchange only with Martin's
suit, and noticed Martin doing the same. It was a bit wearing, this

listening to one person think aloud in ten voices, or was it one voice speaking the thoughts of ten minds?

"A great gut," Pugh said, looking down into the black pit, its veined and warted walls catching stray gleams of headlamps far below. "A cow's bowel. A bloody great constipated intestine."

Martin's counter peeped like a lost chicken. They stood inside the epileptic planet, breathing oxygen from tanks, wearing suits impermeable to corrosives and harmful radiations, resistant to a two-hundred-degree range of temperatures, tear-proof, and as shock-resistant as possible given the soft vulnerable stuff inside.

"Next hop," Martin said, "I'd like to find a planet that has nothing whatever to exploit."

"You found this."

"Keep me home next time."

Pugh was pleased. He had hoped Martin would want to go on working with him, but neither of them was used to talking much about their feelings, and he had hesitated to ask. "I'll try that," he said.

"I hate this place. I like caves, you know. It's why I came in here. Just spelunking. But this one's a bitch. Mean. You can't ever let down in here. I guess this lot can handle it, though. They know their stuff."

"Wave of the future, whatever," said Pugh.

The wave of the future came swarming up the ladder, swept Martin to the entrance, gabbled at and around him: "Have we got enough material for supports? —If we convert one of the extractor-servos to anneal, yes. —Sufficient if we miniblast? —Kaph can calculate stress."

Pugh had switched his intercom back to receive them; he looked at them, so many thoughts jabbering in an eager mind, and at Martin standing silent among them, and at Hellmouth, and the wrinkled plain. "Settled! How does that strike you as a preliminary schedule, Martin?"

"It's your baby," Martin said.

Within five E-days the Johns had all their material and equipment unloaded and operating, and were starting to open up the mine. They worked with total efficiency. Pugh was fascinated and frightened by their effectiveness, their confidence, their independence. He was no use to them at all. A clone, he thought, might indeed be the first truly stable, self-reliant human being. Once adult it would need nobody's help. It would be sufficient to itself physically, sexually, emotionally, intellectually. Whatever he did, any member of it would always receive the support and approval of his peers, his other selves. Nobody else was needed.

Two of the clone stayed in the dome doing calculations and paperwork, with frequent sled-trips to the mine for measurements and tests. They were the mathematicians of the clone, Zayin and Kaph. That is, as Zayin explained, all ten had had thorough mathematical training from age three to twenty-one, but from twenty-one to twenty-three she and Kaph had gone on with math while the others intensified other specialties, geology, mining engineering, electronic engineering, equipment robotics, applied atomics, and so on. "Kaph and I feel," she said, "that we're the element of the clone closest to what John Chow was in his singleton lifetime. But of course he was principally in biomath, and they didn't take us far in that."

"They needed us most in this field," Kaph said, with the patriotic priggishness they sometimes evinced.

Pugh and Martin soon could distinguish this pair from the others, Zayin by gestalt, Kaph only by a discolored left fourth fingernail, got from an ill-aimed hammer at the age of six. No doubt there were many such differences, physical and psychological, among them; nature might be identical, nurture could not be. But the differences were hard to find. And part of the difficulty was that they really never talked to Pugh and Martin. They joked with them, were polite, got along fine. They gave nothing. It was nothing one could complain about; they were very pleasant, they had the standardized American friendliness. "Do you come from Ireland, Owen?"

"Nobody comes from Ireland, Zayin."

"There are lots of Irish-Americans."

"To be sure, but no more Irish. A couple of thousand in all the island, the last I knew. They didn't go in for birth-control, you know, so the food ran out. By the Third Famine there were no Irish left at all but the priesthood, and they were all celibate, or nearly all."

Zayin and Kaph smiled stiffly. They had no experience of either bigotry or irony. "What are you then, ethnically?" Kaph asked, and Pugh replied, "A Welshman."

"Is it Welsh that you and Martin speak together?"

None of your business, Pugh thought, but said, "No, it's his dialect, not mine: Argentinean. A descendant of Spanish."

"You learned it for private communication?"

"Whom had we here to be private from? It's just that sometimes a man likes to speak his native language."

"Ours is English," Kaph said unsympathetically. Why should they have sympathy? That's one of the things you give because you need it back.

"Is Wells quaint?" asked Zayin

"Wells? Oh, Wales, it's called. Yes. Wales is quaint." Pugh switched on his rock-cutter, which prevented further conversation by a synapse-destroying whine, and while it whined he turned his back and said a profane word in Welsh.

That night he used the Argentine dialect for private communication. "Do they pair off in the same couples, or change every night?"

Martin looked surprised. A prudish expression, unsuited to his features, appeared for a moment. It faded. He too was curious. "I think it's random."

"Don't whisper, man, it sounds dirty. I think they rotate."

"On a schedule?"

"So nobody gets omitted."

Martin gave a vulgar laugh and smothered it. "What about us? Aren't we omitted?"

"That doesn't occur to them."

"What if I proposition one of the girls?"

"She'd tell the others and they'd decide as a group."

"I am not a bull," Martin said, his dark, heavy face heating up. "I will not be judged—"

"Down, down, *machismo*," said Pugh. "Do you mean to proposition one?"

Martin shrugged, sullen. "Let 'em have their incest."

"Incest is it, or masturbation?"

"I don't care, if they'd do it out of earshot!"

The clone's early attempts at modesty had soon worn off, unmotivated by any deep defensiveness of self or awareness of others. Pugh and Martin were daily deeper swamped under the intimacies of its constant emotional-sexual-mental interchange: swamped yet excluded.

"Two months to go," Martin said one evening.

"To what?" snapped Pugh. He was edgy lately and Martin's sullenness got on his nerves.

"To relief."

In sixty days the full crew of their Exploratory Mission were due back from their survey of the other planets of the system. Pugh was aware of this.

"Crossing off the days on your calendar?" he jeered.

"Pull yourself together, Owen."

"What do you mean?"

"What I say."

They parted in contempt and resentment.

Pugh came in after a day alone on the Pampas, a vast lava-plain the nearest edge of which was two hours south by jet. He was tired, but refreshed by solitude. They were not supposed to take long trips alone, but lately had often done so. Martin stooped under bright lights, drawing one of his elegant, masterly charts: this one was of the whole face of Libra, the cancerous face. The dome was otherwise empty, seeming dim and large as it had before the clone came. "Where's the golden horde?"

Martin grunted ignorance, crosshatching. He straightened his back to glance around at the sun, which squatted feebly like a great red toad on the eastern plain, and at the clock, which said 18:45. "Some big quakes today," he said, returning to his map. "Feel them down there? Lot of crates were falling around. Take a look at the seismo."

The needle jigged and wavered on the roll. It never stopped dancing here. The roll had recorded five quakes of major intensity back in mid-afternoon; twice the needle had hopped off the roll. The attached computer had been activated to emit a slip reading, "Epicenter 61' N by 4'24" E."

"Not in the Trench this time."

"I thought it felt a bit different from usual. Sharper."

"In Base One I used to lie awake all night feeling the ground jump. Queer how you get used to things."

"Go spla if you didn't. What's for dinner?"

"I thought you'd have cooked it."

"Waiting for the clone."

Feeling put upon, Pugh got out a dozen dinnerboxes, stuck two in the Instobake, pulled them out. "All right, here's dinner."

"Been thinking," Martin said, coming to the table. "What if some clone cloned itself? Illegally. Made a thousand duplicates—ten thousand. Whole army. They could make a tidy power-grab, couldn't they?"

"But how many millions did this lot cost to rear? Artificial placentae and all that. It would be hard to keep secret, unless they had a planet to themselves. . . . Back before the Famines when Earth had national governments, they talked about that: clone your best soldiers, have whole regiments of them. But the food ran out before they could play that game.''

They talked amicably, as they used to do.

"Funny," Martin said, chewing. "They left early this morning, didn't they?''

"All but Kaph and Zayin. They thought they'd get the first payload aboveground today. What's up?''

"They weren't back for lunch.''

"They won't starve, to be sure.''

"They left at seven.''

"So they did." Then Pugh saw it. The air-tanks held eight hours' supply.

"Kaph and Zayin carried out spare cans when they left. Or they've got a heap out there.''

"They did, but they brought the whole lot in to recharge.'' Martin stood up, pointing to one of the stacks of stuff that cut the dome into rooms and alleys.

"There's an alarm signal on every insuit.''

"It's not automatic.''

Pugh was tired and still hungry. "Sit down and eat, man. That lot can look after themselves.''

Martin sat down, but did not eat. "There was a big quake, Owen. The first one. Big enough, it scared me.''

After a pause Pugh sighed and said, "All right.''

Unenthusiastically, they got out the two-man sled that was always left for them, and headed it north. The long sunrise covered everything in poisonous red jello. The horizontal light and shadow made it hard to see, raised walls of fake iron ahead of them through which they slid, turned the convex plain beyond Hellmouth into a great dimple full of bloody water. Around the tunnel entrance a wilderness of machinery stood, cranes and cables and servos and wheels and diggers and robocarts and sliders and control-huts, all slanting and bulking incoherently in the red light. Martin jumped from the sled, ran into the mine. He came out again, to Pugh. "Oh God, Owen, it's down," he said. Pugh went in and saw, five meters from the entrance, the shiny, moist, black wall that ended the tunnel. Newly exposed to air, it looked organic, like visceral tissue. The tunnel entrance, enlarged by blasting and double-tracked for robocarts, seemed unchanged until he noticed thousands of tiny spiderweb cracks in the walls. The floor was wet with some sluggish fluid.

"They were inside," Martin said.

"They may be still. They surely had extra air-cans—"

"Look, Owen, look at the basalt flow, at the roof; don't you see what the quake did, look at it."

The low hump of land that roofed the caves still had the unreal look of an optical illusion. It had reversed itself, sunk down, leaving a vast dimple or pit. When Pugh walked on it he saw that it too was cracked with many tiny fissures. From some a whitish gas was seeping, so that the sunlight on the surface of the gas-pool was shafted as if by the waters of a dim red lake.

"The mine's not on the fault. There's no fault here!"

Pugh came back to him quickly. "No, there's no fault, Martin. Look, they surely weren't all inside together."

Martin followed him and searched among the wrecked machines dully, then actively. He spotted the airsled. It had come down heading south, and stuck at an angle in a pothole of colloidal dust. It had carried two riders. One was half sunk in the dust, but his suit-meters registered normal functioning; the other hung strapped onto the tilted sled. Her imsuit had burst open on the broken legs, and the body was frozen hard as any rock. That was all they found. As both regulation and custom demanded, they cremated the dead at once with the laser-guns they carried by regulation and had never used before. Pugh, knowing he was going to be sick, wrestled the survivor onto the two-man sled and sent Martin off to the dome with him. Then he vomited, and flushed the waste out of his suit, and finding one four-man sled undamaged followed after Martin, shaking as if the cold of Libra had got through to him.

The survivor was Kaph. He was in deep shock. They found a swelling on the occiput that might mean concussion, but no fracture was visible.

Pugh brought two glasses of food-concentrate and two chasers of aquavit. "Come on," he said. Martin obeyed, drinking off the tonic. They sat down on crates near the cot and sipped the aquavit.

Kaph lay immobile, face like beeswax, hair bright black to the shoulders, lips stiffly parted for faintly gasping breaths.

"It must have been the first shock, the big one," Martin said. "It must have slid the whole structure sideways. Till it fell in on itself. There must be gas layers in the lateral rocks, like those formations in the Thirty-first Quadrant. But there wasn't any sign—" As he spoke the world slid out from under them. Things leaped and clattered, hopped and jigged, shouted Ha! Ha! Ha! "It was like this at fourteen

hours," said Reason shakily in Martin's voice; amidst the unfastening
and ruin of the world. But Unreason sat up, as the tumult lessened and
things ceased dancing, and screamed aloud.

Pugh leaped across his spilled aquavit and held Kaph down. The
muscular body flailed him off. Martin pinned the shoulders down.
Kaph screamed, struggled, choked; his face blackened. "Oxy," Pugh
said, and his hand found the right needle in the medical kit as if by
homing instinct; while Martin held the mask he struck the needle home
to the vagus nerve, restoring Kaph to life.

"Didn't know you knew that stunt," Martin said, breathing hard.

"The Lazarus Jab; my father was a doctor. It doesn't often work,"
Pugh said. "I want that drink I spilled. Is the quake over? I can't tell."

"Aftershocks. It's not just you shivering."

"Why did he suffocate?"

"I don't know, Owen. Look in the book."

Kaph was breathing normally and his color was restored, only the
lips were still darkened. They poured a new shot of courage and sat
down by him again with their medical guide. "Nothing about cyanosis
or asphyxiation under 'shock' or 'concussion.' He can't have breathed
in anything with his suit on. I don't know. We'd get as much good out
of *Mother Mog's Home Herbalist.* . . . 'Anal Hemorrhoids,' fy!" Pugh
pitched the book to a crate-table. It fell short, because either Pugh or
the table was still unsteady.

"Why didn't he signal?"

"Sorry?"

"The eight inside the mine never had time. But he and the girl must
have been outside. Maybe she was in the entrance, and got hit by the
first slide. He must have been outside, in the control-hut maybe. He
ran in, pulled her out, strapped her onto the sled, started for the dome.
And all that time never pushed the panic button in his imsuit. Why
not?"

"Well, he'd had that whack on his head. I doubt he ever realized the
girl was dead. He wasn't in his senses. But if he had been I don't know
if he'd have thought to signal us. They looked to one another for
help."

Martin's face was like an Indian mask, grooves at the mouth-
corners, eyes of dull coal. "That's so. What must he have felt, then,
when the quake came and he was outside, alone—"

In answer Kaph screamed.

He came up off the cot in the heaving convulsions of one suffocat-
ing, knocked Pugh right down with his flailing arm, staggered into a

stack of crates and fell to the floor, lips blue, eyes white. Martin dragged him back onto the cot and gave him a whiff of oxygen, then knelt by Pugh, who was just sitting up, and wiped at his cut cheek-bone. "Owen, are you all right, are you going to be all right, Owen?"

"I think I am," Pugh said. "Why are you rubbing that on my face?"

It was a short length of computer-tape, now spotted with Pugh's blood. Martin dropped it. "Thought it was a towel. You clipped your cheek on that box there."

"Is he out of it?"

"Seems to be."

They stared down at Kaph lying stiff, his teeth a white line inside dark parted lips.

"Like epilepsy. Brain damage maybe?"

"What about shooting him full of meprobamate?"

Pugh shook his head. "I don't know what's in that shot I already gave him for shock. Don't want to overdose him."

"Maybe he'll sleep it off now."

"I'd like to myself. Between him and the earthquake I can't seem to keep on my feet."

"You got a nasty crack there. Go on, I'll sit up a while."

Pugh cleaned his cut cheek and pulled off his shirt, then paused.

"Is there anything we ought to have done—have tried to do—"

"They're all dead," Martin said heavily, gently.

Pugh lay down on top of his sleeping-bag, and one instant later was awakened by a hideous, sucking, struggling noise. He staggered up, found the needle, tried three times to jab it in correctly and failed, began to massage over Kaph's heart. "Mouth-to-mouth," he said, and Martin obeyed. Presently Kaph drew a harsh breath, his heartbeat steadied, his rigid muscles began to relax.

"How long did I sleep?"

"Half an hour."

They stood up sweating. The ground shuddered, the fabric of the dome sagged and swayed. Libra was dancing her awful polka again, her Totentanz. The sun, though rising, seemed to have grown larger and redder; gas and dust must have been stirred up in the feeble atmosphere.

"What's wrong with him, Owen?"

"I think he's dying with them."

"Them—But they're dead, I tell you."

"Nine of them. They're all dead, they were crushed or suffocated.

They were all him, he is all of them. They died, and now he's dying their deaths one by one.''

"Oh pity of God," said Martin.

The next time was much the same. The fifth time was worse, for Kaph fought and raved, trying to speak but getting no words out, as if his mouth were stopped with rocks or clay. After that the attacks grew weaker, but so did he. The eighth seizure came at about four-thirty; Pugh and Martin worked till five-thirty doing all they could to keep life in the body that slid without protest into death. They kept him, but Martin said, "The next will finish him." And it did; but Pugh breathed his own breath into the inert lungs, until he himself passed out.

He woke. The dome was opaqued and no light on. He listened and heard the breathing of two sleeping men. He slept, and nothing woke him till hunger did.

The sun was well up over the dark plains, and the planet had stopped dancing. Kaph lay asleep. Pugh and Martin drank tea and looked at him with proprietary triumph.

When he woke Martin went to him: "How do you feel, old man?" There was no answer. Pugh took Martin's place and looked into the brown, dull eyes that gazed toward but not into his own. Like Martin he quickly turned away. He heated food-concentrate and brought it to Kaph. "Come on, drink."

He could see the muscles in Kaph's throat tighten. "Let me die," the young man said.

"You're not dying."

Kaph spoke with clarity and precision: "I am nine-tenths dead. There is not enough of me left alive."

That precision convinced Pugh, and he fought the conviction. "No," he said, peremptory. "They are dead. The others. Your brothers and sisters. You're not them, you're alive. You are John Chow. Your life is in your own hands."

The young man lay still, looking into a darkness that was not there.

Martin and Pugh took turns taking the Exploitation hauler and a spare set of robos over to Hellmouth to salvage equipment and protect it from Libra's sinister atmosphere, for the value of the stuff was, literally, astronomical. It was slow work for one man at a time, but they were unwilling to leave Kaph by himself. The one left in the dome did paperwork, while Kaph sat or lay and stared into his darkness, and never spoke. The days went by silent.

The radio spat and spoke: the Mission calling from ship. "We'll be down on Libra in five weeks, Owen. Thirty-four E-days nine hours I make it as of now. How's tricks in the old dome?''

''Not good, chief. The Exploit team were killed, all but one of them, in the mine. Earthquake. Six days ago.''

The radio crackled and sang starsong. Sixteen seconds lag each way; the ship was out around Planet 11 now. ''Killed, all but one? You and Martin were unhurt?''

''We're all right, chief.''

Thirty-two seconds.

''*Passerine* left an Exploit team out here with us. I may put them on the Hellmouth project then, instead of the Quadrant Seven project. We'll settle that when we come down. In any case you and Martin will be relieved at Dome Two. Hold tight. Anything else?''

''Nothing else.''

Thirty-two seconds.

''Right then. So long, Owen.''

Kaph had heard all this, and later on Pugh said to him, ''The chief may ask you to stay here with the other Exploit team. You know the ropes here.'' Knowing the exigencies of Far Out Life, he wanted to warn the young man. Kaph made no answer. Since he had said, ''There is not enough of me left alive,'' he had not spoken a word.

''Owen,'' Martin said on suit intercom, ''he's spla. Insane. Psycho.''

''He's doing very well for a man who's died nine times.''

''Well? Like a turned-off android is well? The only emotion he has left is hate. Look at his eyes.''

''That's not hate, Martin. Listen, it's true that he has, in a sense, been dead. I cannot imagine what he feels. But it's not hatred. He can't even see us. It's too dark.''

''Throats have been cut in the dark. He hates us because we're not Aleph and Yod and Zayin.''

''Maybe. But I think he's alone. He doesn't see us or hear us, that's the truth. He never had to see anyone else before. He never was alone before. He had himself to see, talk with, live with, nine other selves all his life. He doesn't know how you go it alone. He must learn. Give him time.''

Martin shook his heavy head. ''Spla,'' he said. ''Just remember when you're alone with him that he could break your neck one-handed.''

''He could do that,'' said Pugh, a short, soft-voiced man with a scarred cheekbone; he smiled. They were just outside the dome airlock, programming one of the servos to repair a damaged hauler. They could see Kaph sitting inside the great half-egg of the dome like a fly in amber.

"Hand me the insert pack there. What makes you think he'll get any better?"

"He has a strong personality, to be sure."

"Strong? Crippled. Nine-tenths dead, as he put it."

"But he's not dead. He's a live man: John Kaph Chow. He had a jolly queer upbringing, but after all every boy has got to break free of his family. He will do it."

"I can't see it."

"Think a bit, Martin bach. What's this cloning for? To repair the human race. We're in a bad way. Look at me. My IIQ and GC are half this John Chow's. Yet they wanted me so badly for the Far Out Service that when I volunteered they took me and fitted me out with an artificial lung and corrected my myopia. Now if there were enough good sound lads about would they be taking one-lunged shortsighted Welshmen?"

"Didn't know you had an artificial lung."

"I do then. Not tin, you know. Human, grown in a tank from a bit of somebody; cloned, if you like. That's how they make replacement-organs, the same general idea as cloning, but bits and pieces instead of whole people. It's my own lung now, whatever. But what I am saying is this, there are too many like me these days, and not enough like John Chow. They're trying to raise the level of the human genetic pool, which is a mucky little puddle since the population crash. So then if a man is cloned, he's a strong and clever man. It's only logic, to be sure."

Martin grunted; the servo began to hum.

Kaph had been eating little; he had trouble swallowing his food, choking on it, so that he would give up trying after a few bites. He had lost eight or ten kilos. After three weeks or so, however, his appetite began to pick up, and one day he began to look through the clone's possessions, the sleeping-bags, kits, papers which Pugh had stacked neatly in a far angle of a packing-crate alley. He sorted, destroyed a heap of papers and oddments, made a small packet of what remained, then relapsed into his walking coma.

Two days later he spoke. Pugh was trying to correct a flutter in the tape-player, and failing; Martin had the jet out, checking their maps of the Pampas. "Hell and damnation!" Pugh said, and Kaph said in a toneless voice, "Do you want me to do that?"

Pugh jumped, controlled himself, and gave the machine to Kaph. The young man took it apart, put it back together, and left it on the table.

"Put on a tape," Pugh said with careful casualness, busy at another table.

Kaph put on the topmost tape, a chorale. He lay down on his cot. The sound of a hundred human voices singing together filled the dome. He lay still, his face blank.

In the next days he took over several routine jobs, unasked. He undertook nothing that wanted initiative, and if asked to do anything he made no response at all.

"He's doing well," Pugh said in the dialect of Argentina.

"He's not. He's turning himself into a machine. Does what he's programmed to do, no reaction to anything else. He's worse off than when he didn't function at all. He's not human any more."

Pugh sighed. "Well, good night," he said in English. "Good night, Kaph."

"Good night," Martin said; Kaph did not.

Next morning at breakfast Kaph reached across Martin's plate for the toast. "Why don't you ask for it," Martin said with the geniality of repressed exasperation. "I can pass it."

"I can reach it," Kaph said in his flat voice.

"Yes, but look. Asking to pass things, saying good night or hello, they're not important, but all the same when somebody says something a person ought to answer. . . ."

The young man looked indifferently in Martin's direction; his eyes still did not seem to see clear through to the person he looked toward. "Why should I answer?"

"Because somebody has said something to you."

"Why?"

Martin shrugged and laughed. Pugh jumped up and turned on the rock-cutter.

Later on he said, "Lay off that, please, Martin."

"Manners are essential in small isolated crews, some kind of manners, whatever you work out together. He's been taught that, everybody in Far Out knows it. Why does he deliberately flout it?"

"Do you tell yourself good night?"

"So?"

"Don't you see Kaph's never known anyone but himself?"

Martin brooded and then broke out, "Then by God this cloning business is all wrong. It won't do. What are a lot of duplicate geniuses going to do for us when they don't even know we exist?"

Pugh nodded. "It might be wiser to separate the clones and bring them up with others. But they make such a grand team this way."

"Do they? I don't know. If this lot had been ten average inefficient ET engineers, would they all have been in the same place at the same time? Would they all have got killed? What if, when the quake came and things started caving in, what if all those kids ran the same way, farther into the mine, maybe, to save the one that was farthest in? Even Kaph was outside and went in. . . . It's hypothetical. But I keep thinking, out of ten ordinary confused guys, more might have got out."

"I don't know. It's true that identical twins tend to die at about the same time, even when they have never seen each other. Identity and death, it is very strange. . . ."

The days went on, the red sun crawled across the dark sky, Kaph did not speak when spoken to, Pugh and Martin snapped at each other more frequently each day. Pugh complained of Martin's snoring. Offended, Martin moved his cot clear across the dome and also ceased speaking to Pugh for some while. Pugh whistled Welsh dirges until Martin complained, and then Pugh stopped speaking for a while.

The day before the Mission ship was due, Martin announced he was going over to Merioneth.

"I thought at least you'd be giving me a hand with the computer to finish the rock-analyses," Pugh said, aggrieved.

"Kaph can do that. I want one more look at the Trench. Have fun," Martin added in dialect, and laughed, and left.

"What is that language?"

"Argentinean. I told you that once, didn't I?"

"I don't know." After a while the young man added, "I have forgotten a lot of things, I think."

"It wasn't important, to be sure," Pugh said gently, realizing all at once how important this conversation was. "Will you give me a hand running the computer, Kaph?"

He nodded.

Pugh had left a lot of loose ends, and the job took them all day. Kaph was a good co-worker, quick and systematic, much more so than Pugh himself. His flat voice, now that he was talking again, got on the nerves; but it didn't matter, there was only this one day left to get through and then the ship would come, the old crew, comrades and friends.

During tea-break Kaph said, "What will happen if the Explorer ship crashes?"

"They'd be killed."

"To you, I mean."

"To us? We'd radio SOS all signals, and live on half rations till the rescue cruiser from Area Three Base came. Four and a half E-years away it is. We have life support here for three men for, let's see, maybe between four and five years. A bit tight, it would be."

"Would they send a cruiser for three men?"

"They would."

Kaph said no more.

"Enough cheerful speculations," Pugh said cheerfully, rising to get back to work. He slipped sideways and the chair avoided his hand; he did a sort of half-pirouette and fetched up hard against the dome-hide. "My goodness," he said, reverting to his native idiom, "what is it?"

"Quake," said Kaph.

The teacups bounced on the table with a plastic cackle, a litter of papers slid off a box, the skin of the dome swelled and sagged. Underfoot there was a huge noise, half sound half shaking, a subsonic boom.

Kaph sat unmoved. An earthquake does not frighten a man who died in an earthquake.

Pugh, white-faced, wiry black hair sticking out, a frightened man, said, "Martin is in the Trench."

"What trench?"

"The big fault line. The epicenter for the local quakes. Look at the seismograph." Pugh struggled with the stuck door of a still-jittering locker.

"Where are you going?"

"After him."

"Martin took the jet. Sleds aren't safe to use during quakes. They go out of control."

"For God's sake, man, shut up."

Kaph stood up, speaking in a flat voice as usual. "It's unnecessary to go out after him now. It's taking an unnecessary risk."

"If his alarm goes off, radio me," Pugh said, shut the headpiece of his suit, and ran to the lock. As he went out Libra picked up her ragged skirts and danced a belly-dance from under his feet clear to the red horizon.

Inside the dome, Kaph saw the sled go up, tremble like a meteor in the dull red daylight, and vanish to the northeast. The hide of the dome quivered; the earth coughed. A vent south of the dome belched up a slow-flowing bile of black gas.

A bell shrilled and a red light flashed on the central control board. The sign under the light read Suit Two and scribbled under that, A.G.M. Kaph did not turn the signal off. He tried to radio Martin, then Pugh, but got no reply from either.

When the aftershocks decreased he went back to work, and finished up Pugh's job. It took him about two hours. Every half hour he tried to contact Suit One, and got no reply, then Suit Two and got no reply. The red light had stopped flashing after an hour.

It was dinnertime. Kaph cooked dinner for one, and ate it. He lay down on his cot.

The aftershocks had ceased except for faint rolling tremors at long intervals. The sun hung in the west, oblate, pale-red, immense. It did not sink visibly. There was no sound at all.

Kaph got up and began to walk about the messy, half-packed-up, overcrowded, empty dome. The silence continued. He went to the player and put on the first tape that came to hand. It was pure music, electronic, without harmonies, without voices. It ended. The silence continued.

Pugh's uniform tunic, one button missing, hung over a stack of rock-samples. Kaph stared at it a while.

The silence continued.

The child's dream: There is no one else alive in the world but me. In all the world.

Low, north of the dome, a meteor flickered.

Kaph's mouth opened as if he were trying to say something, but no sound came. He went hastily to the north wall and peered out into the gelatinous red light.

The little star came in and sank. Two figures blurred the airlock. Kaph stood close beside the lock as they came in. Martin's imsuit was covered with some kind of dust so that he looked raddled and warty like the surface of Libra. Pugh had him by the arm.

"Is he hurt?"

Pugh shucked his suit, helped Martin peel off his. "Shaken up," he said, curt.

"A piece of cliff fell onto the jet," Martin said, sitting down at the table and waving his arms. "Not while I was in it, though. I was parked, see, and poking about that carbon-dust area when I felt things humping. So I went out onto a nice bit of early igneous I'd noticed from above, good footing and out from under the cliffs. Then I saw this bit of the planet fall off onto the flyer, quite a sight it was, and after a while it occurred to me the spare aircans were in the flyer, so I leaned on the panic button. But I didn't get any radio reception, that's always happening here during quakes, so I didn't know if the signal was getting through either. And things went on jumping around and pieces of the cliff coming off. Little rocks flying around, and so dusty you couldn't see a meter ahead. I was really beginning to wonder what I'd do for breathing in the small hours, you know, when I saw old Owen buzzing up the Trench in all that dust and junk like a big ugly bat—''

''Want to eat?'' said Pugh.

''Of course I want to eat. How'd you come through the quake here, Kaph? No damage? It wasn't a big one actually, was it, what's the seismo say? My trouble was I was in the middle of it. Old Epicenter Alvaro. Felt like Richter Fifteen there—total destruction of planet—''

''Sit down,'' Pugh said. ''Eat.''

After Martin had eaten a little his spate of talk ran dry. He very soon went off to his cot, still in the remote angle where he had removed it when Pugh complained of his snoring. ''Good night, you one-lunged Welshman,'' he said across the dome.

''Good night.''

There was no more out of Martin. Pugh opaqued the dome, turned the lamp down to a yellow glow less than a candle's light, and sat doing nothing, saying nothing, withdrawn.

The silence continued.

''I finished the computations.''

Pugh nodded thanks.

''The signal from Martin came through, but I couldn't contact you or him.''

Pugh said with effort, ''I should not have gone. He had two hours of air left even with only one can. He might have been heading home when I left. This way we were all out of touch with one another. I was scared.''

The silence came back, punctuated now by Martin's long, soft snores.

''Do you love Martin?''

Pugh looked up with angry eyes: ''Martin is my friend. We've worked together, he's a good man.'' He stopped. After a while he said, ''Yes, I love him. Why did you ask that?''

Kaph said nothing, but he looked at the other man. His face was changed, as if he were glimpsing something he had not seen before; his voice too was changed. ''How can you . . . ? How do you . . . ?''

But Pugh could not tell him. ''I don't know,'' he said, ''it's practice, partly. I don't know. We're each of us alone, to be sure. What can you do but hold your hand out in the dark?''

Kaph's strange gaze dropped, burned out by its own intensity.

''I'm tired,'' Pugh said. ''That was ugly, looking for him in all that black dust and muck, and mouths opening and shutting in the ground. . . . I'm going to bed. The ship will be transmitting to us by six or so.'' He stood up and stretched.

"It's a clone," Kaph said. "The other Exploit team they're bringing with them."

"Is it, then?"

"A twelve-clone. They came out with us on the *Passerine.*"

Kaph sat in the small yellow aura of the lamp seeming to look past it at what he feared: the new clone, the multiple self of which he was not part. A lost piece of a broken set, a fragment, inexpert at solitude, not knowing even how you go about giving love to another individual, now he must face the absolute, closed self-sufficiency of the clone of twelve; that was a lot to ask of the poor fellow, to be sure. Pugh put a hand on his shoulder in passing. "The chief won't ask you to stay here with a clone. You can go home. Or since you're Far Out maybe you'll come on farther out with us. We could use you. No hurry deciding. You'll make out all right."

Pugh's quiet voice trailed off. He stood unbuttoning his coat, stooped a little with fatigue. Kaph looked at him and saw the thing he had never seen before: saw him: Owen Pugh, the other, the stranger who held his hand out in the dark.

"Good night," Pugh mumbled, crawling into his sleeping-bag and half asleep already, so that he did not hear Kaph reply after a pause, repeating, across darkness, benediction.

Masks

Damon Knight

The eight pens danced against the moving strip of paper, like the nervous claws of some mechanical lobster. Roberts, the technician, frowned over the tracings while the other two watched.

"Here's the wake-up impulse," he said, pointing with a skinny finger. "Then here, look, seventeen seconds more, still dreaming."

"Delayed response," said Babcock, the project director. His heavy face was flushed and he was sweating. "Nothing to worry about."

"Okay, delayed response, but look at the difference in the tracings. Still dreaming, after the wake-up impulse, but the peaks are closer together. Not the same dream. More anxiety, more motor pulses."

"Why does he have to sleep at all?" asked Sinescu, the man from Washington. He was dark, narrow-faced. "You flush the fatigue poisons out, don't you? So what is it, something psychological?"

"He needs to dream," said Babcock. "It's true he has no physiological need for sleep, but he's got to dream. If he didn't, he'd start to hallucinate, maybe go psychotic."

"Psychotic," said Sinescu. "Well—that's the question, isn't it? How long has he been doing this?"

"About six months."

"In other words, about the time he got his new body—and started wearing a mask?"

"About that. Look, let me tell you something, he's rational. Every test—"

"Yes, okay, I know about tests. Well—so he's awake now?"

The technician glanced at the monitor board. "He's up. Sam and Irma are with him." He hunched his shoulders, staring at the EEG tracings again. "I don't know why it should bother me. It stands to reason, if he has dream needs of his own that we're not satisfying with the programmed stuff, this is where he gets them in." His face hardened. "I don't know. Something about those peaks I don't like."

Sinescu raised his eyebrows. "You program his dreams?"

"Not program," said Babcock impatiently. "A routine suggestion to dream the sort of thing we tell him to. Somatic stuff, sex, exercise, sport."

"And whose idea was that?"

"Psych section. He was doing fine neurologically, every other way, but he was withdrawing. Psych decided he needed that somatic input in some form, we had to keep him in touch. He's alive, he's functioning, everything works. But don't forget, he spent forty-three years in a normal human body."

In the hush of the elevator, Sinescu said, ". . . Washington."

Swaying, Babcock said, "I'm sorry, what?"

"You look a little rocky. Getting any sleep?"

"Not lately. What did you say before?"

"I said they're not happy with your reports in Washington."

"Goddamn it, I know that." The elevator door silently opened. A tiny foyer, green carpet, gray walls. There were three doors, one metal, two heavy glass. Cool, stale air. "This way."

Sinescu paused at the glass door, glanced through: a gray-carpeted living room, empty. "I don't see him."

"Around the ell. Getting his morning checkup."

The door opened against slight pressure; a battery of ceiling lights went on as they entered. "Don't look up," said Babcock. "Ultraviolet." A faint hissing sound stopped when the door closed.

"And positive pressure in here? To keep out germs? Whose idea was that?"

"His." Babcock opened a chrome box on the wall and took out two surgical masks. "Here, put this on."

Voices came muffled from around the bend of the room. Sinescu looked with distaste at the white mask, then slowly put it over his head.

They stared at each other. "Germs," said Sinescu through the mask. "Is that rational?"

"All right, he can't catch a cold or what have you, but think about it a minute. There are just two things now that could kill him. One is a prosthetic failure, and we guard against that; we've got five hundred people here, we check him out like an airplane. That leaves a cerebro-spinal infection. Don't go in there with a closed mind."

The room was large, part living room, part library, part workshop. Here was a cluster of Swedish-modern chairs, a sofa, coffee table; here a workbench with a metal lathe, electric crucible, drill press, parts bins, tools on wallboards; here a drafting table; here a free-standing wall of bookshelves that Sinescu fingered curiously as they passed. Bound volumes of project reports, technical journals, reference books; no fiction except for *Fire* and *Storm* by George Stewart and *The Wizard of Oz* in a worn blue binding. Behind the bookshelves, set into a little alcove, was a glass door through which they glimpsed another living room, differently furnished: upholstered chairs, a tall philodendron in a ceramic pot. "There's Sam," Babcock said.

A man had appeared in the other room. He saw them, turned to call to someone they could not see, then came forward, smiling. He was bald and stocky, deeply tanned. Behind him, a small, pretty woman hurried up. She crowded through after her husband, leaving the door open. Neither of them wore a mask.

"Sam and Irma have the next suite," Babcock said. "Company for him; he's got to have somebody around. Sam is an old air-force buddy of his, and besides, he's got a tin arm."

The stocky man shook hands, grinning. His grip was firm and warm. "Want to guess which one?" He wore a flowered sport shirt. Both arms were brown, muscular and hairy, but when Sinescu looked more closely, he saw that the right one was a slightly different color, not quite authentic.

Embarrassed, he said, "The left, I guess."

"Nope." Grinning wider, the stocky man pulled back his right sleeve to show the straps.

"One of the spin-offs from the project," said Babcock. "Myoelectric, servo-controlled, weighs the same as the other one. Sam, they about through in there?"

"Maybe so. Let's take a peek. Honey, you think you could rustle up some coffee for the gentlemen?"

"Oh, why, sure." The little woman turned and darted back through the open doorway.

The far wall was glass, covered by a translucent white curtain. They turned the corner. The next bay was full of medical and electronic equipment, some built into the walls, some in tall black cabinets on wheels. Four men in white coats were gathered around what looked like an astronaut's couch. Sinescu could see someone lying on it: feet in Mexican woven-leather shoes, dark socks, gray slacks. A mutter of voices.

"Not through yet," Babcock said. "Must have found something else they didn't like. Let's go out onto the patio a minute."

"Thought they checked him at night—when they exchange his blood, and so on... ?"

"They do," Babcock said. "And in the morning, too." He turned and pushed open the heavy glass door. Outside, the roof was paved with cut stone, enclosed by a green plastic canopy and tinted-glass walls. Here and there were concrete basins, empty. "Idea was to have a roof garden out here, something green, but he didn't want it. We had to take all the plants out, glass the whole thing in."

Sam pulled out metal chairs around a white table and they all sat down. "How is he, Sam?" asked Babcock.

He grinned and ducked his head. "Mean in the mornings."

"Talk to you much? Play any chess?"

"Not too much. Works, mostly. Reads some, watches the box a little." His smile was forced; his heavy fingers were clasped together and Sinescu saw now that the fingertips of one hand had turned darker, the others not. He looked away.

"You're from Washington, that right?" Sam asked politely. "First time here? Hold on." He was out of his chair. Vague upright shapes were passing behind the curtained glass door. "Looks like they're through. If you gentlemen would just wait here a minute, till I see." He strode across the roof. The two men sat in silence. Babcock had pulled down his surgical mask; Sinescu noticed and did the same.

"Sam's wife is a problem," Babcock said, leaning nearer. "It seemed like a good idea at the time, but she's lonely here, doesn't like it—no kids—"

The door opened again and Sam appeared. He had a mask on, but it was hanging under his chin. "If you gentlemen would come in now."

In the living area, the little woman, also with a mask hanging around her neck, was pouring coffee from a flowered ceramic jug. She was smiling brightly but looked unhappy. Opposite her sat someone tall, in gray shirt and slacks, leaning back, legs out, arms on the arms of his chair, motionless. Something was wrong with his face.

"Well, now," said Sam heartily. His wife looked up at him with an agonized smile.

The tall figure turned its head and Sinescu saw with an icy shock that its face was silver, a mask of metal with oblong slits for eyes, no nose or mouth, only curves that were faired into each other. ". . . project." said an inhuman voice.

Sinescu found himself half bent over a chair. He sat down. They were all looking at him. The voice resumed, "I said, are you here to pull the plug on the project." It was unaccented, indifferent.

"Have some coffee." The woman pushed a cup toward him.

Sinescu reached for it, but his hand was trembling and he drew it back. "Just a fact-finding expedition," he said.

"Bull. Who sent you—Senator Hinkel."

"That's right."

"Bull. He's been here himself; why send you? If you are going to pull the plug, might as well tell me." The face behind the mask did not move when he spoke; the voice did not seem to come from it.

"He's just looking around, Jim," said Babcock.

"Two hundred million a year," said the voice, "to keep one man alive. Doesn't make much sense, does it. Go on, drink your coffee."

Sinescu realized that Sam and his wife had already finished theirs and that they had pulled up their masks. He reached for his cup hastily.

"Hundred percent disability in my grade is thirty thousand a year. I could get along on that easy. For almost an hour and a half."

"There's no intention of terminating the project," Sinescu said.

"Phasing it out, though. Would you say phasing it out."

"Manners, Jim," said Babcock.

"Okay. My worst fault. What do you want to know."

Sinescu sipped his coffee. His hands were still trembling. "That mask you're wearing," he started.

"Not for discussion. No comment, no comment. Sorry about that,

don't mean to be rude; a personal matter. Ask me something—''
Without warning, he stood up, blaring, ''Get that damn thing out of
here!'' Sam's wife's cup smashed, coffee brown across the table. A
fawn-colored puppy was sitting in the middle of the carpet, cocking its
head, bright-eyed, tongue out.

The table tipped, Sam's wife struggled up behind it. Her face was
pink, dripping with tears. She scooped up the puppy without pausing
and ran out. ''I better go with her,'' Sam said, getting up.

''Go on; and, Sam, take a holiday. Drive her into Winnemucca, see
a movie.''

''Yeah, guess I will.'' He disappeared behind the bookshelf wall.

The tall figure sat down again, moving like a man; it leaned back in
the same posture, arms on the arms of the chair. It was still. The hands
gripping the wood were shapely and perfect but unreal: there was
something wrong about the fingernails. The brown, well-combed hair
above the mask was a wig; the ears were wax. Sinescu nervously
fumbled his surgical mask up over his mouth and nose. ''Might as well
get along,'' he said, and stood up.

''That's right, I want to take you over to Engineering and R and D,''
said Babcock. ''Jim, I'll be back in a little while. Want to talk to you.''

''Sure,'' said the motionless figure.

Babcock had had a shower, but sweat was soaking through the
armpits of his shirt again. The silent elevator, the green carpet, a little
blurred. The air cool, stale. Seven years, blood and money, five
hundred good men. Psych section, Cosmetic, Engineering, R and D,
Medical, Immunology, Supply, Serology, Administration. The glass
doors. Sam's apartment empty, gone to Winnemucca with Irma.
Psych. Good men, but were they the best? Three of the best had turned
it down. Buried in the files. *Not like an ordinary amputation, this man
has had everything cut off.*

The tall figure had not moved. Babcock sat down. The silver mask
looked back at him.

''Jim, let's level with each other.''

''Bad, huh.''

''Sure it's bad. I left him in his room with a bottle. I'll see him again
before he leaves, but God knows what he'll say in Washington. Listen,
do me a favor, take that thing off.''

''Sure.'' The hand rose, plucked at the edge of the silver mask,
lifted it away. Under it, the tan-pink face, sculptured nose and lips,
eyebrows, eyelashes, not handsome but good-looking, normal-

looking. Only the eyes wrong; pupils too big. And the lips that did not open or move when it spoke. "I can take anything off. What does that prove."

"Jim. Cosmetic spent eight and a half months on that model and the first thing you do is slap a mask over it. We've asked you what's wrong, offered to make any changes you want."

"No comment."

"You talked about phasing out the project. Did you think you were kidding?"

A pause. "Not kidding."

"All right, then open up, Jim, tell me; I have to know. They won't shut the project down; they'll keep you alive but that's all. There are seven hundred on the volunteer list, including two U.S. senators. Suppose one of them gets pulled out of an auto wreck tomorrow. We can't wait till then to decide; we've got to know now. Whether to let the next one die or put him into a TP body like yours. So talk to me."

"Suppose I tell you something but it isn't the truth."

"Why would you lie?"

"Why do you lie to a cancer patient."

"I don't get it. Come on, Jim."

"Okay, try this. Do I look like a man to you."

"Sure."

"Bull. Look at this face." Calm and perfect. Beyond the fake irises, a wink of metal. "Suppose we had all the other problems solved and I could go into Winnemucca tomorrow; can you see me walking down the street, going into a bar, taking a taxi."

"Is that all it is?" Babcock drew a deep breath. "Jim, sure there's a difference, but for Christ's sake, it's like any other prosthesis—people get used to it. Like that arm of Sam's. You see it, but after a while you forget it, you don't notice."

"Bull. You pretend not to notice. Because it would embarrass the cripple."

Babcock looked down at his clasped hands. "Sorry for yourself?"

"Don't give me that," the voice blared. The tall figure was standing. The hands slowly came up, the fists clenched. "I'm in this thing, I've been in it for two years. I'm in it when I go to sleep, and when I wake up, I'm still in it."

Babcock looked up at him. "What do you want, facial mobility? Give us twenty years, maybe ten, we'll lick it."

"No. No."

"Then what?"

"I want you to close down Cosmetic."

"But that's—"

"Just listen. The first model looked like a tailor's dummy, so you spent eight months and came up with this one, and it looks like a corpse. The whole idea was to make me look like a man, the first model pretty good, the second model better, until you've got something that can smoke cigars and joke with women and go bowling and nobody will know the difference. You can't do it, and if you could, what for?"

"I don't— Let me think about this. What do you mean, a metal—"

"Metal, sure, but what difference does that make. I'm talking about shape. Function. Wait a minute." The tall figure strode across the room, unlocked a cabinet, came back with rolled sheets of paper. "Look at this."

The drawing showed an oblong metal box on four jointed legs. From one end protruded a tiny mushroom-shaped head on a jointed stem and a cluster of arms ending in probes, drills, grapples. "For moon prospecting."

"Too many limbs," said Babcock after a moment. "How would you—"

"With the facial nerves. Plenty of them left over. Or here." Another drawing. "A module plugged into the control system of a spaceship. That's where I belong, in space. Sterile environment, low grav, I can go where a man can't go and do what a man can't do. I can be an asset, not a goddamn billion-dollar liability."

Babcock rubbed his eyes. "Why didn't you say anything before?"

"You were all hipped on prosthetics. You would have told me to tend my knitting."

Babcock's hands were shaking as he rolled up the drawings. "Well, by God, this just may do it. It just might." He stood up and turned toward the door. "Keep your—" He cleared his throat. "I mean, hang tight, Jim."

"I'll do that."

When he was alone, he put on his mask again and stood motionless a moment, eye shutters closed. Inside, he was running clean and cool; he could feel the faint reassuring hum of pumps, click of valves and relays. They had given him that: cleaned out all the offal, replaced it with machinery that did not bleed, ooze or suppurate. He thought of the lie he had told Babcock. *Why do you lie to a cancer patient?* But they would never get it, never understand.

He sat down at the drafting table, clipped a sheet of paper to it and with a pencil began to sketch a rendering of the moon-prospector design. When he had blocked in the prospector itself, he began to draw the background of craters. His pencil moved more slowly and stopped; he put it down with a click.

No more adrenal glands to pump adrenaline into his blood, so he could not feel fright or rage. They had released him from all that— love, hate, the whole sloppy mess—but they had forgotten there was still one emotion he could feel.

Sinescu, with the black bristles of his beard sprouting through his oily skin. A whitehead ripe in the crease beside his nostril.

Moon landscape, clean and cold. He picked up the pencil again.

Babcock, with his broad pink nose shining with grease, crusts of white matter in the corners of his eyes. Food mortar between his teeth.

Sam's wife, with raspberry-colored paste on her mouth. Face smeared with tears, a bright bubble in one nostril. And the damn dog, shiny nose, wet eyes . . .

He turned. The dog was there, sitting on the carpet, wet red tongue out—*left the door open again*—dripping, wagged its tail twice, then started to get up. He reached for the metal T square, leaned back, swinging it like an ax, and the dog yelped once as metal sheared bone, one eye spouting red, writhing on its back, dark stain of piss across the carpet, and he hit it again, hit it again.

The body lay twisted on the carpet, fouled with blood, ragged black lips drawn back from teeth. He wiped off the T square with a paper towel, then scrubbed it in the sink with soap and steel wool, dried it and hung it up. He got a sheet of drafting paper, laid it on the floor, rolled the body over onto it without spilling any blood on the carpet. He lifted the body in the paper, carried it out onto the patio, then onto the unroofed section, opening the doors with his shoulder. He looked over the wall. Two stories down, concrete roof, vents sticking out of it, nobody watching. He held the dog out, let it slide off the paper, twisting as it fell. It struck one of the vents, bounced, a red smear. He carried the paper back inside, poured the blood down the drain, then put the paper into the incinerator chute.

Splashes of blood were on the carpet, the feet of the drafting table, the cabinet, his trouser legs. He sponged them all up with paper towels and warm water. He took off his clothing, examined it minutely, scrubbed it in the sink, then put it in the washer. He washed the sink, rubbed himself down with disinfectant and dressed again. He walked through into Sam's silent apartment, closing the glass door behind him. Past the potted philodendron, overstuffed furniture, red-and-yellow painting on the wall, out onto the roof, leaving the door ajar. Then back through the patio, closing the doors.

Too bad. How about some goldfish.

He sat down at the drafting table. He was running clean and cool. The dream this morning came back to his mind, the last one, as he was struggling up out of sleep: *slithery kidneys burst gray lungs blood and hair ropes of guts covered with yellow fat oozing and sliding and oh god the stink like the breath of an outhouse no sound nowhere he was putting a yellow stream down the slide of the dunghole and*

He began to ink in the drawing, first with a fine steel pen, then with a nylon brush. *his heel slid and he was falling could not stop himself falling into slimy bulging softness higher than his chin, higher and he could not move paralyzed and he tried to scream tried to scream tried to scream*

The prospector was climbing a crater slope with its handling members retracted and its head tilted up. Behind it the distant ringwall and the horizon, the black sky, the pinpoint stars. And he was there, and it was not far enough, not yet, for the earth hung overhead like a rotten fruit, blue with mold, crawling, wrinkling, purulent and alive.

Afterword

Theme, if such a thing exists, is the spirit of a story, its ghost, which can be separated from the story only at the cost of the patient's life. What I think is much more interesting and useful is the idea of a story as *mechanism*. What is the story supposed to accomplish? What means are used? Do they work? Etc.

"Masks" was the result of a deliberate effort to make a story about what I call a TP or "total prosthesis"—a complete artificial body. I wanted to do this because it was topical, in the sense that there had been a lot of discussion of this kind of thing and a good deal of R and D on sophisticated artificial limbs. The subject was one which had a deep attraction for me; I had written about it in two early stories called "Ask Me Anything" and "Four in One," and again in a collaboration with James Blish, "Tiger Ride." And, finally, I wanted to do it because it seemed to me that most treatments of the subject in science fiction had been romantic failures, and that to do it realistically would be an achievement.

I read and thought about prosthetic problems until I was sure I knew how my protagonist's artificial body would be built and maintained. I realized that it would take a government-funded effort comparable to the Manhattan Project, so I couldn't put it in the corner of a lab somewhere: the background of the story grew out of this. The other characters were those who had to be there.

Glimpses of scenes and action came to me spontaneously: the first of these was the one which gave the story its title—the silvery mask worn by the protagonist. As I got deeper into the story, I became more and more convinced that the psychic effect of losing the whole body and having it replaced by a prosthetic system had been too casually shrugged off by previous writers, even C. L. Moore in her beautiful "No Woman Born."

The protagonist of my story is the ultimate eunuch: as another character remarks, "This man has had everything cut off." Such a catastrophic loss can be compensated for only by a massive mental tilt. The man in the story has lost the physiological basis of every human emotion, with one exception. He has no heart to accelerate its beat, no gonads, no sweat glands, no endocrines except the pineal: he can't feel love, fear, hate, affection. But he can and must accept his own clean smooth functioning as the norm. When he looks at the sweaty, oozing meat that other people are made of, his own possible emotion is disgust, brought to an intensity we cannot imagine.

Given this, and the fact that the man is intelligent, I saw that the conflict of the story must turn on his effort to conceal the truth about himself, because if it became known the project would be terminated and his life shortened. My problem in writing the story was to hold this back as a revelation, and at the same time to build the story logically, without leaving out anything essential.

The story is a mechanism designed to draw the reader in, provoke his curiosity and interest, involve him in the argument, and give him a series of emotional experiences culminating (I hope) in a double view of the protagonist, from inside and outside, which will squeeze out of him a drop of sympathy and horror.

Sea Change

Thomas N. Scortia

Gleaming ... like a needle of fire ...

Whose voice? He didn't know.

The interstellar ... two of them ...

They were talking all at once then, their voices blending chaotically.

They're moving one out beyond Pluto for the test, someone said.

Beautiful ... We're waiting ... waiting.

That was her voice. He felt coldness within his chest.

That was the terrible part of his isolation, he thought. He could still hear everything. Not just in the Superintendent's office in Marsopolis where he sat.

Everywhere.

All the whispers of sound, spanning the system on pulses of c-cube radio. All the half-words, half-thoughts from the inner planets to the space stations far beyond Pluto.

And the loneliness was a sudden agonizing thing. The loneliness and the loss of two worlds.

Not that he couldn't shut out the voices if he wished, the distant voices that webbed space with the cubed speed of light. But ... might as well shut out all thought of living and seek the mindless foetal state of merely being.

There was the voice droning cargo numbers. He made the small mental change and the tight mass of transistors, buried deep in his metal and plastic body, brought the voice in clear and sharp. It was a Triplanet ship in the twilight belt of Mercury.

He had a fleeting image of flame-shriveled plains under a blinding monster sun.

Then there was the voice, saying, *Okay ... bearing three-ought-six and count down ten to free fall ...*

That one was beyond Saturn ... Remembered vision of bright ribbons of light, lacing a startling blue sky.

He thought, *I'll never see that again.*

And: *Space Beacon Three to MRX two two ... Space Beacon Three ... Bishop to queen's rook four ...*

And there was the soft voice, the different voice: *Matt ... Matt ... Where are you? ... Matt, come in ... Oh, Matt ...*

But he ignored that one.

Instead he looked at the receptionist and watched her fingers dance intricate patterns over the keyboard of her electric typewriter.

Matt . . . Matt . . .

No, no more, he thought. There was nothing there for him but bitterness. The isolation of being apart from humanity. The loneliness. Love? Affection? The words had no meaning in that existence.

It had become a ritual with him, he realized, this trip the first Tuesday of every month down through the silent Martian town to the Triplanet Port. A formalized tribute to something that was quite dead. An empty ritual, a weak ineffectual gesture.

He had known that morning that there would be nothing.

"No, nothing," the girl in the Super's office had said. "Nothing at all."

Nothing for him in his gray robot world of no-touch, no-taste.

She looked at him the way they all did, the ones who saw past the clever human disguise of plastic face and muted eyes.

He waited . . . listening.

When the Super came in, he smiled and said, "Hello, Matt," and then, with a gesture of his head, "Come on in."

The girl frowned silent disapproval.

After they found seats, the Super said, "Why don't you go home?"

"Home?"

"Back to Earth."

"Is that home?"

The voices whispered in his ear while the Super frowned and puffed a black cigar alight.

And: . . . *Matt . . . Matt . . . Knight four to . . . three down . . . two down . . . Out past Deimos, the sun blazing on its sides . . . Matt . . .*

"What are you trying to do?" the Super demanded. "Cut yourself off from the world completely?"

"That's been done already," he said. "Very effectively."

"Look, let's be brutal about it. We don't owe you anything."

"No," he said.

"It was a business arrangement purely," the Super said. "And if this hadn't been done," he gestured at the body Freck wore, "Matthew Freck would have been little more than a page in some dusty official records."

"Or worse," he added.

"I suppose so," Freck said.

"You could go back tomorrow. To Earth. To a new life. No one has to know who you are or what you are unless you tell them."

Freck looked down at his hands, the carefully veined, very human hands and the hard muscled thighs where the cellotherm trousers hugged his legs.

"The technicians did a fine job," he said. "Actually, it's better than my old body. Younger and stronger. And it'll last longer. But . . ."

He flexed his hands sensuously, watching the way the smooth bands of contractile plastic articulated his fingers.

"But the masquerade won't work. We were made for one thing."

"I can't change Company policy," the Super said. "Oh, I know the experiment didn't work. Actually technology is moving too fast. It was a bad compromise anyway. We needed something a little faster, more than human to pilot the new ships. Human reactions, the speed of a nerve impulse wasn't sufficient, electronic equipment was too bulky, and the organic memory units we built for our first cybernetic pilots didn't have enough initiative. That's why we jumped at the chance to use you people when Marshal Jenks first came to us. But we weren't willing to face facts. We tried to compromise . . . keep the human form."

"Well, we gave you what you needed then. You do owe us something in return," he said.

"We lived up to our contract," the Super said. "With you and a hundred like you whom we could save. All in exchange for the ability only you had. It was a fair trade."

"All right, give me a ship then. That's all I want."

"I told you before. Direct hook-up."

"No. If you knew what you were asking . . ."

"Look, one of the interstellars is being tested right this minute. And there are the stations beyond Pluto."

"The stations? That's like the Director all over again. Completely immobile. What kind of a life would that be, existing as a self-contained unit for years on end without the least contact with humanity?"

"The stations are not useless," the Super said. He leaned forward and slapped his palm on the surface of his desk.

"You of all people should know the Bechtoldt Drive can't be installed within the system's heavy gravitational fields. That's why we need the stations. They're set up to install the drive after the ship leaves the system proper on its atomic motors."

"You still haven't answered my question."

"*Stargazer I* is outbound for one of the trans-Plutonian stations now. *Stargazer II* will follow in a few days."

"So?"

"You can have one of them if you want it. Oh, don't get the idea that this is a handout. We don't play that way. The last two ships blew up because the pilots weren't skilled enough to handle the hook-up. We need the best and that's you."

He paused for a long second.

"You may as well know," the Super said. "We've put all our eggs in those two baskets. We've been losing political strength in the past three years, and if either one fails, Triplanet and the other combines stand to lose their subsidies from the government. Then it'll be a century before anyone tries again, if they ever do. We're tired of being tied to a petty nine planets. We're doing the thing you worked for all your life. We're going to the stars now . . . and you can still be a part of that."

"That used to mean something to me," he said, "but after a time, you start losing your identification with humanity and its drives."

When he started to rise, the Super said, "You know you can't operate a modern ship or station, tied down to a humanoid body. It's too inefficient. You've got to become a part of the setup."

"I've told you before. I can't do that."

"What are you afraid of? The loneliness?"

"I've been lonely before," he said.

"What then?"

"What am I afraid of?" He smiled his mechanical smile. "Something you could never understand. I'm afraid of what's happened to me already."

The Super was silent.

"When you start losing the basic emotions, the basic ways of thinking that make you human, well . . . What am I afraid of?

"I'm afraid of becoming more of a machine," he said.

And before the Super could say more, he left.

Outside he zipped up the cellotherm jacket and adjusted his respirator. Then he advanced the setting of the rheostat on the chest of his jacket until the small jewel light above the mechanism glowed in the morning's half-dusk. He had no need for the heat that the clothing furnished, of course, but the masquerade, the pretending to be wholly human would have been incomplete without this vital touch.

All the way back through the pearl-gray light, he listened to the many voices flashing back and forth across the ship lanes. He heard the snatches of commerce from a hundred separate ports and he followed in his mind's eye the swift progress of *Stargazer I* out past the orbit of

Uranus to her rendezvous with the station that would fit her with the Bechtoldt Drive.

And he thought, *Lord, if I could make the jump with her,* and then, *But not at that price, not for what it's cost the others, Jim and Martha and Art and . . . Beth. (Forget the name . . . forget the name . . . lost from you like all the others . . .)*

The city had turned to full life in the interval he had spent in the Super's office and he passed numerous hurrying figures, bearlike in cellotherm clothing and transparent respirators. They ignored him completely and for a moment he had an insane impulse to tear the respirator from his face and stand waiting . . .

Waiting savagely, defiantly for someone to notice him.

The tortured writhings of neon signs glowed along the wide streets and occasionally an electric run-about, balanced lightly on two wheels, passed him with a soft whirr, its headlights cutting a bright swath across his path. He had never become fully accustomed to the twilight of the Martian day. But that was the fault of the technicians who had built his body. In their pathetic desire to ape the human body, they had often built in human limitations as well as human strengths.

He stopped a moment before a shop, idly inspecting the window display of small things, fragile and alien, from the dead Martian towns to the north. The shop window, he realized, was as much out of place here as the street and the individual pressurized buildings that lined it. It would have been better, as someone had suggested, to house the entire city under one pressurized unit. But this was how the Martian settlements had started and men still held to habits more suited to another world.

Well, that was a common trait that he shared with his race. The Super was right, of course. He was as much of a compromise as the town was. The old habits of thought prevailed, molding the new forms.

He thought that he should get something to eat. He hadn't had breakfast before setting out for the port. They'd managed to give him a sense of hunger, though taste had been too elusive for them to capture.

But the thought of food was somehow unpleasant.

And then he thought perhaps he should get drunk.

But even that didn't seem too satisfying.

He walked on for a distance and found a bar that was open and he walked in. He shed his respirator in the airlock and, under the half-watchful eyes of a small fat man, fumbling with his wallet, he pretended to turn off the rheostat of his suit.

Then he went inside, nodded vaguely at the bored bartender and sat at a corner table. After the bartender had brought him a whiskey and water, he sat and listened.

Six and seven... and twenty-ought-three...

... read you...

... and out there you see nothing, absolutely nothing. It's like... Matt... Matt...

... to king's knight four... check in three...

Matt...

And for the first time in weeks, he made the change. He could talk without making an audible sound, which was fortunate. A matter of subverbalizing.

He said silently, *Come on in.*

Matt, where are you?

In a bar.

I'm far out... very far out. The sun's like a pinhole in a black sheet.

I think I'm going to get very drunk.

Why?

Because I want to. Isn't that reason enough? Because it's the one wholly, completely human thing that I can do well.

I've missed you.

Missed me? My voice perhaps. There's little else.

You should be out here with us... with me and Art..., she said breathlessly. *They're bringing the new ones out. The big ships. They're beautiful. Bigger and faster than anything you and I ever rode.*

They're bringing Stargazer I *out for her tests,* he told her.

I know. My station has one of the drives. Station three is handling Stargazer I *now.*

He swallowed savagely, thinking of what the Super had said.

Oh, I wish I were one of them, Beth said.

His hand tensed on the glass and for a moment he thought it would shatter in his fingers. She hadn't said ''on.''

Were... were... I wish I were one of them.

Do you, he said. *That's fine.*

Oh, that's fine, starry eyes, he thought, *I love you and the ship and the stars and the sense of being... I am the ship... I am the station... I am anything but human...*

What's wrong, Matt?

I'm going to get drunk.

There's a ship coming in. Signaling.

The bartender, he saw, was looking at him oddly. He realized that he had been nursing the same drink for fifteen minutes. He raised the glass and very deliberately drank and swallowed.

I've got to leave for a minute, she said.

Do that, he said.

Then: *I'm sorry, Beth. I didn't mean to take it out on you.*

I'll be back, she said.

And he was alone, wrapped in this isolation he had come to know so well. He wondered if such loneliness would eventually drive him to the change that . . . No, that would never be . . . The memory of what that had been like still haunted him.

He would rather have died in that distant cold Plutonian valley, he told himself, than to have ever come to this day. He thought of Jenks and Catherine and David and he envied them the final unthinking blackness that they shared. Even death was better than again facing that frightening loss of humanity he had once suffered.

He sat, looking out over the room, for the first time really noticing his surroundings. There were two tourists at the bar—a fat, weak-chinned man in a plaid, one-piece business suit and a woman, probably his wife, thin, thyroid-looking. They were talking animatedly, the man gesturing heatedly. He wondered what had brought them out so early in the morning.

It was funny, he thought, the image of the fat man, chattering like a nervous magpie, his pudgy hands making weaving motions in the air before him.

He saw that his glass was empty and he rose and went over to the bar. He found a stool and ordered another whiskey.

"I'll break him," the little man was saying in a high, thin voice. "Consolidation or no consolidation . . ."

"George," the woman said gratingly, "you shouldn't drink in the morning."

"You know very well that . . ."

"George, I want to go to the ruins today."

Matt . . . Matt . . .

"They've got the cutest pottery down in the shop on the corner. From the ruins. Those little dwarf figures . . . You know, the Martians."

Only she pronounced it "Mar-chans" with a pitting *ch* sound.

It's the big one, Matt. The Stargazer. *It's coming in. Maybe I'll see it warp. Beautiful . . . You should see the way the sides catch the light from the station's beacon. Like a big needle of pure silver.*

"Pardon me," the woman said, turning on the stool to him. "Do you know what time the tours to the ruins start?"

He tried to smile. He told her and she said, "Thank you."

"I suppose you people get tired of tourists," she said, large eyes questioning.

"Don't be silly," George said. "Got to be practical. Lots of money from tourists."

"That's true," he said.

Matt . . .

"Well," the woman said, "when you don't get away from Earth too often, you've got to crowd everything in."

Matt . . . Uneasy.

"That's true," he told the woman aloud and tried to sip his drink and say silently, *What's wrong?*

Matt, there's something wrong with the ship. The way Art described it that time . . . The field . . . flickering . . .

She started to fade.

Come back, he shouted silently.

Silence.

"I'm in the Manta business back home," George said.

"Manta?" He raised a mechanical eyebrow carefully.

"You know, the jet airfoil planes. That's our model name. Manta. 'Cause they look like a ray, the fish. The jets squirt a stream of air directly over the airfoil. They hover just like a 'copter. But speed? You've never seen that kind of speed from a 'copter."

"I've never seen one," he said.

Beth . . . Beth . . . , his silent voice shouted. For a moment he felt like shouting aloud, but an iron control stopped his voice.

"Oh, I tell you," George said, "we'll really be crowding the market in another five years. The air's getting too crowded for 'copters. They're not safe any longer. Why, the turbulence over Rochester is something . . ."

"We're from Rochester," the thyroid woman explained.

Matt, listen. It's the field generator, I think . . . The radiation must have jammed the pilot's synapses. I can't raise him. And there's no one else aboard. Only instruments.

How far from the station?

Half a mile.

My God, if the thing goes . . .

I go with it! He could feel the fear in her words.

"So we decided now was the time, before the new merger. George would never find the time after . . ."

Try to raise the pilot.

Matt . . . I'm afraid.

Try!

"Is something wrong?" The thyroid woman asked.

He shook his head.

"You need a drink," George said as he signaled the bartender.

Beth, what's the count?

Oh, Matt, I'm scared.

The count . . .

"Good whiskey," George said.

Getting higher . . . I can't raise the pilot.

"Lousiest whiskey on the ship coming in. Those things give me the creeps."

"George, shut up."

Beth, where are you?

What do you mean?

Where are you positioned? Central or to one side?

I'm five hundred yards off station center.

"I told you not to drink in the morning," the woman said.

Any secondary movers? Robot handlers?

Yes, I have to handle the drive units.

All right, tear your auxiliary power pile down.

But . . .

Take the bricks and stack them against the far wall of the station. You're shielded enough against their radiation. Then you'll have to rotate the bulk of the station between you and the ship.

But how . . . ?

Uranium's dense. It'll shield you from the radiation when the ship goes. And break orbit. Get as far away as possible.

I can't. The station's not powered.

If you don't . . .

I can't . . .

Then silence.

The woman and George looked at him expectantly. He raised his drink to his lips, marveling at the steadiness of his hands.

"I'm sorry," he said aloud. "I didn't catch what you said."

Beth, the drive units . . .

Yes?

Can you activate them?

They'll have to be jury-rigged in place. Quick welded.

How long?

Five, maybe ten minutes. But the field. It'll collapse the way the one on the ship's doing.

If you, of all people, can't handle it ... Anyway, you'll have to chance it. Otherwise ...

"I said," George said thickly, "have you ever ridden one of those robot ships?"

"Robot ships?"

"Oh, I know, they're not robots exactly."

"I've ridden one," he said. "After all, I wouldn't be on Mars if I hadn't."

George looked confused.

"George is a little dull sometimes," the woman said.

Beth ...

Almost finished. The count's mounting.

Hurry ...

If the field collapses ...

Don't think about it.

"They give me the creeps," George said. "Like riding a ship that's haunted."

"The pilot is very much alive," he said. "And very human."

Matt, the pile bricks are in place. A few more minutes ...

Hurry ... hurry ... hurry ...

"George talks too much," the woman said.

"Oh, hell," George said, "it's just that ... well, those things aren't actually human any more."

Matt, I'm ready ... Scared ...

Can you control your thrust?

With the remote control units. Just as if I were the Stargazer.

Her voice was chill ... frightened.

All right, then ...

Count's climbing fast ... I'll ... Matt! It's blinding ... a ball of fire ... it's ..

Beth ...

Silence.

"I don't give a damn," George told the woman petulantly. "A man's got a right to say what he feels."

Beth ...

"George, will you shut up and let's go."

Beth ...

He looked out at the bar and thought of flame blossoming in utter blackness and . . .

"They aren't men any more," he told George. "And perhaps not even quite human. But they're not machines."

Beth . . .

"George didn't mean . . ."

"I know," he said. "George is right in a way. But they've got something normal men will never have. They've found a part in the biggest dream that man has ever dared dream. And that takes courage . . . courage to be what they are. Not men and yet a part of the greatest thing that men have ever reached for."

Beth . . .

Silence.

George rose from his stool.

"Maybe," he said. "But . . . well . . ." He thrust out his hand. "We'll see you around," he said.

He winced when Freck's hand closed on his, and for a moment sudden awareness shone in his eyes. He mumbled something in a confused voice and headed for the door.

Matt . . .

Beth, are you all right?

The woman stayed behind for a moment.

Yes, I'm all right, but the ship . . . the Stargazer . . .

Forget it.

But will there be another? Will they dare try again?

You're safe. That's all that counts.

The woman was saying, "George hardly ever sees past his own nose." She smiled, her thin lips embarrassed. "Maybe, that's why he married me."

Matt . . .

Just hang on. They'll get to you.

No, I don't need help. The acceleration just knocked me out for a minute. But don't you see?

See?

I have the drive installed. I'm a self-contained system.

No, you can't do that. Get it out of your mind.

Someone has to prove it can be done. Otherwise they'll never build another.

It'll take you years. You can't make it back.

"I knew right away," the woman was saying. "About you, I mean."

"I didn't mean to embarrass you," he said.

Beth, come back... Beth.

Going out... faster each minute. Matt, I'll be there before anyone else. The first. But you'll have to come after me. I won't have enough power in the station to come back.

"You didn't embarrass me," the thyroid woman said.

Her eyes were large and filmed.

"It's something new," she said, "to meet someone with an object in living."

Beth, come back.

Far out now... accelerating all the while... Come for me, Matt. I'll wait for you out there... circling Centaurus.

He stared at the woman by the bar, his eyes scarcely seeing her.

"You know," the woman said, "I think I could be very much in love with you."

"No," he told her. "No, you wouldn't like that."

"Perhaps," she said, "but you were right. In what you told George, I mean. It does take a lot of courage to be what you are."

Then she turned and followed her husband through the door. Before the door closed, she looked back longingly.

Don't worry, Beth. I'll come. As fast as I can.

And then he sensed the sounds of the others, the worried sounds that filtered through the space blackness from the burned plains of Mercury to the nitrogen oceans of dark Pluto.

And he told them what she was doing.

For moments his inner hearing rustled with their wonder of it.

There was a oneness then. He knew what he must do, the next step he must take.

We're all with you, he told her, wondering if she could still hear his voice. *From now on, we always will be.*

And he reached out, feeling himself unite in a silent wish with all those other hundreds of minds, stretching in a brotherhood of metal across the endless spaces.

Stretching in a tight band of metal, a single organism reaching...

Reaching for the stars.

Day Million

Frederik Pohl

On this day I want to tell you about, which will be about a thousand years from now, there were a boy, a girl and a love story.

Now although I haven't said much so far, none of it is true. The boy was not what you and I would normally think of as a boy, because he was a hundred and eighty-seven years old. Nor was the girl a girl, for other reasons; and the love story did not entail that sublimation of the urge to rape and concurrent postponement of the instinct to submit which we at present understand in such matters. You won't care much for this story if you don't grasp these facts at once. If, however, you will make the effort, you'll likely enough find it jampacked, chockfull and tiptop-crammed with laughter, tears and poignant sentiment which may, or may not, be worth while. The reason the girl was not a girl was that she was a boy.

How angrily you recoil from the page! You say, who the hell wants to read about a pair of queers? Calm yourself. Here are no hot-breathing secrets of perversion for the coterie trade. In fact, if you were to see this girl, you would not guess that she was in any sense a boy. Breasts, two; vagina, one. Hips, Callipygean; face, hairless; supra-orbital lobes, non-existent. You would term her female at once, although it is true that you might wonder just what species she was a female of, being confused by the tail, the silky pelt or the gill slits behind each ear.

Now you recoil again. Cripes, man, take my word for it. This is a sweet kid, and if you, as a normal male, spent as much as an hour in a room with her, you would bend heaven and earth to get her in the sack. Dora (we will call her that; her ''name'' was omicron-Di-base seven-group-totter-oot S Doradus 5314, the last part of which is a color specification corresponding to a shade of green)—Dora, I say, was feminine, charming and cute. I admit she doesn't sound that way. She was, as you might put it, a dancer. Her art involved qualities of intellection and expertise of a very high order, requiring both tremendous natural capacities and endless practice; it was performed in null-gravity and I can best describe it by saying that it was something like the performance of a contortionist and something like classical ballet, maybe resembling Danilova's dying swan. It was also pretty damned sexy. In a symbolic way, to be sure; but face it, most of the things we call "sexy" are symbolic, you know, except perhaps an exhibitionist's open fly. On Day Million when Dora danced, the people who saw her panted; and you would too.

About this business of her being a boy. It didn't matter to her audiences that genetically she was male. It wouldn't matter to you, if you were among them, because you wouldn't know it—not unless you took a biopsy cutting of her flesh and put it under an electron-microscope to find the XY chromosome—and it didn't matter to them because they didn't care. Through techniques which are not only complex but haven't yet been discovered, these people were able to determine a great deal about the aptitudes and easements of babies quite a long time before they were born—at about the second horizon of cell-division, to be exact, when the segmenting egg is becoming a free blastocyst—and then they naturally helped those aptitudes along. Wouldn't we? If we find a child with an aptitude for music we give him a scholarship to Juilliard. If they found a child whose aptitudes were for being a woman, they made him one. As sex had long been dissociated from reproduction this was relatively easy to do and caused no trouble and no, or at least very little, comment.

How much is "very little"? Oh, about as much as would be caused by our own tampering with Divine Will by filling a tooth. Less than would be caused by wearing a hearing aid. Does it still sound awful? Then look closely at the next busty babe you meet and reflect that she may be a Dora, for adults who are genetically male but somatically female are far from unknown even in our own time. An accident of environment in the womb overwhelms the blueprints of heredity. The difference is that with us it happens only by accident and we don't know about it except rarely, after close study; whereas the people of Day Million did it often, on purpose, because they wanted to.

Well, that's enough to tell you about Dora. It would only confuse you to add that she was seven feet tall and smelled of peanut butter. Let us begin our story.

On Day Million Dora swam out of her house, entered a transportation tube, was sucked briskly to the surface in its flow of water and ejected in its plume of spray to an elastic platform in front of her— ah—call it her rehearsal hall. "Oh, shit!" she cried in pretty confusion, reaching out to catch her balance and find herself tumbled against a total stranger, whom we will call Don.

They met cute. Don was on his way to have his legs renewed. Love

was the farthest thing from his mind; but when, absent-mindedly taking a short cut across the landing platform for submarinites and finding
himself drenched, he discovered his arms full of the loveliest girl he
had ever seen, he knew at once they were meant for each other. "Will
you marry me?" he asked. She said softly, "Wednesday," and the
promise was like a caress.

Don was tall, muscular, bronze and exciting. His name was no more
Don than Dora's was Dora, but the personal part of it was Adonis in
tribute to his vibrant maleness, and so we will call him Don for short.
His personality color-code, in Ångstrom units, was 5290, or only a few
degrees bluer than Dora's 5314, a measure of what they had intuitively
discovered at first sight, that they possessed many affinities of taste
and interest.

I despair of telling you exactly what it was that Don did for a
living—I don't mean for the sake of making money, I mean for the
sake of giving purpose and meaning to his life, to keep him from going
off his nut with boredom—except to say that it involved a lot of
traveling. He traveled in interstellar spaceships. In order to make a
spaceship go really fast about thirty-one male and seven genetically
female human beings had to do certain things, and Don was one of the
thirty-one. Actually he contemplated options. This involved a lot of
exposure to radiation flux—not so much from his own station in the
propulsive system as in the spillover from the next stage, where a
genetic female preferred selections and the subnuclear particles making
the selections she preferred demolished themselves in a shower of
quanta. Well, you don't give a rat's ass for that, but it meant that Don
had to be clad at all times in a skin of light, resilient, extremely strong
copper-colored metal. I have already mentioned this, but you probably
thought I meant he was sunburned.

More than that, he was a cybernetic man. Most of his ruder parts had
been long since replaced with mechanisms of vastly more permanence
and use. A cadmium centrifuge, not a heart, pumped his blood. His
lungs moved only when he wanted to speak out loud, for a cascade of
osmotic filters rebreathed oxygen out of his own wastes. In a way, he
probably would have looked peculiar to a man from the 20th century,
with his glowing eyes and seven-fingered hands; but to himself, and of
course to Dora, he looked mighty manly and grand. In the course of his
voyages Don had circled Proxima Centauri, Procyon and the puzzling
worlds of Mira Ceti; he had carried agricultural templates to the planets
of Canopus and brought back warm, witty pets from the pale compan-

ion of Aldebaran. Blue-hot or red-cool, he had seen a thousand stars and their ten thousand planets. He had, in fact, been traveling the starlanes with only brief leaves on Earth for pushing two centuries. But you don't care about that, either. It is people that make stories, not the circumstances they find themselves in, and you want to hear about these two people. Well, they made it. The great thing they had for each other grew and flowered and burst into fruition on Wednesday, just as Dora had promised. They met at the encoding room, with a couple of well-wishing friends apiece to cheer them on, and while their identities were being taped and stored they smiled and whispered to each other and bore the jokes of their friends with blushing repartee. Then they exchanged their mathematical analogues and went away. Dora to her dwelling beneath the surface of the sea and Don to his ship.

It was an idyll, really. They lived happily ever after—or anyway, until they decided not to bother any more and died.

Of course, they never set eyes on each other again.

Oh, I can see you now, you eaters of charcoal-broiled steak, scratching an incipient bunion with one hand and holding this story with the other, while the stereo plays d'Indy or Monk. You don't believe a word of it, do you? Not for one minute. People wouldn't live like that, you say with an irritated and not amused grunt as you get up to put fresh ice in a stale drink.

And yet there's Dora, hurrying back through the flushing commuter pipes toward her underwater home (she prefers it there; has had herself somatically altered to breathe the stuff). If I tell you with what sweet fulfillment she fits the recorded analogue of Don into the symbol manipulator, hooks herself in and turns herself on . . . if I try to tell you any of that you will simply stare. Or glare; and grumble, what the hell kind of love-making is this? And yet I assure you, friend, I really do assure you that Dora's ecstasies are as creamy and passionate as any of James Bond's lady spies, and one hell of a lot more so than anything you are going to find in "real life." Go ahead, glare and grumble. Dora doesn't care. If she thinks of you at all, her thirty-times-great-great-grandfather, she thinks you're a pretty primordial sort of brute. You are. Why, Dora is farther removed from you than you are from the australopithecines of five thousand centuries ago. You could not swim a second in the strong currents of her life. You don't think progress goes in a straight line, do you? Do you recognize that it is an ascending, accelerating, maybe even exponential curve? It takes hell's own time to get started, but when it goes it goes like a bomb. And you, you

Scotch-drinking steak-eater in your Relaxacizer chair, you've just barely lighted the primacord of the fuse. What is it now, the six or seven hundred thousandth day after Christ? Dora lives in Day Million. A thousand years from now. Her body fats are polyunsaturated, like Crisco. Her wastes are hemodialyzed out of her bloodstream while she sleeps—that means she doesn't have to go to the bathroom. On whim, to pass a slow half-hour, she can command more energy than the entire nation of Portugal can spend today, and use it to launch a weekend satellite or remold a crater on the Moon. She loves Don very much. She keeps his every gesture, mannerism, nuance, touch of hand, thrill of intercourse, passion of kiss stored in symbolic-mathematical form. And when she wants him, all she has to do is turn the machine on and she has him.

And Don, of course, has Dora. Adrift on a sponson city a few hundred yards over her head or orbiting Arcturus, fifty light-years away, Don has only to command his own symbol-manipulator to rescue Dora from the ferrite files and bring her to life for him, and there she is; and rapturously, tirelessly they ball all night. Not in the flesh, of course; but then his flesh has been extensively altered and it wouldn't really be much fun. He doesn't need the flesh for pleasure. Genital organs feel nothing. Neither do hands, nor breasts, nor lips; they are only receptors, accepting and transmitting impulses. It is the brain that feels, it is the interpretation of those impulses that makes agony or orgasm; and Don's symbol-manipulator gives him the analogue of cuddling, the analogue of kissing, the analogue of wildest, most ardent hours with the eternal, exquisite and incorruptible analogue of Dora. Or Diane. Or sweet Rose, or laughing Alicia; for to be sure, they have each of them exchanged analogues before, and will again.

Balls, you say, it looks crazy to me. And you—with your after-shave lotion and your little red car, pushing papers across a desk all day and chasing tail all night—tell me, just how the hell do you think you would look to Tiglath-Pileser, say, or Attila the Hun?

8

The City

Theodore R. Cogswell
and Ralph S. Clem

Since about the mid-eighteenth century, mankind has been undergoing what is probably the most profound of all social, economic, and political changes which have occurred in the long span of human history: the process of *urbanization*. Urbanization is a phenomenon which is best defined as the relative shift of people from the countryside to cities, usually through the demographic mechanism of rural to urban migration. This dramatic transformation of society from overwhelmingly rural and agrarian to predominantly urban and industrial, the empirical details and conceptual explanation of which will be traced shortly, has naturally had a major impact upon man's view of himself and upon literature, the principal medium through which these views are expressed.

More than in any other genre, cities have played a critical role in science fiction, principally as the arena in which future societies or individuals act out scenarios representative of a number of themes prevalent in the literature. Beyond the obvious function that the city serves in science fiction as a stage for events is the use of the urban setting of the future as an extrapolation of contemporary (and critically important) social problems. Both of these aspects of the city theme are not unique to science fiction, of course, but their prevalence, it will be argued here, is primarily a reflection of the fact that Western society has become essentially a world of cities.

The magnitude of the growth of cities over the past two centuries escapes most of us, accustomed as we are to thinking of society as urbanized. Yet, as recently as 1800 there were in the world no cities of a million persons, and in that year it has been estimated that only three percent of the earth's inhabitants were city dwellers. By 1970, however, there were some 162 "millionaire" cities (and another 1,725 of over 100,000 in size), and almost one-quarter of the world's population lived in urban areas.* If current trends continue, according to Kingsley Davis, ". . . by the year 2000 there will be one city of over 100 million, two of more than 60 million, and five of more than 30 million!"† Furthermore, there are significant regional disparities in the extent to which societies have become urbanized; in Western Europe, Anglo-America, Japan, Australia, and New Zealand, fully three-quarters of all people reside in cities.††

An explanation of this tremendous growth of cities centers upon the economic, and to some degree the cultural and political, functions which urban areas have historically served. Until modern times, cities existed as service centers for the surrounding rural population, and as such they were in essence parasitic; that is, the city population depended directly upon the rural dwellers not only for food but also for their livelihood. With the advent of the Industrial Revolution, cities were provided with a new economic *raison d'être* which enabled the support of much larger groups of people, and it was primarily the attraction of jobs in the expanding manufacturing sector which gave the impetus to the movement of people into urban areas. Beyond the purely economic rationale for urban growth are other well-known considerations, such as the role of cities as centers of learning and the arts (the lure of the bright lights), as the place in which innovations are most likely to begin (trend-setters), and as the seat of governmental authority and political power (hence Moscow symbolizes the Soviet Union, Washington the United States, and so on).

However, the city as an *idea,* as well as a *place,* has come to mean many different things to many different kinds of people. One major difference is that between those who study cities and those who live, work, play, love, hate, and die in them. Persons who study cities usually develop theories about them. Persons for whom the city becomes a total way of life develop visions about them. This difference between theory and vision is what this chapter, which tries to relate science fiction to urban life, is all about.

*United Nations, *The Determinants and Consequences of Population Trends* (New York: United Nations, 1973), p. 192, table VI.11.

†Kingsley Davis, "Introduction," in *Cities: Their Origin, Growth, and Human Impact* (San Francisco: W. H. Freeman, 1973), p. 3.

††United Nations, *The Determinants and Consequences of Population Trends,* p. 185, table VI.2.

Over time, the city has been an object of study by many different kinds of scholars. The political scientist, the sociologist, the civil engineer, the economist, the geographer, the planner, the historian, the anthropologist—all study and theorize about cities. "Urban theory," then, is simply a potpourri of these different scholarly perspectives. But two major themes seem to be woven throughout these views. We shall call one the "ecological"; the other, the "organizational."

The ecological theme normally emphasizes a setting of people in a relatively small space and studies how the size and density of the city affect its social organization. Indeed, everything that one can think about—communication, education, transportation, social behavior, the status of a culture, political power and authority—is assumed to be an overall result of the size, scale, and magnitude of physical space and the number of people.

The organizational theme, on the other hand, first starts with looking at patterns of social behavior rather than size and density of population. From this point of view, the essence of the study of urban life is to be found in the particular arrangement of human behavior which exists in places called cities. Whereas the ecological theme stresses that changes in urban organization are functions of size, the organizational theme emphasizes that change is a function of differences in organization itself.

But our purpose here is not to assess the relative merits or deficiencies in these two major approaches to the study and theory development of cities but rather to point out a possible lack in both: the lack of an appreciation of and need for an understanding of the *vision* of those who dwell in cities.

Picture yourself as an anthropologist who has just been given a research grant to study the organizational structure and social behavior of a primitive tribe of people in a remote land. The grant allows you enough money to purchase a helicopter with which you hope to hover above the tribe and, from this vantage point, to study and observe the "subjects." You are intellectually armed with *both* ecological and organizational theories of human behavior. With these theories, you will be able to observe the size, density, and scale of the tribe as well as its social patterns of behavior. These observations can be made from your helicopter—and never will you have to come in direct contact with *people!*

Of course, what is missing from your study is an appreciation of the way the people you are observing assign *meaning* to their organizational structure and to their social behavior. What is missing from your study is an understanding of the *vision* through which your subjects are viewing the same things which you are studying.

So it is with modern approaches to the study of the city. What may be needed now is a better way of understanding the city from the vision of those who give it meaning and from the study of different types of vision.

Several different types of urban vision are suggested by the literature of science fiction. The ones mentioned here are not intended to exhaust the possibilities; but they do represent major categories, each implying a decidedly different role for the individual who lives in a city.

The first is the *apocalyptic vision*. This vision is one which captures the city as a place where disaster occurs. Whether the disaster is environmental or human, physical or social is not important. What is important is its emphasis on catastrophe. The role of the individual in this vision is one of anticipating disaster and trying to prepare to survive it. Related to this category is the *tragic vision* of the city. This vision portrays the city as necessary but flawed in some vital way. The city is, by definition, imperfect and will always remain so. The city places barriers to the full development of the human potential—the human being cannot rise above his own creation. The role of the individual here is one of coping—coping with urban problems reflecting the imperfection of the essence of city life. The city as a set of insurmountable problems is a familiar view for all of us.

The extrapolation of literary trends, again representing the views that man holds of the city and urban life, into the future through science fiction has resulted in the almost universal depiction of cities to come as dystopias. Obviously, the manner in which one views cities of the future is conditioned to a large extent by one's perception of present-day urban life. Thus, the city of tomorrow is most often the setting in which the undesirable aspects of contemporary society, presumably allowed to continue unchecked or not amenable to solution, are acted out. Through such scenarios, current social problems such as crime, racial and ethnic antagonisms, pollution, and the like are depicted in extreme form and, in many instances, requiring radical steps to alleviate.

As evidence of the largely dystopian view that science fiction authors hold of urban life, consider this passage from the introduction to one of the better-known anthologies of urban science fiction:

The city in its massiveness, its intricate problems, its concentration of power and resources is indeed overwhelming, and seldom in an awe-inspiring sense, either. It *overwhelms* the eyes and the nose with noise pollution, air pollution and God knows what else; it fosters deep-seated anxieties of every description; and it harbors such an assortment of crimes and acts of violence as to make the mind recoil in outrage and fear.*

Perhaps of even more interest for our purposes here is the recent novel *Dhalgren* by Samuel R. Delany, in which the classic literary theme of the young man entering the city, only to find trials and conditions which eventually force his retreat, is repeated. The Bellona of Delany's story, however, is not only a city of adventure-danger, evil, love, and other standard urban attributes, but also it is a city gone wild, an apocalyptic vision of the collapse of social organization as we know it.†

In many respects, the dystopian view of urban life which so dominates science fiction is, then, merely the projection of the standard approach to city literature into the future. What possible explanation can one offer for this? Most obvious is the fact that for some reason misery, cataclysm, and violence are more marketable than happiness, stability, and peace and cooperation. Because our perceptions of urban life encompass or represent the former rather than the latter, the cities of the future are perfect settings for wildly socially disjunctive events. Perhaps the underlying causal factor in operation here is the pastoral tradition, which despite the fact that today's urbanite on the average is better off than any of his predecessors, urban or rural (if one agrees with Edward Banfield and others),‡ leads such a prominent authority on the urban condition as Lewis Mumford to remark: "If the places where we live and work were really fit for permanent human habitation, why should we spend so much of our time getting away from them."§

The third category is that of the *classical vision*. This perspective sees the city essentially as a beehive, performing necessary but impersonal functions. Trading, transportation, communication, and commerce are examples of these functions. The individual in the city has a role in this vision similar to that of a worker bee, putting out energy and devoting his life to the maintenance and continuity of the city beehive. The city as a conversion process for goods and services is also a familiar picture for most of us.

The fourth major category is a vision which is familiar to most of us

*Roger Elwood, ed., *Future City* (New York: Pocket Books, 1974; originally published in 1973 by Trident Press), p. ix.

†Samuel R. Delany, *Dhalgren* (New York: Bantam Books, 1974).

‡Edward C. Banfield, *The Unheavenly City* (Boston: Little, Brown, 1968). Thus, Banfield states: "By any concernable measure of material welfare the present generation of urban Americans is, on the whole, better off than any other large group of people has ever been anywhere." (pp. 3–4)

§Lewis Mumford, *The Urban Prospect* (New York: Harcourt, Brace and World, 1968), p. 9.

but is, in fact, shared by relatively few people. This is the *romantic vision,* which captures the essence of the city as a place where the amenities of civilization are available to its inhabitants. The fine arts—music, art, sculpture—"high culture," and knowledge abound only in cities, according to this view, and the role of the individual is one of developing access to ever higher levels of cultural and aesthetic satisfaction.

The fifth category is the *utopian vision.* It involves thinking about the city as a distinctive and higher order of moral development and civilization. Indeed, it is through the city that human beings can transcend their own imperfections and shortcomings. This view suggests the city as fraternity with a focus for energy being contemplation about moral development and the individual as an intellectual. The images of St. Augustine's *The City of God* and Sir Thomas More's *Utopia* are associated with this vision.

Whether we like it or not, cities have become the principal abode for modern man. The question now before us concerns what shape and characteristics the future city will hold. In unique ways, the stories in this chapter touch on some of these major urban visions. Developing alternative urban worlds, they dramatize these visions and force us to come to terms with the wide range of meanings which human beings assign to their cities. "Billenium" by J. G. Ballard portrays the effect of high-density existence on the lives of human beings. In "A Happy Day in 2381" Robert Silverberg presents an overtly utopian view of the future city, where social adaptation has altered contemporary views on such critical concerns as privacy and sexual behavior.

BIBLIOGRAPHY

Asimov, Isaac, *Caves of Steel,* 1954 (Doubleday)
Ballard, J. G., *Chronopolis,* 1971 (Putnam) (in *Chronopolis and Other Stories*)
———, *The Concentration City,* 1967 (Kape) (in *The Disaster Area*)
Blish, James, *Cities in Flight,* 1970 (Avon)
Brunner, John, *The Sheep Look Up,* 1972 (Ballantine)
Calvino, Italo, *Invisible Cities,* 1974 (Harcourt)
Clem, Ralph; Greenberg, Martin Harry; and Olander, Joseph, *The City 2000 A.D.: Urban Life Through Science Fiction,* 1976 (Fawcett)

Delany, Samuel R., *Dhalgren,* 1974 (Bantam)
Elwood, Roger, *Future City,* 1974 (Pocket Books)
MacLean, Katherine, *Missing Man,* 1975 (Putnam)
Priest, Christopher, *The Inverted World,* 1974 (Harper)
Silverberg, Robert, *The World Inside,* 1971 (Doubleday)
Wells, H. G., *When the Sleeper Awakes*

Billenium

J. G. Ballard

All day long, and often into the early hours of the morning, the tramp of feet sounded up and down the stairs outside Ward's cubicle. Built into a narrow alcove in a bend of the staircase between the fourth and fifth floors, its plywood walls flexed and creaked with every footstep like the timbers of a rotting windmill. Over a hundred people lived in the top three floors of the old rooming house, and sometimes Ward would lie awake on his narrow bunk until 2 or 3 a.m. mechanically counting the last residents returning from the all-night movies in the stadium half a mile away. Through the window he could hear giant fragments of the amplified dialogue booming among the rooftops. The stadium was never empty. During the day the huge four-sided screen was raised on its davit and athletics meetings or football matches ran continuously. For the people in the houses abutting the stadium the noise must have been unbearable.

Ward, at least, had a certain degree of privacy. Two months earlier, before he came to live on the staircase, he had shared a room with seven others on the ground floor of a house in 755th Street, and the ceaseless press of people jostling past the window had reduced him to a state of chronic exhaustion. The street was always full, an endless clamor of voices and shuffling feet. By six-thirty, when he woke, hurrying to take his place in the bathroom queue, the crowds already jammed it from sidewalk to sidewalk, the din punctuated every half minute by the roar of the elevated trains running over the shops on the opposite side of the road. As soon as he saw the advertisement describing the staircase cubicle (like everyone else, he spent most of his spare time scanning the classifieds in the newspapers, moving his lodgings an average of once every two months) he had left despite the higher rental. A cubicle on a staircase would almost certainly be on its own.

However, this had its drawbacks. Most evenings his friends from the library would call in, eager to rest their elbows after the bruising crush of the public reading room. The cubicle was slightly more than four and a half square meters in floor area, half a square meter over the statutory maximum for a single person, the carpenters having taken advantage, illegally, of a recess beside a nearby chimney breast. Consequently Ward had been able to fit a small straight-backed chair into the interval between the bed and the door, so that only one person at a time need sit on the bed—in most single cubicles host and guest had to sit side by side on the bed, conversing over their shoulders and changing places periodically to avoid neck strain.

"You were lucky to find this place," Rossiter, the most regular visitor, never tired of telling him. He reclined back on the bed, gesturing at the cubicle. "It's enormous, the perspectives really zoom. I'd be surprised if you hadn't got at least five meters here, perhaps even six."

Ward shook his head categorically. Rossiter was his closest friend, but the quest for living space had forged powerful reflexes. "Just over four and a half, I've measured it carefully. There's no doubt about it."

Rossiter lifted one eyebrow. "I'm amazed. It must be the ceiling then."

Manipulating the ceiling was a favorite trick of unscrupulous landlords—most assessments of area were made upon the ceiling, out of convenience, and by tilting back the plywood partitions the rated area of a cubicle could be either increased, for the benefit of a prospective tenant (many married couples were thus bamboozled into taking a single cubicle), or decreased temporarily on the visit of the housing inspectors. Ceilings were crisscrossed with pencil marks staking out the rival claims of tenants on opposite sides of a party wall. Someone timid of his rights could be literally squeezed out of existence—in fact, the advertisement "quiet clientele" was usually a tacit invitation to this sort of piracy.

"The wall does tilt a little," Ward admitted. "Actually, it's about four degrees out—I used a plumb line. But there's still plenty of room on the stairs for people to get by."

Rossiter grinned. "Of course, John. I'm just envious, that's all. My room's driving me crazy." Like everyone, he used the term "room" to describe his tiny cubicle, a hangover from the days fifty years earlier when people had indeed lived one to a room, sometimes, unbelievably, one to an apartment or house. The microfilms in the architecture catalogs at the library showed scenes of museums, concert halls, and other public buildings in what appeared to be everyday settings, often virtually empty, two or three people wandering down an enormous gallery or staircase. Traffic moved freely along the center of streets, and in the quieter districts sections of sidewalk would be deserted for fifty yards or more.

Now, of course, the older buildings had been torn down and replaced by housing batteries, or converted into apartment blocks. The great banqueting room in the former City Hall had been split horizontally into four decks, each of these cut up into hundreds of cubicles.

As for the streets, traffic had long since ceased to move about them. Apart from a few hours before dawn when only the sidewalks were crowded, every thoroughfare was always packed with a shuffling mob of pedestrians, perforce ignoring the countless "Keep Left" signs suspended over their heads, wrestling past each other on their way to home and office, their clothes dusty and shapeless. Often "locks" would occur when a huge crowd at a street junction became immovably jammed. Sometimes these locks would last for days. Two years earlier Ward had been caught in one outside the stadium; for over forty-eight hours he was trapped in a gigantic pedestrian jam containing over twenty thousand people, fed by the crowds leaving the stadium on one side and those approaching it on the other. An entire square mile of the local neighborhood had been paralyzed, and he vividly remembered the nightmare of swaying helplessly on his feet as the jam shifted and heaved, terrified of losing his balance and being trampled underfoot. When the police had finally sealed off the stadium and dispersed the jam he had gone back to his cubicle and slept for a week, his body blue with bruises.

"I hear they may reduce the allocation to three and a half meters," Rossiter remarked.

Ward paused to allow a party of tenants from the sixth floor to pass down the staircase, holding the door to prevent it jumping off its latch. "So they're always saying," he commented. "I can remember that rumor ten years ago."

"It's no rumor," Rossiter warned him. "It may well be necessary soon. Thirty million people packed into this city now, a million increase in just one year. There's been some pretty serious talk at the Housing Department."

Ward shook his head. "A drastic revaluation like that is almost impossible to carry out. Every single partition would have to be dismantled and nailed up again; the administrative job alone is so vast it's difficult to visualize. Millions of cubicles to be redesigned and certified, licenses to be issued, plus the complete resettlement of every tenant. Most of the buildings put up since the last revaluation are designed around a four-meter module—you can't simply take half a meter off the end of each cubicle and then say that makes so many new cubicles. They may be only six inches wide.'' He laughed. ''Besides, how can you live in just three and a half meters?''

Rossiter smiled. ''That's the ultimate argument, isn't it? They used it twenty-five years ago at the last revaluation, when the minimum was cut from five to four. It couldn't be done they all said, no one could stand living in only four square meters; it was enough room for a bed and suitcase, but you couldn't open the door to get in.'' Rossiter chuckled softly. ''They were all wrong. It was merely decided that from then on all doors would open outward. Four square meters was here to stay.''

Ward looked at his watch. It was seven-thirty. ''Time to eat. Let's see if we can get into the food bar across the road.''

Grumbling at the prospect, Rossiter pulled himself off the bed. They left the cubicle and made their way down the staircase. This was crammed with luggage and packing cases so that only a narrow interval remained around the bannister. On the floors below the congestion was worse. Corridors were wide enough to be chopped up into single cubicles, and the air was stale and dead, cardboard walls hung with damp laundry and makeshift larders. Each of the five rooms on the floors contained a dozen tenants, their voices reverberating through the partitions.

People were sitting on the steps above the second floor, using the staircase as an informal lounge, although this was against the fire regulations, women chatting with the men queueing in their shirtsleeves outside the washroom, children diving around them. By the time they reached the entrance Ward and Rossiter were having to force their way through the tenants packed together on every landing, loitering around the notice boards or pushing in from the street below.

Taking a breath at the top of the steps, Ward pointed to the food bar on the other side of the road. It was only thirty yards away, but the throng moving down the street swept past like a river at full tide, crossing them from right to left. The first picture show at the stadium started at nine o'clock, and people were setting off already to make sure of getting in.

''Can't we go somewhere else?'' Rossiter asked, screwing his face up at the prospect of the food bar. Not only would it be packed and take them half an hour to be served, but the food was flat and unappetizing. The journey from the library four blocks away had given him an appetite.

Ward shrugged. "There's a place on the corner, but I doubt if we can make it." This was two hundred yards upstream; they would be fighting the crowd all the way.

"Maybe you're right." Rossiter put his hand on Ward's shoulder. "You know, John, your trouble is that you never go anywhere, you're too disengaged, you just don't realize how bad everything is getting."

Ward nodded. Rossiter was right. In the morning, when he set off for the library, the pedestrian traffic was moving with him toward the downtown offices; in the evening, when he came back, it was flowing in the opposite direction. By and large he never altered his routine. Brought up from the age of ten in a municipal hostel, he had gradually lost touch with his father and mother, who lived on the east side of the city and had been unable, or unwilling, to make the journey to see him. Having surrendered his initiative to the dynamics of the city he was reluctant to try to win it back merely for a better cup of coffee. Fortunately his job at the library brought him into contact with a wide range of young people of similar interests. Sooner or later he would marry, find a double cubicle near the library, and settle down. If they had enough children (three was the required minimum) they might even one day own a small room of their own.

They stepped out into the pedestrian stream, carried along by it for ten or twenty yards, then quickened their pace and side-stepped through the crowd, slowly tacking across to the other side of the road. There they found the shelter of the shop fronts, slowly worked their way back to the food bar, shoulders braced against the countless minor collisions.

"What are the latest population estimates?" Ward asked as they circled a cigarette kiosk, stepping forward whenever a gap presented itself.

Rossiter smiled. "Sorry, John, I'd like to tell you but you might start a stampede. Besides, you wouldn't believe me."

Rossiter worked in the Insurance Department at the City Hall, had informal access to the census statistics. For the last ten years these had been classified information, partly because they were felt to be inaccurate, but chiefly because it was feared they might set off a mass attack of claustrophobia. Minor outbreaks had taken place already, and the official line was that world population had reached a plateau, leveling off at twenty thousand million. No one believed this for a moment, and Ward assumed that the 3 percent annual increase maintained since the 1960s was continuing.

How long it could continue was impossible to estimate. Despite the gloomiest prophecies of the Neo-Malthusians, world agriculture had managed to keep pace with the population growth, although intensive cultivation meant that 95 percent of the population was permanently trapped in vast urban conurbations. The outward growth of cities had at last been checked; in fact, all over the world former suburban areas were being reclaimed for agriculture and population additions were confined within the existing urban ghettos. The countryside, as such, no longer existed. Every single square foot of ground sprouted a crop of one type or other. The one-time fields and meadows of the world were now, in effect, factory floors, as highly mechanized and closed to the public as any industrial area. Economic and ideological rivalries had long since faded before one overriding quest—the internal colonization of the city.

Reaching the food bar, they pushed themselves into the entrance and joined the scrum of customers pressing six deep against the counter.

"What is really wrong with the population problem," Ward confided to Rossiter, "is that no one has ever tried to tackle it. Fifty years ago shortsighted nationalism and industrial expansion put a premium on a rising population curve, and even now the hidden incentive is to have a large family so that you can gain a little privacy. Single people are penalized simply because there are more of them and they don't fit conveniently into double or triple cubicles. But it's the large family with its compact, space-saving logistic that is the real villain."

Rossiter nodded, edging nearer the counter, ready to shout his order. "Too true. We all look forward to getting married just so that we can have our six meters."

Directly in front of them, two girls turned around and smiled. "Six square meters," one of them, a dark-haired girl with a pretty oval face, repeated. "You sound like the sort of young man I ought to get to know. Going into the real estate business, Henry?"

Rossiter grinned and squeezed her arm. "Hello, Judith. I'm thinking about it actively. Like to join me in a private venture?"

The girl leaned against him as they reached the counter. "Well, I might. It would have to be legal, though."

The other girl, Helen Waring, an assistant at the library, pulled Ward's sleeve. "Have you heard the latest, John? Judith and I have been kicked out of our room. We're on the street right at this minute."

"What?" Rossiter cried. They collected their soups and coffee and edged back to the rear of the bar. "What on earth happened?"

Helen explained. "You know that little broom cupboard outside our cubicle? Judith and I have been using it as a sort of study hole, going in there to read. It's quiet and restful, if you can get used to not breathing. Well, the old girl found out and kicked up a big fuss, said we were breaking the law and so on. In short, out." Helen paused. "Now we've heard she's going to let it as a single."

Rossiter pounded the counter ledge. "A broom cupboard? Someone's going to live there? But she'll never get a license."

Judith shook her head. "She got it already. Her brother works in the Housing Department."

Ward laughed into his soup. "But how can she let it? No one will live in a broom cupboard."

Judith stared at him somberly. "You really believe that, John?"

Ward dropped his spoon. "No, I guess you're right. People will live anywhere. God, I don't know who I feel more sorry for—you two, or the poor devil who'll be living in that cupboard. What are you going to do?"

"A couple in a place two blocks west are subletting half their cubicle to us. They've hung a sheet down the middle and Helen and I'll take turns sleeping on a camp bed. I'm not joking, our room's about two feet wide. I said to Helen that we ought to split up again and sublet one half at twice our rent."

They had a good laugh over all this and Ward said goodnight to the others and went back to his rooming house.

There he found himself with similar problems.

The manager leaned against the flimsy door, a damp cigar butt revolving around his mouth, an expression of morose boredom on his unshaven face.

"You got four point seven two meters," he told Ward, who was standing out on the staircase, unable to get into his room. Other tenants stepped past onto the landing, where two women in curlers and dressing gowns were arguing with each other, tugging angrily at the wall of trunks and cases. Occasionally the manager glanced at them irritably. "Four seven two. I worked it out twice." He said this as if it ended all possibility of argument.

"Ceiling or floor?" Ward asked.

"Ceiling, whaddya think? How can I measure the floor with all this junk?" He kicked at a crate of books protruding from under the bed.

Ward let this pass. "There's quite a tilt on the wall," he pointed out. "As much as three or four degrees."

The manager nodded vaguely. "You're definitely over the four. Way over." He turned to Ward, who had moved down several steps to allow a man and woman to get past. "I can rent this as a double."

"What, only four and a half?" Ward said incredulously. "How?"

The man who had just passed him leaned over the manager's shoulder and sniffed at the room, taking in every detail in a one-second glance. "You renting a double here, Louie?"

The manager waved him away and then beckoned Ward into the room, closing the door after him.

"It's a nominal five," he told Ward. "New regulation, just came out. Anything over four five is a double now." He eyed Ward shrewdly. "Well, whaddya want? It's a good room, there's a lot of space here, feels more like a triple. You got access to the staircase, window slit—" He broke off as Ward slumped down on the bed and started to laugh. "Whatsa matter? Look, if you want a big room like this you gotta pay for it. I want an extra half rental or you get out."

Ward wiped his eyes, then stood up wearily and reached for the shelves. "Relax, I'm on my way. I'm going to live in a broom cupboard. 'Access to the staircase'—that's really rich. Tell me, Louie, is there life on Uranus?"

Temporarily, he and Rossiter teamed up to rent a double cubicle in a semiderelict house a hundred yards from the library. The neighborhood was seedy and faded, the rooming houses crammed with tenants. Most of them were owned by absentee landlords or by the city corporation, and the managers employed were of the lowest type, mere rent collectors who cared nothing about the way their tenants divided up the living space, and never ventured beyond the first floors. Bottles and empty cans littered the corridors, and the washrooms looked like sumps. Many of the tenants were old and infirm, sitting about listlessly in their narrow cubicles, wheedling at each other back to back through the thin partitions.

Their double cubicle was on the third floor, at the end of a corridor that ringed the building. Its architecture was impossible to follow, rooms letting off at all angles, and luckily the corridor was a cul-de-sac. The mounds of cases ended four feet from the end wall and a partition divided off the cubicle, just wide enough for two beds. A high window overlooked the areaways of the building opposite.

Possessions loaded onto the shelf above his head, Ward lay back on his bed and moodily surveyed the roof of the library through the afternoon haze.

"It's not bad here," Rossiter told him, unpacking his case. "I know there's no real privacy and we'll drive each other insane within a week, but at least we haven't got six other people breathing into our ears two feet away."

The nearest cubicle, a single, was built into the banks of cases half a dozen steps along the corridor, but the occupant, a man of seventy, was deaf and bedridden.

"It's not bad," Ward echoed reluctantly. "Now tell me what the latest growth figures are. They might console me."

Rossiter paused, lowering his voice. "Four percent. *Eight hundred million extra people in one year*—just less than half the Earth's total population in 1950."

Ward whistled slowly. "So they will revalue. What to? Three and a half?"

"Three. From the first of next year."

"Three square meters!" Ward sat up and looked around him. "It's unbelievable! The world's going insane, Rossiter. For God's sake, when are they going to do something about it? Do you realize there soon won't be room enough to sit down, let alone lie down?"

Exasperated, he punched the wall beside him, on the second blow knocked in one of the small wooden panels that had been lightly papered over.

"Hey!" Rossiter yelled. "You're breaking the place down." He dived across the bed to retrieve the panel, which hung downward supported by a strip of paper. Ward slipped his hand into the dark interval, carefully drew the panel back onto the bed.

"Who's on the other side?" Rossiter whispered. "Did they hear?"

Ward peered through the interval, eyes searching the dim light. Suddenly he dropped the panel and seized Rossiter's shoulder, pulled him down onto the bed.

"Henry! Look!"

Rossiter freed himself and pressed his face to the opening, focused slowly and then gasped.

Directly in front of them, faintly illuminated by a grimy skylight, was a medium-sized room, some fifteen feet square, empty except for the dust silted up against the skirting boards. The floor was bare, a few strips of frayed linoleum running across it, the walls covered with a drab floral design. Here and there patches of the paper had peeled off and segments of the picture rail had rotted away, but otherwise the room was in habitable condition.

Breathing slowly, Ward closed the open door of the cubicle with his foot, then turned to Rossiter.

"Henry, do you realize what we've found? Do you realize it, man?"

"Shut up. For Pete's sake keep your voice down." Rossiter examined the room carefully. "It's fantastic. I'm trying to see whether anyone's used it recently."

"Of course they haven't," Ward pointed out. "It's obvious. There's no door into the room. We're looking through it now. They must have paneled over this door years ago and forgotten about it. Look at that filth everywhere."

Rossiter was staring into the room, his mind staggered by its vastness.

"You're right," he murmured. "Now, when do we move in?"

Panel by panel, they pried away the lower half of the door, nailed it onto a wooden frame so that the dummy section could be replaced instantly.

Then, picking an afternoon when the house was half empty and the manager asleep in his basement office, they made their first foray into the room, Ward going in alone while Rossiter kept guard in the cubicle.

For an hour they exchanged places, wandering silently around the dusty room, stretching their arms out to feel its unconfined emptiness, grasping at the sensation of absolute spatial freedom. Although smaller than many of the subdivided rooms in which they had lived, this room seemed infinitely larger, its walls huge cliffs that soared upward to the skylight.

Finally, two or three days later, they moved in.

For the first week Rossiter slept alone in the room, Ward in the cubicle outside, both there together during the day. Gradually they smuggled in a few items of furniture: two armchairs, a table, a lamp fed from the socket in the cubicle. The furniture was heavy and Victorian; the cheapest available, its size emphasized the emptiness of the room. Pride of place was taken by an enormous mahogany wardrobe, fitted with carved angels and castellated mirrors, which they were forced to dismantle and carry into the house in their suitcases. Towering over them, it reminded Ward of the microfilms of Gothic cathedrals, with their massive organ lofts crossing vast naves.

After three weeks they both slept in the room, finding the cubicle unbearably cramped. An imitation Japanese screen divided the room adequately and did nothing to diminish its size. Sitting there in the evenings, surrounded by his books and albums, Ward steadily forgot the city outside. Luckily he reached the library by a back alley and avoided the crowded streets. Rossiter and himself began to seem the only real inhabitants of the world, everyone else a meaningless by-product of their own existence, a random replication of identity which had run out of control.

It was Rossiter who suggested that they ask the two girls to share the room with them.

"They've been kicked out again and may have to split up," he told Ward, obviously worried that Judith might fall into bad company. "There's always a rent freeze after revaluation, but all the landlords know about it so they're not reletting. It's getting damned difficult to find a room anywhere."

Ward nodded, relaxing back around the circular redwood table. He played with a tassel of the arsenic-green lampshade, for a moment felt like a Victorian man of letters, leading a spacious, leisurely life among overstuffed furnishings.

"I'm all for it," he agreed, indicating the empty corners. "There's plenty of room here. But we'll have to make damn sure they don't gossip about it."

After due precautions, they let the two girls into the secret, enjoying their astonishment at finding this private universe.

"We'll put a partition across the middle," Rossiter explained, "then take it down each morning. You'll be able to move in within a couple of days. How do you feel?"

"Wonderful!" They goggled at the wardrobe, squinting at the end-less reflections in the mirrors.

There was no difficulty getting them in and out of the house. The turnover of tenants was continuous and bills were placed in the mail rack. No one cared who the girls were or noticed their regular calls at the cubicle.

However, half an hour after they arrived neither of them had un-packed her suitcase.

"What's up, Judith?" Ward asked, edging past the girls' beds into the narrow interval between the table and wardrobe.

Judith hesitated, looking from Ward to Rossiter, who sat on his bed, finishing off the plywood partition. "John, it's just that . . ."

Helen Waring, more matter of fact, took over, her fingers straightening the bedspread. "What Judith's trying to say is that our position here is a little embarrassing. The partition is—"

Rossiter stood up. "For heaven's sake, don't worry, Helen," he assured her, speaking in the loud whisper they had all involuntarily cultivated. "No funny business, you can trust us. This partition is as solid as a rock."

The two girls nodded. "It's not that," Helen explained, "but it isn't up all the time. We thought that if an older person were here, say Judith's aunt—she wouldn't take up much room and be no trouble, she's really awfully sweet—we wouldn't need to bother about the partition—except at night," she added quickly.

Ward glanced at Rossiter, who shrugged and began to scan the floor.

"Well, it's an idea," Rossiter said. "John and I know how you feel. Why not?"

"Sure," Ward agreed. He pointed to the space between the girls' beds and the table. "One more won't make any difference."

The girls broke into whoops. Judith went over to Rossiter and kissed him on the cheek. "Sorry to be a nuisance, Henry." She smiled at him. "That's a wonderful partition you've made. You couldn't do another one for Auntie—just a little one? She's very sweet but she is getting on."

"Of course," Rossiter said. "I understand. I've got plenty of wood left over."

Ward looked at his watch. "It's seven-thirty, Judith. You'd better get in touch with your aunt. She may not be able to make it tonight."

Judith buttoned her coat. "Oh, she will," she assured Ward. "I'll be back in a jiffy."

The aunt arrived within five minutes, three heavy suitcases soundly packed.

"It's amazing," Ward remarked to Rossiter three months later. "The size of this room still staggers me. It almost gets larger every day."

Rossiter agreed readily, averting his eyes from one of the girls changing behind the central partition. This they now left in place as dismantling it daily had become tiresome. Besides, the aunt's subsidiary partition was attached to it and she resented the continuous upsets. Ensuring she followed the entrance and exit drills through the camouflaged door and cubicle was difficult enough.

Despite this, detection seemed unlikely. The room had obviously been built as an afterthought into the central well of the house and any noise was masked by the luggage stacked in the surrounding corridor. Directly below was a small dormitory occupied by several elderly women, and Judith's aunt, who visited them socially, swore that no sounds came through the heavy ceiling. Above, the fanlight let out through a dormer window, its lights indistinguishable from the hundred other bulbs burning in the windows of the house.

Rossiter finished off the new partition he was building and held it upright, fitting it into the slots nailed to the wall between his bed and Ward's. They had agreed that this would provide a little extra privacy.

"No doubt I'll have to do one for Judith and Helen," he confided to Ward.

Ward adjusted his pillow. They had smuggled the two armchairs back to the furniture shop as they took up too much space. The bed, anyway, was more comfortable. He had never got completely used to the soft upholstery.

"Not a bad idea. What about some shelving around the wall? I've got nowhere to put anything."

The shelving tidied the room considerably, freeing large areas of the floor. Divided by their partitions, the five beds were in line along the rear wall, facing the mahogany wardrobe. In between was an open space of three or four feet, a further six feet on either side of the wardrobe.

The sight of so much space fascinated Ward. When Rossiter mentioned that Helen's mother was ill and badly needed personal care he immediately knew where her cubicle could be placed—at the foot of his bed, between the wardrobe and the side wall.

Helen was overjoyed. "It's awfully good of you, John," she told him, "but would you mind if Mother slept beside me? There's enough space to fit an extra bed in."

So Rossiter dismantled the partitions and moved them closer together, six beds now in line along the wall. This gave each of them an interval of two and a half feet wide, just enough room to squeeze down the side of their beds. Lying back on the extreme right, the shelves two feet above his head, Ward could barely see the wardrobe, but the space in front of him, a clear six feet to the wall ahead, was uninterrupted.

Then Helen's father arrived.

Knocking on the door of the cubicle, Ward smiled at Judith's aunt as she let him in. He helped her swing out the made-up bed which guarded the entrance, then rapped on the wooden panel. A moment later Helen's father, a small gray-haired man in an undershirt, braces tied to his trousers with string, pulled back the panel.

Ward nodded to him and stepped over the luggage piled around the floor at the foot of the beds. Helen was in her mother's cubicle, helping the old woman to drink her evening broth. Rossiter, perspiring heavily, was on his knees by the mahogany wardrobe, wrenching apart the frame of the central mirror with a jimmy. Pieces of the wardrobe lay on his bed and across the floor.

"We'll have to start taking these out tomorrow," Rossiter told him. Ward waited for Helen's father to shuffle past and enter his cubicle. He had rigged up a small cardboard door, and locked it behind him with a crude hook of bent wire.

Rossiter watched him, frowning irritably. "Some people are happy. This wardrobe's a hell of a job. How did we ever decide to buy it?"

Ward sat down on his bed. The partition pressed against his knees and he could hardly move. He looked up when Rossiter was engaged and saw that the dividing line he had marked in pencil was hidden by the encroaching partition. Leaning against the wall, he tried to ease it back again, but Rossiter had apparently nailed the lower edge to the floor.

There was a sharp tap on the outside cubicle door—Judith returning from her office. Ward started to get up and then sat back. "Mr. Waring," he called softly. It was the old man's duty night.

Waring shuffled to the door of his cubicle and unlocked it fussily, clucking to himself.

"Up and down, up and down," he muttered. He stumbled over Rossiter's tool bag and swore loudly, then added meaningly over his shoulder: "If you ask me there's too many people in here. Down below they've only got six to our seven, and it's the same size room."

Ward nodded vaguely and stretched back on his narrow bed, trying not to bang his head on the shelving. Waring was not the first to hint that he move out. Judith's aunt had made a similar suggestion two days earlier. Since he left his job at the library (the small rental he charged the others paid for the little food he needed) he spent most of his time in the room, seeing rather more of the old man than he wanted to, but he had learned to tolerate him.

Settling himself, he noticed that the right-hand spire of the wardrobe, all he had been able to see for the past two months, was now dismantled.

It had been a beautiful piece of furniture, in a way symbolizing this whole private world, and the salesman at the store told him there were few like it left. For a moment Ward felt a sudden pang of regret, as he had done as a child when his father, in a mood of exasperation, had taken something away from him and he knew he would never see it again.

Then he pulled himself together. It was a beautiful wardrobe, without doubt, but when it was gone it would make the room seem even larger.

A Happy Day in 2381

Robert Silverberg

Here is a happy day in 2381. The morning sun is high enough to reach the uppermost fifty stories of Urban Monad 116. Soon the building's entire eastern face will glitter like the sea at dawn. Charles Mattern's window, activated by the dawn's early photons, deopaques. He stirs. God bless, he thinks. His wife stirs. His four children, who have been up for hours, now can officially begin the day. They rise and parade around the bedroom, singing:

> "God bless, God bless, God bless!
> God bless us every one!
> God bless Daddo, God bless Mommo, God bless you and me!
> God bless us all, the short and tall,
> Give us fer-til-i-tee!"

They rush toward their parents' sleeping platform. Mattern rises and embraces them. Indra is eight, Sandor is seven, Marx is five, Cleo is three. It is Charles Mattern's secret shame that his family is so small. Can a man with only four children truly be said to have reverence for life? But Principessa's womb no longer flowers. The medics have said she will not bear again. At twenty-seven she is sterile. Mattern is thinking of taking in a second woman. He longs to hear the yowls of an infant again; in any case, a man must do his duty to God.

Sandor says, "Daddo, Siegmund is still here. He came in the middle of the night to be with Mommo."

The child points. Mattern sees. On Principessa's side of the sleeping platform, curled against the inflation pedal, lies fourteen-year-old Siegmund Kluver, who had entered the Mattern home several hours after midnight to exercise his rights of propinquity. Siegmund is fond of older women. Now he snores; he has had a good workout. Mattern nudges him. ''Siegmund? Siegmund, it's morning!'' The young man's eyes open. He smiles at Mattern, sits up, reaches for his wrap. He is quite handsome. He lives on the 787th floor and already has one child and another on the way.

''Sorry,'' says Siegmund. ''I overslept. Principessa really drains me. A savage, she is!''

''Yes, she's quite passionate,'' Mattern agrees. So is Siegmund's wife, Mattern has heard. When she is a little older, Mattern plans to try her. Next spring, perhaps.

Siegmund sticks his head under the molecular cleanser. Principessa now has risen from bed. She kicks the pedal and the platform deflates swiftly. She begins to program breakfast. Indra switches on the screen. The wall blossoms with light and color. ''Good morning,'' says the screen. ''The external temperature, if anybody's interested, is 28°. Today's population figures at Urbmon 116 are 881,115, which is +102 since yesterday and +14,187 since the first of the year. God bless, but we're slowing down! Across the way at Urbmon 117 they added 131 since yesterday, including quads for Mrs. Hula Jabotinsky. She's eighteen and has had seven previous. A servant of God, isn't she? The time is now 0620. In exactly forty minutes Urbmon 116 will be honored by the presence of Nicanor Gortman, the visiting sociocomputator from Hell, who can be recognized by his outbuilding costume in crimson and ultraviolet. Dr. Gortman will be the guest of the Charles Matterns of the 799th floor. Of course we'll treat him with the same friendly blessmanship we show one another. God bless Nicanor Gortman! Turning now to news from the lower levels of Urbmon 116—''

Principessa says, ''Hear that, children? We'll have a guest, and we must be blessworthy toward him. Come and eat.''

When he has cleansed himself, dressed, and eaten, Charles Mattern goes to the thousandth-floor landing stage to meet Nicanor Gortman. Mattern passes the floors on which his brothers and sisters and their families live. Three brothers, three sisters. Four of them younger than he, two older. One brother died, unpleasantly, young. Jeffrey. Mattern rarely thinks of Jeffrey. He rises through the building to the summit. Gortman has been touring the tropics and now is going to visit a typical urban monad in the temperate zone. Mattern is honored to have been named the official host. He steps out on the landing stage, which is at the very tip of Urbmon 116. A force-field shields him from the fierce winds that sweep the lofty spire. He looks to his left and sees the western face of Urban Monad 115 still in darkness. To his right, Urbmon 117's eastern windows sparkle. Bless Mrs. Hula Jabotinsky and her eleven littles, Mattern thinks. Mattern can see other urbmons in the row, stretching on and on toward the horizon, towers of super-stressed concrete three kilometers high, tapering ever so gracefully. It is as always a thrilling sight. God bless, he thinks. God bless, God bless, God bless!

He hears a cheerful hum of rotors. A quickboat is landing. Out steps a tall, sturdy man dressed in high-spectrum garb. He must be the visiting sociocomputator from Hell.

"Nicanor Gortman?" Mattern asks.

"Bless God. Charles Mattern?"

"God bless, yes. Come."

Hell is one of the eleven cities of Venus, which man has reshaped to suit himself. Gortman has never been on Earth before. He speaks in a slow, stolid way, no lilt in his voice at all; the inflection reminds Mattern of the way they talk in Urbmon 84, which Mattern once visited on a field trip. He has read Gortman's papers: solid stuff, closely reasoned. "I particularly liked 'Dynamics of the Hunting Ethic,'" Mattern tells him while they are in the dropshaft. "Remarkable. A revelation."

"You really mean that?" Gortman asks, flattered.

"Of course. I try to keep up with a lot of the Venusian journals. It's so fascinatingly alien to read about hunting wild animals."

"There are none on Earth?"

"God bless, no," Mattern says. "We couldn't allow that! But I love reading about such a different way of life as you have."

"It is escape literature for you?" asks Gortman.

Mattern looks at him strangely. "I don't understand the reference."

"What you read to make life on Earth more bearable for yourself."

"Oh, no. No. Life on Earth is quite bearable, let me assure you. It's what I read for *amusement*. And to obtain a necessary parallax, you know, for my own work," says Mattern. They have reached the 799th level. "Let me show you my home first." He steps from the dropshaft and beckons to Gortman. "This is Shanghai. I mean, that's what we call this block of forty floors, from 761 to 800. I'm in the next-to-top level of Shanghai, which is a mark of my professional status. We've got twenty-five cities altogether in Urbmon 116. Reykjavík's on the bottom and Louisville's on the top."

"What determines the names?"

"Citizen vote. Shanghai used to be Calcutta, which I personally prefer, but a little bunch of malcontents on the 775th floor rammed a referendum through in '75."

"I thought you had no malcontents in the urban monads," Gortman says.

Mattern smiles. "Not in the usual sense. But we allow certain conflicts to exist. Man wouldn't be man without conflicts, even here!"

They are walking down the eastbound corridor toward Mattern's home. It is now 0710, and children are streaming from their homes in groups of three and four, rushing to get to school. Mattern waves to them. They sing as they run along. Mattern says, "We average 6.2 children per family on this floor. It's one of the lowest figures in the building, I have to admit. High-status people don't seem to breed well. They've got a floor in Prague—I think it's 117—that averages 9.9 per family! Isn't that glorious?"

"You are speaking with irony?" Gortman asks.

"Not at all." Mattern feels an uptake of tension. "We *like* children. We *approve* of breeding. Surely you realized that before you set out on this tour of—"

"Yes, yes," says Gortman, hastily. "I was aware of the general cultural dynamic. But I thought perhaps your own attitude—"

"Ran counter to norm? Just because I have a scholar's detachment, you shouldn't assume that I disapprove in any way of my cultural matrix."

"I regret the implication. And please don't think I show disapproval of your matrix either, although your world is quite strange to me. Bless God, let us not have strife, Charles."

"God bless, Nicanor. I didn't mean to seem touchy."

They smile. Mattern is dismayed by his show of irritation.

Gortman says, "What is the population of the 799th floor?"

"805, last I heard."

"And of Shanghai?"

"About 33,000."

"And of Urbmon 116?"

"881,000."

"And there are fifty urban monads in this constellation of houses."

"Yes."

"Making some 40,000,000 people," Gortman says. "Or somewhat more than the entire human population of Venus. Remarkable!"

"And this isn't the biggest constellation, not by any means!" Mattern's voice rings with pride. "Sansan is bigger, and so is Boswash!

And there are several bigger ones in Europe—Berpar, Wienbud, I think two others. With more being planned!''

''A global population of—''

''—75,000,000,000,'' Mattern cries. ''God bless! There's never been anything like it! No one goes hungry! Everybody happy! Plenty of open space! God's been good to us, Nicanor!'' He pauses before a door labeled 79915. ''Here's my home. What I have is yours, dear guest.'' They go in.

Mattern's home is quite adequate. He has nearly ninety square meters of floor space. The sleeping platform deflates; the children's cots retract; the furniture can easily be moved to provide play area. Most of the room, in fact, is empty. The screen and the data terminal occupy two-dimensional areas of wall that once had to be taken up by television sets, bookcases, desks, file drawers, and other encumbrances. It is an airy, spacious environment, particularly for a family of just six.

The children have not yet left for school; Principessa has held them back, to meet the guest, and so they are restless. As Mattern enters, Sandor and Indra are struggling over a cherished toy, the dream-stirrer. Mattern is astounded. Conflict in the home? Silently, so their mother will not notice, they fight. Sandor hammers his shoes into his sister's shins. Indra, wincing, claws her brother's cheek. ''God *bless*,'' Mattern says sharply. ''Somebody wants to go down the chute, eh?'' The children gasp. The toy drops. Everyone stands at attention. Principessa looks up, brushing a lock of dark hair from her eyes; she has been busy with the youngest child and has not even heard them come in.

Mattern says, ''Conflict sterilizes. Apologize to each other.''

Indra and Sandor kiss and smile. Meekly Indra picks up the toy and hands it to Mattern, who gives it to his younger son Marx. They are all staring now at the guest. Mattern says to him, ''What I have is yours, friend.'' He makes introductions. Wife, children. The scene of conflict has unnerved him a little, but he is relieved when Gortman produces four small boxes and distributes them to the children. Toys. A blessful gesture. Mattern points to the deflated sleeping platform. ''This is where we sleep. There's ample room for three. We wash at the cleanser, here. Do you like privacy when voiding waste matter?''

''Please, yes.''

''You press this button for the privacy shield. We excrete in this. Urine here, feces here. Everything is reprocessed, you understand. We're a thrifty folk in the urbmons.''

''Of course,'' Gortman says.

Principessa says, "Do you prefer that we use the shield when we excrete? I understand some outbuilding people do."

"I would not want to impose my customs on you," says Gortman.

Smiling, Mattern says, "We're a post-privacy culture, of course. But it wouldn't be any trouble for us to press the button if—" He falters. "There's no general nudity taboo on Venus, is there? I mean, we have only this one room, and—"

"I am adaptable," Gortman insists. "A trained sociocomputator must be a cultural relativist, of course!"

"Of course," Mattern agrees, and he laughs nervously.

Principessa excuses herself from the conversation and sends the children, still clutching their new toys, off to school.

Mattern says, "Forgive me for being overobvious, but I must bring up the matter of your sexual prerogatives. We three will share a single platform. My wife is available to you, as am I. Avoidance of frustration, you see, is the primary rule of a society such as ours. And do you know our custom of nightwalking?"

"I'm afraid I—"

"Doors are not locked in Urbmon 116. We have no personal property worth mentioning, and we all are socially adjusted. At night it is quite proper to enter other homes. We exchange partners in this way all the time; usually wives stay home and husbands migrate, though not necessarily. Each of us has access at any time to any other adult member of our community."

"Strange," says Gortman. "I'd think that in a society where there are so many people, an exaggerated respect for privacy would develop, not a communal freedom."

"In the beginning we had many notions of privacy. They were allowed to erode, God bless! Avoidance of frustration must be our goal, otherwise impossible tensions develop. And privacy is frustration."

"So you can go into any room in this whole gigantic building and sleep with—"

"Not the whole building," Mattern interrupts. "Only Shanghai. We frown on nightwalking beyond one's own city." He chuckles. "We do impose a few little restrictions on ourselves, so that our freedoms don't pall."

Gortman looks at Principessa. She wears a loinband and a metallic cup over her left breast. She is slender but voluptuously constructed, and even though her childbearing days are over she has not lost the sensual glow of young womanhood. Mattern is proud of her, despite everything.

Mattern says, "Shall we begin our tour of the building?"

They go out. Gortman bows gracefully to Principessa as they leave. In the corridor, the visitor says, "Your family is smaller than the norm, I see."

It is an excruciatingly impolite statement, but Mattern is tolerant of his guest's faux pas. Mildly he replies, "We would have had more children, but my wife's fertility had to be terminated surgically. It was a great tragedy for us."

"You have always valued large families here?"

"We value life. To create new life is the highest virtue. To prevent life from coming into being is the darkest sin. We all love our big bustling world. Does it seem unendurable to you? Do we seem unhappy?"

"You seem surprisingly well adjusted," Gortman says. "Considering that—" He stops.

"Go on."

"Considering that there are so many of you. And that you spend your whole lives inside a single colossal building. You never do go out, do you?"

"Most of us never do," Mattern admits. "I have traveled, of course—a sociocomputator needs perspective, obviously. But Principessa has never been below the 350th floor. Why should she go anywhere? The secret of our happiness is to create self-contained villages of five or six floors within the cities of forty floors within the urbmons of a thousand floors. We have no sensation of being overcrowded or cramped. We know our neighbors; we have hundreds of dear friends; we are kind and loyal and blessworthy to one another."

"And everybody remains happy forever?"

"Nearly everybody."

"Who are the exceptions?" Gortman asks.

"The flippos," says Mattern. "We endeavor to minimize the frictions of living in such an environment; as you see, we never refuse a reasonable request, we never deny one another anything. But sometimes there are those who abruptly can no longer abide by our principles. They flip; they thwart others; they rebel. It is quite sad."

"What do you do with flippos?"

"We remove them, of course." Mattern says. He smiles, and they enter the dropshaft once again.

Mattern has been authorized to show Gortman the entire urbmon, a tour that will take several days. He is a little apprehensive; he is not as familiar with some parts of the structure as a guide should be. But he will do his best.

"The building," he says, "is made of superstressed concrete. It is constructed about a central service core two hundred meters square. Originally, the plan was to have fifty families per floor, but we average about 120 today, and the old apartments have all been subdivided into single-room occupancies. We are wholly self-sufficient, with our own schools, hospitals, sports arenas, houses of worship, and theaters."

"Food?"

"We produce none, of course. But we have contractual access to the agricultural communes. I'm sure you've seen that nearly nine tenths of the land area of this continent is used for food-production; and then there are the marine farms. There's plenty of food, now that we no longer waste space by spreading out horizontally over good land."

"But aren't you at the mercy of the food-producing communes?"

"When were city-dwellers not at the mercy of farmers?" Mattern asks. "But you seem to regard life on Earth as a thing of fang and claw. We are vital to them—their only market. They are vital to us—our only source of food. Also we provide necessary services to them, such as repair of their machines. The ecology of this planet is neatly in mesh. We can support many billions of additional people. Someday, God blessing, we will."

The dropshaft, coasting downward through the building, glides into its anvil at the bottom. Mattern feels the oppressive bulk of the whole urbmon over him, and tries not to show his uneasiness. He says, "The foundation of the building is four hundred meters deep. We are now at the lowest level. Here we generate our power." They cross a catwalk and peer into an immense generating room, forty meters from floor to ceiling, in which sleek turbines whirl. "Most of our power is obtained," he explains, "through combustion of compacted solid refuse. We burn everything we don't need, and sell the residue as fertilizer. We have auxiliary generators that work on accumulated body heat, also."

"I was wondering about that," Gortman murmurs.

Cheerily Mattern says, "Obviously 800,000 people within one sealed enclosure will produce an immense quantity of heat. Some of this is directly radiated from the building through cooling fins along the outer surface. Some is piped down here and used to run the generators.

In winter, of course, we pump it evenly through the building to maintain temperature. The rest of the excess heat is used in water purification and similar things.''

They peer at the electrical system for a while. Then Mattern leads the way to the reprocessing plant. Several hundred schoolchildren are touring it; silently they join the tour.

The teacher says, ''Here's where the urine comes down, see?'' She points to gigantic plastic pipes. ''It passes through the flash chamber to be distilled, and the pure water is drawn off here—follow me, now—you remember from the flow chart, about how we recover the chemicals and sell them to the farming communes—''

Mattern and his guest inspect the fertilizer plant, too, where fecal reconversion is taking place. Gortman asks a number of questions. He seems deeply interested. Mattern is pleased; there is nothing more significant to him than the details of the urbmon way of life, and he had feared that this stranger from Venus, where men live in private houses and walk around in the open, would regard the urbmon way as repugnant or hideous.

They go onward. Mattern speaks of air-conditioning, the system of dropshafts and liftshafts, and other such topics.

''It's all wonderful,'' Gortman says. ''I couldn't imagine how one little planet with 75,000,000,000 people could even survive, but you've turned it into—into—''

''Utopia?'' Mattern suggests.

''I meant to say that, yes,'' says Gortman.

Power production and waste disposal are not really Mattern's specialties. He knows how such things are handled here, but only because the workings of the urbmon are so enthralling to him. His real field of study is sociocomputation, naturally, and he has been asked to show the visitor how the social structure of the giant building is organized. Now they go up, into the residential levels.

''This is Reykjavík,'' Mattern announces. ''Populated chiefly by maintenance workers. We try not to have too much status stratification, but each city does have its predominant populations—engineers, academics, entertainers, you know. My Shanghai is mostly academic. Each profession is clannish.'' They walk down the hall. Mattern feels edgy here, and he keeps talking to cover his nervousness. He tells how each city within the urbmon develops its characteristic slang, its way of dressing, its folklore and heroes.

"Is there much contact between cities?" Gortman asks.

"We try to encourage it. Sports, exchange students, regular mixer evenings."

"Wouldn't it be even better if you encouraged intercity nightwalking?"

Mattern frowns. "We prefer to stick to our propinquity groups for that. Casual sex with people from other cities is a mark of a sloppy soul."

"I see."

They enter a large room. Mattern says, "This is a newlywed dorm. We have them every five or six levels. When adolescents mate, they leave their family homes and move in here. After they have their first child they are assigned to homes of their own."

Puzzled, Gortman asks, "But where do you find room for them all? I assume that every room in the building is full, and you can't possibly have as many deaths as births, so—how—?"

"Deaths do create vacancies, of course. If your mate dies and your children are grown, you go to a senior citizen dorm, creating room for establishment of a new family unit. But you're correct that most of our young people don't get accommodations in the building, since we form new families at about two percent a year and deaths are far below that. As new urbmons are built, the overflow from the newlywed dorms is sent to them. By lot. It's hard to adjust to being expelled, they say, but there are compensations in being among the first group into a new building. You acquire automatic status. And so we're constantly overflowing, casting out our young, creating new combinations of social units—utterly fascinating, eh? Have you read my paper, 'Structural Metamorphosis in the Urbmon Population'?"

"I know it well," Gortman replies. He looks about the dorm. A dozen couples are having intercourse on a nearby platform. "They seem so young," he says.

"Puberty comes early among us. Girls generally marry at twelve, boys at thirteen. First child about a year later, God blessing."

"And nobody tries to control fertility at all."

"*Control fertility?*" Mattern clutches his genitals in shock at the unexpected obscenity. Several copulating couples look up, amazed. Someone giggles. Mattern says, "Please don't use that phrase again. Particularly if you're near children. We don't—ah—think in terms of control."

"But—"

"We hold that life is sacred. Making new life is blessed. One does one's duty to God by reproducing." Mattern smiles. "To be human is to meet challenges through the exercise of intelligence, right? And one challenge is the multiplication of inhabitants in a world that has seen the conquest of disease and the elimination of war. We could limit births, I suppose, but that would be sick, a cheap way out. Instead we've met the challenge of overpopulation triumphantly, wouldn't you say? And so we go on and on, multiplying joyously, our numbers increasing by three billion a year, and we find room for everyone, and food for everyone. Few die, and many are born, and the world fills up, and God is blessed, and life is rich and pleasant, and as you see we are all quite happy. We have matured beyond the infantile need to place insulation between man and man. Why go outdoors? Why yearn for forests and deserts? Urbmon 116 holds universes enough for us. The warnings of the prophets of doom have proved hollow. Can you deny that we are happy here? Come with me. We will see a school now."

The school Mattern has chosen is in a working-class district of Prague, on the 108th floor. He thinks Gortman will find it particularly interesting, since the Prague people have the highest reproductive rate in Urban Monad 116, and families of twelve or fifteen are not at all unusual. Approaching the school door, they hear the clear treble voices singing of the blessedness of God. Mattern joins the singing; it is a hymn he sang too, when he was their age, dreaming of the big family he would have:

> "And now he plants the holy seed,
>   That grows in Mommo's womb,
> And now a little sibling comes—"

There is an unpleasant and unscheduled interruption. A woman rushes toward Mattern and Gortman in the corridor. She is young, untidy, wearing only a flimsy gray wrap; her hair is loose; she is well along in pregnancy. "Help!" she shrieks. "My husband's gone flippo!" She hurls herself, trembling, into Gortman's arms. The visitor looks bewildered.

Behind her there runs a man in his early twenties, haggard, blood-shot eyes. He carries a fabricator torch whose tip glows with heat. "Goddam bitch," he mumbles. "Allatime babies! Seven babies already and now number eight and I gonna go off my *head!*" Mattern is appalled. He pulls the woman away from Gortman and shoves the visitor through the door of the school.

"Tell them there's a flippo out here," Mattern says. "Get help, fast!'' He is furious that Gortman should witness so atypical a scene, and wishes to get him away from it.

The trembling girl cowers behind Mattern. Quietly, Mattern says, "Let's be reasonable, young man. You've spent your whole life in urbmons, haven't you? You understand that it's blessed to create. Why do you suddenly repudiate the principles on which—''

"Get the hell away from her or I gonna burn you too!''

The young man feints with the torch, straight at Mattern's face. Mattern feels the heat and flinches. The young man swipes past him at the woman. She leaps away, but she is clumsy with girth, and the torch slices her garment. Pale white flesh is exposed with a brilliant burn-streak down it. She cups her jutting belly and falls, screaming. The young man jostles Mattern aside and prepares to thrust the torch into her side. Mattern tries to seize his arm. He deflects the torch; it chars the floor. The young man, cursing, drops it and throws himself on Mattern, pounding in frenzy with his fists. "Help me!'' Mattern calls. "Help!''

Into the corridor erupt dozens of schoolchildren. They are between eight and eleven years old, and they continue to sing their hymn as they pour forth. They pull Mattern's assailant away. Swiftly, smoothly, they cover him with their bodies. He can dimly be seen beneath the flailing, thrashing mass. Dozens more pour from the schoolroom and join the heap. A siren wails. A whistle blows. The teacher's amplified voice booms, "The police are here! Everyone off!''

Four men in uniform have arrived. They survey the situation. The injured woman lies groaning, rubbing her burn. The insane man is unconscious; his face is bloody and one eye appears to be destroyed. "What happened?'' a policeman asks. "Who are you?''

"Charles Mattern, sociocomputator, 799th level, Shanghai. The man's a flippo. Attacked his pregnant wife with the torch. Attempted to attack me.''

The policemen haul the flippo to his feet. He sags in their midst. The police leader says, rattling the words into one another, "Guilty of atrocious assault on woman of childbearing years currently carrying unborn life, dangerous antisocial tendencies, by virtue of authority vested in me I pronounce sentence of erasure, carry out immediately. Down the chute with the bastard, boys!'' They haul the flippo away. Medics arrive to care for the woman. The children, once again singing, return to the classroom. Nicanor Gortman looks dazed and shaken. Mattern seizes his arm and whispers fiercely, "All right, those things happen sometimes. But it was a billion to one against having it happen where you'd see it! It isn't typical! It isn't typical!''

They enter the classroom.

The sun is setting. The western face of the neighboring urban monad is streaked with red. Nicanor Gortman sits quietly at dinner with the members of the Mattern family. The children, voices tumbling one over another, talk of their day at school. The evening news comes on the screen; the announcer mentions the unfortunate event on the 108th floor. ''The mother was not seriously injured,'' he says, ''and no harm came to her unborn child.'' Principessa murmurs, ''Bless God.'' After dinner Mattern requests copies of his most recent technical papers from the data terminal and gives them to Gortman to read at his leisure. Gortman thanks him.

''You look tired,'' Mattern says.

''It was a busy day. And a rewarding one.''

''Yes. We really traveled, didn't we?''

Mattern is tired too. They have visited nearly three dozen levels already; he has shown Gortman town meetings, fertility clinics, religious services, business offices. Tomorrow there will be much more to see. Urban Monad 116 is a varied, complex community. And a happy one, Mattern tells himself firmly. We have a few little incidents from time to time, but we're *happy*.

The children, one by one, go to sleep, charmingly kissing Daddo and Mommo and the visitor good night and running across the room, sweet nude little pixies, to their cots. The lights automatically dim. Mattern feels faintly depressed; the unpleasantness on 108 has spoiled what was otherwise an excellent day. Yet he still thinks that he has succeeded in helping Gortman see past the superficialities to the innate harmony and serenity of the urbmon way. And now he will allow the guest to experience for himself one of their techniques for minimizing the interpersonal conflicts that could be so destructive to their kind of society. Mattern rises.

''It's nightwalking time,'' he says. ''I'll go. You stay here . . . with Principessa.'' He suspects that the visitor would appreciate some privacy.

Gortman looks uneasy.

''Go on,'' Mattern says. ''Enjoy yourself. People don't deny happiness to people, here. We weed the selfish ones out early. Please. What I have is yours. Isn't that so, Principessa?''

"Certainly," she says.

Mattern steps out of the room, walks quickly down the corridor, enters the dropshaft and descends to the 770th floor. As he steps out he hears sudden angry shouts, and he stiffens, fearing that he will become involved in another nasty episode, but no one appears. He walks on. He passes the black door of a chute access door and shivers a little, and suddenly he thinks of the young man with the fabricator torch, and where that young man probably is now. And then, without warning, there swims up from memory the face of the brother he had once had who had gone down that same chute, the brother one year his senior, Jeffrey, the whiner, the stealer, Jeffrey the selfish, Jeffrey the unadaptable, Jeffrey who had had to be given to the chute. For an instant Mattern is stunned and sickened, and he seizes a doorknob in his dizziness.

The door opens. He goes in. He has never been a nightwalker on this floor before. Five children lie asleep in their cots, and on the sleeping platform are a man and a woman, both younger than he is, both asleep. Mattern removes his clothing and lies down on the woman's left side. He touches her thigh, then her breast. She opens her eyes and he says, "Hello. Charles Mattern, 799."

"Gina Burke," she says. "My husband Lenny."

Lenny awakens. He sees Mattern, nods, turns over and returns to sleep. Mattern kisses Gina Burke lightly on the lips. She opens her arms to him. He shivers a little in his need, and sighs as she receives him. God bless, he thinks. It has been a happy day in 2381, and now it is over.

9

Utopias and Dystopias

Frederik Pohl,
Martin Harry Greenberg,
and Joseph D. Olander

Clever people and butchers, Alexis Zorba reminds us in the novel *Zorba the Greek,* have a lot in common—they "weigh everything." It is interesting that this comment is made by a Greek, since formal philosophy was developed by the Greeks approximately two thousand years ago. Since that time fields of philosophy have been defined and categorized. One conventional breakdown of philosophy, for example, includes the "fields" of logic, epistemology, metaphysics, aesthetics, ethics, politics, and poetics. Despite the variety of ways by which philosophy can be defined, two major traditions of "philosophizing" can be traced throughout the intellectual history of the Western world—the *analytic* tradition and the *speculative* tradition. The former stresses the methods by which we can deal with uncertainty and acquire knowledge; the latter, the examination of values and ideals like goodness, beauty, and justice.

We are now living during a time when our scientific analytical abilities to deal with uncertainty, and our technological capabilities to transform our physical and social worlds, are at an all-time high. Ironically, pessimism about our ability to enter the future with our present—and serious—problems solved is at an equally all-time high. Part of the reason for this paradox may be the emphasis we have placed upon our need to analyze the world and the neglect of our need to speculate about our world and, in so doing, discover meaning in it which will satisfy basic conscious and subconscious psychological needs. Can we integrate analytical and speculative modes of thinking so that our scientific and technological powers can be guided by major values which affirm human life, give purpose to our institutions, convey meaning to individuals, and nurture the physical world?

One of the challenges—and benefits—science fiction implies as an art form is an opportunity for reflection about the balance between analysis and speculation. The powers of science and technology, for example, are portrayed—and expanded—in this literature, to be sure; but there is also speculation about the purposes of such powers and about their impact upon human beings and human civilization. This quality is not unique to science fiction; in fact, science fiction can be linked to a tradition of discourse which we have come to know as "utopian literature and thought."

The word "utopia," of course, comes from the work by Sir Thomas More, published in 1516. It is a pretty word; indeed, it is one which almost did not come to exist. More's first thought for a name for the island visited by his fictional protagonist, Ralph Hythlodaye, was "Nusquama."* Although the word "utopia" was coined at this time, utopian literature predates More's efforts. The classical prelude to More's famous work probably begins with Plato's *Republic* and *Critias*. Xenophon's *Cryopaedia* and Plutarch's *Lycurgus* are also utopian in nature.

But this is the traditional way of pinpointing the beginning of the utopian tradition, and a major part of this approach is the assumption that the utopian tradition began with the Greeks and is peculiar to Western civilization. Although an examination of this assumption is beyond the scope of this general introduction, it should be noted that East Asian civilization also gave birth to a utopian tradition which was approximately contemporaneous with that of Classical Greece. During the fifth century B.C., Confucius devoted his life to amplifying utopian themes. His theory of the "Grand Commonwealth," contained in the *Li Chi* (*Book of Rites*), is a utopian conception of the just state. Mencius, a later disciple, wrote about utopian notions of human nature in his *Meng Tzu*. At about the same time, the disciples of Lao Tzu wrote the famous *Tao Te Ching,* which contains a formula for the development of the ideal community. A utilitarian by philosophic position, Mo Tzu, sometime during the fourth century B.C., developed a utopian ideal for good government in his *Mo Tzu*. Somewhat later (179–104

---

*If More had not been persuaded to change the roots of his coinage from Greek to Latin, would we now be speaking of "Nusquamas" and "Dysquamas"?

B.C.), Tung Chungshu articulated a theory of social harmony in his *Interpretations of the Spring and Autumn*. This tradition of utopian literature and thought recedes until, during the seventeenth century, Huang Tsunghsi revives it in his *A Treatise on Political Science*. The most sophisticated expression of this tradition in early modern Chinese history is K'ang Yuwei's *Great Commonwealth,* published in 1885. The utopian legacy of East Asian civilization is rich with comparative and cross-cultural insight for the systematic study of utopian literature and thought.

But the more familiar form of delineating the evolution of utopian literature after the classical prelude is to point to those early utopias, beginning with More's *Utopia,* which used a voyage to an imaginary place as the basic vehicle for social commentary. These early practitioners made great use of itinerant sailors, laying their societies on previously unknown islands or barely explored continents like South America. Some of the best examples of these utopists include Johann Valentin Andreae, *Christianopolis* (1619); Francis Bacon, *The New Atlantis* (1627); Tommaso Campanella, *City of the Sun* (1637); Joannes Bisselius, *Icaria* (1637); Samuel Gott, *Nova Solyma* (1648); James Harrington, *Oceana* (1656); Jonathan Swift, *Gulliver's Travels* (1726); and Etienne Cabet, *Le Voyage en Icarie* (1842).

Most of these utopias, like their classical counterparts, are distinguished by their attempt to explicate the past or to criticize the present rather than to anticipate the future. More recent utopists, during the latter half of the nineteenth century, can be said to have begun a tradition of utopias which aim to anticipate the future. Included in this tradition are Edward Bulwer Lytton, *The Coming Race* (1871); Samuel Butler, *Erewhon* (1872); William Henry Hudson, *A Crystal Age* (1887); Edward Bellamy, *Looking Backward* (1888); and William Morris, *News from Nowhere* (1890).

Beginning with H. G. Wells at the turn of the century and continuing to the present time, the utopian tradition witnesses changes in the techniques of utopian commentary through literature. Some utopists in this category prefer to explore utopian themes by displacing their utopias in time. Among these writers are H. G. Wells, *The Time Machine* (1895), *A Modern Utopia* (1905), *Men Like Gods* (1922), *The Shape of Things To Come* (1933); George Stewart, *Earth Abides* (1949); Arthur C. Clarke, *Childhood's End* (1953); Walter M. Miller, Jr., *A Canticle for Leibowitz* (1959); Anthony Burgess, *The Wanting Seed* (1962); Aldous Huxley, *Island* (1962); Robert A. Heinlein, *Farnham's Freehold* (1964); Frederik Pohl, *The Age of the Pussyfoot* (1969).

Still other writers found it fruitful to explore utopian themes on other planets. Included among these writers are Arthur C. Clarke, *Against the Fall of Night* (1953); Robert A. Heinlein, *Revolt in 2100* (1953); James Blish, *A Case of Conscience* (1959); Joanna Russ, *And Chaos Died* (1970); and Ursula K. Le Guin, *The Dispossessed* (1974). Yet other writers pursued utopian themes by establishing parallel worlds for their explorations; e.g., Aldous Huxley, *Ape and Essence* (1948); Roger Zelazny, *Lord of Light* (1967); and Joanna Russ, *The Female Man* (1975). Although the techniques for articulating utopian themes have undergone some changes since the late nineteenth century, the process remains essentially the same. For the diagnostic feature of all utopias and dystopias is the evident disenchantment of the writer with society, leading the reader to want to make changes in the world.

But the trouble with this sort of diagnosis is that it rests on an assumption about the intentions of the writer. This is a risky business; good writers write for a complexity of reasons. Even their own statements about their motives are not always to be trusted.* And a great deal of writing, especially science fiction writing, contains some elements of social comment. Edgar Rice Burroughs's ''Barsoom'' series is full of utopian and dystopian aspects: casual, offhand, and heavy-fisted though they are, his description of the grave, graceful society of Helium in *A Princess of Mars* is exactly utopian, as his passages on the worship of the god Tur in *The Master Mind of Mars* are dystopian. To be sure, these sections are submerged in a much greater volume of action and adventure; but they are there, and undoubtedly contributed considerably to the popularity of Burroughs's work.

A utopia, then, may simply be a writer's personal vision of an ideal world. It need not be a workable world at all; one definition of the word ''utopian'' is ''impractical.'' But it is a world that one might like to try living in, if only for a change, to test out its assumptions. It need not even be a prescription for all of humanity, for some utopias are parochial. Samuel R. Delany's *Dhalgren* is a utopia of the counterculture; Joanna Russ's *The Female Man,* a utopia of the radical-feminist.

Except for the fanatics and the certifiably insane, few people expect ever to live an ideal. The utopia is rarely to be taken as a prescription for immediate consumption; but it is a statement about a kind of life

---

*Obviously George Orwell wrote *1984* as a protest against state power of all kinds. His whole work shows the strength, and the progressive growth, of his feelings about this. Yet we have his own word, in an interview shortly before his death, that the reason he wrote *1984* was for the money. He knew he was seriously ill and wished to provide for his family by writing a best-selling potboiler.

that would be better than the one we have—one which could be achieved if people have the will to achieve it.

If the function of the utopia is to show us what a fine life we might have, so that we can strive toward it, the function of the dystopia is to show us what misery we may all-unknowing be in, so that we can escape it. The dystopia is not a new literary invention, although it is normally associated with contemporary science fiction. It is already recognizable in *Gulliver's Travels* (1726); the Lilliputians and Blefuscans are Swift's own England and France, taken one small step farther; the Laputans his projection of a society of irrelevant intellectuals. Both are nearly the archetypal examples of what Kingsley Amis has called "the comic inferno," but structurally they are not quite the same. Lilliput is satirical exaggeration; Laputa is satirical extrapolation. The one caricatures what is; the other warns of what may be.

As H. G. Wells is the foremost utopist of modern times, so his *When the Sleeper Awakes* was the first—and among the best—of full-fledged dystopias. *Sleeper* is cautionary literature. It warns against the concentration of money-power and is surprisingly, almost eerily, exact in forecasting the "managerial revolution" half a century before Burnham. Wells had no such examples in the real world before him when he wrote the book; money-power was in the hands of entrepreneur-capitalist individuals, not managerial soviets. But, in the novel, ownership counts for no more than does ownership of a few shares of IT&T today. *Sleeper* owns everything there is, but it is his employee-executives who wield all the power, even over him.

Dystopias, then, are important elements in the modern evolution of the utopian tradition. Some of the best elements in this tradition include Evgeniy Zamyatin, *We* (1921?); Aldous Huxley, *Brave New World* (1932); George Orwell, *1984* (1949); Kurt Vonnegut, Jr., *Player Piano* (1952); Ray Bradbury, *Fahrenheit 451* (1953); Frederik Pohl and Cyril M. Kornbluth, *The Space Merchants* (1957); Anthony Burgess, *A Clockwork Orange* (1962); Robert Sheckley, *The Tenth Victim* (1966); and John Brunner, *Stand on Zanzibar* (1968).

Of course, it is not only in science fiction that fiction can be used to explore dystopian themes or to caution the reader. Indeed, it is challenging to think about so-called mainstream literature in terms of potential dystopian elements. Upton Sinclair and Harriet Beecher Stowe are only two of a great gallery of impassioned American novelists who have used their white-hot pens to crusade; and there is nothing of science fiction in *The Jungle* or *Uncle Tom's Cabin*.

But the science fiction dystopia gives an opportunity to display not only the evil-that-is but also the evil-that-may-be-coming. The projection into the future does not diminish the effectiveness of social criticism. It can enhance it. To write of evils as they are may fail in convincing anyone who is not already convinced, for familiarity breeds numbness. But to carry today's evil a step farther, showing where it may terribly lead, can break through the anesthesia of habit and give a fresh, new insight into what is wrong.

So with Aldous Huxley. Angry at the workings of that Gresham's Law of Culture, by which mass-produced trash drives out the single, sacred individual soul, he wrote of a world of cloned* people and mass-produced minds in *Brave New World*.

So, too, with George Orwell. Setting aside his expressed "reasons" for writing *1984,* what does the book do? It carries a known process to its conclusion: state interference in private lives becomes total. Orwell did not have to displace his setting thirty-odd years into the future to speak out against statism. He could have written another *Coming Up for Air* or *The Road to Wigan Pier.* But he had already written them. They had been well received and had in fact made his reputation in literary circles; but they had made hardly any impression at all on the world at large, and he must have come to realize that his preaching was being heard only by the already saved. *1984* reached an immensely larger audience much more effectively than anything he had written before. It does not say anything Orwell had not said in earlier work, but it says it in a way that compels attention because of its impact, and at the same time permits the reader to tolerate it because it is displaced in time.

It is this quality of being "displaced in time" that characterizes most science fictional utopias and dystopias. In fact, the most frequent classification used for describing alternative future worlds is utopian-dystopian. Many typologies have been developed for analyzing utopian literature and thought. Frank E. Manuel describes some of these as ". . . the soft and the hard, the static and the dynamic, the sensate and the spiritual, the aristocratic and the plebeian, the utopia of escape and the utopia of realization, the collectivist and individualistic utopias."†

Regardless of the kinds of typologies which can be developed about this literature, it may be more significant to recognize that utopias and

---

*He said "Bokanovskified," not "cloned," because the process of cloning had not been discovered yet—but for all the intents and purposes of his novel they are the same thing.

†"Introduction," in Frank E. Manuel, ed., *Utopias and Utopian Thought* (Boston: Beacon Press, 1967), p. viii.

dystopias allow for reflection on our own nature and on the nature of our collective concerns. They constitute "ordering visions" by which we can assess and assign meaning to the physical and social worlds in which we live.

One major vision which relates to the overall purpose of this book is the mythic vision. For as long as humans have existed up until modern times, myths have provided us with an opportunity, similar to that given to us by utopian and dystopian science fiction, for thinking about our nature and our collective concerns. The rise of science and technology, however, has been accompanied by a depreciation of the importance of myths in our individual and social lives. This book raises the question of whether science and technology have generated a new set of myths for modern man—myths which are captured and most effectively portrayed in the literature we have come to know as science fiction. Is science fiction more or less useful—either at the level of psychological truth which gives us meaning or at the level of cautionary or normative models for our social worlds—in dealing with present and future worlds? In this sense, it may provide a format for our thinking about ways to achieve a better world or to avoid a worse one.

Certainly, over a hundred science fiction writers have developed utopian and dystopian visions for us to ponder, especially the three represented in this section: Hugo Gernsback, Cyril M. Kornbluth, and Fritz Leiber. Gernsback, engineer and scientist, developed visions of utopian futures in which technology and science assure happiness for us. One of his visions is portrayed in "New York A.D.: 2660." However, Kornbluth, newsman and poet, and Leiber, Shakespearean actor and candidate for the ministry, had sharp insights into the pockets of decay behind the stainless-steel surfaces of twentieth-century society and reveal them for all of us in stories like "Coming Attraction" and "The Luckiest Man in Denv." Like all good science fiction—and like all good myths—they should stimulate reflection about our collective dreams and nightmares.

BIBLIOGRAPHY

Bellamy, Edward, *Looking Backward: 2000–1887,* 1888 (many editions)
Blish, James, and Knight, Norman L., *A Torrent of Faces,* 1967 (Ace)
Brackett, Leigh, *The Long Tomorrow,* 1955 (Doubleday)

Bradbury, Ray, *Fahrenheit 451,* 1953 (Ballantine)
Brunner, John, *Stand on Zanzibar,* 1968 (Ballantine)
————, *The Sheep Look Up,* 1972 (Ballantine)
Budrys, A. J., *Who?,* 1958 (Pyramid)
Burgess, Anthony, *A Clockwork Orange,* 1963 (Norton)
Clarke, Arthur C., *Childhood's End,* 1953 (Ballantine)
Dick, Philip K., *Eye in the Sky,* 1957 (Ace)
Gunn, James, *The Joymakers,* 1961 (Bantam)
Huxley, Aldous, *Brave New World,* 1946 (Harper & Row)
————, *Island,* 1962 (Bantam)
Jones, Raymond F., *Renaissance,* 1951 (Gnome Press)
Kateb, George, *Utopia and Its Enemies,* 1963 (Free Press of Glencoe)
Kornbluth, C. M., *The Syndic,* 1953 (Doubleday)
Levin, Ira, *This Perfect Day,* 1920 (Fawcett)
Miller, Walter M., Jr., *A Canticle for Leibowitz,* 1959 (Lippincott)
Moore, C. L., *Doomsday Morning,* 1957 (Doubleday)
Nolan, William F., and Johnson, George Clayton, *Logan's Run,* 1969 (Dell)
Orwell, George, *Nineteen Eighty-Four,* 1949 (Harcourt, Brace)
Pohl, Frederik, and Kornbluth, C. M., *The Space Merchants,* 1953 (Ballantine)
———— and ————, *Gladiator-at-Law,* 1955 (Ballantine)
Reynolds, Mack, *Looking Backward, From The Year 2000,* 1973 (Ace)
Roshwald, Mordecai, *Level 7,* 1959 (McGraw-Hill)
Sheckley, Robert, *The Status Civilization,* 1968 (Dell)
Shute, Nevil, *On the Beach,* 1957 (Morrow)
Simak, Clifford D., *City,* 1952 (Gnome Press)
Skinner, B. F., *Walden Two,* 1948 (Macmillan)
Tucker, Wilson, *The Long Loud Silence,* 1952 (Rinehart)
Vance, Jack, *To Live Forever,* 1956 (Ballantine)
Vidal, Gore, *Messiah,* 1965 (Little, Brown)
Vonnegut, Kurt, Jr., *Player Piano,* 1951 (Scribner's)
Wells, H. G., *A Modern Utopia,* reissued 1967 (University of Nebraska Press)
Wolfe, Bernard, *Limbo,* 1952 (Random House)
Zamiatin, Yevgeny, *We,* 1921 (Bantam)

New York A.D.:2660

Hugo Gernsback

Being much interested in sports she desired to know presently how the modern New Yorker kept himself in condition and for his answer Ralph stopped at a corner and they entered a ta-l, flat-roofed building. They took off their coasters, stepped into the electromagnetic elevator and ascended the fifty-odd stories in a few seconds. At the top, they found a large expanse on which were stationed dozens of flyers of all sizes. There was a continuous bustle of departing and arriving aerial flyers and of people alighting and departing.

As soon as Ralph and Alice appeared a dozen voices began to call: *"Aerocab, sir, Aerocab, this way please!"* Ralph, ignoring them, walked over to a two-seated flyer and assisted his companion to the seat; he then seated himself and said briefly to the "driver," *"National Playgrounds."* The machine, which was very light and operated entirely by electricity, was built of metal throughout; it shot up into the air with terrific speed and then took a northeasterly direction at a rate of ten miles per minute, or 600 miles per hour.

From the great height at which they were flying it was not hard to point out the most interesting structures, towers, bridges, and wonders of construction deemed impossible several centuries ago.

In less than ten minutes they had arrived at the National Playgrounds. They alighted on an immense platform and Ralph, leading Alice to the edge, where they could see the entire playgrounds, said:

"These National Playgrounds were built by the city in 2490, at the extreme eastern end of what used to be Long Island, a few miles from Montauk. An immense area had been fitted up for all kinds of sports, terrestrial and aquatic as well as aerial. These municipal playgrounds are the finest in the world and represent one of New York's greatest achievements. The City Government supplied all the various sport paraphernalia and every citizen has the right to use it, by applying to the lieutenants in charge of the various sections.

"There are playgrounds for the young as well as for the old, grounds for men, grounds for women, grounds for babies to romp about in. There are hundreds of baseball fields, thousands of tennis courts, and uncounted football fields and golf links. It never rains, it is never too hot, it is never too cold. The grounds are open every day in the year, from seven in the morning till eleven at night. After sunset, the grounds and fields are lighted by thousands of iridium wire spirals, for those who have to work in the daytime.

"As a matter of fact all the great baseball, tennis, and football contests are held after sundown. The reason is apparent. During the daytime, with the sun shining, there is always one team which has an advantage over the other, on account of the light being in their eyes. In the evening, however, with the powerful, stationary light overhead, each team has the same conditions and the game can be played more fairly and more accurately."

Ralph and his companion strolled about the immense grounds watching the players and it was not long before he discovered that she, like himself, was enthusiastic about tennis. He asked her if she would care to play a game with him and she acquiesced eagerly.

They walked over to the dressing building where Ralph kept his own sport clothes. Since the girl had no tennis shoes, he secured a pair for her in the Arcade, and they sauntered over to one of the courts.

In the game that followed, Ralph, an expert at tennis, was too engrossed in the girl to watch his game. Consequently, he was beaten from start to finish. He did not see the ball, and scarcely noticed the net. His eyes were constantly on Alice, who, indeed, made a remarkably pretty picture. She flung herself enthusiastically into her game, as she did with everything else that interested her. She was the true sport-lover, caring little whether she won or not, loving the game for the game itself.

Her lovely face was flushed with the exercise, and her hair curled into damp little rings, lying against her neck and cheeks in soft clusters. Her eyes, always bright, shone like stars. Now and again, they met Ralph's in gay triumph as she encountered a difficult ball.

He had never imagined that anyone could be so graceful. Her lithe and flexible figure was seen to its best advantage in this game requiring great agility.

Ralph, under this bombardment of charms, was spellbound. He played mechanically, and, it must be admitted, wretchedly. And he was so thoroughly and abjectly in love that he did not care. To him, but one thing mattered. He knew that unless he could have Alice life itself would not matter to him.

He felt that he would gladly have lost a hundred games when she at last flung down her racket, crying happily: "Oh, I won, I won, didn't I?"

"You certainly did," he cried. "You were wonderful!"

"I'm a little bit afraid you let me win," she pouted. "It really wasn't fair of you."

"You were fine," he declared. "I was hopelessly outclassed from the beginning. You have no idea how beautiful you were," he went on, impulsively. "More beautiful than I ever dreamed anyone could be."

Before his ardent eyes she drew back a little, half pleased, half frightened, and not a little confused.

Sensing her embarrassment he instantly became matter-of-fact.

"Now," he said, "I am going to show you the source of New York's light and power."

A few minutes later, after both had changed their shoes, they were again seated in an aerocab and a twenty-minute journey brought them well into the center of what was formerly New York state.

They alighted on an immense plain on which twelve monstrous Mcteoro-Towers, each 1,500 feet high, were stationed. These towers formed a hexagon inside of which were the immense *Helio-Dynamophores,* or Sun-power-generators.

The entire expanse, twenty kilometers square, was covered with glass. Underneath the heavy plate-glass squares were the photo-electric elements which transformed the solar heat *direct* into electric energy.

The photo-electric elements, of which there were 400 to each square meter, were placed in large movable metal cases, each containing 1,600 photo-electric units.

Each metal case in turn was movable, and mounted on a kind of large tripod in such a manner that each case from sunrise to sunset presented its glass plate directly to the sun. The rays of the sun, consequently, struck the photo-electric elements always vertically, never obliquely. A small electric motor inside of the tripod moved the metal case so as to keep the plates always facing the sun.

In order that one case might not take away the light from the one directly behind it, all cases were arranged in long rows, each sufficiently far away from the one preceding it. Thus shadows from one row could not fall on the row behind it.

At sunrise, all cases would be almost vertical, but at this time very little current was generated. One hour after sunrise, the plant was working to its full capacity; by noon all cases would be in a horizontal position, and by sunset, they again would be in an almost vertical position, in the opposite direction, however, from that of the morning. The plant would work at its full capacity until one hour before sunset.

Each case generated about one hundred and twenty kilowatts almost as long as the sun was shining, and it is easily understood what an enormous power the entire plant could generate. In fact, this plant supplied all the power, light, and heat for entire New York. One-half of the plant was for day use, while the other half during daytime charged the chemical gas-accumulators for night use.

In 1909 Cove of Massachusetts invented a thermo-electric Sun-power-generator which could deliver ten volts and six amperes, or one-sixtieth kilowatt in a space of twelve square feet. Since that time inventors by the score had busied themselves to perfect solar generators, but it was not until the year 2469 that the Italian 63A 1243 invented the photo-electric cell, which revolutionized the entire electrical industry. This Italian discovered that by derivatives of the Radium-M class, in conjunction with Tellurium and Arcturium, a photo-electric element could be produced which was strongly affected by the sun's ultra-violet rays and in this condition was able to transform heat *direct* into electrical energy, without losses of any kind.

After watching the enormous power plant for a time Alice remarked:

"We, of course, have similar plants across the water but I have never seen anything of such magnitude. It is really colossal. But what gives the sky above such a peculiar black tint?"

"In order not to suffer too great losses from atmospheric disturbances," Ralph explained, "the twelve giant Meteoro-Towers which you notice are working with full power as long as the plant is in operation. Thus a partial vacuum is produced above the plant and the air consequently is very thin. As air ordinarily absorbs an immense amount of heat, it goes without saying that the Helio-Dynamophore plant obtains an immensely greater amount of heat when the air above is very clear and thin. In the morning the towers direct their energy toward the East in order to clear the atmosphere to a certain extent, and in the afternoon their energy is directed toward the West for the same purpose. For this reason, this plant furnishes fully thirty per cent more energy than others working in ordinary atmosphere."

As it was growing late they returned to the city, traversing the distance to Ralph's home in less than ten minutes.

Alice's father arrived a few minutes later, and she told him of the delightful time she had had in the company of their distinguished host.

Shortly after they had dined that evening Ralph took his guests down to his *Tele-Theater*. This large room had a shallow stage at one end, with proscenium arch and curtain, such as had been in use during the whole history of the drama. At the rear of the room were scattered a number of big upholstered chairs.

When they had seated themselves, Ralph gave Alice a directory of the plays and operas that were being presented that night.

"Oh, I see they are playing the French comic opera, *La Normande,* at the National Opera tonight," she exclaimed. "I have heard and read much of it. I should like to hear it so much."

"With the greatest of pleasure," Ralph replied. "In fact, I have not heard it myself. My laboratory has kept me so busy, that I have missed the Opera several times already. There are only two performances a week now."

He walked over to a large switchboard from which hung numerous cords and plugs. He inserted one of the plugs into a hole labeled "National Opera." He then manipulated several levers and switches and seated himself again with his guests.

In a moment, a gong sounded, and the lights were gradually dimmed. Immediately afterward, the orchestra began the overture.

A great number of loud-speaking telephones were arranged near the stage, and the acoustics were so good that it was hard to realize that the music originated four miles away at the National Opera House.

When the overture was over, the curtain rose on the first act. Directly behind it several hundred especially constructed Telephots were arranged in such a manner as to fill out the entire space of the shallow stage. These Telephots were connected in a series and were all joined together so cleverly that no break or joint was visible in the rear part of the stage. The result was that all objects on the distant stage of the National Opera were projected full size on the composite Telephot plates on the Tele-Theater stage. The illusion was so perfect in all respects that it was extremely hard to imagine that the actors on the Telephot stage were not real flesh and blood. Each voice could be heard clearly and distinctly, because the transmitters were close to the actors at all times and it was not necessary to strain the ear to catch any passages.

Between the acts Ralph explained that each New York playhouse now had over 200,000 subscribers and it was as easy for the Berlin and Paris subscribers to hear and see the play as for the New York subscriber. On the other hand, he admitted that the Paris and Berlin as well as the London playhouses had a large number of subscribers, local as well as long distance, but New York's subscription list was by far the largest.

"Can you imagine," mused Alice, "how the people in former centuries must have been inconvenienced when they wished to enjoy a play? I was reading only the other day how they had to prepare themselves for the theater hours ahead of time. They had to get dressed especially for the occasion and even went so far as to have different clothes in which to attend theaters or operas. And then they had to ride or perhaps walk to the playhouse itself. Then the poor things, if they did not happen to like the production, had either to sit all through it or else go home. They probably would have rejoiced at the ease of our Tele-Theaters, where we can switch from one play to another in five seconds, until we find the one that suits us best.

"Nor could their sick people enjoy themselves seeing a play, as we can now. I know when I broke my ankle a year ago, I actually lived in the Tele-Theater. I cannot imagine how I could have dragged through those dreary six weeks in bed without a new play each night. Life must have been dreadful in those days."

"Yes, you are right," Ralph said. "Neither could they have imagined in their wildest dreams the spectacle I witnessed a few days ago.

"I happened to be passing this room and I heard such uproarious laughter that I decided to see what caused it all. Entering unnoticed, I found my ten-year-old nephew 'entertaining' half-a-dozen of his friends. The little rascal had plugged into a matinee performance of *Romeo and Juliet* playing at the Broadway—in English of course. He then plugged in at the same time into *Der Spitzbub,* a farce playing that evening in Berlin, and to this, for good measure, he added *Rigoletto* in Italian, playing at the Gala in Milan.

"The effect was of course horrible. Most of the time, nothing but a Babel of voices and music could be heard; but once in a while a single voice broke through the din, followed immediately by another one in a different language. The funniest incident was when, at the Broadway, Juliet called: 'Romeo, Romeo, where art thou, Romeo?,' and a heavy comedian at the Berlin Theatre howled: *'Mir ist's Wurst, schlagt ihn tot!'*

"Of course, everything on the stage was blurred most of the time, but once in a while extremely ludicrous combinations resulted between some of the actors at the various theaters, which were greeted with an uproar by the youngsters."

As he concluded the anecdote the curtain rose once more, and the audience of three settled back to enjoy the second act of the opera.

Later, when it was all over, they went down to the street floor at Ralph's suggestion, where they put on their Tele-motor-coasters, preparatory to seeing more of New York—this time by night.

The party proceeded to roll down Broadway, the historic thoroughfare of New York. Despite the fact that it was 11 o'clock at night, the streets were almost as light as at noonday. They were illuminated brilliantly by the iridium spirals, hanging high above the crossings. These spirals gave forth a pure, dazzling-white light of the same quality as sunlight. This light moreover was absolutely cold, as all electrical energy was transformed into light, none being lost in heat. Not a street was dark—not even the smallest alley.

James 212B 422, as well as his daughter, lingered over the superb displays in the various stores and they entered several to make a few purchases. Alice was much impressed with the automatic-electric packing machines.

The clerk making the sale placed the purchased articles on a metal platform. He then pushed several buttons on a small switchboard, which operated the "size" apparatus to obtain the dimensions of the package. After the last button was pressed, the platform rose about two feet, till it disappeared into a large metal, box-like contrivance. In about ten to fifteen seconds it came down again bearing on its surface a neat white box with a handle at the top, *all in one piece.* The box was not fastened with any strings or tape, but was folded in an ingenious manner so that it could not open of its own accord. Moreover, it was made of *Alohydrolium,* which is the lightest of all metals, being one-eighth the weight of aluminum.

The automatic packing machine could pack anything from a small package a few inches square up to a box two feet high by three feet long. It made the box to suit the size of the final package, placed the articles together, packed them into the box which was not yet finished, folded the box after the handle had been stamped out, stenciled the firm's name on two sides and delivered it completely packed, all within ten to fifteen seconds.

The box could either be taken by the purchaser or the clerk would stencil the customer's name and address into the handle, place a triangular packet-post stamp on the box and drop it into a chute beside the counter. It was carried down into the *Packet-Post Conveyor,* which was from seventy-five to one hundred feet below the level of the street, where it landed on a belt-like arrangement moving at the rate of five miles an hour. The action was entirely automatic and the chute was arranged with an automatic shutter which would only open when there was no package immediately below on the moving belt. This precluded the possibility of packages tumbling on top of each other and in this way blocking the conveyor tube.

When the package had landed on the conveyor belt it traveled to the nearest *distributor office,* where the post office clerk would take it from the belt and see if it was franked correctly. The stamp was then machine cancelled and after the clerk had noted the address he routed it to the sub-station nearest to the addressee's home. Next he clamped onto the package an automatic metal "rider" which was of a certain height, irrespective of the size of the package.

The package with its rider was placed on an express conveyor belt traveling at the rate of 25 miles an hour. This express belt, bearing the package, moved at an even speed, and never stopping, passed numerous sub-stations on the way. At the correct sub-station the rider came against a contact device stretching across the belt at right angles, at a certain height. This contact arrangement closed the circuit of a powerful electromagnet placed in the same line with the contact, a few feet away from the express belt. The electromagnet acted immediately on the metal package (Alohydrolium is a magnetic metal), drawing it in a flash into the sub-station from the belt. If there was another package right behind the one so drawn out, it was handled in the same manner.

After the package had arrived at the sub-station it was dispatched to its final destination. Another rider was attached to it and the package placed on a local conveyor belt passing by the house to which it was addressed. On arriving at the correct address its rider would strike the contact overhead, which operated the electromagnet, pulling the package into the basement of the house, where it fell on the platform of an electric dumb-waiter. The dumb-waiter started upward automatically and the package was delivered at once.

By this method a package could be delivered in the average space of forty minutes from the time of purchase. Some packages could be delivered in a much shorter time and others which had to travel to the city limits took much longer.

"How wonderful!" Alice exclaimed after Ralph had explained the system. "It must have taken decades to build such a stupendous system."

"No, not quite," was the reply. "It was built gradually by an enormous number of workers. The tubes are even now extended almost daily to keep pace with the growth of the city."

From the stores Ralph took his guests to the roof of an aerocab stand and they boarded a fast flyer.

"Take us about 10,000 feet up," Ralph instructed the driver.

"You haven't much time," the man answered; "at 12 o'clock all cabs must be out of the air."

"Why?"

"Today is the 15th of September, the night of the aerial carnival, and it's against the law to go up over New York until it's over. You have twenty-five minutes left, however, if you wish to go up.''

"I forgot all about this aerial carnival," said Ralph, "but twenty-five minutes will be time enough for us if you speed up your machine."

The aerial flyer rose quickly and silently. The objects below seemed to shrink in size and within three minutes the light became fainter.

In ten minutes an altitude of twelve thousand feet had been reached, and as it became too cold, Ralph motioned to the driver not to rise further.

The spectacle below them was indescribably beautiful. As far as the eye could see was a broad expanse studded with lights, like a carpet embroidered with diamonds. Thousands of aerial craft, their powerful searchlights sweeping the skies, moved silently through the night, and once in a while an immense transatlantic aerial liner would swish by at a tremendous speed.

Most beautiful of all, as well as wonderful, were the *Signalizers*. Ralph pointed them out to his guests, saying:

"In the first period of aerial navigation large electric lamps forming figures and letters were placed on housetops and in open fields that the aerial craft above might better find their destinations. To the traffic flying 5,000 feet or higher such signals were wholly inadequate, as they could not be correctly read at such a distance. Hence the signalizers. These are powerful searchlights of the most advanced type, mounted on special buildings. They are trained skyward and shoot a powerful shaft of light directly upward. No aerial craft is allowed to cross these light shafts. Each shaft gives a different signal; thus the signalizer in Herald Square is first white; in ten seconds it changes to red and in another ten seconds it becomes yellow. Even an aerial liner at sea can recognize the signal and steer directly into the Herald Square pier, without being obliged to hover over the city in search of it. Some signalizers have only one color, flashing from time to time. Others more important use two searchlights at one time, like the one at Sandy Hook. This signalizer has two light shafts, one green and one red; these do not change colors, nor do they light periodically."

From on high Ralph's guests marveled at these signalizers, which pierced the darkness all around them. It was a wonderful sight and the weird beauty of the colored shafts thrilled Alice immeasurably.

"Oh, it is like a Fairyland," she exclaimed. "I could watch it forever."

But presently the aerocab was descending rapidly and in a few minutes the strong light from below had obliterated the light shafts. As the craft drew closer the streets could be seen extending for miles like white ribbons and the brilliantly lighted squares stood out prominently. They landed, at the stroke of twelve, and Ralph found three unoccupied chairs on the top of one of the public buildings and only then did they notice that hundreds of people were seated, watching the sky expectantly.

At the last stroke of twelve, all the lights below went out and simultaneously the light shafts of all the searchlights. Everything was plunged in an utter darkness.

Suddenly overhead at a great height the flag of the United States in immense proportions was seen. It was composed of 6,000 flyers, all together in the same horizontal plane. Each flyer was equipped with very powerful lights on the bottom, some white, some red, others blue. Thus an immense flag in its natural colors was formed and so precisely did the flyers co-operate that, although they all were at least 50 feet from each other, the appearance to those below was that of an unbroken silk flag, illuminated by a searchlight. The immense flag began to move. It passed slowly overhead, describing a large circle, so that the entire population below obtained a perfect view.

Everyone applauded the demonstration. Then as suddenly as it had appeared the flag vanished and all was once more in darkness. Ralph explained to his guests that the lights of each one of the aerial flyers had been shut off simultaneously in preparation for the next spectacle.

All at once there was seen an enormous colored circle which revolved with great rapidity, becoming smaller and smaller, as though it were shrinking. Finally it became a colored disc, whirling rapidly on its axis. In a few seconds, the edge opened and a straight line shot out, the disc unrolling like a tape measure. After a few minutes more, there remained nothing of the disc. It had resolved itself into a perfectly straight many-hued line, miles long. Then the lights went out again. The next spectacle was a demonstration of the solar system. In the center a large sun was seen standing still. Next to the "sun" a small red round globe spun rapidly about it, representing the planet Mercury. Around both the sun and the "planet" Mercury revolved another globe, blue in color; this was Venus. Then followed a white orb, the "Earth" with the moon turning about it. Next came the red planet Mars with its two small moons, then green Jupiter and its moons, and Saturn in yellow. Uranus was orange and lastly came Neptune in pink, all globes and their moons traveling in their proper orbits around the "sun." While the spectacle was in progress a white "comet" with a long tail traveled across the paths of the planets, turned a sharp corner around the "sun," its tail always pointing away from that body, recrossed the orbits of the "planets" again on the other side and lost itself in the darkness.

Several other spectacles were presented, each more superb than the one preceding it. The carnival closed with a light-picture of the Planet Governor. This was exhibited for fully five minutes during which time the applause was continuous.

"We have never seen such a marvelous spectacle," James 212B 422 declared. "You Americans still lead the world. Upon my word, the old saying that 'nothing is impossible in America,' still holds good."

It was after one when they reached the house, and Ralph suggested a light lunch before they retired for what remained of the night. The others assented and Ralph led the way to the *Bacillatorium*.

The Bacillatorium, invented in 2509 by the Swede 1A 299, was a small room, the walls and bottom of which were composed of lead. On each of the four sides were large vacuum bulbs on pedestals. These tubes, a foot in height and about six inches thick and two feet in diameter, were each equipped with a large concave Radio-arcturium cathode. The glass of the tube in front of the cathode had a double wall, the space between being filled with helium gas.

The rays emanating from the cathode, when the tube was energized with high oscillatory currents, were called *Arcturium Rays* and would instantly destroy any bacilli exposed to them for a few seconds. Arcturium Rays, like X rays, pass through solid objects, and when used alone burned the tissue of the human body. It was found, however, that by filtering arcturium rays through helium no burns would result, but any germ or bacillus in or on the body would be killed at once.

The Bacillatorium was prescribed by law and each citizen ordered to use it at least every other day, thus making it impossible for the human body to develop contagious diseases. As late as the twentieth century more than half the mortality was directly attributable to diseases communicated by germs or bacilli.

The Bacillatorium eradicated such diseases. The arcturium rays, moreover, had a highly beneficial effect on animal tissue and the enforced use of the Bacillatorium extended the span of human life to between one hundred and twenty and one hundred and forty years, where in former centuries three score and ten was the average.

Coming Attraction

Fritz Leiber

The coupe with the fishhooks welded to the fender shouldered up over the curb like the nose of a nightmare. The girl in its path stood frozen, her face probably stiff with fright under her mask. For once my reflexes weren't shy. I took a fast step toward her, grabbed her elbow, yanked her back. Her black skirt swirled out.

The big coupe shot by, its turbine humming. I glimpsed three faces. Something ripped. I felt the hot exhaust on my ankles as the big coupe swerved back into the street. A thick cloud like a black flower blossomed from its jouncing rear end, while from the fishhooks flew a black shimmering rag.

"Did they get you?" I asked the girl.

She had twisted around to look where the side of her skirt was torn away. She was wearing nylon tights.

"The hooks didn't touch me," she said shakily. "I guess I'm lucky."

I heard voices around us:

"Those kids! What'll they think up next?"

"They're a menace. They ought to be arrested."

Sirens screamed at a rising pitch as two motor police, their rocket-assist jets full on, came whizzing toward us after the coupe. But the black flower had become an inky fog obscuring the whole street. The motor police switched from rocket assists to rocket brakes and swerved to a stop near the smoke cloud.

"Are you English?" the girl asked me. "You have an English accent." Her voice came shudderingly from behind the sleek black satin mask. I fancied her teeth must be chattering. Eyes that were perhaps blue searched my face from behind the black gauze covering the eyeholes of the mask.

I told her she'd guessed right.

She stood close to me. "Will you come to my place tonight?" she asked rapidly. "I can't thank you now. And there's something else you can help me about."

My arm, still lightly circling her waist, felt her body trembling. I was answering the plea in that as much as in her voice when I said, "Certainly."

She gave me an address south of Inferno, an apartment number and a time. She asked me my name and I told her.

"Hey, you!"

I turned obediently to the policeman's shout. He shooed away the small clucking crowd of masked women and barefaced men. Coughing from the smoke that the black coupe had thrown out, he asked for my papers. I handed him the essential ones.

He looked at them and then at me. "British Barter? How long will you be in New York?"

Suppressing the urge to say, "For as short a time as possible." I told him I'd be here for a week or so.

"May need you as a witness," he explained. "Those kids can't use smoke on us. When they do that, we pull them in."

He seemed to think the smoke was the bad thing. "They tried to kill the lady," I pointed out.

He shook his head wisely. "They always pretend they're going to, but actually they just want to snag skirts. I've picked up rippers with as many as fifty skirt snags tacked up in their rooms. Of course, sometimes they come a little too close."

I explained that if I hadn't yanked her out of the way she'd have been hit by more than hooks. But he interrupted. "If she'd thought it was a real murder attempt, she'd have stayed here."

I looked around. It was true. She was gone.

"She was fearfully frightened," I told him.

"Who wouldn't be? Those kids would have scared old Stalin himself."

"I mean frightened of more than 'kids.' They didn't look like kids."

"What did they look like?"

I tried without much success to describe the three faces. A vague impression of viciousness and effeminacy doesn't mean much.

"Well, I could be wrong," he said finally. "Do you know the girl? Where she lives?"

"No," I half lied.

The other policeman hung up his radiophone and ambled toward us, kicking at the tendrils of dissipating smoke. The black cloud no longer hid the dingy façades with their five-year-old radiation flash burns, and I could begin to make out the distant stump of the Empire State Building, thrusting up out of Inferno like a mangled finger.

"They haven't been picked up so far," the approaching policeman grumbled. "Left smoke for five blocks, from what Ryan says."

The first policeman shook his head. "That's bad," he observed solemnly.

I was feeling a bit uneasy and ashamed. An Englishman shouldn't lie, at least not on impulse.

"They sound like nasty customers," the first policeman continued in the same grim tone. "We'll need witnesses. Looks as if you may have to stay in New York longer than you expect."

I got the point. I said, "I forgot to show you all my papers," and handed him a few others, making sure there was a five-dollar bill in among them.

When he handed them back a bit later, his voice was no longer ominous. My feelings of guilt vanished. To cement our relationship, I chatted with the two of them about their job.

"I suppose the masks give you some trouble," I observed. "Over in England we've been reading about your new crop of masked female bandits."

"Those things get exaggerated," the first policeman assured me. "It's the men masking as women that really mix us up. But, brother, when we nab them, we jump on them with both feet."

"And you get so you can spot women almost as well as if they had naked faces," the second policeman volunteered. "You know, hands and all that."

"Especially all that," the first agreed with a chuckle. "Say, is it true that some girls don't mask over in England?"

"A number of them have picked up the fashion," I told him. "Only a few, though—the ones who always adopt the latest style, however extreme."

"They're usually masked in the British newscasts."

"I imagine it's arranged that way out of deference to American taste," I confessed. "Actually, not very many do mask."

The second policeman considered that. "Girls going down the street bare from the neck up." It was not clear whether he viewed the prospect with relish or moral distate. Likely both.

"A few members keep trying to persuade Parliament to enact a law forbidding all masking," I continued, talking perhaps a bit too much.

The second policeman shook his head. "What an idea. You know, masks are a pretty good thing, brother. Couple of years more and I'm going to make my wife wear hers around the house."

The first policeman shrugged. "If women were to stop wearing masks, in six weeks you wouldn't know the difference. You get used to anything, if enough people do or don't do it."

I agreed, rather regretfully, and left them. I turned north on Broadway (old Tenth Avenue, I believe) and walked rapidly until I was beyond Inferno. Passing such an area of undecontaminated radioactivity always makes a person queasy. I thanked God there weren't any such in England, as yet.

The street was almost empty, though I was accosted by a couple of beggars with faces tunneled by H-bomb scars, whether real or of make-up putty I couldn't tell. A fat woman held out a baby with webbed fingers and toes. I told myself it would have been deformed anyway and that she was only capitalizing on our fear of bomb-induced mutations. Still, I gave her a seven-and-a-half-cent piece. Her mask made me feel I was paying tribute to an African fetish.

"May all your children be blessed with one head and two eyes, sir."

"Thanks," I said, shuddering, and hurried past her.

". . . There's only trash behind the mask, so turn your head, stick to your task: Stay away, stay away—from—the—girls!"

This last was the end of an anti-sex song being sung by some religionists half a block from the circle-and-cross insignia of a femalist temple. They reminded me only faintly of our small tribe of British monastics. Above their heads was a jumble of billboards advertising predigested foods, wrestling instruction, radio handies and the like.

I stared at the hysterical slogans with disagreeable fascination. Since the female face and form have been banned on American signs, the very letters of the advertiser's alphabet have begun to crawl with sex—the fat-bellied, big-breasted capital *B,* the lascivious double *O.* However, I reminded myself, it is chiefly the mask that so strangely accents sex in America.

A British anthropologist has pointed out that, while it took more than five thousand years to shift the chief point of sexual interest from the hips to the breasts, the next transition, to the face, has taken less than fifty years. Comparing the American style with Moslem tradition is not valid; Moslem women are compelled to wear veils, the purpose of which is to make a husband's property private, while American women have only the compulsion of fashion and use masks to create mystery.

Theory aside, the actual origins of the trend are to be found in the antiradiation clothing of World War III, which led to masked wrestling, now a fantastically popular sport, and that in turn led to the current female fashion. Only a wild style at first, masks quickly became as necessary as brassieres and lipsticks had been earlier in the century.

I finally realized that I was not speculating about masks in general, but about what lay behind one in particular. That's the devil of the things; you're never sure whether a girl is heightening loveliness or hiding ugliness. I pictured a cool, pretty face in which fear showed only in widened eyes. Then I remembered her blond hair, rich against the blackness of the satin mask. She'd told me to come at the twenty-second hour—10 P.M.

I climbed to my apartment near the British Consulate; the elevator shaft had been shoved out of plumb by an old blast, a nuisance in these tall New York buildings. Before it occurred to me that I would be going out again, I automatically tore a tab from the film strip under my shirt. I developed it just to be sure. It showed that the total radiation I'd taken that day was still within the safety limit. I'm no phobic about it, as so many people are these days, but there's no point in taking chances.

I flopped down on the daybed and stared at the silent speaker and the dark screen of the video set. As always, they made me think, somewhat bitterly, of the two great nations of the world. Mutilated by each other, yet still strong, they were crippled giants poisoning the planet with their respective dreams of an impossible equality and impossible success.

I fretfully switched on the speaker. By luck, the newscaster was talking excitedly of the prospects of a bumper wheat crop, sown by planes across a dust bowl moistened by seeded rains. I listened carefully to the rest of the program (it was remarkably clear of Russian telejamming), but there was no further news of interest to me. And, of course, no mention of the moon, though everyone knows that America and Russia are racing to develop their primary bases into fortresses capable of mutual assault and the launching of alphabet bombs toward Earth. I myself knew perfectly well that the British electronic equipment I was helping trade for American wheat was destined for use in spaceships.

I switched off the newscast. It was growing dark, and once again I pictured a tender, frightened face behind a mask. I hadn't had a date since England. It's exceedingly difficult to become acquainted with a girl in America, where as little as a smile often can set one of them yelping for the police—to say nothing of the increasingly puritanical morality and the roving gangs that keep most women indoors after dark. And, naturally, the masks, which are definitely not, as the Soviets claim, a last invention of capitalist degeneracy, but a sign of great psychological insecurity. The Russians have no masks, but they have their own signs of stress.

I went to the window and impatiently watched the darkness gather. I was getting very restless. After a while a ghostly violent cloud appeared to the south. My hair rose. Then I laughed. I had momentarily fancied it a radiation from the crater of the Hell-bomb, though I should instantly have known it was only the radio-induced glow in the sky over the amusement and residential area south of Inferno.

Promptly at twenty-two hours I stood before the door of my unknown girl friend's apartment. The electronic say-who-please said just that. I answered clearly, "Wysten Turner," wondering if she'd given my name to the mechanism. She evidently had, for the door opened. I walked into a small empty living room, my heart pounding a bit.

The room was expensively furnished with the latest pneumatic hassocks and sprawlers. There were some midgie books on the table. The one I picked up was the standard hard-boiled detective story in which two female murderers go gunning for each other.

The television was on. A masked girl in green was crooning a love song. Her right hand held something that blurred off into the foreground. I saw the set had a handie, which we haven't in England as yet, and curiously thrust my hand into the handie orifice beside the screen. Contrary to my expectations, it was not like slipping into a pulsing rubber glove, but rather as if the girl on the screen actually held my hand.

A door opened behind me. I jerked out my hand with as guilty a reaction as if I'd been caught peering through a keyhole.

She stood in the bedroom doorway. I think she was trembling. She was wearing a gray fur coat, white-speckled, and a gray velvet evening mask with shirred gray lace around the eyes and mouth. Her fingernails twinkled like silver.

It hadn't occurred to me that she'd expect us to go out.

"I should have told you," she said softly. Her mask veered nervously toward the books and the screen and the room's dark corners. "But I can't possibly talk to you here."

I said doubtfully, "There's a place near the Consulate...."

"I know where we can be together and talk," she said rapidly. "If you don't mind."

As we entered the elevator I said, "I'm afraid I dismissed the cab."

But the cab driver hadn't gone, for some reason of his own. He jumped out and smirkingly held the front door open for us. I told him we preferred to sit in back. He sulkily opened the rear door, slammed it after us, jumped in front and slammed the door behind him.

My companion leaned forward. "Heaven," she said.

The driver switched on the turbine and televisor.

"Why did you ask if I were a British subject?" I said, to start the conversation.

She leaned away from me, tilting her mask close to the window. "See the moon," she said in a quick, dreamy voice.

"But why, really?" I pressed, conscious of an irritation that had nothing to do with her.

"It's edging up into the purple of the sky."

"And what's your name?"

"The purple makes it look yellower."

Just then I became aware of the source of my irritation. It lay in the square of writhing light in the front of the cab beside the driver.

I don't object to ordinary wrestling matches, though they bore me, but I simply detest watching a man wrestle a woman. The fact that the bouts are generally "on the level," with the man greatly outclassed in weight and reach and the masked females young and personable, only makes them seem worse to me.

"Please turn off the screen," I requested the driver.

He shook his head without looking around. "Uh-uh, man," he said. "They've been grooming that babe for weeks for this bout with Little Zirk."

Infuriated, I reached forward, but my companion caught my arm. "Please," she whispered frightenedly, shaking her head.

I settled back, frustrated. She was closer to me now, but silent, and for a few moments I watched the heaves and contortions of the powerful masked girl and her wiry masked opponent on the screen. His frantic scrambling at her reminded me of a male spider.

I jerked around, facing my companion. "Why did those three men want to kill you?" I asked sharply.

The eyeholes of her mask faced the screen. "Because they're jealous of me," she whispered.

"Why are they jealous?"

She still didn't look at me. "Because of him."

"Who?"

She didn't answer.

I put my arm around her shoulders. "Are you afraid to tell me?" I asked. "What *is* the matter?"

She still didn't look my way. She smelled nice.

"See here," I said laughingly, changing my tactics, "you really should tell me something about yourself. I don't even know what you look like."

I half playfully lifted my hand to the band of her neck. She gave it an astonishingly swift slap. I pulled it away in sudden pain. There were four tiny indentations on the back. From one of them a tiny bead of blood welled out as I watched. I looked at her silver fingernails and saw they were actually delicate and pointed metal caps.

"I'm dreadfully sorry," I heard her say, "but you frightened me. I thought for a moment you were going to . . ."

At last she turned to me. Her coat had fallen open. Her evening dress was Cretan Revival, a bodice of lace beneath and supporting the breasts without covering them.

"Don't be angry," she said, putting her arms around my neck. "You were wonderful this afternoon."

The soft gray velvet of her mask, molding itself to her cheek, pressed mine. Through the mask's lace the wet warm tip of her tongue touched my chin.

"I'm not angry," I said. "Just puzzled and anxious to help."

The cab stopped. To either side were black windows bordered by spears of broken glass. The sickly purple light showed a few ragged figures slowly moving toward us.

The driver muttered, "It's the turbine, man. We're grounded." He sat there hunched and motionless. "Wish it had happened somewhere else."

My companion whispered, "Five dollars is the usual amount."

She looked out so shudderingly at the congregating figures that I suppressed my indignation and did as she suggested. The driver took the bill without a word. As he started up, he put his hand out the window and I heard a few coins clink on the pavement.

My companion came back into my arms, but her mask faced the television screen, where the tall girl had just pinned the convulsively kicking Little Zirk.

"I'm so frightened," she breathed.

Heaven turned out to be an equally ruinous neighborhood, but it had a club with an awning and a huge doorman uniformed like a spaceman, but in gaudy colors. In my sensuous daze I rather liked it all. We stepped out of the cab just as a drunken old woman came down the sidewalk, her mask awry. A couple ahead of us turned their heads from the half-revealed face as if from an ugly body at the beach. As we followed them in I heard the doorman say, "Get along, Grandma, and cover yourself."

Inside, everything was dimness and blue glows. She had said we could talk here, but I didn't see how. Besides the inevitable chorus of sneezes and coughs (they say America is fifty per cent allergic these days), there was a band going full blast in the latest robop style, in which an electronic composing machine selects an arbitrary sequence of tones into which the musicians weave their raucous little individualities.

Most of the people were in booths. The band was behind the bar. On a small platform beside them a girl was dancing, stripped to her mask. The little cluster of men at the shadowy far end of the bar weren't looking at her.

We inspected the menu in gold script on the wall and pushed the buttons for breast of chicken, fried shrimps and two Scotches. Moments later, the serving bell tinkled. I opened the gleaming panel and took out our drinks.

The cluster of men at the bar filed off toward the door, but first they stared around the room. My companion had just thrown back her coat. Their look lingered on our booth. I noticed that there were three of them.

The band chased off the dancing girls with growls. I handed my companion a straw and we sipped our drinks.

"You wanted me to help you about something," I said. "Incidentally, I think you're lovely."

She nodded quick thanks, looked around, leaned forward. "Would it be hard for me to get to England?"

"No," I replied, a bit taken aback. "Provided you have an American passport."

"Are they difficult to get?"

"Rather," I said, surprised at her lack of information. "Your country doesn't like its nationals to travel, though it isn't quite as stringent as Russia."

"Could the British Consulate help me get a passport?"

"It's hardly their—"

"Could you?"

I realized we were being inspected. A man and two girls had paused opposite our table. The girls were tall and wolfish-looking, with spangled masks. The man stood jauntily between them like a fox on its hind legs.

My companion didn't glance at them, but she sat back. I noticed that one of the girls had a big yellow bruise on her forearm. After a moment they walked to a booth in the deep shadows.

"Know them?" I asked. She didn't reply. I finished my drink.

"I'm not sure you'd like England," I said. "The austerity's altogether different from your American brand of misery."

She leaned forward again. "But I must get away," she whispered.

"Why?" I was getting impatient.

"Because I'm so frightened."

There was chimes. I opened the panel and handed her the fried shrimps. The sauce on my breast of chicken was a delicious steaming compound of almonds, soy and ginger. But something must have been wrong with the radionic oven that had thawed and heated it, for at the first bite I crunched a kernel of ice in the meat. These delicate mechanisms need constant repair and there aren't enough mechanics.

I put down my fork. "What are you really scared of?" I asked her.

For once her mask didn't waver away from my face. As I waited I could feel the fears gathering without her naming them, tiny dark shapes swarming through the curved night outside, converging on the radioactive pest spot of New York, dipping into the margins of the purple. I felt a sudden rush of sympathy, a desire to protect the girl opposite me. The warm feeling added itself to the infatuation engendered in the cab.

"Everything," she said finally.

I nodded and touched her hand.

"I'm afraid of the moon," she began, her voice going dreamy and brittle, as it had in the cab. "You can't look at it and not think of guided bombs."

"It's the same moon over England," I reminded her.

"But it's not England's moon any more. It's ours and Russia's. You're not responsible. Oh, and then," she said with a tilt of her mask, "I'm afraid of the cars and the gangs and the loneliness and Inferno. I'm afraid of the lust that undresses your face. And"—her voice hushed—"I'm afraid of the wrestlers."

"Yes?" I prompted softly after a moment.

Her mask came forward. "Do you know something about the wrestlers?" she asked rapidly. "The ones that wrestle women, I mean. They often lose, you know. And then they have to have a girl to take their frustration out on. A girl who's soft and weak and terribly frightened. They need that, to keep them men. Other men don't want them to have a girl. Other men want them just to fight women and be heroes. But they must have a girl. It's horrible for her."

I squeezed her fingers tighter, as if courage could be transmitted— granting I had any. "I think I can get you to England," I said.

Shadows crawled onto the table and stayed there. I looked up at the three men who had been at the end of the bar. They were the men I had seen in the big coupe. They wore black sweaters and close-fitting black trousers. Their faces were as expressionless as dopers. Two of them stood about me. The other loomed over the girl.

"Drift off, man," I was told. I heard the other inform the girl, "We'll wrestle a fall, sister. What shall it be? Judo, slapsie or kill-who-can?"

I stood up. There are times when an Englishman simply must be maltreated. But just then the foxlike man came gliding in like the star of a ballet. The reaction of the other three startled me. They were acutely embarrassed.

He smiled at them thinly. "You won't win my favor by tricks like this," he said.

"Don't get the wrong idea, Zirk," one of them pleaded.

"I will if it's right," he said. "She told me what you tried to do this afternoon. That won't endear you to me, either. Drift."

They backed off awkwardly. "Let's get out of here," one of them said loudly as they turned. "I know a place where they fight naked with knives."

Little Zirk laughed musically and slipped into the seat beside my companion. She shrank from him, just a little. I pushed my feet back, leaned forward.

"Who's your friend, baby?" he asked, not looking at her.

She passed the question to me with a little gesture. I told him.

"British," he observed. "She's been asking you about getting out of the country? About passports?" He smiled pleasantly. "She likes to start running away. Don't you, baby?" His small hand began to stroke her wrist, the fingers bent a little, the tendons ridged, as if he were about to grab and twist.

"Look here," I said sharply. "I have to be grateful to you for ordering off those bullies, but—"

"Think nothing of it," he told me. "They're no harm except when they're behind steering wheels. A well-trained fourteen-year-old girl could cripple any one of them. Why, even Theda here, if she went in for that sort of thing . . ." He turned to her, shifting his hand from her wrist to her hair. He stroked it, letting the strands slip slowly through his fingers. "You know I lost tonight, baby, don't you?" he said softly.

I stood up. "Come along," I said to her. "Let's leave."

She just sat there. I couldn't even tell if she was trembling. I tried to read a message in her eyes through the mask.

"I'll take you away," I said to her. "I can do it. I really will."

He smiled at me. "She'd like to go with you," he said. "Wouldn't you, baby?"

"Will you or won't you?" I said to her. She still just sat there.

He slowly knotted his fingers in her hair.

"Listen, you little vermin," I snapped at him. "Take your hands off her."

He came up from the seat like a snake. I'm no fighter. I just know that the more scared I am, the harder and straighter I hit. This time I was lucky. But as he crumped back I felt a slap and four stabs of pain in my cheek. I clapped my hand to it. I could feel the four gashes made by her dagger finger caps, and the warm blood oozing out from them.

She didn't look at me. She was bending over Little Zirk and cuddling her mask to his cheek and crooning, "There, there, don't feel bad, you'll be able to hurt me afterward."

There were sounds around us, but they didn't come close. I leaned forward and ripped the mask from her face.

I really don't know why I should have expected her face to be anything else. It was very pale, of course, and there weren't any cosmetics. I suppose there's no point in wearing any under a mask. The eyebrows were untidy and the lips chapped. But as for the general expression, as for the feelings crawling and wriggling across it . . .

Have you ever lifted a rock from damp soil? Have you ever watched the slimy white grubs?

I looked down at her, she up at me. "Yes, you're so frightened, aren't you?" I said sarcastically. "You dread this little nightly drama, don't you? You're scared to death."

And I walked right out into the purple night, still holding my hand to my bleeding cheek. No one stopped me, not even the girl wrestlers. I wished I could tear a tab from under my shirt and test it then and there, and find I'd taken too much radiation, and so be able to ask to cross the Hudson and go down New Jersey, past the lingering radiance of the Narrows Bomb, and so on to Sandy Hook to wait for the rusty ship that would take me back over the seas to England.

The Luckiest Man in Denv

C. M. Kornbluth

May's man Reuben, of the eighty-third level, Atomist, knew there was something wrong when the binoculars flashed and then went opaque. Inwardly he cursed, hoping that he had not committed himself to anything. Outwardly he was unperturbed. He handed the binoculars back to Rudolph's man Almon, of the eighty-ninth level, Maintainer, with a smile.

"They aren't very good," he said.

Almon put them to his own eyes, glanced over the parapet, and swore mildly. "Blacker than the heart of a crazy Angelo, eh? Never mind; here's another pair."

This pair was unremarkable. Through it, Reuben studied the thousand setbacks and penthouses of Denv that ranged themselves below. He was too worried to enjoy his first sight of the vista from the eighty-ninth level, but he let out a murmur of appreciation. Now to get away from this suddenly sinister fellow and try to puzzle it out.

"Could we—?" he asked cryptically, with a little upward jerk of his chin.

"It's better not to," Almon said hastily, taking the glasses from his hands. "What if somebody with stars happened to see, you know? How'd *you* like it if you saw some impudent fellow peering up at you?"

"He wouldn't dare!" said Reuben, pretending to be stupid and indignant, and joined a moment later in Almon's sympathetic laughter.

"Never mind," said Almon. "We are young. Some day, who knows? Perhaps we shall look from the ninety-fifth level, or the hundredth."

Though Reuben knew that the Maintainer was no friend of his, the generous words sent blood hammering through his veins; ambition fired him for a moment.

He pulled a long face and told Almon: "Let us hope so. Thank you for being my host. Now I must return to my quarters."

He left the windy parapet for the serene luxury of an eighty-ninth-level corridor and descended slow-moving stairs through gradually less luxurious levels to his own Spartan floor. Selene was waiting, smiling, as he stepped off the stairs.

She was decked out nicely—too nicely. She wore a steely hued corselet and a touch of scent; her hair was dressed long. The combination appealed to him, and instantly he was on his guard. Why had she gone to the trouble of learning his tastes? What was she up to? After all, she was Griffin's woman.

"Coming *down?*" she asked, awed. "Where have you been?"

"The eighty-ninth, as a guest of that fellow Almon. The vista is immense."

"I've never been . . ." she murmured, and then said decisively: "You belong up there. And higher. Griffin laughs at me, but he's a fool. Last night in chamber we got to talking about you, I don't know how, and he finally became quite angry and said he didn't want to hear another word." She smiled wickedly. "I was revenged, though."

Blank-faced, he said: "You must be a good hand at revenge, Selene, and at stirring up the need for it."

The slight hardening of her smile meant that he had scored, and he hurried by with a rather formal salutation.

Burn him for an Angelo, but she was easy enough to take! The contrast of the metallic garment with her soft, white skin was disturbing, and her long hair suggested things. It was hard to think of her as scheming something or other; scheming Selene was displaced in his mind by Selene in chamber.

But what was she up to? Had she perhaps heard that he was to be elevated? Was Griffin going to be swooped on by the Maintainers? Was he to kill off Griffin so she could leech onto some rising third party? Was she perhaps merely giving her man a touch of the lash?

He wished gloomily that the binoculars-problem and the Selene-problem had not come together. That trickster Almon had spoken of youth as though it were something for congratulation; he hated being young and stupid and unable to puzzle out the faulty binoculars and the warmth of Griffin's woman.

The attack alarm roared through the Spartan corridor. He ducked through the nearest door into a vacant bedroom and under the heavy steel table. Somebody else floundered under the table a moment later, and a third person tried to join them.

The firstcomer roared: "Get out and find your own shelter! I don't propose to be crowded out by you or to crowd you out either and see your ugly blood and brains if there's a hit. Go, now!"

"Forgive me, sir. At once, sir!" the latecomer wailed; and scrambled away as the alarm continued to roar.

Reuben gasped at the "sirs" and looked at his neighbor. It was May! Trapped, no doubt, on an inspection tour of the level.

"Sir," he said respectfully, "if you wish to be alone, I can find another room."

"You may stay with me for company. Are you one of mine?" There was power in the general's voice and on his craggy face.

"Yes, sir. May's man Reuben, of the eighty-third level, Atomist."

May surveyed him, and Reuben noted that there were pouches of skin depending from cheekbones and the jawline—dead-looking, coarse-pored skin.

"You're a well-made boy, Reuben. Do you have women?"

"Yes, sir," said Reuben hastily. "One after another—I *always* have women. I'm making up at this time to a charming thing called Selene. Well-rounded, yet firm, soft but supple, with long red hair and long white legs—"

"Spare me the details," muttered the general. "It takes all kinds. An Atomist, you said. That has a future, to be sure. I myself was a Controller long ago. The calling seems to have gone out of fashion—"

Abruptly the alarm stopped. The silence was hard to bear.

May swallowed and went on: "—for some reason or other. Why don't youngsters elect for Controller any more? Why didn't you, for instance?"

Reuben wished he could be saved by a direct hit. The binoculars, Selene, the raid, and now he was supposed to make intelligent conversation with a general.

"I really don't know, sir," he said miserably. "At the time there seemed to be very little difference—Controller, Atomist, Missiler, Maintainer. We have a saying, 'The buttons are different,' which usually ends any conversation on the subject."

"Indeed?" asked May distractedly. His face was thinly filmed with sweat. "Do you suppose Ellay intends to clobber us this time?" he asked almost hoarsely. "It's been some weeks since they made a maximum effort, hasn't it?"

"Four," said Reuben. "I remember because one of my best Servers was killed by a falling corridor roof—the only fatality and it had to happen to my team!"

He laughed nervously and realized that he was talking like a fool, but May seemed not to notice.

Far below them, there was a series of screaming whistles as the interceptors were loosed to begin their intricate, double basketwork wall of defense in a towering cylinder about Denv.

"Go on, Reuben," said May. "That was most interesting." His eyes were searching the underside of the steel table.

Reuben averted his own eyes from the frightened face, feeling some awe drain out of him. Under a table with a general! It didn't seem so strange now.

"Perhaps, sir, you can tell me what a puzzling thing, that happened this afternoon, means. A fellow—Rudolph's man Almon, of the eighty-ninth level—gave me a pair of binoculars that flashed in my eyes and then went opaque. Has your wide experience—"

May laughed hoarsely and said in a shaky voice: "That old trick! He was photographing your retinas for the blood-vessel pattern. One of Rudolph's men, eh? I'm glad you spoke to me; I'm old enough to spot a revival like that. Perhaps my good friend Rudolph plans—"

There was a thudding volley in the air and then a faint jar. One had got through, exploding, from the feel of it, far down at the foot of Denv.

The alarm roared again, in bursts that meant all clear; only one flight of missiles and that disposed of.

The Atomist and the general climbed out from under the table; May's secretary popped through the door. The general waved him out again and leaned heavily on the table, his arms quivering. Reuben hastily brought a chair.

"A glass of water," said May.

The Atomist brought it. He saw the general wash down what looked like a triple dose of xxx—green capsules which it was better to leave alone.

May said after a moment: "That's better. And don't look so shocked, youngster; you don't know the strain we're under. It's only a temporary measure which I shall discontinue as soon as things ease up a bit. I was saying that perhaps my good friend Rudolph plans to substitute one of his men for one of mine. Tell me, how long has this fellow Almon been a friend of yours?"

"He struck up an acquaintance with me only last week. I should have realized—"

"You certainly should have. One week. Time enough and more. By now you've been photographed, your fingerprints taken, your voice recorded and your gait studied without your knowledge. Only the retinascope is difficult, but one must risk it for a real double. Have you killed your man, Reuben?"

He nodded. It had been a silly brawl two years ago over precedence at the refectory; he disliked being reminded of it.

"Good," said May grimly. "The way these things are done, your double kills you in a secluded spot, disposes of your body, and takes over your role. We shall reverse it. You will kill the double and take over *his* role.''

The powerful, methodical voice ticked off possibilities and contingencies, measures and countermeasures. Reuben absorbed them and felt his awe return. Perhaps May had not really been frightened under the table; perhaps it had been he reading his own terror in the general's face. May was actually talking to him of backgrounds and policies. ''Up from the eighty-third level!'' he swore to himself as the great names were uttered.

''My good friend Rudolph, of course, wants the five stars. You would not know this, but the man who wears the stars is now eighty years old and failing fast. I consider myself a likely candidate to replace him. So, evidently, must Rudolph. No doubt he plans to have your double perpetrate some horrible blunder on the eve of the election, and the discredit would reflect on me. Now what you and I must do—''

You and I—May's man Reuben and May—up from the eighty-third! Up from the bare corridors and cheerless bedrooms to marble halls and vaulted chambers! From the clatter of the crowded refectory to small and glowing restaurants where you had your own table and servant and where music came softly from the walls! Up from the scramble to win this woman or that, by wit or charm or the poor bribes you could afford, to the eminence from which you could calmly command your pick of the beauty of Denv! From the moiling intrigue of tripping your fellow Atomist and guarding against him tripping you to the heroic thrust and parry of generals!

Up from the eighty-third!

Then May dismissed him with a speech whose implications were deliriously exciting. ''I need an able man and a young one, Reuben. Perhaps I've waited too long looking for him. If you do well in this touchy business, I'll consider you very seriously for an important task I have in mind.''

Late that night, Selene came to his bedroom.

''I know you don't like me,'' she said pettishly, ''but Griffin's such a fool and I wanted somebody to talk to. Do you mind? What was it like up there today? Did you see carpets? I wish I had a carpet.''

He tried to think about carpets and not the exciting contrast of metallic cloth and flesh.

''I saw one through an open door,'' he remembered. ''It looked odd, but I suppose a person gets used to them. Perhaps I didn't see a very good one. Aren't the good ones very thick?''

''Yes,'' she said. ''Your feet sink into them. I wish I had a *good* carpet and four chairs and a small table as high as my knees to put things on and as many pillows as I wanted. Griffin's such a fool. Do you think I'll ever get those things? I've never caught the eye of a general. Am I pretty enough to get one, do you think?''

He said uneasily: "Of course you're a pretty thing, Selene. But carpets and chairs and pillows—" It made him uncomfortable, like the thought of peering up through binoculars from a parapet.

"I want them," she said unhappily. "I like you very much, but I want so many things and soon I'll be too old even for the eighty-third level, before I've been up higher, and I'll spend the rest of my life tending babies or cooking in the creche or the refectory.''

She stopped abruptly, pulled herself together and gave him a smile that was somehow ghastly in the half-light.

"You bungler," he said, and she instantly looked at the door with the smile frozen on her face. Reuben took a pistol from under his pillow and demanded, "When do you expect him?''

"What do you mean?" she asked shrilly. "Who are you talking about?''

"My double. Don't be a fool, Selene. May and I—" he savored it—"May and I know all about it. He warned me to beware of a diversion by a woman while the double slipped in and killed me. When do you expect him?''

"I really *do* like you," Selene sobbed. "But Almon promised to take me up there and I *knew* when I was where they'd see me that I'd meet somebody really important. I really do like you, but soon I'll be too old—''

"Selene, listen to me. Listen to me! You'll get your chance. Nobody but you and me will know that the substitution didn't succeed!''

"Then I'll be spying for you on Almon, won't I?" she asked in a choked voice. "All I wanted was a few nice things before I got too old. All right, I was supposed to be in your arms at 2350 hours.''

It was 2349. Reuben sprang from bed and stood by the door, his pistol silenced and ready. At 2350 a naked man slipped swiftly into the room, heading for the bed as he raised a ten-centimeter poniard. He stopped in dismay when he realized that the bed was empty.

Reuben killed him with a bullet through the throat.

"But he doesn't look a bit like me," he said in bewilderment, closely examining the face. "Just in a general way.''

Selene said dully: "Almon told me people always say that when they see their doubles. It's funny, isn't it? He looks just like you, really.''

"How was my body to be disposed of?''

She produced a small flat box. "A shadow suit. You were to be left here and somebody would come tomorrow."

"We won't disappoint him." Reuben pulled the web of the shadow suit over his double and turned on the power. In the half-lit room, it was a perfect disappearance; by daylight it would be less perfect. "They'll ask why the body was shot instead of knifed. Tell them you shot me with the gun from under the pillow. Just say I heard the double come in and you were afraid there might have been a struggle."

She listlessly asked: "How do you know I won't betray you?"

"You won't, Selene." His voice bit. "You're *broken*."

She nodded vaguely, started to say something, and then went out without saying it.

Reuben luxuriously stretched in his narrow bed. Later, his beds would be wider and softer, he thought. He drifted into sleep on a half-formed thought that some day he might vote with other generals on the man to wear the five stars—or even wear them himself, Master of Denv.

He slept healthily through the morning alarm and arrived late at his regular twentieth-level station. He saw his superior, May's man Oscar of the eighty-fifth level, Atomist, ostentatiously take his name. Let him!

Oscar assembled his crew for a grim announcement: "We are going to even the score, and perhaps a little better, with Ellay. At sunset there will be three flights of missiles from Deck One."

There was a joyous murmur and Reuben trotted off on his task.

All forenoon he was occupied with drawing plutonium slugs from hypersuspicious storekeepers in the great rock-quarried vaults, and seeing them through countless audits and assays all the way to Weapons Assembly. Oscar supervised the scores there who assembled the curved slugs and the explosive lenses into sixty-kilogram warheads.

In mid-afternoon there was an incident. Reuben saw Oscar step aside for a moment to speak to a Maintainer whose guard fell on one of the Assembly Servers, and dragged him away as he pleaded innocence. He had been detected in sabotage. When the warheads were in and the missilers seated, waiting at their boards, the two Atomists rode up to the eighty-third's refectory.

The news of a near-maximum effort was in the air; it was electric. Reuben heard on all sides in tones of self-congratulation: "We'll clobber them tonight!"

"That Server you caught," he said to Oscar. "What was he up to?"

His commander stared. "Are you trying to learn my job? Don't try it, I warn you. If my black marks against you aren't enough, I could always arrange for some fissionable material in your custody to go astray."

"No, no! I was just wondering why people do something like that."

Oscar sniffed doubtfully. "He's probably insane, like all the Angelos. I've heard the climate does it to them. You're not a Maintainer or a Controller. Why worry about it?"

"They'll brainburn him, I suppose?"

"I suppose. *Listen!*"

Deck One was firing. One, two, three, four, five, six. One, two, three, four, five, six. One, two, three, four, five, six.

People turned to one another and shook hands, laughed and slapped shoulders heartily. Eighteen missiles were racing through the stratosphere, soon to tumble on Ellay. With any luck, one or two would slip through the first wall of interceptors and blast close enough to smash windows and topple walls in the crazy city by the ocean. It would serve the lunatics right.

Five minutes later an exultant voice filled most of Denv.

"Recon missile report," it said. "Eighteen launched, eighteen perfect trajectories. Fifteen shot down by Ellay first-line interceptors, three shot down by Ellay second-line interceptors. Extensive blast damage observed in Griffith Park area of Ellay!"

There were cheers.

And eight Full Maintainers marched into the refectory silently, and marched out with Reuben.

He knew better than to struggle or ask futile questions. Any question you asked of a Maintainer was futile. But he goggled when they marched him onto an upward-bound stairway.

They rode past the eighty-ninth level and Reuben lost count, seeing only the marvels of the upper reaches of Denv. He saw carpets that ran the entire length of corridors, and intricate fountains, and mosaic walls, stained-glass windows, more wonders than he could recognize, things for which he had no name.

He was marched at last into a wood-paneled room with a great polished desk and a map behind it. He saw May, and another man who must have been a general—Rudolph?—but sitting at the desk was a frail old man who wore a circlet of stars on each khaki shoulder.

The old man said to Reuben: "You are an Ellay spy and saboteur."

Reuben looked at May. Did one speak directly to the man who wore the stars, even in reply to such an accusation?

"Answer him, Reuben," May said kindly.

"I am May's man Reuben, of the eighty-third level, an Atomist," he said.

"Explain," said the other general heavily, "if you can, why all eighteen of the warheads you procured today failed to fire."

"But they did!" gasped Reuben. "The Recon missile report said there was blast damage from the three that got through and it didn't say anything about the others failing to fire."

The other general suddenly looked sick and May looked even kindlier. The man who wore the stars turned inquiringly to the chief of the Maintainers, who nodded and said: "That was the Recon missile report, sir."

The general snapped: "What I said was that he would *attempt* to sabotage the attack. Evidently he failed. I also said he is a faulty double, somehow slipped with great ease into my good friend May's organization. You will find that his left thumbprint is a clumsy forgery of the real Reuben's thumbprint and that his hair has been artificially darkened."

The old man nodded at the chief of the Maintainers, who said: "We have his card, sir."

Reuben abruptly found himself being fingerprinted and deprived of some hair.

"The f.p.'s check, sir," one Maintainer said. "He's Reuben."

"Hair's natural, sir," said another.

The general began a rearguard action: "My information about his hair seems to have been inaccurate. But the fingerprint means only that Ellay spies substituted his prints for Reuben's prints in the files—"

"Enough, sir," said the old man with the stars. "Dismissed. All of you. Rudolph, I am surprised. All of you, go."

Reuben found himself in a vast apartment with May, who was bubbling and chuckling uncontrollably until he popped three of the green capsules into his mouth hurriedly.

"This means the eclipse for years of my good friend Rudolph," he crowed. "His game was to have your double sabotage the attack warheads and so make it appear that my organization is rotten with spies. The double must have been under posthypnotic, primed to admit everything. Rudolph was so sure of himself that he made his accusations before the attack, the fool!"

He fumbled out the green capsules again.

"Sir," said Reuben, alarmed.

"Only temporary," May muttered, and swallowed a fourth. "But you're right. You leave them alone. There are big things to be done in your time, not in mine. I told you I needed a young man who could claw his way to the top. Rudolph's a fool. He doesn't need the capsules because he doesn't ask questions. Funny, I thought a coup like the double affair would hit me hard, but I don't feel a thing. It's not like the old days. I used to plan and plan, and when the trap went *snap* it was better than this stuff. But now I don't feel a thing.''

He leaned forward from his chair; the pupils of his eyes were black bullets.

"Do you want to *work?*" he demanded. "Do you want your world stood on its head and your brains to crack and do the only worthwhile job there is to do? Answer me!''

"Sir, I am a loyal May's man. I want to obey your orders and use my ability to the full.''

"Good enough,'' said the general. "You've got brains, you've got push. I'll do the spadework. I won't last long enough to push it through. You'll have to follow. Ever been outside of Denv?''

Reuben stiffened.

"I'm not accusing you of being a spy. It's really all right to go outside of Denv. I've been outside. There isn't much to see at first—a lot of ground pocked and torn up by shorts and overs from Ellay and us. Farther out, especially east, it's different. Grass, trees, flowers. Places where you could grow food.

"When I went outside, it troubled me. It made me ask questions. I wanted to know how we started. Yes—started. *It wasn't always like this.* Somebody built Denv. Am I getting the idea across to you? *It wasn't always like this!*

"Somebody set up the reactors to breed uranium and make plutonium. Somebody tooled us up for the missiles. Somebody wired the boards to control them. Somebody started the hydroponics tanks.

"I've dug through the archives. Maybe I found something. I saw mountains of strength reports, ration reports, supply reports, and yet I never got back to the beginning. I found a piece of paper and maybe I understood it and maybe I didn't. It was about the water of the Colorado River and who should get how much of it. How can you divide water in a river? But it could have been the start of Denv, Ellay, and the missile attacks.''

The general shook his head, puzzled, and went on: "I don't see clearly what's ahead. I want to make peace between Denv and Ellay, but I don't know how to start or what it will be like. I think it must mean not firing, not even making any more weapons. Maybe it means that some of us, or a lot of us, will go out of Denv and live a different kind of life. That's why I've clawed my way up. That's why I need a young man who can claw with the best of them. Tell me what you think.''

''I think,'' said Reuben measuredly, ''it's magnificent—the salvation of Denv. I'll back you to my dying breath if you'll let me.''

May smiled tiredly and leaned back in the chair as Reuben tiptoed out.

What luck, Reuben thought—what unbelievable luck to be at a fulcrum of history like this!

He searched the level for Rudolph's apartment and gained admission.

To the general, he said: ''Sir, I have to report that your friend May is insane. He has just been raving to me, advocating the destruction of civilization as we know it, and urging me to follow in his footsteps. I pretended to agree—since I can be of greater service to you if I'm in May's confidence.''

''So?'' said Rudolph thoughtfully. ''Tell me about the double. How did that go wrong?''

''The bunglers were Selene and Almon. Selene because she alarmed me instead of distracting me. Almon because he failed to recognize her incompetence.''

''They shall be brainburned. That leaves an eighty-ninth-level vacancy in my organization, doesn't it?''

''You're very kind, sir, but I think I should remain May's man— outwardly. If I earn any rewards, I can wait for them. I presume that May will be elected to wear the five stars. He won't live more than two years after that, at the rate he is taking drugs.''

''We can shorten it,'' grinned Rudolph. ''I have pharmacists who can see that his drugs are more than normal strength.''

''That would be excellent, sir. When he is too enfeebled to discharge his duties, there may be an attempt to rake up the affair of the double to discredit you. I could then testify that I was your man all along and that May coerced me.''

They put their heads together, the two saviors of civilization as they knew it, and conspired ingeniously long into the endless night.

10

Apocalypse
Jack Williamson and David Ketterer

In many ways *The Time Machine* by H. G. Wells provides a kind of science fiction paradigm. Certainly, most of the themes presented in the preceding sections could be illustrated by aspects of that book. But the Time Traveller's most affecting and familiar experience, perhaps the most mythopoeic passage in Wells's entire work, concerns a dying world and intimations of its end. It is imaged in terms of an eclipse of the sun. The Time Traveller is situated on a "desolate beach." Human life emerged from the sea and might appropriately be conceived, both here and in Nevil Shute's *On the Beach,* as ending where it began. Indeed, one might adopt the title of J. G. Ballard's well-known novel and credit Wells with creating "the terminal beach" myth.

The end of the world or universe is commonly referred to as the apocalypse. This accurate but limited sense of the word can be paralleled by the limited sense many people have of science fiction. Thanks to the cinematic exploitation of science fiction, the notion is current that the genre is essentially about world destruction, or at least the threat of world destruction narrowly averted. Of course, this theme does have an honorable tradition within science fiction and should, perhaps, be related to the myth of Atlantis. Nineteenth-century examples would include Mary Shelley's *The Last Man* (1826), in which the human race succumbs to plague; Poe's "The Conversation of Eiros and Charmion" (1839), in which Earth's atmosphere is denitrogenated by a passing comet; Félicien Champsaur's *Le dernier homme* (1886), which combines Mary Shelley's title with Poe's fatal atmospheric alteration; and another Wells story, "The Star" (1897), where the threat is world collision. Camille Flammarion's *Le fin du monde* (1893) deserves special attention in this context. After discussing at length a compendium of possibilities, Flammarion has Earth die gradually of old age.

Stories in which the world and the universe finally and irrevocably end are very rare. Even Samuel Beckett has not been able to imagine a state of absolute nothingness. Even when confronted with an apparent end of the world, a reader's sense of what comes next continues to operate. But whether something follows or not, concurrent with the end of the world is the experience of revelation—the truth or point of it all. The Greek original of the word "apocalypse" means, in fact, revelation. If nothing is assumed to follow the demise of man, then we are granted the revelation that, in purely human terms, life is meaningless. This is the ultimately pessimistic conclusion of *The Time Machine*. Even if man was to change his ways and evolve more positively, his career is terminally linked to the fate of the cosmos.

The best known and perhaps *the best* exemplification of the dual destructive/revelatory nature of the apocalypse myth is Arthur C. Clarke's "The Nine Billion Names of God." (It is in fact so well known that it seemed redundant to anthologize the story yet again.) For three centuries, the monks in a Tibetan lamasary have been engaged in cataloging all the possible names of God. They believe that when the list is complete the purpose of human creation will have been fulfilled and the universe will end. A computer is obtained to radically speed up the process. As the project nears completion, the two engineers who have come with the computer fear the reaction of the monks when the expected results do not ensue and decide to quietly slip away. At the appropriate time, they look up to discover that "Overhead, without any fuss, the stars were going out." Simultaneously, then, this beautifully understated story brings down the curtain on the universe and reveals the true purpose of man's existence. The religious factor puts Clarke's apocalypse in company with the Book of Revelation, where it is the unseen realms of Heaven and Hell that are revealed; thus the truth of the Biblical explanation of the spiritually meaningful nature of human existence is corroborated.

There is a potent visionary tradition in science fiction which looks forward to a semi-secularized version of the triumphant Biblical revelation. The universe is headed for a unified state of supreme consciousness, some kind of transcendent Over Mind. This myth is variously embodied in the work of Poe (particularly his cosmology *Eureka*), in Shaw's *Man and Superman* and *Back to Methuselah,* in Stapledon's

Star Maker, and in much of the science fiction of Arthur C. Clarke. Poe intuits an alternately expanding and contracting universe. At the point of ultimate contraction, or unity, man will become what he truly is—God. Shaw, Stapledon, and Clarke move this idea more directly into the realm of science fiction by allying it with the notion of evolution. The process is clearly illustrated in the film version of *2001: A Space Odyssey.* Mankind is presently in its infancy. Consciousness will evolve through various physical and cybernetic forms into an independent state of oneness with the universe. This is the ultimate science fiction vision of Heaven. There does not seem to be a comparable "spiritual" vision of Hell.

The revelation provided by visionary or mystical science fiction puts an end to the physical universe as we presently know it. There are other kinds of revelations which are not visionary in the same sense but which similarly destroy the universe as we presently know it and which therefore belong in any consideration of apocalypse in science fiction. These are revelations of a broadly philosophical nature. To write a story revealing that human reality actually derives from some unsuspected alien experiment, that it is some kind of front or imposture, dream or illusion, that men are actually robots or aliens, is to end the known world.

Such stories fall, in terms of emphasis, into three groups depending upon the angle of the radical rationale involved. Such stories may radically reinterpret the nature of reality directly, as is the case in Borges's "Tlön, Ugbar, Orbis Tertius." Or they may apocalyptically transform reality more indirectly by radically redefining the nature of man or, and this is the third possibility, by discovering the existence of a hitherto unsuspected outside manipulator who is responsible for everything.

Often a neat placing of a particular story is impossible. For example, Nigel Kneale's television serial *Quartermass and the Pit,* subsequently filmed as *Five Million Years to Earth,* is concerned with the revelation that in prehistoric times remnants of a dying Martian culture engrafted their identity onto man's ancestors—we are actually Martians! This story involves, in turn, the alien manipulator concept, the discovery of the true nature of man and hence the true nature of reality. To see the way in which the philosophical sense of apocalypse is actually a translation of the religious or visionary apocalypse, it is only necessary to interpret the categories, man, reality, and outside manipulator, as body and soul, Heaven and Earth, and God.

The strong appeal of apocalyptic fiction must lie partly in the way it dramatizes some of the less comfortable implications of modern science to tease or deny some of our deepest desires. We need to know ourselves, but Freud discovered that we don't—and Fred Pohl's hero, in "The Tunnel Under the World," finds that he is not the man he thinks he is, but an almost miscroscopic puppet, manipulated to relive one insane day again and again.

We yearn to know "reality," but the physicists and the psychologists and the linguists seem to agree that each of us creates his own unique universe, shaped from sense impressions and verbal symbols that are no better than distorted reflections of some presumed actuality forever beyond our grasp. We feel a shock of truth when apocalyptic fiction demonstrates again that our senses can't be trusted or that the symbols of language are never equal to the things symbolized. Pohl's hero finds that his whole world is a table-top model.

We hunger for permanence, but science reveals our universe as flux. Life and mind as we know them are incidental phenomena in the energy flow from atomic fusion in the core of a star. Even the seemingly stable crust of our planet is now shown to be flowing, continually formed at the mid-ocean ridges and continually . shown to be flowing, continually formed at the mid-ocean ridges and continually swallowed back into the semifluid mantle. A thousand apocalyptic stories since Wells's *Time Machine* have been set in worlds as mortal as we are, revealing us as a changing and endangered species, lifted for only a moment on the crest of our evolutionary wave. Stapledon projects the rise and fall of many future human races.

Longing for some eternal cosmic significance, we're at first dismayed when the scientists find that we are no longer the favored darlings of an everlasting God, shaped in his image and heirs to endless life, but ephemeral midges instead, adrift in a universe vast beyond our understanding, where divine benevolence has been replaced by statistical chance and divine law by Heisenberg's principle of uncertainty. These chastening themes from science are echoed by such writers as Ballard, Delany, and Vonnegut.

Two authors present their versions of apocalypse in the stories below. Roger Joseph Zelazny, born on May 13, 1937, at Euclid, Ohio, began winning awards with his brilliant science fiction in the mid-1960s. George Alec Effinger, known as Piglet to his friends, is one of the able young writers who have been honing their arts at Damon

Knight's Milford conferences and the various Clarion science fiction workshops.

Science fiction has given us many another version of apocalypse. Robert Sheckley's "Specialist," in Chapter 4 of this volume, is a fine example. For the bipedal Pusher, certainly, an ugly old world closes and a dazzling new one opens. For us as readers it scarcely matters that his new universe is one repudiated long ago by modern science, a benign cosmos, visibly purposeful, sanely ordered for the benefit of life. Robert A. Heinlein has given us at least three apocalyptic visions, in "Goldfish Bowl," "They," and "The Year of the Jackpot." The first two assault our old certainties about the world around us, one with a disturbing notion from Charles Fort, the other with a haunting suggestion of paranoid solipsism. The third builds logically toward its appalling conclusion from a simple fact of nature and common sense: when waves with differing periods are running together, their crests must sometimes coincide.

Zelazny's "The Game of Blood and Dust" is a very brief tale, but another telling challenge to our smug superiority. In search of the actuality beneath his symbolism, we might take his players as metaphors for the immense but blind historic forces that overwhelm the deeds and desires of all individual men in such theories as those of Marx, Spengler, and Arnold Toynbee. Effinger's "All the Last Wars at Once" has been called black humor, but his satiric vision of the end of the world comes too near our everyday experience to be very funny.

Memorable pieces of apocalyptic fiction to amuse us or chide us or perhaps disturb us, these stories reflect the coldest conclusions of scientific philosophy, as well as newspaper headlines of the sort we prefer to ignore. Zelazny jolts us with his warning that we may be pawns in a game we never suspect. Effinger catches us off guard with his half-joking hint that the end of everything may be nearer than we like to think.

The ultimate effect of apocalyptic fiction is not to leave us mired in the desolate self-pity of those who are unstrung by a sense of the hopeless "human condition," but rather, by exposing some of our oldest and most infantile illusions, to aid our emotional maturity. The essential truth beneath its fantastic surface can be as bracing as a cold shower. However hauntingly it may tantalize our fond desires or gnaw at our smug assumptions about the importance of ourselves and the permanence of our universe, it makes captivating reading.

When we speak of the myth or theme of apocalypse in science fiction, we are defining the outer limits of the genre, establishing a boundary of significance within which science fiction as a whole operates. Since the present volume is concerned with the myths of science fiction, this is hardly the place to move from apocalypse as myth to apocalypse as structure. But this is the place to point out that myths of apocalypse have a tendency to turn into myths of genesis and thus to contain and give meaning to whatever comes in between. Perhaps the popular notion that science fiction is about the end of the world is not so wrong after all. The end of one world is often the beginning of another.

BIBLIOGRAPHY

Anderson, Poul, *Tau Zero,* 1970 (Doubleday)
Ballard, J. G., *The Crystal World,* 1966 (Farrar, Straus & Giroux)
—, "Voices of Time," 1960
Blish, James, *The Triumph of Time,* 1958 (Avon)
—, *Black Easter,* 1968 (Doubleday)
Christopher, John, *No Blade of Grass,* 1957 (Simon and Schuster)
Clarke, Arthur C., *Childhood's End,* 1953 (Houghton Mifflin)
—, *2001: A Space Odyssey,* 1968 (New American Library)
—, "The Nine Billion Names of God," 1953
Delany, Samuel R., *The Einstein Intersection,* 1967 (Ace)
Dick, Philip K., *The Three Stigmata of Palmer Eldrich,* 1965 (Doubleday)
Heinlein, Robert A., "The Year of the Jackpot," 1952
Le Guin, Ursula K., *The Lathe of Heaven,* 1971 (Scribner's)
Lovecraft, H. P., "The Shadow out of Time," 1936
Pohl, Frederik, "The Tunnel Under the World," 1955
Shelley, Mary, *The Last Man,* 1826 (various editions)
Shute, Nevil, *On the Beach,* 1957 (Morrow)
Silverberg, Robert, "When We Went to See the End of the World," 1972
Spinrad, Norman, "The Big Flash," 1969
Stapledon, Olaf, *Last and First Men,* 1930 (Methuen)
—, *Star Maker,* 1937 (Methuen)
Vonnegut, Kurt, Jr., *Cat's Cradle,* 1963 (Holt)
—, *The Sirens of Titan,* 1959 (Dell)
Wells, H. G., *The Time Machine,* 1895 (various editions)

Williamson, Jack, "Born of the Sun," 1934
__, *Darker Than You Think,* 1948 (Fantasy Press)
Wyndham, John, *The Day of the Triffids,* 1951 (Doubleday)

The Game of Blood and Dust

Roger Zelazny

> "I am Blood. I go first."
> "I am Dust—I follow you."

They drifted toward the Earth, took up stations at its Trojan points.

They regarded the world, its two and a half billions of people, their cities, their devices.

After a time, the inhabitant of the forward point spoke:

"I am satisfied."

There was a long pause, then, "It will do," said the other, fetching up some strontium-90.

Their awarenesses met above the metal.

"Go ahead," said the one who had brought it.

The other insulated it from Time, provided antipodal pathways, addressed the inhabitant of the trailing point: "Select."

"That one."

The other released the stasis. Simultaneously, they became aware that the first radioactive decay particle emitted fled by way of the opposing path.

"I acknowledge the loss. Choose."

"I am Dust," said the inhabitant of the forward point. "Three moves apiece."

"And I am Blood," answered the other. "Three moves. Acknowledged."

"I choose to go first."

"I follow you. Acknowledged."

They removed themselves from the temporal sequence and regarded the history of the world.

Then Dust dropped into the Paleolithic and raised and uncovered metal deposits across the south of Europe.

"Move one completed."

Blood considered for a timeless time then moved to the second century B.C. and induced extensive lesions in the carotids of Marcus Porcius Cato where he stood in the Roman Senate, moments away from another "Carthago delenda est."

"Move one completed."

Dust entered the fourth century A.D. and injected an air bubble into the bloodstream of the sleeping Julius Ambrosius, the Lion of Mithra.

"Move two completed."

Blood moved to eighth century Damascus and did the same to Abou Iskafar, in the room where he carved curling alphabets from small, hard blocks of wood.

"Move two completed."

Dust contemplated the play.

"Subtle move, that."

"Thank you."

"But not good enough, I feel. Observe."

Dust moved to seventeenth century England and, on the morning before the search, removed from his laboratory all traces of the forbidden chemical experiments which had cost Isaac Newton his life.

"Move three completed."

"Good move. But I think I've got you."

Blood dropped to early nineteenth century England and disposed of Charles Babbage.

"Move three completed."

Both rested, studying the positions.

"Ready?" said Blood.

"Yes."

They reentered the sequence of temporality at the point they had departed.

It took but an instant. It moved like the cracking of a whip below them . . .

They departed the sequence once more, to study the separate effects of their moves now that the general result was know. They observed:

The south of Europe flourished. Rome was founded and grew in power several centuries sooner than had previously been the case. Greece was conquered before the flame of Athens burned with its greatest intensity. With the death of Cato the Elder the final Punic War was postponed. Carthage also continued to grow, extending her empire far to the east and the south. The death of Julius Ambrosius aborted the Mithraist revival and Christianity became the state religion in Rome.

.

The Carthaginians spread their power throughout the middle east. Mithraism was acknowledged as their state religion. The clash did not occur until the fifth century. Carthage itself was destroyed, the westward limits of its empire pushed back to Alexandria. Fifty years later, the Pope called for crusades. These occured with some regularity for the next century and a quarter, further fragmenting the Carthaginian empire while sapping the enormous bureaucracy which had grown up in Italy. The fighting fell off, ceased, the lines were drawn, an economic depression swept the Mediterranean area. Outlying districts grumbled over taxes and conscription, revolted. The general anarchy which followed the wars of secession settled down into a dark age reminiscent of that in the initial undisturbed sequence. Off in Asia Minor, the printing press was not developed.

"Stalemate till then, anyway," said Blood.

"Yes, but look what Newton did."

"How could you have known?"

"That is the difference between a good player and an inspired player. I saw his potential even when he was fooling around with alchemy. Look what he did for their science, single-handed— everything! Your next move was too late and too weak."

"Yes. I thought I might still kill their computers by destroying the founder of International Difference Machines, Ltd."

Dust chuckled.

"That was indeed ironic. Instead of an IDM 120, the *Beagle* took along a young naturalist named Darwin."

Blood glanced along to the end of the sequence where the radioactive dust was scattered across a lifeless globe.

"But it was not the science that did it, or the religion."

"Of course not," said Dust. "It is all a matter of emphasis."

"You were lucky. I want a rematch."

"All right. I will even give you your choice: Blood or Dust?"

"I'll stick with Blood."

"Very well. Winner elects to go first. Excuse me."

Dust moved to second century Rome and healed the carotid lesions which had produced Cato's cerebral hemorrhage."

"Move one completed."

Blood entered eastern Germany in the sixteenth century and induced identical lesions in the Vatican assassin who had slain Martin Luther.

"Move one completed."

"You are skipping pretty far along."

"It is all a matter of emphasis."

"Truer and truer. Very well. You saved Luther. I will save Babbage. Excuse me."

An instantless instant later Dust had returned.

"Move two completed."

Blood studied the playing area with extreme concentration. Then, "All right."

Blood entered Chevvy's Theater on the evening in 1865 when the disgruntled actor had taken a shot at the President of the United States. Delicately altering the course of the bullet in midair, he made it reach its target.

"Move two completed."

"I believe that you are bluffing," said Dust. "You could not have worked out all the ramifications."

"Wait and see."

Dust regarded the area with intense scrutiny.

"All right, then. You killed a president. I am going to save one—or at least prolong his life somewhat. I want Woodrow Wilson to see that combine of nations founded. Its failure will mean more than if it had never been—and it *will* fail. —Excuse me."

Dust entered the twentieth century and did some repair work within the long-jawed man.

"Move three completed."

"Then I, too, shall save one."

Blood entered the century at a farther point and assured the failure of Leon Nozdrev, the man who had assassinated Nikita Khrushchev.

"Move three completed."

"Ready, then?"

"Ready."

They reentered the sequence. The long whip cracked. Radio noises hummed about them. Satellites orbited the world. Highways webbed the continents. Dusty cities held their points of power throughout. Ships clove the seas. Jets slid through the atmosphere. Grass grew. Birds migrated. Fishes nibbled.

Blood chuckled.

"You have to admit it was very close," said Dust.

"As you were saying, there is a difference between a good player and an inspired player."

"You were lucky, too."

Blood chuckled again.

They regarded the world, its two and a half billions of people, their cities, their devices...

After a time, the inhabitant of the forward point spoke:
"Best two out of three?"
"All right. I am Blood. I go first."
"... And I am Dust. I follow you."

All the Last Wars at Once

George Alec Effinger

We interrupt this p—
—upt this program to—
—terrupt our regularly scheduled programming to bring you this
bulletin pieced together from the archives of the General Motors Corporation.

"Good afternoon. This is Bob Dunne, NBC News in New Haven,
Connecticut. We're standing here in the lobby of the Hotel Taft in New
Haven, where the first international racial war has just been declared.
In just a few seconds, the two men responsible will be coming out of
that elevator. (Can you hear me?)

"—elevator. Those of you in the western time zones are probably
already—"

The elevator doors opened. Two men emerged, smiling and holding
their hands above their heads in victorious, self-congratulatory boxers'
handshakes. They were immediately mobbed by newsmen. One of the
two men was exceptionally tall, and black as midnight in Nairobi. The
other was short, fat, white, and very nervous. The black man was
smiling broadly, the white man was smiling and wiping perspiration
from his face with a large red handkerchief.

"—C News. The Negro has been identified as the representative of
the people of color of all nations. He is, according to the mimeographed flyer distributed scant minutes ago, Mary McLeod Bethune
Washington, of Washington, Georgia. The other man with him is
identified as Robert Randall La Cygne, of La Cygne, Kansas, evidently the delegate of the Caucasian peoples. When, and by whom,
this series of negotiations was called is not yet clear.

"At any rate, the two men, only yesterday sunk in the sticky obscurity of American life, have concluded some sort of bargaining that threatens to engulf the entire world in violent reaction. The actual content of that agreement is still open to specu—"

"—or at any later date."

A close-up on Washington, who was reading from a small black notebook.

"We have thus reached, and passed, that critical moment. This fact has been known and ignored by all men, on both sides of the color line, for nearly a generation. Henceforth, this situation is to be, at least, honest, if bloodier. Bob and I join in wishing you all the best of luck, and may God bless."

"Mr. Washington?"

"Does this necessarily mean—"

"—iated Press here, Mr. Washing—"

"Yes? You, with the hat."

"Yes, sir. Vincent Reynolds, UPI. Mr. Washington, are we to understand that this agreement has some validity? You are aware that we haven't seen any sort of credentials—"

Washington grinned. "Thank you. I'm glad you brought that up. Credentials? Just you wait a few minutes, and listen outside. Ain't no stoppin' when them rifles start poppin'!"

"Mr. Washington?"

"Yes?"

"Is this to be an all-out, permanent division of peoples?"

"All-out, yes. Permanent, no. Bob and I have decided on a sort of statute of limitations. You go out and get what you can for thirty days. At the end of the month, we'll see what and who's left."

"You can guarantee that there will be no continuation of hostilities at the end of the thirty days?"

"Why, sure! We're all growed up, now, ain't we? Sure, why, you can trust *us!*"

"Then this is a war of racial eradication?"

"Not at all," said Bob La Cygne, who had remained silent, behind Washington's broad seersucker back. "Not at all what I would call a war of eradication. 'Eradicate' is an ugly term. 'Expunge' is the word we arrived at, isn't it, Mary Beth?"

"I do believe it is, Bob."

Washington studied his notebook for a few seconds, ignoring the shouting newsmen around him. No attempt was made by the uniformed guards to stop the pushing and shoving, which had grown somewhat aggravated. Then he smiled brightly, turning to La Cygne. They clasped hands and waved to the flashing bulbs of the photographers.

"No more questions, boys. You'll figure it all out soon enough; that's enough for now." The two men turned and went back into the waiting elevator.

(Tock tockatock tocka tock tock) "And now, the Six O'Clock Report (tocka tock tocka tocka), with (tockatock) Gil Monahan."

(Tocka tocka tock tock tocka)

"Good evening. The only story in the news tonight is the recently declared official hostilities between members of all non-Caucasian races and the white people of the world. Within minutes of the original announcement, open warfare broke out in nearly every multiracially populated area in the U.S. and abroad. At this moment the entire globe is in turmoil; the scene everywhere flickers between bloody combat in the streets and peaceful lulls marked by looting and destruction of private property.

"What has happened, in effect, is a thirty-day suspension of all rational codes of conduct. The army and National Guard are themselves paralyzed due to their own internal conflicts. A state of martial law has been declared by almost all governments, but, to our knowledge, nowhere has it been effectively enforced.

"There seems to be absolutely no cooperation between members of the opposite sides, on any level. Even those who most sympathized with the problems of the other are engaged in, using Mary McLeod Bethune Washington's terms, 'getting their own.' Interracial organizations, social groups, and even marriages are splintering against the color barrier.

"We have some reports now from neighboring states that may be of importance to our viewers, concerning the conditions in these areas at the present time. A state of emergency has been declared for the following municipalities in New Jersey: Absecon, Adelphia, Allendale, Allenhurst, Allentown, Allenwood, Alloway, Alpha... Well, as my eye travels over this list of some eight or nine hundred towns I notice that only a few *aren't* listed, notably Convent Station and Peapack. You can pretty well assume that things are bad *all* over. That goes for the New York, Pennsylvania, and Connecticut regions as well.

"We have some footage that was shot in Newark about ten minutes after the New Haven declaration. It's pretty tense out there now. The expert analysts in the news media are astounded that the intense polarization and outbreaks of rioting occurred so quickly. Let's take a look at those films now.

"Apparently there's some diffi—

"I don't know, what can . . . experiencing ourselves some of this interference with . . . refusal to even . . .

"—rifying. They're running around out there like maniacs, shooting and—

"—flames and the smoke is—you can see the clouds against the sky, between the buildings like waves of—"

It was a pink mimeographed factsheet. Frowning, he stuffed it into his pocket. "Factsheet," eh? It had been several days since Stevie had heard a fact that he could trust.

Nobody was saying *anything* worth listening. The factsheets had begun the second day with the expected clutter of charges and accusations, but soon everyone realized that this wasn't going to be that kind of war. Nobody gave a good goddamn *what* happened to anyone else. On the third day the few angry allegations that were made were answered with "our own sources do not indicate that, in fact, any such incident actually occurred" or with a curt "T.S., baby!" or, finally, no reply at all. Now the factsheets just bragged, or warned, or threatened.

Stevie was hitchhiking, which was a dangerous thing to do, but no more dangerous than sitting in an apartment waiting for the blazing torches. He felt that if he were going to be a target, a moving target offered the better odds.

He carried a pistol and a rifle that he had liberated from Abercrombie & Fitch. The hot morning sun gleamed on the zippers of his black leathers. He stood by the side of the parkway, smiling grimly to himself as he waited for a ride. Every car that came around the curve was a challenge, one that he was more than willing to accept. There wasn't much traffic lately, and for that Stevie was sorry. He was really getting to dig this.

A car approached, a late model black Imperial with its headlights burning. He set himself, ready to dodge into the ditch on the side of the road. Stevie stared through the windshield as the car came nearer. He let out his breath suddenly: it was a white chick. It looked like she had liberated the car; maybe she was looking for someone to team up with. Even if she was a dog, it would beat hitching.

The Imperial passed him, slowed, and stopped on the road's shoulder. The chick slid over on the seat, rolling down the window on the passenger's side and shouting to him.

"Hurry up, you idiot. I don't want to sit here much longer."

He ran to the car, pulling open the door to get in. She slammed it shut again, and Stevie stood there confused.

"What the hell—"

"Shut up," she snapped, handing him another pink factsheet. "Read this. And hurry it up."

He read the factsheet. His throat went dry and he began to feel a buzz in his head. At the top of the page was the familiar, fisted Women's Lib symbol. In regulation incendiary rhetoric below it, a few paragraphs explained that it had now been decided by the uppermost echelon to strike now for freedom. During the period of severe disorientation, women the world over were taking the opportunity to beat down the revisionist male supremist pigs. Not just the oppressed racial minorities can express their militancy, it said. The female popular liberation front knew no color boundaries. Who did they think they were kidding? Stevie thought.

"You're gonna get plugged by some black bitch, you know that?" he said. He looked up at her. She had a gun pointed at him, aimed at his chest. The buzz in his head grew louder.

"You wanna put that sheet back on the pile? We don't have enough to go around," she said.

"Look," said Stevie, starting to move toward the car. The girl raised the pistol in a warning. He dove to the ground, parallel to the car, and rolled up against the right front wheel. The girl panicked, opening the door to shoot him before he could get away. Stevie fired twice before she sighted him, and she fell to the grassy shoulder. He didn't check to see if she were dead or merely wounded; he took her pistol and got in the car.

"My fellow Americans." The voice of the President was strained and tired, but he still managed his famous promiseless smile. The picture of the Chief Executive was the first to disturb the televisions' colored confetti snow for nearly two weeks.

"We are met tonight to discuss the intolerable situation in which our nation finds itself. With me this evening"—the President indicated an elderly, well-dressed Negro gentleman seated at a desk to the left of the President's—"I have invited the Rev. Dr. Roosevelt Wilson, who will speak to you from his own conscience. Rev. Wilson is known to many of you as an honest man, a community leader, and a voice of collaboration in these times of mistrust and fiscal insecurity."

Across the nation, men in dark turtlenecks ran down searing channels of flame, liberated television sets in their gentle grasp, running so that they might see this special telecast. Across the nation men and women of all persuasions looked at Wilson and muttered, "Well, isn't he the clean old nigger!"

Rev. Wilson spoke, his voice urgent and slow with emotion. "We must do everything that our leaders tell us. We cannot take the law into our own hands. We must listen to the promptings of reason and calmth, and find that equitable solution that I'm sure we all desire."

The TV Broadcast had been a major accomplishment. Its organization had been a tribute to the cooperation of many dissatisfied men who would rather have been out liberating lawn furniture. But the message of these two paternal figures of authority was more important.

"Thank you, Dr. Wilson," said the President. He stood, smiling into the camera, and walked to a large map that had been set up to his right. He took a pointer in one hand.

"This," he said, "is our beleaguered nation. Each green dot represents a community where the violence that plagues us has gone beyond containable limits." The map was nearly solid green, the first time the USA had been in that condition since the early seventeenth century. "I have asked for assistance from the armed forces of Canada, Mexico and Great Britain, but although I mailed the requests nearly two weeks ago I have yet to receive a reply. I can only assume that we are on our own.

"Therefore, I will make one statement concerning official government policy. As you know, this state of affairs will technically come to an end in about fifteen days. At that time, the government will prosecute *severely* anyone connected with any further disruptions of Federal activities. This is not merely an empty threat; it con—"

A young black man ran before the camera, turning to shout an incoherent slogan. Rev. Wilson saw the pistol in the boy's hand and stood, his face contorted with fear and envy. "The business of America *is* business!" he screamed, and then dropped back into his seat as the black militant shot. The President clutched his chest and cried, "We *must* not . . . lose . . ." and fell to the floor.

The cameras seemed to swing at random, as men rushed about confusedly. From somewhere a white man appeared, perhaps one of the technicians, with his own pistol. He hurried to the desk shouting, "For anarchy!" and shot Dr. Wilson point-blank. The white assassin turned, and the black assassin fired at him. The two killers began a cautious but noisy gun battle in the studio. Here most viewers turned off their sets. "In very poor taste," they thought.

The sign outside: SECOND NATIONAL BANK OF OUR LORD, THE ENGINEER. UNIVERSAL CHURCH OF GOD OR SOME SORT OF COSMIC EMBODIMENT OF GOOD.

Above the entrance to the church fluttered a hastily made banner. The masculine symbol had been crudely painted on a white sheet; the white flag indicated that the worshippers were white males and that blacks and women were "welcome" at their own risk. The population was now split into four mutually antagonistic segments. The separate groups began to realize that there was some point in keeping their members together in little cadres. The streets and apartment buildings were death traps.

Inside the church the men were silent in prayer. They were led by an elderly deacon, whose inexperience and confusion were no greater or less than any in the congregation.

"Merciful God," he prayed, "in whatever Form the various members of our flock picture You, corporal Entity or insubstantial Spirit, we ask that You guide us in this time of direst peril.

"Brother lifts sword against brother, and brother against sister. Husband and wife are torn asunder against Your holiest ordainments. Protect us, and show us our proper response. Perhaps it is true that vengeance is solely Yours; but speak to us, then, concerning Limited Cautionary Retaliation, and other alternatives. We would see a sign, for truly we are lost in the mires of day-to-day living."

The deacon continued his prayer, but soon there began a series of poundings on the door. The deacon stopped for just a second, looking up nervously, his hand straying to his sidearm. When nothing further happened he finished the prayer and the members of the congregation added, if they chose, their amens.

At the end of the service the men rose to leave. They stood at the door, in no hurry to abandon the sanctuary of the church. At last the deacon led them out. It was immediately noticed that a yellow factsheet had been nailed to the outside of the door. The Roman Catholics of the neighborhood had decided to end the centuries-long schism. Why not now, when everybody else was settling their differences? A Final Solution.

A bullet split wood from the door frame. The men standing on the stoop jumped back inside. A voice called from the street, "You damn commie atheist Protestants! We're gonna wipe you out and send your lousy heretic souls straight to Hell!" More gunfire. The stained glass windows of the church shattered, and there were cries from inside.

"They got one of the elders!"

"It's those crummy Catholics. We should have got them when we had the chance. Damn it, now they got us holed up in here."

The next day a blue factsheet was circulated by the Jewish community explaining that they had finally gotten tired of having their gabardine spat on, and that everybody'd just have to watch out. Around the world the remaining clusters of people fractured again, on the basis of creed.

It was getting so you didn't know *who* you could trust.

Stevie was heading back toward the city when the car went. It made a few preliminary noises, shaking and rattling slower, and then it stopped. For all he knew it might simply have been out of gas. There were eight days left in the prescribed thirty, and he needed a ride.

He took the rifle and the two pistols from the Imperial and stood by the side of the road. It was a lot more dangerous to hitch now than it had been before, for the simple reason that the odds were that anyone who happened by would probably be on the other side of *one* of the many ideological fences. He was still confident, though, that he would be safely picked up, or be able to wrest a car away from its owner.

There was very little traffic. Several times Stevie had to jump for cover as a hostile driver sped by him, shooting wildly from behind the wheel. At last an old Chevy stopped for him, driven by a heavy white man whom Stevie judged to be in his late fifties.

"Come on, get in," said the man.

Stevie climbed into the car, grunting his thanks and settling warily back against the seat.

"Where you going?" asked the man.

"New York."

"Um. You, uh, you a Christian?"

"Hey," said Stevie, "right now we ain't got any troubles at all. We can just drive until we get where we're going. We only have eight days, right? So if we leave off the questions, eight days from now *both* of us'll be happy."

"All right. That's a good point, I guess, but it defeats the whole purpose. I mean, it doesn't seem to enter into the spirit of things."

"Yeah, well, the spirit's getting a little tired."

They rode in silence, taking turns with the driving. Stevie noticed that the old man kept staring at the rifle and two pistols. Stevie searched the car as best he could with his eyes, and it looked to him as though the old man was unarmed himself. Stevie didn't say anything.

"You seen a factsheet lately?" asked the man.

"No," said Stevie. "Haven't seen one in days. I got tired of the whole thing. *Now* who's at it?"

The old man looked at him quickly, then turned back to the road. "Nobody. Nothing new." Stevie glanced at the man now, studying his face curiously. Nothing new.

After a while the man asked him for some bullets.

"I didn't think that you had a gun," said Stevie.

"Yeah. I got a .38 in the glove compartment. I keep it there, well, I'm less likely to use it."

"A .38? Well, these shells wouldn't do you any good, anyhow. Besides, I don't really want to give them up yet."

The man looked at him again. He licked his lips, appearing to make some decision. He took his eyes off the road for a moment and lunged across the seat in a dive for one of the loaded pistols. Stevie slammed the edge of his hand into the older man's throat. The man choked and collapsed on the seat. Stevie switched off the engine and steered the car to the side of the road, where he opened the door and dumped the still body.

Before he started the car again, Stevie opened the glove compartment. There was an unloaded revolver and a crumpled factsheet. Stevie tossed the gun to the ground by the old man. He smoothed out the wrinkled paper. The youth of the world, it proclaimed, had declared war on everyone over the age of thirty years.

"How you coming with that factsheet?"

The thin man in the green workshirt stopped typing and looked up. "I don't know. It's hard making out your crummy handwriting. Maybe another fifteen minutes. Are they getting restless out there?"

The man in the jacket gulped down some of his lukewarm coffee. "Yeah. I was going to make an announcement, but what the hell. Let 'em wait. They had their vote, they know what's coming. Just finish that factsheet. I want to get it run off and put up before them goddamn Artists beat us to it."

"Look, Larry, them queers'll never think of it in the first place. Calm down."

The man in the workshirt typed in silence for a while. Larry walked around the cold meeting hall, pushing chairs back in place and chewing his cigar nervously. When the stencil was finished, the man in the workshirt pulled it out of the typewriter and handed it to Larry. "All right," he said, "there it is. Maybe you better go read it to them first. They been waiting out there for a couple of hours now."

"Yeah, I guess so," said Larry. He zipped up his green jacket and waited for the man in the workshirt to get his coat. He turned off the lights and locked the door to the hall. Outside was a huge crowd of men, all white and all well into middle age. They cheered when Larry and the other man came out. Larry held up his hands for quiet.

"All right, listen up," he said. "We got our factsheet here. Before we go and have it run off, I'm going to let you hear it. It says just like what we voted for, so you all should be pretty satisfied."

He read the factsheet, stopping every now and then to wait through the applause and cheers of the men. He looked out at the crowd. They're all brawny veteran-types, he thought. That's what we are: we're Veterans. We been through it all. We're the ones who know what's going on. We're the Producers.

The factsheet explained, in simple language unlike the bitter diatribes of other groups, that the laborers—the Producers—of the world had gotten fed up with doing all the work while a large portion of the population—the goddamn queer Artists—did nothing but eat up all the fruits of honest nine to five work. Artists contributed nothing, and wasted large amounts of our precious resources. It was simple logic to see that the food, clothing, shelter, money and recreational facilities that were diverted from the Producers' use was as good as thrown into the garbage. The Producers worked harder and harder, and got back less and less. Well then, what could you expect to happen? Everything was bound to get worse for everybody.

The men cheered. It was about time that they got rid of the parasites. No one complained when you burned off a leech. And no one could complain when you snuffed out the leechlike elements of normal, organized, Productive society.

Larry finished reading the sheet and asked for questions and comments. Several men started talking, but Larry ignored them and went on speaking himself.

"Now, this doesn't mean," he said, "that we gotta get everybody that doesn't work regular hours like we do. You see that some of the people are hard to tell whether they're Producers like us, or just lousy addict Artists. Like the people that make TV. We can use them. But we have to be careful, because there's a lot of Artists around who are trying to make us think that they're really Producers. Just remember: if you can use it, it's not Art."

The crowd cheered again, and then it began to break up. Some of the men stood around arguing. One of the small groups of Producers that was slowly walking to the parking lot was deeply involved in debating the boundaries separating Artists and Producers.

"I mean, where are we going to stop?" said one. "I don't like the way this divisioning is going. Pretty soon there won't be any groups left to belong to. We'll all be locked up in our homes, afraid to see anybody at all."

"It's not doing us any good," agreed another. "If you go out and get what you want, I mean, take something from a store or something, why, everybody knows you got it when you bring it home. Then *you're* the target. I got less now than when this all started."

A third man watched the first two grimly. He pulled out a factsheet of his own from the pocket of his jacket. "That's commie talk," he said. "You're missing the point of the whole thing. Let me ask you a question. Are you right- or left-handed?"

The first man looked up from the factsheet, puzzled. "I don't see that it makes any difference. I mean, I'm basically left-handed, but I write with my right hand."

The third man stared angrily, in disbelief.

Bang.

YANG and YIN: Male and female. Hot and cold. Mass and energy. Smooth and crunchy. Odd and even. Sun and moon. Silence and noise. Space and time. Slave and master. Fast and slow. Large and small. Land and sea. Good and evil. On and off. Black and white. Strong and weak. Regular and filter king. Young and old. Light and shade. Fire and ice. Sickness and health. Hard and soft. Life and death.

If there *is* a plot, shouldn't you know about it?

One more hour.

Millions of people hid in their holes, waiting out the last minutes of the wars. Hardly anyone was out on the streets yet. No one shouted their drunken celebrations that little bit ahead of schedule. In the night darkness Stevie could still hear the ragged crackings of guns in the distance. Some suckers getting it only an hour from homefree.

The time passed. Warily, people came out into the fresher air, still hiding themselves in shadows, not used yet to walking in the open. Guns of the enthusiasts popped; they would never get a chance like this again, and there were only fifteen minutes left. Forty-second Street chromium knives found their lodgings in unprotected Gotham throats and shoulders.

Times Square was still empty when Stevie arrived. Decomposing corpses sprawled in front of the record and porno shops. A few shadowy forms moved across the streets, far away down the sidewalk.

The big ball was poised. Stevie watched it, bored, with murderers cringing around him. The huge lighted New Year's globe was ready to drop, waiting only for midnight and for the kissing New Year's VJ-Day crowds. There was Stevie, who didn't care, and the looters, disappointed in the smoked-out, gunfire black, looted stores.

It said it right up there: 11:55. Five more minutes. Stevie pushed himself back into a doorway, knowing that it would be humiliating to get it with only five minutes left. From the vague screams around him he knew that some were still finding it.

People were running by now. The square was filling up. 11:58 and the ball was *just* hanging there: the sudden well of people drew rapid rifle-fire, but the crowd still grew. There was the beginning of a murmur, just the hint of the war-is-over madness. Stevie sent himself into the stream, giving himself up to the release and relief.

11:59. . . . The ball seemed . . . to tip . . . and *fell!* 12:00! The chant grew stronger, the New York chant, the smugness returned in all its sordid might. "We're Number One! We're Number One!" The cold breezes drove the shouting through the unlit streets, carrying it on top of the burnt and fecal smells. It would be a long time before what was left would be made livable, but We're Number One! There were still sporadic shots, but these were the usual New York Town killers, doing the undeclared and time-honored violence that goes unnoticed.

We're Number One!

Stevie found himself screaming in spite of himself. He was standing next to a tall, sweating black. Stevie grinned; the black grinned. Stevie stuck out his hand. "Shake!" he said. "We're Number One!"

"We're Number One!" said the black. "I mean, it's *us!* We gotta settle all this down, but, I mean, what's left is *ours!* No more fighting!"

Stevie looked at him, realizing for the first time the meaning of their situation. "Right you are," he said with a catch in his voice. "Right you are, Brother."

"Excuse me."

Stevie and the black turned to see a strangely dressed woman. The costume completely hid any clue to the person's identity, but the voice was very definitely feminine. The woman wore a long, loose robe decorated fancifully with flowers and butterflies. Artificial gems had been stuck on, and the whole thing trimmed with cheap, dimestore "gold-and-silver" piping. The woman's head was entirely hidden by a large, bowl-shaped woven helmet, and from within it her voice echoed excitedly.

"Excuse me," she said. "Now that the preliminary skirmishes are over, don't you think we should get on with it?"

"With what?" asked the black.

"The Last War, the final one. The war against ourselves. It's senseless to keep avoiding it, now."

"What do you mean?" asked Stevie.

The woman touched Stevie's chest. "There. Your guilt. Your frustration. You don't really feel any better, do you? I mean, women don't really hate men; they hate their own weaknesses. People don't really hate other people for their religion or race. It's just that seeing someone different than you makes you feel a little insecure in your own belief. What you hate is your own doubt, and you project the hatred onto the other man."

"She's right!" said the black. "You know, I wouldn't mind it half so much if they'd hate me because of *me;* but nobody ever took the trouble."

"That's what's so frustrating," she said. "If anyone's ever going to hate the *real* you, you know who it'll have to be."

"You're from that Kindness Cult, aren't you?" the black said softly.

"Shinsetsu," she said. "Yes."

"You want us to meditate or something?" asked Stevie. The woman dug into a large basket that she carried on her arm. She handed each of them a plump cellophane package filled with a colorless fluid.

"No," said the black as he took his package. "Kerosene."

Stevie held his bag of kerosene uncertainly, and looked around the square. There were others dressed in the *Shinsetsu* manner, and they were all talking to groups that had formed around them.

"Declare war on myself?" Stevie said doubtfully. "Do I have to publish a factsheet first?" No one answered him. People nearby were moving closer so they could hear the *Shinsetsu* woman. She continued to hand out the packages as she spoke.

Stevie slipped away, trying to get crosstown, out of the congested square. When he reached a side street he looked back: already the crowd was dotted with scores of little fires, like scattered piles of burning leaves in the backyards of his childhood.

Notes on the Contributors

BRIAN ALDISS is an important figure in science fiction in two respects, as the author of one of the leading histories of science-fiction—*Billion Year Spree* (1973), and as one of the field's premier authors—*The Long Afternoon of Earth* (1962), *Greybeard* (1964), *Cryptozoic!* (1968), and the complex *Barefoot in the Head* (1970).

POUL ANDERSON has been an important writer of science fiction for almost thirty years. He has produced a wide variety of science fiction and fantasy, from his superb *Brain Wave* (1954) to the fascinating *Fire Time* (1974). Most of his work fits into a larger "Future History" framework, and he has developed a number of memorable series characters, including the intergalactic agent Dominic Flandry and that model capitalist of the future, Nicholas van Rijn.

ISAAC ASIMOV, born in Russia in 1920, came to this country at the age of three. He was educated at Columbia University, and took his doctorate in chemistry in 1948, after which he taught at the Boston University School of Medicine. Asimov has been a professional writer from the age of eighteen, publishing books that span the fields of anatomy, biology, chemistry, mathematics, astronomy, geography, and history. Perhaps best known for his science fiction, Asimov has also written children's books, college textbooks, histories, and books on classic literature, including annotated versions of *Paradise Lost* and *Don Juan*. More recently he has written guides to Shakespeare and the Bible, as well as joke books and satire.

J. G. BALLARD has been one of the most important figures in modern science fiction since the publication of his first story "Prima Belladonna" in 1956. A master of the short story form, he has been

459

collected many times, a few of his more notable collections being *Bellenium* (1962), *Terminal Beach* (1964), *The Disaster Area* (1967), and *Chronopolis and Other Stories* (1971). He is even better known for his novels of personal and societal disintegration and for his "experimental" works.

The late JAMES BLISH (1921–1975) was one of the first "serious" critics of science fiction (writing as William Atheling, Jr.), as well as a pioneer of the treatment of previously neglected themes in the *genre,* including his Hugo Award winning novel *A Case of Conscience* (1958), one of the first important attempts to address profound religious questions from within the science fiction community. Other notable contributions include his "Okie" series (collected as *Cities in Flight,* 1970); the "Pantropy" series (collected as *The Seedling Stars,* 1957); and the novel *A Torrent of Faces* (with Norman L. Knight, 1967).

The late JOHN CAMPBELL, JR. is credited by most historians as the father of modern science fiction through his influence as editor of the field's leading magazine, *Astounding.* A producer of space opera as a young writer, he employed the name "Don A. Stuart" for his more important efforts examining the impact of technology on people. A controversial figure in the fifties and sixties because of his championing of dianetics and the "Dean Drive," his real impact on the field has yet to be fully explored and explained.

TERRY CARR is one of the most important editors in science fiction, working with both original material (his *Universe* series) and reprinted stories (*The Best Science Fiction of the Year* series and many others, including the sadly neglected *On Our Way to the Future,* 1970). His editorial talents have obscured the fact that he is also an outstanding writer of science fiction—witness such fine stories as "The Dance of the Changer and the Three," "Ozymandias," "They Live On Levels," and "Touchstone."

THOMAS D. CLARESON is Professor of English at the College of Wooster, and received his doctorate from the University of Pennsylvania. He teaches in the fields of American Literature and nineteenth and twentieth century literature. Since 1959 he has edited *Extrapolation: The Newsletter of the MLA Seminar on Science Fiction.* He has written and edited a number of critical works including *SF: The Other Side of Realism* and *A Spectrum of Worlds.*

One of the best-known modern science-fiction writers, ARTHUR C. CLARKE will also be remembered for his contributions to the popularization of the possibilities of spaceflight in such books as *The Exploration of Space* (1951) and *The Exploration of the Moon* (1957). In science fiction he is best known for his novels *Childhood's End* (1953), *The City and the Stars* (1956), *Rendezvous with Rama* (1973), and the novel and screenplay *2001: A Space Odyssey,* certainly the most important science fiction film of all time.

RALPH S. CLEM is Assistant Professor of International Relations at Florida International University, Miami. He received his Ph.D. degree from Columbia University, and is the author or editor of several books and articles on the geography of the Soviet Union. In 1976 he edited, together with Martin Harry Greenberg and Joseph Olander, *The City 2000 A.D.,* an anthology of science fiction stories on urban themes.

THEODORE R. COGSWELL is a member of the English faculty at Keystone Junior College, La Plume, Pennsylvania. He took his B.A. at the University of Colorado in 1948 and his M.A. at the University of Denver in 1949. In addition to teaching, he also writes both science fiction and fantasy. His works include *The Other Cheek, The Third Eye,* and *The Wall Around the World.*

L. SPRAGUE DE CAMP is a self-employed writer with a B.S. degree in Aeronautical Engineering from California Institute of Technology and an M.S. degree in Engineering and Economics from Stevens Institute of Technology. He is the author of a large number of books and articles about science, including *The Ancient Engineers* and *The Day of the Dinosaur.* His numerous science fiction works include *Lest Darkness Fall* and *Rogue Queen.* With his wife, Catherine, he has written the *Science Fiction Handbook.*

The multi-layered novels and stories of PHILIP K. DICK are famous all over the world for he is as well known in countries such as France and Germany (and until recently, better appreciated) as he is in the United States. The recent intense critical interest in his work is richly deserved because few writers as prolific as he have produced as important a body of work. Among his best works are the Hugo-winning *The Man in the High Castle* (1962), *Flow My Tears, The Policeman Said* (1974), *The Three Stigmata of Palmer Eldritch* (1965), and the powerful *Ubik* (1969).

Best known as the author of the *Dorsai Trilogy,* GORDON R. DICKSON has been producing first-rate science fiction and fantasy since 1950. He won the Hugo Award in 1965 for his story "Soldier Ask Not" (later expanded into a novel that forms part of his *Trilogy*), but he is better known as the author of one of the most famous computer stories ever written, "Computers Don't Argue."

GEORGE ALEC EFFINGER is one of the most interesting and talented young writers in science fiction. "Piglet" Effinger's first novel, *What Entropy Means to Me* (1972) was nominated for a Nebula Award. His haunting and often poetic short stories such as "At the Bran Factory" and "How It Felt" can be found in his collection *Irrational Numbers* (1976).

CHARLES ELKINS, born on April 1, 1940, received his B.A. from the University of California at Berkeley in 1964 and his Ph.D. from Southern Illinois University in 1972, after serving with the Peace Corps in Afghanistan from 1964 to 1966. His main interests are sociology of literature, nineteenth and twentieth century literature, popular culture, and science fiction. Elkins is presently Associate Professor in the Department of English, Florida International University, Miami, working in the area of the sociology of science fiction.

Though he had never heard of birth, PHILIP JOSÉ FARMER was, nevertheless, born. This microcosmic event was ignited on January 26, 1918—three months before the Red Baron was shot down and about 6,000 years before the creation of the universe (Jahweh's time). Farmer has used these significant events more or less in his fiction. At the age of four Farmer moved from his native state of Indiana to Illinois, where he has lived to this day except for a fourteen-year sojourn as a technical writer for various defense-space industries. His first science fiction story, "The Lovers," which appeared in *Startling Stories* magazine in 1952, is credited with breaking the sex taboo against mature dealing with sex in American science fiction. In recent years Farmer has been using in his writing themes and characters from pop and pulpit mythology (Tarzan, Doc Savage, Sherlock Holmes, Leopold Bloom, the Shadow, et al.). His main achievements are a thirty-five-year marriage, two children, four grandchildren, and a desire to write the greatest science fiction novel ever. Only time will tell if any of these are worthwhile.

BEVERLY FRIEND is Assistant Professor of Communications and Journalism, Oakton Community College, Morton Grove, Ill. She is editor of *SFRA Newsletter,* author of *SF: the Classroom in Orbit,* and contributing author to *Many Futures, Many Worlds* and *Voices for the Future.* The author of articles on science fiction in *English Journal, Extrapolation,* and *Media and Method,* Dr. Friend is currently book reviewer for the *Chicago Daily News,* the *Chicago Sun Times,* and *Delaps F&SF Review.* She has also conducted lectures and workshops on science fiction and the teaching of science fiction for the National Council of Teachers of English, the Chicago Area College English Association, the Midwest Modern Language Association, and at many high schools and universities throughout the country.

MARTIN HARRY GREENBERG was born in Miami Beach, Florida, in 1941. He received degrees from the University of Miami, and his doctorate in political science from the University of Connecticut. He is the co-editor of a number of science fiction text anthologies, including *Political Science Fiction* (1974), *Introductory Psychology Through Science Fiction* (2nd ed., 1977), and *The City 2000 A.D.: Urban Life Through Science Fiction* (1976), as well as a number of trade anthologies. He is also co-editor of the Twenty-First Century Authors Series of monographs on leading science fiction writers. Professor Greenberg is presently the Director of Graduate Studies at the University of Wisconsin-Green Bay.

JAMES E. GUNN was born in Kansas City, Missouri, in 1923, received his B.S. degree in journalism in 1947, and his M.A. in English from the University of Kansas in 1951. He is both writer and critic. He has written a number of short stories and novels, including *The Joy Makers, The Immortals,* and *The Listeners.* He is a Professor of English and Journalism at the University of Kansas, specializing in the teaching of fiction writing and science fiction. He is also the author of *Alternate Worlds, the Illustrated History of Science Fiction* (1975), a superb history of science fiction.

DAVID HARTWELL is the general editor for the Gregg Press Science Fiction series, editor of *The Little Magazine,* and the consulting editor in science fiction for Berkley Publishing Corp. He is a partner in Dragon Press, Publisher and Bookseller; and publisher of Entwhistle Books, Berkley Books, and Berkley/Putnam Books. Presently residing in Pleasantville, New York, with his wife, Patricia, and daughter,

Alison, Hartwell teaches a science fiction course at Stevens Institute of Technology. He also writes reviews and essays, and is working on a novel.

Born in England in 1942, DAVID KETTERER is presently an Associate Professor of English at Concordia University, Montreal. His articles have appeared in numerous periodicals, including the *Journal of American Studies, PMLA,* and *Texas Studies in Literature and Language.* He is the author of *New Worlds for Old,* a critical study of the relationship of the apocalyptic imagination in science fiction and American literature.

C. M. KORNBLUTH died in 1958 at the age of 35, by which time he had been a professional science fiction writer for almost twenty years. A dark, satirical and caustic writer, Kornbluth has been described as the Lenny Bruce of science fiction. Because he collaborated with Frederik Pohl (*The Space Merchants,* 1952, and several others) and Judith Merril, his talent and importance have tended to be obscured, although he is now receiving the attention from critics that he so richly deserves. His solo efforts include the novel *The Syndic* (1953), and many fine short stories, including several regarded as classics—"The Little Black Bag," "The Silly Season," and the now controversial "The Marching Morons."

DAMON KNIGHT's influence in science fiction covers all aspects of the field—editor (the *Orbit* series); writer (he is a master of the short story); and critic (winner of the 1976 Pilgrim Award of the Science Fiction Research Association for his book *In Search of Wonder*). Much of his best writing can be found in *The Best of Damon Knight* (1975).

Widely acclaimed as the premier science fiction writer of the seventies, URSULA K. LE GUIN is as effective in the fantasy field as she is in science fiction. A multiple winner of the Hugo Award—she won both the Hugo and the Nebula for her novel *The Dispossessed,* one of the most influential novels ever published in the field. Despite her international reputation outside of the *genre,* she has often defended the virtues of science fiction against the attacks of its critics.

FRITZ LEIBER is as well known for his fantasy as he is for his science fiction. In the latter *genre* his novels, *Gather, Darkness!* (1950), *The Big Time* (1961), the Hugo-winning *The Wanderer* (1964), and the wild *A Specter Is Haunting Texas* (1969), are particularly noteworthy. He is also a fine short story writer, and his *The Best of Fritz Leiber* (1974) belongs on the shelves of every science fiction reader.

Although he has been categorized as a "hard science" writer, LARRY NIVEN is actually at home with many different types of science fiction. He has written a popular series of stories and novels within a consistent future history framework (the stories collected as *Tales of Known Space*, 1975); exciting and humorous space opera (*The Mote in God's Eye*, with Jerry Pournelle, 1974); and the Hugo- and Nebula-winning *Ringworld* (1970), one of the seminal works in modern science fiction.

A medical doctor, ALAN E. NOURSE has based a number of his novels and stories on medical themes (*Star Surgeon*, 1960 and *The Mercy Men*, 1968) as well as the widely reprinted "Nightmare Brother" and "Brightside Crossing." His stories can be found in the collections *Tiger by the Tail* (1961) and *PSI High and Others* (1965).

JOSEPH D. OLANDER was born and raised in Hazelton, Pennsylvania. After service in the United States Air Force he received degrees from Rollins College and a doctorate in political science from the University of Indiana. He has co-edited a number of science fiction text anthologies, including *Sociology Through Science Fiction* and *American Government Through Science Fiction*. He was a co-editor of *Run to Starlight* (1975), the only science fiction anthology ever selected as an "Outstanding Book of the Year" by the *New York Times Book Review*. He is a co-editor of the Twenty-First Century Authors Series. Professor Olander is presently on leave from Florida International University, serving as a Special Assistant to the Commissioner of Education for the State of Florida.

FREDERIK POHL is one of the seminal figures in the history of modern science fiction. Born and raised in New York and active in the early development of science fiction fandom, Pohl was an important literary agent specializing in science fiction prior to his reemergence as a writer. He is best known as the co-author (with the late C. M. Kornbluth) of *The Space Merchants* (1953). Other notable works include *Slave Ship* (1957), *Drunkard's Walk* (1961), *The Age of the Pussyfoot* (1969), and (with Kornbluth), *Gladiator-at-Law* (1955). He ranks as one of the influential editors in the history of science fiction, both for his *Star Science Fiction* series of original anthologies and for his work as editor of the magazines *If* and *Galaxy Science Fiction* (1962–1969).

PAMELA SARGENT received her B.A. and M.A. from the State University of New York at Binghamton, where she majored in classical philosophy. She has published over twenty short stories in *Fantasy & Science Fiction, New Worlds, Universe, Wandering Stars, Amazing, Fellowship of the Stars, Ten Tomorrows, Two Views of Wonder,* and other magazines and anthologies. She is the editor of *Women of Wonder, Bio-Futures,* and *More Women of Wonder* (all published by Vintage Books). She is the author of a novel, *Cloned Lives* (Fawcett-Gold Medal), and is completing a second novel for Fawcett.

For a long time THOMAS SCORTIA was considered one of "the bright young writers in science fiction," in spite of the fact that he wrote in many fields and produced relatively few stories in science fiction. Most of his best work can be found in his collection *Caution Inflammable!* (1975), including "Woman's Rib," "By the Time I Get to Phoenix," and his famous "Sea Change." In recent years he has written a number of very successful suspense novels with Frank Robinson, most notably *The Towering Inferno.*

ROBERT SHECKLEY is one of the great but unappreciated talents of the fifties. The caustic and ingenious short stories of Robert Sheckley can be found in (among many) *Untouched by Human Hands* (1954), *Citizen in Space* (1956), and *Can You Feel Anything When I Do This?* (1971). Few writers have been as consistently good with the demanding short story form. Few groups, social movements, or institutions have escaped his satirical pen (typewriter). Happily, he is still producing excellent science fiction.

ROBERT SILVERBERG is the editor or author of over sixty science fiction books, including the Nebula award-winning *A Time of Changes* (1971). One of science fiction's most prolific authors early in his career, he has developed into an outstanding craftsman since the late sixties. Other noteworthy titles include *Thorns* (1967), *Hawksbill Station* (1968), *Tower of Glass* (1970), *Downward to the Earth* (1970), *The Book of Skulls* (1972), and *Dying Inside* (1972). In addition, he has become one of the outstanding anthologists in the field. Born in New York, he now lives in Oakland, California.

The first great mystery talent in science fiction, CORDWAINER SMITH was actually Professor Paul Linebarger of Johns Hopkins University. His mystical stories of the "Lords of the Instrumentality" captured the imagination of readers all over the world. His beautiful short story "The Ballad of Lost C'mell" can be found in *The Science Fiction Hall of Fame* (1970). His novel *Norstrilia* (1975) was published after his death.

THEODORE STURGEON, the author of *More Than Human* (winner of the International Fantasy Award in 1954), needs little introduction to science fiction readers, but it is not generally realized that he was the most widely reprinted writer in science fiction up until the mid-sixties. He has examined the meaning of love and friendship in most of his work, especially in the short stories collected in *E Pluribus Unicorn* (1953), *A Touch of Strange* (1958), and *Sturgeon Is Alive and Well* (1971). Despite the last title, he has been relatively unproductive in recent years.

Much better known for his horror/supernatural tales than for his science fiction, DONALD WANDREI belongs to that group of individuals (including August Derleth and Robert Bloch) who both emulated and kept alive the work of H. P. Lovecraft. His most memorable work appeared in the late and lamented magazine *Weird Tales*.

PATRICIA S. WARRICK is Associate Professor of English at the University of Wisconsin-Fox Valley. Her undergraduate degree was in chemistry, and her master's and doctorate, in English. She has co-edited a number of science fiction test anthologies, including *Political Science Fiction, Psychology Through Science Fiction,* and *The New Awareness*. She has also written essays on contemporary fiction. Her particular area of concentration is cybernetic science fiction.

JACK WILLIAMSON is a native Southwesterner, born in Arizona Territory in 1908; a pioneer in science fiction, publishing his first story in 1928; a one-time Air Force weather forecaster stationed in the northern Solomons in 1945; the creator of a comic strip, *Beyond Mars,* which ran in the New York *Sunday News* in the 1950s; a professor of English at Eastern New Mexico University since 1960, teaching science fiction as well as linguistics and James Joyce. His novels include *The Legion of Space, Darker Than You Think, The Humanoids,* and *The Moon Children*. He has received the First Fandom Hall of Fame Award, the

Pilgrim Award from the Science Fiction Research Association, and the Grand Master Nebula from the Science Fiction Writers of America. Fascinated all his life with the drama of science in our evolving world, he now writes a weekly newspaper column forecasting the life of mankind in our next century.

GEORGE ZEBROWSKI is the author of more than thirty stories and essays appearing in *Fantasy & Science Fiction, Galaxy/If, Amazing, Current Science,* and other magazines, as well as in many anthologies, including *Nebula Awards 7, Immortal, New Constellations, Strange Bedfellows,* and *New Worlds Quarterly.* His first novel, *The Omega Point,* has appeared in six foreign editions; other novels include *The Star Web, Ashes and Stars* (the first volume of the trilogy in which *The Omega Point* is the middle book), *Mirror of Minds* (the last volume), the long work *Macrolife,* and *Free Space;* his collected stories appear in *The Monadic Universe and Other Stories.* He is the editor of *Human-Machines* (with Thomas N. Scortia); *Faster Than Light* (with Jack Dann); and *Tomorrow Today.* He has taught science fiction at SUNY/BINGHAMTON (Harpur College), where he also studied philosophy; as a lecturer he has appeared at colleges and universities and professional gatherings. He was editor of the *SFWA Bulletin* from 1970–1975. He lives and writes in upstate New York, resisting to date the lemming-like urge of his fellow writers to move to California.

One of the great science fiction stars of the late sixties and early seventies, ROGER ZELAZNY has successfully merged the mythologies of several cultures with science fiction. His many readers may debate their favorite novels but the powerful *Lord of Light* (1967) will be at the top of most lists. Other outstanding works include *This Immortal* (1966), *The Dream Master* (1966), *Isle of the Dead* (1969), and the collection *The Doors of His Face, The Lamps of His Mouth and Other Stories* (1971).

Index

COLLEGE OF MARIN

3 2555 00106075 0

DATE DUE

Demco, Inc. 38-293